Professional Front Office Management

Professional Front Office Management

Robert H. Woods, Ph.D.

Jack D. Ninemeier, Ph.D.

David K. Hayes, Ph.D.

Michele A. Austin

PEARSON
Prentice
Hall

Upper Saddle River, New Jersey 07458

Library of Congress Cataloging-in-Publication Data

Professional front office management / Robert H. Woods . . . [et al.].
 p. cm.
Includes index.
ISBN 0-13-170069-3
1. Hotel management. I. Woods, Robert H.
TX911.3.M27P82 2006
747.94068–dc22

2005035717

Director of Development: Vernon R. Anthony
Senior Editor: Eileen McClay
Managing Editor-Editorial: Judy Casillo
Editorial Assistant: Marion Gottlieb
Executive Marketing Manager: Ryan DeGrote
Senior Marketing Coordinator: Elizabeth Farrell
Marketing Assistant: Les Roberts
Director of Manufacturing and Production: Bruce Johnson
Managing Editor-Production: Mary Carnis
Production Liaison: Jane Bonnell
Production Editor: Shelley L. Creager, *TechBooks/GTS*
Manufacturing Manager: Ilene Sanford
Manufacturing Buyer: Cathleen Petersen
Senior Design Coordinator: Miguel Ortiz
Cover Designer: Carey Davies
Cover Image: Uripos/eStock Photo
Composition: *TechBooks/GTS Companies,* York, PA Campus
Manager of Media Production: Amy Peltier
Media Production Project Manager: Lisa Rinaldi
Printer/Binder: Courier Westford

Text photo credits appear on pages 663–664, which constitute a continuation of this copyright page.

Pearson Education Ltd.
Pearson Education Singapore Pte. Ltd.
Pearson Education Canada, Ltd.
Pearson Education—Japan

Pearson Education Australia Pty. Limited
Pearson Education North Asia Ltd.
Pearson Educación de Mexico, S.A. de C.V.
Pearson Education Malaysia Pte. Ltd.

10 9 8 7 6 5 4 3 2 1
ISBN 0-13-170069-3

We dedicate this book to its readers (students and industry employees), the hospitality faculty members and trainers who teach them, practicing industry professionals in the front office departments of hotels throughout the world, and guests who will benefit as the practices described make their hotel experiences more enjoyable. We hope this book helps in some way to make travel safe and fun for all travelers!

Brief Contents

Companion website available at www.prenhall.com/woods

Contents

Companion website available at www.prenhall.com/woods

Authors' Remarks

The Peninsula Hong Kong has been cited as one of the world's very best hotels in many international surveys for many years. Just a few of the many awards received through January 2005, are the following:

- **Conde Nast Traveler (UK):** 2005 Gold List—The Best Hotels in the World for Service (January 2005)
- **TripAdvisor Traveler's Choice (USA):** No.1—Overall Hotel List for 2004—Asia & South Pacific (January 2005)
- **Travel + Leisure (USA):** No. 1 in Hong Kong—T+L 500—The Greatest Hotels in the World (January 2005)
- **Conde Nast Traveler (USA):** 2005 Gold List—World's Best Places to Stay (January 2005)
- **Luxury Travel Magazine (Australia):** No. 1 Best of the Best Awards—The Best Overseas Hotel (December 2004)
- **The Leading Hotels of the World (USA):** Commitment to Quality Awards—Best in Asia (November 2004)
- **Business Traveller Awards Asia-Pacific 2004 (Asia/HK):**

    No. 2—Best Business Hotel in the World

    No. 2—Best Business Hotel in Asia-Pacific

    No. 1—Best Business Hotel in Hong Kong (October 2004)

- **Time Magazine (Asia/HK):** No. 1—Readers' Travel Choice Awards 2004—Favorite Business Hotel (October 2004)

- **Travel + Leisure (USA):** World's Best Business Hotels—No. 1 in Hong Kong (September 2004)
- **Forbes Magazine (USA):** World's Best Hotel Bars—Felix (July 2004)
- **Celebrated Living (USA):** American Airlines first class in-flight magazine—No. 1—Top Five Hotels in Asia (June 2004)
- **Zagat Survey (USA):**

  No. 2—Top Hotels in the World

  No. 1—Top Places by Country—China (April 2004)

- **Restaurant Magazine (UK):** The 50 Best Restaurants in the World—Felix (April 2004)—the only restaurant in Asia included in the list
- **Conde Nast Traveler (USA):** No. 1—Best By Food (January 2004)

To review current awards and accolades received by The Peninsula Hong Kong, check out its Web site: www.peninsula.com.

Not everyone can be fortunate enough to manage one of the world's very best hotels. Every hotel manager can, however, help to implement and maintain the type of organizational culture that Jan Michael Svoboda says is absolutely critical for The Peninsula Hong Kong hotel to be successful: one in which the best-possible service is emphasized and in which hotel employees are genuinely respected.

Foreword

The authors of this book requested that I provide some perspective on several topics. Doing so is a pleasure, because I have enjoyed my 20-year career—so far—in the hotel industry. During that time, I have developed some viewpoints and I am happy to share them with others.

The world of hotel management is exciting, and I know this because of the many experiences I have had while working in the hospitality industry in Vienna, Rome, New York City, Macau, Singapore, Hong Kong, and Bangkok. The lodging industry, like most others today, is global in nature. Hotels are located almost everywhere, and many events in one part of the world have an impact on properties in all other parts of the world. For example, businesses (and persons who travel for business) are influenced by global economies, and people who travel for pleasure do so with increasing or decreasing frequency based on world events.

I am fortunate to be a member of the management team of what some observers would say is an exemplary hotel. So what makes a hotel excellent? I can assure you that there are no secrets to operating a world-class hotel. Capital (i.e., financial resources) is essential for building the infrastructure and furnishing it with the contents that are required to meet the needs and desires of the world's most discriminating guests. However, the ongoing philosophy of excellence that must be practiced by all staff members all the time is also absolutely critical, and often excellence is more difficult to facilitate than is the acquisition of capital.

Readers of this book will gain insights into the management and operation of the front office department. In many ways, the front office is the hub of the hotel because of the important communication and coordination role that its staff assumes between the guests and the hotel's departments, managers, and staff. Is the front office the most important department? Not really, because all departments and functions within them are of critical importance or they would not be designed into the hotel's organizational structure. The front office department is, however, a focal point where many guests' needs are identified and where the hotel's pursuit of excellence can be honed as guests' needs are quickly and appropriately addressed.

There is no doubt that a successful hotel is made so in large measure by its staff members. They must have a passion to serve their guests and to perform their jobs at the highest possible levels all of the time. This observation is easy to think about and the philosophy of service that it expresses is easy to write about; however, the consistent delivery of service that meets guests' standards is incredibly difficult to achieve.

Hoteliers must begin the journey to an ongoing emphasis on the highest level of service by first determining what guests want and need. Then they must design the facilities, services, and product offerings and procedures to deliver them. The "right" staff members must be selected and be given a proper orientation to the hotel, to its mission, and to its philosophy of service excellence. At The Peninsula Hong Kong, all of our staff receive extensive training early in their tenure on the job. Initial training can last many months (or longer), but training never ends and it is always given a priority.

What else besides (1) a marketing emphasis to discover guests' needs, (2) the design of procedures to deliver desired products and services, (3) selection of appropriate employees and development of proper orientation practices, and (4) ongoing training and professional development is required for a hotel to be as good as it can be? There are many things, but my first response to this question is simple: It is absolutely necessary for hoteliers to have and to show a genuine respect for all employees.

Hotels are labor intensive. Machines cannot be used to replace the staff members required to perform all the work necessary to please guests. In our hotel, for example, we have 300 rooms and approximately 720 employees: a 2.4 to 1 ratio of employees to rooms. This ratio may seem high, and it is much greater than that of many properties in other segments of the industry. Yes, we are interested in productivity and costs, but we are also concerned about satisfying our guests. The delivery of service is the primary role played by our staff members; each of them either directly serves guests or provides services to another staff member (an internal guest!) who directly serves the guests. Our hotel, then, depends on our staff members for success.

A hotelier's relationship with employees should be built around genuine respect. We know that our staff have employment alternatives, and we want them to experience an on-job environment in which they can truly enjoy their work. Managers who treat their staff members with respect and dignity serve as role models who mirror the desired relationship between employees and guests. Many of our staff members have a cultural background that emphasizes a sincere attitude of "service to others." Nevertheless, what the management team does (or doesn't do) helps to emphasize (or discourage) the appropriate levels of service delivery that our guests expect when they register at our hotel—time after time after time!

I have learned that most guests can easily discern when the service they receive is genuine and when it is delivered as a standard operating procedure by someone who is doing something "because it says so in my job description." The hotel's management team can establish the foundation of employee selection, orientation, and training and can develop processes and procedures that enable staff to properly serve *some of our guests some of the time.* However, our staff members are in constant interaction with our guests, even more so than are many of our managers. Therefore, it is their attitude of the "genteel host" that must influence their words, thoughts, and actions to provide service that is beyond the norm to *all of our guests all of the time.*

Much has been written over the past decade or so about the concept of quality in the hotel industry. However, the notion of consistently delivering products and services desired by guests that meet or exceed their standards is not new to many hoteliers. For years, managers in successful properties have been practicing the art and science of focusing on the guests while managing the business.

If you have read this far, you might be surprised that there has been no mention of profit as an element in hotel success. Of course, a proper return on the owners' investment is necessary to remain viable and competitive and to sustain business growth. We know, however, that our hotel's financial goals are best addressed by thinking about our guests initially and then by addressing revenue goals and associated cost obligations.

It is said over and over again that the hotel business is a people business. This is true, but the people referred to must include both the guests and the employees. Both must be satisfied for the hotel to be successful. An effective hotel manager recognizes this and facilitates the work of staff members so that they can focus their priorities on their guest service responsibilities.

It's no surprise that people—guests and employees—are different. They have different needs, react differently to common situations, and have different expectations and opinions about what they experience. Hotel managers know about these differences and use established and creative approaches as they interact with the guests being served and with the employees providing the services. Successful hoteliers apply their experience and intuition as they determine the "best" tactics to use in ongoing interactions with guests and employees.

Hoteliers must enjoy interacting with people because this will be their most important responsibility. Those in the front office department must especially like the "people" aspects of their work. As you'll learn in this book, modern technology can provide a significant asset to front office decision makers. There is, therefore, less need for manual number crunching. The time managers save can be devoted to assisting guests directly and to helping their staff members to better do so. Much has changed during my career in the hotel business. However, the need to be concerned about guests and employees has been constant and will continue to be very important during the careers of the young people who will be part of the next generation of hoteliers.

Yes, the hotel business is exciting. There are and will continue to be significant opportunities for persons with interests ranging from interacting with guests (in the front office department) to working with machinery (in the engineering department) to preparing elaborate meals (in the food and beverage department). A common element runs through these and every other hotel department: the contribution that hoteliers and their organizations make to ensure that the travel experience is pleasurable, comfortable, and safe for their guests.

Jan Michael Svoboda
Hotel Manager
The Peninsula Hong Kong
Hong Kong Special Administrative Region
People's Republic of China

Preface

The front office department in a hotel of any size is the hub of the property's communication and operations systems, and its location in the hotel is among the first seen by hotel guests and others entering the lobby area. Its staff members, which include van drivers, parking lot and door attendants, and front desk agents, will probably be the first hotel representatives to meet and greet guests. The front desk is, indeed, the coordinating center for relationships between guests and hotel departments and for relationships among staff members who provide products and services for the guests.

Professionals in today's front office department must consistently use a blend of people skills to provide hospitable service and technology skills as they make reservations, register guests, and check out guests at the end of their stay. Front office managers must know and apply a wide range of professional work practices and skills to make decisions about room sales to and pricing decisions for individual and group travelers. They must also determine which reports will be of most use for their own planning and monitoring purposes, and they must generate historical and current data and future estimates of business information for all of their hotel's department heads.

Professional Front Office Management provides basic background information about and practical examples of the work roles and responsibilities of front office managers and their staff members. The book is an up-to-date benchmark of information about today's technology that provides a foundation on which future innovations will be based.

Hotels do not just open their front doors and allow guests to register. In today's increasingly competitive environment, it is important for hoteliers to carefully consider the needs of their guests and to develop plans that best meet those needs. Two chapters in this text address how the front office plans and delivers quality guest services, which form the basis of many operating procedures used by front office personnel.

Professional Front Office Management addresses technology in several chapters as it describes the property management system (PMS). The PMS is a computerized system, typically interfaced with several subsystems, used by front office personnel to manage reservations, room rates, room assignments, and many other service functions. "Yesterday" guests made reservations directly with the hotel or through a travel agent. Today, hotels' Internet Web sites and third-party Internet providers have dramatically changed the way reservations are made. Front office managers must recognize that the costs associated with using alternative distribution channels (i.e., sources for reservations) have an impact on the profitability of hotel room sales. Details about the ways that guest reservations can be made are presented in a chapter devoted to the topic.

Hotel guests and consumers in general are becoming more litigious; they increasingly use the court system to settle disputes. Front office managers, working with legal advisors, must establish procedures that comply with applicable laws, and front desk staff must consistently follow these procedures to minimize their property's legal liability. For example, front office staff must honor contracts, collect monies owed by current guests, notify and protect guests in times of emergencies, and help to avoid identity theft. Security issues are also of concern to front office staff. Consider, for example, the need to manage disturbances, to implement special precautions during times of increased terrorism alerts, and to protect guests' anonymity during their stay. The responsibility of front office employees goes far beyond checking in and checking out hotel guests, and chapters addressing legal and security issues related to the front office are included.

Professional Front Office Management provides a comprehensive treatment of topics in the context of the department's primary responsibility to "connect" the property and its employees with the guests. Readers will find that this book equally emphasizes the front office's responsibility to provide guest service, facilitate the work of employees in other departments as they provide service, and use technology to meet the needs of guests and other hotel employees.

FOCUS ON THE READERS

Professional Front Office Management was written to address the needs of postsecondary hospitality students, hospitality faculty members, and hospitality industry employees.

Postsecondary Hospitality Students

Hospitality management students enrolled in the ever-increasing number of universities, four-year and community colleges, and technical institutes that offer programs frequently express professional and vocational interests in becoming a hotel general manager. This is a reasonable expectation for many students and an admirable goal. Students can follow different tracks through an organization and throughout their career to attain professional goals. However, because the front office department is of such critical importance to a hotel, students desiring positions in top management should know a great deal about front office operations, and this book helps them to do so. First, the book details the overall functions of the department and the roles and responsibilities of persons working in most positions within the department. This information can help students confirm that a career in the hotel segment of the hospitality industry is desirable for them. Second, much of the information in the book is long-lived, for example, the emphasis on quality, on guest service, and on ways that various hotel departments depend on front office staff for service and information. The fast pace of technological change likely means that some of the current information about automated systems will become dated. However, the role that technology plays in the front office and the ways in which it is used are an integral part of the decision-making process that will stand the test of time.

Some readers will use this book as they take courses for which it is applicable. Others doing research in libraries for hospitality-related projects will likewise find it useful. Serious hospitality management students who are beginning to build a library of basic reference works while they are still in school will find a place for this book on their professional bookshelves.

Hospitality Faculty Members

Hospitality faculty want their students to have the best-available professional resources. This book, with its practical content and helpful supplemental materials, will facilitate learning. Instructors will find the book easy to read and to be an informative resource for use in the classroom and for external projects. As they master the subject matter in this book, students will begin to know about and understand the world of hotel management from the perspective of the front office department. They will learn how front office staff interact with guests and facilitate communication among employees and between employees and guests, and they will have an increased understanding of the technology that helps this interaction and communication to occur. Faculty will know that their efforts to make the best hospitality learning resources available to their students have been successful.

Hospitality Industry Employees

Many hotel employees who are interested in furthering their careers within the industry recognize the importance of participation in professional development and continuing activities. Some are fortunate and can enroll in community-based educational programs. Others, however, do not have access to such opportunities; instead, they must learn on their own. The authors envision that hotel general managers and front office managers who have copies of *Professional Front Office Management* will make it available to those whom they are mentoring. Also, today's world of Amazon.com and other Internet booksellers makes hospitality resources such as this book readily available to persons just about anywhere in the world.

There is another way that this book can help practicing industry professionals: It can be used to resolve problems. Instead of using the book in the traditional way of reading it cover to cover, front office managers and others can read or review applicable sections of the book as needed to gain suggestions for resolving specific problems.

ORGANIZATION OF THE BOOK

In the early planning stages of this book, we considered and discussed several organizational models. Each in its own way seemed rational, but the format we adopted was thought to be the most organizationally sound.

In Part I (Context of Front Office Operations), we provide an overview of the lodging industry to indicate where the hotel segment fits in to the vast hospitality industry (Chapter 1). Hotels, like organizations in all other parts of the hospitality industry, must emphasize quality guest service. Tactics that enable front office personnel to do so effectively are described in Chapter 2. Chapter 3 provides an overview of the front office department—its role and responsibilities in the hotel, the staff positions that are required, and some human resources-related concerns.

Part II of the book (How Technology Helps Front Office Operations) describes a hotel's property management system (Chapter 4) and how it is used to forecast data (Chapter 5) and manage revenue (Chapter 6). Chapter 7 discusses the various ways by which reservations can be made, with special emphasis on those involving technology, especially the Internet and the third-party Internet providers. The final chapter in this section (Chapter 8) reviews data-generating subsystems such as telephones, recodable locks, in-room vending, pay-per-view services and other systems that may or may not be interfaced with the PMS.

Part III of the book (Front Office and the Guest Cycle) focuses directly on guests and how reservations, reception, and room assignments are managed (Chapter 9). A discussion about how front office staff deliver guest service (Chapter 10) and how guest charges, payments, and check-out procedures are managed is also included (Chapter 11). A final chapter in this section (Chapter 12) describes the night audit and the management of seemingly innumerable reports that can be generated by the PMS.

In Part IV of the book (Special Concerns of the Front Office), the topic of the front office and the law is discussed in detail (Chapter 13). The final chapter describes how front office personnel interact with employees in every department of the hotel (Chapter 14).

CHAPTER ELEMENTS THAT FACILITATE LEARNING

Each chapter in *Professional Front Office Management* uses a variety of components to facilitate learning. Each component is educational and is designed to hold the readers' interest and make the book an "easy read." Some chapter elements illustrate how the content applies to the "real world." Other elements alert readers to additional information, including that available on the Internet, or allow readers to assess their comprehension of the subject matter presented.

Chapter Outline

Each chapter begins with an outline that provides a detailed overview of the chapter's content. Readers can skim it as they preview the chapter, or they can use it to locate specific information of interest.

Chapter Roadmap

The innovative graphic called a *chapter roadmap* appears at the beginning of every chapter and at the beginning of every major section within a chapter. The roadmap from Chapter 1, Overview of the Lodging Industry, is reproduced below.

Note that the roadmap identifies each of the major topics in the chapter and presents a learning objective applicable to each. The purpose of the roadmap is to provide context for the chapter: What does the chapter cover? What has been addressed to this point? What is the current section about? How does the current topic relate to those yet to be discussed in the chapter?

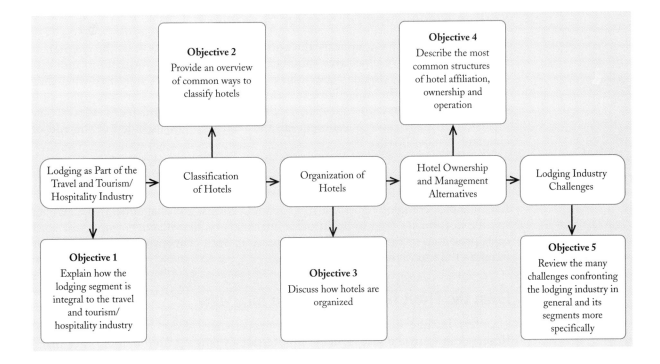

Chapter Preview

The preview in each chapter summarizes important information that will be presented in the chapter. The chapter preview explains why information in the chapter is critical to the job of a front office manager.

The FOM in Action: The Challenge

A case study introduces a problem, or challenge, relevant to the role of the front office manager (FOM). Readers are asked to consider the case study as they read through the chapter.

The FOM in Action: A Solution

At the conclusion of the chapter, the case study continues. In this section, readers learn one possible solution that might be useful to the front office manager in the case study.

Front Office Semantics

This chapter feature defines keywords when they are first used in the book. The definitions are important to those learning about the industry, because over time, industry-specific jargon and other business-related terms have evolved and have become part of the everyday language of hotel managers. For example, what is RevPar? This and many other terms are defined throughout the book. Terms are also listed in the sequence used at the end of each chapter, and they are combined into a full glossary at the end of the book.

Section Review and Discussion Questions

This innovative element appears the end of each major section in the chapter. It reviews the section's objective, summarizes the section's information, and lists discussion questions. Readers can use this chapter element to reinforce what they have just learned (the objective and summary) and to test their comprehension (by answering discussion questions). The format of this element allows easy inclusion of many more questions than the relatively few included at the end of chapters in most books.

Chapter Graphics

Each chapter contains figures, such as reports, forms, and diagrams, that illustrate specific documents used by front office managers or that illustrate important concepts presented in the chapter. Several photos in each chapter help readers to better visualize the situations being discussed.

From the Front Office: Front-Line Interview

Chapters include an interview with an experienced front office staff member. Readers can learn the perspectives of professionals ranging from a front office manager to a front desk agent to a concierge. Throughout the interviews, a common theme becomes apparent: the need to consistently provide quality service.

Modern Front Office Issues and Tactics

News events related to the front office are included in each chapter. For example, Chapter 14 includes descriptions of how front office staff can help prevent identity theft and how a power outage at the Bellagio Hotel in Las Vegas affected the hotel's front office staff.

Information Sidelights

Examples that supplement topics discussed in the chapter are presented throughout. For example, readers will learn that in some international hotels serving airports with late-night departures, it is necessary to clean rooms for arriving guests during the very early morning hours (1:00 a.m. to 4:00 a.m.), not during the traditional mid-morning schedule of a housekeeping department.

Front Office and the Internet

An end-of-chapter section lists Web site addresses for readers to consult if they wish to learn more about the topics discussed in the chapter.

Real-World Activities

This end-of-chapter element suggests out-of-class projects and assignments that allow students to learn more about the chapter's topics and to synthesize information presented in the chapter.

SOME FINAL THOUGHTS

Our work as authors in developing this book was made much easier by efforts expended by many persons behind the scenes. We thank Vernon Anthony and Ann Brunner, Pearson Prentice Hall for, respectively, suggesting that we undertake this writing task and for helping us with details as the project evolved.

We are indebted to Jan Michael Svoboda, Hotel Manager, The Peninsula Hong Kong—truly one of the world's greatest hotels. In his foreword to this book, Jan Michael expresses the need for all staff members to consistently practice a philosophy of excellence and service. This simply stated, but incredibly difficult-to-achieve goal, establishes the context within which *Professional Front Office Management* has been written.

We also thank our text reviewers for their valuable input: Moe Ammar, Monterey Peninsula College; James Groves, University of Missouri; Sandra Grunwell, Western Carolina University; Bo Hu, Oklahoma State University; Peter Ricci, University of Central Florida; Chris Roberts, University of Massachusetts; Larry Ross, Florida Southern College; Susan Stafford, SUNY Tompkins Cortland Community College; and Charles R. Stockman, Lakeland College.

Our long-time associate, Debbie Ruff, is also acknowledged for her word processing assistance and for helping us with numerous technical problems that are beyond our ability to comprehend, let alone to resolve.

Finally, our spouses are publicly thanked for their support and encouragement through a relatively long process of research and writing that made us unavailable for other priorities.

R. H. W.
J. D. N.
D. K. H.
M. A. A.

1

Overview of the Lodging Industry

Chapter Outline

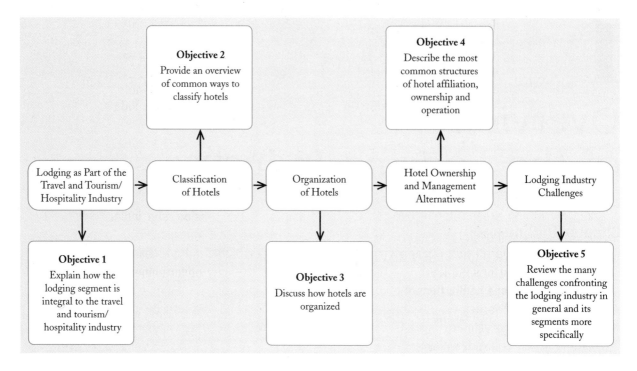

CHAPTER ROADMAP

Chapter Preview

Whether you travel for business or for pleasure, whether you simply want a safe and clean place to rest or a unique lodging experience, or whether you seek to pay a modest price or have the ability to splurge, the vast lodging industry has accommodation alternatives available. This chapter provides an overview of the industry and provides the context within which hotel managers and their staff in all departments, including the front office, work. The industry has evolved from a shared sleeping room in houses located along trade routes to modern properties of all types, many of which are described in this chapter.

Today's hotel organizations research the needs of the travelers they want to attract and, in the process, differentiate their properties from others. Nevertheless, successful hotels have many common characteristics. One of these is the availability of highly professional, knowledgeable, and experienced managers who recognize the importance of providing the appropriate level of guest service at a price that provides value for guests and profits for owners or shareholders. These managers increasingly use technology wherever it is cost-effective to do so, and they "walk and talk" the philosophy of quality. They also recognize that their success is driven by the contributions of their employees; therefore, they use human relations tactics to empower staff and to encourage employees to find pride and success in the workplace.

A hotel (or any other business organization) is only as good as its employees. In this book, we will focus on management of the front office—the hotel's communication center. Its efforts are important to property success, as are those of all other departments, but the front office plays a special role in coordinating the work of other departments.

Every hotel, regardless of size, has a front office (or a person whose work responsibilities involve those associated with the front office). Details about how this department works and what specific staff members do differ among organizations. However, basic work processes (the topic of this book) and the department's goal (to please the guests) are the same. What are the responsibilities of people who work in the front office? What do they do? The answers to these and related questions will be addressed throughout this book. The first step in understanding the role of the front office is to obtain basic background information about the lodging industry and learn the types of properties that use front office personnel to serve guests.

The FOM in Action: The Challenge

Lorine is a front office manager (FOM) who has worked in lodging organizations ranging from a 125-room, limited-service property to an 800-room, full-service hotel (her current workplace). During her long career she has worked for independent hotel owners, management companies, and franchisor-operated properties. She was, therefore, a perfect candidate to volunteer for the education committee of her state's lodging association. The committee had taken on the challenge of scheduling a representative to speak at the hospitality program of each postsecondary school within the state.

In a one-hour presentation at a local school, Lorine reviewed the wide range of professional opportunities available in the lodging industry. At the end of the session, she indicated that time was available for questions. The first question addressed to her had two parts: "It's good that there are so many opportunities in so many segments of the lodging industry. But how can we decide if it is better to work for a large organization or a small one? Also, you mentioned that the industry has been kind to many of its entrepreneurs. What are the pros and cons of starting your own hospitality business?"

If you were Lorine, how would you respond to these insightful questions?

LODGING AS PART OF THE TRAVEL AND TOURISM/HOSPITALITY INDUSTRY

Roadmap 1.1 indicates that we will begin our exploration of the lodging industry by describing how it fits into the broader **travel and tourism industry,** and the **hospitality industry.**

FRONT OFFICE SEMANTICS

Travel and tourism industry: All businesses that cater to the needs of the traveling public.

Hospitality industry: Businesses that provide accommodations (lodging) and foodservices for people when they are away from their homes.

Travel and Tourism: The Big Picture

Figure 1.1 provides an overview of the types of organizations that compose the travel and tourism industry. This brief review of industry segments and the types of organizations within them will help you to learn where hotels fit in the broader industry of which they are a part. As you review Figure 1.1, note that there are three major segments. One (hospitality) includes the accommodations (lodging) sector that will be discussed in depth in the remainder of this chapter. Transportation services includes companies that operate airplanes, rental cars, trains, ships, and other ways that people travel between their homes, businesses, and destinations. The third

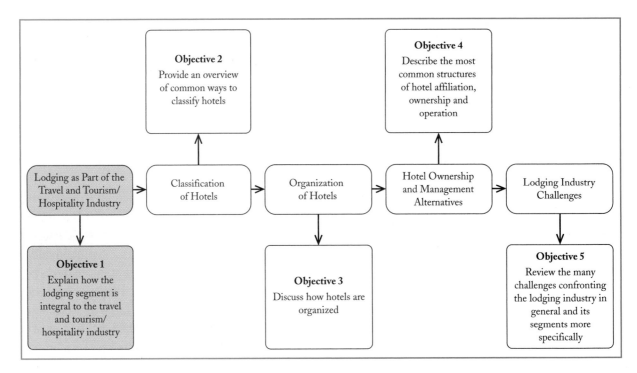

ROADMAP 1.1

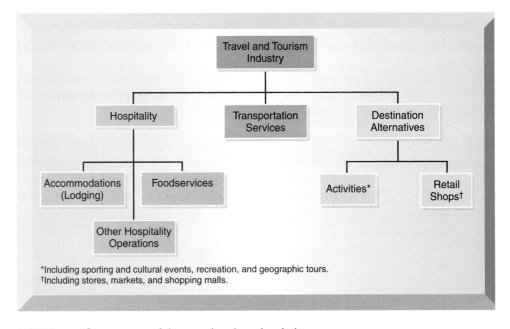

FIGURE 1.1   Components of the travel and tourism industry.

Source: Ninemeier, J., and J. Perdue. 2005. *Hospitality operations: Careers in the world's greatest industry,* p. 4. Upper Saddle River, NJ: Pearson Education, Inc. Reprinted by permission.

All types of lodging are designed for people to sleep comfortably away from home.

sector, destination alternatives, includes activities such as sporting and cultural events, recreation, and geographic tours, along with retail shops such as stores, markets, and shopping malls.

In the United States, the travel and tourism industry is the third largest retail industry, following the automotive and food stores industries. It is the nation's largest service industry and one of the country's largest employers. It is also the first, second, or third largest employer in 30 states.[1]

Hospitality Industry

Figure 1.2 suggests the range of organizations that comprise the hospitality industry. Let's look at the hospitality industry more closely.

Accommodations (Lodging) Segment

Where can people sleep safely when they are away from home? Several types of organizations are part of in the accommodations (lodging) segment of the hospitality industry:

- *Hotels.* **Hotels** may be large or small, relatively inexpensive or highly priced. Guests may drive up to the front door of their room or take an elevator up many stories to their room. Properties may or may not offer foodservices, and they may be located along a highway, or in a city or suburb, or at an airport

---

[1]American Hotel & Lodging Industry. Lodging industry profile. Retrieved September 10, 2005, from http://www.ahla.com.

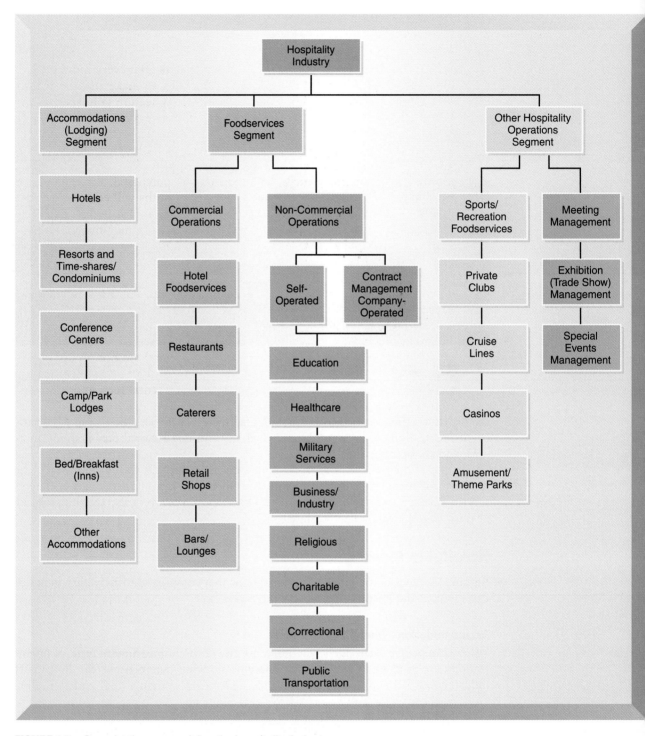

FIGURE 1.2   Organizations comprising the hospitality industry.

Adapted from Ninemeier, J., and J. Perdue. 2005. *Hospitality operations: Careers in the world's greatest industry,* p. 7. Upper Saddle River, NJ: Pearson Education, Inc. Reprinted by permission.

location. Although at least one type of hotel (called *extended-stay*) markets to those desiring accommodations for several weeks or longer, most hotels generally rent rooms for one week or less.

- *Resorts and time-shares/condominiums.* Most **resorts** offer everything provided by a **full-service hotel** plus additional attractions to make them a primary destination for travelers. For example, resorts may feature golf, spas, skiing, horseback riding, tennis, and oceanfronts to entertain guests for several days or longer. **Time-share properties** (also called *interval-ownership properties*) allow persons to purchase partial-year ownership of a lodging property (usually in one-week intervals). Typically, purchase prices differ depending on the month or season for which the time-share is purchased; for example, in Florida, a week's ownership during the winter months will cost more than a week's ownership in July. The buyer (or others whom the buyer designates) will have access to a room in that property during that same time period every year. Organizations such as Resort Condominiums International (RCI) have established global networks to allow owners to trade their ownership on an annual basis with someone else in another property in another part of the world at the same time or another time of the year. Point systems are also becoming popular; they allow time-share owners to use traditional lodging properties for their time-share.

  Condominium (condo) complexes may allow owners to place their unit on the complex's rental plan when they (the owners) are not occupying the unit. A management company markets the condominium complex (including owners' units) on a rental plan, collects guest rental fees, and hires personnel to provide housekeeping and other services during and between guest visits. In turn, the management company is paid a fee taken from the condo rental income. The remaining income from guest rental fees is paid to the unit owners.

- *Conference centers.* Professionals in **conference centers** (also called *professional development centers* or *executive education centers*) assist organizations by planning meetings. Many conference centers are operated by postsecondary institutions and employ professional staff who work with associations and large companies to develop and offer specialized programs. These centers may also offer programs to individuals who desire to learn about a general topic. Large corporations may have in-house conference facilities in their headquarters or other offices. Foodservices range from coffee breaks to full, sit-down meals. Some conference centers offer sleeping rooms. If they do not, one or more nearby hotels are typically available, and transportation between the center and the hotels is provided.

- *Camp/park lodges.* Many states and the federal government offer sleeping accommodations for visitors to parks and other nature conservation areas in **camp/park lodges** that are much more formalized than a "tent and campfire." Sometimes operated by management companies, these facilities offer accommodations that are comparable to those offered elsewhere in the area.

- *Bed and breakfast inns.* **Bed and breakfast inns** (often called *B&Bs*) are generally very small (one to several guestrooms) properties owned and managed by persons living on-site. Guests sleep in a room that is part of the owner's house and generally receive a breakfast meal, the cost of which is included in the room's rental price. These businesses are the modern-day equivalent of the home owner of earlier times who provided food and a night's rest to travelers before they continued on their journey.

- *Other accommodations.* Other types of businesses provide sleeping accommodations for travelers: youth hostels, campgrounds, working ranches, wilderness lodges and ranches. There are two relatively new types of hotels. **Condotels** are hotels with several floors dedicated to condominium units; condo owners in these properties typically have access to the hotel's amenities. In a stretch of the definition of *hotels*, entrepreneurs now offer "daytime sleeping salons"—dimly lighted rooms with a white-noise machine and sleeping "pods"(dome-covered chairs featuring nature sounds and headphones). Nap sessions are sold in 15-minute increments.

FRONT OFFICE SEMANTICS

Hotel: For-profit business that rents sleeping rooms and often provides other amenities such as food and beverage services, swimming pools and exercise rooms, meeting spaces, business centers, and concierge services. Also referred to as *motel, motor hotel,* or *motor inn.*

Resort: Full-service hotel with additional attractions to make it a primary destination for travelers.

Full-service hotel: Hotel that offers guests an extensive range of food and beverage products and services.

Time-share property: Lodging property that sells a part ownership (e.g., one week within a specified time period) in a unit within the property. Also called *interval ownership property.*

Condominium: Lodging property in which units are individually owned. In some condominium properties, units can be placed into a rental pool with resulting guest fees split between the owner and the company managing the units. Also called *condo.*

Conference center: Specialized hospitality operation specifically designed for and dedicated to the needs of small- and medium-size meetings of from 20 to 100 people.

Camp/park lodge: Sleeping accommodations in parks and other nature conservation areas owned by governmental agencies and often operated by for-profit management companies.

Bed and breakfast inn: Very small (one to several guestrooms) property owned and managed by person living on-site. These businesses typically offer at least one meal daily. Also called *B&B.*

Condotel: Hotel with several floors dedicated to condominium units. Condo owners typically have access to the property's amenities.

Foodservices Segment

Travelers must, of course, eat while they are away from home. They often do so in many of the same foodservice operations used by community residents who are dining out for business or social purposes. A wide variety of foodservice businesses generate profits from the sale of their products and services to travelers and area residents. These are referred to as **commercial foodservice operations.** In contrast, there is another type of foodservice: **noncommercial foodservice** operations, which are not in business primarily to generate profits from food and beverage products. Instead, they are offered by organizations, such as schools and hospitals, which exist to educate and provide health services, respectively, but in the process provide foodservice to their constituents (e.g., students, patients, employees). These two types of operations are part of the foodservices segment of the hospitality industry.

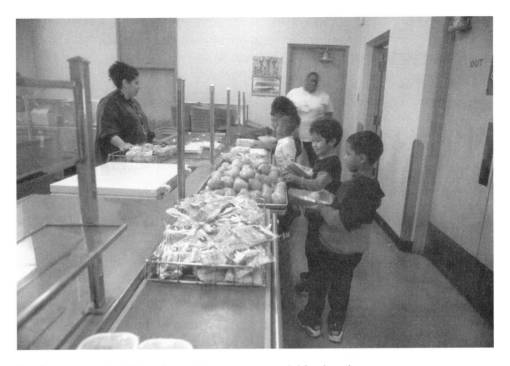

An elementary school's lunchroom is a noncommercial foodservice.

FRONT OFFICE SEMANTICS

Commercial foodservice operation: Foodservices offered in hotels and restaurants and other organizations whose primary financial goal involves generation of profits from the sale of food and beverage products.

Noncommercial foodservice operation: Foodservice operation whose financial goal does not involve generating profits from the sale of food and beverage products. Also called *institutional foodservices* and *on-site foodservices*.

Figure 1.2 identifies several types of commercial foodservice businesses: hotel foodservices, **restaurants, caterers,** retail shops, and **bars** and **lounges.**

FRONT OFFICE SEMANTICS

Restaurant: For-profit foodservice operation whose primary business involves the sale of food and beverage products to individuals and small groups of guests.

Caterer: For-profit business that produces food for groups at off-site locations. Some caterers have banquet space available for on-site use by groups desiring foodservices.

Bar: For-profit business serving alcoholic beverages to guests seated at a counter (bar). Limited table service may be available.

Lounge: For-profit business serving alcoholic beverages to guests seated at tables. A small counter (bar) may be available.

Noncommercial foodservice operations are not typically available to the traveling public, although those available to persons using public transportation such as airplanes and trains are an exception. Noncommercial operations include programs operated by educational institutions that offer meals to primary, high school, and postsecondary students, and by health care facilities that offer meals to hospital patients and residents in nursing homes and retirement communities. Military services feed their troops, business and industry provide meals to employees at work, and religious and charitable organizations provide foodservices to their own members and those within the community who need assistance.

There are two basic ways that noncommercial foodservices can be operated:

- They may be **self-operated;** that is, the organization may employ a foodservice director and staff to manage and operate the program.
- They may be operated by a **contract management company;** that is, the organization may negotiate and contract with a for-profit management company to provide the foodservices for the organization.

FRONT OFFICE SEMANTICS

Self-operated noncommercial foodservices: Type of noncommercial foodservices operation in which the program is managed and operated by the organization's employees.

Contract management company-operated noncommercial foodservices: Type of noncommercial foodservices operation in which the program is managed and operated by a for-profit management company.

Other Hospitality Operations Segment

In addition to accommodations (lodging) and foodservices businesses, there are other operations that are considered part of the hospitality industry:

- Sports and recreation foodservices
- Private clubs
- Cruise lines
- Casinos
- Amusement and theme parks
- Meeting management businesses
- Exhibition (trade show) management
- Special events management

SECTION REVIEW AND DISCUSSION QUESTIONS

Section Objective: Explain how the lodging segment is integral to the travel and tourism/hospitality industry.

Section Summary: The travel and tourism industry consists of three segments: hospitality, transportation services, and destination alternatives. Within the hospitality segment, there are three basic types of organizations: accommodations (lodging), foodservices, and other hospitality operations. Hotels are one type of lodging organization that provide products and services for travelers to and residents of a community.

Discussion Questions:

1. What are some characteristics that all businesses in the travel and tourism industry have in common?

2. What are some additional characteristics that all organizations in the hospitality industry share?
3. What are specific elements that all businesses in the accommodations (lodging) segment of the hospitality industry have in common?

CLASSIFICATION OF HOTELS

Hotels are one type of organization in the accommodations (lodging) segment of the hospitality industry. The many types of hotels can be classified to make discussion and study easier. As Roadmap 1.2 indicates, common hotel classifications will be considered in this section.

Methods of Classification

As shown in Figure 1.3, common classifications of lodging properties are location, rate, and size. In 2003, most U.S. hotels were in suburban and highway locations, were low- to mid-priced ($30 to $59.99), and had fewer than 75 rooms. This description of an "average" hotel may be of interest to those aspiring to careers in the lodging industry. Even though there are many excellent positions available in the industry, the number of large properties with high **rack rates** in large city centers or exotic locations is relatively small.

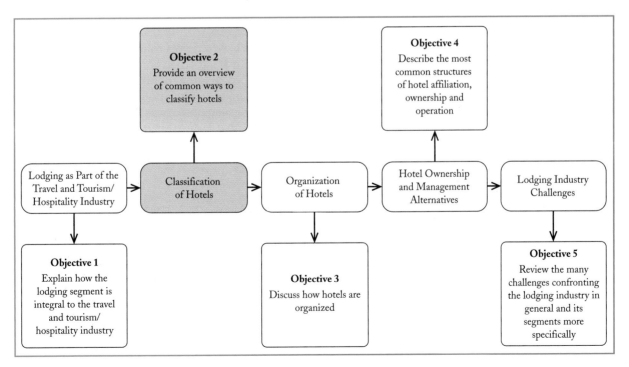

ROADMAP 1.2

By location	By rate	By size
Urban	Under $30	Under 75 rooms
Suburban	$30–$44.99	75–149 rooms
Highway	$45–$59.99	150–299 rooms
Airport	$60–$85	300–500 rooms
Resort	More than $85	More than 500 rooms

Note: These classifications are used by the American Hotel & Lodging Association (AH&LA); check out current statistics applicable to each classification on AH&LA's home page: www.ahla.com.

FIGURE 1.3   Common ways to classify hotels.

FRONT OFFICE SEMANTICS

Rack rate: Price at which a hotel sells its rooms when no discounts of any kind are offered to the guest. Often shortened to *rack.*

Lodging properties are also frequently classified by guestroom rental charges. Classifications fall along a range such as that suggested in Figure 1.4. However, these classifications do not correlate easily with the rate structure suggested in Figure 1.3. It is difficult to classify hotels strictly by rack rates, because room charges vary significantly in different geographic regions. For example, the most expensive hotel available in a small, northern, Midwest town in the United States may be half (or less) of the rate charged for the least expensive, safe, and clean hotel room in a major East Coast or West Coast city.

LODGING INDUSTRY CHARACTERISTICS

Hotels in any classification typically share several common characteristics.

- *Emphasis on safety, cleanliness, and service.* Few guests consider only the room and physical attributes of the property when making a decision to rent a room. Safety and cleanliness are important considerations, as is the friendliness (hospitality) of the hotel's employees. In contrast to retail sales where products are tangible (e.g., clothes or televisions), hotel sales involve intangible aspects in the purchase decision of potential guests.
- *Inseparability of manufacture and sales.* It is not possible to separate the "manufacture" (production) of a guestroom with its "sale." A room exists and is sold at the

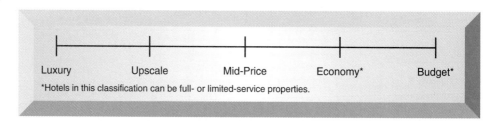

FIGURE 1.4   Range of hotels classified by guestroom rental charges.

Source: Ninemeier, J., and J. Perdue. 2005. *Hospitality operations: Careers in the world's greatest industry,* p. 62. Upper Saddle River, NJ: Pearson Education, Inc. Reprinted by permission.

same site. In contrast, clothes or televisions are manufactured at one site and sold at another. The hotel's staff must be experts at both manufacture and sales.

- *Perishability.* If a guestroom is not rented on a specific date, the revenue is lost forever. In contrast, clothes or televisions can be sold tomorrow if they are not sold today.
- *Repetitiveness.* The steps required to register a guest checking into a hotel are basically the same every time the guestroom is sold. These routines (operating procedures) allow for some standardization. At the same time, however, they create challenges. It is always important to focus on a guest's individual needs, and standardization can provide less opportunity for staff creativity in the decision-making process.
- *Labor intensive.* In many industries, technology and equipment have replaced people in some work activities, but in the lodging industry this has occurred to a lesser degree. For example, technology is being used in the front office and the sales and accounting departments where many tasks are highly automated. Although technology could be used even more (e.g., automated check-in and check-out systems are available), many segments of the traveling public desire and are willing to pay for services that must be delivered by employees. As well, the two hotel departments with the greatest number of staff members (food and beverage and housekeeping) provide fewer opportunities for technology to reduce labor hours.

Classification by Features and Guest Focus

Another way to classify hotels is to consider the types of guests who use them. A system using this approach is shown in Figure 1.5. Let's look more closely at each of the types of hotels and the guests who most frequently visit them.

Full-Service Hotels

Full-service hotels in the United States trace their origins to pre-Revolutionary times. Taverns were often the only locations where travelers and local citizens could consume meals and beverages away from home. Today, in most cities full-service hotels have assumed the tavern's original role of hosting local public and civic events. They also enjoy a significant **market share** of organizations that house travelers from out of town.

FRONT OFFICE SEMANTICS

Market share: Percentage of a total market (typically in dollars spent) captured by an industry segment or property.

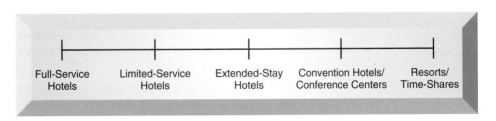

FIGURE 1.5   Hotel classification by type of guests using them.

The costs of staying in or using the products and services provided by a full-service hotel vary widely from fairly inexpensive to extremely expensive. Nevertheless, most industry observers identify full-service hotels as being in either the mid-price, upscale, or luxury segments of the lodging industry.

Mid-price full-service hotels are popular. Holiday Inns, the largest chain within this segment, is credited by most observers with founding the hotel franchise concept in the United States. In many smaller cities, one or more mid-price full-service hotels serve as community centers to host the area's business-related meetings, local political gatherings, weddings, anniversary parties, and other celebratory events. Mid-price properties appeal to travelers who desire the services offered by a full-service hotel, but who also desire rental rates only slightly higher than their limited-service hotel alternatives.

FRONT OFFICE SEMANTICS

Mid-price full-service hotel: Lodging property offering three meals daily, a lounge, a swimming pool, and limited meeting and banquet spaces.

Guests of mid-price hotels expect to find a restaurant that serves three meals per day, a lounge, a swimming pool, and designated spaces for meetings or meal functions. These hotels are often found on interstate highway exchanges, near airports, or in downtown areas of small cities. Major hotel brands in the mid-price full-service market include InterContinental's Holiday Inns, Choice's Clarion brand, and Cendant's Howard Johnson and Ramada Inn brands. In addition, many Best Western hotels offer full-service amenities.

Upscale full-service hotels are generally located in large cities, adjacent to casinos or international airports, or near significantly large tourist destinations. These properties typically offer more guestrooms and meeting spaces than the average mid-price hotel.

FRONT OFFICE SEMANTICS

Upscale full-service hotel: Lodging property offering the amenities of mid-price hotels and additional services such as a gift shop, concierge, exercise facility, high-speed Internet access, and many guest services.

Upscale full-service hotels offer all the amenities of mid-price properties. In addition, they provide special services such as an on-site gift shop, full- or part-time **concierge,** and a comprehensive exercise facility. A variety of related guest services may include extensive room service offerings, on-premise laundry and dry cleaning services, and recreational facilities appropriate for the location (e.g., tennis, golf, and horseback riding, and motorized and nonmotorized water sports, for properties located on a beach).

FRONT OFFICE SEMANTICS

Concierge: Individual or individuals within a full-service hotel responsible for providing guests with detailed information about local dining and attractions as well as assisting with related guest needs.

Upscale full-service hotel companies in the United States have been successful in building **name recognition** and **brand loyalty.** As a result, many have expanded their properties internationally. In fact, for some of the largest U.S. hotel companies, the number of new hotels developed internationally has exceeded the number of their new hotels built in the United States.

FRONT OFFICE SEMANTICS

Name recognition: Ability of guests or potential guests to remember and associate with a hotel's (or restaurant's) name.

Brand loyalty: Interest of guests or potential guests to revisit and recommend a hotel (or restaurant).

The upscale full-service hotel segment is large and includes some of the best-known names in the hotel business: Hyatt, Radisson, Westin, and full-service Sheraton, Hilton, and Marriott properties. These hotels range in size from smaller properties with 200 to 500 rooms to 1,000-plus room properties located in downtown areas such as New York, Chicago, and Atlanta.

When people discuss the very best hotels in the world, they are talking about **luxury full-service hotels.** These properties can be located in a resort area if they target vacation travelers, in the heart of a major city if they serve upscale business travelers, or in locations that appeal to both leisure and business travelers. Luxury full-service hotels cater to clientele who demand the highest levels of products and services and who are willing to pay premium prices for these products and services.

FRONT OFFICE SEMANTICS

Luxury full-service hotel: Lodging property offering the amenities of upscale full-service hotels and additional features that appeal to clientele who desire the best and are willing to pay premium prices.

MODERN FRONT OFFICE ISSUES AND TACTICS

How Much Do You Want to Pay for a Hotel Room?

If money is no problem, there are lodging options beyond luxury suites. For example, villas offer the privacy of a luxurious home along with hotel amenities, activities, and services. How about one of the following:

- The One and Only Ocean Club in the Bahamas. This property has three ocean-front villas with outdoor tubs and infinity-edge pools. Villas come with a butler and cost $4,000 to $5,000 per day (summer rates).
- Little Dick's Bay on Virgin Gorda (British Virgin Islands). Villas feature oversized living and dining areas, private pools, and outdoor showers. Nightly rates are $1,500 (two bedrooms) and $2,000 (three bedrooms).
- Jumby Bay Resort (Antigua). Summer rates begin at $1,500 per day for two, including all meals and alcoholic beverages.
- Starwood Santa Marina Resort and Villas (Greek island of Mykonos). Guests can choose two- to four-bedroom villas costing $1,600 to $6,000 nightly in June.
- Sandy Lane (Barbados). This is a five-bedroom villa starting at $8,000 per night.
- The Greenbriar (West Virginia). This property offers privately owned "estate homes" with rates running from $2,000 to $4,000 daily in summer, including breakfast and dinner.

One of the most unusual and priciest packages did not give the guest a room but the *entire* Millenium Resort Scotsdale, McCormick Ranch (125 deluxe guestrooms). For a minimum price of $100,000 dollars, the winner of an eBay auction, along with 250 guests, had exclusive access to the entire resort from August 27–30, 2004. The package included unlimited food and beverages and private use of the resort's ballroom, tennis courts, sand volleyball courts, swimming pool, cabana bar, and award-winning restaurant.

Typical room rates in luxury full-service hotels range from several hundred to several thousand dollars per night. Although independent hotels dominate this market, brands include world-famous names such as the Four Seasons, Marriott's Ritz-Carlton, Starwood's St.Regis, and the Hong Kong-based Regal Hotels group.

What do guests expect at luxury full-service properties? Quite simply, the very best. Luxury hotel guests desire and are willing to pay for superlative accommodations, food, beverages, banquets, meetings, and activities. Depending on the location and the clientele they serve, luxury full-service properties offer a wide range of products and services.

WHAT DO GUESTS EXPECT AT LUXURY FULL-SERVICE HOTELS?

Guests expect the very best at luxury full-service hotels. Items and services such as the following are common:

- Concierge services 24 hours a day.
- Extensive in-room amenities such as monogrammed terry-cloth bathrobes and other complimentary products
- Personalized shopping services to replace lost or forgotten travel necessities such as clothing, luggage, or personal care items
- Complimentary towels and drinks at poolside or on the beach
- Personal chefs available to prepare guest-selected menus
- Private and confidential check-in services
- In-suite offices complete with in-room fax and clerical personnel available 24 hours a day
- Complimentary child-care services
- Gourmet restaurants that offer a variety of regional and international cuisines and that maintain extensive and exceptional wine lists
- Complimentary international newspapers
- Multiline telephones near the bed, on work desks, and in bathrooms
- Laundry and tailoring services 24 hours a day
- Health and recreation facilities that include extensive spa services
- Twice (or more) daily housekeeping services
- Complimentary use of luxury autos with unlimited mileage

Full-service hotels attract an important type of guest who does not typically represent a large client base for other types of hotels: the local resident who uses the property's restaurants and meeting facilities. Because full-service hotels have meeting space, local business associations, service clubs, and social groups (e.g., chambers of commerce and Rotary and Lions clubs), may use meeting space regularly. Also, local residents may attend weddings, anniversary parties, company holiday parties, and political gatherings in full-service hotels. Even though local residents rarely rent guestrooms from the full-service hotel, their use of the property's meeting and dining spaces often represents a large portion of the hotel's annual food and beverage and meeting room rental revenues.

People who rent guestrooms at full-service hotels typically are part of a group meeting or are individual travelers who want unique services. In a successful full-service hotel, group business often accounts for a third (or more) of the total number of guest **room nights** each year.

FRONT OFFICE SEMANTICS

Room night: Single night use of a guestroom. A group using 10 rooms for 5 nights generates 50 room nights. The number is used as an indicator of group size and quantifies the group's importance to the hotel.

Full-service hotels are popular with corporate and leisure travelers. **Business travelers** appreciate the fact that many full-service hotels are in excellent locations, and they enjoy the convenience of the informal and formal meetings that can be held there. Business travelers may be on an expense account, and the slightly higher prices charged by full-service hotels can be justified by the additional services and amenities available.

FRONT OFFICE SEMANTICS

Business traveler: Person who travels primarily for business reasons. Such guests often have an expense account to defray reasonable travel costs.

Many **leisure travelers** are attracted by the added elegance of full-service hotels. This is especially true of upscale and luxury vacation travelers. For many of these individuals, a night, a week, or even longer in a high quality full-service hotel is an experience to be remembered for a lifetime.

FRONT OFFICE SEMANTICS

Leisure traveler: Person who travels primarily for personal reasons. Such guests use private funds for travel expenses and are often sensitive to the prices charged.

Limited-Service Hotels

Limited-service hotels developed as a direct result of consumer demand, and at the beginning of the twenty-first century, they were the largest and fastest growing segment of the lodging industry. For many travelers, a simple, clean, and safe room located near their desired destination (or on the way to it) is all that is required.

FRONT OFFICE SEMANTICS

Limited-service hotel: Lodging property that offers no or very limited foodservices; sometimes a complimentary breakfast is served, but there is no restaurant with table service.

Features that make limited-service properties a unique segment of the hotel industry include their relatively small size, the large proportion affiliated with a franchise brand, the room rental charges, and guest services that are offered.

Most limited-service properties are small; average size consists of fewer than 150 rooms. Nearly all are affiliated with a franchise brand. The most distinguishing features of the limited-service hotel segment, however, are its price and service segmentation. Although there is no industry standard, some observers group limited-service hotels into three categories: budget (economy), mid-price, and upscale.

Budget (economy) limited-service hotels were among the first to be developed in the United States. Popular brands include Accor's Motel 6, Choice's Econo Lodge, and Cendant's Super 8. These brands are attractive to owners and investors because they are relatively inexpensive to build and simple to operate. Travelers are attracted by low room rates and, often, convenient locations.

FRONT OFFICE SEMANTICS

Budget (economy) limited-service hotel: Lodging property within the limited-service segment that offers low-priced guestrooms and few, if any, amenities other than a complimentary continental breakfast or coffee service.

Traveler amenities offered by these budget hotels are few. They are not likely to have swimming pools, meeting spaces, or food and beverage facilities (although many offer a complimentary morning coffee service or limited **continental breakfast**). Successful budget hotels offer clean and safe rooms, low prices, and few frills.

FRONT OFFICE SEMANTICS

Continental breakfast: Morning meal that includes coffee, juices, and pastries. An upscale continental breakfast may include additional items such as fruit, hot and cold cereals, and milk and yogurt. Most limited-service hotels offer a complimentary continental breakfast as a guest amenity.

Mid-price limited-service hotels offer amenities at prices that are below those of most full-service hotels. In addition to the features found at budget hotels, mid-price hotels typically offer amenities such as these:

- **Frequent-traveler programs**
- Swimming pools
- Larger bathroom areas
- In-room coffeemakers
- In-room irons, ironing boards, and hair dryers
- Upgraded complimentary continental breakfasts
- Complimentary morning newspapers
- Complimentary local telephone calls

FRONT OFFICE SEMANTICS

Mid-price limited-service hotel: Lodging property within the limited-service segment that offers selected property and within-room upgrade amenities for room rates that are higher than budget (economy) hotels within the limited-service segment.

Frequent-traveler program: Program developed to reward a hotel company's guests with free room nights, frequent-flyer airline miles, and other awards as an incentive to book rooms at a property within the brand.

Popular mid-price brands include Marriott's Fairfield Inn, Hilton's Hampton Inn, InterContinental's Holiday Inn Express, Carlson Country Inns & Suites, and Choice's Comfort Inn. Mid-price hotels make up the largest portion of the limited-service market, and each brand has developed its own loyal clientele.

Some travelers do not want to pay for the restaurants, lounges, gift shops and meeting spaces found at full-service hotels; they do, however, desire the comfort and amenities offered at the finest full-service properties. For these guests, **upscale limited-service hotels** provide the comfort, convenience, and in many cases, the elegance these travelers desire.

FRONT OFFICE SEMANTICS

Upscale limited-service hotel: Lodging property within the limited-service segment that offers a wide range of property and within-room amenities designed to provide high levels of comfort, convenience, and elegance.

Popular upscale brands include Marriott's TownePlace Suites, U.S. Franchise System's Hawthorn Hotels and Suites, and Candlewood's Candlewood Suites. In many markets, these properties target their sales efforts to the extended-stay guest, the transient corporate market, or both.

Upscale limited-service hotels typically offer all of the guest services and amenities offered at mid-price properties as well as one or more of the following:

- Substantially upgraded room furnishings and decor
- Multipurpose suites
- Hot breakfasts in addition to continental breakfasts
- Upgraded in-room amenities, (soaps, shampoos and other toiletries)
- Personal shopping and laundry services
- High-speed Internet access
- In-room safes
- On-premise laundry facilities
- On-premise convenience stores

Traditionally, hotel guests have been classified as either with a **group** (often defined as 10 or more rooms reserved per night) or as a **transient** (traveling alone). These classifications are useful when examining the characteristics of the limited-service hotel guest.

FRONT OFFICE SEMANTICS

Group (type of guest): Large number of guests sharing a common characteristic who are staying at a property at the same time. Groups may receive special rates, amenities, and privileges because of the increased revenue that they generate. Also called *tour group.*

Transient (guest): Guest who is not part of a group. Transient guests can be subdivided by traveler demographics to gain more detailed information about the type of guests staying at a property.

Many group travelers enjoy the convenience and generally lower costs offered by limited-service hotels. Tour bus operators find that many clients want to eat in well-known, popular, local restaurants when traveling and do not want to pay the price required to stay at a full-service hotel. These travelers also want to visit local attractions rather than spend time in elaborate hotel facilities. For groups such as these, limited-service hotels offer great value.

Other groups that routinely prefer limited-service hotels include visiting sports teams, religious and fraternal organizations, and social groups. Another important source of business for many limited-service properties arises from large groups staying in full-service convention hotels. A nearby limited-service hotel may be asked to house the groups' **overflow** and would likely find it advantageous to do so.

FRONT OFFICE SEMANTICS

Overflow (hotel): Guestrooms that are part of a larger group booking that cannot be accommodated by a single hotel. Room rates for overflow rooms are often established at a rate similar to that of the hosting hotel.

Transient guests rent the largest number of guestrooms offered by limited-service hotels. Traditionally, these guests are classified as corporate or leisure travelers. Nearly all the limited-service hotel brands market to both types of guests. A hotel's location, amenities offered, and pricing structure significantly affect its ability to attract such guests.

Corporate travelers travel on business or because of their jobs. Limited-service properties have been successful in attracting corporate travelers who

- are self-employed and want to control travel costs,
- work for the government, military, or a nonprofit organization that establishes **per diem** levels,
- must stay in one location for several days,
- want to stay at or near the specific location of a limited-service hotel, or
- are attracted by the highway locations of many limited-service hotels.

FRONT OFFICE SEMANTICS

Corporate traveler: Guest who is traveling on business or because of his or her job.

Per diem: Fixed dollar amount per day that a traveler will be reimbursed for a hotel room, meals, or both; the amount is determined by the traveler's employer and may differ by travel destination.

Leisure travelers are traveling for pleasure or other nonwork-related activities. Examples include vacationers, family members attending family events, and highway travelers enroute to and from their destinations. Leisure travelers are an important part of the customer base of most limited-service hotels. Increasingly, these guests are loyal to a specific brand because of a frequent-traveler program benefit. As the Internet becomes more accessible, travelers are using it to book their own room reservations. Price plays an important part in these guests' decisions about where to stay, as does location and perception of brand quality.

HOW WOULD YOU CLASSIFY THESE HOTELS?

Hotel rooms can be exotic and unusual. Consider the following:

- *Earth-ships.* Solar homes called earth-ships built of mostly recycled materials (including earth-rammed automobile tires) can be rented near Taos, New Mexico. No supplemental utilities are needed, and food grows inside the homes. (www.earthship.org)
- *Dive hotel.* Want to live 21 feet below the sea's surface in a mangrove location near Key Largo, Florida? Guests scuba dive to the lodge, enter a "wet" room at the bottom (air pressure keeps the water from rising), and enter a habitat with television, telephone, air conditioning, and a kitchen. Large windows allow guests to view undersea life. (www.jul.com)
- *Cave bed and breakfast.* A large suite (1,700 square feet) carved out of solid rock sits under a cliff and has a view of the surrounding area. (www.bbonline.com/nm/kokopelli)
- *Tree house.* This guestroom is located 50 feet off the ground in a gigantic cedar tree. It has two double beds, a kitchen, dining room, and bath. Animals in the surrounding area provide viewing pleasure. (www.cedarcreektreehouse.com)
- *Covered wagon or teepee housing.* These options are available at a ranch hostel. Bathroom facilities are separate. (www.vashonhostel.com)
- *Ice hotel.* This hotel located near Fairbanks, Alaska, has eight rooms, a bar, and an ice sculpture gallery. Guests can soak in outdoor springs—weather permitting. (www.chenahotsprings.com)

- *Lighthouse.* This bed and breakfast in Minnesota features a room overlooking the shores of Lake Superior. Guests become assistant lighthouse keepers for the night and check the rotation of the light and chart passing boats and weather patterns. (www.lighthousebb.org)

Extended-Stay Hotels

The **extended-stay hotel** segment began when Marriott's Residence Inn brand was established in the United States in the 1980s. This segment is growing quickly, having expanded nearly fivefold between 1995 and 2002. Sometimes **all-suite hotels** are classified as extended-stay properties. When these properties that offer only **suites** are included, the extended-stay segment represents approximately 10 percent of the entire hotel market.

FRONT OFFICE SEMANTICS

Extended-stay hotel: Mid-price limited-service hotel marketing to guests desiring accommodations for extended time periods (generally a week or longer).

All-suite hotel: Lodging property in which all guestrooms are suites.

Suite: Hotel guestroom in which the living area is separated from the sleeping area.

A typical extended-stay hotel consists of 80 to 100 medium to very large suites. Many offer a fitness center and a swimming pool or spa. The guestrooms are usually 350 (or more) square feet in size and typically include a living area, recliner-type chair, coffee table, television with remote control and cable, voice mail with free local calls, and a computer data port. Foodservice amenities include a separate kitchen with a coffeemaker, refrigerator, microwave, cooking and dining utensils, a stove, and a dining table with chairs. The sleeping area generally has a king- or queen-size bed and a dresser; also, there may be an additional pull-out sleeper sofa in the suite.

The objective of an extended-stay facility is to make guests feel as at home as possible during their (extended) stay. This is accomplished by the exterior and interior architecture of the hotel facility itself, by the design of guestrooms and suites, and by the service levels provided by the hotel's staff.

The advantages of staying in an extended-stay hotel instead of, for example, an apartment include regular housekeeping services, complimentary breakfasts (in many properties), and free use of amenities such as a swimming pool and exercise facilities. In addition, an extended-stay hotel guest does not incur the cost of utility deposits (e.g., telephone, electricity, gas, water, and cable) normally incurred by an apartment dweller. Extended-stay guests, especially those who are not sure how long they will be in the community, appreciate the lack of long-term leases. For many guests, then, advantages of staying in a hotel outweigh a cost per night that may be somewhat higher than the costs of an apartment.

Why might a guest need or want to stay at a hotel for a long period of time? Consider, for instance, a family whose home has been damaged by a fire. The family probably did not intend to become long-term guests, but it is likely to be several weeks (or more) before the family home is repaired. Consider a retired couple who stays for several months in the same hotel to enjoy recreational activities, restaurants, and shopping. Other typical guests may be privately employed subcontractors, corporate employees on extended assignments, people relocating or building or remodeling a home, and travelers on long-term vacations. Whether they stay because

Groups use hotel facilities for meeting of various types.

of circumstances, choice, or work, long-term guests look for the specific features offered by hotels in the extended-stay segment.

Convention Hotels and Conference Centers

Convention hotels are specifically designed to meet the lodging and meeting needs of large groups, whereas conference centers are designed for the meeting-related needs of small groups. This singular focus on group activities most distinguishes these two types of facilities from other segments in the lodging industry.

FRONT OFFICE SEMANTICS

Convention hotel: Lodging property with extensive and flexible meeting and exhibition spaces that markets to associations, corporations, and other groups bringing people together for meetings.

The needs of group travelers visiting a hotel or conference center differ markedly from those of individual travelers. Group travelers typically require adequate function space, breakout rooms for small-group activities, large dining areas, and group entertainment and activity areas.

The most common facility requirement for group gatherings is an adequate number of appropriately sized **function rooms.** Convention hotels contain thousands (and sometimes hundreds of thousands!) of square feet of space that can easily be separated into function rooms of almost any size needed by any group. For example, a large ballroom may be capable of seating several thousand persons. At the other extreme, a small **hospitality suite** can provide selected group members with a quiet getaway after a busy day of meetings.

FRONT OFFICE SEMANTICS

Function room: Public space—including meeting rooms, conference areas, and ballrooms (which can be subdivided into smaller spaces)—for banquets, meetings, or other group rental purposes.

Hospitality suite: Private guestroom of sufficient size to provide meeting space and food and beverage service for a small group of guests.

A convention hotel or conference center must also provide breakout rooms for a group. Consider a group of 1,000 attendees who must meet at 8:00 a.m. for a general session. Later, they must break into 10 groups of 100 for special sessions. The property hosting this group must have the facilities available to seat the 1,000 attendees in one area, as well as 10 additional breakout rooms with capacity for at least 100 persons in each room.

Groups also require special services that are often provided only by convention hotels and conference centers. Before a meeting begins, staff at a convention hotel or conference center help with guestroom reservations, schedule function spaces, plan meals and related functions, and coordinate many other activities. Before the meeting, services may include help in planning transportation to and from the facility, local entertainment activities, and sightseeing excursions. During the meeting, convention hotel or conference center professionals assist the group with welcoming and registering attendees. Function rooms must be set and refreshed, and audiovisual, sound, and lighting needs must be addressed. Added services may be scheduling and coordinating speakers and managing recognition or certification procedures related to meeting attendance. Food and beverage services and dining area decorations must be planned and provided. (The quality of food and beverage service is often a deciding factor when a meeting planner selects a facility.) After the meeting has concluded, convention hotel or conference center staff total and document the charges incurred. They know that timely and professional billing and collection activities are critical to a meeting's financial success and to rebooking the group's future meetings.

Three of the largest markets for group meetings are associations, government and nonprofit organizations, and corporations. **Professional associations** meet because of the common interest of their members. For example, the American Culinary Federation (ACF) is the association for professional chefs and culinarians, and the Hospitality Sales and Marketing Association International (HSMAI) is the professional association for those involved in the industry's sales and marketing efforts. Nearly every profession has formed a group for its members. Professional associations typically hold annual conventions, quarterly or monthly meetings, professional development and awards meetings, and training sessions.

FRONT OFFICE SEMANTICS

Professional association: Group of persons who affiliate to promote common interests (which may or may not include business).

There are thousands of business groups whose members have formed a **trade association** to advance their own business and industry goals. Examples in the hospitality industry include the National Restaurant Association (NRA) and the American Hotel & Lodging Association (AH&LA). Groups such as these may have national, regional, and state **chapters,** all of which may convene meetings.

FRONT OFFICE SEMANTICS

Trade association: Group of persons who affiliate because of common business or industry concerns.

Chapter (association): Group that is a subset of an association. Chapters are often formed on the basis of geography (e.g., a state association chapter is a subset of a national association).

The market for government meetings is also large. Government agencies and employees at the federal, state, and local levels meet for training, policy development, and planning purposes. There are also a wide variety of nonprofit organizations that advance a cause of interest to the membership. Examples include the United Auto Workers (a labor union) and the Sierra Club (a group that advances environmental causes).

Businesses meet in convention hotels and conference centers to provide training, to introduce new products to sales personnel, to plan strategies, and to reward employees or customers. Transportation, lodging, and dining expenses related to meetings for business purposes may be tax deductible. Many companies plan meetings to allow attendees to mix business with pleasure. Meeting sites are selected that can service meetings and provide minivacations for employees and customers.

Resorts and Time-Shares

Resorts exist in nearly every part of the world. In many instances, they are open year-round. In other cases, a resort is operated as a **seasonal hotel.**

FRONT OFFICE SEMANTICS

Seasonal hotel: Hotel whose revenues and expenditures vary greatly depending on the time (season) of the year. For example, ski resorts are busy in winter months and lake resorts in the northern part of the United States are busy in summer months. Many seasonal resorts are open for only part of the year.

A ski resort is one type of seasonal property.

Many travelers like to visit exciting places and to engage in recreational or leisure activities that are not possible in their everyday lives. Resorts, unlike their hotel counterparts, are often a traveler's destination, rather than a resting place on the way to a destination. Tourists represent a large percentage of the guests visiting resorts, but they are joined by people who are attending corporate meetings and conventions. Groups often hold their meetings in resort locations, and this allows participants (and, increasingly, their families) to mix business with pleasure during their stay. Resorts are a unique segment of the hotel market because of the seasonality of their business (in many locations), a dependence on location, and the availability of leisure activities beyond those normally provided by a hotel.

Sometimes guests enjoy their stay at a resort or in an area so much that they want to return frequently. Because of this market of guests who return frequently, some developers build time-share properties. In addition, some owners convert all or part of their properties to time-shares. Buyers of a time-share do not typically occupy the same room during each visit. Instead, they know that a room of a specific type will be available. Most time-shares have been built on ocean-front property, near mountains (for skiing), or around lakes (for water-related sports).

Time-sharing involves the right to use specific weeks of a resort during a specific time period. Essentially, it is the prepurchase of future vacation weeks. Most vacation ownerships consist of either a **deeded interest** or a **leased interest** for a specific number of years. In the United States, virtually all time-shares are deeded interests; in effect, buyers purchase access to real estate that is owned outright forever. Time-share ownership is an absolute right that can be sold or passed on to the owner's heirs. Therefore, a time-share owner may legally use, sell, rent, give away, donate, or will a time-share much as the owner of a private home or other real estate property might do. By contrast, a leased interest in a time-share is like renting an apartment, except the right to use the space is restricted to a specific week (or weeks) during the year. When the lease expires, the right to control the space reverts to the resort's owners.

FRONT OFFICE SEMANTICS

Deeded interest (time-share): Ownership in perpetuity that can be sold or passed on to the owner's heirs.

Leased interest (time-share): Right limited to a length of time (e.g., 10 years); when the lease expires, ownership (access) expires.

Exchanging ownership on an occasional or more frequent basis can bring variety and flexibility to vacation experience. Now that well-known hotel operators such as Disney, Hilton, and Marriott offer time-share alternatives, the option to exchange units is a major reason many people consider purchasing a time-share. Potential advantages to time-share ownership include these:

- Savings from not paying high guestroom rental rates for days the time-share unit is used
- Opportunity to trade time intervals with others through exchange programs
- Potential for financial gain from the appreciation of real estate values (time-share ownerships can be sold)

Guests who use resorts and time-shares do so primarily for pleasure and are attracted to a specific property because of its location, reputation and property, and local activities.

SECTION REVIEW AND DISCUSSION QUESTIONS

Section Objective: Provide an overview of common ways to classify hotels.

Section Summary: Hotels can be classified by location, by rate, and by size. They can also be classified by considering the types of guests who use them: full-service hotels, limited-service hotels, extended-stay hotels, convention hotels and conference centers, and resorts and time-shares.

Discussion Questions:

1. What types of factors do you consider when you make a decision about staying at a lodging property?
2. What impact, if any, does the purpose of your visit (to the property or the community) have on your decision?
3. What are your expectations as a guest staying at a full-service hotel, a limited-service hotel, an extended-stay property, a convention hotel or conference center, or a resort or time-share?
4. If you were the manager of a full-service hotel and thought you were losing market share to a nearby limited-service property, what practical tactics might you use to increase the sale of your guestrooms?

ORGANIZATION OF HOTELS

As the number of rooms in a hotel increases, the number of staff members required increases and positions become more specialized. It is difficult to generalize about the organization of hotels or a department such as front office within them. Two hotels of the same size, and even operated by the same company, may use different positions, include different tasks within positions or establish different reporting relationships in efforts to most effectively serve their guests. As noted in Roadmap 1.3, the information in this section will give you an idea of who does what in a front office. In the process, this section provides an introduction to staff members' responsibilities and activities, which will be described in detail in subsequent chapters of the book.

Let's begin by reviewing the **organization charts** for hotels of three sizes: a small property with fewer than 75 rooms, a large hotel with 350 rooms, and a mega hotel with 3,000 rooms.

FRONT OFFICE SEMANTICS

Organization chart: Diagram depicting the departments in an organization along with (usually) the management and nonmanagement positions within each department.

Small, Limited-Service Hotel

Figure 1.6 is an organization chart for a limited-service property with approximately 75 rooms. The property owner may be the general manager who performs many functions involved with marketing and sales, human resources, and purchasing. In larger properties, these functions are assigned to specialized positions. A bookkeeper or

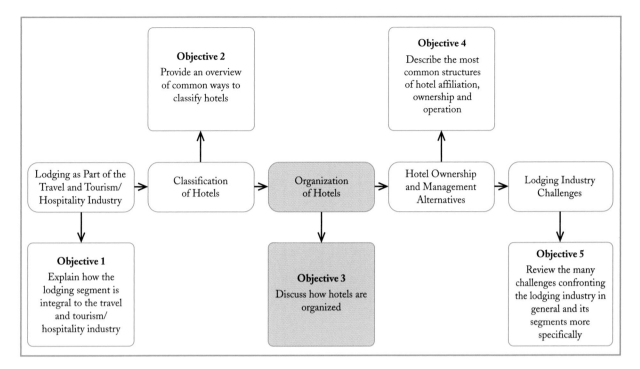

ROADMAP 1.3

accountant (typically working part time) may complete financial reports and tax returns. One or more maintenance persons are available for routine maintenance and repair tasks. (Work that requires extensive knowledge or specialized equipment is outsourced.) A front office manager supervises the staff working at the front desk. These entry-level employees perform duties such as reservations, and guest registration and payment, and they may have other service responsibilities that require full-time staff members in larger properties. A housekeeping supervisor directs the work of entry-level staff who clean the hotel's guestrooms and public spaces.

Large, Full-Service Hotel

Figure 1.7 shows the formal organization of a large, full-service hotel. With its increased sized, specialists **(department heads)** become necessary to perform front

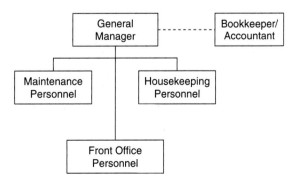

FIGURE 1.6   Organization chart for small, limited-service hotel.

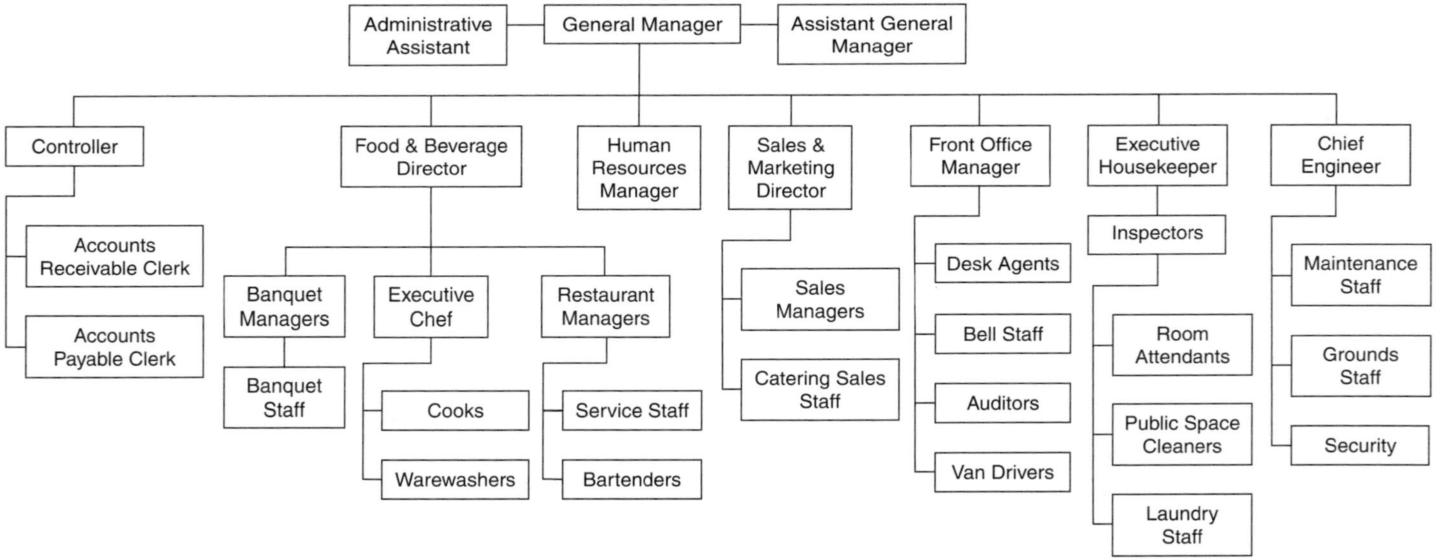

FIGURE 1.7 Organization chart for large (350 room), full-service hotel.

Source: Hayes, D. K., and J. D. Ninemeier. 2004. *Hotel Operations Management*, p. 24. Upper Saddle River, NJ: Pearson Prentice Hall. Reprinted by permission.

office functions and housekeeping, food and beverage, safety and security, engineering and maintenance, marketing and accounting, and other functions. Department heads, in turn, often require assistance from **managers** and **supervisors** who manage the day-to-day work of entry-level staff members.

FRONT OFFICE SEMANTICS

Department head: Individual responsible to a higher-level executive such as hotel general manager or resident manager for all property activities related to a specific function such as front office, food and beverage, accounting, human resources, sales and marketing, housekeeping, maintenance and engineering, and security.

Manager: Staff member who directs the work of supervisors.

Supervisor: Staff member who directs the work of entry-level employees.

When reviewing Figure 1.7 notice how the responsibilities and activities of front office personnel have become more specialized. Instead of one (or a few) employees basically performing all required tasks, there are now desk agents **bell services attendants,** auditors, and van drivers.

FRONT OFFICE SEMANTICS

Bell services attendant: Entry-level hotel employee who assists guests with luggage and who may deliver newspapers, dry cleaning, and other guest-related incidentals to guestrooms. Also called *bell staff.*

Mega Hotel

Figure 1.8A, 1.8B and 1.8C are the organization charts for a mega hotel with several thousand guestrooms. The number and type of positions have increased significantly from the chart of the 350-room property depicted in Figure 1.7. Note, for example, that a rooms division director is responsible to a resident manager (who reports to the property's general manager). The rooms division director, in turn, directs the work of an executive housekeeper, a front office manager, and a night manager. The front office manager directs the work of an assistant front office manager, a **PBX (telephone)** supervisor, and a reservations supervisor. Figure 1.8 also identifies the positions supervised by the assistant front office manager (i.e., front office supervisor, uniformed services manager, and head cashier) and the positions that are the ultimate responsibility of the night manager (i.e., night supervisor, **night auditors,** and night clerks). Figure 1.8 also indicates that the responsibilities of the uniformed services manager include supervising the work of the concierge staff, bell services manager (who is responsible for bell services attendants), door and parking attendants, and van drivers.

FRONT OFFICE SEMANTICS

PBX (private broadcast exchange): System in the hotel used to process incoming, internal, and outgoing telephone calls.

Night auditor: Front office employee who performs the daily review of guest transactions recorded by the front office.

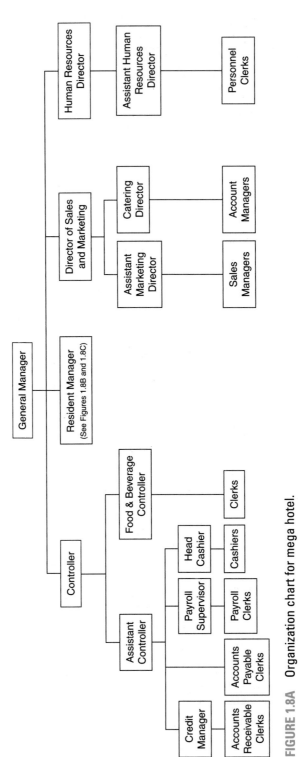

FIGURE 1.8A Organization chart for mega hotel.

Adapted from Hayes, D. K., and J. D. Ninemeier. 2004. *Hotel Operations Management*, pp. 25–27. Upper Saddle River, NJ: Pearson Prentice Hall. Reprinted by permission.

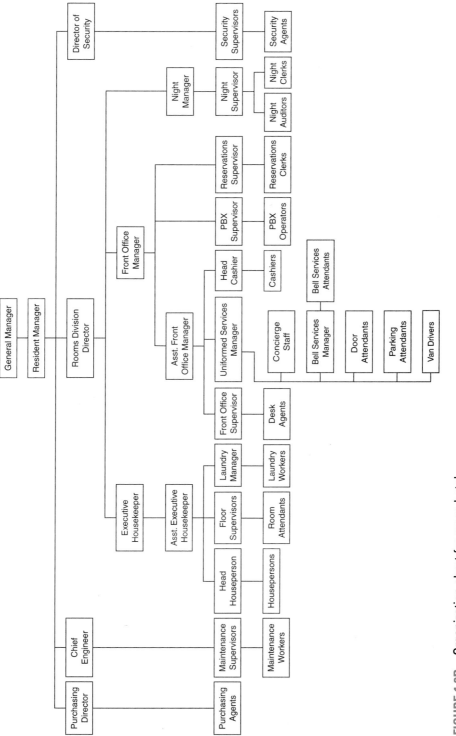

FIGURE 1.8B Organization chart for mega hotel.

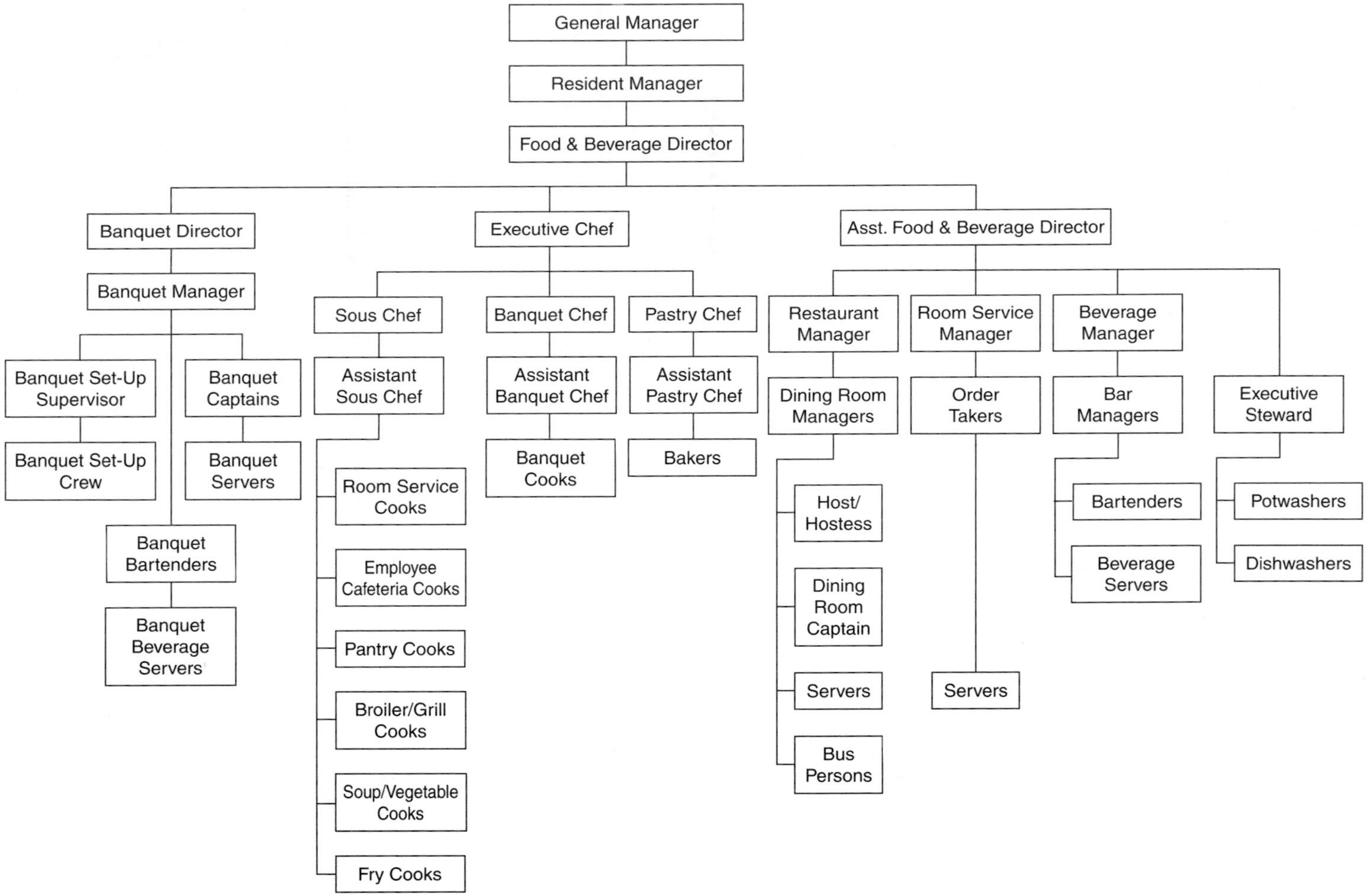

FIGURE 1.8C Organization chart for mega hotel.

HOTEL LINE AND STAFF DEPARTMENTS

Line departments are those involved in the hotel's chain of command. Managers in these departments make direct operating decisions that affect the success of the property. The front office and food and beverage departments are examples of line departments.

Staff departments provide specialized and technical assistance to managers in line departments. Typical staff departments in a hotel include purchasing, human relations, and accounting. Purchasing staff buy items needed by line menu planners; human resources personnel provide staff needed by managers of line departments and provide technical advice about labor laws and training; accounting personnel develop accounting systems, collect financial information, record data in financial statements, and make recommendations to (but do not make decisions for) line decision makers.

FRONT OFFICE SEMANTICS

Line department: Hotel division that is in the chain of command and directly responsible for generating revenues (such as front office and food and beverage department) or for property operations (such as housekeeping and maintenance and engineering).

Staff department: Hotel division such as human resources, purchasing, and accounting that provides technical, supportive assistance to managers of line-departments.

SECTION REVIEW AND DISCUSSION QUESTIONS

Section Objective: Discuss how hotels are organized.

Section Summary: Hotels, regardless of size (number of rooms), are organized by functions that include general hotel management, front office, control (accounting), engineering and maintenance, housekeeping, and marketing and sales. In small properties, one staff member has responsibilities that will likely be split among several managers in a larger property. For example, the front office manager in a small property may be responsible for the front desk, cashier, uniformed services, night audit, PBX, and reservations activities, but these activities would represent specialized positions in larger properties. Similarly, small-property managers must assume purchasing and human resources duties that would be performed by specialists in larger operations.

Discussion Questions:
1. From the perspective of a department manager, what are the advantages and disadvantages of working in a large property with specialized management positions? What are the advantages and disadvantages of working as a department head in a small property where many responsibilities must be combined into one position?
2. Review the section of Figure 1.8 that addresses the general responsibilities of the front office manager. What are the ideal experience and education require-

ments for someone in this position? To what extent must the front office manager know and be able to perform the various tasks performed by those in subordinate positions?

3. Assume a person has experience as a front office manager in a small, limited-service hotel (see Figure 1.6). What might be a starting position and a career plan for this individual if he or she begins to work in a mega hotel?

HOTEL OWNERSHIP AND MANAGEMENT ALTERNATIVES

A motorist driving along the highway sees a building with a sign indicating that it is a hotel in a popular **hotel chain.** The name is recognizable because of an extensive nationwide advertising campaign. The driver's thought is likely to be, "That hotel company purchased some land and built another hotel to operate in this location." In fact, that is not likely the case. More likely, an independent investor or company hired a developer to build the property on owned (or leased) land and signed an agreement with those who own the brand to operate the hotel in a manner consistent with that brand's standards. In many cases, the investor retains a third party to manage the hotel.

FRONT OFFICE SEMANTICS

Hotel chain: Group of hotels with the same brand name.

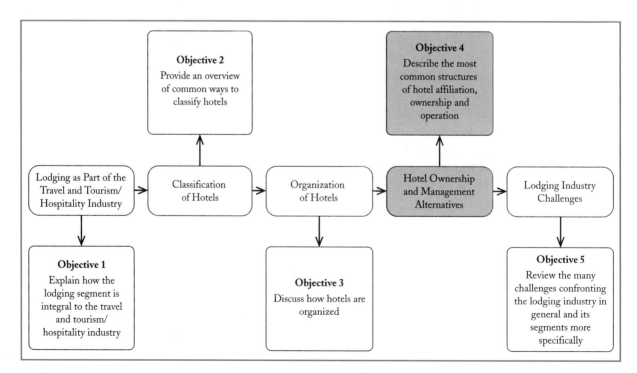

ROADMAP 1.4

Best Western is a well-known hotel brand.

Roadmap 1.4 indicates that this chapter's overview of the lodging industry now continues with a discussion of hotel ownership and management alternatives, the most common of which are illustrated in Figure 1.9. Let's look at Figure 1.9 closely. First, note that a hotel may or may not be affiliated with a **franchise.**

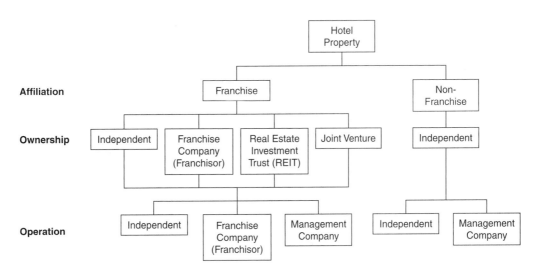

FIGURE 1.9   Hotel ownership and management alternatives.

Adapted from Hayes, D. K., and J. D. Ninemeier. 2004. *Hotel Operations Management*, p. 22. Upper Saddle River, NJ: Pearson Prentice Hall. Reprinted by permission.

FRONT OFFICE SEMANTICS

Franchise: Arrangement whereby one party (the brand) allows another party (the hotel's owners) to use its logo, name, systems, and resources in exchange for a fee.

If a property is affiliated with a franchise, it may be owned by an **independent operator** or by other entities such as a **franchisor,** a **real estate investment trust (REIT)** or a **joint venture.**

FRONT OFFICE SEMANTICS

Independent operator: Entrepreneur who owns or operates one or a few hospitality properties. Sometimes referred to as owning a *mom-and-pop property.*

Franchisor: Company that manages the brand and sells the right to use the brand name. Some franchisors own and operate hotels as well as sell use of the brand name to others.

Real estate investment trust (REIT): Public corporation that sells stock to raise money (capital) that is then used to purchase real estate, including hotels.

Joint venture: Partnership composed of organizations such as corporations, governments, or other entities, that is formed to develop a lodging brand or property.

The franchised hotel can be operated by the independent operator, the franchise company (franchisor), or by a **management company.**

FRONT OFFICE SEMANTICS

Management company: Organization that operates one or more hotels for a fee. Sometimes called a *contract company* or a *contract management company.*

Figure 1.9 also indicates that a hotel property may not be franchised; it can be operated without affiliation to a franchisor. Nonfranchised properties are typically owned by one or more persons (independents) who operate the property or retain the services of a management company for day-to-day operation.

DO YOU WANT TO OWN A HOTEL?

If you want to own a hotel, you have several alternatives:

- You can own a single-unit property that is not affiliated with any brand. Some single-unit properties have been in business for years, are extremely successful, and may be the preeminent hotel in a community or area.
- You can own a single-unit property affiliated with a brand. Properties that are part of a hotel chain are most prevalent. Brand affiliations—whether international, nationwide, regional, or even located within a smaller area—are successful because of name recognition. Also, business financing may be easier to obtain when a proposed hotel will be affiliated with a brand.
- You can own multiunit properties affiliated with the same brand. Some businesspersons own several hotels and affiliate all of them with the same brand. Often this makes managing the hotels easier, because the expectations of the brand's owners are well-known.

- You can own multiunit properties affiliated with different brands. An owner who has more than one hotel in the same market area may believe that a business decision to build two hotels with the same brand in that area would not be a good one. Or, an owner may have both limited- and full-service hotels, and the same brand is not available for both types of properties.
- You can own one or more properties that are or are not affiliated with a franchise and have the properties operated by someone else. For a fee, some brands will offer management services to hotel owners. Also, management companies that do not own brands or hotels provide management services for a fee.

SECTION REVIEW AND DISCUSSION QUESTIONS

Section Objective: Describe the most common structures of hotel affiliation, ownership, and operation.

Section Summary: A specific hotel property may (or may not) be affiliated with a franchise. If it is, it may be owned by an independent, a franchisor, a REIT, or a joint venture. If it is not franchised, the property is typically owned by an independent. Franchised properties can be operated by an independent, a franchisor, or a management company. Nonfranchised properties are operated by an independent or a management company.

Discussion Questions:
1. If you want to own a hotel, what factors should you consider as you decide whether to affiliate with a franchise company or remain nonaffiliated?
2. If you are an independent hotel owner, what factors will help you decide whether to operate it independently or to affiliate with a management company?
3. What, if any, impact does a specific hotel's affiliation, ownership, or operation have on an individual guest?

LODGING INDUSTRY CHALLENGES

Significant challenges now confront the hotel industry. As noted in Roadmap 1.5, this chapter concludes with a discussion of some of the operating, marketing, technological, and economic challenges faced by all segments of the lodging industry. These are previewed in Figure 1.10.

Broad-Based Challenges (All Segments)

Operating Issues

- *Labor shortages.* Hoteliers in almost every geographic location consider labor shortages among the most difficult challenges they face. In some instances, hotel expansion is limited not by capital (money) but by human resources.

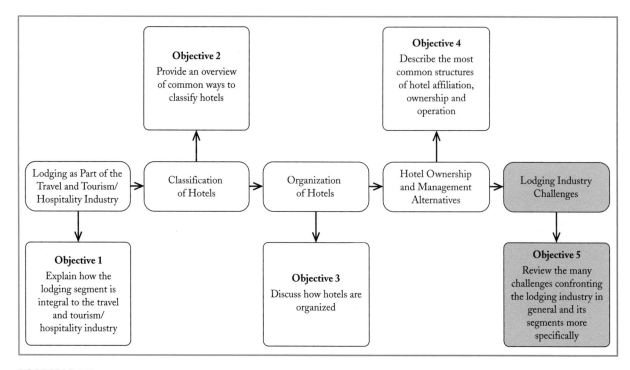

ROADMAP 1.5

- *Cost containment.* Hoteliers are increasingly challenged to find ways to reduce costs without sacrificing the quality standards that have been established to meet their guests' expectations. The challenge to "do more with less" requires managers to think about ways of operating more effectively and to examine possibilities for cost savings that do not affect guests' perception of value.

Type of challenge	Specific concerns
Operating	• Labor shortages • Cost containment
Marketing	• Increased competition • Market segmentation and overlapping brands • Increased guest sophistication and desire for amenities
Technological	• Third-party wholesalers • Interactive reservation systems • Guestroom innovations • Data mining • Yield management
Economic	• Dependence on a nation's economy • Globalization • Terrorism and safety

FIGURE 1.10   Challenges confronting the lodging industry.

- *Increased competition.* Hoteliers everywhere indicate that their community is **overbuilt**: There are too many hotel rooms available relative to the guests desiring to rent them. Tactics that involve price-cutting to provide greater guest value reduce profit further.

FRONT OFFICE SEMANTICS

Overbuilt: Condition that exists when there are too many hotel guestrooms available for the number of travelers wanting to rent them.

Marketing Issues

- *Market segmentation and overlapping brands.* **Market segmentation** is increasing as lodging chains focus on ever-decreasing niches of travelers. Additionally, brands overlap. Some observers are concerned that franchisors may expand their number of brands to the point that investors who purchase from the same franchisor may be in direct competition with themselves! Also, as the number of brands increases, the ability of consumers to differentiate between them decreases.

FRONT OFFICE SEMANTICS

Market segmentation: Efforts to focus on a highly defined (smaller) group of travelers.

- *Increased guest sophistication.* Consumers have become more sophisticated, and so have the types of products and services that they desire. Amenities such as business centers, exercise and recreational facilities, and guestroom innovations increase costs. If amenities are not selected carefully, they may not appeal to the guests being served by a specific property.

MODERN FRONT OFFICE ISSUES AND TACTICS

Whose Hotel Is That, Anyway?

Hotels offer frequent-guest programs to encourage travelers to return to the hotels' brands. However, a study by Phoenix Marketing International has indicated that no member of the Hilton H. Honors, Radisson Gold Rewards, or Starwood Preferred Guest Programs could identify all of the Hilton, Radisson, or Starwood hotel brands participating in the respective programs. By contrast, organizations with greater member awareness were LaQuinta, Red Roof, Wyndham, and Hyatt. Perhaps by coincidence, the latter organizations have fewer brands than the previously mentioned groups. According to this study, 32 percent of the 4,000 hotel frequent-guests surveyed indicated that the hotel frequent-guest program influenced them all most or some of the time. Therefore, it is important for hotel frequent-guest programs to effectively communicate the lodging brands that participate in their programs.

Source: Phoenix Marketing International. Identity problem for some of the hotel industry's biggest frequent guest programs: Members cannot correctly identify all of the hotel brands within. Retrieved June 24, 2004, from http://www.hotel-online.com.

Technological Issues

The challenge of keeping up with the fast pace of technology is difficult and expensive.

- *Third-party wholesalers.* Hotel room availability and pricing information can be seen by potential guests on thousands of Web sites, as hotels sell inventory to wholesalers. Determining the number of rooms to assign to third parties and the price these wholesalers will be charged has become an increasingly complex challenge.
- *Interactive reservation systems.* Guests can now use the Internet to make reservations directly with a hotel.
- *Guestroom innovations.* Multiple telephone lines, Internet access, interactive opportunities for ordering room service, and guestroom check-out are examples of amenities that guests increasingly desire but that are expensive to install and implement.
- *Data mining.* The technology of **data mining** allows marketing and sales personnel to find new ways to use guest-related data.

FRONT OFFICE SEMANTICS

Data mining: Using technology to analyze guest-related and other data to make better marketing decisions.

- *Yield management.* The semicomputerized process of **yield management** allows managers to match guest demand with room rates. High demand allows no discounts or lessened discounts from rack rates; low demand results in higher discounts from rack rates.

FRONT OFFICE SEMANTICS

Yield management: Demand forecasting system designed to maximize revenue by holding room rates high during times of high guestroom demand and by decreasing room rates during times of lower guestroom demand.

Economic Issues

- *Dependence on a nation's economy.* When a nation's economy is good, business travel generally increases. **Hotel occupancy rates** and rack rates increase, which results in higher profit levels. The reverse is also true: Business travel slows when the economy slows, and occupancy and rack rates decrease. Discounts are offered to increase occupancy, which yields lower revenues and decreased profits.

FRONT OFFICE SEMANTICS

Hotel occupancy rate: Ratio of guestrooms sold (including complimentary rooms) to guestrooms available for sale in a given time period. Always expressed as a percentage, the formula for occupancy rate is as follows:

Number of guestrooms sold ÷ Number of guestrooms available

- *Globalization.* **Globalization** has affected the lodging industry dramatically, because it influences the extent to which people travel within a country and around the world. It is not only the economy of the country where lodging properties are located, but the economies of countries worldwide, that are playing an increasingly greater role in the financial success of the properties.

FRONT OFFICE SEMANTICS

Globalization: Condition in which countries throughout the world and communities within them are becoming increasingly interrelated.

- *Terrorism and safety.* Fear of travel after the attacks on the World Trade Center and the Pentagon on September 11, 2001, and worldwide concerns about **terrorism** have brought safety issues to the forefront of every segment of the hotel industry. The issue of terrorism, though beyond hoteliers' control, will be of significant concern for the foreseeable future.

FRONT OFFICE SEMANTICS

Terrorism: Threat of danger and actual harm caused by persons for political or religious reasons.

Segment-Specific Challenges

Some challenges are important to specific segments of the lodging industry. These challenges are outlined in Figure 1.11.

Segment	Challenges
Full-service hotels	• Increased competition from limited-service hotels • Increased costs to operate foodservices • Rising construction costs • Difficulties in developing a unified Internet marketing strategy
Limited-service hotels	• Increased guest expectations (budget and mid-price properties) • Fewer profitable locations • Brand proliferation • Conflicts between franchisors and franchisees
Extended-stay hotels	• Too many hotels within segment • Overreliance on corporate travel • Competing in a multicompetitor environment
Convention hotels and conference centers	• High construction costs • Competition from nontraditional sources • Use of meeting technology
Resorts and time-shares	• Lagging productivity gains • Increased expectations about social and local economic responsibilities • Transnational competition • Developing creative time-share marketing exchange programs

FIGURE 1.11   Segment-specific challenges.

Full-Service Hotels

The maturity of the full-service hotel segment yields the advantages of highly preferred property locations, long-established operating procedures, and significant brand recognition. Nevertheless, the segment faces considerable challenges:

- *Increased competition from limited-service hotels.* The limited-service hotel segment is expanding rapidly. As a result, full-service hotels must compete with other full-service hotels and with newer (and often more modern) limited-service properties. For example, many older full-service hotels are not wired so that guests have high-speed Internet access for their computers. The cost of rewiring a property to provide this access can be immense. New, limited-service hotels, however, are routinely wired with **CAT 5 cable** (or higher quality) at little additional installation expense.

FRONT OFFICE SEMANTICS

CAT 5 cable: Category five cable; the preferred cable quality to use when providing certain forms of high-speed Internet access to a standard computer.

Complimentary (but limited) breakfast programs, larger guest bathrooms, availability of suites, and locations near emerging business areas are additional features that make limited-service hotels a challenge to full-service properties.

- *Increased costs required to operate foodservices.* It has always been difficult for a full-service hotel to make a significant profit from its food and beverage operations. This is especially true today, as labor costs often increase more quickly than do food costs. Some hotel managers address rising operating costs by leasing foodservices, increasing prices on menus, reducing service levels, or curtailing operating hours. However, it is the presence of foodservice that makes this segment of the hotel industry distinctive. Providing quality food and beverage services at prices that guests will readily accept is a critical challenge confronting full-service hotel managers.

- *Rising construction costs.* Hotel construction costs rise each year. The costs of furnishing a quality guestroom at a full-service hotel are generally no higher than those of furnishing a room at an extended-stay or a limited-service property with an **average daily rate (ADR)** in the same range. It is, however, more expensive to build a full-service hotel of any size than to construct an equal number of rooms in another type of hotel.

FRONT OFFICE SEMANTICS

Average daily rate (ADR): Average selling price of all guestrooms for a given time period. The formula for ADR is as follows:

Total room revenue ÷ Total number of rooms sold

Real estate costs are generally higher for full-service hotels because more land is needed for foodservice facilities, meeting and banquet spaces, parking, and the other amenities typically provided.

- *Difficulties in developing a unified Internet marketing strategy.* Full-service hoteliers face a unique challenge as they deal with the Internet. The many travelers who seek the lowest cost lodging rates consult the Internet. Limited-service hotels have been the major beneficiaries of the increased use of the Internet to book room reservations. Travelers simply log on to one of the many booking sites available (or even the Web site of a hotel brand) to find the property that offers the lowest rate for desired dates. The result has been a downward pressure on ADR as hotels seek to secure their share of the available market. Limited-service hotels appeal to cost-conscious travelers, so these properties benefit most from comparison shopping. In other segments of the lodging market (e.g., resort and convention hotels), the Internet's impact in reducing room rates has been less pronounced.

Limited-Service Hotels

- *Increased guest expectations (budget and mid-price properties).* The first limited-service hotels were readily accepted because of their good locations and moderate room rates. As the segment became more mature, some brand managers upgraded their organization's services and amenities (sometimes substantially). Today's guests in limited-service hotels have high expectations, even in the budget segment. Some hotels struggle to meet increasing guest expectations and brand requirements while maintaining profitable operations. In the future, guests' wants and expectations will likely increase even more; this will result in even greater managerial challenges and pressures on profit levels.

- *Fewer profitable locations.* The best real estate location for a limited-service hotel is near an interstate highway entrance or exit, a highly developed shopping or office complex, a popular recreational area, a high-density population center, or a significant local tourist attraction or other **demand generator.** Each hotel's competitors look for the same locations, so the demand for choice building sites often exceeds availability. The result is often inflated real estate costs and associated property taxes and, consequently, excessive building and operating costs.

FRONT OFFICE SEMANTICS

Demand generator: Organization, entity, or location that creates a significant need for hotel services. Examples are large businesses, tourist sites, sports stadiums, educational facilities, and manufacturing plants.

- *Brand proliferation.* When consumers clearly understand the defining characteristics of a brand name and when the demand for that brand's products is high, there is a win–win situation for consumers and for the brand. If, however, consumers are not clear about what a brand stands for (or even worse, are not familiar with a brand's defining attributes), neither the consumer nor the brand is well served.

    In the limited-service hotel business, **brand proliferation** has reached the point that consumer confusion will likely affect the segment. Unless consumers are certain about what they will receive when they select one brand over another, they are less likely to try the brand. Brand managers must attempt to influence consumers by actions such as reducing room rates, spending significant dollars on advertising and marketing, and creating highly discounted introductory room rates.

FRONT OFFICE SEMANTICS

Brand proliferation: Oversaturation of the market with different brands.

- *Conflicts between franchisors and franchisees.* Franchisors must ensure that all franchisees uphold the organization's standards of operation. Hotel owners and operators (franchisees) desire to affiliate with strong brands that will help them sell more rooms and maximize the value of their assets. Hotel operators are keenly concerned about how their franchisor manages their brand's image and operations. However, most brand managers are not directly responsible for hotel operations (they manage brand images not hotel properties). Thus, conflicts can arise about how to best position the brand in the marketplace and about what each operating hotel within the brand should do to assist in the effort. For example, assume the managers of a limited-service brand believe that their guests want irons and ironing boards in guestrooms. Assume also that no such standard exists. Brand managers believe that such an upgraded standard is desirable. Hotel owners and operators who must bear the substantial cost of buying and installing the irons and ironing boards may, however, disagree.

  The issue of who pays for brand-mandated programs and amenities is common to all segments of the hotel industry. However, such concerns are stronger in limited-service properties because of the historic strength of franchisors in setting and enforcing brand standards.

Extended-Stay Hotels

- *Too many hotels within segment.* When the first extended-stay hotels were developed in the mid 1980s, they met with immediate success. The next 15 years saw tremendous building and development within the segment, and in many areas, the segment became overbuilt. Two factors have caused a virtual halt to the extended-stay segment's growth in revenue per available room **(RevPar)** during the early 2000s: (1) the tragedy of September 11, 2001, and its resulting impact on travel, and (2) development of so many brands that consumers had difficulty recognizing which represented an extended-stay alternative. Hotel owners and managers in this market segment will likely have difficulty in finding markets that are not overbuilt and in locating lenders willing to risk financing.

FRONT OFFICE SEMANTICS

RevPar (revenue per available room): Average revenue generated by each guestroom during a given time period. The formula for RevPar is

$$\text{Occupancy \% } (\times) \text{ ADR} = \text{RevPar}$$

- *Overreliance on corporate travel.* Many extended-stay guests travel because of their work. When business is good, there are many travelers. When the economy slows, however, so does business travel. During a slow economy, the extended-stay segment, which is so dependent on business travel, suffers more than other segments of the hotel industry.

- *Competing in a Multicompetitor environment.* Nearly every hotel must compete with other hotels for guests. Extended-stay hotels are unique, however, because they face more than the normal number of competitors as they seek business from potential guests. Naturally, the extended-stay hotel must compete with other extended-stay properties. However, its most serious challenge may come from the apartment industry, which has the facilities to compete for the long-term traveler's business. In markets where apartment units are in great supply and where demand is less than supply, apartment owners who decide to target the extended-stay traveler can create significant challenges.

Convention Hotels and Conference Centers

- *High construction costs.* Convention hotels are usually much larger and, therefore, more expensive to construct than other hotels. Convention hotels require more land, more sleeping and function rooms, larger dining and food production areas, and, in many cases, extensive guest-service areas such as swimming pools and fitness center. In addition, if a convention hotel or conference center is located in a popular geographic area (e.g., a ski or beach location), the cost of property and its taxes are likely to be especially high.

- *Competition from non traditional sources.* Convention hotels and conference centers compete for business with similar properties, but they also may compete with other types of facilities. For example, limited-service hotels may have only one or two small function rooms; however, that is sufficient for small groups that need function rooms and sleeping rooms. So the larger hotels and conference centers may not book such small-group clients. Many convention hotels also face competition from city- and county-funded conference centers. A city may build a convention center that offers many of the facilities and services found within the area's convention hotels. Traditional convention hotels and conference centers in the area may experience a decline in business.

- *Use of meetings technology.* Today, advances in meeting technology offer tremendous opportunities to improve meeting services. The challenge is to keep up with rapidly changing technology. Consider high-speed Internet access. More and more groups request this service, so it simply must be available to attract and retain business. However, the cost of supplying the service to an older hotel or conference center can be significant.

    Globally, the number of hotels offering **Wi-Fi** (short for wireless fidelity) has risen from about 2,500 in 2003 to about 6,000 in 2004 (the majority of these hotels are in the United States). That number is expected to jump to more than 35,000 by 2008. Overall, the number of Wi-Fi users is also growing rapidly, from 12 million globally in 2003 to an estimated 707 million by 2008. Clearly, hotel guests want the freedom and flexibility offered by Wi-Fi technology. They want to use their laptops anywhere within the hotel, on its grounds, or even at the nearby beach.

FRONT OFFICE SEMANTICS

Wi-Fi (wireless fidelity): Internet access technology that does not use a building's wiring system when providing users Internet access.

Technological advances related to services are also significant. In the past, a hotel employee may have been called on to change a bulb in an overhead projector. Today, that same employee may need to connect multiple computers to a digital display board to allow multiscreen projection of a PowerPoint presentation. Those that manage and train employees to service the meetings business must continually increase their skill levels.

Resorts and Time-Shares

• *Lagging productivity gains.* All segments of the lodging industry require labor for guest services. Unfortunately, the industry has not enjoyed the productivity gains achieved by other industries. Productivity issues especially affect resort hotels that depend on skilled and unskilled persons in many different positions. Also, properties that hire many staff members at the beginning of a season and dismiss them at its end have special problems. The cost of recruiting and developing highly trained staff members can also create productivity problems.

If the resort and time-share segment (and the entire hotel industry) is to meet its potential, managers must devote more attention to finding ways to improve employee productivity. Then they can better use existing staff and create opportunities to employ more individuals at competitive wages.

• *Increased expectations about social and economic responsibilities.* Some locations such as those in Hawaii or Mexico can benefit from projects that yield an additional resort or time-share in an already developed tourism region. Many tourists, however, want to visit pristine or exclusive areas that are remote or exotic and where little, if any, development has occurred. Although their intentions are not to harm these areas, many tourists put demands on local labor, food supplies, and natural resources that can significantly change the areas. These changes can spoil the attributes that attracted the tourists initially. Increased demand can also cause the prices for resources to exceed the abilities of residents to afford them.

Those who build and manage resorts and time-shares are increasingly being held responsible for the potentially negative impacts that development can have on local residents and the natural environment. Responsible managers work with local officials so that the quality of life enjoyed by local residents is improved by area development.

• *Transnational competition.* Resort and time-share guests come from all over the world and from a variety of cultural backgrounds and income levels. Now they can choose from more world-class properties operated by fewer **transnational companies.**

FRONT OFFICE SEMANTICS

Transnational company: Organization with its headquarters in one country but with company operations in several other countries.

Some governments decentralize the operation of tourism-related sites by contracting with private companies to manage the sites' resort and tourism components. Governments also help fund tourism development to boost their own local economies. The number of countries hosting resort development or operations companies has increased, while the number of companies that compete on a worldwide scale has dwindled.

• *Developing creative time-share marketing and exchange programs.* Time-share purchasers are popular with relatively young (45-to 55-year old) buyers. Some observers, however, are concerned about whether the industry can develop programs to address potential drawbacks to time-share purchases such as relatively high initial purchase costs, overly aggressive sales techniques, and poor resale values during downturns in the economy.

Since the September 11, 2001, terrorist attacks, the time-share industry has learned it is relatively **recession**-proof. While hotel occupancies dwindled to virtually nothing, and airlines canceled many flights, people who owned time-shares continued to use them for vacations. After the terrorist attacks and the recession that followed, some time-share owners exchanged their access to properties far from home to properties within driving distance of their homes.

FRONT OFFICE SEMANTICS

Recession: Period of downturn in a nation's economy.

From the Front Office: Front-Line Interview

Marti Hoffman
Guest Services Manager
Fairfield Resorts Grand Desert Hotel
Las Vegas, Nevada

Only in Las Vegas!

Marti earned an undergraduate degree in business with an emphasis in information systems. She has held positions in direct sales or customer service for 15 years. She has three years of experience in the hospitality industry, the last two of which have involved front office manager responsibilities. Her present position is with a 599-room time-share property.

1. **What are the most important responsibilities in your present position?**
   My primary responsibility is to ensure that our guests are satisfied, and we do this by exceeding their expectations. First, we focus on hiring the "right" hospitality professionals (people with some with related experience). Then, we train our new staff members in a program that I am constantly improving. Like all professionals in my position, my on-going responsibilities relate to making decisions about how to best use the always limited human and fiscal resources we have available to us. It is a significant challenge to attain goals that focus on consistent delivery of quality services that our guests expect and deserve.

2. **What are the biggest challenges that confront you in your day-to-day work and in the long-term operation of your property's front office?**
   My most significant daily challenges relate to people: hotel staff and our guests. One example that involves both employees and guests involves service recovery when a guest becomes dissatisfied. Some guests will speak first to entry-level employees and then ask for the manager (me). Others will want to speak initially with the manager (me). I always hope my response will be similar to that of staff members if they were the initial point of contact. This typically is

the case because, first, we try to select front-line employees who genuinely want to please our guests. Second, our staff members have been trained in procedures to effectively deliver guest service in the first place and to effectively respond to guest service issues if they arise. I like to address the challenges of service recovery on the relatively rare occasions when they occur. I set self-imposed goals relating to how quickly I can turn the service from a bad experience to a good one without giving the house away! After all, a win–win result is the most satisfying result to the guests as well as to the property and me.

Long-term operating challenges of our property's front office involve human resources and technology. It is important to keep our staff members refreshed and enthusiastic about the work they do in general and their guest contact responsibilities more specifically. Technology is also a challenge because, as in most properties, not all systems are interfaced. I know that the time-share industry and our suppliers are working aggressively to address this issue. Our situation is compounded by the need to manage and track points based on time-share and exchange commitments. It is a challenge to keep up with the changing needs of our customers (both vacation exchange companies and our guests), and I hope tomorrow's technology will allow information flow to occur seamlessly.

3. What is your most unforgettable front office moment?
Lots of things happen in Las Vegas that probably don't happen frequently elsewhere. I vividly recall a potentially serious problem that arose when one of our guests called the front desk. He had used his room phone to meet someone from a private escort service. By the time the escort arrived and knocked on his door, the guest had changed his mind. He told her so from behind his locked door and asked her to leave. Instead, she became upset, began pounding on the door and phoned her "bodyguard" to assist in collecting the fee ($300) that was agreed on. Our guest had become frightened and called the front desk for assistance. While this was happening, the escort was making so much noise in the corridor outside the guestroom that we started to receive calls at the front desk from guests in nearby rooms.

I called a staff member from our security department, and we went to the room. We suggested to our guest that it would be in his best interest to pay the agreed-on fee. After some discussion and a voiced concern that police may need to be called to resolve the matter, this is what he did. The situation was over; the escort received payment, the bodyguard did not need to visit the hotel to further exacerbate the situation, and the guest learned a valuable lesson.

4. What advice do you have for those studying about or considering a career in front office or hotel management?
Be sure that its something you really want to do. Find an entry-level, no-experience-necessary position in any department: food and beverage, maintenance, housekeeping, front desk. You'll find that working in the hotel industry is something that you will either love or hate, and you won't know which attitude you'll have without first experiencing it.

During my experience here in Las Vegas, I have met some University of Nevada Las Vegas students who have worked at our property to complete an internship or in an entry-level job. At the end of the semester, most confirmed that they wanted to pursue a career in the lodging industry. However, some decided to change their major because they knew the industry wasn't for them. It is good that they had this initial experience so they could better direct their efforts to a career they would enjoy.

Hoteliers must love interacting with all kinds of people. They must have a service attitude, an aptitude for solving problems, and the ability to embrace the diversity that they will encounter daily. This is why I love the industry. There are never two days the same. Never! If you like an organized routine, this is not the job for you. But if you like ever-changing challenges that allow you to be creative, and if you enjoy interacting with guests and employees (this is a labor-intensive industry), the hotel industry offers a career you're likely to enjoy.

SECTION REVIEW AND DISCUSSION QUESTIONS

Section Objective: Review the many challenges confronting the lodging industry in general and its segments more specifically.

Section Summary: Figure 1.10 lists challenges confronting the lodging industry, and Figure 1.11 notes challenges confronting specific segments of the industry.

Lodging industry challenges include those relating to operating concerns such as labor shortages and increased competition, marketing concerns such as market segmentation and overlapping brands, technological concerns such as third-party wholesalers, and economic issues such as globalization and terrorism and safety. Segment-specific challenges are numerous for each segment, but two concerns affect all segments: increased costs and marketing issues related to competition and guest expectations or confusion about the crowded marketplace.

Discussion Questions:
1. Which of the challenges confronting the lodging industry do you think are most significant? Why?
2. How do you think the wants, needs, and desires of guests in each segment of the lodging industry will change, and how will these changes likely affect that segment of the industry?
3. How, if at all, is an increased use of technology likely to help hoteliers resolve the most significant challenges that confront them?

The FOM in Action: A Solution

The lodging industry consists of many different types of properties that are owned and operated in several different ways, and the properties can be affiliated with a franchisor's brand or remain unaffiliated. What are the advantages and disadvantages to working for a large lodging organization and a small one? What are the rewards and risks of being an entrepreneur and owning one or more properties?

Lorine, the FOM who was asked these questions after making a presentation at a postsecondary school, had been asked these questions before. Therefore, she was prepared to provide a well-organized response, which is summarized here.

Large lodging organization

Possible advantages
- Greater opportunity to advance and relocate
- Prestige associated with a name
- Less employment risk
- Potential for larger compensation and greater benefits
- Legal protection (Small employers may be exempt from some labor regulations.)
- More structured and effective training

Possible disadvantages
- Less control over one's work
- Belief that one may be just a "number"
- Less access to senior executives

Small lodging organization

Possible advantages

- Employees who are likely to know each other
- Greater variety of duties for employees
- Executives who tend to be more approachable
- More responsibilities for employees
- More companywide involvement
- Less bureaucracy (fewer rules and regulations)
- Potential for a job that will grow as the company grows

Possible disadvantages

- Limited benefits
- Possibility of less training
- Fewer opportunities for promotion

Entrepreneur rewards and risks

Possible rewards

- Ability to make more money
- Freedom to work when you want to
- Power to make your own decisions
- Absence of bureaucracy
- Ability to make quick decisions
- Opportunities to take risks and realize great rewards
- Reduced tax liabilities (because of small-business deductions)
- Functioning as your own boss
- Avoidance of boredom

Possible risks

- No assured level of compensation
- Need to work long hours (especially during business start-up)
- More difficulty in getting objective feedback from others
- Lack of financial resources enjoyed by an established organization
- Inadequate support when making decisions
- Personal financial losses and the need to repay losses
- Lack of corporate benefits and perks
- Need to report to many "bosses," including guests and governmental regulatory agencies
- Constant attention to being a self-starter and to remaining motivated
- A demanding schedule

FRONT OFFICE SEMANTICS LIST

Travel and tourism industry
Hospitality industry
Hotel
Resort
Full-service hotel
Time-share property
Condominium
Conference center
Camp/park lodge
Bed and breakfast inn (B&B)
Condotel
Commercial foodservice operation
Noncommercial foodservice operation
Restaurant

Caterer
Bar
Lounge
Self-operated noncommercial foodservices
Contract management company-operated noncommercial foodservices
Rack rate
Market share
Mid-price full-service hotel
Upscale full-service hotel
Concierge
Name recognition
Brand loyalty
Luxury full-service hotel

Room night
Business traveler
Leisure traveler
Limited-service hotel
Budget (economy) limited-service hotel
Continental breakfast
Mid-price limited-service hotel
Frequent-traveler program
Upscale limited-service hotel
Group (type of guest)
Transient (guest)
Overflow (hotel)
Corporate traveler
Per diem
Extended-stay hotel

All-suite hotel
Suite
Convention hotel
Function room
Hospitality suite
Professional association
Trade association
Chapter (association)
Seasonal hotel
Deeded interest (time-share)
Leased interest (time-share)
Organization chart
Department head
Manager
Supervisor

Bell services attendant
PBX (private broadcast exchange)
Night auditor
Line department
Staff department
Hotel chain
Franchise
Independent operator
Franchisor
Real estate investment trust (REIT)
Joint venture
Management company
Overbuilt

Market segmentation
Data mining
Yield management
Hotel occupancy rate
Globalization
Terrorism
CAT 5 cable
Average daily rate (ADR)
Demand generator
Brand proliferation
RevPar (revenue per available room)
Wi-Fi (wireless fidelity)
Transnational company
Recession

FRONT OFFICE AND THE INTERNET

Many Web sites allow you to keep up with the latest news about the fast-paced lodging industry. These Web sites change frequently (often each weekday), so review them regularly to remain current.

Check out one or more of the following sites:

- www.hotelnewsresource.com
- www.hospitalitynet.org
- www.hotel-online.com
- www.ahla.com
- www.hotelbusiness.com

REAL-WORLD ACTIVITIES

1. What are some similarities between work performed (1) by a restaurant manager and a hotel manager; (2) by an amusement or theme park manager and a hotel manager, and (3) by a private club manager and a hotel manager?
2. What factors might be of interest to you as a hotel owner considering affiliation with a hotel franchise organization? Why do you think that hotel franchises have grown so quickly in the United States?
3. Review the broad-based and segment-specific challenges to the lodging industry discussed in this chapter. Which do you think are the most important? Why? Are there elements that most of these challenges have in common?
4. What are the pros and cons of beginning one's hotel management career in a large hotel and in a smaller property?
5. If possible, talk with one or more front office managers or front desk agents. Determine the types of training provided to entry-level staff. (If you are able to contact a front desk agent, ask about additional topics that would have been helpful to study to more effectively prepare for the job.)

2

Front Office and the Guests: Planning for Quality Service

Chapter Outline

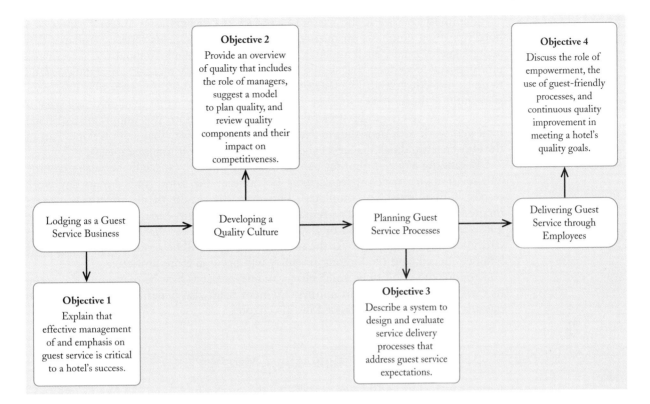

CHAPTER ROADMAP

Chapter Preview

A hotel is much more than a building with guestrooms, function areas for preparing and serving meals and beverages and for facilitating meetings. Successful hotels today differentiate themselves from their less successful counterparts with an ongoing and significant emphasis on guest service. Creative advertising, the property's brand name, or a discount incentive may be sufficient to encourage guests' first visits. However, what occurs between the time guests reach the hotel's parking lot or front door and the time they depart influences (1) their perception of the hotel, (2) their interest in returning to it (or even to another hotel of the same brand), and (3) what they say about their lodging experience to friends, family, and others.

Guest-friendly tactics should be incorporated into work processes and standard operating procedures. The front office manager (FOM) might specify how a front desk agent should meet and greet guests at the time of registration. For example, "Greet the guests by name, welcome them to the hotel, complete all registration tasks efficiently, smile, look each guest directly in the eye, and inform each guest that any hotel employee can be contacted for assistance at any time." However, the concept of the hotelier as a genteel host (i.e., refined and polite) who genuinely wants to please guests and who is empowered to perform in an extraordinary way to do so, goes beyond the dialogue and training needed to meet the goals established by the FOM in this example.

The most consistent and exemplary service is delivered as an integral aspect of a hotel's ongoing emphasis on quality. A focus on quality yields service standards that address guests' needs. Such a focus also yields an understanding about the "best" work processes and procedures that should be used to consistently meet service standards (and to do so cost-effectively). The realization that traditional work processes may need revision and that the emphasis must be on pleasing the guests rather than on doing what is easiest or least costly can be stressful to hotel staff. Therefore, it is important that hotel managers work with their staff to design quality into the way that work is done. Part of the effort is attitudinal: managers and their staff must *want* to please guests.

Beginning a quality journey can be time-consuming, especially because planning and revisions to work processes must be done at the same time day-to-day work responsibilities must be completed. However, the results of an effectively implemented and ongoing quality program can be significant. First, the majority of the guests' needs will be met. Second, a mechanism to address the unique needs of specific guests will be in place. At the same time, errors will be omitted, operating costs will be reduced, and the lodging property will become more profitable.

Sounds too good to be true? How can guests' needs best be met while the hotel, its owners, its managers and nonmanagement team also benefit? These and related questions issues will be discussed in this chapter.

The FOM in Action: The Challenge

Candida has just begun her new position as the FOM in a 125-room, extended-stay property. She supervises a staff of approximately 10 full- and part-time front desk agents. Before accepting the position, Candida knew that two of her initial challenges would be to address the relatively low ratings guests gave the front office over the past several months and the increasing rate of employee turnover.

Her predecessor, who had been with the property for about six years, had worked his way up from an entry-level position as a front desk agent. When he became FOM, he quickly alienated several staff members who had been his peers until the promotion. His attitude appeared to be basically, "I worked my way to the top; I am now the boss; you must do what I tell you to do."

During Candida's employment interview, the general manager expressed great concern about guests' ratings and about the problem of low morale and high turnover. He summed it up by saying, "I guess it's hard to be nice to your guests when your own boss is not nice to you."

What should Candida do to improve employee morale and to more consistently please guests?

LODGING AS A GUEST SERVICE BUSINESS

What do you want when you stay at a hotel? What are the most important factors that influence whether it was a good or bad experience? Consumers, including you and all other hotel guests, typically are looking for **value** when they select and pay for lodging accommodations. Roadmap 2.1 indicates that the lodging business is a service business, and this topic introduces the chapter.

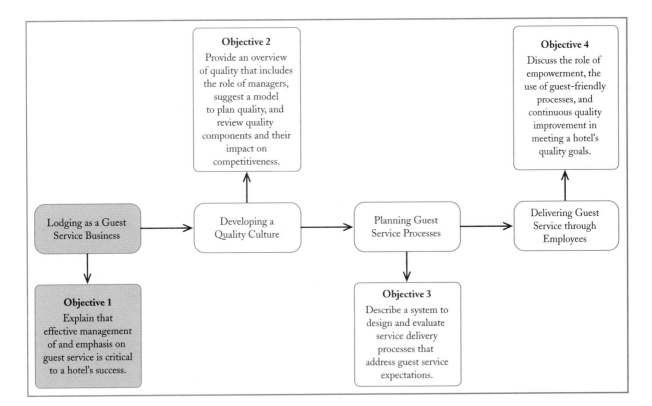

ROADMAP 2.1

FRONT OFFICE SEMANTICS

Value: Relationship between what one pays for something and what is received in return. Value is the relationship between the quality and price of the product or service.

Many elements contribute to the "value equation" for renting a hotel room, for example, the need for the property to be in an acceptable location, cleanliness, safety, and amenities in line with what has been promised and what is being paid. However, guests also expect a level of **service** that meets their needs and that adequately addresses any problems they encounter during their stay. The level of service affects the atmosphere of hospitality that encourages guests to be comfortable and contributes to their enjoyment while staying at the hotel.

FRONT OFFICE SEMANTICS

Service (hotel): Process of helping guests by addressing their wants and needs with respect and dignity in a timely manner.

Let's assume that you are checking into a new and beautiful hotel with a multi-storied **atrium.** The lobby has marble floors and a cascading waterfall. The flowers

If a hotel is impeccably maintained and service levels are high, guest satisfaction will be high.

and plants are attractive, as are the modern (and obviously expensive) furniture, fixtures, and design features.

FRONT OFFICE SEMANTICS

Atrium: Large, central, and open lobby area of a hotel designed to project an ornate and spectacular reception for guests and others entering the property.

You arrive at the beautiful wood, glass, and marble front desk expecting a welcome that is in concert with the quality of your first impressions of the environment. However, the two front desk agents are busy in a personal conversation that continues until your irritation prompts you to say, "Excuse me, are you able to help me?"

This example, emphasizes a point: The hotel environment that can make you think, "Wow, this will be great!," can quickly turn into a question of, "Is this what my stay in this hotel is going to be like?" Although it is expensive to create the lobby atmosphere just described, it is often easier to secure the funding to create such an environment than it is to have staff members available who genuinely and consistently want to please their guests.

So in some cases your first impression is *not* a lasting impression. The beauty of the hotel environment was quickly spoiled by the lack of a good impression of guest service. Unfortunately, even if the first impression (the environment) was excellent and the second impression (a hospitable welcome) also was favorable, what about all of the other service encounters that will occur during your stay? What does (or does not) happen as luggage is brought to your guestroom? As your telephone calls are routed through the hotel operator? As you contact the front desk agent, perhaps many times during your stay? All of these and related opportunities for interaction with hotel employees will have a significant and lasting impact on your impression of the total hotel experience.

It is not only the service attitude of the front office staff that is important; rather, hotel employees in every department must be part of the hotel's service delivery team. The attitude that guest service is the highest priority must start at the top of the organization with the hotel's general manager and the **executive committee.** This attitude must be incorporated into the hotel's **organizational culture** and must be seen in the actions of every employee, in every department, all the time.

FRONT OFFICE SEMANTICS

Executive committee: Short for executive operating committee—members of the hotel's management team (generally department heads) responsible for top leadership and overall administration of the property.

Organizational culture: Pattern of shared beliefs and values that affect norms of behavior and that significantly influence the behavior of the organization's members.

Today's hotel guests desire good service, and they are willing to pay for it. Effective managers, including those in the front office, continually ask this question: "What is best for our guests?" One of the primary responsibilities of managers is to address this question, and the effort is never completed because guests' needs change over time. If managers make decisions considering their guests' needs a priority, their hotel is likely to be successful. In contrast, when managers focus on maximizing revenue, minimizing costs, and doing what is easiest or what has always been done, guest service will likely suffer as will the long-term (and possibly short-term) financial health of the property.

Successful hotels maintain an infrastructure of quality within which they develop, implement, and evaluate strategies to consistently meet guest service expectations. Fortunately, the basics of a quality service system are not difficult to understand or implement. Unfortunately, however, these basics often require changing "the way things are done" in the hotel as existing **work processes** are studied, as planning evolves, and as new work processes are implemented. Even more difficult for many hotel managers is the need to rethink the role of their nonmanagement staff members, including those in the front office, as they recognize that all employees are an integral part of the hotel's guest service team.

FRONT OFFICE SEMANTICS

Work processes: Series of tasks (steps) undertaken to achieve a specific purpose. A typical employee must have the knowledge and skills necessary to perform several work processes.

Effective delivery of guest service results from an emphasis on quality throughout the hotel. The next section of this chapter discusses the basics of quality.

SECTION REVIEW AND DISCUSSION QUESTIONS

Section Objective: Explain that effective management of and emphasis on guest service is critical to a hotel's success.

Section Summary: Consumers desire value when they select a hotel. They expect that what they pay for their hotel experience will be worth the product (room) and service that they receive in exchange for payment. Successful hotels differentiate themselves from others by the extent to which they have defined and meet the service needs of their guests.

Discussion Questions:
1. How important to you is the perception of the service you will receive when you select a hotel? To what extent is service a factor that you evaluate at the conclusion of your hotel experience?
2. Can you think of examples of actions by hotel staff members that suggest they recognize the importance of guest service? In contrast, what types of employee actions suggest that service is not an important consideration?
3. Assume you are an FOM who wants to increase the quality of guest service at the front desk. What tactics might you use and what might you say to defend this "new" approach to a front desk agent with many years of experience who is comfortable doing things as they have always been done?

DEVELOPING A QUALITY CULTURE

Quality provides the context within which work processes that emphasize guest service should be planned and implemented. It is important, therefore, to understand the basics of quality. As Roadmap 2.2 shows, the process of developing a quality culture is the next topic in this chapter.

What Is Quality?

A working definition of **quality** is easy to state but, much more difficult to achieve: Quality is the consistent delivery of products and services according to expected standards.

FRONT OFFICE SEMANTICS

Quality: Consistent delivery of products and services according to expected standards.

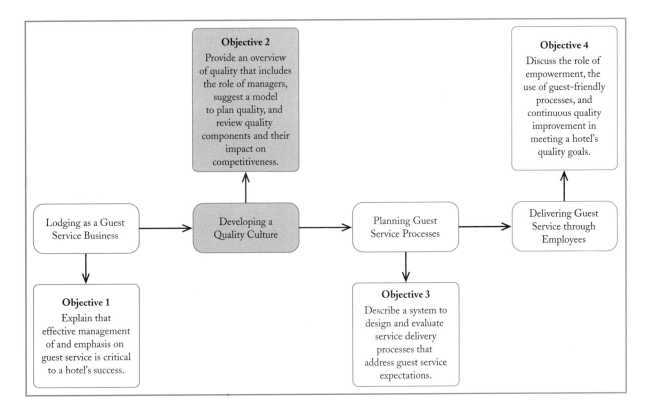

ROADMAP 2.2

Let's look at the components of the definition more closely:

• *Consistent.* The component of consistency implies that standards are always met. In practice, consistency is a goal toward which FOMs and other hotel managers move but never totally attain. People make errors as they design service delivery processes and as they follow procedures that the processes require. Sometimes the procedures yield unacceptable outcomes. In addition, the guests' expectations about quality service (what it is and how it should be delivered) may vary. **Defects** can be minimized, however, through tactics such as proper planning, employee training, and providing staff members with the proper equipment to do their jobs. The extent to which quality is attained (defects are reduced) can be measured as work processes are implemented to meet standards.

FRONT OFFICE SEMANTICS

Defect: Outcome arising from a failure to meet standards. A defect can be as simple as an accounting error by a front desk agent or as significant as an agent's failure to take proper action when an obviously intoxicated guest is observed in the hotel's public areas.

• *Delivery of products and services.* This element in the definition of quality requires specific focus on the guest and a commitment to consistently deliver service to all guests at levels that meet or exceed established quality standards.

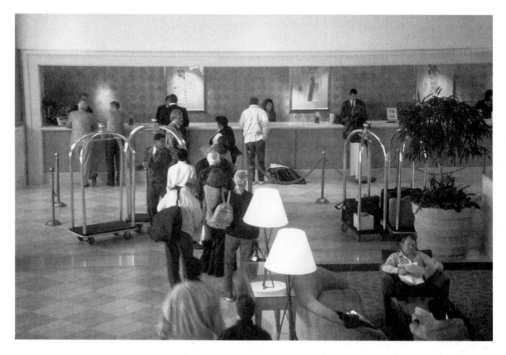

The same level of quality is expected if the front office is assisting one guest or many guests.

Front desk agents sell products: the hotel's guestrooms, meeting spaces, and other amenities. As well, they provide service by successfully addressing the wants and needs of guests during their visits. The "right" products and services cannot be delivered until those desired by guests have been identified, and work processes that yield desired products and services cannot be developed until these outputs (desired products and services) are known.

- *According to expected standards.* With few exceptions, standards must be developed by the property, because they are not imposed by the government, the hospitality industry, professional associations, or other external organizations. The local fire department may regulate the number of persons that can occupy a hotel's meeting room (occupancy standard). It is the FOM, however, who establishes standards about how long guests should be expected to wait in line for registration and about how front desk agents should address guest complaints. For example, FOMs can develop a staffing guide to schedule front desk agents according to the forecasted number of guests who will register and check out. FOMs can provide training to define the process to handle guest complaints and **empower** their employees to make decisions about corrective action. Service standards should be established by managers with the help of their employees to best recognize the needs of the hotel's guests.

FRONT OFFICE SEMANTICS

Empowerment: Act of granting authority to employees to make key decisions within the employees' areas of responsibility.

What is the cost of quality? Quality is not free. Rather, quality involves these costs:

- Prevention—the cost of doing things correctly the first time
- Appraisal—the cost of confirming that things are done correctly the first time
- Failure (or rework)—the cost of not doing things correctly the first time

---

GUIDING PRINCIPLES FOR QUALITY

- Top-level managers must emphasize quality.
- Emphasis on quality must be an integral part of an organization's culture. For example, a manager in one department cannot emphasize a philosophy of quality if quality is not valued in other departments throughout the organization. A hotel is comprised of subsystems (departments); what happens in one affects the others, and how staff in one department treat guests affects guests' perceptions about the entire property.
- Most problems are caused by managers (not by their employees). For example, managers may use recruitment and selection procedures that bring the wrong people to a job, or they may use faulty techniques in orienting and training new employees. Often managers adopt improper supervision principles that result in work errors and high levels of employee turnover. Thus the recruitment, training, and supervision cycle continues through successive "generations" of staff members. As this occurs, it becomes more difficult (even impossible) to maintain the emphasis on quality that was envisioned when owners and managers initially considered the role of the property.
- Two principles of quality cannot be delegated: the responsibility of hotel managers to help employees be successful, and the leadership necessary for the quality philosophy to be integrated throughout the property.
- Quality takes time, effort, and everyone's participation.
- The quality plan should be the hotel's business plan.
- An emphasis on quality is not a program that begins and ends at a specified time. Rather, quality is a philosophy that affects the actions of hotel managers and staff members at all times.

Role of Hotel Senior Managers in Quality

Executive committee members, including the FOM, play a role in developing and implementing guest service processes that emphasize quality. These senior managers must be committed to and share the vision that guest service will always be a high priority. They must consistently "walk and talk" the philosophy of guest service. These senior leaders must provide the support, time, money, and training needed to ensure that process improvement projects are undertaken and will be successful. They must also provide the necessary training, equipment, tools, and other resources that will assist employees in consistently performing work tasks that meet standards. The hotel's senior leaders must also establish employee appraisal systems that reward employees who consistently meet standards designed to maximize guest service.

Another important task of senior managers is to empower staff members to make *nonroutine* decisions to meet their guests' needs. They should do so in recognition of the following basic beliefs:

- The person doing the job generally best knows how to do the job.
- Problem solving and decision making should be done at the lowest capable level in the organization.

- People (staff members) are the hotel's greatest resource.
- Employees will generally meet expectations if they have been empowered to do so and, with encouragement, will exceed them. (Empowerment is discussed in the concluding section of this chapter.)

Senior leaders must also establish systems that allow defects to be measured. For example, a properly constructed and administered guest survey system that allows hotel managers to determine and track guest input about service levels must be available and in use. This system will enable managers and others to identify where, if at all, additional work process study and revision is required. (The guest survey process will be reviewed briefly later in this chapter and in depth in Chapter 10.)

Incentives for front desk agents provide employee motivation, which can assist FOMs in exceeding their goals.

FOCUS ON FOMS WHO EMPHASIZE QUALITY

FOMs who emphasize quality

- consistently give high priority to guest service;
- know that they do not have all the answers and accept the opinions, comments, and suggestions of others who create or deliver service in the organization and in the department;
- consider guest service to be the hotel's competitive advantage;
- recognize that if staff members are not directly serving the guests, they should be serving someone who is;
- solicit the commitment and assistance of all staff members;
- include quality as part of their department's planning efforts and identify quality- and service-related goals to help drive the department's planning efforts;
- work to ensure that quality is a critical part of the front office culture;
- use teamwork and **cross-functional teams** for process planning;
- provide ongoing training;
- empower their staff (i.e., employees are given the responsibility for quality and are not just simply told what is expected);
- link rewards to guest satisfaction and to financial results;
- facilitate **continuous quality improvement (CQI);** and
- consider quality to be the hotel's guiding principle that will evolve as the hotel and the FOM and staff travel on their quality journeys.

FRONT OFFICE SEMANTICS

Cross-functional team: Group of employees representing different departments within the hospitality operation that work together to resolve problems.

Continuous quality improvement (CQI): Ongoing efforts within the hotel to better meet (or exceed) guests' expectations and to find ways to perform work with better, less costly, and faster methods.

How Managers Plan for Quality

Figure 2.1 reviews the planning tools that hotel managers, including FOMs, should use to identify goals, to work toward their attainment, and to measure results. The accompanying example focuses on business travelers. As you review Figure 2.1, refer to the definitions of these terms: **vision, mission statement, long-range plan, business plan, marketing plan,** and **operating budget.**

FRONT OFFICE SEMANTICS

Vision: Abstract idea about what the hospitality operation would be like if it was ideally effective.

Mission statement: More focused picture of what the hospitality operation wants to do and how it will do it.

Long-range plan: Statement of goals and the activities that will be undertaken to attain them that a hospitality operation will use during the next three to five years in efforts to move toward attainment of its mission.

Business plan: Plan of goals and activities that will be addressed within the next 12 months to move the organization toward attainment of its mission.

Marketing plan: Calendar of specific activities designed to meet the operation's revenue goals.

Operating budget: Financial plan that estimates the amount of revenue to be generated, the expenses to be incurred, and the amount of profit, if any, to be realized.

Planning tools such as those identified in Figure 2.1 are developed by members of the hotel's executive committee. The FOM and other department managers should work with staff to consider how they can best use the resources allocated to them to support the property's planning efforts. As you review Figure 2.1, note the example of plans designed to yield an increase in the hotel's meeting business. To accomplish this goal, sales and marketing staff will need to develop and implement creative sales campaigns and other tactics. However, the campaigns cannot be successful without assistance from other departments, including the front office. Some responsibilities of FOMs are informational; for example, they must provide accurate forecasts about the number of guestrooms likely to be available for use by meeting attendees when meetings are sold and booked for specific times. FOMs must also interact with the director of sales and marketing and, in some cases, the property's general manager, to establish room rates for individual travelers during these periods. Knowledge of the rates will help sales and marketing personnel determine the "worth" of meeting business that they are able to attract to the hotel at that time.

Other responsibilities of the FOM in helping to attract meeting business directly relate to the emphasis on quality and guest service. Consider, for example, hotel guests

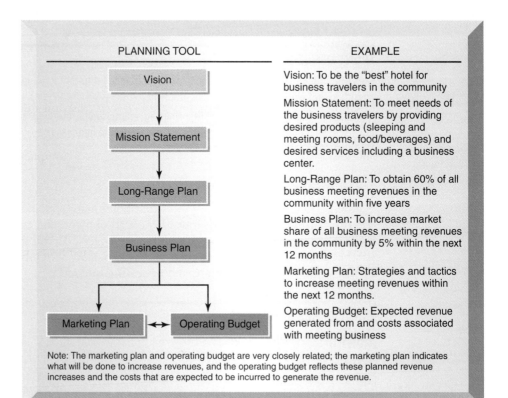

FIGURE 2.1 Basic planning tools.

Source: Ninemeier, J., and J. Perdue. 2005. *Hospitality operations: Careers in the world's greatest industry,* p. 43. Upper Saddle River, NJ: Pearson Education, Inc. Reprinted by permission.

who are impressed with service quality at a property during earlier visits and who recommend the property as a meeting site for their business or a service organization to which they belong. Consider also meeting attendees who receive excellent service and suggest the property as a site for a future conference of another group with which they are affiliated. Also, the quality of service provided by reservations staff who process incoming calls from prospective meeting attendees will help ensure that the maximum number of attendees will stay at the property rather than elect to look somewhere else.

To this point, our example has focused on actions the front office staff can take to help the hotel meet its goal of increased revenues from business meetings. At the same time these actions are implemented, FOMs will likely be involved in planning other activities that address the needs of other business travelers. For example, FOMs might plan ways to increase average daily rates by conducting how-to sessions and rewarding front desk agents who sell guestrooms at higher rates, and by advocating improvements in the hotel's business center based on feedback from business travelers.

Each department in the hotel, including the front office, must be committed to and involved in planning for the emphasis on quality, that is, the consistent delivery of products and services according to expected standards. Experienced managers know that, after the basics of a room rental are addressed (e.g., clean and safe rooms in a preferred location), the level (quality) of service will be high on the list of expectations for travelers. Guests will not likely accept a room that does not meet their cleanliness, safety, or location concerns, so the level of anticipated service becomes an important factor that will influence hotel selection from among the properties that a guest will consider. As will be reaffirmed throughout this text, the front office department is the hub through which communication and guest service is delivered to guests.

Model for Quality

Figure 2.2 provides an overview of how an emphasis on quality can help a hotel become and remain more competitive. As you review Figure 2.2, note the role of top-level leadership (the general manager and all others on the executive committee, including the FOM) as they emphasize the need for quality and work process improvement, with a focus on guests.

Emphasis on quality will yield guest satisfaction that, in turn, will increase hotel revenue. How will revenue increase? As stated earlier in this chapter, guests want and will pay for the appropriate level of service. They will see value in a higher room rate because they are willing to pay for products and services that meet their requirements. **Incremental** (additional) **sales** will occur during their visits. Other increases in revenue will result from **repeat business** (returning guests) and an increased guest base generated from positive **word-of-mouth advertising** provided by guests who are pleased with their hospitality experience.

FRONT OFFICE SEMANTICS

Incremental sales: Sales of products and services to guests in addition to those that would otherwise have been generated.

Repeat business: Revenues generated from guests returning to the hotel as a result of positive experiences on previous visits.

Word-of-mouth advertising: Informal conversations between persons as they discuss their positive or negative experiences at a hotel.

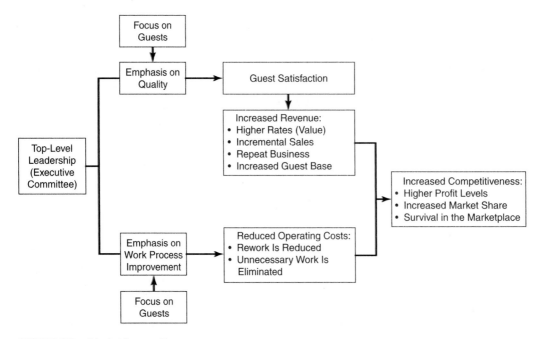

FIGURE 2.2   Model for quality.

Figure 2.2 also illustrates the role of senior leadership as they emphasize work process improvements that focus on guests. As defects in processes are removed, operating costs can be reduced because, for example, rework is reduced and unnecessary work is eliminated. Figure 2.2 shows that senior leaders who emphasize quality by focusing on guests are effective: Increased revenue and reduced operating costs increase the property's competitiveness. The hotel enjoys higher profit levels, increased market share, and long-term survival in the marketplace.

SECTION REVIEW AND DISCUSSION QUESTIONS

Section Objective: Provide an overview of quality that includes the role of managers, suggest a model to plan quality, and review quality components and their impact on competitiveness.

Section Summary: Quality is the consistent delivery of products and services according to expected standards. Hotel managers must share their vision of and emphasize the philosophy of quality. They must provide the support, time, money, training, and other resources necessary to plan for and implement quality work processes. As they find ways to increase guest satisfaction and remove defects from work processes, revenues will increase, operating costs will decrease, and the property will be competitive and successful.

Discussion Questions:

1. Figure 2.1 and its discussion provide an example of a hotel team that is planning ways to increase its business from business travelers and meetings. What are

tactics (other than those noted in the text) that the FOM can use to assist in this effort?

2. Assume that you are an FOM and have just returned from a workshop about the importance of quality when delivering guest service at the front desk. Assume also that you want to renew a guest service emphasis in your department. Develop an outline of the points you would make in a presentation of your plan to your staff.

3. The text suggests that it is not possible for one department in a hotel to emphasize total quality and emphasize guest service without participation of other hotel departments? Do you agree? Why or why not?

PLANNING GUEST SERVICE PROCESSES

This chapter's working definition of quality (i.e., the consistent delivery of products and services according to expected standards) emphasizes service. Guests renting hotel rooms desire an expected standard of service as well as physical access to a clean and safe room as part of their lodging experience. More and more guests are willing to pay the cost of renting rooms in properties that meet (or exceed) their service expectations. As suggested in Roadmap 2.3, it is now time to consider the details of how processes that address guest service expectations are designed and evaluated.

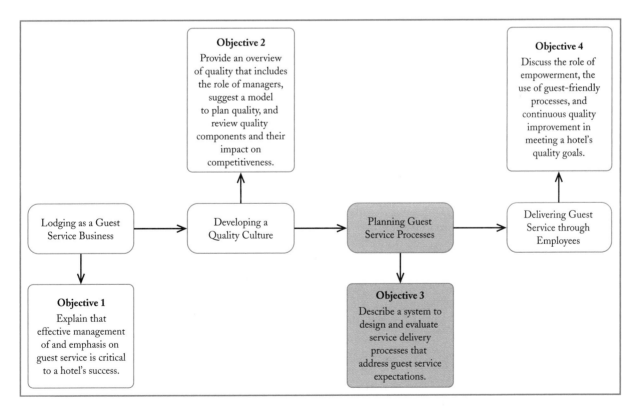

ROADMAP 2.3

A leisure traveler may have different expectations from those of a business traveler.

Recognizing Basic Concerns

Two points are important in this discussion of service. First, service is not the same as servility (to assist someone of a better social class). The Ritz-Carlton Hotel Company emphasizes this point as well as any other hospitality organization with its motto: "We Are Ladies and Gentlemen Serving Ladies and Gentlemen." The best front office employees are those who genuinely enjoy working with others (employees on their team) and helping others (their guests), and they treat their peers and guests with respect and dignity.

Second, the definition of service emphasizes helping guests by addressing their wants and needs, but what do guests want? A businessperson and a family registering at a hotel represent two different types of guests. At their most basic level, however, they want the same things. All guests want a clean room in a safe environment and contact with the property's staff that is, at a minimum, respectful and polite. Then the businessperson's wants might expand to high-speed Internet access in the guestroom and use of the property's business center, and the family might be interested in the swimming pool, use of a roll-away bed, and access to babysitting services.

All properties must meet the basic needs and additional expectations of their guests at a price that represents a value to the guests. As guest expectations increase (e.g., the desire for more luxurious guestrooms and public spaces and for more personalized services that require a greater **employee-to-room ratio**), charges will likely need to be increased to enable the hotel to supply the resources required to meet these higher-level expectations.

FRONT OFFICE SEMANTICS

Employee-to-room ratio: Number of employees relative to the number of rooms. For example, a 500-room, luxury, full-service property may have 500 employees: a 1:1 employee-to-room ratio. A 100-room, limited-service property may have only 25 employees: a 1:4 employee-to-room ratio.

THE GENTEEL HOST!

How would you treat a special friend or relative that you invite to your home? Your answer will help explain how guests visiting a hotel should be treated. The earliest travelers were offered meals and a safe night's rest by families living near trade routes. Families invited travelers into their home for today's equivalent of lodging and foodservices.

Guests in your home do not have to pay for their night's lodging, for meals during their visit, or for your considerate service. Paying guests in a hotel deserve similar service. A hotel's basic vision and mission, along with the policies and procedures about how they should be delivered, must incorporate a service emphasis.

Do the terms *customer* and *guest* mean the same thing? Perhaps they do in a dictionary; however, in the world of hospitality, hotel staff who treat their visitors as *guests* will likely be more successful than competitors who treat their visitors as *customers*. The tradition of a hotelier as a genteel host is just as relevant today as it was in the earliest history of the lodging industry.

If you were registering at a hotel, would you want to be greeted by a front desk agent reading a newspaper or doing homework and who said, "Just a moment, please," while you waited? In response to your question about room location, would you want to be told, "It's that way" (indicated by a pointed finger)? If you and other guests experience such interactions that indicate lack of basic respect and courtesy, you are not likely to return to the property. As well, friends and family members will likely learn about the unacceptable visit.

Perhaps you think that these extreme violations of basic courtesy do not happen in any lodging property, and certainly not in a "good" hotel. Accept a challenge: Ask any **road warrior** for examples of service in "good" hotels that violated basic courtesy standards. You likely will hear many "war stories" from each person you interview.

FRONT OFFICE SEMANTICS

Road warrior: Term used to describe business travelers who travel frequently.

Fortunately, service does not involve significant financial resources beyond the manager's control or complex standard operating procedures that are too detailed to execute consistently. Rather, service involves an attitude and a philosophy that are within a manager's control.

WHAT ARE YOUR SERVICE EXPECTATIONS?

Think about your own service expectations and use them to benchmark, plan, and evaluate basic service procedures. Consider the guest registration process. Guests will likely have formed some impressions about the hotel before they reach the reception area. For example, they will have seen the building's exterior and some of its public spaces, and they may have had contact with representatives of the property if reservations were made directly with hotel personnel. They may have been assisted by members of the hotel's staff as they were transported by the hotel's van, and they may have observed employees unload luggage, park cars, and assist guests into the hotel's lobby. Nevertheless, first impressions about guest service are formed during the actual registration process with front desk agents.

What would you want to occur when you checked in to a hotel? Your responses probably include the following:

- No (or a short) wait time at the front desk
- Correct reservation information (e.g., dates of room occupancy and room rate)
- A friendly welcome that includes eye contact, a smile, and acknowledgment of your name (e.g., "Welcome to our hotel, Ms. Gonzalez.")
- The proper room available (e.g., queen-size bed, mountain view, nonsmoking)
- Correct answers to your questions (e.g., "What time does the restaurant open for breakfast?" "How late is room service available this evening?")
- Accurate directions to your room
- An invitation for assistance by the bell services attendant (if applicable)
- Suggestions about where to park your car (if applicable; e.g., closest to room access)

Not surprisingly, these and related questions are common to first-time guests. The FOM's own service desires can, at their most basic level, help to anticipate guest registration expectations and can drive the development of procedures to respond to them. The FOM's experience can also help identify the training that front desk agents need to properly register guests and suggest how registration service levels should be evaluated (e.g., the extent to which front desk staff meet service standards as part of the guest registration process).

How can the FOM determine the expectations of the guests? Once discovered, how can service delivery processes be designed to more consistently deliver what the guests want? These questions will be addressed in the next section.

MODERN FRONT OFFICE ISSUES AND TACTICS

How Well Do Hotel Companies Treat Their Guests Online?

The Customer Respect Group is an international research and consulting firm that studies how companies treat their customers online. It assigns a *customer respect index* rating to each company on a scale of 0 to 10 (10 = highest score). A representative sample of adult Internet users are interviewed, and applicable Web sites are analyzed. Attributes used to judge the online customer experience relate to simplicity (ease of navigation), responsiveness (quick and thorough responses to inquiries), privacy, attitude (customer focus of the site), transparency (open and honest policies), and principles (extent to which the company values and respects customer data).

Hotel organizations receiving the company's highest ratings in spring, 2004, were Marriott International, Hyatt Hotels & Resorts, Starwood Hotels & Resorts, Radisson Hotels & Resorts, and Caesar's Entertainment.

More than 50 percent of users who abandoned Web sites in the three months previous to the study cited a lack of simplicity as the main reason why they did so. Seventy percent of respondents said they would go to a competitor if a Web site was difficult to use.

A hotel organization's Web site is an ever-increasing source of information for potential guests who use the sites to make reservations (see Chapter 7). Some good advice: Make sure your Web site is easy to use and that the process required to make a reservation is understandable and fast (fewest possible keystrokes).

Adapted from Online Customer Respect Survey Studies. How hotel companies treat their customers online. Hotel Online Special Report. Retrieved April 2, 2004, from http://www.hotel-online.com/News/PR2004_2nd/Apr04_OnlineRespect.html.

Determining Guests' Service Expectations

What do guests want and what do they need? Some FOMs and other managers ask questions as they interact with guests: "What did you like about your visit?" "What would have made your visit more enjoyable?" Hard-copy questionnaires (comment cards) are sometimes provided to guests when they register as part of a packet of information. Questionnaires also may be placed in guestrooms or other locations and may be available at the front desk.

Common systems invite guests to complete the form and leave it at the front desk or in the guestroom at the time of departure. Some comment cards are designed to be mailed to a corporate office. Increasingly, lodging properties of all sizes are implementing electronic surveys on the hotel's guestroom television channel or contacting willing guests by e-mail to collect information about guest preferences. In some properties, senior managers (including those with front office responsibilities) routinely talk with guests as they check out to learn more about what they liked and what they would have wanted during their visit. (A nice touch: In smaller properties, the manager may help guests with their luggage as they depart.)

Ongoing input from guests is necessary to assess whether processes that deliver service need to be revised or redesigned. Hoteliers require such information to identify which and how guest service systems can be improved.

Many hoteliers recognize that it is far better to become aware of guest problems at the time they occur, so that they can be corrected quickly in a way that is least troublesome to guests. In doing so, staff members implement their service pledge to help guests. At the same time, their service attitude may contribute toward repeat business for the property and within the brand. Many managers perceive guest-reported "problems" as opportunities to initiate or improve a long-term relationship with the guest.

Obviously, guest-related problems cannot be resolved until they are identified. For several reasons, guests may *not* alert the FOM and other hotel managers to a problem they are experiencing:

- The problem occurred immediately before or at the time of check-out. No problems occurred during the guest stay.
- The guest did not believe the problem could be resolved.
- The guest did not want to wait for the problem to be resolved.
- The guest did not want to repack and move to another guestroom.
- The guest may have thought that the problem was integral to the hotel. (For example, hotel policy regarding check-in time was much later than the guest's arrival time.)
- The problem was judged to be minor.
- The guest did not want to be considered a troublemaker.
- The guest considered the problem to be justification to try another hotel in the future.

- The guest did report the problem (e.g., on a guest comment card left in a guestroom), but the problem was not brought to the attention of hotel staff on a timely basis (while the guest was still registered at the hotel).
- The guest did report the problem to a hotel staff member who did not take responsibility for it and did not bring it to the attention of the appropriate manager.

Some hoteliers take proactive actions to ensure that their guest's stay is satisfactory:

- A front desk agent may call the guestroom some time (e.g., a half hour) after check-in to ensure that the room condition is acceptable and that no guest-related supplies are needed.
- A front desk agent may contact a guest on the first or second day of a longer stay.
- Front desk and other hotel staff can be encouraged to communicate with guests as they encounter them in the lobby or throughout the property.
- A card titled "For Immediate Attention Please" can be left in the guestroom, so that the room attendant can pick it up during the daily room-cleaning process.
- A toll-free telephone number can be made available for immediate guest concerns.
- A staff member with dedicated responsibility for guest contact may phone the guestroom and talk with the guest or leave a message related to correcting any problems the guest may be experiencing.

Managers have another way to collect information about guests: They can ask their employees. It is ironic but true that many times line-level employees know more about the likes and dislikes of guests than do their department heads or supervisors. Consider, for example, guests complaining about long registration lines when they check in; they routinely note their frustration to front office staff. If you want to know what guests desire and what they dislike, ask the employees who provide the products and services to them. (Details about guest survey processes are presented in Chapter 10.)

MODERN FRONT OFFICE ISSUES AND TACTICS

Now the Whole World Will Know!

In the past, a pleased or disappointed hotel guest might relay his or her experiences to a few friends, business associates, family members, and others willing to listen. Today, however, the whole world could know! Internet Web sites (e.g., www.epinions.com and www.tripadvisor.com) encourage hotel guests to recount their experiences for public viewing by anyone visiting the site. Will a series of favorable ratings increase a hotel's business? Will a series of less-than-favorable comments reflect negatively on a hotel? It is probably too early to say. It is possible, however, that tomorrow's travelers will increasingly consider information from these and related sites as they make hotel selections.

Establishing Quality Processes that Yield *Exemplary Guest Service*

Figure 2.3 provides an overview of the impact that guest needs and desires should have on the revision of a work process and on the measurement of the improved guest satisfaction levels that result. The figure considers the process of guest registration. It addresses the concerns that all guests desire fast and efficient check-in to reduce waiting time and that they want no defects (errors) during the process.

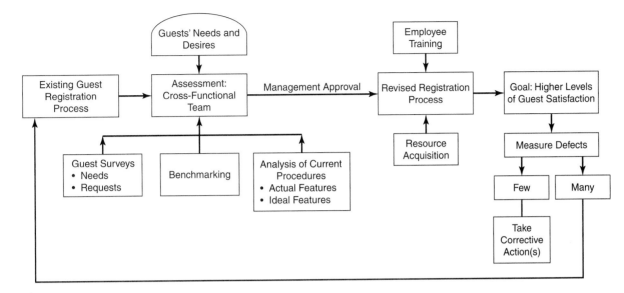

FIGURE 2.3 Overview of registration process revision with emphasis on quality guest service.

Designing Work Processes

Let's look at Figure 2.3. Assume that an informal process evaluation (cursory review of results of some guest surveys, observations by the FOM and his or her team, and conversations with guests) have suggested that improvements in the registration process can be helpful.

- The existing guest registration process is formally analyzed to help answer this question: What process can be used for guest registration that will minimize guests' waiting time and will help to reduce errors? A cross-functional team of hotel employees (perhaps from the front office, housekeeping, maintenance and engineering, and accounting departments) can review input from guests (surveys and conversations), study **benchmarking** information, and analyze current registration procedures. Note that benchmarking efforts might involve review of registration practices described in articles in trade magazine or on the Internet, discussions with FOMs in other hotels, observations by members of the cross-functional team as they register at other hotels, and visits to other properties (perhaps those of the same brand).

FRONT OFFICE SEMANTICS

Benchmarking: Search for best practices and an understanding of how they are achieved in efforts to determine how well a hospitality organization is doing.

- The study of how registration now occurs (actual features) and a comparison to ideal features may yield suggestions about possible revisions to the registration process. The sum of all inputs (guest surveys, benchmarking, and comparisons between actual and ideal features) will likely yield process changes that better ensure the goals of minimizing wait time and reducing registration errors.

- After management approves the revised procedures, the procedures are incorporated into the revised registration process.
- Once defined, procedures are incorporated into employee training programs and should be used consistently to register guests. Any necessary resources (e.g., equipment or supplies) should be obtained.
- Will the goal (higher levels of guest satisfaction with the registration process) be attained more consistently? It is impossible to know unless an evaluation system is developed and implemented. The number of defects can be assessed by, for example, guest survey data and FOM interviews with hotel guests. If evaluation of the revised registration process suggests only few problems, minor corrective actions may be taken. For example, assume that the average length of a guest's wait in the registration line has been reduced significantly; the only time that a wait is excessive is when there are large numbers of guests to be checked in at the same time. Also assume that these times are generally known and that the front desk is fully staffed in anticipation of the large volume of business. Corrective actions might include setting up (1) a temporary registration center in another area of the lobby (if computers that interface with the hotel's electronic property management system are available (see Chapter 4) or (2) a complimentary refreshment station in the area of the registration line, which may reinforce the hotel's service emphasis. What if evaluation of the revised registration process indicates that more there are more defects or suggests that problems in the previous process have not been addressed effectively? Then, as illustrated in Figure 2.3, the steps in process revision need to be repeated.

Steps in the registration process development are cyclical. Over time, input from guest surveys, additional benchmarking, and analysis of current procedures by another cross-functional team may yield still further improvements in the registration process and, in turn, higher levels of guest satisfaction.

QUESTIONS GUIDE REVISIONS OF WORK PROCESSES

Answering the following questions can help to revise work processes:

- Why are we doing this?
- Why does this happen?
- What is likely to happen (in the short term and in the long term) because of the actions we are considering?
- Why don't all managers and all employees always emphasize the goal of satisfying guests?
- Why do we review and approve the work of employees many times?
- Why do managers "fight fires" instead of creating value for guests?
- Why can't our business culture encourage staff to reveal favorable and unfavorable information?
- Why are the actions of the managers sometimes inconsistent with their goals?

Process Revision Is Ongoing

Assume that processes for guest registration and problem resolution were initially developed with a focus on guests. Over time, though, guest preferences are likely to change. Input from guest surveys and other sources may suggest that changes in processes will benefit the guests. Technologies will evolve and, perhaps, new and improved work processes may become useful. These processes may affect what guests desire and how products and services can be delivered most effectively. As these events indicate, work processes that are in current use always need to be evaluated and modified.

Evaluating Work Processes

Processes used today to deliver service to guests may need revision tomorrow. Soliciting feedback from guests and from the staff members who interact with them can be an effective tactic of obtaining input about the need for change. One method to quantify guest perceptions about service is to measure defects. However, even with a goal of **zero defects,** there will be times when service standards are not met.

FRONT OFFICE SEMANTICS

Zero defects: Goal of no guest-related complaints that is established when guest service processes are implemented.

Guests' needs and concerns are addressed when processes are developed. Therefore, ongoing measurement of guest responses to processes can provide information about how well the processes satisfy guests. Figure 2.4 provides an overview of how the measurement (count) of defects helps to evaluate a process.

Let's look at Figure 2.4. Note that input from guests suggested there were approximately 12 service complaints about the original registration process per 1,000 rooms. Assume that this defect rate was judged excessive, and a new process was implemented using the tactics noted in the previous section of this chapter. A subsequent evaluation then determined that there were approximately 8 service defects per 1,000 rooms. Some FOMs would likely believe that this reduction in complaints was significant (and it is) and would look elsewhere to determine how guests could be better served. Other FOMs might continue to evaluate the registration process because the process has been identified on the guest comment card or other survey system that is in use. However, they might discount concerns from these sources because they have already addressed them. An FOM with a zero defect goal will likely pay serious attention to other ways that the new process can be revised. (This will especially be so if analysis of other processes indicates that the number of defects remains higher for the registration process than for other processes that are the responsibility of the FOM.) In Figure 2.4 note that further revisions in the registration process reduced the defect rate still further (to 6 service defects per 1,000 rooms).

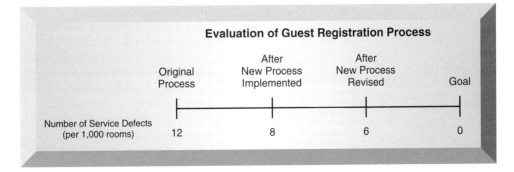

FIGURE 2.4   Counting defects to evaluate service processes.

The process of analyzing defects with the goal of eliminating them should be ongoing and will help the FOM and his or her department move further along the journey toward quality service (zero defects). Some observers may question the use of a zero defect goal, because it is not reasonably attainable. Isn't it likely that if 200 guests are checked in on an average day, there will be some defects each week, month, and year? If a goal is not attainable, won't establishing that goal lead to frustration and stress? In fact, a perception of success should occur with any reduction in the number of defects (e.g., from 12 to 6 per 1,000 rooms). Front office staff can, in fact, be rewarded for their efforts to reduce the number of defects during the guest registration process. Then the challenge becomes how can the defect rate be lowered from less than 6 defects per 1,000 rooms? Ongoing efforts may yield still fewer defects and improved scores on guest surveys.

Managing Work Processes

The discussion in this section of the chapter presented a practical and commonsense method to determine service needs of guests and to incorporate them into the work processes used to serve the guests. Steps in the method are reviewed in Figure 2.5. Professional FOMs recognize their responsibility to use a quality management approach such as that illustrated in Figure 2.5 as an integral part of their job. They want their department to be the best that it can be. To achieve this goal, they know that they must accept reports of service defects to be opportunities for service improvement.

Enhancing Moments of Truth

Moments of truth are opportunities that guests have to form an impression about a lodging organization. A moment of truth may involve an employee (e.g., excellent or rude service), but human interaction is not essential. Consider, for example, the negative impressions formed when guests walk through a hotel lobby furnished with shabby furniture and heavily stained carpeting. Contrast this with the positive first impressions created by a large vase of fresh, beautiful flowers at the check-in desk. Consider also the **wow factor** created when one of these fresh flower stems is offered to guests as part of the registration process.

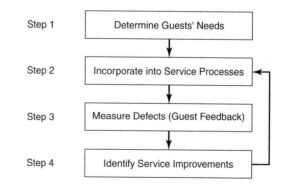

FIGURE 2.5   Review of revision procedures for work processes.

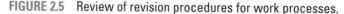

FRONT OFFICE SEMANTICS

Moment of truth: Any (and every) time a guest has an opportunity to form an impression about the hospitality organization. Moments of truth can be positive or negative and may, but do not have to, involve the property's staff members.

Wow factor: Feeling guests have as they experience an unanticipated extra during their visit to a hospitality operation.

Hoteliers want their guests to experience positive moments of truth. Some of these occur through planning (e.g., an efficient guest registration process), but they can also be spontaneous (e.g., an empowered front desk agent pleases a guest who has just made an out-of-the-ordinary request). Unfortunately, negative moments of truth occur frequently in many properties. Many of these can be anticipated or, at least, should not be a surprise to an FOM. For example, complaints about long waits for registration at the front desk should be expected if an inadequate number of employees were scheduled for a work shift. Others are unanticipated, such as a guest's reaction to a front desk agent about a wake-up call received an hour later than requested.

Professional FOMs and their teams plan work processes designed to yield positive guest experiences. Through an organized planning system, processes are in place for guest reservations and registration, for luggage transport to rooms, for guest security and safety, for guest check-out, and for other guest-property interactions. Nevertheless, guests in such hotels will encounter (sometimes by chance), other moments of truth that can be favorable or unfavorable. These moments will have a significant influence on the guest's total perception of the visit. Many of these moments involve employees of departments other than the front office. What these staff members do (or do not do) will influence guests' perceptions as will the words and actions of front office employees. All employees in all departments must work together to ensure that guests' perceptions about their visit to the property will be positive and will be repeated.

This chapter's simple definition of quality (i.e, consistent delivery of products and services according to expected standards) is difficult to attain. To be effective, FOMs must ensure that service-focused procedures have been developed and are in use to minimize the number of service failures. When failures do occur, FOMs try to correct the problem while the guests are still at the hotel, and they learn from the experiences to reduce future service failures.

SECTION REVIEW AND DISCUSSION QUESTIONS

Section Objective: Describe a system to design and evaluate front office service delivery processes that address guest service expectations.

Section Summary: Initially, processes to deliver guest service should have been planned with the guests' wants and needs in mind. Over time, changes in processes may become necessary. Potential changes might be identified through input from guest surveys (comment cards) and management interviews with guests and employees. Use of a cross-functional team to consider ways to revise processes can help reduce the number of service defects. Ongoing evaluation (count of defects) will likely yield additional process revisions. Moments of truth may be planned and unplanned and can be favorable or unfavorable. The sum of the planned processes and moments of truth affect guests' perceptions of quality service at the hotel.

Discussion Questions:

1. What are your typical reactions when you visit a hotel and experience problems? What factors determine whether you will inform the staff? What are your thoughts, from the perspectives of an FOM and a guest, to money-back guarantees if your stay is not free of troubles or if problems are not resolved?

2. What do you think are the best methods for a cross-functional team to use in assessing whether a service process should be revised? Why do you prefer these methods?

3. Consider the following guest-related problems:

   • Long waits in registration lines at the front desk
   • Reservation errors (e.g., incorrect spelling of a guest's name or improper registration or check-out dates)
   • Inoperative television in guestroom
   • Excessive plumbing noises in guestroom caused by pipes in the walls or ceilings

   Assume that you are an FOM conducting a guest service training program for front desk agents and that the trainees identify these issues as common problems. What would you suggest they say to guests who express concerns? What longer-term processes can be implemented to address the issues?

DELIVERING GUEST SERVICE THROUGH EMPLOYEES

After viewing a video emphasizing quality service, one manager was heard saying to another, "I wish my hotel had staff like those in the video." The video showed a series of situations in which a trained front desk agent (1) provided a hospitable greeting, (2) suggested an upgraded (and higher priced) room that improved the guest's experience, (3) displayed knowledge of the hotel, (4) answered all the guest's questions, (5) helped peers when they became especially busy, and (6) met or exceeded guests' service expectations. Why couldn't (didn't) the manager viewing the training video employ, train, and enable staff members who consistently performed these relatively simple and common-sense actions? What kind of service was the manager's staff providing if they did not do what was shown in the video? People who stayed at this lodging operation might also be asking these questions: "What's wrong with the staff? Why does their supervisor allow these things to happen? If I as a guest know the negative impact that a staff member's actions (or inactions) have on business, why can't those who work here and who have a vested interest in the business's success see it as well and do something about it?"

As noted in Roadmap 2.4, this last section of the chapter addresses the delivery of service. This is important because the quality of service provided to guests in every hospitality operation is affected most by the staff members who provide the service. They, in turn, use work processes that, traditionally, have been developed by managers. (However, hotel employees are increasingly being asked to contribute to process development and are more frequently empowered to make decisions in non-routine situations.) If the employee's role is critical in service delivery, what role does

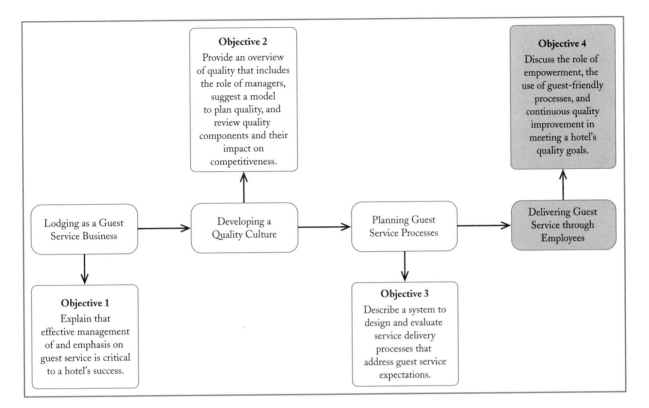

ROADMAP 2.4

the manager play? It has been said that most problems in lodging operations are caused by the manager. Can this be true? The observation runs contrary to the thinking of the traditional manager who believes, "I wish I could find good employees. Then my operating problems would be solved, my guests would be happy, and my business would be profitable." In fact, the manager effectively (or ineffectively) recruits, orients, trains, motivates, and empowers staff members to serve guests. The manager establishes and maintains (or does not establish and maintain) the philosophy about the critical importance of guest service.

Managers cannot delegate the **accountability** they receive from their own boss to their subordinates. Instead, managers are held responsible for the extent to which the property is successful. As emphasized throughout this chapter and this book, service is an essential ingredient in the success of all lodging organizations.

FRONT OFFICE SEMANTICS

Accountability: Obligation created when a staff member is delegated duties and responsibilities from higher levels of management.

FOMs must understand their own role in helping to establish and maintain the guest service priority for those whom they supervise. They must recognize that what they do (and don't do) and what they say (and don't say) may be the most significant factors in determining the extent to which service is emphasized in the department. What else can FOMs do to ensure that their employees know and consistently practice effective guest service skills? What tactics can be used to make sure guest service is and remains a top priority of all staff members in the hotel? FOMs should empower staff with service authority, ensure that guest-friendly processes are in use, and emphasize continuous quality improvement. These are the topics of the remainder of this chapter.

MODERN FRONT OFFICE ISSUES AND TACTICS

The Guest Is Always Right (Kind Of)

A survey done with hotel guests by Orbitz (the travel Web site) yielded some interesting findings that are probably well-known by experienced hoteliers:

- Approximately 25 percent of respondents threw towels on the floor and used more towels than necessary.
- Approximately 60 percent of respondents removed complimentary toiletry items when they departed, and almost 20 percent have taken or have considered taking toiletries from a housekeeper's cart. Approximately 18 percent of respondents indicated that they took guestroom towels.
- Many respondents brought extra people into guestrooms without registering them (29 percent), smoked in a nonsmoking room (12 percent), and brought pets into rooms (11 percent).
- About 30 percent of males ages 18 to 34 years admitted using, or considered using, the swimming pool at another property.

Adapted from *What we do in hotels when no one is looking: "Hotel habits" survey.* Hotel Online Special Report. Retrieved April 2, 2004, from http://www.hotel-online.com/News/PR2004_2nd/Apr04_HotelHabits.html.

Empower Staff with Service Authority

The concept of empowerment suggests that FOMs should facilitate—not direct—the delivery of service by their employees. Staff members who are in contact with guests require the ability to make quick decisions that focus on guests' needs as they arise. As it is not possible to anticipate what every guest will want all the time, it is not possible to develop and teach procedures that recognize how to consistently meet (or exceed) the expectations of every guest. Front office employees can be empowered to help guests with reasonable out-of-the-ordinary service requests after they (1) learn about their service mission, (2) receive the training and obtain the resources required to meet the needs of most guests, and (3) show ongoing interest in providing exceptional guest service.

Several management strategies help support the empowerment of front office personnel:

- *Accepting the philosophy that supports empowerment.* FOMs who think that employees don't care, only want to perform to minimum levels of expectations, and don't want to make creative decisions, will find it difficult to implement an empowerment tactic. Managers must gradually reduce the level of their supervision for qualified staff and encourage them to exercise the authority (power) that they have received.
- *Pointing staff in the right direction.* Informing front office employees about their primary goal (e.g., to provide guests with a memorable experience that

Well-trained FOMs can empower their staffs to provide consistent guest service.

exceeds their expectations) is a necessary first step. Establishing standards for performance and helping employees understand the wants, needs, desires, and perceptions of guests are critical.

- *Recognizing the role of the guest.* Guests demand that products and services meet predetermined quality standards that incorporate their needs, expectations, and desires. Achieving these standards should be the personal responsibility of each member of the front office team. All staff members must understand their obligation to satisfy guests and must exercise the necessary authority to do so. Guests are the final inspectors and, as the definition of acceptability may differ for guest, so also should the methods (work processes) used to achieve an acceptable level of satisfaction.

- *Removing the barriers that inhibit pride in work.* Most front office employees want to perform their jobs to the best of their abilities. They should be praised when they achieve expected results, represented by the attainment of standards. Managers help to build pride when they design work systems that allow their employees to succeed and when they effectively communicate goals and assignments to their staff.

- *Monitoring work to ensure that standards are attained consistently.* FOMs must ensure that their staff's own professional and personal needs are met to the extent practical. They must support staff decision making and must provide the training and coaching that is a prerequisite to staff empowerment. If measurable standards are in place, it becomes relatively easy to assess the quality of work outputs.

For empowerment to be effective, FOMs must follow these guidelines:

- Treat employees like adults.
- Respect employees as individuals.
- Recognize that employees can make significant contributions to the department and the hotel.
- Ask for and use employees' suggestions.
- Trust staff members.
- Allow employees to find pride and joy in the workplace.

The need for employee empowerment will not go away. Instead, it must become further ingrained into the organizational culture of all departments in the hotel. Managers and employees working together can accomplish more together than they can independently. The empowerment effort is a critical strategy to help the hotel please guests and, in the process, to remain competitive.

Ensure that Guest-Friendly Processes Are Used

The initial section of this chapter discussed the importance of quality and described how quality might best be ensured as work processes are developed. A later section of the chapter emphasized the need to address guests' wants, needs, and desires as processes are developed and implemented. This need may seem obvious, however, other factors such as the following too often supersede concerns about the guests as work processes are designed and implemented: "How have we always done it?" "What is the easiest, cheapest, or fastest?" "What will meet with the least employee resistance?"

Today's FOMs do not wait until problems become significant before they are addressed. "Yesterday," one tactic to prioritize problems was to consider that the squeaky wheel should get the grease. Today, processes should be evaluated continually, and guests and the employees who serve them should be queried on an ongoing basis about how to do things better. Each step taken on the quality journey allows the hotel to more consistently meet guest needs and, as a result, to better attain its own financial and other goals.

Emphasize Continuous Quality Improvement

Guests and lodging operations change constantly, so hotels become better or worse; they do not stay the same. Current emphasis on "better, faster, cheaper" is important. The first two factors (better and faster), however, should be assessed with guests' needs in mind. The third factor (cheaper) is a meaningful goal as long as it occurs by eliminating error and rework from the hotel's products and services rather than by reducing value from the guests' perspective.

The concept of continuous quality improvement (CQI) relates to the efforts required of all hotel managers and staff to reduce defects (in other words, to get better). As problems are identified, they should be resolved and corrected in such a way that they cannot reoccur. Managers practice CQI as they and their employees address both the largest problems (e.g., guest complaints about service) and the smallest problems (e.g., a burned out lightbulb in a lobby lamp). In both cases, processes should be implemented that recognize goals (meeting quality standards) and that remove defects from the work processes. This is CQI in action. As the CQI effort occurs, each improvement in a process results in fewer defects. Another step on the property's journey toward excellence has been taken.

WHAT MAKES SERVICE SPECIAL?

Service is an attitude as much or more than it is a skill. Front office employees provide special service to their guests as they

- acknowledge guests on arrival and thank them for visiting;
- smile;
- maintain eye contact;
- reflect a genuine interest in providing quality service;
- consider every guest to be unique;
- create a warm environment of hospitality;
- strive for excellence in guest service skills;
- act courteously, politely, and attentively;
- determine what guests *really* want and need, and address those wants and needs;
- pay more attention to guests than to machines and co-workers; and
- genuinely thank guests for their business and invite them to return.

MODERN FRONT OFFICE ISSUES AND TACTICS

Technology and the Hotel Room of the Future

Now that most hotels provide high-speed Internet access (and those that don't will), is the emphasis on technology over? Not at all.

Hoteliers are testing and implementing new high-tech devices and software that will allow the use of handheld computers to register guests at curbside. Minibars are being developed that will know a guest's food and beverage preferences. Thermostats are available that adjust guestroom temperature when guests are in the room, and digital movies are available on demand. Biometric scanners such as those that use iris identification technology can provide more secure access to guestrooms. What about altering the firmness of mattresses and changing art work in the room based on guest preferences? (The latter can be done with flat-screen monitors.) Today, and certainly tomorrow, hotels will use impersonal equipment to deliver highly personalized guest experiences.

Adapted from Stanford, K. *High wired: The hotel room of the future.* Hotel Online Special Report. Retrieved April 2, 2004, from http://www.hotel-online.com/News/PR2004_2nd/Apr04_HighWiredRoom.html.

SECTION REVIEW AND DISCUSSION QUESTIONS

Section Objective: Discuss the role of empowerment, the use of guest-friendly processes, and continuous quality improvement (CQI) in meeting a hotel's quality goals.

Section Summary: Service is delivered by employees. FOMs must, therefore, empower staff with service authority, ensure that guest-friendly processes that address what's best for guests are in continuous use, and emphasize CQI tactics in their departments.

Discussion Questions:

1. This chapter suggests that most problems in a hotel or other hospitality operation are created (or are allowed to continue) by the manager, *not* by subordinate employees. Do you agree or disagree? Why?
2. Describe the types of front desk employees who should and should not be empowered to make creative decisions about guest service.
3. How should an FOM address a front office employee who resists change, who wants to continue to do things the way they have always been done, and who considers guest service to be an important (but not the most important) responsibility?

From the Front Office: Front-Line Interview

Eric Wolfer
Front Office Manager
Hyatt Regency Cincinnati (488 rooms)
Cincinnati, Ohio

Just Another Busy Weekend!

Eric received his undergraduate degree in hotel, restaurant, and institutional management from the University of Delaware. While in college, he held several part-time positions in the hospitality industry, including restaurant food server and front desk agent. He completed rooms and food and beverage internships with Hilton hotels, Marriott hotels, and a small chain of time-share properties in Colorado. After graduation, Eric entered the corporate management training program with Hyatt in Cincinnati. After completing the six-month training program, he became the assistant FOM and was promoted to his current position of FOM.

1. What are the most important responsibilities in your present position?

My most important responsibility is to please all of our guests and to consistently exceed their expectations. It is critical to ensure that every guest is satisfied. We do this by properly training and motivating our Front Office staff. Other important responsibilities include scheduling, payroll, daily reports, organization of incoming groups, and handling special requests.

2. What are the biggest challenges that confront you in your day-to-day work and in the long-term operation of your property's front office?

Some of the biggest challenges I face daily are guest satisfaction issues such as complaints, communication, last minute changes, and special requests for incoming guests. The front desk is the focal point of the hotel, and guests who encounter a problem, even if it is in a restaurant or with room service or housekeeping, typically inform us. Sometimes these problems can be small and they can be addressed by a front desk agent. Sometimes, however, they require the attention of the FOM. No matter how small or large a problem is, it is always important to listen closely to the guest, to show genuine concern, to apologize, and to take care of the problem.

Another challenge relates to last-minute changes that can involve a single guest or a 500-person group. Regardless of the number of guests affected, it is vital to be smart and to act appropriately to get the job done. Many issues arise on any given day that can be challenging and hectic. As a manager, you must stay calm and create an action plan to take care of the situation.

In the long term, my biggest challenges are maintaining proper staffing levels and keeping employees motivated. In the hotel industry, the level of business changes constantly. Busy months may be followed by slow months. Sometimes it is a challenge to retain good employees during the slow months if there are fewer work hours available. It is important to be honest with your employees so that they know what to expect during slow times and can better plan for them.

Other long-term challenges are training and coaching employees. Every employee is different and requires a different level of attention during the training process. I try to spend the proper amount of training time with each employee before expecting that employee to do the job alone. If this is not done, employees become frustrated. Training is an ongoing process. There are always areas for improvement, and it is valuable to work with employees on new tasks to keep them motivated and to learn from their ideas.

3. What is your most unforgettable front office moment?
It was the third day of my training program at the front desk for Hyatt Regency Cincinnati, and it happened to be Red Hot Weekend in the city. On Saturday, there was the Ohio State versus University of Cincinnati football game. The final baseball games of the season were being played at Cinergy Field (the Reds' baseball stadium), and an Oktoberfest event was being held in town.

As a result, the city was extremely busy. Hundreds of people checked into the hotel on Friday to stay for one night; then a whole new crowd checked in on Saturday. The hotel was sold out all weekend. The time for Friday night check-out was noon Saturday, and guests with Saturday evening reservations began arriving Saturday morning. There were no rooms available because the hotel was full. This meant we had to check out one set of guests and check in another set of guests in only a few hours.

It was quite incredible the way the staff worked together, and we managed to get the job done. It was a great experience, and I now realize this was not, by any means, an out-of-the-ordinary event. However, that was my first experience during a busy weekend as a front desk agent of a full-service hotel, and it was a moment I will not forget.

4. What advice do you have for those studying about or considering a career in front office or hotel management?
Take advantage of every opportunity offered by your school. Within the hotel and restaurant management program, there are likely to be a variety of clubs available to students. I would highly recommend joining one of them to gain the experience and networking that comes with it. Find a club that suits you the best and join it. If there are two that you like, join both of them! Clubs offer a great opportunity to become more involved in what you are studying, and you will gain a better idea about what to expect in careers.

Also, be sure to work in the industry (specifically front desk), if you want to become an FOM. Hands-on experience will be the best test of whether this is really the career you want, and you will gain valuable skills and industry knowledge. Internships may be available with different hospitality companies. Complete at least one internship before graduating, even it is not a formal requirement. It will allow you to gain exposure to different departments throughout a hotel, and you can learn how they all work together. As an intern, you will be involved in activities such as meetings, training, and other activities that are part of a hotel manager's workday.

The FOM in Action: A Solution

What strategies and tactics can a new FOM such as Candida use to improve guest service ratings for the front office and to improve the morale of front desk agents who did not like their previous supervisor? The new FOM should begin by acknowledging an important philosophy: The guest is the reason for my job. The FOM also must understand that the employees' attitudes toward guest service are influenced by what the FOM does (and does not do) and says (and does not say).

A good place to start is with a group meeting to initiate the process of reestablishing a professional relationship with all members of the front office team. Discussion can include the following issues:

- What can I (the FOM) do to help?
- What do employees like (dislike) about their jobs?
- What do the guests like (dislike) about their visits to the property?

- What can I (the FOM) do to help staff better respond to guest needs?
- What are some actions that front office staff can take when they are empowered to better serve guests?

As the new FOM, Candida can serve as a role model by treating guests and employees with respect and dignity in the way that she would like to be treated by her boss. Other activities may help her during the first phase of the improvement strategy.

- Schedule a series of staff meetings to develop a mission statement about what the department is attempting to accomplish and how it intends to accomplish it.
- Observe carefully during the initial days on the job, analyze previous evaluations by guests, and interview present guests to identify what guests liked and disliked about their lodging experience. This information may suggest training needs that should be addressed quickly.

- Obtain group input in revising work processes to better meet the needs of the guests. Front desk agents must do what is necessary (within reason) to please the guest.
- Encourage the staff to make suggestions and reward them for doing so. For example, dinner and movie passes might be given to all front desk agents who work more than a specified number of hours weekly for each month in which the guest comment ratings are at or above a specified level.

A second phase of the new FOM's improvement strategy might involve staff in discussions about how to make the department and the hotel an employer-of-choice within the community, that is, a place where employees want to work. Meetings and formal conversations that address this issue will likely yield responses that, over time, can be addressed.

As Candida implements improvement strategies, employee morale and guest service evaluations will change positively.

FRONT OFFICE SEMANTICS LIST

Value	Continuous quality	Word-of-mouth advertising
Service (hotel)	improvement (CQI)	Employee-to-room ratio
Atrium	Vision	Road warrior
Executive committee	Mission statement	Benchmarking
Organizational culture	Long-range plan	Zero defects
Work processes	Business plan	Moment of truth
Quality	Marketing plan	Wow factor
Defect	Operating budget	Accountability
Empowerment	Incremental sales	
Cross-functional team	Repeat business	

FRONT OFFICE AND THE INTERNET

- Market Metrix is a market research organization that serves the hospitality industry. It publishes a quarterly report (*Market Metrix Hospitality Index*) that addresses customer satisfaction about organizations in the hotel, airline, and rental car industries. To learn more about the company and to see quarterly reports for the last several periods, go to www.marketmetrix.com.

- The *Mobil Travel Guide* and its star rating system are useful to many travelers in selecting hotel accommodations. Factors used to award stars can be a helpful foundation to managers who want to benchmark quality, physical facility, and property amenities. To view this information, go to www.mobiltravelguide.com. When you arrive at this site, click on Latest Star Ratings and then click on Lodging Stars to see a general description of properties earning one to five stars. You can learn about services, facilities, guestroom details, and specialized facility details for each property rating.

- To view an extensive library of general information about quality and quality management, go to www.mapnp.org/library/quality/quality.htm. You will find an extensive listing of quality and related topics that can be researched for a wide range of information. This is a good one-site source for a virtual library about quality that is useful for hoteliers.

- The Ritz-Carlton is the only lodging organization that has won the coveted Malcolm Baldrige National Quality Award (two times). To learn more about this organization and its quality journey, go to www.ritzcarlton.com. When you arrive at the site, click on About Us. You can learn about the company's awards, gold standards, quality philosophy, and leadership center (which is a resource center that helps leading organizations to benchmark business practices).

- John Self, a lecturer at the Collins School of Hospitality Management at California State Polytechnic Institute, has developed a series of brief customer service articles that provide suggestions about tactics useful to hotel managers. To view this site, go to www.sideroad.com/cs.

REAL-WORLD ACTIVITIES

1. Some people say that the best way to ensure happy guests is to give them a deeply discounted or even complimentary guestroom. Hotels cannot, obviously, do this routinely and remain in business. Comment on the role of price as travelers select properties, anticipate service levels, and evaluate their experiences after they depart.

2. Front desk agents, like employees in any other business, will have bad days. If you are an FOM talking with an employee who is having a bad day, what could you say that will benefit the staff member and, at the same time, encourage him or her to continue providing exemplary levels of service for guests?

3. Assume you are a hotel guest. Take an imaginary tour through a lobby and other public areas. Along the way, note examples of positive and negative moments of truth that can occur and indicate how they may affect your perception of the property.

4. When some FOMs train new front desk agents, they request that the employees wear a badge stating "trainee." What message does this give to guests checking in? What is your opinion of the tactic? What are the pros and cons of requiring new staff members to wear a trainee badge? Do you think guests will be more forgiving if the level of service from a trainee is less than that expected or typically received?

5. In what situations would you as an FOM allow (empower) experienced front desk agents to make decisions in response to unusual requests from guests? Give examples of situations that extend beyond the boundaries of the level of empowerment that you would permit.

3

Overview of the Front Office Department

Chapter Outline

FRONT OFFICE FUNCTIONS AND RESPONSIBILITIES
  Primary Function: Coordinate Guest Services
  Specific Activities: Deliver Guest Services
  Front Office Responsibilities
FRONT OFFICE ORGANIZATION
  Small Hotel (75 Rooms)
  Large Hotel (350 Rooms)
  Mega Hotel (3,000 Rooms)
FRONT OFFICE POSITIONS
  Management Positions
  Nonmanagement Positions
HUMAN RESOURCES MANAGEMENT (ENTRY-LEVEL PERSONNEL)
  Recruitment and Selection
  Orientation and Training
  Motivation and Leadership
  Staffing and Scheduling

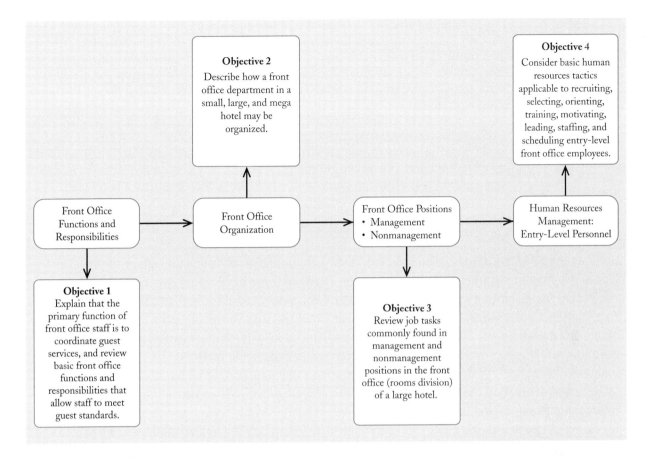

CHAPTER ROADMAP

Chapter Preview

Chapter 1 provided an overview of the industry to which hotels belong and an explanation of the organization within which front office personnel work. Chapter 2 emphasized the importance of guest service and reviewed procedures to develop quality processes that help front office (and other employees) work in a way that consistently meets standards desired by guests. Now in this chapter, we are ready to discuss the specifics of front office management as we answer these questions: What are the responsibilities of a hotel's front office department? How is the front office organized and what positions typically make up the department? What work activities (job tasks) are performed by those in front office positions?

Although much will be said in this book about technology and how it helps front office personnel, service is delivered by *people*. Employees are the department's most important resource, and basic principles of human resources management must be used consistently to ensure that the best employees are available, and that they are performing effectively. The concluding section of this chapter addresses basic tactics for staff recruitment and selection, for orientation and training, for motivating and supervising, and for staffing and scheduling.

Which department in a hotel is most important? Experienced hoteliers know that all departments are important. Each department is responsible for different functions, all of which, in one way or another, affect guests. Work outputs frequently flow to and through the front office on the way to pleasing the guests. It is with guest focus in mind that the concept of the "front office as the hub of the hotel" becomes relevant.

As a result of reading this chapter, you should have an idea about why an entire book on hospitality management can be devoted to one department (front office) in one type of property (hotel). The role of the front office is absolutely critical to the property's success. It is where guest service begins, where guest service is focused during a guest's stay at the property, and, where the service experience is concluded.

The FOM in Action: The Challenge

Raoul is the FOM in a large destination resort in Hawaii. The resort is part of a chain that has similar properties in other locations throughout the Pacific. Raoul has enjoyed working with several young front desk agents who are from the local area. Several began working at the property while in high school, have remained for several years after graduation, and have expressed an interest in the lodging industry. This is good news for Raoul because, like his competitors throughout the area, he is experiencing a shortage of highly qualified staff members for almost all lodging positions.

During a performance appraisal session for one of these employees, Raoul asked, "Kimo, have you thought about your professional future? You've told me that you enjoy your front office position and want to learn more and be promoted. What are your plans to do this?"

Kimo responded: "I have been thinking about a lodging career. If you have time now, can we talk about it? What is your advice about what I should do? How can you and the hotel help me to plan and advance in my career?"

What are some general suggestions that Raoul should make to Kimo?

FRONT OFFICE FUNCTIONS AND RESPONSIBILITIES

What exactly do employees in the front office department do? As Roadmap 3.1 indicates, this is the topic of this first section of the chapter. Historically, the department has been referred to as the front office or the front desk. However, the functions of this department extend far beyond the hotel lobby and the front desk at which guests have had face-to-face contact with a front desk agent during registration and checkout. Today, technology allows guests to register at a hotel while in the shuttle van from the airport, at curbside at the hotel entrance, or at a **kiosk** in the lobby. Guests can check out using their guestroom's television. In these instances, direct personal contact with the front desk agent is no longer necessary.

FRONT OFFICE SEMANTICS

Kiosk: Small electronic unit (machine) located in a hotel lobby that allows guests with proper identification to register or check out of the hotel without the need to interact with a front desk agent.

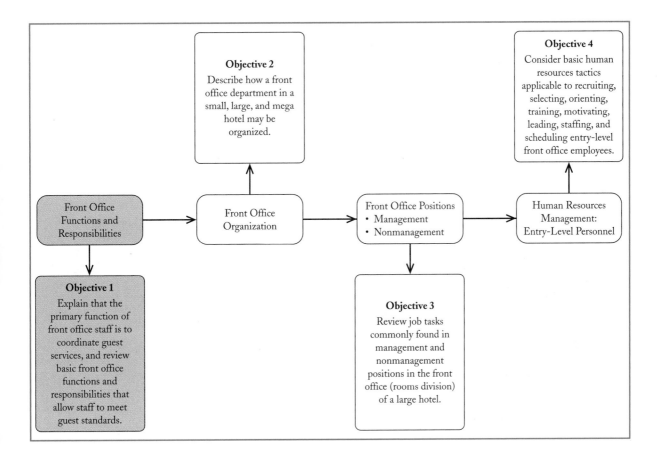

ROADMAP 3.1

Primary Function: Coordinate Guest Services

What is the primary function of the front office? A lengthy answer involves the many activities discussed throughout this book. A more concise response, however, relates to the front office as the hotel's primary point of contact with guests. Therefore, the front office manager (FOM) must coordinate the work of other departments to ensure that each guest's stay is an enjoyable and value-filled experience, which helps to help promote repeat business and positive word-of-mouth advertising.

The role of the front office in interacting with guests and coordinating the services of other departments with a focus on the guests has prompted some organizations to change its name. For example, instead of the term *front office,* some properties prefer the term *guest services.* Staff members working at the front desk in these properties are no longer called *front desk clerks* or *front desk agents*; instead, they are referred to as *guest service agents.*

Figure 3.1 reemphasizes the service-related function of the front office department. When reviewing Figure 3.1, note that front office staff members provide service directly to guests, for example, when reservations are made, as guests register and depart from the property, and as guests request service during their stay.

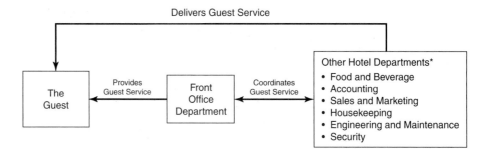

*Two departments (human resources and purchasing) are omitted; they provide services to other departments that, in turn, provide service to the guests.

FIGURE 3.1   Front office department: Centralizing and coordinating the hotel's guest service function.

Details about the interactions between the front office and other hotel departments will be presented in Chapter 14. However, to introduce the role of the front office department in coordinating guest services, examples by department are previewed in Figure 3.2. The examples show guest service delivered directly by each department and indicate how that service is coordinated by front office personnel.

To this point, the chapter has emphasized the significant role of the front office in directly providing service to guests and in coordinating services provided by other departments. To carry out this role effectively, the FOM and staff must engage in specific activities which are reviewed next.

Department	Example of direct service delivered by department	Coordinated by front office
Food and beverage	À la carte dining	Charges to guestroom routed to front office for entry in guest **folio**
Accounting	Modifications to guest charges after departure	Original room and other charges maintained during the guest's stay
Sales and marketing	Planning of meetings and functions	Guest concerns during event routed through the front desk
Housekeeping	Cleaning of guestrooms and public areas	Guestroom linen requests made to front desk personnel
Engineering and maintenance	In-room maintenance during guest stay	Request for guestroom maintenance made to front desk staff
Security	Management of guest-related security issues	Telephone request for security assistance made to front desk staff

FIGURE 3.2   Examples of coordination: The front office and other hotel departments.

FRONT OFFICE SEMANTICS

Folio: Detailed list of guestroom and other charges authorized by the guest or legally imposed by the hotel.

MODERN FRONT OFFICE ISSUES AND TACTICS

Amenities for Budget Business Travelers

In the "old days," business travelers typically paid a higher price than other travelers for hotel rooms, products, and services; in return, they expected and received higher levels of service. Today, however, many business travelers are budget minded and, of necessity, hotels must downsize amenities that business travelers receive for the reduced prices that they pay. In the view of many business travelers, hoteliers have forgotten the basics of customer service. Hoteliers recognize that their business travelers want to save money, but they believe that these guests must, therefore, adjust their expectations accordingly.

Corporate travel managers acknowledge that their employees are demanding and that a large percentage of these travelers believe they should receive a higher level of service than leisure travelers. Their reasoning is this: They tend to travel in good times and bad times (although not as frequently in bad times), and they often book hotel rooms on short notice, thereby filling rooms that would otherwise go unsold.

Creative hoteliers must discover practical ways to meet the expectations of business travelers in line with the reduced revenues they generate for hotels.

Adapted from Elliott, C. 2004. When business class means second class. *New York Times.* Business Travel Section, July 20.

Specific Activities: Deliver Guest Services

Figure 3.3 reviews specific activities of front office personnel that enable the department to meet guests' needs. Each of the activities is integral to the front office department's role in delivering guest service:

- *Revenue management:* Establishes guestroom rates.
- *Reservations management:* Arranges (reserves) a room for guests before their arrival.

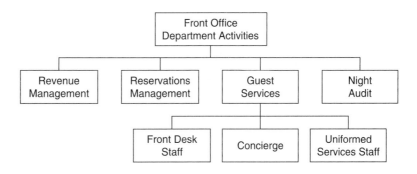

FIGURE 3.3 Front office activities.

Adapted from Hayes, D. K., and J. D. Ninemeier. 2004. *Hotel Operations Management,* p. 177. Upper Saddle River, NJ: Pearson Prentice Hall. Reprinted by permission.

- *Guest services:* Assists with registration and service requests during guests' stay and helps guests settle charges as they depart. Concierge and **uniformed services employees,** including bell services attendants, may also help with specific guest service functions. (Concierge personnel are considered part of the uniformed services staff at some properties.)
- *Night audit:* Uses automated systems (typically) to review the accuracy and completeness of each day's accounting transactions and to close that day's information in preparation for posting the next day's transactions.

FRONT OFFICE SEMANTICS

Uniformed services employee: Person in the front office department who provides personalized services to guests. Positions include bell staff (porters), door and parking attendants, van drivers, and in some hotels, concierge personnel.

Night audit: Process of reviewing for accuracy and completeness the accounting transactions from one day to conclude, or close, that day's sales information in preparation for posting transactions of the next day.

Front Office Responsibilities

The responsibilities of the front office department relate to the activities just described. Assigned personnel must ensure that the activities are carried out consistently and effectively in a manner that meets established performance standards.

Let's look at the most general front office responsibilities. Consider this brief discussion as a preview of information that will be presented in subsequent chapters:

- *Managing the property management system.* The front office manager maintains the **property management system (PMS),** which is the computerized system used by the hotel to manage room revenue, room rates, reservations and room assignments, guest histories, and accounting information. As well, the PMS performs many other guest service and management information-related functions. Essentially, it records who comes to the hotel, what they spend while they are there, and how (and what) they pay when they leave. The functions of a PMS are described in detail in Chapter 4.

FRONT OFFICE SEMANTICS

Property management system (PMS): The computer hardware and programs used to record guest reservations and requests and to manage the prices charged for rooms and other services. The system also records and stores hotel sales data and other historical information useful in decision making for effective hotel management.

- *Revenue and reservations management.* The front office has the responsibility to maximize the hotel's revenue per available room (RevPar). To do so requires staff to implement tactics to increase the occupancy percentage and the average daily rate (ADR). Revenue management is discussed in Chapter 6.

- *Management of guest services.* The front office focuses directly on the delivery of service to the guests while they are at the hotel. Examples include handling

Modern property management systems speed the processing of guest reservations and free desk agents to focus on improving guest services.

luggage, taking and routing guests' messages, and handling guest concerns and disputes as they arise. Information about this responsibility is introduced in this chapter and described in detail in Chapter 10.

MODERN FRONT OFFICES ISSUES AND TACTICS

Hotel Souvenirs: A New Profit Center?

Are guests always right? What many guests refer to as "taking souvenirs" is called *pilfering* by hotels. Losses as a result of hotel theft total an estimated $100 million per year. Towels are the items taken most often, but toiletries, ashtrays, bathrobes, and bath mats are also frequently removed. Many hotels expect guests to remove unopened toiletries and related amenities even though they do not provide much marketing value. (These are not items that travelers typically show to their friends and family.)

What tactics can resolve and address this problem? Items that can easily "walk away" like televisions, paintings, lamps, and alarm clocks are often securely attached to the wall or furniture to make them more difficult to steal. Many properties offer amenities for sale. Guests can purchase bedding, towels, bathrobes, and individually numbered room glasses. This type of program can be successful in terms of generating revenue and reducing the number of pilfered items.

Adapted from Gilden, J. 2004. Hotels might call "souvenirs" stolen. *Chicago Tribune* online edition, July 18. Retrieved July 18, 2004, from http://www.chicagotribune.com.

• *Guest accounting.* The front office is responsible for accounting tasks related to guest stays. Different and changing room rates, room charges during a visit, and adjustments to room charges at time of departure make what otherwise seems to be a straightforward responsibility more challenging. Accounting aspects of front office management are discussed in Chapter 12.

- *General data management.* The front office collects data relating to guests and to the effective management of the hotel. Such data are used by departments throughout the property. Chapters 4 and 8 discuss data management tactics in-depth.

SECTION REVIEW AND DISCUSSION QUESTIONS

Section Objective: Explain that the primary function of front office staff is to coordinate guest services, and review basic front office activities and responsibilities that allow staff to meet guest service standards.

Section Summary: The primary role of the front office department relates to its function as the hotel's primary point of contact with guests. The front office fulfills this role by interacting directly with guests and by coordinating the services of other departments with a focus on guests. Specific activities that assist in delivery of guest services relate to revenue management, reservations, guest services while guests are at the property, and night audit. Specific responsibilities of front office personnel that relate to these activities include managing the property management system (PMS), revenue and reservations management, management of guest services, accounting tasks for guests, and general data management.

Discussion Questions:
1. What is your reaction to the idea of renaming the front office department the guest services department? If you were a hotel general manager, might you make this change? Why?
2. Figure 3.2 includes examples of direct services delivered by hotel departments that are coordinated by front office personnel. What are other examples?
3. Can you describe any activities that are the responsibility of the FOM but do *not* have a direct or indirect impact on guests? Can you think of any other hotel department that has a greater impact on guest service? If so, explain your answer.

FRONT OFFICE ORGANIZATION

Now that we have reviewed the primary function and important activities and responsibilities of the front office department, Roadmap 3.2 suggests that it is time to consider how the department is organized to effectively meet its obligations. Not surprisingly, the organizational structure depends, in great part, on the size of the property. Many, but not all, responsibilities must be performed regardless of the

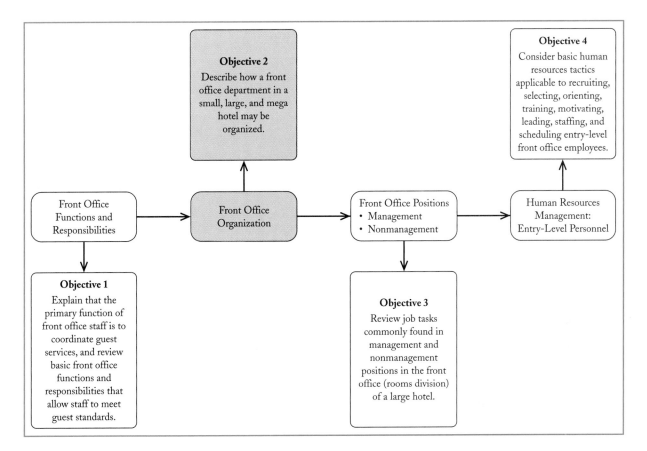

ROADMAP 3.2

hotel's size (number of rooms). For example, the five front office responsibilities noted in the previous section (managing the PMS, revenue and reservations, guest services, guest accounting, and general data management) relate to effective management of all types of hotels. Other considerations include the availability of specific uniformed services staff such as door and parking attendants, bell services attendants, and concierge personnel. Property size and the type of guests to which the property is marketed influence whether these staff will be available.

How can a small property with fewer front office employees perform the same basic activities as their larger counterparts with more employees? One basic tactic involves the use of more generalist positions in small properties. For example, in a very small property, the hotel's general manager may function as the FOM and may frequently perform the duties of a front desk agent. By contrast, in a large property, there may be four or more levels of employees between the general manager and the front desk agent, including resident manager, FOM, assistant FOM, and front desk manager. Individuals in these specialized positions may perform fewer different tasks than the generalists in smaller properties. Nevertheless, supervisors and managers in these larger properties probably will be able to perform many of the tasks done by their **subordinates,** because they will likely have had experience in subordinate positions during their career progression. Many properties **cross-train** persons in several related positions so that they can gain experience and so that staff are available at all times to perform all necessary tasks.

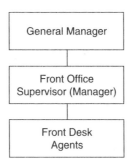

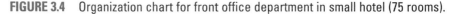

FIGURE 3.4   Organization chart for front office department in small hotel (75 rooms).

FRONT OFFICE SEMANTICS

Subordinate: Person whose work is directly supervised or controlled by an individual of higher rank or position.

Cross-train: Tactic of training persons for more than one position so that they can assist wherever they are needed.

Small Hotel (75 Rooms)

Figure 3.4 shows the organization chart for the front office department in a small hotel of approximately 75 rooms. The property's small size allows for a simple structure: A general manager supervises a front office supervisor (manager) who, in turn, directs the work of the front desk agents. All (or almost all) of the tasks done by the greater number of employees in a large hotel (350 rooms) and in a mega hotel (more than 3,000 rooms) will be performed by the general manager, front office supervisor (manager), or front desk agents in a small property.

MODERN FRONT OFFICES ISSUES AND TACTICS

Who Owns Small Hotels?

Although they make up less than 1 percent of the U.S. population, Asian-Indian Americans own approximately 37 percent of hotels in the United States, including half of the nation's economy lodging properties, which are typically small. The hotel industry seems to be attractive to Asian-Indian immigrants for several reasons: operating a hotel need not be complicated, hotel owners need not have significant proficiency in the English language, and family members can help. In addition, there can be significant positive cash flow along with reasonable profits after taxes, interest, and depreciation.

Hospitality is a significant part of the culture of Asian-Indian Americans. An ancient phrase, "The guest is like God," suggests their attitude about the business. Hotel owners work long hours, must learn every aspect of the business, must manage operating costs while delivering product and service quality, and must reinvest in the business. These are among the traits shared by Asian-Indian Americans who experience success in the hotel industry.

What's next? Some observers believe the next generation will acquire larger assets with bigger developers and will participate in joint ventures with townships and cities. In doing so, Asian-Indian Americans will continue to play a significant role in the hotel industry of the United States.

Adapted from Newton, B. 2004. Hotels fuel the dream for many Indian-Americans. *The Virginian-Pilot*, July 18.

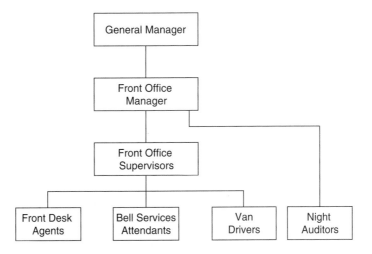

FIGURE 3.5 Organization chart for front office department in large hotel (350 rooms).

Large Hotel (350 Rooms)

Figure 3.5 shows a possible organization chart for a front office department in a hotel with 350 rooms. Note that the general manager supervises the work of an FOM who, in turn, directs the work activities of the front office supervisors and night auditors. The front office supervisor is responsible for several types of entry-level employees: front desk agents, bell services attendants, and van drivers.

In a large hotel, activities involving reservations, registration, service to guests during their stay, and guest accounting are likely assumed by the FOM and front desk agents. End-of-day accounting tasks are performed by night auditors, and selected aspects of guest service are shared between bell services attendants and van drivers.

Mega Hotel (3,000 Rooms)

Figure 3.6 shows a possible organization chart for the rooms division in a very large hotel. Note the significant differences between the staffing structure of this property and the two smaller properties just discussed:

- In a mega hotel, the general manager supervises a resident manager (sometimes called a rooms manager or director of the rooms division) who, in turn, directs the work of an FOM as well as the executive housekeeper and, in many cases, the director of security.

- In a very large property, the front office may be considered part of the rooms division, and the FOM supervises three positions: reservations manager, assistant FOM, and PBX manager. (Recall that PBX refers to private branch exchange, the hotel's internal telephone/communications system.)

- The reservations manager directs the work of reservations agents; the PBX manager is responsible for PBX operators.

- The assistant FOM supervises two managers: manager of the front desk (who supervises cashiers and front desk agents) and manager of uniformed services

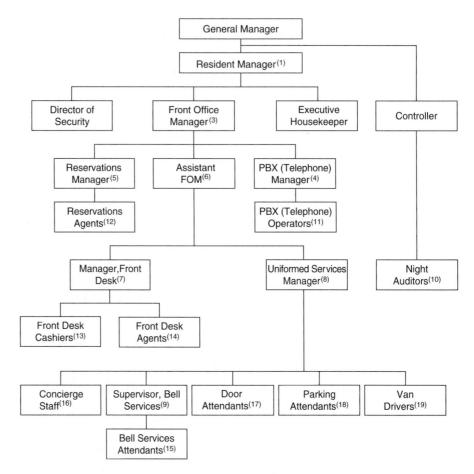

Number after each position title refers to the listing of job tasks in Figures 3.8 and 3.9.

FIGURE 3.6 Organization chart for rooms division in a mega hotel (3,000 rooms).

(who is responsible for the concierge staff, supervisor of bell services, door attendants, parking attendants, and van drivers).

• In large hotels, night auditors may be the responsibility of the controller's (accountant's) office, which reports to the general manager. This type of organization centralizes responsibilities for serving guests in the rooms division and for financial management in the accounting division.

The work of all of the staff members in these specialized positions represents the property's response to this question: What positions are needed to consistently and effectively deliver quality services for our guests that meet (or exceed) the quality standards established by the hotel?

The organization chart illustrated in Figure 3.6 is oversimplified in efforts to explain how positions become more specialized as hotels become larger. In fact, there is no "typical" organizational structure, and the one used by a specific property

A property's size will often determine the scope of an FOM's responsibilities.

has probably evolved over time and is currently perceived to best meet the needs of the property. In some large properties, the responsibilities for reservations of transient guests may rest with the marketing and sales department, and there may be a rooms control manager (also called rooms controller) within the front desk department who manages room blocks for group reservations after they are booked. Some properties create specialized positions of night front desk supervisor and night front desk agents. There may also be a manager (or supervisor) of night auditors. In spite of these and many other variations, Figure 3.6 represents the basics of an organizational structure that shows the range of front office responsibilities in a very large property.

The next section reviews job tasks for many of the positions illustrated in Figure 3.6. Recall that in smaller properties, fewer persons perform wider ranges of activities. Recall also that someone in a property of any size must be responsible for each of the most basic activities that will be identified.

SECTION REVIEW AND DISCUSSION QUESTIONS

Section Objective: Describe how a front office department in a small, large, and mega hotel may be organized.

Section Summary: Basic front office responsibilities must be performed regardless of the hotel's size (number of rooms). Smaller properties use generalist positions in which the incumbent performs work tasks that would be separated into different positions in larger properties. A very large hotel may be organized so that a resident manager supervises the work of the director of security, the FOM, and the executive housekeeper. The FOM, in turn, directs the work of the reservations manager, the assistant FOM, and the PBX manager. The assistant FOM supervises the front desk manager and uniformed services manager.

Discussion Questions:

1. Assume that an experienced front office supervisor in a small hotel (75 rooms) wants to transfer to a mega hotel. In what position might this front office supervisor begin in the large property? Why?
2. Assume you are beginning to work in the hotel industry in an entry-level, uniformed services position (door or parking attendant or van driver). What might be a **career ladder** that would allow you to gain necessary experience and skills so that eventually you would be director of the rooms division?
3. Which management position in the rooms division of a mega hotel might require the widest range of knowledge, skills, and experience to manage the diverse number of tasks in subordinate positions? Explain your choice.

FRONT OFFICE SEMANTICS

Career ladder: Plan that projects successively more responsible professional positions within an organization or industry. Career ladders allow an employee to plan and schedule developmental activities judged necessary to assume higher level positions.

FRONT OFFICE POSITIONS

Now that we have discussed how the front office is organized, we note that Roadmap 3.3 considers the need to review specific positions within the department positions.

One way to classify front office positions is to consider whether persons working within the position must supervise others. For the purposes of the discussion in this section, these will be referred to as management positions. Although most management positions are **salaried,** they are not necessarily so. Some managers are paid a **wage** in compensation for their services.

FRONT OFFICE SEMANTICS

Salary: Pay calculated at a weekly, monthly, or annual rate rather than at an hourly rate.

Wage: Pay calculated on an hourly basis.

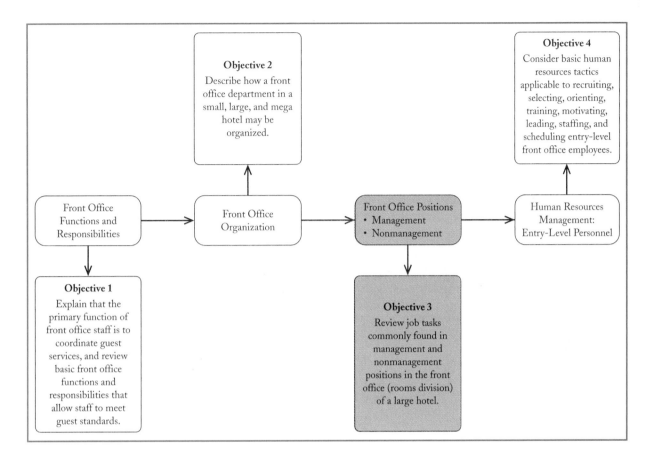

ROADMAP 3.3

Positions that do not require an incumbent to manage the work of others are referred to as nonmanagement positions. Most typically, these are **entry-level positions** in which the incumbent is paid a wage.

FRONT OFFICE SEMANTICS

Entry-level position: Position that requires little previous experience in or knowledge of job tasks and whose incumbents do not direct the work of other staff members.

This section reviews job tasks, skills, and traits of front office personnel in management and nonmanagement positions.

Management Positions

What do managers in front office positions do? Not surprisingly, some of their responsibilities, activities, and skills are similar to those of their management peers in other departments of the hotel. Many of these are listed in Figure 3.7. As you review Figure 3.7, note the emphasis on guest service, management of employees, and control of factors that address the attainment of financial goals. Communication skills, knowledge about ways to maximize guest and employee safety, and legal aspects of management responsibilities are also listed. Note that there is, in fact, a **universal process of management.** Most, if not all, of the responsibilities, activities, and skills

Management Responsibilities

- Deal effectively with the hotel's and the department's internal and external customers. Identify and resolve all guest concerns to ensure high levels of guest satisfaction in the delivery of services.
- Remain calm and alert during emergency situations or heavy property activity (e.g., heavy occupancy or in-house meetings). Serve as a leader and role model for other employees.
- Make decisions and take action based on previous experience. Use good judgment to determine useful procedures for unusual situations.
- Communicate effectively both orally and in writing to provide clear direction to staff members. Observe staff performance and create a work environment that fosters the professional development and growth of employees. Monitor workloads and make staffing recommendations accordingly.
- Provide clear directions, instruction, and guidance. Attend a variety of meetings and conduct staff meetings to ensure timely and effective communication and coordination within and between departments.
- Know labor-related legislation and applicable collective agreements, human resources policies, and procedures sufficiently to ensure correct application and adherence as staff are supervised.
- Organize and prioritize work to meet deadlines.
- Supervise staff including recruitment, training, counseling, performance evaluation, and discipline.
- Access and input information using a (increasingly) complex, automated PMS.
- Possess mathematical skills necessary to develop financial management tools, to complete management forecasts, and to monitor payroll controls.
- Logically and independently plan, organize, and complete work in a timely manner.
- Evaluate work quality, read materials, and review documents; receive instructions and learn about inquiries from guests, staff, and management peers.
- Keep immediate supervisor informed of all problems or unusual events.
- Protect the property's assets.
- Comply with all policies and procedures.

Management Activities

- Develop and recommend short- and long-term goals, and establish and implement specific strategies to achieve them.
- Develop, recommend, and implement policies and procedures and ensure that all guidelines are followed.
- Develop, recommend, and implement departmental standards and improvements to standards that support the business plan and increase guest satisfaction.
- Prepare, recommend, and implement budgets. Monitor progress throughout the fiscal period and take corrective action as necessary.
- Research and recommend new products, automation, and services to improve operations and service delivery processes.
- Monitor employee performance. Ensure that workloads are fairly distributed while recognizing experience and skill levels of employees. Ensure appropriate staffing levels for business conditions.
- Prepare operating reports for management review.
- Prepare letters, memos, and reports.
- Remain alert throughout the duration of the shift and remain calm during emergency situations.
- Know and follow all safety and emergency procedures.
- Maintain staff attendance and payroll records.
- Emphasize employee development by coaching staff, by offering training to those who are qualified, and by assigning qualified mentors to employees who request them.
- Conduct regular staff meetings.
- Manage daily staffing to ensure that all necessary positions are filled, and guest service standards are maintained.
- Serve as the property's manager on duty as requested.
- Train, cross-train, and develop employees for promotions.
- Resolve guest complaints to benefit guests and the property.
- Perform tasks as assigned by higher-level management.

FIGURE 3.7 General management responsibilities, activities, and skills: all front office managers.

Managerial Skills

- Has appropriate written and oral communication skills.
- Can sell concepts and ideas to management peers and employees.
- Demonstrates team-building experience.
- Builds morale and motivates employees.
- Uses an appropriate management (leadership) style.
- Can serve as a mentor to inspire, train, and develop staff members for promotion.
- Instills a guest service and can-do attitude in all employees.
- Coaches employees to resolve problems and conflicts.
- Uses a calm, organized approach to all situations.
- Uses time management skills and organizational skills.
- Applies appropriate knowledge of technology.
- Uses strong guest service skills.
- Applies listening and follow-up skills
- Practices follow-up skills.
- Applies strong budgetary, forecasting, and cost-control skills.
- Follows and enforces company policies and procedures.
- Resolves problems.
- Assumes responsibility; is accountable.
- Understands and follows security and safety requirements.
- Maintains courteous, friendly, and professional work environment.
- Provides overall direction, coordination, and ongoing evaluation of operations.
- Uses creative problem-solving skills.
- Evaluates alternatives to determine an action plan.
- Thinks creatively.
- Understands basic asset management.
- Has the manual dexterity to use computer keyboard and calculator.
- Walks and stands a significant amount of time during a work shift.
- Maintains attendance in conformance with standards.
- Maintains a neat, clean, and well-groomed appearance.

FIGURE 3.7   *(continued)*

noted in Figure 3.7 apply to those in management positions in other segments of the hospitality industry and to many for-profit and not-for-profit businesses and organizations of any type.

FRONT OFFICE SEMANTICS

Universal process of management: Concept that, at the most basic level, the principles of planning, organizing, coordinating, staffing, controlling, and evaluating are the same (or similar) in any type of business or organization.

Some management responsibilities and activities are unique to the rooms division and to the management positions within it. Job tasks for common front office management positions are noted in Figure 3.8. (Note that the positions in Figures 3.8 and 3.9 are keyed to the organization chart for the mega hotel shown in Figure 3.6.)

There are, of course, many ways to organize a hotel, its departments, and the positions within them. For example, the organization chart in Figure 3.6 indicates

Text continued on page 108.

Resident Manager[1]

Facilitates the work of those with direct management obligations for security, front office operations, and housekeeping to ensure that these departments consistently deliver the highest levels of guest service and attain revenue and expense goals.

- Directs the work of the director of security, FOM, and executive housekeeper; interacts with human resources personnel regarding recruitment, selection, orientation, training, and performance appraisals tactics for these top-level department managers.
- Analyzes operating costs and coordinates development of department operating budgets.
- Reviews PMS reports to monitor revenue generation, yield management forecasts, expense management, and payroll controls.
- Prepares operating reports for the general manager.
- Coordinates service and guest expectation and experience information with other department heads; works with staff to plan for and implement corrective actions that address issues related to responsibilities.
- Facilitates implementation of corrective actions within responsible departments when negative variances occur.
- Assumes manager-on-duty coverage in absence of the general manager.
- Performs room and ground inspections.
- Encourages use of positive tactics in guests relations.
- Ensures that corrective actions resolve guest complaints.
- Oversees security concerns: helps ensure a safe environment for guests and staff members and helps to protect hotel assets.

Front Office Manager[3]

Directs the work of the reservations manager, assistant FOM, and PBX manager and enables them to consistently provide exemplary service for guests and resolve problems encountered by guests.

- Oversees all administrative tasks regarding the front office.
- Analyzes operating costs and coordinates development of the department's operating budget.
- Works with managers to determine, plan, and implement necessary training for subordinate personnel.
- Determines reports to be generated and assists in data analysis and revenue management decision making.
- Monitors and follows through on all group needs and demands. (Works closely with housekeeping, engineering, catering, and convention services staff.)
- Maintains documentation of and billing for guestroom relocations.
- Assumes manager-on-duty coverage in absence of the general manager.

PBX (Telephone) Manager[4]

Responsible for operation of the PBX (telephone) department and its staff.

- Manages the work of PBX operators.
- Prepares reports including all sales conversions, room rates, and related financial and employee productivity indicators.
- Interacts with human resources staff regarding recruitment, selection, orientation, performance appraisal, and discipline, if necessary.
- Ensures that all hotel policies and procedures are followed.
- Performs duties of PBX operator when staffing difficulties arise.
- May assume manager-on-duty coverage.

The number after each position refers to the organization chart in Figure 3.6.

FIGURE 3.8   Overview of job tasks for common front office management positions.

Reservations Manager[5]

Responsible to increase guestroom revenues and guest satisfaction levels by facilitating the work of reservation agents.

- Supervises the work of reservations agents, including interactions with human resources staff regarding recruitment, selection, orientation, performance appraisal, and discipline, if applicable.
- Ensures completion of daily assignments by subordinate staff.
- Analyzes operating costs regularly.
- Reviews daily, weekly, and other reports to monitor revenues, rate, and yield management forecasts and expense management, including payroll controls.
- Monitors and evaluates marketing trends and makes recommendations about future goals.
- Develops and implements controls of guestroom inventory.
- Reviews short- and long-term occupancy and revenue forecasts; identifies deficiencies and takes appropriate corrective action.
- Develops, recommends, and implements, as applicable, rate and yield structures for guestroom inventory and for central reservation strategies with third-party sources.
- Confirms that current information about guestroom status is maintained and effectively communicated.
- Responds to guest communications; takes necessary action to resolve identified issues.
- Ensures compliance with applicable service guarantees.
- Manages and follows up on executive reservations.
- Prepares weekly staffing schedules based on forecasts; monitors business volume workloads.
- May assume manager-on-duty coverage.

Assistant Front Office Manager[6]

Facilitates the work of the manager of the front desk and manager of uniformed services to ensure that these departments consistently deliver the highest levels of guest service and attain revenue and expense goals.

- Directs the work of the manager of front desk and manager of uniformed services.
- Interacts with human resources personnel regarding recruitment, selection, orientation, training, and performance appraisals for these managers.
- Coordinates budget development for these departments.
- Assists in analyzing PMS data and in selected revenue management activities.
- Prepares operating reports.
- Coordinates services and guest expectation and expense information with other department heads; works with staff to plan for and implement corrective actions that addresses issues related to his or her responsibilities.

Front Desk Manager[7]

Responsible for managing, directing, and evaluating the activities of front desk cashiers and front desk agents. Facilitates their work to ensure that the appropriate level of guest service is provided and that departmental revenue goals are attained.

- Provides input to the selection of front desk agents and cashiers.
- Trains and cross-trains front desk agents and cashiers.
- Participates in performance appraisals of front desk agents and cashiers.
- Maintains master-key control during each shift.
- Verifies that accurate room status information is maintained and properly communicated.
- Resolves guest problems.
- Updates group information. Maintains, monitors, and prepares group requirements and relays information to appropriate personnel.
- Completes reports on credit limits and potential room revenues.
- Receives information from the previous shift manager; provides details to the oncoming shift manager.
- Maintains a professional environment within the department.

FIGURE 3.8   *(continued)*

Front Desk Manager (*continued*)

- Schedules front desk cashiers.
- Checks cashiers in and out and verifies bank deposits at the end of each shift.
- Ensures that all paperwork and credit card vouchers are correct and balanced.
- Enforces all cash-handling, check-cashing, and credit policies.

Uniformed Services Manager[8]

Responsible to facilitate the work of concierge staff, door and parking attendants, van drivers, and the supervisor of bell services and directs their work to ensure the appropriate level of guest service.

- Directs the work of the supervisor of bell services, concierge staff, door and parking attendants, and van drivers. Interacts with human resources staff regarding recruitment, selection, orientation, performance appraisal, and discipline, if necessary.
- Prepares operating budgets for department; analyzes negative variances and takes corrective action as necessary.
- Analyzes guest service reports and plans and implements staff training programs as necessary.
- Schedules staff.

Supervisor, Bell Services[9]

Responsible for managing, directing, and evaluating the work of bell services attendants and facilitates their work to ensure the appropriate level of guest service.

- Manages the bell services department and its team of bell services staff.
- Provides quality bell services to guests to help ensure their satisfaction and return.
- Plans and coordinates department areas to meet requirements of VIP, group, banquet, and transient guests.
- Develops policies and procedures to remain on the cutting edge of industry standards.
- Develops, implements, and conducts training programs within the department to increase the level of professionalism, proficiency, and courtesy of employees.
- Sells department services to groups for baggage pulls and deliveries to maximize the hotel's profitability.

FIGURE 3.8   *(continued)*

that the night auditor is a **direct report** to the controller. In some hotels, this position may report to the FOM. As a second example, note that the organization chart in Figure 3.6 does not separate positions applicable to the night shift. In some very large properties, there may be a separate night shift manager who reports to the FOM. The night shift manager directs the work of a night shift supervisor, and night shift clerks (and even the night auditor) may report to the night shift supervisor.

Regardless of the hotel's size or exact organization, numerous activities exist that must be done by someone. The discussion in Figure 3.8 identifies activities in relation to specialized positions, but these activities could be grouped into one position in different ways.

FRONT OFFICE SEMANTICS

Direct report: Employee's immediate supervisor; also called *superordinate.*

The specific job tasks noted for each of the front office management positions in Figure 3.8 may be included in a **job description** for the position. This description may include **job specifications** that identify the personal qualities (e.g., education, experience, and other **bona fide occupational qualifications**) that are judged necessary for successful performance within a position.

FRONT OFFICE SEMANTICS

Job description: List of tasks that an employee working in a specific position must be able to perform effectively.

Job specification: List of personal qualities judged necessary for successful performance of the tasks required by the job description.

Bona fide occupational qualification (BOQ): Qualification to perform a job that is judged reasonably necessary to safely or adequately perform all tasks within the job.

An interesting trend is that hotel organization charts, including sections applicable to the front office, are becoming more **flat.**

FRONT OFFICE SEMANTICS

Flat (organization chart): Combination of positions within an organization to reduce the number of management layers in efforts to improve communication, increase operating efficiencies, and reduce costs.

For example, as technology applications allow FOMs to "do more with less," the number of management positions and the managers within them may be reduced. Some observers of the hotel industry note the irony that technology has had a very significant influence on hotel departments with the fewest number of people (e.g., front office, accounting, and marketing and sales). In contrast, departments with the largest number of staff members (e.g., food and beverage, and housekeeping) have been unable to significantly reduce the number of positions and staff members by adapting technology to departmental operations.

Nonmanagement Positions

What kind of general responsibilities and skills are important for those in nonmanagement positions in the front office? Figure 3.9 provides some answers to this question. As noted in the discussion about management positions, the general responsibilities and skills listed apply to other hotel positions, to positions in other segments of the hospitality industry, and to positions in most profit and nonprofit businesses and organizations.

Figure 3.10 provides an overview of job tasks for common nonmanagement positions in the front office. (Recall that the positions are keyed to the rooms division for the mega hotel outlined in Figure 3.6). The job specifications for many of these positions often require a minimal amount of education and experience. They are, then, entry-level positions. Contrary to a common stereotype, an entry-level position is not the same as a dead-end position. Individuals who want a career in the hotel industry may begin while they are in high school or in a postsecondary program. Over time, especially with proper mentoring, they may gain experience in several positions and plan a career ladder that will allow them to move up in the front office department and into general management positions within a hotel organization.

Text continued on page 115.

General responsibilities and skills required for nonmanagement employees

- Wears appropriate uniform, if applicable, at all times.
- Works to comply with the hotel's hospitality (guest service) commitment.
- Has oral and writing skills appropriate for the position with basic language fluency applicable to peers and property guests.
- Is citizen of country or has valid work permit.
- Complies with written and oral directions.
- Pays attention to details.
- Can handle multiple tasks concurrently (if appropriate).
- Is knowledgeable about the property, its revenue-producing outlets, and its amenities.
- Willing to work a variety of day and night and weekend shifts if needed.
- Lives in the local area or within commuting distance.
- Willing to stand for long periods of time.
- Uses excellent people skills.
- Uses computer for selected work tasks.
- Has appropriate physical stamina for a work environment that can be fast paced and stressful.
- Has a genuine interest in helping guests and employee peers.
- Has a strong work ethic.
- Complies with the hotel's policies and does routine work according to standardized processes.
- Maintains a clean and safe work area.

FIGURE 3.9   General responsibilities and skills: Nonmanagement staff.

Properly fitting and well-designed uniforms are an important part of creating a professional image at the front desk.

Night Auditor[10]

Responsible for the daily review of guest-related financial transactions recorded by the front office staff.

- Ensures that correct charges for room rentals and purchases at hotel outlets are charged (posted) to correct guest accounts.
- Processes credit card and guest charge vouchers.
- Receives and records guest payments.
- Maintains daily count information on walk-in reservations.
- Records and makes wake-up calls.
- Transfers authorized guest charges and deposits to group master accounts.
- Verifies accuracy of all account postings and balances.
- Monitors effectiveness of discounts and other advertising and promotion efforts.
- Develops "today" and "to-date" reports of room revenues, occupancy rates, and other statistics requested by the controller.
- Prepares a summary of revenue by types (cash, check, credit card).
- May perform guest registration and check-out procedures.
- Prepares high-balance credit reports.
- Prepares housekeeper's report showing status of check-outs, stays, and vacant and out-of-order rooms for the night just ended.

PBX (Telephone) Operator[11]

Responsible to professionally answer and route telephone calls throughout the property, provide accurate information, and promote the highest levels of guest satisfaction.

- Professionally answers and routes telephone calls throughout the property.
- Ensures that guest-related issues are resolved.
- Makes sure that correct information and instructions are given to guests and that follow-up calls to guests are completed as necessary.
- Enters guest wake-up calls as requested; ensures that these calls are placed in a timely manner; and conducts follow-up calls on incomplete wake-up attempts.
- Inputs and retrieves text and voice messages correctly.
- Routes emergency calls to appropriate departments; follows hotel requirements regarding the contact of officials for emergencies; and completes accurate records of emergency calls. Remains calm and is able to calm callers while providing information that helps ensure their safety.
- Answers the department's general phone when necessary.

Reservations Agent[12]

Responsible to provide efficient and friendly service and information for guests and potential guests making room reservations, while at the same time maximizing room revenues.

- Processes guestroom reservations from the hotel sales office, direct inquiries, third-party sources, correspondence, and guests at the front desk.
- Responds to guests' requests efficiently and courteously.
- Registers and assigns rooms that accommodate special requests wherever possible.
- Knows room locations, types of rooms available, and room rates.
- Answers guests' questions about the property and its products and services.
- Arranges for special guest services by inputting information for front desk, bell services attendants, housekeeping, concierge, or other departments.
- Stays current on developments within the property.

The number after each position refers to the organization chart in Figure 3.6.

FIGURE 3.10   Overview of job tasks for common nonmanagement positions in front office.

Reservations Agent (*continued*)

- Adheres to proper credit, check-cashing, and cash-handling policies and procedures. Monitors reservations to ensure adherence to credit limits and verifies accuracy of guest information.
- Verifies information about guest's name, address, and payment method. Completes shift closing requirements.
- Uses effective selling techniques to sell upgraded rooms and to promote other services and amenities.
- Efficiently operates the PMS system. Maintains assignment of guestrooms.
- Logically plans, organizes, and completes work in a timely manner.
- Keeps supervisor informed of all problems or unusual events and refers difficult situations to supervisor's attention.
- Complies with property's policies and procedures.
- Complies with all departmental service guarantees.
- Assists in preregistration and blocking of rooms for reservations. Takes (confirms) same-day reservations and future reservations and follows appropriate cancellation procedures.
- Keeps up with safety and emergency procedures. Maintains the cleanliness and neatness of the front desk area. Reports unusual activity to management.
- Maintains information about travel agent commissions.
- Offers area overflow hotels when necessary.
- Enters reservations into the PMS made by phone (transient guest) or from delegate (group) meeting lists.
- Provides reservation information to front desk personnel.
- Processes advance deposits on reservations.
- Provides input to room revenue and occupancy forecasts.
- Prepares arrival lists for use of front office personnel.
- Prepares guest confirmations for mailing as necessary.
- Maintains records for no-show accounts.

Front Desk Cashier[13]

Responsible to maintain control of operating funds in the hotel vault and for transactions at the cashier's station at the front desk.

- Maintains cash banks.
- Posts revenue charges to guest folios.
- Receives and processes guest payments at check-out time.
- Interacts with accounting department for credit card and direct-billing accounts.
- Performs banking services for guests.
- Transfers guest balances to other accounts as applicable.
- Manages safe-deposit boxes for guests.

Front Desk Agent[14]

Responsible for the efficient registration and check-out of transient and group guests, for exceeding guests' expectations about the resolution of hotel visit and travel challenges, and provides information and assistance to guests during their stay.

- Provides courteous guest service by responding promptly and efficiently to inquiries, requests, and complaints.
- Uses selling skills and hotel sales programs to maximize revenue and occupancy levels.
- Makes room assignments and provides keys to the guests; is familiar with the location and types of guestrooms throughout the property.
- Obtains guest signatures on registration cards and credit cards, obtains approval and form of payment information as part of the registration process.
- Issues and logs parking vouchers.
- Delivers messages, faxes, and packages to guests in a timely and professional manner.
- Maintains information and communication sources such as log book, guest services directory, and franchise directories.
- Keeps records and reports as outlined in the hotel's policies and procedures manual; maintains order and cleanliness at the front desk.

FIGURE 3.10   *(continued)*

Front Desk Agent (*continued*)

- Handles accounting of money, receipts, guest accounts, and credit through operation of the electronic data machine (register), and completes reports required to ensure that company funds are secure. Maintains access to safe-deposit boxes.
- Keeps current about the company's marketing programs, special rates, and promotions and presents and explains them to guests.
- Operates the telephone console and uses appropriate telephone etiquette when taking incoming calls.
- Processes incoming and outgoing reservation and cancellation requests received by mail, telephone, in person, and from the organization's central reservation center.
- Complies with the hotel's safety and security rules and instructions in performing work efficiently while protecting self, fellow workers, and hotel property.
- Ensures 100 percent guest satisfaction at the time of check-in, check-out, and during guest stays.
- Ensures that all guests are evacuated in the event of a fire. (Calls each guest by telephone, knocks on room door of guests who do not answer the telephone, and assists disabled guests.)
- Handles guest complaints and reassures guests that complaints will be addressed.
- Runs shift reports and completes duties located on the shift list.
- Works closely with housekeeping staff to ensure that room status reports are current.
- Coordinates requests for guestroom maintenance.

FIGURE 3.10   *(continued)*

A front desk agent's responsibilities may include cashier, PBX, or concierge duties—or all three.

Bell Services Attendant[15]

Responsible to assist guests with luggage and parcels. May also serve as door or parking attendant and van driver.

- Helps guests by transporting luggage to their rooms.
- Shows guests around their rooms; explains equipment such as television, lighting, air-conditioning, and Internet access hookups.
- Describes hotel facilities such as the restaurant, swimming pool, and exercise facilities; shows guests where these facilities are located, if requested.
- Parks guests' cars and helps guests to secure taxis.
- Runs errands for guests including taking and picking up dry cleaning.
- Posts letters and messages.
- Provides directions.
- Answers questions (e.g., about local attractions and shopping).
- Assists guests with luggage needs at check-out.
- Delivers guest-related items such as flowers, parcels, and messages.
- Knows about and can assist with emergency guest evacuation.

Concierge[16]

Responsible to provide individualized and requested special services to guests.

- Provides world-class service for and is responsive to every guest request in a professional manner.
- Provides accurate and current information to guests about the hotel and city.
- Assists guests in the purchase of tickets for entertainment, athletic, and other events.
- Provides detailed services and assists individuals designated as preregistered and VIP guests.
- Maintains a house bank of a predetermined amount and posts charges to guests' accounts; balances house bank each shift.
- Maintains accurate logs of mail, packages, parcels, and miscellaneous items for delivery or pickup.
- Takes reservations for all of the hotel's food and beverage outlets and inputs data into the computerized restaurant reservations system.
- Maintains proper telephone etiquette and displays a professional attitude at all times.
- Coordinates, maintains, and disseminates information to managers of specific outlets regarding food and beverage functions and events (e.g., birthdays, anniversaries, and dinner parties) that require special preparations.
- Provides information about, reserves, and obtains services of babysitters.
- Performs special services for VIPs: ensures that they receive a note from the concierge department, inspects rooms before arrival, places special gifts, and escorts VIPs to their rooms.
- Handles guest complaints.
- Assists with guests' special business-related needs.

Note: Some hotels have VIP or concierge floors that provide private registration, lobby (reading), meeting, and refreshment areas for those paying a higher room rate. This area may be supervised by a concierge staff member.

Door Attendant[17]

Responsible for providing hospitable greetings to and providing necessary services for guests as they arrive, enter, and leave the hotel. May perform duties of parking lot attendant or van driver.

- Greets arriving guests; opens automobile doors.
- Assists with guests' luggage.
- Opens lobby doors for guests as they arrive at and depart from the hotel.
- Summons taxis; opens taxi doors for guests.
- Provides travel instructions.

FIGURE 3.10   *(continued)*

Parking Attendant[18]

Responsible for parking and retrieving automobiles for hotel guests. May perform duties of door attendant or van driver.

- Greets arriving guests.
- Assists guests, including disabled guests, to enter or leave their vehicle (e.g., assist with wheelchairs).
- Parks guests' vehicles in designated parking areas and returns vehicles at guests' request in a safe and timely manner.
- Responds to general requests for hotel information and directs guests to the appropriate areas of the hotel.
- Monitors the general area and cleans as necessary to ensure the vehicle unloading and parking areas are neat and orderly.
- Assists guests with luggage; opens lobby doors for guests.
- Provides assistance to parking guests (gives directions, explains charges, reports vehicles needing garage service, and provides general information); refers unusual customer-related problems to supervisor.
- Inspects parking passes, if applicable, to ensure validity.
- Inspects vehicles in parking lots for appropriate parking decals, if applicable.

Note: Many hotels lease parking services and facilities to an external vendor. When this occurs, persons in positions such as parking lot attendant and cashier are not hotel employees.

Van Driver[19]

Responsible for transporting guests and employees to and from the property. May perform duties of door and parking lot attendant.

- Must be able to drive all hotel vehicles (buses, shuttle carts, VIP limousines, vans).
- Follows only designated routes for vehicles on or off property.
- Fills out daily log that includes mileage, incidents and accidents, gas use, vehicle defects and problems.
- Assists guests with luggage as they enter and leave the van.
- Complies with all hotel policies and standard operating procedures.
- Works as a team member to yield a positive experience for guests and employees.
- Maintains uniform, grooming, and conduct standards.
- Works a flexible 24/7 schedule according to the needs of the department.
- Protects the assets of the hotel.

FIGURE 3.10   *(continued)*

MODERN FRONT OFFICE ISSUES AND TACTICS

Who Needs a Front Desk?

Le Meridien Cyber Port in Hong Kong has a number of innovations that emphasize a can do philosophy. The goal is to please all of the guests all of the time, and the word *no* is not one in common use.

Le Meridien Cyber Port does not have a typical reception desk. The property uses e-mail and the Internet to send registration forms to guests, or guests can check in from locations on the property (e.g., a restaurant). After a guest initially checks in, he or she need never do it again. The property's wireless check-in, or seamless check-in, works through personal digital assistants (PDAs) and laptops. Guests do not have to sign forms or provide registration details. Even restaurant staff can check guests into the property.

The hotel does maintain a reception desk, although it is not used for check-in purposes. Some guests prefer to go to the desk to pay their bill at check-out time. The property believes in flexibility and giving the guests what they want. For example, guests can check in at 3:00 a.m. and leave at 3:00 a.m. the next morning at their convenience. When guests check in and check out at all times of the day, does this cause problems for the hotel? Most guests arrive and depart at "normal" times. Therefore, all the hotel must do is devote a limited number of rooms to a 24-hour check-in room block.

The property has significant high-tech capabilities. Nevertheless, staff recognize that although technology drives guest service, it is not guest service. The purpose of technology is to give staff more time with guests, not to reduce the time staff has available with guests.

Adapted from Shellum., S. Le Meridien's first art+ tech property in Asia aims to raise the benchmark; typical reception desk has been vanished. Hotel Online Special Report. Retrieved July 3, 2004, from http://www.hotel-online.com/News/PR2004_3rd/Jul04_Cyberport.html.

SECTION REVIEW AND DISCUSSION QUESTIONS

Section Objective: Review job tasks commonly found in management and non-management positions in the front office (rooms division) of a large hotel.

Section Summary: Incumbents in many management and nonmanagement positions within the front office department have many of the same basic types of responsibilities and require the same types of knowledge and skills as do peers in other hotel departments, and even in other hospitality and nonhospitality businesses and organizations. There are, however, specific responsibilities based on job tasks that are unique to front office positions. Knowledge of these job tasks can be helpful to front office personnel in entry-level positions who want to follow a career ladder as they advance within the front office department and to other departments in the hotel.

Discussion Questions:
1. Assume that you are a human resources specialist hiring people for entry-level positions in the front office. How would you use current job descriptions for these positions? What advice would you give to applicants about career opportunities within the department and the hotel?
2. Review Figure 3.7 about general management responsibilities, activities, and skills. Then, think about the concept of the universal process of management. What additional responsibilities, activities, and skills are important for all managers, regardless of the department, hotel, or other organization in which they work?
3. What positions shown in the organization chart for a mega hotel (Figure 3.6) are most logical for cross-training in different career tracks? Why?

HUMAN RESOURCES MANAGEMENT (ENTRY-LEVEL PERSONNEL)

Roadmap 3.4 highlights the need for front office employees to be managed effectively. Use of basic principles of human relations is essential as hoteliers, including FOMs, interact with employees in entry-level positions. This section reviews principles that

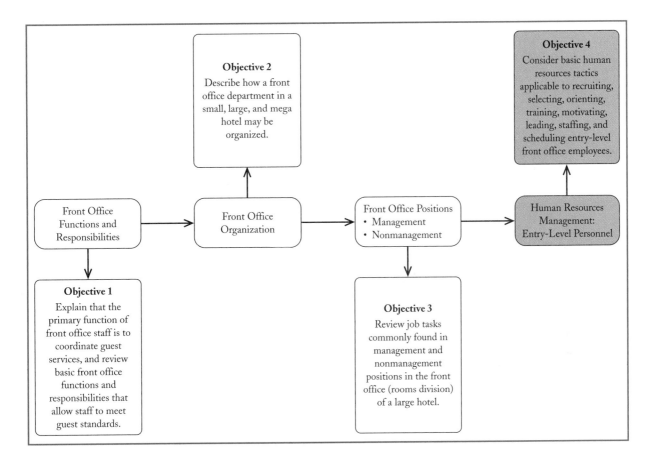

ROADMAP 3.4

can be helpful in recruiting and selecting, orientating and training, motivating and supervising, and staffing and scheduling entry-level personnel in the front office.

Recruitment and Selection

The process of **recruitment** refers to activities designed to alert potential job applicants to employment opportunities within the hotel.

FRONT OFFICE SEMANTICS

Recruitment: Activities designed to attract qualified applicants for vacant positions within the hotel.

In large hotels with human resources departments, much of the responsibility for recruitment is assigned to specialists within that department. In smaller properties without a human resources department, recruitment becomes another responsibility of the FOM, who interacts with the supervisor to whom the employee will report. The number of vacancies for a position depends on the **turnover rate** for that position.

FRONT OFFICE SEMANTICS

Turnover rate: Measure of the proportion of a workforce that is replaced during a designated time period (e.g., month, quarter, or year). Number of employees separated ÷ number of employees in the workforce = employee turnover rate.

FOMs in hotels of all sizes can successfully use **internal recruiting** tactics. When **external recruiting** must be undertaken, managers in large properties have an ally in the human resources department. As noted, however, managers in small properties must assume this responsibility themselves.

FRONT OFFICE SEMANTICS

Internal recruiting: Tactics to identify and attract currently employed staff members for job vacancies that represent promotions or lateral transfers to similar positions in the same organization.

External recruiting: Tactics designed to attract persons who are not current hotel employees for vacant positions in the organization.

Many managers appreciate the benefits of internal recruiting. Presently employed staff members who understand the work environment (including the relationship between management and employees) might know others who would enjoy working in the organization. Some properties, especially those with high turnover rates, offer financial incentives to staff members who refer applicants who are subsequently employed and remain with the organization for a specified time period.

A wide range of external recruiting tactics can be used. Some traditional tactics are newspaper ads, promotion at career fairs, and postings with employment divisions of state labor agencies. Other recruitment tactics are less traditional.[1]

- Meeting with school guidance counselors
- Seeking out senior citizens
- Assuring that uniform requirements do not have a negative effect on job applicants
- Adding an employment section to the hotel's Web site
- Using current employee endorsements in employment ads

After applicants for vacant front office positions have been recruited, the **selection** process evaluates applicants to determine those most likely to be successful in the position. An organized and objective selection process is preferable to the **warm-body syndrome.**

FRONT OFFICE SEMANTICS

Selection: Process of evaluating job applicants to determine those more qualified (or potentially qualified) for vacant positions.

Warm-body syndrome: Often used but ineffective selection technique that involves hiring almost anyone who applies for the vacant position, without regard to qualifications.

---

[1]These and many other recruitment tactics are reviewed in Hayes, D., and J. Ninemeier. 2001. *Fifty One-Minute Tips for Recruiting Employees. Building a Win–Win Environment.* Menlo Park, CA: Crisp Publications.

Candidates for a front office position should have a good attitude, knowledge of computer programs, and general mathematical skills.

The "best" candidates for any front office position are those who are most able to interact with hotel guests and team peers. Many hotel observers note that "problem" employees are most typically those who have attitude problems and are unable to professionally interact with their supervisor and peers. These employees generally have the knowledge and skills necessary to successfully perform required job tasks, but they do not have the desire to do so.

Front office applicants can be screened with several traditional selection tools.

- *Preliminary screening, including review of the applicant's application form.* The form used for front office personnel will likely be the same as that used for applicants for positions in other departments. Application forms should be developed carefully and reviewed by a qualified attorney to make sure they are not prejudicial to any class of applicants covered by Equal Employment Opportunity guidelines or related laws.

- *Employment interviews.* In large hotels, an initial screening interview will likely be conducted by a representative of the human resources department as a final step in the screening process. Applicants judged potentially eligible are then referred to the front office department for an interview with the FOM, the supervisor with whom the applicant would work, or both. In small properties, initial interviews are often conducted by the applicable department head. Sometimes (and this is desirable) the position's supervisor is involved in the interview process.

- *Employment tests.* These selection tools can be useful especially when an applicant with experience is desired. For example, if a properly trained reservations agent must be able to do word processing, a test could be conducted to determine an applicant's word processing proficiency. If a night auditor with knowledge of a specific software package is desired, knowledge or skills tests could be developed to allow applicants to demonstrate their competence with the required system.

- *Reference checks.* References may be checked to confirm employment dates and positions held.

- *Review of other requirements.* Van drivers may be required to have and maintain a specific type of state driver's license. Cashiers handling money may require **bonding;** processing of paperwork with an insurance company will determine if bonding is possible for an applicant.

- *Drug screening* (if done by the hotel). The FOM should discuss the use of drug tests for applicants with human resources managers, who likely will have obtained legal advice about the appropriateness of and procedures for this screening tactic.

FRONT OFFICE SEMANTICS

Bonding: Purchasing an insurance policy against the possibility that an employee will steal.

After the screening process is complete, applicants judged to be most qualified for and to be potentially successful in the position might be reinterviewed, or offered a position. At this point, the new front office employee will be looking for confirmation that his or her decision to accept a position was a good one. The FOM's actions—and inactions—will have an impact on the new employee's first impressions about the job, which are formed at the time of orientation and training.

Orientation and Training

Orientation is the process of providing basic information about the hotel that should be known by all employees. Effective orientation programs are organized and well planned. They should not be conducted in an inconsistent, haphazard fashion that depends on the interest of the manager assigned to conduct the orientation or on how busy the hotel is when the orientation is scheduled.

FRONT OFFICE SEMANTICS

Orientation: Process of providing basic information about the hotel that should be known by all of its employees.

In large properties, orientation is typically the responsibility of the human resources department. As evidence of very high turnover rates, some properties conduct orientation classes for new employees several times weekly.

The orientation process should address items that every employee needs to know, regardless of position or department. Important topics include:

- Overview of the hotel and a presentation of its mission statement
- Importance of effective guest service and the emphasis on teamwork
- Review of the hotel's most important policies and procedures
- Detailed discussion about compensation, including fringe benefits and pay periods
- Guest and employee safety and security concerns
- Review of union relations issues (if applicable)
- Tour of all hotel areas, including visits to different types of rooms and, perhaps, a meal in a hotel restaurant
- Other topics applicable to the specific property

Many hotels provide an **employee handbook** to new staff members during their orientation.

FRONT OFFICE SEMANTICS

Employee handbook: Written policies and procedures related to employment at a hotel. Sometimes called an *employee manual.*

Many general managers recognize the importance of an effective orientation program to initiate the relationship between the property and the new employee. They take an active part in the orientation that includes much more than a short speech of welcome. The general manager who takes time to meet all new employees shows respect for them and indicates the dignity with which employees are treated. In the process, the manager is setting the stage for an **employer-of-choice** environment, which will yield highly motivated employees who will help the hotel attain its guest service, financial, and other goals.

FRONT OFFICE SEMANTICS

Employer-of-choice: Concept that the hospitality operation is a preferred place of employment within the community by those who have alternative employment opportunities.

In some hotels a follow-up orientation session is held several weeks (or longer) after the initial orientation. This allows employees to provide input about their initial job experiences. Their information can be used to help revise and improve the hotel's orientation program.

After the new front office employee has received general information about the property during orientation, the **induction** process begins. Induction acquaints the new employee with specific information that should be known by all employees in the front office department.

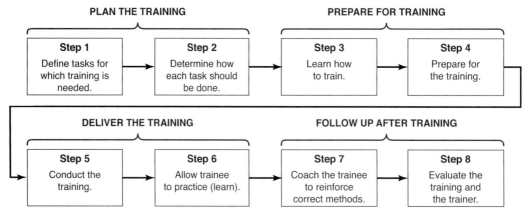

FIGURE 3.11 Steps for effectively training front office personnel.

FRONT OFFICE SEMANTICS

Induction: Process of informing new employees about matters related to the department in which they will work. Induction is done after the orientation process is completed.

During induction, the new employee meets his or her peers, obtains a more detailed tour of the front office (e.g., front desk area and workstations), and learns about policies and procedures unique to the department (e.g., policies about work-schedule requests and procedures to follow when calling in about an assigned work shift).

After the induction process is completed, training can begin. On-the-job training is a common method to prepare new front office employees for their positions. It also can be a useful technique to retrain and provide new information and skills to experienced employees. For example, a currently employed front desk clerk may need to learn how to use new equipment, or an experienced reservations agent may need to learn revised procedures to handle reservations made by third-party agents.

The concept of on-the-job training is excellent: A knowledgeable and trained person teaches another person how to correctly perform job tasks. In practice, however, the training method is widely misused. Common sense suggests that (1) even an experienced employee needs to learn *how* to train; (2) training takes time away from other activities the trainer would do; and (3) preparation must be undertaken to plan and organize the training and how it will be delivered. Unfortunately, some FOMs perceive on-the-job training to be tag-along training. In other words, they believe that any employee who knows how to perform required job tasks can train others, because training merely involves showing the trainee how to do the required work.

A well-designed training program for front office personnel, or for those in any other department of the hotel, involves the steps identified in Figure 3.11. Let's look at Figure 3.11 more closely:

- *Step 1: Define tasks for which training is needed.* Tasks to be performed by a person working in a position should be identified in a current job description. The job description is a selection tool should be explained to job applicants so that they know the details of the work they will be doing if they are selected.

- *Step 2: Determine how each task should be done.* For routine, recurring tasks, standard operating procedures should be available. For example, how exactly is the computer used to check in guests with a reservation? Basic operating procedures are provided by the software manufacturer, but specific procedures should be developed by the FOM and his or her team.
- *Step 3: Learn how to train.* Even the best-intentioned and experienced FOM or supervisor will not "magically" know how to train. Every hotel should at least have available an **off-the-shelf** train-the-trainer program to teach what should and should not be done as the training process evolves.

FRONT OFFICE SEMANTICS

Off-the-shelf: Term relating to a generic product (such as a training resource) that is developed for general use rather than for a unique property.

- *Step 4: Prepare for the training.* A training schedule should be developed and training-related questions should be addressed as part of the preparation process. Here are some examples: How much time should be allocated for training the new employee to perform each task up to standard? Should different trainers be used to teach different tasks or should one trainer be used to teach all tasks? When can training be offered to be least disruptive to other staff members and most helpful to the new employee? What kind of equipment, supplies, and other resources are needed to train each task?
- *Step 5:* Conduct the training. Many steps may be appropriate when training is conducted. Figure 3.12 lists examples.
- *Step 6: Allow trainee to practice (learn).* Some tasks done by front office employees are difficult to learn (perhaps because they are difficult to teach!). Many employees need practice time to perform tasks correctly at desired output (speed) standards. Practice time should be provided in a risk-free situation that does not affect guest service.
- *Step 7: Coach the trainee to reinforce correct methods.* The goal of coaching is to help staff members and the hotel team to reach the highest levels of performance.

---

1. Explain and demonstrate job tasks to trainee.
2. Maintain a patient and appropriate pace throughout the training session.
3. Make sure the trainee understands each job task and procedure.
4. Encourage the trainee to ask questions.
5. Check for understanding by asking open-ended questions.
6. Take up only one point at a time.
7. Follow an orderly sequence using the job breakdown as a guide.
8. Provide only the amount of information or instruction that can be mastered in one session.
9. Make sure that all instructions are clear, concise, and complete.
10. Try to make the session interesting.
11. Have all equipment and tools available for the trainee.
12. Show the trainee how to do the task correctly.
13. Remind the trainee to look at effectiveness from the point of view of guests and other staff.

FIGURE 3.12 Training delivery tactics for front office employees.

In effect, training is never finished. If, for example, a front office employee performs a new task correctly, the correct procedure should be reinforced. ("Janet, you did an excellent job.") If a task is not being done correctly, corrective action is required. ("Janet, you've almost got it; there is just one additional procedure that you should use.")

- *Step 8: Evaluate the training and the trainer.* Ideally, the effectiveness of the training can be evaluated easily because the trainee can now perform tasks that meet quality and quantity standards. It is also important to evaluate the content of the training program, the methods of delivery, and the trainer. If rapport has been established among the trainer, department head, and the trainee, the discussion will likely be honest, professional, and frank. Sometimes evaluation of the trainer can occur during a performance appraisal session. In other larger hotels, trainees may be asked to submit evaluations anonymously to the human resources department.

To this point, the discussion has focused on individualized, on-the-job training tactics. However, there are times when group training is useful. As the name implies, group training involves providing instruction to several (or more) employees who need the same information at the same time. Examples of topics for group training are **upselling,** an explanation of new hotel policies, and rollout of a new **frequent-guest program** for hotel guests. The eight-step training process presented in Figure 3.11 also applies to group training.

FRONT OFFICE SEMANTICS

Upsell: Tactic used to increase the hotel's average daily rate by inviting guests to rent a higher-priced room with better and/or more amenities (e.g., view, complimentary breakfast, and newspaper) than provided with a lower-priced room.

Frequent-guest program: Promotional effort administered by a hotel brand that rewards travelers each time they stay at that specific brand's affiliated hotels. Typical rewards include free-night stays, room upgrades, and complimentary hotel services.

Motivation and Leadership

One of the FOM's most important leadership activities is to **motivate** employees. Motivated employees will want to do their jobs correctly. They will have a relationship of mutual respect with their supervisor; in the process, both the employee and the organization (e.g., front office department) will benefit.

FRONT OFFICE SEMANTICS

Motivate: Process of appealing to a person's inner drive to attain a goal.

Employer-of-choice properties pay special attention to the organizational culture that promotes a win–win relationship for the employee and employer. Fortunately, there are many inexpensive and commonsense tactics that can be used to motivate front office employees. Figure 3.13 reviews some of them. A participative management style, the practice of total quality management leadership (see Chapter 2), and the empowerment of staff members are among useful strategies to gain motivated staff members.

Strategy 1:	**Follow sound management advice.**
Tactic 1:	Serve first and lead second.
Tactic 2:	Learn your turnover costs.
Tactic 3:	Eliminate workers who won't.
Tactic 4:	Eliminate managers who can't.
Tactic 5:	Manage your guests.
Strategy 2:	**Provide effective orientation.**
Tactic 6:	Understand the role of starting wages.
Tactic 7:	Inform employees about their total compensation.
Tactic 8:	Explain the long-term benefits of staying.
Tactic 9:	Share your vision.
Tactic 10:	Motivate entry-level employees.
Tactic 11:	Conduct an entrance interview.
Tactic 12:	Create career ladders.
Strategy 3:	**Train correctly.**
Tactic 13:	Invest in training.
Tactic 14:	Encourage employees to try your hotel.
Tactic 15:	Train trainers to train.
Tactic 16:	Reward your trainers.
Tactic 17:	Relieve trainers of other job duties.
Tactic 18:	Conduct preshift training.
Strategy 4:	**Manage a professional hotel.**
Tactic 19:	Strictly enforce a zero-tolerance harassment policy.
Tactic 20:	Create a culturally diverse workforce.
Tactic 21:	Make employee safety a top priority.
Tactic 22:	Ensure reasonable accommodations for disabled employees.
Tactic 23:	Share financial information with employees.
Strategy 5:	**Supervise like you want to be supervised.**
Tactic 24:	Enforce on-time policies fairly and consistently.
Tactic 25:	Be careful not to overschedule.
Tactic 26:	Give employees a personal copy of their work schedule.
Tactic 27:	Seek out employee assistance programs.
Tactic 28:	Invite fast-track employees to attend management meetings.
Tactic 29:	Implement a program titled "catch the employee doing something right."
Tactic 30:	Conduct an exit interview with employees who leave.
Strategy 6:	**Encourage effective communication.**
Tactic 31:	Hold employee-focused meetings for nonmanagement staff.
Tactic 32:	Communicate the benefits of your hotel.
Tactic 33:	Create an employee retention committee.
Tactic 34:	Recognize employee birthdays.
Tactic 35:	Make daily "howdy" rounds.
Strategy 7:	**Manage a friendly hotel.**
Tactic 36:	Use employee recognition programs.
Tactic 37:	Build a great team and praise it often.
Tactic 38:	Write a personal letter to parents of teenage employees.
Tactic 39:	Share scheduling responsibilities with employees.
Tactic 40:	Reward employees who work on nonscheduled days.
Tactic 41:	Invite family members of new employees to visit the hotel.
Tactic 42:	Make the hotel a fun place to work.

FIGURE 3.13 Common sense tactics to motivate front office employees.

Strategy 8: **Help your employees succeed.**
    Tactic 43:   Identify state-approved (licensed) child-care options.
    Tactic 44:   Reward success in each employee.
    Tactic 45:   Recognize your employees' elder-care responsibilities.
    Tactic 46:   Don't punish your best for being good.
    Tactic 47:   Go to lunch.
    Tactic 48:   Help employees learn about public transportation systems.

Adapted from Hayes, D., and J. Ninemeier. 2001. *Fifty One-Minute Tips for Retaining Employees. Building a Win–Win Environment,* Menlo Park, CA: Crisp Publications.

FIGURE 3.13 *(continued)*

FOMs must be good leaders, but what is a good leader? Entire books and bookshelves are devoted to this question. Nevertheless, a short list of effective leadership traits can be developed. An effective FOM must meet the following challenges:

- Have a good understanding of the hotel's values and be able to translate these values into practice. In other words, the FOM must be able to implement the front office's share of the property's mission statement.
- Have an objective and measurable vision of the future for the hotel
- Help others develop the knowledge and skills needed to attain the hotel's vision. This is done, in part, through orientation, training, and follow-up coaching activities.
- Use the empowerment process to help others move toward the vision by enabling them to use discretion in addressing guests' needs
- Develop a team of staff members who are committed to the hotel's success
- Achieve a reputation for quality meets or exceeds guests' expectations

Effective FOMs vary their **leadership styles** according to the specific employee and the situation. Figure 3.14 introduces four basic leadership styles. Let's look at each of these leadership styles more carefully and review how and when they can be used to manage employees in common front office positions.

FRONT OFFICE SEMANTICS

Leadership style: Mix of attitudes and behaviors that a supervisor can use to direct the work of employees.

- *Autocratic managers.* Autocratic FOMs like to make decisions and solve problems without getting information from affected employees. They give instructions unilaterally and expect employees to follow them. Sometimes these FOMs use a structured set of awards (to encourage employees to follow orders) and punishments (to discipline employees when orders are not followed). Front office employees can easily become dependent on FOMs who are autocratic. They may act only under FOM supervision, and they have little opportunity to make decisions as work evolves. Autocratic managers emphasize the work and getting it done. They are more concerned about the hotel and the front office department and less concerned about the employees.

Type	Overview of leadership type	Target employee for leadership type
Autocratic manager	FOM retains as much power and decision-making authority as possible. FOM makes decisions without consulting employees. Orders are given to and must be obeyed by employees without their input.	New employees who must quickly learn work tasks; difficult-to-supervise employees who do not respond to other styles; temporary employees
Bureaucratic manager	FOM "manages by the book." Emphasis is on doing things specified by rules, policies, regulations, and standard operating procedures. FOM relies on higher levels to resolve problems not addressed by the rules.	Employees who must follow set procedures; employees working with dangerous equipment or under special conditions
Democratic manager	FOM involves employees in aspects of the job that affect them. Employee input is solicited. Employees participate in the decision-making process and are delegated the authority to make decisions.	Employees with high levels of skill or extensive experience; employees who need to make significant changes in work assignments; employees who want to voice complaints; employee groups with common problems
Laissez-faire manager	FOM maintains a hands-off policy and delegates by default much decision-making authority. FOM gives little direction and allows extensive levels of freedom.	Highly motivated employees such as staff technical specialists; consultants

FIGURE 3.14 Leadership styles for front office managers.

- *Bureaucratic managers.* Bureaucratic FOMs "manage by the book," with an emphasis on enforcing rules. Problems not addressed by the rules are referred to higher levels of management in the hotel. The bureaucratic manager is more of a police officer than a leader. Because the emphasis is on rules, not cooperation, rules become more important than work outcomes.
- *Democratic managers.* Democratic FOMs want to include employees in the decision-making activities that affect them. They focus on subordinates and the role that they play in the hotel, and they search for ways to help employees find satisfaction in their jobs. There are some potential disadvantages to the democratic approach. For example, decision making is likely to take longer, and mistakes are more likely to occur. Also, once this style has been used in the front office, it is difficult for employees to accept another approach (e.g., when a new FOM has a different leadership style).
- *Laissez-faire managers.* Laissez-faire FOMs use a hands-off approach and do as little supervising as possible. Front office employees make decisions with little, if any, supervisory input. This approach can only be used with highly motivated and experienced staff.

It is doubtful whether any FOM uses one of the four leadership styles exclusively. In an ideal situation, the FOM would know each employee and would be able to use the leadership style appropriate to the specific employee in the specific situation. However, few, if any, supervisors can switch between different leadership styles. Several factors influence the type of leadership style actually used:

- *Manager's personal background.* Every FOM brings unique knowledge, experience and common sense to a job situation, and those factors influence how FOMs feel about their job and their employees.

- *Characteristics of employees.* Some employees desire decision-making responsibility; others do not. Some agree with the property's goals; others may not. The different backgrounds and attitudes of employees should be considered as leadership approaches are determined.

- *Relationship between manager and employees.* The degree of confidence that an FOM has in employees will affect the leadership style that is selected. When there is trust and acceptance, a democratic approach may be useful. When these elements are lacking, an autocratic approach may be appropriate, but it may lead to conflict between the FOM and employees.

- *Job situation itself.* The culture of the hotel, the makeup of employee groups, and the type of work to be done all affect the choice and effectiveness of leadership styles. The size of the work group must be considered, because it is more difficult to use group decision-making approaches as the size of the group increases. The effectiveness of communication and amount of cooperation between hotel departments is of concern. If not satisfactory, the FOM may be uncertain about the goals of the property and may be inclined to use less participative approaches in decision making. Consider also the type of work and the magnitude and kinds of problems to be resolved. In some situations, employee input will be helpful but in others, employee input may not be useful to FOMs.

Basic knowledge about leadership styles and the conditions under which they are likely to be useful can help FOMs to be more effective. Although FOMs cannot be psychologists, they can use background knowledge and common sense to improve their abilities to supervise front office employees.

Staffing and Scheduling

FOMs face significant challenges as they plan and implement tactics for employee **staffing.** A key challenge is to have the correct number of qualified staff members available in every necessary position to meet the property's daily business needs, while consistently meeting guest service standards. Unfortunately, staffing needs can change on an hourly basis. Scheduling more staff members than necessary leads to lowered productivity and, in turn, to higher than necessary operating costs.

FRONT OFFICE SEMANTICS

Staffing: Basic management activity that involves finding the right people for the job.

FOMs consider staffing requirements, as they determine what work must be done and as they group similar tasks into positions. They are also involved in staffing activities as they develop job descriptions and job specifications to more specifically identify what must be done and the types of skills and experience that will most likely yield a successful staff member. (Recall that FOMs in larger properties receive assistance in these staffing activities from the human resources department.) An extended definition of staffing includes the orientation, induction, and training activities designed to prepare a staff member for employment at the property and, more specifically, in the front office department.

How many staff members in what positions are needed to work at what times in a front office department? This question must be answered specifically by FOMs in each hotel, but general principles can assist in the decision-making process. For example, does a front desk agent need to be present at all times? Yes, at least in a large property, because guests register, check out, and want service issues resolved at all hours of the day and night. Must a PBX operator be available 24/7? Perhaps in a very large hotel; definitely not in a small property. In the small property a position titled "night desk agent" may be in place. A staff member in this position can be trained to perform the duties of the front desk agent, to operate the switchboard, to serve as the concierge (e.g., to recommend late-night dining alternatives), and, to perform night audit tasks as well. This example reinforces a point made earlier in the chapter: Someone must be available in a hotel to perform a wide variety of front office tasks. In smaller properties, positions become more generalized, and an employee in a specific position must be able to perform a wide range of duties. Although cross-training is important in large properties, it is of *significant* importance in small hotels.

Let's consider an example of staffing needs in a large property. Must a manager of uniformed services be available every hour of every day? The answer is no for all but the very largest hotels. However, someone must be available on-site or at least **on-call,** to address any nonroutine matters related to the position.

FRONT OFFICE SEMANTICS

On-call: Agreement between a hotel employer and a staff member that the staff member, although not formally scheduled to work, will remain available to work, to answer questions, or to do both, if necessary, during a specified time period.

Front office employees in **variable labor positions** must be scheduled according to the forecasted volume of business. Employees in **fixed labor positions** do work that is not directly affected by business volume. These employees can be scheduled according to times when their work should be done, and these times may not correlate with when guests are arriving, visiting, or departing from the hotel.

FRONT OFFICE SEMANTICS

Variable labor position: Position that must be staffed according to the volume of business. Examples are front desk agents and staff members working in uniformed services positions.

Fixed labor position: Position that involves work tasks not directly tied to the level of business volume. Examples are management positions such as FOM and uniformed services manager.

As FOMs determine the number of front office staff members needed for a specific work shift, they consider many factors:

• *Number of guest arrivals and departures.* The experience of front office schedule planners will suggest the number of front desk agents needed to register and check out guests. Perhaps, for example, they schedule on the basis of one front desk agent for every 75 guests per shift. If 150 guests are scheduled to register or check out, two staff members (150 guests ÷ 75 guests per shift) are scheduled. If travelers on a tour bus or sports fans on a chartered plane are scheduled to arrive at the same time, additional front desk personnel and bell services attendants will be needed for the times of peak arrival and check-out.

Managers in large properties that have several workstations behind the front desk may be able to schedule four, five, or even more agents to work at key times. In contrast, the FOM in a small property with relatively few front desk workstations can (1) schedule front desk agents according to the number of workstations and (2) schedule others to assist with supportive tasks (e.g., making room keys, answering the telephone, and providing directions) to minimize the time that agents are away from their workstations. Entry-level positions are also affected by the estimated number of guest arrivals and departures: front desk cashiers, bell services attendants, door and parking attendants, van drivers, and PBX operators.

FOMs likely know from experience at the specific property when the peaks and valleys of guest registration and departure occur. These times are influenced by factors such as airline schedules, posted check-in times, room availability, and posted start and end times for in-house group events. Consider, for example, a large group that has scheduled an opening reception and dinner on the evening preceding a conference. Most of the attendees will probably arrive in the afternoon rather than in the early evening. FOMs are usually aware of arrival and departure trends that help with staffing plans. For example, business travelers may typically arrive in the evening and depart in the early morning. Transient guests may arrive earlier and depart later in the day.

• *Occupancy rate.* The number of guests occupying rooms also affects front office staffing and scheduling patterns. When occupancy rate increases, there are likely to be more guest requests for PBX, bell, door, and parking attendants; and concierge services. As well, guest service requests that require action by front desk staff will be greater. For example, in many smaller properties front office staff deliver requested towels and extra bedding to guestrooms. Additional staff may be needed for these and related tasks as occupancy increases.

• *Number of available workstations and availability of equipment.* Consider, for example, the front office that only has two workstations for front desk agents or equipment to accommodate only two telephone operators. In these cases, the FOM must schedule with these limitations in mind. Now consider a hotel that offers an amenity of van service to the airport every half hour. The hotel has one van, so only one van driver is scheduled. Experience will suggest a correlation between the number of guests departing and those needing airport transportation. If there is only one van and the number of departing guests is greater than the van's capacity, the short-range solution is to rent another vehicle and request that an on-call van driver be assigned a work shift or to pay taxi fees for guests. The longer-term solution is to consider the need, for a second van while assessing its impact on capital and operating costs and, just as importantly, on guest satisfaction levels.

OCCUPANCY FORECASTS DRIVE EMPLOYEE SCHEDULES

Room occupancy forecasts based on PMS data and other information are an important scheduling tool. FOMs use these forecasts when they develop schedules for employees in front desk and uniformed services positions. Forecasted occupancy information is used by other departments for the same purposes. For example, how many rooms must be cleaned by housekeeping staff? The estimated number of guests departing on a specific date will help answer this question. How many production personnel and servers will be needed in the àla carte dining room? The estimated guest count, less those attending banquet events within the property, will help food and beverage schedule planners, who also use separate forecasting systems to estimate the number of walk-in guests who will visit the property's restaurants.

Generation and distribution of room occupancy forecasts is another example of why the front office department is the communication hub of the hotel.

After the number of employees needed for front office positions is estimated for specific shifts, a schedule can be developed. In a relatively small property (see Figure 3.4), the general manager, perhaps working with the front office supervisor, may develop the work schedule for the front office staff (which consists of, primarily, front desk agents). In a larger property (see Figure 3.5), the FOM is typically assigned the employee scheduling task. In a very large property (see Figure 3.6), several management personnel will likely be involved in schedule planning:

- The front desk supervisor will schedule the work of front desk agents.
- The PBX manager will schedule the PBX operators.
- The reservations manager may schedule the work of reservation agents.
- The supervisor of bell services may schedule bell services attendants.
- The uniformed services manager may develop schedules for door and parking attendants, van drivers, and concierge staff.

The list of factors to consider as specific employees are scheduled for specific shifts can be lengthy. Here are some examples:

- *Employee interest and history of work shifts.* Some employees are hired for **full-time** positions and may have always worked specific shifts. Others are hired for **part-time** work and may work only during peak registration or check-out hours. Although occasional exceptions may require changes in these schedules, employment agreements and work experience precedents must be considered.
- *Employee experience and training.* New staff members, especially those in training, will only be able to supplement or assist the work tasks of experienced staff. If employees have been cross-trained, they can perform work tasks normally

done by persons in different positions, which may reduce staffing needs during times of low occupancy. Many FOMs schedule their best staff members during the busiest times.

FRONT OFFICE SEMANTICS

Full-time employee: Staff member who works several days (or more) each week for up to 40 hours each week.

Part-time employee: Staff member who works fewer than 40 hours weekly. Some part-time employees may work on-call and work on an infrequent basis as needed.

- *Employee requests.* FOMs should have a system in place that allows employees to request time away from their jobs for personal reasons such as vacations, special family occasions, or religious holidays. Requests that were made on a timely basis and are in accord with the requirements of hotel policies should be met. Doing so helps to reinforce the employer-of-choice concept that is so important to employee morale and retention. Failure to do so (except on an infrequent or emergency basis) will have negative effects on the department and property in both the short term and long term.
- *Legal factors.* Workplace laws must be considered as employees are scheduled. For example, there are restraints related to the work shifts and work activities of minors. The Family and Medical Leave Act of 1993 (FMLA) entitles covered employees to take up to three months of unpaid leave for specified reasons. The Fair Labor Standards Act (FLSA) addresses wage rates that must be paid to certain staff members who work more than 40 hours in a workweek.

Hotel policies applicable to the entire property should be followed as employee schedules are completed and circulated. Perhaps, for example, schedules indicate work shifts on a Sunday through Saturday basis and are announced one or two weeks ahead of the first date in the schedule. Perhaps schedules are posted on the employee bulletin board in the employee locker room or dining room. Perhaps they are provided with payroll checks. More large properties are now using a computerized **intranet** system that employees can access from specified computer terminals in front desk or back-of-house (nonpublic) areas.

FRONT OFFICE SEMANTICS

Intranet: Designated segment of an organization's Internet site where access and use is restricted to specifically identified individuals (such as employees or managers).

It is important to have procedures for developing and disseminating information about employee schedules that are consistent and fair. Employee input to the process should be solicited, and FOMs should be open to suggestions that improve the way schedules are developed and circulated.

From the Front Office: Front-Line Interview

Paul Reggio
Director of Support Services
The Hotel at Auburn University (248 rooms)
Auburn, Alabama

Here's to the Bride and Groom!

Paul received a degree in hospitality management from the University of Southern Mississippi in 1999 while working full time at several restaurants and catering facilities. After graduation, he worked for the Ritz-Carlton in its preopening offices in New Orleans. He rapidly moved through positions in the front office and guest services and became the operations manager of the Iberville Suites (a four-diamond hotel that is part of the Ritz-Carlton, New Orleans).

Since July, 2003, Paul has worked with the West Paces Hotel Group as the director of support services at The Hotel at Auburn University. His responsibilities include the housekeeping, laundry and engineering departments.

1. **What are the most important responsibilities in your present position?**
   My most important responsibility is leading the ladies and gentlemen for whom I am responsible by creating a vision and purpose for what they are trying to accomplish. I am also responsible for creating standard operating procedures and training manuals, controlling labor costs, measuring efficiency and productivity, and coaching and counseling my team members.

2. **What are the biggest challenges that confront you in your day-to-day work and in the long-term operation of your property's front office?**
   Staffing is one of the largest challenges. Without the appropriate staffing, you will overwork your staff. This will contribute to a higher turnover rate that can, in turn, tempt one to make poor hiring decisions. Front office personnel are also under pressure to turn rooms quickly because they want to accommodate all guests with whatever requests they have. For example, when guests arrive for an early check-in, they want a room to be ready for them. However, if there has been a high occupancy level the previous night, it can be difficult to provide a room early.

3. **What is your most unforgettable front office moment?**
   When I was working in the front office at the Ritz-Carlton, New Orleans, I learned that we had a bride and groom checking in for their wedding night. We prepared their room prior to arrival with champagne and chocolate-covered strawberries. The door attendant knew what time they were to arrive and what type of car they were coming in, so he was able to greet them by name from the first interaction. The check-in was flawless. When the couple went out for dinner, the concierge drew a bubble bath with red rose pedals and placed another bottle of champagne next to the tub. Throughout their stay they were greeted by name and given extra-special treatment. After they checked out they went on their honeymoon. When they returned from their honeymoon to retrieve their car, they stopped by the front desk to tell me that their one night at the Ritz-Carlton was the most memorable experience of the entire trip.

4. **What advice do you have for those studying about or considering a career in front office or hotel management?**
   Work experience is crucial to good job placement when you are beginning your career. Although education is very important to your future in the hospitality industry, it is imperative to show your commitment and drive by obtaining first-hand experience in a working environment. You also need to remember that your ladies and gentlemen are your most important resource. If you cannot create a positive working environment and listen to what your employees are saying, you will not be successful.

SECTION REVIEW AND DISCUSSION QUESTIONS

Section Objective: Consider basic human resources tactics applicable to recruiting, selecting, orienting, training, motivating, leading, staffing, and scheduling entry-level front office employees.

Section Summary: FOMs must use basic principles of human resources management as they facilitate the work of entry-level front office employees. Their goal is to help the hotel and front office become an employer-of-choice in the community. Large properties have human resources departments with specialists to help with recruitment, selection, orientation, and training of employees. Managers in small properties must perform these tasks without centralized assistance. Hoteliers can use external and internal recruiting tactics to attract the largest number of applicants for vacant positions. They can screen applicants by studying application forms, by conducting employment interviews and tests, and by performing a basic reference check to confirm employment dates and positions held. Orientation provides information that all hotel employees must know, and induction alerts employees to department-specific information.

New employees must be trained for the front office. A well-designed, eight-step process applies to both individualized and group training.

FOMs can use a wide range of common sense tactics to motivate front office employees. When possible, the leadership style of FOMs should be adapted to the individual needs of those being supervised.

Basic principles of staffing and scheduling are important to plan work tasks that are integral to work positions. PMS data tempered by the judgment, experience, and skills of the schedule planner should be used to match the business volume with the number of front office employees needed (for variable labor positions) and to determine the best time for those in fixed labor positions to perform required work.

Discussion Questions:

1. What, if any, role should an individual who will be the immediate supervisor of a new front office employee play in recruitment, selection, orientation, and training of the new staff member? Why?
2. Review the common sense tactics to motivate front office employees (see Figure 3.13). Which of these tactics would you like to be used by your supervisor? What additional common sense (and low-cost) tactics would you suggest based on the perspective of an entry-level staff member?
3. Assume that you are an FOM developing a set of policies applicable to employee schedule requests. What issues would you address in your policy statements? What input, if any, would you solicit from your staff members as you develop these policies?

The FOM in Action: A Solution

As a mentor, what advice might you give to a young staff member who shows promise and expresses an interest in a career in your department and with your property? This is an excellent challenge, because too often FOMs are confronted with the opposite situation: An unmotivated staff member has no interest in a long-term career but just wants do the job rather than apply creativity and talents to please the guests.

Raoul, the FOM at the Hawaiian resort, might begin his response to Kimo by identifying steps in planning a career:

- Recognize that careers can be planned. You do not need to rely on luck to obtain positions in the same or different organizations in the same or another industry.
- Consider personal interests and try to find a position that allows you to do the type of work you like. For example, careers in the lodging industry involve interacting with many people (employees and guests), and Kimo enjoys interacting with people. Kimo also likes the challenge of doing something different throughout each shift, and he enjoys working with computers.
- Consider alternatives. Raoul should advise Kimo to talk to many employees in the hotel, to

attend community career fairs, and to think about work responsibilities that would be in harmony with his personal interests. Other factors to consider include position and career rewards, the chance to learn more through training while on the job, and, formal education and training opportunities in the community.

Raoul should give Kimo time to think about these suggestions. Then, if Kimo is still interested, they can draft a professional development plan. For example, Kimo might rotate between various front office positions, and he can be assigned special projects to learn more about specific aspects of the department. Subsequent performance appraisals can assess the extent to which previous plans have been attained and address plans for further development.

Significant time will be required from Raoul to assist Kimo with the process just described. However, this time will be well spent, because Kimo will likely remain a motivated employee who will contribute to the front office team. In addition, some of Kimo's peers may take an interest in the Kimo's professional development process. If this occurs, Raoul's team will be well-suited to meet the ever-changing needs of guests.

FRONT OFFICE SEMANTICS LIST

Kiosk	Salary	Flat (organization chart)
Folio	Wage	Recruitment
Uniformed services employee	Entry-level position	Turnover rate
Night audit	Universal process of management	Internal recruiting
Property management system (PMS)	Direct report	External recruiting
Subordinate	Job description	Selection
Cross-train	Job specification	Warm-body syndrome
Career ladder	Bona fide occupational qualification (BOQ)	Bonding
		Orientation

Employee handbook	Frequent-guest program	Variable labor position
Employer-of-choice	Motivate	Fixed labor position
Induction	Leadership style	Full-time (employee)
Off-the-shelf	Staffing	Part-time (employee)
Upsell	On-call	Intranet

FRONT OFFICE AND THE INTERNET

You can use the Internet to learn more about the topics of this chapter.

- Type *hotel guest service* into your favorite search engine. Guest service sections of home pages for an almost uncountable number of hotels will be shown. Click on several of these and note the variety and types of guest services and amenities that originate from or are delivered by personnel in the front office department.

- Type *hotel job descriptions* into your favorite search engine. You will discover many Web sites that provide sample job descriptions for hotel positions, including those in the front office. You will also discover executive search and personnel recruiting firms that use job descriptions to seek applicants for hotel-related positions worldwide.

- Type *hotel front office manager* into your favorite search engine to learn details about the job of a front office manager. Job descriptions for vacant FOM positions in hotels around the world will be shown. You can learn about written and video references that provide additional education and training about the work undertaken by FOMs.

- Type *hotel training* into your favorite search engine. Thousands of Web sites provide information about and examples of off-the-shelf training resources directly applicable to hotel and front office management.

- Check out a great hospitality resource to learn about a wide variety of topics (www.hotel-online.com). When you arrive at the site, scroll down to the bottom of the page where you will find this instruction: To search, enter a word or phrase below and click on "Find it Fast." Type in words of interest such as *front office manager* or *motivation*.

REAL-WORLD ACTIVITIES

1. If possible, interview one or more hotel general managers or front office managers. Ask them to prioritize the responsibilities of their front office staff. (Where does guest service occur on the list?) Ask them for examples of times when front office staff provided exemplary guest service. Ask if they attempt to determine whether an applicant for a front office position has the proper guest service philosophy? Discuss the tactics used in their hotel to train front office staff about guest service responsibilities.

2. Assume that you have a career goal to be general manager in a large property. Assume also that it is important for an incumbent in this position to have significant knowledge, skills, and experience in front office responsibilities. Would you

prefer to begin work in a small, large, or mega hotel? Why? What are the advantages and disadvantages to beginning your career in a large or small property?

3. The text and Figure 3.14 review basic information about four leadership styles that front office managers may use as they facilitate the work of their employees. Which of these leadership styles do you think would be best for your superordinate to use in interacting with you? Why? Do you think that leadership styles preferred by those entering the hotel industry today might clash with the styles used by seasoned industry managers?

4. The chapter reviews topics that all hotel employees should know about and that, therefore, should be included in hotel orientation programs. One of these topics is guest service. Prepare an outline of the content for an orientation session on guest services that you would develop for your hotel.

5. The chapter makes references to the concept of employer-of-choice. Tactics are noted that managers, including those with front office responsibilities, can use to help make the hotel a preferred place of employment in the community. What are some stereotypes about the hotel industry that persons without knowledge may have? What tactics could you, as an FOM, use to address these stereotypes in an effort to help your property become an employer-of-choice?

4

Front Office Property Management System

Chapter Outline

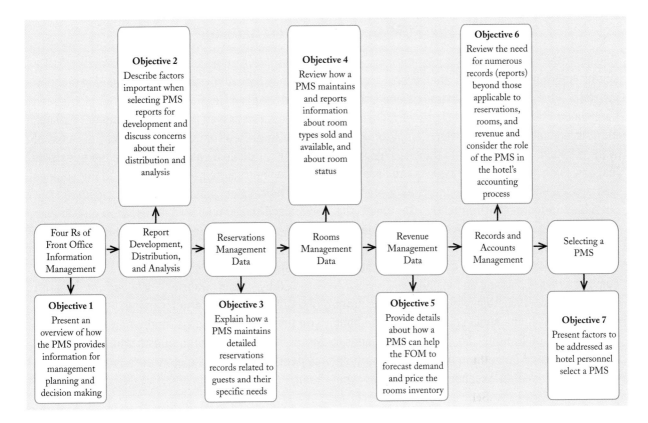

CHAPTER ROADMAP

Chapter Preview

A hotel's property management system (PMS) is the major source of information collection in every hotel. As a result, it is of indispensable help to front office managers (FOMs). Used properly, the PMS collects and reports data in ways that drive the management-planning and decision-making processes in the front office department and throughout the hotel.

This chapter examines the function of the PMS in detail. Which PMS reports are of value? How often should reports be generated? Who should receive them? This chapter answers these and related questions.

PMS reports summarize historical information that can help FOMs better understand and forecast future activities. This allows them to improve the tactics used to manage reservations, room types, and room status and, in the process, to increase revenue. Maintaining basic hotel records and generating and storing many of the hotel's accounting transactions are also important PMS functions. The chapter concludes with an in-depth look at how FOMs should evaluate specific PMS features and functions to determine which of the many available systems best suit their hotel's needs.

The FOM in Action: The Challenge

Guests at the Lexington Lodge love the new high-speed Internet connections that were recently installed in the hotel's 110 guestrooms and chalets. Located on a lake in the upper Northwest, the lodge attracts upscale leisure travelers, many of whom want to remain in contact with their business colleagues. Even though these travelers and their families are vacationing at the lodge, they e-mail and download documents frequently. So when the hotel's retiring general manager and chief maintenance engineer decided to install high-speed Internet connections in each guestroom, the hotel's employees were pleased and excited.

Libby, the FOM, received rave reviews from guests. However, the same could not be said about the reaction of Gabriel, the hotel's new general manager. He had come from a smaller property in the area and was an excellent administrator who had extensive guest service and cost-control skills. However, he had almost no background in technology. According to Gabriel, after the high-speed Internet system was installed, telephone revenues began to drop off sharply. In addition, the cost of providing troubleshooting advice for the guests as they configured their laptops to match the settings of the hotel's designated Internet provider was significant. The 800 number that assisted guests with their hookups was free to guests, but it was not free to the lodge! As system use increased, so did the cost of providing guest assistance.

"Libby," said Gabriel, "We've got to start charging for this Internet service. How much do you think we can charge, and when can you program the PMS to charge guests who log on to the system so we are absolutely sure we collect from them?"

FOUR Rs OF FRONT OFFICE INFORMATION MANAGEMENT

As shown in Roadmap 4.1, this chapter begins with an overview of how the PMS provides information to FOMs for planning and decision making. Front office managers must supervise the daily work of front desk staff to attain optimal guest satisfaction levels and to maximize room revenues and profits. To do so, FOMs must identify and respond to their guests' special requests, needs, problems, issues, and concerns. They must also facilitate the efforts of front office personnel as they train, schedule, empower, coach, counsel, and resolve staff-related problems. In addition to fulfilling their responsibilities to hotel guests and employees, FOMs must manage information. To do so allows FOMs to monitor and control daily revenues and expenses and to ensure that proper procedures and required controls are in place.

The hotel business, in its earliest days, was relatively uncomplicated. As shown in Figure 4.1, FOMs could do an effective job if they simply understood these four basics:

- Desires of their guests
- Rooms and services available for sale
- Prices to be charged for rooms and services
- Accounting and data management methods required for proper record keeping

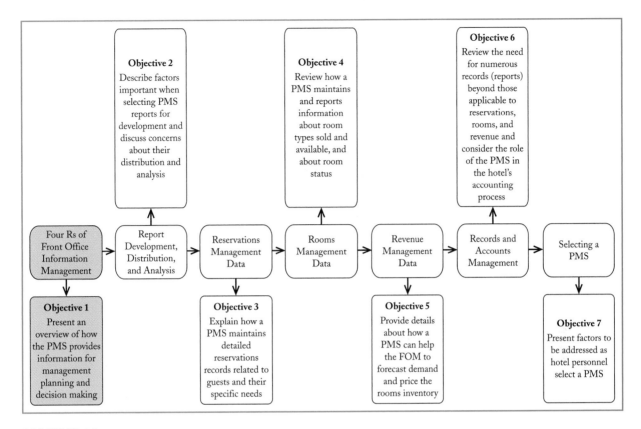

ROADMAP 4.1

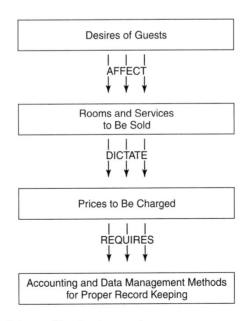

FIGURE 4.1 Yesterday's front office fundamentals.

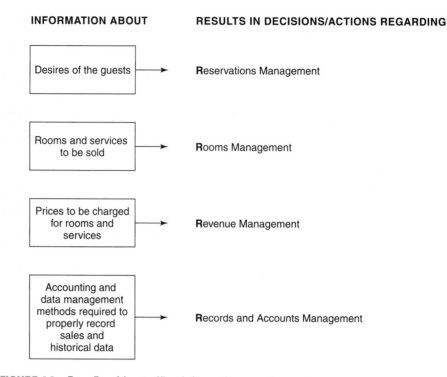

FIGURE 4.2   Four Rs of front office information management.

Effective management of today's technologically advanced front office still requires the proper collection and maintenance of data to address these four front office fundamentals. Today's FOMs, however, use a sophisticated property management system (PMS) to assist them in managing massive amounts of data. Despite rapidly developing enhancements for virtually every PMS available, each system must still address the FOM's fundamental need for information related to reservations, rooms, revenue, and records and accounts—the four Rs of front office information management. Figure 4.2 shows how a modern PMS assists FOMs in processing data related to the four Rs.

FOMs make many decisions every day that affect their hotel's success. Much of their decision making is affected by the way they manage the PMS. The following examples illustrate each of the four Rs in action.

R1—Reservations Management

The Indianapolis 500 (Indy 500) is a significant event for all hoteliers in the Indianapolis area. The crowds attending the race are huge, and each available guestroom in every hotel is extremely valuable for its revenue-generating potential. A sellout the day before the race is routine, because most guests want to be in town the night before the race. Some guests, however, want to be in town before, during, and after the race. These guests represent more attractive business for a hotel than their one-night-only counterparts.

What actions can be taken to ensure that a hotel in the Indianapolis area consistently sells to longer-stay and, therefore, preferred potential guests during the Indy 500?

Chevy American Revolution 400 NASCAR race in Richmond, VA is an example of a special event that can generate high revenue for hoteliers.

Assume that an FOM could estimate the number of, and then identify, guests who want to rent a room for at least three nights while in town for the auto race. The FOM could then accept reservations only from these guests and refuse reservations for others wanting to rent a room for only one night. The situation is complicated by the fact that reservations are not taken solely by the hotel's employees. Franchised hotels have toll-free telephone numbers that potential guests can use to make a reservation. In addition, there are thousands of Internet sites at which a potential guest could make a reservation at the hotel. All of these reservation sources must be coordinated. A quality PMS will do that, in part by allowing FOMs to establish and enforce a minimum length of stay (**MLOS**) for any day they desire.

FRONT OFFICE SEMANTICS

MLOS (minimum length of stay): Designation that instructs reservationists to decline a reservation request from any guest who will not reserve a room for the minimum number of days allowed as predetermined by the hotel.

The FOM may place a three, four, or even longer MLOS on rooms during the period immediately before and after the race. However, if the FOM overestimates the demand for room reservations with the planned MLOS, the hotel may deny too many reservation attempts for stays shorter than the MLOS. This could result in empty rooms that could have been sold if the MLOS requirement had been reduced. An effective PMS provides information about reservation-booking patterns that allows an FOM to adjust MLOS requirements easily and quickly and to send that information to all possible reservation-booking sites.

R2—Rooms Management

Assume that a hotel sells all 400 of its rooms on a Tuesday night because of a large conference being held at the hotel on Monday, Tuesday, and Wednesday. On Wednesday, however, most conference guests check out at noon during their last meeting break. As a result, nearly 400 rooms occupied on Wednesday morning become vacant (and ready to be cleaned) at noon on Wednesday. Not surprisingly, many Wednesday night guests arriving at 3:00 p.m. (the hotel's posted check-in time) learn that their rooms are not ready for them, even though all of the hotel's available housekeepers are busy cleaning the rooms vacated at noon.

How can front desk agents remain updated about the availability of clean guestrooms so that no guest is checked into a room that has not been properly cleaned and inspected? How can agents know as soon as clean rooms are available so that they can assign them to the growing crowd in the hotel's lobby? (Note that some guests will not understand that the stated check-in time is not guaranteed, nor will they care about the hotel's problems arising from the extensive number of noontime check-outs.)

A hotel's front office staff interacts with every department in the hotel. Therefore, its PMS must interface with many other data- and information-generating systems (see Chapter 8 for an in-depth examination of PMS interfaces).

FRONT OFFICE SEMANTICS

Interface: Term used to describe the process that allows one data-generating system to share its information electronically with another system.

An effective PMS serves as an important communication device. In this case, a computer terminal in the executive housekeeper's office may allow him or her to input data about cleaned and inspected rooms urgently needed by the front office staff. Sophisticated PMS systems have telephone interfaces that permit housekeepers or room inspectors to enter room status changes (e.g., from "needs cleaning" to "has been cleaned") directly into the PMS by use of the guestroom telephone.

R3—Revenue Management

Three months from now there will be a national attorney's conference that will significantly increase local demand for hotel rooms. One hotel anticipates that the demand for rooms with king-size beds will be much greater than for rooms with two queen-size beds. As a result, the hotel is likely to sell all of its rooms with king-size beds very quickly, leaving it with only rooms with two beds.

What decisions should be made about the relative prices guests should be charged for these two different types of rooms?

If RevPar is to be maximized, the desires of guests for a specific room type must be considered. Guests' desires should factor into the ultimate pricing decisions made about that room type. The higher the demand for a specific room type during a specific time period, the greater potential the hotel has to increase RevPar for that room type during that time period.

FRONT OFFICE SEMANTICS

Room type: Term used to designate specific guestroom configurations. For example, smoking versus nonsmoking, king bed versus queen or double beds, and suite versus regular sleeping room. Commonly abbreviated (e.g., K for king and NS for nonsmoking). Availability of the proper room type is often important to guests as they decide whether to rent a room.

Data held in a hotel's PMS are critical to the decision-making activities required to maximize RevPar. The PMS helps forecast demand for the hotel's rooms, allows FOMs to rapidly adjust room rates, and performs sophisticated mathematical calculations that result in RevPar maximization strategies.

R4—Records and Accounts Management

Ms. Larson, Ms. Thompson, Ms. Jankowski, and Ms. Daley shared a room on Friday and Saturday night while attending a craft show in town. Their room cost $199 per night, plus locally applicable sales and **occupancy taxes.** *While staying in the room they watched one movie that cost $12.99. During check-out, they announce that they would each like to pay a fourth of the guestroom rental charge; however, because Ms. Daley did not watch the movie, they would like to split that charge only three ways. Ms. Larson would like to pay cash, Ms. Thompson would like to pay by personal check, Ms. Jankowski wants to pay by credit card, and Ms. Daley has offered her debit card to pay for her share of the charges.*

How can these charges be computed and recorded quickly and accurately so that other guests in line to check out are not delayed?

FRONT OFFICE SEMANTICS

Occupancy tax: Money collected from guests and paid by a hotel to a local taxing authority. Room revenue (room sales) generated by a hotel determines the amount collected and paid out. In some areas, this tax is known as the *bed tax.*

It is possible to manually compute and record the payments of the women described in this example. However, a PMS that can easily and quickly allow the front desk agent to establish, receive, and record the proper payment from each guest will be of great value. Note that although only one room was sold, a **guest history** should be automatically created in the PMS for each of the four individuals who stayed at the hotel.

FRONT OFFICE SEMANTICS

Guest history: Record maintained in the PMS that details information about a guest's previous hotel stay or stays. A useful guest history includes information related to guest name, address, previous dates of stays, room preferences, room rates paid, form of payment, and any other information judged important by the FOM and recordable in the PMS.

As the four examples have shown, the value of an effective and well-managed PMS is enormous. Without it, the ability of the FOM to properly address the advanced technological issues faced daily would be severely limited, and the profitability potential of the hotel would be greatly diminished.

SECTION REVIEW AND DISCUSSION QUESTIONS

Section Objective: Present an overview of how the PMS provides information for management planning and decision making.

Section Summary: The PMS is the primary tool used by the FOM to generate data about the four Rs of front office information management: reservations management, rooms management, revenue management, and records and accounts management. This information is critical to effective management planning and decision making for the front office department and throughout the hotel.

Discussion Questions:
1. This section provided examples of PMS applications related to reservations, rooms, revenue, and records and accounts management. Can you think of other situations in which the PMS provides data to help FOMs make decisions regarding the four Rs?
2. How can other departments in the hotel use PMS data about reservations, rooms, revenue, and records and accounts management? Give specific examples.
3. How might the FOM and other hotel managers use guest history information that has been entered in the PMS?

PMS REPORT DEVELOPMENT, DISTRIBUTION, AND ANALYSIS

The hotel's PMS is the major storage and retrieval site of critical information for the front office. Therefore, current and relevant **PMS reports** enable the best managerial decision making. A modern PMS allows FOMs to select from, literally, hundreds of possible reports. As indicated in Roadmap 4.2, this section of the chapter focuses on the development, distribution, and analysis of PMS reports.

FRONT OFFICE SEMANTICS

PMS report: Specific set of data or information taken from a hotel's property management system.

The FOM, working in concert with the hotel's general manager and others, must determine which PMS reports should be generated and analyzed by front office and other decision makers. For example, assume that a specific PMS report estimates the following day's ADR. This information may be critical to the decision making of the hotel's **revenue manager,** but will be of much less importance to the hotel's food and beverage director.

FRONT OFFICE SEMANTICS

Revenue manager: Individual within a hotel's accounting department responsible for decision making necessary to maximize the property's long-term RevPar.

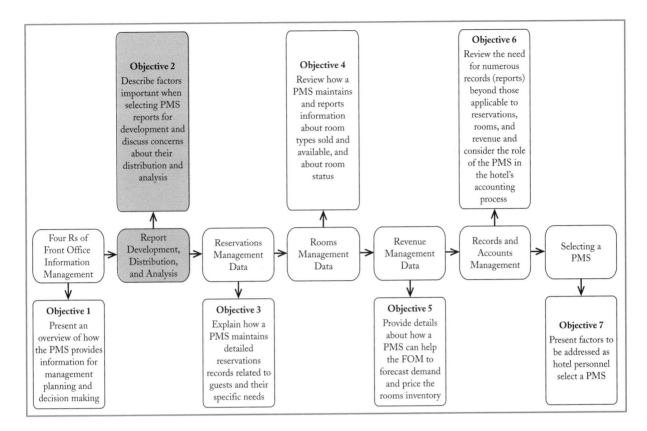

ROADMAP 4.2

Now consider the situation in which a hotel sells all of its rooms on a specific weekday night. The PMS report that estimates that night's **house count** will be of critical importance to the food and beverage director who must estimate the number of guests expected in the hotel's dining rooms that evening and the next morning. Revenue managers may be less interested in this PMS report, because today's house count is not likely to affect decisions about how to establish and manage future room rates.

FRONT OFFICE SEMANTICS

House count: Total number of guests staying in a hotel on a specific night.

Selection of Most Useful Reports

The type and amount of information retrievable from a well-managed, modern PMS is immense. It is unlikely that any FOM would (or could) regularly review all of the reports generated by the PMS. The reports that can be generated by most systems can be classified into one or more of the four information areas (four Rs) already discussed: reservations management, rooms management, revenue management, and records and accounts management.

A single item of data may be contained in one, several, or even all four of the fundamental information areas. Consider, for example, Mr. Swan's hotel visit. If he made a reservation and stayed at a hotel for even one night, information about

Using the correct PMS reports can provide critical information regarding the types of guest staying at a property.

him would be found in PMS reports related to the management of *reservations*. Stored information would, include, at minimum, when Mr. Swan's reservation was made, who made it, and how it was received (e.g., by telephone, mail, fax, or Internet). *Rooms* management information about the Swan reservation would include the specific room type requested, guestroom number, when and how many electronic room keys were provided, and when the room was cleaned and made ready for the next guest. *Revenue* management components of the PMS would consider detailed information about the Swan reservation to establish the rate he should be charged for his room type and the rates to be charged to other guests arriving on the same date. *Records and accounts* information about the Swan reservation and subsequent stay would include how much Mr. Swan paid for his room, how he paid (e.g., cash, credit card, debit card, or traveler's check), what hotel purchases he made during his stay, and the time of day when he checked out of the hotel.

So Mr. Swan's reservation and subsequent stay would affect all four areas of PMS information, and specific data from one area would be incorporated in another area. Let's consider one item: the room type requested by Mr. Swan. This information will be recorded in four areas:

- Reservations management: to document the room type requested by Mr. Swan
- Rooms management: to ensure that the exact room type requested will be available when Mr. Swan arrives

- Revenue management: to determine the total amount of revenue forecasted for the day Mr. Swan will arrive
- Records and accounts management: to document how long Mr. Swan will occupy the room, which indicates the amount he will be charged

Later sections of this chapter and other chapters detail the PMS information and reports available to FOMs and suggest how these reports can be used. Producing, distributing, and reviewing reports involve a real cost to the hotel in both money and staff time; therefore, only the reports that are most useful to management should be selected for recurring production and distribution.

Distribution of Reports

The PMS is a powerful tool that can assist the FOM and his or her staff as well as other hotel managers. Consider, for example, a typical full-service hotel with departments that include general manager (overall property management), front office, food and beverage, accounting, maintenance and engineering, housekeeping, and sales and marketing. Figure 4.3 illustrates the flow of reports from the PMS to these departments.

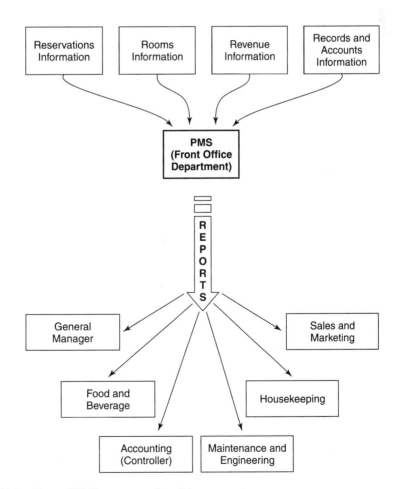

FIGURE 4.3 Flow of PMS reports to hotel departments.

The general manager will likely want daily information about the hotel's overall occupancy rate and its ADR and RevPar. The food and beverage director will want to know about the nature of the hotel's guests (e.g., families, couples, or business travelers). House counts as well as estimated arrival and check-out times will be important because they may affect food and beverage sales patterns. The accounting staff will want to know about guests who have exceeded their established credit limits and if cashier drawers at the front desk were **over** or **short** on each shift.

FRONT OFFICE SEMANTICS

Over: Situation in which cashiers have more money in their cash drawer than the official revenue records indicate. A cashier with $10 more in the cash drawer than the PMS record indicates is said to be $10 *over*.

Short: Situation in which cashiers have less money in their cash drawer than the official revenue records indicate. A cashier with $10 less in the cash drawer than the PMS record indicates is said to be $10 *short*.

The maintenance and engineering staff will want to know about rooms that cannot be sold because they are in need of repair, and housekeeping needs to know about guests who checked out of the hotel so these rooms can be cleaned and readied for the next guests. The sales and marketing staff must know, on a regular basis, the dates on which room discounts should be offered and future dates for which the hotel has already sold out. These few examples indicate that every managerial position and every department in the hotel need information maintained in and reported by the PMS to make informed operating decisions.

In addition to their content, frequency of distribution is an important factor in distribution of PMS reports. Although virtually any report can be created at any time, most reports are generated annually, monthly, weekly, or daily. Some reports are created more than once a day—in some cases every hour or even several times per hour. Figure 4.4 details some characteristics of PMS reports based on the frequency of distribution.

The PMS is a powerful decision-making tool that is used by nearly all hotel managers, supervisors, and even some employees. Accurate information that is properly evaluated improves decision making. Effective FOMs provide themselves and their colleagues with accurate and timely information needed for decision making by carefully selecting and promptly distributing appropriate PMS reports. After they are produced and received, the PMS reports must be analyzed properly.

Report Analysis

Managers in every department benefit from a careful analysis of PMS reports applicable to their areas of responsibility. Any manager with access to a computer terminal connected to the PMS can generate a specific report selected from a report list and display it on the computer screen. If no direct access to the PMS is available, managers must rely on a hard copy (i.e., printed copy) of the reports of interest to them. Hard copies are typically prepared by the night auditor and are distributed to the appropriate managers.

For example, consider a 200-room, limited-service hotel. It is unlikely that the chief engineer will have direct access to the PMS, even though he or she probably has

Type of report	Characteristics
Annual	• Summarize monthly data • Provide data for measuring hotel performance against forecasted or budgeted results • Provide data for measuring hotel performance against similar hotels in the area
Monthly	• Summarize weekly data • Assist in forecasting staffing requirements for departments • Provide data for monthly financial reporting
Weekly	• Summarize daily data • Provide consistent updating of information important to specific hotel departments • Help revenue manager forecast future sales levels and establish room rates
Daily	• Summarize hourly data • Provide snapshots of the previous day's performance • Allow for modification of staffing requirements, if necessary
Hourly (when needed)	• Update staff on occupied rooms • Summarize room types still available for sale • Track reservation-booking patterns and allow daily occupancy forecasting

FIGURE 4.4   Frequency characteristics of PMS reports.

a computer in the office, because each PMS connection is expensive to establish and maintain. Therefore, only managers with a recurring and significant need for PMS data will be directly connected to the system. In this example, the chief engineer will likely request and receive several daily maintenance-related reports, including one that indicates rooms that are currently **out of order (OOO).** Figure 4.5 is a sample report printed from PMS data files.

FRONT OFFICE SEMANTICS

Out of order (OOO): Room that is unrentable for reasons other than routine cleaning. The industry standard notation for this room is OOO.

The PMS report in Figure 4.5 is titled "Today's Work Order," and it gives the reader the following information:

   A. Business date on which the report was generated
   B. Shift on which the report was prepared
   C. Initials of the individual who generated the report
   D. Room number that is out of order
   E. Room type (codes used are specific to each hotel)
   F. Date(s) for which the room should not be sold.
   G. OOO status of the room. (In this report, the Y indicates that "yes" the room is OOO, is in need of attention, and should not be sold.)

A

Today's Work Order

Business Date: 06/01/2006 B Shift 1 C User: CL

Room	Room Type	From	To	Out of Order	Entered Date	Reason	Notes J	Department K	Individual L
176	SBDO	05/28/06	06/02/06	Y	05/28/06	OTHER	DUE TO WATER DAMAGE FROM RAIN LEAKAGE IN PATIO DOOR PER DIANNE	FRONT DESK/FRONT OFFICE	DOYLE, CAROL
D	E	F		G	H	I			

Total Rooms: 1 M

Total Work Orders 1 N

Date/Time of printing 06/01/2006 02:18 pm Software Version 5.3006 Page 1 of 1

FIGURE 4.5 Sample work order—000 rooms report.

H. Date the room was placed in OOO status.

I. Reason the room was placed in OOO status.

J. Notes that identify the room's specific problem.

K. Department that placed the room in OOO status

L. Name of staff member who placed the room in OOO status

M. Total number of rooms that were in OOO status at the time of this report

N. Number of **work orders** prepared to notify maintenance personnel that the room requires attention.

FRONT OFFICE SEMANTICS

Work order: Form used to initiate and document a request for maintenance.

With a current list of OOO rooms, the chief engineer can assess priorities and assign staff to quickly repair rooms that are unrentable or that could detract from a guest's perception of the hotel.

In most cases, report analysis requires that the FOM and other readers understand what has happened in the past, so that they can influence or predict what will happen in the future. For example, assume an FOM reviews a PMS report that identifies the number of **walk-ins** who arrived at the hotel on each of the past 10 Saturday nights.

FRONT OFFICE SEMANTICS

Walk-in: Guest wanting to rent a room who arrives at the hotel without an advance reservation.

Assume also that the PMS's walk-in report indicates that the average number of walk-ins each Saturday was 25. Using this past (historical) information, the FOM can better estimate (forecast) the number of walk-ins the hotel is likely to receive this coming Saturday. Based on this estimate, the FOM can establish an appropriate selling price for the hotel's remaining available rooms.

Understanding Past Performance

In the hotel business, the best prediction of what will happen in the future often relates to what has happened in the past. Therefore, maintenance and use of historical data are critical parts of a FOM's job, and the PMS is used for these purposes. Nearly all FOMs can discover what has happened in the past. Better FOMs know what is happening now. The best FOMs can predict, with great accuracy, what will happen in the future. Because of the tremendous amount of information available through the PMS, the challenge is to decide precisely what historical data should be collected and analyzed.

In some cases, the hotel's general manager or one of several department heads will want specific historical data. Consider Jodi Guild, the director of sales at a 400-room, full-service property. She controls the advertising budget for the hotel and wants to know where her hotel's guests come from. The PMS report in Figure 4.6 indicates the states whose residents generate the most business for the hotel. Information for this report is found in the guest history portion of the PMS data files.

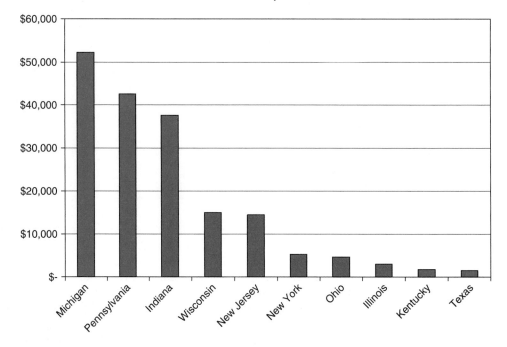

Top-10 Revenue States Jan 1 thru Mar 31 200X
PMS Report #141

FIGURE 4.6 PMS report showing a hotel's Top-10 revenue states.

In addition to the information in this PMS report, Jodi might seek other data: the ADR paid by guests from each of these states, average length of stay, room type selected, number of guests in each room, or days of the week guests visited. Clearly, with this type of information, Jodi will be better prepared to decide where hotel advertising dollars should be spent. Such historical data are probably not important to Jodi on a daily basis, so she is unlikely to need a daily updated report of the Top-10 revenue states. A monthly or even quarterly report would probably be sufficient. In contrast, the executive housekeeper needs a daily list of the occupied rooms and may request hourly reports of the rooms from which guests have checked out so the rooms can be cleaned.

Although other managers will request data with a frequency that assists their decision making, FOMs must regularly analyze the historical data that will be of most use to them. The first questions FOMs must ask are simple: How many rooms will be sold today? This week? This year? The answers to these questions are critical, as room sales provide the revenue that the hotel requires to pay its expenses and to return a profit to its owners. In addition, staffing decisions require knowing the number of guests who will be staying in the hotel. For professional FOMs, their "best guess" of the projected number of rooms to be sold must be short on "guess" and long on "best"!

Forecasting Future Performance
Of the many future events that interest FOMs, room sales is the most important. When FOMs predict the number of rooms that will be sold in a specified time period, they have created a rooms **forecast.**

FRONT OFFICE SEMANTICS

Forecast: Estimate of future sales activity.

There is a difference between **revenue** and **sales** (number of rooms sold). Consider Lea, an FOM whose Monday business consisted of $60,000 in revenue because her hotel sold 400 rooms at an ADR of $150.

FRONT OFFICE SEMANTICS

Revenue: Money the hotel collects from the sale of rooms or from the sale of the hotel's products and services.

Sales: Number of units (such as guestrooms) sold.

Generally, FOMs are interested in maximizing both revenue and the number of rooms sold, because when the maximum number of rooms is sold at the highest possible ADR, RevPar is maximized. By accurately forecasting future demand (sales) and revenue, FOMs can make the rate and sales decisions needed to maximize RevPar. In addition, an understanding of anticipated revenues and number of rooms sold helps FOMs and other managers to schedule the correct number of staff at the right time.

Assume in Lea's hotel that one front desk agent can properly (according to standards) check in 50 guests during a shift. If Lea forecasts 200 check-ins on a specific **shift,** she would need four front desk agents (200 guests ÷ 50 guests per front desk agent) for that shift. Without a room sales forecast, she might schedule too few or too many staff members. A **sales history** can be properly maintained if PMS records are accurate.

FRONT OFFICE SEMANTICS

Shift: Eight-hour period of time. In the hotel business, the most common shifts are 7:00 a.m. to 3:00 p.m., 3:00 p.m. to 11:00 p.m., and 11:00 p.m. to 7:00 a.m. (sometimes referred to as *night audit* or *graveyard* shift).

Sales history: Record of past sales activity for a specific period of time.

A review of sales histories helps FOMs make accurate predictions of future sales. Figure 4.7 lists some of the advantages FOMs gain as they accurately estimate the number of rooms they will sell in a future time period.

- Accurate revenue estimates
- Better guest service because of improved staffing decisions
- Lowered labor costs because employees can be scheduled more accurately according to productivity standards
- Improved budgeting abilities
- Increased operational efficiencies
- Improved profit margins (revenues minus costs)
- Maximized owner (shareholder) profits

FIGURE 4.7 Advantages of precise guestroom sales forecasts.

The PMS is an efficient tool for maintaining a hotel's historical data. The chapters that follow show how various types of histories improve the decision making of FOMs. The best FOMs "see" into the future as they predict room sales and the number of guests who will occupy them. In other words, they create accurate sales forecasts. As the PMS maintains the sales history data necessary to create accurate sales forecasts, it is the primary tool that allows FOMs to see the future.

SECTION REVIEW AND DISCUSSION QUESTIONS

Section Objective: Describe factors that are important when selecting PMS reports for development and discuss concerns about the distribution and analysis of these reports.

Section Summary: The FOM must work with the hotel's general manager, department heads, and others to determine the type and frequency of PMS reports that should be generated to best help management decision makers. The types of data and the amount of information retrievable from a modern PMS are immense, but all reports can be classified into one or more of four fundamental information areas, the four Rs: reservations, rooms, revenue, and records and accounts.

The manager of each hotel department must determine the specific information required for effective decision making and must determine the frequency with which this information will be best used. Then, PMS reports can be generated.

The best prediction of what will happen in the future often relates to what has happened in the past. Accurate historical information about room revenues and sales is critical for making decisions about the future. PMS reports help managers to forecast future performance by estimating room revenues and sales. Based on this information, FOMs and other hotel managers can improve guest service, lower labor costs, and improve the revenue of owners or shareholders.

Discussion Questions:

1. What tactics can an FOM use to interact with department heads and other hotel managers to assess their needs for PMS reports? What is the best way that the FOM can provide service to these colleagues?
2. Assume that you are a front desk agent. What kinds of operating-related information would you like to have at the beginning of your shift that could be provided in PMS reports?
3. Assume you are a hotel's controller. What are several of the most important PMS reports that could help you to assist the FOM in developing next year's budget for the front office department?

RESERVATIONS MANAGEMENT DATA

The way room reservations are made contributes to accurate sales forecasting by FOMs. As indicated in Roadmap 4.3, the modern PMS is an asset in this process because it can accurately maintain detailed reservation records related to guests and

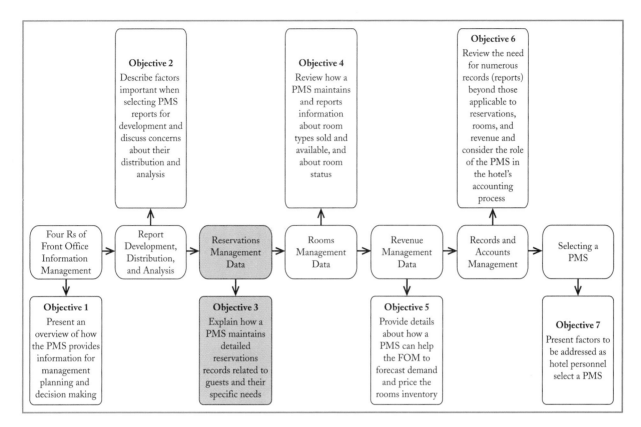

ROADMAP 4.3

to their specific reservation requests. The data-collection process must be examined carefully because of its impact on FOMs as they forecast sales and work to maximize RevPar.

Guest Information

Guests supply specific information when they make a hotel reservation. Depending on the method used to make a reservation, the amount of data collected can range from extensive to minimal. Although each PMS is formatted somewhat differently, basic information related to the guest and guest requests must be collected. Figure 4.8 shows a data screen that appears on a typical PMS when a guest calls a hotel directly to request a new reservation. The screen contains the data **fields** that relate directly to the guest; these fields are labeled by letter:

A. *Adults:* Number of adults staying in the room
B. *Child:* Number of children staying in the room
C. *Frequent Traveler ID:* Identification for frequent-traveler programs that hotels maintain to reward guests who frequently use a specific hotel or hotel brand. This field allows the hotel to credit the traveler's account for the stay.
D. *Last Name:* Very important field in which proper spelling is critical
E. *First Name*

```
           1
Account: 139675        Arr/Dep Info          Status: Reserved                    Balance: .00

┌──────────────────────────────────────────────────────────────────────────────────────────┐
│ STAY INFORMATION:                                                                          │
│ Arrival:    00/00/00    2        Adults:      A      Rate Plan:          7       Room:    10│
│ Nights:           0     3         Child:      B      Room Type:          8  Suppress Rate:11│
│ Departure:  00/00/00    4    No. of Rooms:    6      Room Rate:   .00     9                 │
│ GTD/CXL:                5                                                                   │
└──────────────────────────────────────────────────────────────────────────────────────────┘

┌──────────────────────────────────────────────────────────────────────────────────────────┐
│ GUEST INFORMATION:                                                                         │
│ Frequent Travel ID:              C                                                         │
│ Last Name:                       D      Company:                                         H │
│ First Name:                      E      Address:                                         I │
│ Phone:                           F      City, St ZIP:                                    J │
│ Caller:                          G      E-Mail:                                          K │
└──────────────────────────────────────────────────────────────────────────────────────────┘

┌────────────────────────────────┐  ┌──────────────────────────┐  ┌──────────────────────┐
│ GUARANTEE INFORMATION:  12     │  │ TRACKING:  13            │  │ OPTIONS:  14         │
│ Gtd/Pmt:                       │  │ Source:       Geo:       │  │ Confirm:             │
│ Deposit:          Due Date:    │  │ Track:        Open:      │  │ Exempt:    N         │
│ Credit Card:    /      $.00    │  │ ID:                      │  │ Vip:                 │
│ Card Holder:                   │  │ Vehicle:             M   │  │ No Post:             │
└────────────────────────────────┘  └──────────────────────────┘  └──────────────────────┘

┌────────────────────────────────┐  ┌──────────────────────────────────────┐
│ ASSOCIATED ACCOUNTS:  15       │  │ NOTES:      L                        │
│ Group:                         │  │                                      │
│ A/R:                           │  │                                      │
│ T/A 1:              Comm:      │  │                                      │
│ T/A 2:              Comm:      │  │                                      │
└────────────────────────────────┘  └──────────────────────────────────────┘

  Reserve: 06/01/06    Cxl:         00/00/0
  00/00/00
  16                   17
```

FIGURE 4.8   Reservation screen.

F. *Phone:* Telephone number, which is a way to contact the guest before arrival if necessary and allows for creation of PMS reports that track the geographic (by area code) source of reservations

G. *Caller:* Name of the person making the reservation (Frequently, this individual is not the person who will be staying in the hotel.)

H. *Company:* Organization the traveler works for (if a business traveler)

I. *Address.* Guest's home or business address

J. *City, St ZIP:* City, state, and zip code, which help with guest contact and are useful in generating reports about the origination of business

K. *E-Mail:* An increasingly popular electronic means for communicating with guests

L. *Notes:* Open field that can be used for special guest requests or other guest-related information that would be helpful when the guest arrives. Examples are requests for a specific floor or type of room, requests for late check-out or early check-in, and specific information regarding the guest's payment of charges.

M. *Vehicle:* Registration required by some hotels when guests register at check-in (but not typically when the reservation is made)

FRONT OFFICE SEMANTICS

Field: Data-entry location in a PMS. For example, the reservation screen on a PMS contains a *field* for the guest's name and another field for the guest's telephone number (along with many other fields). Data for these fields are typically entered at the time the reservation is made and may be modified at the time of guest registration. Fields are sometimes referred to as *data fields*.

Guest Request Information

In addition to specific information about the guest, a room reservation typically includes an extensive amount of information about the guest's specific reservation requests. Figure 4.8 shows the following fields, labeled by number:

1. *Account:* Also known as a **confirmation number;** identifies the specific reservation within the PMS

2. *Arrival:* Date the guest will arrive

3. *Nights:* Number of nights the guest will stay

4. *Departure:* Date the guest will leave

5. *GTD/CXL:* In this PMS, a field activated when a reservation has been completed (GTD) or canceled (CXL)

6. *No. of Rooms:* One or more. Guests may reserve more than one room at a time.

7. *Rate Plan:* Special rate. Hotels often negotiate or offer special rates to some guests, and these are identified by code numbers or letters. For example, a rate plan called *AAA* may be used to identify the rate to be charged to members of the American Automobile Association (AAA). The proper use of the rate plan feature simplifies the reservation process and allows tracking of activities of various groups.

8. *Room Type:* several types usually offered based on bed size (e.g., king, queen, and double) and other features such as location, smoking or nonsmoking, and in-room amenities

---

FRONT OFFICE SEMANTICS

Confirmation number: Number (or combination of numbers and letters) that identifies a specific guest reservation.

---

9. *Room Rate:* Per night charge for the room. Typically rate does not include applicable taxes.

10. *Room:* Number (if known) of the specific room reserved

11. *Suppress Rate:* Field checked if the guest making the reservation prefers that the room charge not show on the folio

12. *Guarantee Information:* Some form of payment to guarantee reservation. Payment may be cash, credit card, or an **advance deposit.** This section of the reservation screen allows the hotel to collect the information required for the guest's payment.

FRONT OFFICE SEMANTICS

Advance deposit: Partial or full payment made for guestroom rental before the guest's arrival.

---

13. *Tracking:* Section used to record the following information:
    - *Source:* Whether the reservation was made by telephone, fax, e-mail, letter, or other form of communication
    - *Track:* Type of guest (business, leisure, or other designated type)
    - *ID:* Driver's license number (sometimes required of guests based on hotel policy)
    - *Vehicle:* License tag information (sometimes required of guests based on hotel policy)
    - *Geo:* State, county, or city
    - *Open:* Field that may be used by the hotel to collect its own property-specific information of interest

14. *Options:* Section that notes the following information:
    - *Confirm:* Checked if the guest wishes to receive written confirmation of the reservation. If so, the PMS automatically prints a confirmation letter addressed to the guest.
    - *Exempt:* Used for individuals who are exempt from specific hotel taxes
    - *VIP:* Used to identify very important guests
    - *No Post:* Used to waive (not **post**) specific guest charges.

FRONT OFFICE SEMANTICS

Post: To enter data (including guest charges) into the PMS to create a permanent record of the information. Posting may be done automatically or manually. Used as in, "Please *post* this room charge to Mr. Walker's folio."

---

15. *Associated Accounts:* Section is used to record the following information:
    - *Group:* Name of the group (if any) with which the guest is associated
    - *A/R:* Place for routing charges to a specific accounts receivable (A/R) account
    - *TA/1 and T/A2:* Place for recording to whom the hotel will pay any travel agent (TA) commission that is due

- *Comm:* Percentage amount of the guest's charge to be paid as a TA commission. Typical TA commissions range from 5 percent to 15 percent of the guest's total, pretax sleeping room charges.
16. *Reserve:* Date the reservation was made
17. *Cxl:* Date on which reservation cancellation was recorded

Names of specific fields vary based on the PMS in use. Nevertheless, all systems collect extensive information about guests and their reservation requests in the reservation screen. Even a modestly priced PMS allows FOMs to create a large number of reports (many of which will be reviewed throughout this text), and because of these reports, managers' decision-making abilities are enhanced.

SECTION REVIEW AND DISCUSSION QUESTIONS

Section Objective: Explain how a PMS maintains detailed reservations records related to guests and their specific needs.

Section Summary: A reservation screen for a typical PMS allows the FOM to gather specific information about guests, including data that are necessary to reserve the appropriate room type for required dates and to collect payment. Data entered into the PMS are used to develop many reports that enhance management decision making.

Discussion Questions:
1. This section mentions several special requests commonly made by guests. Can you think of other requests that might be posed?
2. How should the front desk agent taking the reservation respond to a request such as this: "I know the hotel's check-in time is at 2:00 p.m., but my flight arrives at 11:00 a.m. and I can be there by noon. May I please have my room early?"
3. Can you think of room features that a front desk agent might upsell to a guest at the time a reservation is made?
4. How should the FOM determine exactly what information should be required from guests at the time they make room reservations?

ROOMS MANAGEMENT DATA

Revenue from room sales represents the largest single source of revenue for most hotels; therefore the ability of FOMs to manage rooms-related information is critical. As Roadmap 4.4 shows, the PMS provides FOMs the information they need. The PMS maintains and reports information about the kinds of rooms (room types) sold and available to be sold, and about the readiness of the rooms for immediate guest occupancy **(room status).**

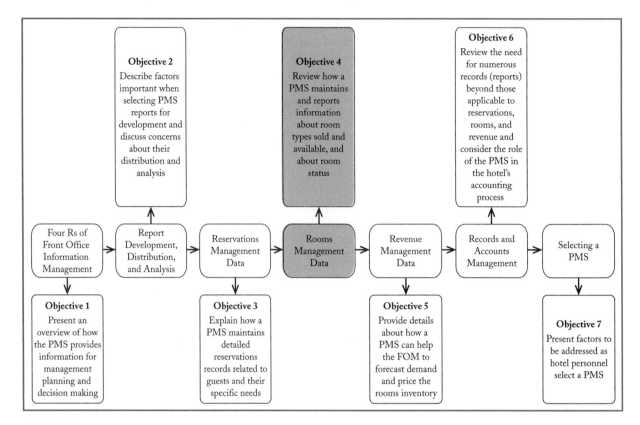

ROADMAP 4.4

FRONT OFFICE SEMANTICS

Room status: Up-to-date (actual) condition (e.g., occupied, vacant, dirty, or clean) of all the hotel's individual guestrooms.

Room Type

Most hotels offer guests more than one type of room. FOMs must manage not only the number of rooms available to sell but, as well, the types of rooms available for sale. When a PMS is initially programmed, all of the hotel's available room types are entered into the system's database. For example, if a 400-room hotel elects to designate 250 of its rooms as nonsmoking, that information would be entered, by specific room number, into the PMS. As a result, the hotel's FOM and his or her staff could review a selected PMS report to learn the number of nonsmoking rooms sold and the number available for sale on any specific day.

The names of room types used in the hotel industry are as varied as are the hotels that make up the industry. A hotel built on a beach would likely designate rooms facing the beach as *beach front* or *beach view* and would probably sell them for a higher ADR than counterpart rooms not facing the beach. In this beach property, rooms on another side of the building can still sound attractive: "Would you enjoy a room with a mountain view (or garden view)?" Obviously, a hotel located near an airport in the Midwest would not use such room types, but the property would likely have its own way of designating its largest, best, and most desirable rooms.

An accurate forecast of the number of occupied rooms will help staff provide guests with high-quality service.

Even though specific room types vary by hotel, some designations of room type are commonly used by most hotels. They are generally based on a specific room's bed type, location or other room feature. Figure 4.9 lists some of the most commonly used room types and their definitions.

Depending on the hotel's location and unique features, the hotel room types may be designated by a variety of special characteristics. The following characteristics commonly qualify for a separate room type: existence of designated business amenities, in-room high-speed Internet access **(HIA),** in-room refrigerators or safes, and desirable locations within the hotel itself (e.g., pool front and pool view).

FRONT OFFICE SEMANTICS

HIA (high-speed Internet access): Technology required to allow hotel guests to access the Internet at download speeds much higher than those that can be achieved with traditional telephone dial-up systems.

FOMs and their general managers create room types when they believe that different rooms have different perceived value to guests and that, as a result, some room types can be sold to guests at a higher ADR than others. In addition, a room type of higher perceived value may be used to **upgrade** special guests or guests who have experienced some difficulty with their hotel stay.

FRONT OFFICE SEMANTICS

Upgrade: To assign a guest to a more expensive (or desirable) room type than the room type to which the guest was originally assigned.

Room type	Definitions regarding bed type
Single (twin)	Room that contains a single-person (standard/twin) bed
Double	Room that contains one double bed
Double-double	Room that contains two double beds
Queen	Room that contains a queen-size bed
King	Room that contains a king-size bed
Sofa sleeper	Room that contains a sofa sleeper
	Definitions regarding location
Adjoining rooms	Rooms that are next to each other but do not have a connecting door
Connecting rooms	Rooms that have individual entrance door but also share a common interior door, which allows guests to enter each room from inside either room
Beach front	Room that allows direct access to the beach (or other desirable hotel location)
Beach view	Room that gives the occupants a direct view of the beach (or other desirable hotel location)
Restricted floor	Room that is located in a section of the hotel that is accessible only to specifically designated guests
	Definitions regarding features
Barrier free	Special room that is easily accessible to those with limited physical abilities (In the past, referred to as *handicapped*)
Smoking/nonsmoking	Rooms designating smoking status. Some hotels use the terms *smoking permitted* and *no smoking permitted* to identify these rooms.
Suite	Typically a large room with the sleeping area separated by a wall or partial wall. A whirlpool suite has an in-room whirlpool tub or hot-tub. A parlor suite has a large, separate living room (parlor) area suitable for entertaining.

FIGURE 4.9   Room types and standard definitions.

FOMs and their staff must know all of the different room types the hotel property offers.

Different room types need not sell at different ADRs. For example, few hotels would sell rooms that allow smoking at a different price than rooms that do not allow smoking, even though most hotels in the United States offer these two different room types. Similarly, a hotel whose guestroom windows face east and west may or may not charge the same for rooms with sunrise views as for rooms with sunset views.

In all cases, the hotel's PMS must be programmed to identify the various room types offered for sale. Typically, this is done by a coding system unique to each PMS. For example, in one PMS, the code NDD may refer to a nonsmoking, double-double room. In a different PMS, the coding might identify the same room as DD, because in that system SM is used to designate a room where smoking *is* permitted. Therefore, it would code a smoking-permitted, double-double as SMDD.

FOMs must make sure that the room types and the codes used to define them make sense for their hotel, and the codes must be well understood by front office personnel who take reservations and make specific room assignments. Experienced FOMs will not allow new front desk agents to work alone at the desk until they have memorized (or at least have an easily accessible list of) all the hotel's codes for room type. If well-defined codes for room type are programmed into the PMS, front office personnel can more easily keep up-to-date on the status of their rooms and make better decisions about managing them.

Room Status

When the PMS has been programmed properly with hotel-specific codes for room type, FOMs will know about the long-term availability of the room types they can manage and sell. Short-term availability of room types, however, is affected by each room's status. As with room types, each PMS may have its own coding system to communicate room status. Figure 4.10 lists the hotel industry's most common terms for room status.

The importance of using the PMS to continually manage the room status in hotels cannot be overemphasized. Consider guest reaction to two of the many mistakes that can occur when room status is *not* managed properly:

- *Guest assigned to an uncleaned room.* Few errors are as embarrassing for professional FOMs or their staffs as having a guest return to the front desk for a new room assignment because the room originally assigned has not been cleaned. If the status of "cleaned and vacant" and "on-change" rooms is not properly managed, this mistake is easy to make.

Term	Meaning
Clean and vacant	Room is vacant, has been cleaned, and can be assigned to a guest
Occupied	Room is registered to a current guest
On-change	Room is vacant but not yet cleaned
Do not disturb	Room is occupied but has not been cleaned due to the guest's request not to be disturbed
Sleep-out (sleeper)	Room is reported as occupied, but the room was not used (bed not used, no personal belongings in room), and the guest is not present
Stayover	Guest will stay in the room at least one more night
Due out	Guest has indicated this is the last day the room will be used
Check-out	Guest has departed
Out of order	Room is unrentable and, therefore, unassignable at this time
Lock-out	Guest has items in the room but will be denied access until approved to reenter by management
Late check-out	Guest requested and was given an extension of the regular check-out time

FIGURE 4.10   Room status terminology.

• *Guest assigned to an occupied room.* This error is widely regarded as the most serious room assignment mistake that can be made by a front desk agent; yet, it can occur if room status is not properly maintained. When this mistake is made, the hotel staff appears incompetent and unprofessional. Think of the embarrassment of the new guest assigned to the occupied room (who now feels like a trespasser) and the anger and surprise of the guests initially assigned the room (who likely feel insecure). Every FOM wants to avoid this scene.

SECTION REVIEW AND DISCUSSION QUESTIONS

Section Objective: Review how a PMS maintains and reports information about room types sold and available, and about room status.

Section Summary: An effectively developed and maintained PMS system provides front office personnel who makes reservations with up-to-date and accurate information about the number of rooms of each room type that are available for sale. The PMS also provides current information about the status of rooms that are and should be available for sale in the hotel at any specific time.

Discussion Questions:

1. What are ways that a front desk agent can use information about room status to assign rooms to guests who have just reached the front desk to begin the registration process?
2. For a future, specific date, a guest is requesting a specific room type that the PMS system indicates will be unavailable. What, if anything, can a front desk agent do in this situation?

REVENUE MANAGEMENT DATA

Based on an understanding of reservations, the room types available to be sold, and the short-term readiness for sale of those rooms, FOMs can use the PMS to make revenue management decisions. Roadmap 4.5 indicates that the PMS helps FOMs forecast demand and price rooms inventory.

To see how data about the first three Rs (reservations, rooms, and revenue) in the front office information system interact to influence decision making, consider Allisha Miller, the FOM at a 300-room hotel. To simplify the example, let's assume that Allisha has only two room types in her rooms inventory: 150 of her available rooms are DD (double-double rooms) and 150 are K (king-size bed) rooms. Typically, both of these room types are offered for sale at $100 per weekend night. However, Allisha offers rate discounts when she feels it is in the hotel's best interest to do so. (Generally, an occupancy rate of 50 percent or less suggests a need for a discount tactic.) At noon on a specific day, the PMS occupancy report indicates there will be a 50 percent occupancy rate for the night (150 total rooms sold). Two different situations that could exist, however, when Allisha reviews an additional PMS report that shows the specific room types reserved (sold) for the day.

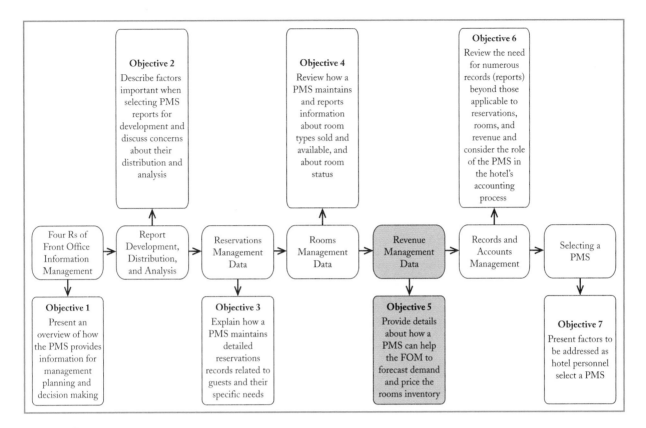

ROADMAP 4.5

Situation A

Room type	Total rooms available	Rooms sold
DD	150	140
K	150	10
	Total sold	150

Occupancy rate = 150 rooms ÷ 300 rooms = 50 percent

Situation B

Room type	Total rooms available	Rooms sold
DD	150	75
K	150	75
	Total sold	150

Occupancy rate = 150 rooms ÷ 300 rooms = 50 percent

In Situation A, discounting rooms with king-size beds may be an appropriate strategy to maximize RevPar. However, there is a strong demand for (and, therefore, no compelling reason for discounting) double-double rooms. With only 10 DD rooms remaining to sell, Allisha would likely instruct her reservations and sales staff not to discount them. In Situation B, however, Allisha may want to accept discounted rates for both room types, because demand on this day for both types is moderate and equal.

Effective FOMs depend on their PMS to provide critical reservation and room type information to help them forecast demand and properly price the hotel's inventory of rooms. When you consider that even a medium-size hotel can have dozens of room types with each selling at a different rate, you can recognize the benefits of detailed PMS record keeping and reports.

Forecasting Demand

If FOMs always knew when demand for their rooms would be strong, their decision making would be simplified. Although FOMs should stay informed about major seasons and events that will likely affect occupancy rates, they can best monitor demand by consulting PMS reports about reservation activity. Reports of this type typically evaluate demand for the coming 12-month period (or longer). From report data, FOMs can monitor **booking pace** and forecast demand.

FRONT OFFICE SEMANTICS

Booking pace: Term that refers to the amount of future demand for rooms (or for hotel services such as catering). Often shortened to *pace*.

FOMs monitor forecasts so that they can alert staff about the arrival of large groups.

To illustrate the importance of pace information, let's again consider the FOM Allisha Miller and her 300-room property:

- It is May 1 and Allisha's PMS can produce pace reports for each of the upcoming 12 months.
- Allisha reviews a pace report for October (6 months in the future). The PMS reports that the current number of guestrooms already reserved (sold) for October is 1,860, or 20 percent of available rooms (1,860 rooms ÷ [300 rooms × 31 days] = 20 percent occupancy).
- Last year, on May 1, the number of rooms already reserved for the month of October was 465, or 5 percent (465 rooms ÷ [300 rooms × 31 days] = 5 percent occupancy).
- By the end of October last year, the hotel had sold 6,510 rooms and achieved an occupancy of 70 percent for that month (6,510 rooms ÷ [300 rooms × 31 days] = 70 percent occupancy). In fact, the month was one of the hotel's best that year.

Allisha must now evaluate whether the rates this October, when compared with data for forecasted rooms and actual rooms for last October, should be discounted, remain the same, or be increased. Although many variables affect the determination of appropriate room rates, the *demand* for Allisha's rooms is strong and is clearly outpacing the past year's demand. Demand information will be critical as Allisha makes decisions about how to maximize her property's RevPar by minimizing room rate discounts that are not likely to be necessary to help fill her rooms.

FOMs must continually monitor PMS reports about booking pace reports. Based on a thorough understanding of future demand, FOMs can effectively price rooms to achieve maximum revenues, because increased demand typically yields increased ADRs.

Pricing Inventory

In a perfect world, FOMs would sell all of their rooms every day at rack rate. Unfortunately, the hotel world is not perfect; therefore, most FOMs offer travelers discounts on room rates on nights with weak demand to increase occupancy rates. The next two chapters will examine how FOMs monitor room demand and make pricing decisions on room rates to maximize RevPar. For purposes of the current discussion, recognize that the PMS serves several important pricing-related functions:

- Reporting overall ADRs for selected historical periods (e.g., yesterday, last week, last month, and last quarter)
- Reporting overall ADRs for selected historical days (e.g., all past Mondays, Wednesdays, or Fridays)
- Reporting overall ADRs for selected historical periods by room type (e.g., kings, double-doubles, and suites sold during selected time periods)
- Reporting future ADRs based on current booking pace reports for the first three functions
- Maintaining the FOM's current discount and pricing strategy for every future date that a reservation can be made and for every room type

The PMS can generate data such as these to "advise" an FOM about appropriate pricing strategies based on the hotel's specific historical bookings and the hotel's current booking pace. The PMS can then "recommend" pricing models to be used based on time of year, day of week, and forecasted demand by room type.

SECTION REVIEW AND DISCUSSION QUESTIONS

Section Objective: Provide details about how a PMS can help the FOM to forecast demand and price the rooms inventory.

Section Summary: The PMS tracks the number of each type of room available for sale at any point in time, from the current moment to a future date limited by the length of the period for which reservations are taken. Current and future data can be compared with historical data to help FOMs determine pricing strategies such as increasing, maintaining, or decreasing prices based on room availability.

Discussion Questions:
1. Review Allisha Miller's reservation data in Situation A. What factors should she consider as she determines the amount of the discount, if any, to be offered for guestrooms with king-size beds? Should the same discount be offered to *any* guest inquiring about reserving this type of room?
2. Assume that Allisha currently has only relatively few double-double rooms available for sale at a future date. What factors should she consider as she determines whether room selling prices should be increased?

RECORDS AND ACCOUNTS MANAGEMENT

The fourth of the four Rs of front office information management involves records and accounts, as noted in Roadmap 4.6. Like reservations, rooms, and revenue management, in all but the smallest properties, the management of a hotel's records and financial accounts can only be done effectively with a modern PMS. The need for FOMs to have a solid understanding of the records and accounting components of their jobs is so important that Chapters 11 and 12 are devoted to this topic.

Records Management

It might seem that FOMs who regularly review PMS data related to their reservations, rooms, and revenues will have considered all the facts necessary to make major decisions. In fact, the PMS generates much information that is not directly related to these topics but is often critical to management decision making. The best PMS provides this additional and valuable information in timely and easy-to-review formats and reports.

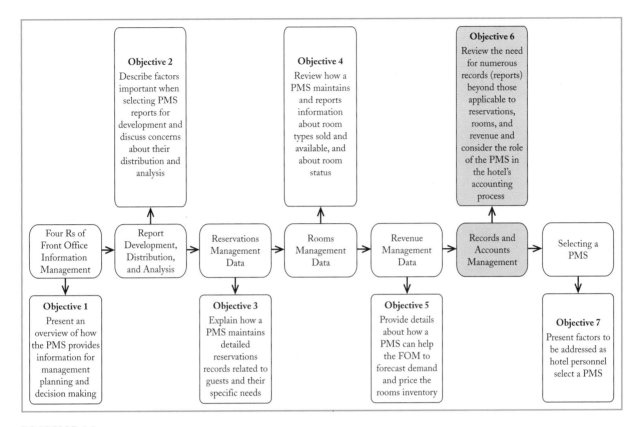

ROADMAP 4.6

Let's return to our example of Allisha Miller and her 300-room hotel. Consider the number of additional hotel records that might be of value, including reports such as those listed in Figure 4.11. A sophisticated PMS can generate dozens of such reports based on management's specific needs and requests. The number of reports is limited only by the imagination of the system's programmers and the skill level of the hoteliers advising them. One of the most important factors to consider when evaluating a specific PMS is the number and quality of useful records that can be produced in a functional format. A modern PMS can maintain a wide range of hotel statistics and records. Of these, the most important are the many records related to the hotel's financial accounts.

Accounts Management

The word *account* means to record and report. Because the PMS serves as the hotel's major information collection and report center, it plays a crucial role in the hotel's accounting processes.

In the most simple case, the PMS records the charges and collection of payments for the rooms and services sold by the hotel. A guest reserving and staying in one room for a total rate of $150 for a night and charging a $25 meal consumed in the hotel's dining room to the room would expect to pay one bill at check-out. The PMS

Report	Use
1. Number of new frequent-traveler members enrolled at the front desk in the past six months	To evaluate the effectiveness in enrolling new members
2. Travel agent reports	To determine travel agents who have generated the most business for the hotel
3. In-house lists	In a crisis, to notify emergency workers about rooms that are currently occupied
4. Cancellation lists	To identify guests who have canceled a reservation for (but not on) a specific day
5. Peak arrival reports	To better schedule staff by identifying the times of day when front office check-in activity is greatest
6. Peak departure reports	To better schedule staff by identifying the times of day when front office check-out activity is greatest
7. Reservation activity reports	To better schedule staff by identifying the times of the day when call-in or walk-in reservation activity is greatest
8. Room change list	To identify guests who have requested (or have been given) a room different than the one they were originally assigned and to identify reasons for the change
9. Revenue by day of week	To summarize the revenue generated by the hotel by day of the week
10. Occupancy by room type	To identify the hotel's most popular and best-selling room types

FIGURE 4.11   Ten selected PMS reports related to hotel records.

records both the room sale ($150) and the meal ($25) to create a total bill of $175. The PMS records the guest's **form of payment** when the bill is paid.

FRONT OFFICE SEMANTICS

Form of payment: Method that guests use to pay their bills (e.g., credit card, debit card, cash, check).

A simple accounting report for this transaction would include both the room and food sale and a record of the bill's final payment, but any hotel's daily accounting transactions are much more complex than this simple example. Large hotels create literally thousands of complex sales and payment transactions each day. Therefore, the ability of a PMS to properly record and accurately report these accounting functions must be equal to the task. Although the complexity of the accounting function of a PMS in a large hotel is much greater than that of smaller hotels, every PMS performs essentially the same accounting functions, and these are conceptualized in Figure 4.12.

Note in Figure 4.12 that guest charges (they are only charges until paid) arise from one of two broad sources:

- *Room charges.* Room charges are always posted in the PMS; these include the rate guests are charged for the room and applicable taxes. Typically, on the guest's folio the rate paid for the room is shown separately from the taxes to be paid. In the PMS, separate records of room charges and tax charges are maintained.

- *Non-room charges.* In addition to guestroom charges, the PMS records non-room charges. Hotels allow guests to purchase goods and services and charge these purchases to their rooms, for example, pay-per-view movies, telephone toll charges, and food and beverages. Some resort hotels impose use fees for golf, tennis, or selected water activities (e.g., boats and water skis). Guests are typically allowed to charge these items to their rooms, and the charges must be posted in the PMS.

Additional sources of non-room revenues in full-service hotels include charges for meeting room rental (considered separate from sleeping room revenue), audiovisual equipment rental, and any special setup or service charges related to the sale and use of meeting space.

When all room and non-rooms charges have been entered into the PMS, the system performs two major functions, as shown in Figure 4.12:

- *Creation of guest folios (bills).* As defined earlier in this chapter, *folio* is the industry term used to identify the charges assessed to a hotel guest. Persons not staying in the hotel (e.g., a local couple eating in the hotel's dining room) would receive a *bill*. The total of all folios and bills (that represent the hotel's revenues) must be recorded in the PMS.

- *Updating the hotel's accounting records.* A primary function of the PMS is to maintain accurate accounting records. Therefore, every room and non-room sale must be recorded, and the database related to total sales and payment records must be updated.

The PMS is usually not the same as the hotel's **back-office accounting system.**

FRONT OFFICE SEMANTICS

Back-office accounting system: Automated (or manual) system of data collection and reporting used by a hotel to summarize and document its financial activity and position.

For example, in most cases a hotel's payment to a supplier who provides table-cloths for banquets would be documented in the hotel's back-office accounting

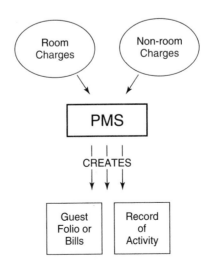

FIGURE 4.12   PMS accounting functions.

system. This payment (accounting transaction) would not likely be recorded in the PMS. Traditionally, PMS manufacturers have not developed systems that are easily interfaced with back-office accounting systems. Now, however, more manufacturers are working to develop these interfaces, and in the near future hoteliers will likely be using a system that integrates all of the hotel's financial information.

SECTION REVIEW AND DISCUSSION QUESTIONS

Section Objective: Review the need for numerous records (reports) beyond those applicable to reservations, rooms, and revenue and consider the role of the PMS in the hotel's accounting system.

Section Summary: FOMs can select a wide range of PMS reports in addition to those that are helpful with reservations, rooms, and revenue management. First, however, FOMs must consider the types of data relationships that will help them to make critical business decisions. This task is difficult given the seemingly innumerable reports that can be generated. Few, if any, PMSs interface completely with and can replace a back-office accounting system. Rather, the contributions that PMSs make related to room and non-room charges complement data about other hotel financial transactions in the back-office accounting system.

Discussion Questions:

1. Figure 4.11 reviews selected PMS reports related to hotel records. Can you think of additional reports—other than those related to rooms, reservations, and revenues—that could be of interest to you as an FOM?

2. What are the traditional reasons why manufacturers have not developed an effective interface between a PMS and a property's back-office system? What factors are influencing a convergence of these technologies today?

SELECTING A PMS

The importance of a dependable and cost-effective PMS system for the management of a hotel's front office is clear. FOMs must rely on the PMS to help them with every aspect of their rooms-related decision-making responsibilities. Therefore, the selection of the best PMS system is critical. As Roadmap 4.7 indicates, the chapter concludes with a discussion of the factors involved in selecting a PMS.

In many cases, a hotel's franchisor may dictate that a specific PMS (usually developed by the franchisor) be used. This ensures that the PMS in each hotel within the chain can be interfaced with the franchisor's PMS monitoring system. Franchisors prefer this arrangement because they are typically paid a royalty fee based on room (and other) revenues achieved by each hotel within the chain. By mandating that franchisees use a specific PMS, franchisors can interface with that PMS and directly monitor revenues and sales. The interface also helps ensure that the hotel is paying all of its applicable franchise and royalty fees according to the terms of its franchise agreement.

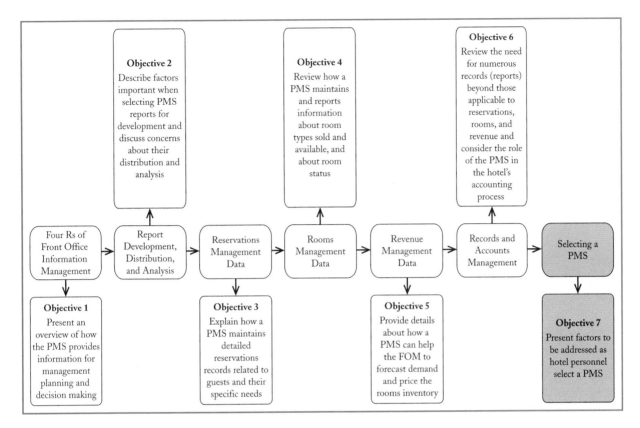

ROADMAP 4.7

Whether selected by a hotel or dictated by a hotel's franchisor, the quality of a PMS can be evaluated by examining hotel-specific characteristics related to the system. Some of the most important characteristics relate to the system's operating hardware; others relate to software. Some FOMs believe that the best approach to use when selecting a PMS is to compare purchase prices of various systems; The lowest priced system then becomes the most attractive. Although cost is always a consideration in the purchase of any important hotel item, FOMs should evaluate a PMS based on many characteristics, including these:

- *Reliability.* The cost of a PMS is much less significant than is its reliability, which is the single most important concern. The PMS is a computer system and, like any other computer system, it may become inoperable at times (i.e., "crash" or "go down").

  Think of selecting transportation for a trip. If the trip is to be made by car, the worst-case scenario may be that the car's engine stops and delays the trip. The traveler may incur significant additional costs for repair and experience inconvenience. If the form of transportation is an airplane the worst-case scenario is engine failure. In this case, the traveler may experience cata- strophic consequences. Seasoned FOMs agree that the PMS is more like an airplane than an automobile. Imagine, for example, the difficulty that would arise in a 1,600-room convention hotel if, at 3:00 p.m. on the day that 1,000 guests are scheduled to arrive, the PMS goes down. In this scenario, think of the information the front office agents would *not* know: who was in the hotel, who was coming to the hotel, which rooms were occupied, which rooms were clean, and which rooms were in need of cleaning. It is difficult to imagine a more challenging scenario for this hotel's FOM, especially if the 1,000 arriving guests are now waiting in the lobby!

The PMS can fail because of hardware problems, software glitches, or power failures. A desirable PMS includes a battery or generator backup capable of operating the system if the hotel loses power due to a weather-related event or other circumstances beyond its control. For example, in 2003, a serious power outage affected much of the U.S. East Coast and Midwest. In some areas of the United States the possibility exists for energy blackouts and brownouts caused by a less than modern electric generating and relaying grid that is operating significantly beyond its planned power-producing capacity.

- *Cost of operation.* The hardware (e.g., computers, printers, and backup disc drives) used by the PMS should be replaceable at reasonable costs. Costs for operating supplies such as paper and print cartridges should also be reasonable. Systems that require special ink cartridges, special paper, or custom-made replacement hardware parts that cannot be obtained economically, readily, and locally should be avoided. If such systems cannot be avoided, the true operating costs must be factored into the total cost of the system.

- *Ease of installation.* Hotels operate 24 hours a day, 7 days a week, so any disruption in the continuous operation of its PMS can affect the hotel and its guests. Before selecting a new PMS, the FOM should thoroughly investigate the amount of downtime involved in the installation of the new system. In addition, recall that all of a hotel's existing historical data must be loaded into the new system. If not, historical information helpful in the management of the hotel will be lost. The time required to program and completely install a new system will vary based on the complexity of the PMS and the size of the hotel. Installation time and its actual costs are, however, common considerations in the selection of a new PMS.

- *Ease of use.* New front office employees must learn how to use the PMS. The ease with which they can learn the system is a factor in reducing training costs and increasing the pace at which new employees become comfortable operating the system. Potential buyers of a PMS should be able to test-drive the system through simulations. Then it is the job of the FOM to select a PMS that is intuitively logical and, as a result, easy for employees to learn how to use.

- *Ease of interface integration.* Information needed by FOMs to professionally and profitably manage the front office comes from a variety of sources. For example, if a guest in a hotel room makes a long-distance telephone call, the charges must be posted to the guest's folio. In any PMS the charges could be posted manually. In a large hotel, however, with thousands of phone calls made daily, manual posting of charges would be time-consuming, subject to data-entry error, and simply unnecessary in today's advanced technological age. By interfacing data from the hotel's **call accounting system** with the PMS, phone charges can be easily established and posted to the proper folio immediately after the guest completes the call.

FRONT OFFICE SEMANTICS

Call accounting system: System in a hotel used to establish telephone charges, document calls made, and determine the amount to be assessed to guests for use of the telephone.

Interfaced information systems have numerous advantages. In many cases, however, a specific PMS may not be capable of interfacing with all other information-generating subsystems in the hotel. Therefore, FOMs must ensure that a PMS can be interfaced with all of the hotel's critical, preexisting, information-generating systems (interfacing is discussed in Chapter 8.) When a PMS is selected for a new hotel, it will dictate the choices available when selecting other information-generating subsystems. Clearly, the best PMS is one that can interface with the hotel industry's best and most popular ancillary hardware and software products.

- *Maintenance requirements.* Like any other item of hotel equipment, the PMS must be properly maintained to operate efficiently. The cost of effective **preventive maintenance** programs for each PMS will vary. The FOM must determine and understand the time and money required to minimize downtime and to maximize system efficiencies by providing routine, ongoing cleaning and maintenance.

FRONT OFFICE SEMANTICS

Preventive maintenance: Maintenance activities designed to minimize maintenance costs and prolong the life of equipment.

- *Ease and frequency of upgrading and updating.* Technology related to front office management advances at a fast pace. Hardware and software upgrades are routinely issued by manufacturers, and most of these significantly improve the operational effectiveness of a PMS. Difficulties can arise, however, when a system's hardware component is not adequate to effectively operate new software systems. When selecting PMS-related hardware, FOMs should anticipate significant increases in demand for memory and speed.

  PMS software upgrades must be easy to install and should minimize system downtime. If a PMS manufacturer is keeping up with the hotel industry's changing demands for information, newer versions of the system's software will be issued on a regular and fairly frequent basis. Therefore, FOMs should inquire about the frequency with which a specific PMS has upgraded its system in the past and about plans for future improvements or versions.

- *Quality and availability of support services.* A PMS is a computerized system and, as such, is subject to the same hardware malfunctioning issues, software glitches, and potentially damaging intrusive viruses as is any other computer linked to the outside environment by the Internet. In addition, because many other computerized systems interface with the PMS, difficulties may be caused by one or more of these interfaces. Support-services personnel available to FOMs must be easily accessed (typically via a toll-free telephone number or e-mail), reasonably priced (or provided as part of the system's purchase price), and above all, knowledgeable about what will need to be done at the property to resolve problems and to quickly get the system back into proper operation. Access to support services must be offered on 24/7 basis, including holidays.

The FOM must thoroughly understand the features and the limitations of the PMS in use. A well-designed and properly functioning PMS helps an FOM to excel. A poorly designed or frequently malfunctioning system causes tremendous difficulties at the front desk and throughout the entire front office and hotel. The principles and practices of effective front office management detailed in this text assume the presence of a well-designed, up-to-date, and effective PMS administered by a trained and talented FOM. The chapters that follow explain (1) how FOMs can use the PMS to collect and manage information about their hotels and (2) how the PMS serves as a powerful tool to effectively manage the front office and other hotel departments.

SECTION REVIEW AND DISCUSSION QUESTIONS

Section Objective: Present factors to be addressed as hotel personnel select a PMS.

Section Summary: Factors to consider as a PMS is selected include reliability, cost of operation, ease of installation, ease of use, ease of interface integration, maintenance requirements, ease and frequency of upgrading and updating, and quality and availability of support services. Although purchase price is an obvious concern, it is not the most important consideration.

Discussion Questions:
1. Given the information you learned about training in Chapter 3, what are some factors you would consider as you develop a PMS training program for a new front desk agent?
2. What supplier services would you, as an FOM, want as you select a PMS and the supplier who will provide it for you?

From the Front Office: Front-Line Interview

Julie Coker
General Manager
Hyatt Lodge (218 rooms)
Oak Brook, Illinois

Let It Snow! Let It Snow!

Julie received her associate of science degree in hotel and restaurant management and her bachelor of science degree in hospitality management from Johnson and Wales University. She began her Hyatt career in 1989 as a corporate management trainee. After completing that program, she held various rooms division positions, including assistant front office manager, front office manager, assistant/executive housekeeper, hotel assistant manager, and convention services floor manager. Her first management committee position was rooms executive at the Hyatt Deerfield (300 rooms). She also served as rooms executive at the Hyatt Regency Cincinnati and helped open the Hyatt Regency McCormick Place (Chicago), where she served as rooms executive. She was promoted to her present general manager position 10 years after joining the company.

1. **What are the most important responsibilities in your present position?**
   Maintaining the best possible relationships with owners, guests, and employees and managing financial aspects of the hotel and its operation.

2. **What are the biggest challenges that confront you in your day-to-day work and in the long-term operation of your property's front office?**
   Hiring quality candidates: Recruiting, hiring, and training staff members who have the right customer-service skill set is a significant challenge. In addition, our guests are discriminating and demanding; this requires us to become more creative as we determine the best ways to address their changing wants and needs.

3. **What is your most unforgettable front office moment?**

During the winter of 1993, there was huge snowstorm in Chicago, and O'Hare airport was closed. I was the front office manager at Hyatt Regency O'Hare at the time. We began the day with 200 arrivals. I left for home about 6:30 a.m. and was called back about an hour later because we now had an additional 800 arrivals, and the hotel was sold out. When I returned to work there was a long line of people that stretched from the front desk outside the front doors. Guests were arriving on our airport shuttles and literally standing in line from that point. For the next two hours, we checked guests in to more than 800 rooms. About 90 percent of the guests had dinner in our restaurant or ordered room service. To conclude the evening, we entered about 700 wake-up calls for the next morning.

We all pulled together as a team to serve our guests. Despite the circumstances, our guests were happy to have a place to stay, and they appreciated our efforts. We made an otherwise difficult situation tolerable. This was one of my best days at Hyatt.

4. **What advice do you have for those studying about or considering a career in front office or hotel management?**

You must enjoy what you do, and you must have a passion for guest service. You have to be able to put yourself in the guests' shoes. You must be flexible, willing to learn and to accept criticism, able to lead as well as follow, and committed to holding your staff accountable. Don't be afraid to take chances, think "outside the box," and try new things. Consistently practice sound financial management principles and operate the business as if it were your own. Our employee workforce and guests are ever-changing and diverse. As a result, diversity must be a part of our business strategy. To hire and retain quality candidates and to meet the ever-changing needs of our guests, we must value each other's differences and achieve a truly diverse workforce. We have to promote inclusion. Every day is different as is every guest, and our daily challenge is to exceed guests' expectations.

The FOM in Action: A Solution

What should the FOM do when changes in technology can enhance guest services but, at the same time, be misunderstood by others in the organization? Sometimes simply determining the problem to be solved can be the FOM's biggest challenge. In the case of Lexington Lodge, communication, not high-speed Internet access, is the real issue. It appears that Gabriel, the new general manager, may not have realistic expectations about the capability of the front office system. He must be informed about the potential and the limitations of the property's PMS as they relate to the new guest-service enhancement: high-speed Internet connections.

Recall that a hotel's PMS needs an interface for automatic posting of charges to a guest folio. It is highly unlikely that Lexington Lodge's PMS has a direct interface with the high-speed Internet provider, or that the PMS can even detect high-speed Internet use in the guestroom.

High-speed Internet access can be provided in a variety of ways—through existing telephone lines, newly installed or existing coaxial cable, or wireless hot spots. The technologies are most often implemented specifically to bypass the hotel's telephone call accounting system to increase available bandwidth. Unfortunately, this does result in lower telephone revenues, because guests no longer incur charges for using the older and slower dial-up Internet connections. Devices that allow for guest-initiated Internet connections can be issued from the front desk, but many hotels have found the required procedures are cumbersome, and most guests find them to be burdensome. The hotel industry is quickly moving away from viewing high speed Internet access as a guest enhancement for which additional charges may be assessed, toward the view that it is an amenity that most guests expect to receive at no extra charge.

At Lexington Lodge, any solution to be implemented must begin with information-sharing sessions between Libby, the FOM, and Gabriel. Libby should understand the goals that Gabriel has set for her department, and Gabriel must understand the limitations associated with the new guest enhancement and the ability of the PMS to address his concerns. Only by working together can the general manager and the FOM meet their expectations and achieve the hotel's overall goals. In general, FOMs will likely have more specialized knowledge about required technology than will other managers. Technology-savvy managers have an obligation to continually inform others in the hotel, including their own superiors and subordinates, about the impact of technology as it becomes more enhanced and advanced.

FRONT OFFICE SEMANTICS LIST

MLOS (minimum length
  of stay)
Interface
Room type
Occupancy tax
Guest history
PMS report
Revenue manager
House count
Over
Short

Out of order (OOO)
Work order
Walk-in
Forecast
Revenue
Sales
Shift
Sales history
Field
Confirmation number
Advance deposit

Post
Room status
HIA (high-speed Internet
  access)
Upgrade
Booking pace
Form of payment
Back-office accounting system
Call accounting system
Preventive maintenance

FRONT OFFICE AND THE INTERNET

Many companies manufacture, market, and support PMS systems. Among them are the following:

Web address	Company or product
www.alohapos.com	Aloha technologies
www.galaxyhotelsystems.com	Galaxy Hotel Systems
www.micros.com/products/hotels/	MICROS-Fidelio
www.msisolutions.com	Multi-Systems
www.innsystems.net	INNSystems
www.remcosoftware.com	NiteVision
www.innfinity.com	INNfinity
www.execu-tech.com	Execu/Tech

REAL-WORLD ACTIVITIES

1. Go to several of the PMS Web site addresses noted above. Look at the sites from a marketing perspective. Why, for example, do manufacturers claim their systems to be the best? What features are promoted as unique? What reasons are suggested for selecting a specific PMS instead of others?

2. If applicable, contact a local hotel's general manager or FOM and ask these questions:

   - What are the most important PMS reports you use for rooms, reservations, revenues, and records and accounts management?
   - What other reports are of significant interest to you?
   - What are the best features and the least desirable features of the PMS you are using?

3. If applicable, contact an executive housekeeper or a food and beverage director in a local hotel. What types of information generated by the PMS are of most use to them? How frequently do they receive the reports? What procedures are in place at the property for a department head to request a new (not previously issued) PMS report?

4. Develop a list of special room requests that the following types of guests might have:

   - Businessperson
   - Couple with one child
   - Couple with several children
   - Delegate attending conference to be held at the property
   - Person stating need for special accommodations because of disability
   - Persons visiting hotel as part of a tour-bus group

5. What, if any, laws or other regulations apply to increasing room rates above those posted (rack rates) in your local area or state?

5

Managing Forecast Data

Chapter Outline

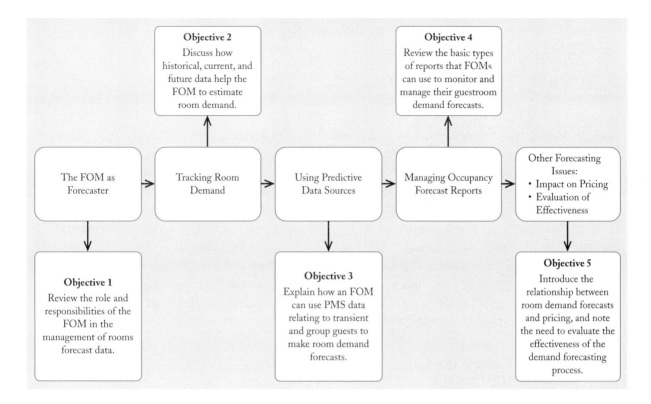

CHAPTER ROADMAP

Chapter Preview

One of the most important tasks confronting front office managers involves forecasting demand for the hotel's guestrooms. When forecasts are accurate, they can establish and maintain the hotel's room pricing structure to maximize RevPar. This chapter focuses on how FOMs gather and monitor information needed to make accurate demand forecasts.

One of the best ways for FOMs to predict future room demand is to examine past demand. FOMs use PMS data to establish and analyze their hotel's guest reservation, arrival, and departure patterns. Current PMS data also provide clues about the demand patterns of guests who have reserved rooms but who have not yet arrived.

FOMs also evaluate predictive data about individual and group reservations when assessing future room demand. Information about individual reservations is obtained internally, primarily with the PMS. Sources of external predictive data relating to individual reservations are also of value, and two major compilers of industry-related data are examined in the chapter: Smith Travel Research (STR) and TravelCLICK. Group reservation activity is best monitored by assessing group history and cutoff dates (when blocked rooms are returned to the hotel's general rooms inventory); therefore, these two concepts are also reviewed in the chapter.

Pickup is an industry term that refers to reservation activity. Techniques to monitor short- and long-term pickup are presented in the chapter. Experienced FOMs ultimately use all available information to produce and evaluate their occupancy forecasts.

The FOM in Action: The Challenge

"Renee, please recall that I need your estimate of next October's transient revenue by Tuesday," said Josephine McCullough, general manager of the 175-room Santa Clara Suites. "I've got to blend your information with the numbers from the sales department and then send everything to Mr. Zollars by next Friday."

Renee Monteagudo is the FOM at the Santa Clara and Mr. Zollars is the regional manager for Holyfield Management, the management group that operates the Santa Clara. Transient revenue, as defined by Renee's company, is that generated by any reservation for 10 or fewer guests and, on most months, for the Santa Clara, transient revenue is about 60 percent of the hotel's total room

revenue. Sometimes, however, it is much higher, and sometimes it is much lower.

When the sales department books nearly all of the rooms, the hotel does well, but the percentage of transient business then falls far below 60 percent. If there are no groups in-house, transient business represents 100 percent of the hotel's revenues. Renee realizes that Josephine doesn't want to know just the percentage of revenues from transient sales; her boss requires the total dollar amount as well.

It is only February, so October is eight months away. "How can I tell Josephine what's going to happen in October," thought Renee, "when I'm not even positive about what's going to happen next month?"

THE FOM AS FORECASTER

Chapter 4 described the PMS and how it helps FOMs to perform a variety of tasks, one of the most essential of which involves forecasting room demand. Despite its valuable assistance, however, the PMS is not the crucial component in a hotel's forecasting efforts. As suggested in Roadmap 5.1, the crucial component is the FOM who, literally, must be able to see the future. In the past, hotel managers emphasized the need for forecasting techniques only on nights when the hotel expected a **sellout.**

FRONT OFFICE SEMANTICS

Sellout: Night on which a hotel expects to achieve 100 percent occupancy.

Today, it is easier for FOMs to use forecasting data at any time, not only in periods of exceptionally high demand. FOMs can, with a few computer keystrokes, modify room rates carried in their PMS and publish these modified rates worldwide through the **Global Distribution System (GDS)** and Internet. As a result, the time required for FOMs to inform travel professionals and individual travelers about new room rates is measured in seconds.

FRONT OFFICE SEMANTICS

Global Distribution System (GDS): System of companies (Sabre, Galileo, Apollo, Amadeus, and Worldspan) that connects hotels offering rooms for sale with individuals and travel professionals worldwide who will potentially purchase them.

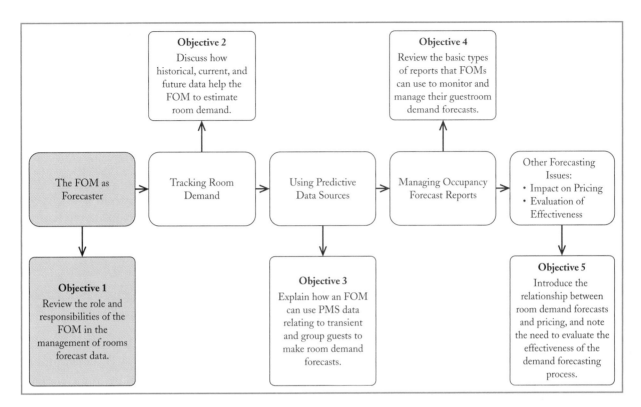

ROADMAP 5.1

Careful study of a PMS's forecast-related reports allows FOMs to adjust room rates according to occupancy.

Date: Jan.	1	2	3	4	5	6	7
Day	Mon.	Tues.	Wed.	Thurs.	Fri.	Sat.	Sun.
Rooms available	300	300	300	300	300	300	300
Forecast of room demand	180	180	180	240	300	300	90
Occupancy forecast	60%	60%	60%	80%	100%	100%	30%

FIGURE 5.1   Occupancy forecast for the Altoona Hotel.

Savvy FOMs continually monitor and adjust their room rates to reflect the realities of actual room demand. Consider, for example, the data shown in a forecast of room demand at the Altoona Hotel shown in Figure 5.1. For the first seven days in January, the FOM at the Altoona Hotel has created an **occupancy forecast** that ranges from a low of 30 percent on Sunday night to a high of 100 percent on Friday and Saturday nights.

FRONT OFFICE SEMANTICS

Occupancy forecast: Estimate of future occupancy stated as a percentage of rooms available.

The computation of the occupancy forecast percentage is similar to the computation of an actual occupancy percentage:

$$\frac{\text{Forecast of room demand}}{\text{Rooms available}} = \text{Occupancy forecast \%}$$

$$\frac{\text{Rooms sold}}{\text{Rooms available}} = \text{Actual occupancy \%}$$

Some PMS systems generate **availability forecasts** rather than occupancy forecasts to evaluate room demand.

FRONT OFFICE SEMANTICS

Availability forecast: Estimate of the number of rooms that remain to be sold.

Figure 5.2 details the same January data for the Altoona Hotel shown in Figure 5.1 in the format of an availability forecast.

Date: Jan.	1	2	3	4	5	6	7
Day	Mon.	Tues.	Wed.	Thurs.	Fri.	Sat.	Sun.
Rooms available	300	300	300	300	300	300	300
Forecast of rooms available	120	120	120	60	0	0	210
Availability forecast	40%	40%	40%	20%	0%	0%	70%

FIGURE 5.2   Availability forecast for the Altoona Hotel.

Whereas the occupancy forecast tells FOMs how many rooms are *projected to be sold*, the availability forecast tells FOMs about the rooms that *remain to be sold*.

Rooms available to sell (100%) − Occupancy forecast % = Availability forecast %

and

Rooms available to sell (100%) − Availability forecast % = Occupancy forecast %

Some FOMs use both systems. They rely on occupancy forecasts to analyze demand for dates far into the future, and they evaluate availability forecasts for dates that are near (within one or two weeks). Regardless of the preferred forecast system, FOMs must estimate demand to match room rates with the number of travelers willing to pay those rates.

Most PMSs include forecasting programs or components that provide necessary historical and current data. However, ultimate responsibility for making and acting on forecasts rests with FOMs. The following paragraph is typical of the marketing material FOMs encounter when they select forecasting components integrated within a PMS or other systems that are built to interface with an existing PMS.

The "Forecast Tool" brings together the industry's most sophisticated tools for forecasting, analysis, and rate quotation in a fully integrated, easy-to-use design. Our "Forecast Tool" guides transient reservation agents and group sales managers in offering rates and dates that maximize RevPar.

PMS forecasting modules may indeed "guide" hotel staff as they sell rooms, but FOMs ultimately makes the best occupancy forecasts and, therefore, maximize RevPar. Effective FOMs follow these guidelines:

- Recognize the unique property features that affect demand for the hotel
- Know about special citywide events in the area that affect room demand
- Understand the demand for competitive hotels in the area
- Consider the opening or closing of competitive hotels in the area
- Include weather, road construction, season of the year, and any other relevant factors in demand assessments
- Adjust forecasts quickly when confronted with significant events that affect demand (e.g., power outages and airport or highway closings)

Sophisticated PMS forecast programs can manage the data that help FOMs forecast room demand. These programs are improving rapidly, but they will always be forecasting tools for FOMs' use. They will never replace the skill and experience of FOMs.

SECTION REVIEW AND DISCUSSION QUESTIONS

Section Objective: Review the role and responsibilities of the FOM in the management of rooms forecast data.

Section Summary: Modern PMSs provide data that an FOM can use to forecast room occupancy (percentage of rooms sold) and availability (percentage of rooms available to sell). However, the data are only one source of input to the FOM's decisions about room selling rates, and the data must be tempered with the FOM's skill and experience.

Discussion Questions:
1. What are the advantages and disadvantages of using occupancy forecasts to estimate room demand?
2. What are the advantages and disadvantages of using availability forecasts to estimate room demand?
3. Do you think that PMS data will ever replace the need for an FOM's judgment, skill, and experience in decisions about room pricing? Why or why not?

TRACKING ROOM DEMAND

How can FOMs best **track** and then forecast room demand? As noted in Roadmap 5.2, FOMs must rely on **historical, current,** and **future** data.

FRONT OFFICE SEMANTICS

Track: Hotel term meaning to monitor or to examine.

Historical data: Data related to events that have already occurred. Sometimes referred to as *actual data*.

Current data: Data related to events that are entered into the PMS but have yet to occur. For example, a room reservation can be entered into the PMS on Thursday for the following Friday night.

Future data: Data related to events that have yet to occur and will not be found in the PMS. Although unknown, the data can be estimated.

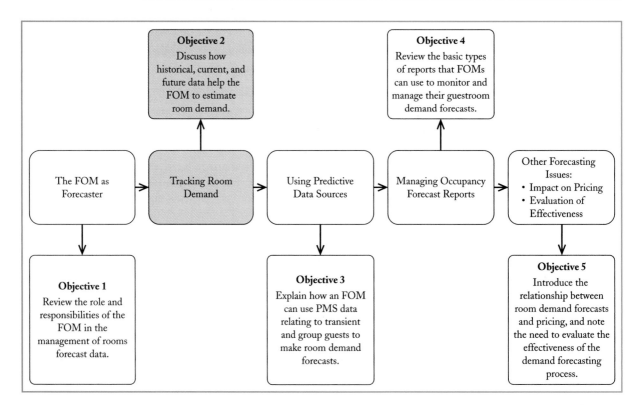

ROADMAP 5.2

FOMs rely on their own skills and experience to create usable demand forecasts. They analyze relevant historical and current data and estimate other information applicable to the future.

Computation of Occupancy Forecast

Before studying how FOMs use historical data in making demand forecasts, it is important to understand how the actual occupancy forecast is computed. Let's again consider the 300-room Altoona Hotel. Figure 5.3 shows the detailed method used by a PMS to compute one day's actual occupancy forecast. Let's review how the forecast is developed line by line:

Line 1:   Identifying the number of rooms in the hotel (300)

Line 2:   Subtracting out-of-order rooms (0)

Line 3:   Determining net room availability (300)

Line 4:   Subtracting **stayover** rooms (40)

Line 5:   Subtracting rooms for which a current reservation exists (150)

Line 6:   Determining the number of rooms sold or reserved (190)

Line 7:   Adjusting the forecast for anticipated reservation **no-shows** (15)

Line 8:   Adjusting the forecast for anticipated **early departures** (5)

Line 9:   Adjusting the forecast for **overstays** (10)

Line 10: Determining the number of rooms forecasted to be sold or reserved after adjustments (180)

Date:	Jan. 1		
Day:	Mon.		
Total rooms available:		300	Line 1
(−) Out-of-order rooms		0	Line 2
Net availability		**300**	Line 3
(−) Stayovers		40	Line 4
(−) Reservations (arrivals)		150	Line 5
Rooms sold or reserved		**190**	Line 6
Forecasted adjustments:			
(−) Reservation no-shows		15	Line 7
(−) Early departures		5	Line 8
(+) Overstays		10	Line 9
Total forecast sold or reserved after adjustments		**180**	Line 10
Occupancy forecast		**60%**	Line 11
Net rooms availability		120	Line 12
Net availability		40%	Line 13

FIGURE 5.3   Occupancy forecast for the Altoona Hotel—Monday, Jan. 1.

Line 11: Dividing the total number of rooms forecasted to be sold or reserved after adjustments (line 10) by net availability (line 3) to yield the occupancy forecast (60 percent)

Line 12: Calculating net rooms availability (120)

Line 13: Dividing net rooms availability (line 12) by net availability (line 3) to yield net availability percentage (40 percent)

FRONT OFFICE SEMANTICS

Stayover: Guest who is not scheduled to check out of the hotel on the day his or her room status is assessed. This guest will be staying and using the room at least one more day.

No-show: Guest who makes a room reservation but fails to cancel the reservation or arrive at the hotel on the date of the reservation.

Early departure: Guest who checks out of the hotel before his or her originally scheduled check-out date.

Overstay: Guest who checks out of the hotel after his or her originally scheduled check-out date.

Note that Figure 5.3 also indicates an availability forecast percentage (40 percent in line 13), which is the inverse of the occupancy forecast percentage (60 percent in line 11).

In a more realistic example, room use and availability would be forecast by room type (see Chapter 4), as well as for the total number of hotel rooms available. However, the procedures used by FOMs are the same whether forecasting room type availability or total room availability.

Much of the data in Figure 5.3 are maintained by the PMS, for example, the number of rooms available, number of out-of-order rooms, and number of reservations currently booked. Data for the three forecast adjustments (no-shows, early departures, and overstays), however, describe events that will occur in the future. Therefore, "real" (actual) data for these adjustments do not exist. Instead, they must be forecast by the FOM, and this is relatively easy to do if the FOM has carefully tracked the hotel's historical data related to these adjustments.

No-shows

Every hotel experiences some no-show guests. For many reasons, guests change their plans and fail to contact the hotel for a **cancellation number.**

FRONT OFFICE SEMANTICS

Cancellation number: Series of numbers, letters, or both that identifies the cancellation of a specific hotel reservation.

Estimates about no-shows are important when forecasting, because each no-show represents a room that appears to be sold to a guest but will not be occupied by that guest. As a result, FOMs must track no-shows. For example, if historical PMS data show that, on average, 1 of 50 confirmed room reservations will be a no-show, then the FOM might estimate 10 no-shows on a day when the hotel has 500 confirmed reservations (500 rooms ÷ 50 rooms = 10 no-show rooms).

Forecasting the number of no-shows is the first of many examples in this text that demonstrate how FOMs who use a well-designed PMS can improve their job performance. Assume, for example, that an FOM is reviewing historical data to forecast no-shows. By selecting a specific PMS no-show report, the FOM can identify the property's historical no-show averages for last night, last week, last month, the average of the last 10 similar days (e.g., Saturdays, Wednesdays, or Mondays), the same date in the prior year, and an average day on the same month in the prior year.

The types of reports selected by the FOM will influence no-show projections. Depending on the type of hotel, factors such as day of week, season, and room type (to name just a few) may affect the no-show rate. The challenge for an FOM is to select and evaluate the "right" historical data rather than just "any" historical data.

Determination of precisely how to best track no-show data for a specific hotel (i.e., to assess which specific historical trends to monitor) depends on the hotel's unique characteristics. To generalize that the *best* way to forecast no-shows in *all* hotels is to use the *average* no-show number for the last two weeks (or other time period) trivializes the distinctive insight that an FOM can bring to the process of estimating no-shows. Instead, an accurate estimate of no-shows requires an FOM's talent, intuition, and experience, along with accurate data from the PMS.

Early Departures

PMS data related to early departures are also important in tracking and forecasting room demand. When estimating the number of early departures, FOMs can access many historical records; they are limited only by the limits of their PMS.

Early departures are affected by a variety of factors, ranging from changes in travel plans (e.g., a meeting ending earlier than expected or a change in an airline schedule) to difficulties with the hotel (e.g., an upset guest checks out early). The estimated number of early departures can only be properly evaluated in conjunction with total occupancy (stayovers). As seen in Figure 5.4, early departures, when calculated as a percentage of stayover rooms, can remain fairly constant, even while the actual number of early departures varies widely. Clearly, the Altoona Hotel's FOM should forecast a different number of early departures when the hotel expects a larger number of stayovers from the previous night than when it does not.

Date	Expected stayovers	Actual early departures	Early departure (%)
Jan. 1 (Sun.)	10	1	10%
Jan. 2 (Mon.)	100	10	10%
Jan. 3 (Tues.)	200	20	10%
Jan. 4 (Wed.)	250	25	10%
Jan. 5 (Thurs.)	250	50	20%
Jan. 6 (Fri.)	200	20	10%
Jan. 7 (Sat.)	200	20	10%
Jan. 8 (Sun.)	10	1	10%
Jan. 9 (Mon.)	100	10	10%
Jan. 10 (Tues.)	200	20	10%
Jan. 11 (Wed.)	250	25	10%
Jan. 12 (Thurs.)	250	50	20%
Jan. 13 (Fri.)	200	20	10%
Jan. 14 (Sat.)	200	20	10%
Total/average	2,420	292	12%

FIGURE 5.4 Stayover report for the Altoona Hotel—January 1–14 (total rooms = 300).

The analysis of early departures in Figure 5.4 presents an additional challenge as the FOM uses historical data. Note that, despite the relatively consistent early departure percentage, the actual number of early departures ranges from a low of 1 (on Jan. 1 and Jan. 8) to a high of 50 (on Jan. 5 and Jan. 12). In most cases, the number of early departures increases as the number of anticipated stayovers increases. Therefore, the Altoona Hotel's FOM must not use the average early departure percentage (12 percent) on a day when, historically, the *actual* number of early departures varies greatly from that percentage. Professional FOMs know that historical data about early departures should be reviewed carefully and closely, especially on days when a sellout or near sellout is expected.

Overstays

The PMS provides historical data about the number of guests who extend their stay beyond their original check-out date. These data should be carefully reviewed and monitored by FOMs. The most accurate forecast of overstays frequently requires the consideration of room type. For example, assume that the 300-room Altoona Hotel consists of the room types listed in Figure 5.5.

Assume also that the hotel's reservations, no-shows, and early departures have been forecast for a day one week from today. The FOM estimates that 10 overstays are likely. According to the occupancy forecast formula in Figure 5.3, the 10 additional overstay rooms should be added to the number of hotel rooms sold. If the hotel were in a sellout (or near sellout) situation, it would likely face difficulty if the 10 overstays were in the eight WH room types and two BR room types. Why? On a sellout night at least some of the guests with reservations arriving that day will likely have reserved a WH room and may be ever a BR suite. These arriving guests will find that the room types they reserved are unavailable, because the guests in those rooms decided to extend their stays. Imagine the difficulties arising if one of the bridal suites is not available to a bride and groom checking in that day (especially if they are holding their 500-person wedding reception at the hotel!). To avoid potential difficulties such as these, many FOMs carefully monitor the historical number of overstays by room total and by selected room type.

Use of Current and Future Data

Historical PMS data are valuable because room demand often follows fairly predictable patterns. For example, in most business hotels, room demand for Sunday

Room type	PMS code	No. of rooms
Nonsmoking king	NK	50
Smoking-permitted king	K	50
Nonsmoking double-double	NDD	100
Smoking-permitted double-double	DD	50
Nonsmoking whirlpool	NWH	40
Smoking whirlpool	WH	8
Bridal suites	BR	2
Total rooms		**300**

FIGURE 5.5   Hotel Altoona room types.

By considering the historical data of an event, FOMs can help maximize their hotel's RevPar.

night is less than on Tuesday nights. This historical pattern will likely hold true and help to yield accurate demand forecasts, *unless* current data and estimates of future data dictate otherwise.

Later in this chapter, you will see how a complete demand forecast is assembled. For now, recognize that the use of historical data alone is generally an ineffective way to estimate room demand. Consider, for example, the data in Figure 5.6. In this situation, if the FOM considered only historical data, he or she could be tempted to estimate room demand for the next Saturday night at approximately 200 rooms (66.6 percent occupancy).

	Report Run Date: *Monday, 7:00 a.m.*	
Time period	**Actual rooms sold**	**Occupancy (%)**
Actual last Saturday	195	65%
Average last four Saturdays	205	68%
Average Saturdays in last quarter	188	63%
Average Saturday **YTD**	199	66%
Saturday one year ago	202	67%
Saturday two years ago	185	62%
On-the-books (current)	260	87%

FIGURE 5.6 Actual room usage at the Altoona Hotel—Saturday analysis (total rooms = 300).

FRONT OFFICE SEMANTICS

YTD (year to date): Numbers that include all relevant data for the current year. For example, a YTD ADR of $95 indicates a cumulative average ADR of $95 to this point in the current year.

On-the-books: Hotel term for cumulative current data. The term is used most often in reference to reservation data. For example, a 300-room hotel with reservations for 200 rooms on a given (future) date is said to have 200 reservations *on-the-books.* (The term originated when hotel reservation data were stored in a bound reservation book rather than in a software program.)

Note, however, that the number of rooms already on-the-books for this Saturday (260) suggests demand that is stronger than that indicated by the historical data. Therefore, FOMs must always monitor current data as well as historical data before assembling demand forecasts.

Figure 5.7 illustrates that FOMs also need future data to accurately forecast occupancy (room demand). In fact, an FOM's ability to accurately assess future data is the most critical determinant of an accurate demand forecast. The importance of future data in forecasting can be demonstrated by the following real-life situations routinely faced by FOMs:

- An airport hotel in the U.S. Northeast normally discounts heavily (sometimes as much as 50 percent off rack rate) on Sunday night, because historically it sells an average of only 100 rooms on that night. At noon on Sunday, January 1, the 400-room property has 105 reservations on-the-books. However, Internet users can go online and see rates for the hotel offered at up to a 50 percent discount. The weather forecast is for heavy snowstorms, and in the past, such storms have significantly delayed flights or closed the airport. On these nights, the hotel usually experiences a sellout as airlines seek housing for their **distressed passengers** and accommodations for delayed flight crews. Additional rooms are also sold to stranded travelers (those who missed connections) and to travelers with tickets on outbound flights originating in the city (but delayed until the next day).

  In this case, should the FOM *eliminate* heavy discounts on the rooms available on Sunday night? Most FOMs would answers "yes" and would monitor the weather to make future data predictions based on their own experience and intuition. Discounts would be reduced or eliminated to take advantage of anticipated future data.

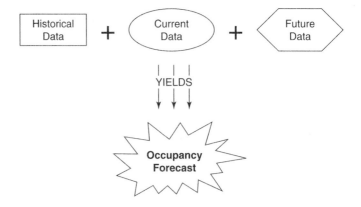

FIGURE 5.7   Data required for occupancy forecasts.

FRONT OFFICE SEMANTICS

Distressed passenger: Guest housed at a hotel due to air travel delays. In some cases, the cost of housing is borne by the airline on which the guest was traveling.

- A mid-size city in the U.S. West is home to a large university that plays football on Saturdays in the fall. Such days create a sellout situation in the city, because the visiting team's students and fans fill the area's hotel rooms. For the past several years, no hotels in the area have offered discounts on rooms for football Saturdays. The new football schedule for next year has just been released. On one Saturday, the university will play a much smaller school located only 20 minutes away from the city. Its football program has not been strong, and it attracts few fans.

   On non-football Saturdays in the fall, the Claremont Hotel, located near the campus, offers a family package that includes a room, reduced prices on dinner in the dining room, and tickets to the local zoo. The program is advertised to local families by a posting on the city's **convention and visitors bureau (CVB)** Web site. Should the date the university plays the new opponent be included on the family package list of available dates? (Currently it is not.)

FRONT OFFICE SEMANTICS

Convention and visitors bureau (CVB): Organization generally funded by taxes levied on overnight hotel guests that seeks to increase the number of visitors to the area it represents.

   Most FOMs would answer yes. Although the booking pace for that date should be monitored, all signs point to reduced demand that will necessitate some room discounting. In anticipation of reduced demand, the best FOMs take decisive actions—even actions not normally taken—as they consider future patterns of room demand.

- The 500-room Crystal Hotel is attached to the convention center in a large city in the U.S. South. Typically the hotel achieves a 60 percent occupancy on Friday and Saturday nights. It does so by heavily promoting a weekend getaway **package** to local city residents that includes rooms at 30 percent off rack rate.

FRONT OFFICE SEMANTICS

Package: Group of hospitality services (e.g., hotel rooms, meals, and airfare) sold for one price. For example, a Valentine's Day getaway package to Las Vegas offered by a travel agent might include airfare, lodging, meals, and show tickets for two people at one inclusive price.

   The hotel's FOM learns from the local CVB that the city will host the statewide, three-day, physicians' convention in three years. This will be the first time the group has met in this city. The group's meetings will be held at the convention center on the third weekend in November. Because of its proximity to the convention center, the Crystal Hotel will likely be a desirable location for attendees. Rooms will sell at rack rate. Should the FOM designate the

Through use of current and future data, FOMs are better able to make decisions that improve guest service.

weekend of the physicians' convention as one in which the weekend getaway package should not be offered?

Most talented FOMs would answer yes. They would eliminate the package for that weekend because the physicians will likely fill the hotel. This decision would be made despite the facts that (1) there are no historical PMS data related to the physicians' convention; (2) the PMS shows that not a single current reservation now exists for the date on which the convention will be held; and (3) the date in question is three years away.

As can be seen from these few examples, if FOMs are to make accurate forecasts of room demand they must carefully consider historical, current, and future data.

SECTION REVIEW AND DISCUSSION QUESTIONS

Section Objective: Discuss how historical, current, and future data help the FOM to estimate room demand.

Section Summary: An occupancy forecast considers the net number of rooms available on a specific date and deducts from that number the estimated number of stayovers and the actual number of reservations. The forecast must also be adjusted by deducting the estimated number of no-shows and early departures and by adding the estimated number of overstays. The PMS provides current data about the number of reservations, and historical data can be used in estimating the remaining variables (stayovers, reservation no-shows, early departures, and overstays). Experienced FOMs use PMS reports to estimate future demand based on the impact of these factors on past room sales. On-the-books (current demand) data must be factored into the forecast as must future data related to anticipated business increases or decreases caused by, for example, holidays (which may reduce demand) and activities in the community (which may increase demand).

Discussion Questions:

1. Select several hotels within your area. What types of factors are likely to increase and decrease their room demand on specific dates?
2. What, if any, tactics can an FOM use when he or she notices that the number of no-shows is increasing?
3. Assume that an FOM knows in advance that the hotel is likely to be sold out during a specific time period. What, if any, tactics can the FOM use to help ensure that guests who reserve rooms several days before the sellout period will not become overstays?

USING PREDICTIVE DATA SOURCES

FOMs must properly apply historical, current, and future forecast data to sell guestrooms. Every hotel has unique characteristics that influence forecasting. In addition, the types of guests a hotel serves affect an FOM's choice of predictive data and techniques and strategies for their use. As Roadmap 5.3 indicates, it is important to understand the use of predictive data sources.

In the hotel industry, individual guests are classified several ways. Most commonly, FOMs consider guests as transient travelers or as part of a **group.**

FRONT OFFICE SEMANTICS

Group: Guests who have a hotel reservation as a part of a larger, multiguest reservation. Examples include domestic and international tour groups, associations, conventioneers, corporate groups, and individual members of sports teams.

The techniques used and resources available to assist FOMs in predicting the actions of these two types of guests are different. When the FOM predicts the behavior of transient guests, he or she evaluates reservations individually. In contrast, it is the group's reservation **block** that is of interest to FOMs.

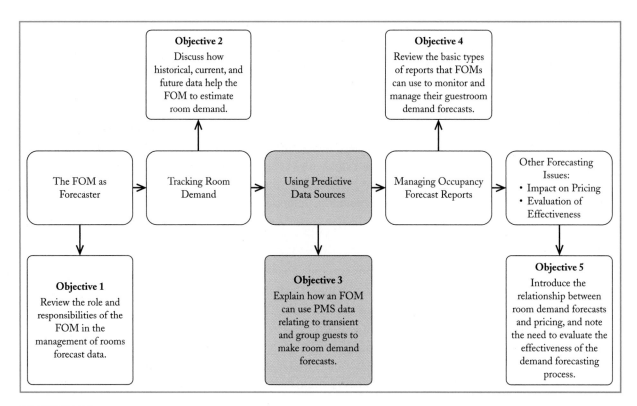

ROADMAP 5.3

FRONT OFFICE SEMANTICS

Block: Rooms reserved exclusively for members of a specific group. A block consists of all rooms held (reserved) by the hotel for the exclusive use of that group. To set aside rooms in this manner effectively creates a "block" of reservations for the group. Sometimes referred to as a *group block*.

To predict the actions and behaviors of transient guests, FOMs use information from internal and external sources. When predicting the actions of groups, FOMs consider that group's specific **group history** as well as the number of rooms the group has already reserved at the hotel (its booking pace).

FRONT OFFICE SEMANTICS

Group history: Number of rooms blocked for and ultimately used by a group during similar events held in the past.

Transient Guests

Most FOMs predict the booking activity of transient guests by use of historical and current data. Accurate predictions of future data, however, are also critical. FOMs can increase their knowledge of future data by examining **trend lines,** which are based on internal and external data sources.

FRONT OFFICE SEMANTICS

Trend line: Documentation (usually displayed on a graph or chart) of changes in data values. Trend lines may show increases, decreases, or no change in comparative data values.

Internal Data

FOMs can predict the reservation behavior of transient guests by analyzing several important internal trend lines. Specific data important to a particular hotel are influenced by the property's unique characteristics; however, most FOMs evaluate internal trend lines relative to these data:

- Occupancy percentage
- Room count
- Reservation activity
- Cancellation activity
- No-shows
- Arrivals
- Early departures
- Stayovers

To see how internal data are used, consider Figure 5.8, which contains data about the Altoona Hotel's transient occupancy the past year and this year. It is time for the FOM to predict July's transient guest occupancy. Data analysis indicates that the FOM should expect an *increase* in transient occupancy this July in comparison with last July based on the current trend of this year's monthly increases over the same months last year. Although the amount, if any, of actual increase will not be known until the end of July, a prediction of a 2 percent to 3 percent increase in transient guest occupancy appears reasonable.

Figure 5.9 shows the information in Figure 5.8 in a bar graph. Note that the linear trend line identified in the figure could easily be extended for the months beyond June, even if last year's data from July and subsequent months are not added to the chart. Of course, when such data are added, the predictive validity of the trend line is enhanced.

The mathematics involved in these projections may be of interest to some, but most FOMs are content to allow their PMS to make the calculations. If a PMS does not provide a forecasting feature, FOMs who are familiar with Microsoft Excel can

Month	Last year	This year	Difference
January	51.5	53.7	2.2
February	53.8	55.1	1.3
March	60.2	63.3	3.1
April	62.4	65.1	2.7
May	59.7	62.3	2.6
June	60.4	62.9	2.5
July	62.5	?	

FIGURE 5.8   Transient guest occupancy percentage analysis for the Altoona Hotel.

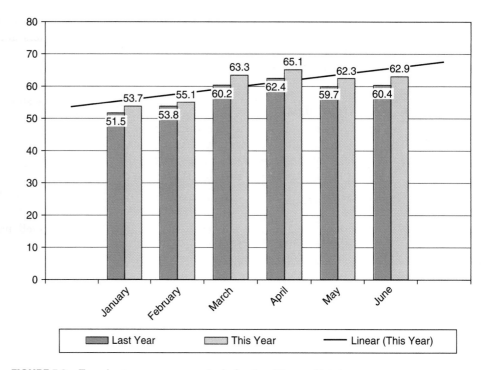

FIGURE 5.9 Transient occupancy analysis for the Altoona Hotel.

use its charting capacity to compute trend-line projections. (See the "Add Trendline" feature under the "Chart" option on the toolbar in most versions of Excel.)

In the past, few FOMs had the mathematical and statistical background required to create sound data forecasts based on trends. Today's FOMs can easily do so. Effective FOMs select the right internal data for analysis; then they use their own skills and experience to interpret (project) future values for that data.

External Data

The events of September 11, 2001, clearly demonstrated that hotels are affected by external as well as internal factors. FOMs must understand how local, national, and international events, along with the economy and national and regional travel trends, are likely to affect their business.

Several sources compile and publish data trends for the hotel industry. In years past, hotel accounting firms such as Leventhal and Horwath (L&H) and Arthur Andersen compiled annual trend data primarily from their own clients and then published the data. These firms no longer exist but accounting firms such as Price Waterhouse and hospitality consulting firms such as Yesawich, Pepperdine, Brown & Russell (YPB&R) compile trend data. The data are distributed at no cost, reported in the hospitality trade press, or sold to hoteliers who want the information. Unfortunately, data from these and related sources are usually of little predictive value to FOMs, because the data are not specific enough to assist in forecasting sales for *their* properties. For example, it is not very helpful in predicting future revenue, for an FOM to learn that national hotel sales increased 5 percent, but his or her state experienced a 5 percent overall decline in occupancy.

Fortunately, some sources of external trend data can be of tremendous value to FOMs as they create occupancy forecasts. Two compilers and distributors whose published data should be reviewed regularly are Smith Travel Research (STR) and TravelCLICK. Founded in 1985 by Randy Smith, STR (often called as STAR) is the older, more comprehensive, and better known of these two organizations. As an independent third party, STR collects and distributes summaries of hotel data related to historical performance. Although STR does not forecast future trends, professional FOMs use STR data to do so.

Each month STR collects performance data on more than 23,000 hotels, which represents more than 2.8 million rooms. The data are provided by hotel chain head-quarters, management companies, owners, and independent hotels. Data are audited for accuracy and checked for adherence to STR reporting guidelines. STR personnel also collect daily performance data from more than 18,000 hotels each week. The data collected include number of hotel rooms available to sell, number of rooms sold, and total room revenue. Using these data, STR personnel compute a variety of hotel statistics such as these:

- Property occupancy percentage
- Property ADR
- Property RevPar
- Property percentage change from prior period
- **Competitive set** occupancy percentage
- Competitive set ADR
- Competitive set RevPar
- Competitive set percentage change from prior period
- **STR index** scores
- Index change scores

FRONT OFFICE SEMANTICS

Competitive set: Group of competing hotels to which an individual hotel's operating performance is compared. Often referred to as the *comp set*.

STR index: Comparative measure of a specific hotel's operating performance.

STR also publishes several reports:

- Trend report—summarizes monthly room sales for a specific hotel and its competitive set
- Monthly STAR—summarizes monthly room sales for the hotel's local market
- Daily detail by week—summarizes a hotel's daily performance by week
- Daily detail by month—summarizes monthly performance on a by-day basis
- Weekday/weekend report—summarizes a hotel's weekday versus weekend performance

To understand how FOMs use STR reports, let's review the terms *competitive set* and *STR index*. Assume the Altoona Hotel, which was introduced earlier, achieved an occupancy rate of 60 percent for a specific month. The FOM wants to know if

STR reports allow FOMs to compare hotel data with similar hotels in the area.

that is "good" performance. The city in which the Altoona Hotel is located has 24 additional hotels. STR data for the Altoona Hotel and the city average are displayed in Figure 5.10.

In Scenario 1, the Altoona hotel has outperformed the "average" hotel in the city: Its 60 percent occupancy rate is substantially higher than the 40 percent occupancy rate achieved by the average hotel (which includes data from the Altoona). In Scenario 2, the Altoona performed exactly the same as the average hotel, and in Scenario 3, the average hotel outperformed the Altoona by 20 occupancy percentage points (80% − 60% = 20%).

Each of these three scenarios indicates different performance levels and may provide the Altoona's FOM with valuable information. However, many FOMs would be less concerned about comparing the property to the city average and more concerned

Occupancy Data for the Month of: November	
Property	**Occupancy (%)**
Altoona Hotel	60%
City average (all 25 hotels including the Altoona)	
Scenario 1	40%
Scenario 2	60%
Scenario 3	80%

FIGURE 5.10   Occupancy data for the Altoona Hotel and city in which it is located.

about comparing its performance to similar hotels in the city. If, for example, the Altoona is a full-service hotel that offers many upscale amenities, it may not be critical to know how it is performing compared with limited-service, budget hotels in the city. The Altoona client is not likely to be a client of these budget properties. To make STR data more useful, the FOM can select and compare data from competitive hotels (the competitive set) whose performance would, theoretically, mirror that of the Altoona.

A competitive set consists of a group of four or more properties selected by management of an individual hotel or that hotel's parent company. The competitive set enables FOMs to compare their property's performance with the aggregate performance of their direct competitors. According to STR policy, a single hotel can represent a maximum of 35 percent of the reporting rooms of any competitive set; STR sets this limit to protect each property's proprietary data. The hotel itself may or may not be included in its competitive set, depending on the STR reports the hotel receives. The weekday/weekend, daily detail by month, and daily detail by week competitive set reports always exclude the subject hotel.

To fully understand the STR index, consider the data presented in Figure 5.11. The figure shows data about the Altoona hotel's occupancy and that of its competitive set along with index information. STR uses indexes to measure a property's performance in three key areas: occupancy, ADR, and RevPar. An index is computed by dividing the performance of the subject hotel by the performance of the competitive set hotels:

$$\frac{\text{Performance of subject hotel}}{\text{Performance of competitive set hotels}} = \text{Index}$$

An index of 100 indicates that the property has captured its fair share of business; it is performing on par (equally) with its competitive set. This is the case in Scenario 2. An index greater than 100 indicates a property is capturing more than its fair share (Scenario 1), whereas an index below 100 indicates the property is capturing less than its fair share (Scenario 3).

STR data are used for a variety of purposes, including the improvement of forecast accuracy. Let's consider the occupancy data in Figure 5.12, which are from a section of a STR trend report (monthly rooms sales) showing occupancy data for the Altoona Hotel for a 12-month period. The data show that the Altoona Hotel, like its competitive set, has experienced an occupancy decline through the last three months ending. October, 200Z, compared with 200X (-5.0 percent for the Altoona and -14.2 percent for the competitive set; see line 16). However, its occupancy is up

Occupancy Data for the Month of: November		
Property	**Occupancy (%)**	**Index**
Altoona Hotel	60%	
Competitive set (six selected hotels, including the Altoona)		
Scenario 1	40%	133.3
Scenario 2	60%	100.0
Scenario 3	80%	66.6

FIGURE 5.11   Occupancy and index data: The Altoona Hotel and competitive set.

Line	Year	Month	Property	Occupancy Change (%)	Comp set	Occupancy Change (%)	Index	Occupancy Change (%)
1	200Y	Oct.	47.8	47.5	65.0	3.2	73.5	43.0
2	200Y	Nov.	35.1	72.1	51.2	−4.1	68.6	79.6
3	200Y	Dec.	27.9	72.2	41.4	−3.7	67.4	78.8
4	200Z	Jan.	29.2	111.6	53.1	2.1	55.0	107.5
5	200Z	Feb.	39.0	54.8	59.3	−5.6	65.8	64.1
6	200Z	March	45.0	45.6	61.6	7.1	73.1	36.1
7	200Z	April	51.7	39.7	52.6	−8.5	98.3	52.9
8	200Z	May	36.4	−10.3	53.8	−17.2	67.7	8.3
9	200Z	June	43.7	43.3	54.6	−6.7	80.0	53.6
10	200Z	July	38.4	−8.8	47.9	−11.3	80.2	2.8
11	200Z	Aug.	44.7	1.4	53.9	−17.6	82.9	23.0
12	200Z	Sept.	40.8	−20.8	48.7	−15.2	83.8	−6.6
13	200Z	Oct.	50.2	5.0	58.2	−10.5	86.3	17.4
Three months—ending Oct.								
14		200X	40.6	3.5	59.4	−9.5	68.4	2.3
15		200Y	47.7	17.5	62.6	5.4	76.2	11.5
16		200Z	45.3	−5	53.7	−14.2	84.4	10.8
YTD—ending Oct.								
17		200X	38	−18.5	59.7	−7.6	63.7	−11.7
18		200Y	36.2	−4.7	59.5	−0.3	60.8	−4.6
19		200Z	41.9	15.7	54.3	−8.7	77.2	27
Twelve months—ending Oct.								
20		200X	34.3	−23.9	57.8	−6.9	59.3	−18.3
21		200Y	33.2	−3.2	57.6	−0.3	57.6	−2.9
22		200Z	40.2	21.1	53	−8	75.8	31.6

FIGURE 5.12   STR trend report showing occupancy data for the Altoona Hotel.

21.1 percent for the 12 months ending October, 200Z (see line 22). Its competitive set for the same period is down 8.0 percent from the prior 12-month period (also reported in line 22). Note also that the competitive set that includes the Altoona has experienced a monthly occupancy decline compared with the prior year in 10 of the 13 months for which data are presented (see lines 2, 3, 5, 7, 8, 9, 10, 11, 12, and 13).

When the FOM projects November (and beyond) room demand at the Altoona, he or she can make several conclusions from the data in Figure 5.12:

• The Altoona will, in all likelihood, experience room demand in November this year that is less than in November last year.

• The reduced demand is experienced by hotels in the competitive set as well as by the Altoona. Therefore, reduced demand is more likely to be an effect of economic conditions than a result of a poor sales effort by Altoona staff.

• The rate at which occupancy is declining at the competitive set hotels exceeds that of the Altoona; thus, the Altoona's sales staff is probably doing the things required to keep the property competitive.

• Competitive set hotels will, in all likelihood, review the room rates charged.

The portion of the STR trend report presented in Figure 5.12 is just one example of the quantity and quality of data available to FOMs. Careful review of the data will improve their forecasting abilities and room-pricing decisions. As you can see, the term *competitive set* is appropriate, because the management teams at competitive hotels will use the data from STR and other sources to make strategic decisions to best position their hotels for success.

TravelCLICK is a research organization that compiles external data about transient guests. FOMs use the data to estimate room demand. The company was formed in response to the ever-growing use of **e-distribution channels.**

FRONT OFFICE SEMANTICS

E-distribution channel: Generic term used to indicate all electronic (e)methods of advertising and selling guestrooms. Also known as *e-commerce.*

Because individual travelers and travel professionals increasingly use the Internet to book rooms, hotels and hotel companies must make strategic decisions about partnering with and supporting specific GDS companies and individual travel-related Web sites. In 2003, hotel bookings comprised one quarter of all consumer Internet travel transactions and exceeded $10 billion dollars. Total hotel e-commerce (GDS and Internet) sales exceeded $22 billion.

TravelCLICK'S "RateVIEW," "Phaser," and other reports assist FOMs in comparing their room pricing (and availability) to that of their competitors. TravelCLICK reports the advertised selling prices of rooms listed on nearly 100 individual and hotel company-operated sites on the GDS. In many cases, the information about rates and availability is less than 24 hours old. TravelCLICK reports include the following information:

- Identification of top revenue-producing Web sites
- Identification of top revenue-producing travel agents using the GDS
- Listings of top **feeder markets**
- Summaries of room rate
- Patterns of arrival
- Length of stay data
- ADR data
- Comparisons to data from hotel-selected competitive sets

FRONT OFFICE SEMANTICS

Feeder market: Geographic location that includes a significant number of travelers using a hotel's services. Used as in, "St. Louis is a top *feeder market* for our ski resort."

In the future, it is likely that additional sources of external data will be available to assist FOMs in demand forecasting. They must, therefore, stay current by monitoring the industry's data resources.

Group Guests

Predictive data are also available to help FOMs forecast room demand for groups. Group business is a significant portion of the total room volume in many, especially larger, hotels. In fact, many properties generate 50 percent or more of total room demand from groups. Although no standard definition for *group* exists in the industry, many hotels and hotel companies consider any entity reserving 10 or more guestrooms at one time to have made a **group reservation.** In smaller hotels, group reservations are made by the FOM. In larger properties, the director of sales **(DOS)** or a member of the sales and marketing staff will likely be responsible for group reservations.

FRONT OFFICE SEMANTICS

Group (reservation): Any entity that reserves 10 or more guestrooms at one time.

DOS (director of sales): Person with overall responsibility for a hotel's sales efforts. Sometimes called *DOSM (director of sales and marketing).*

The reservation patterns of travelers who are part of a group must be considered separately from patterns of transient travelers. When evaluating group activity, most FOMs find that the two best predictive sources of room demand are group history and group booking pace.

Group History

A useful group history includes information about the group's previous date or dates of stay, room preferences, room rates paid, form of payment, and any other information desired by the DOS or FOM. Unlike a history of a transient guest, however, a history of a group probably does not exist in the hotel's PMS, because in many cases a group's previous stay will not have been in the same hotel. Sometimes groups do meet at the same hotel year after year or on a rotational basis, and group data will be available. However, when this is not the case, the FOM may have to rely on group history information provided by other hotels or by the group itself.

Figure 5.13 details the group history of an organization requesting a group room block at the Altoona Hotel. The group has met at the Altoona for three consecutive years. Note that in 2005, the **peak arrival day** (the day when most attendees arrive) was Wednesday because 71 rooms were **picked up** on that day. By contrast, only 18 new rooms for the group were sold to the group on Thursday (89 rooms − 71 rooms), 32 new rooms were added on Friday (121 rooms − 89 rooms), and 34 additional rooms (155 rooms − 121 rooms) were sold on Saturday. So Saturday was the group's **peak night,** because no other night had a larger number of rooms sold to the group.

FRONT OFFICE SEMANTICS

Peak arrival day: Day for which most rooms in a group block are sold.

Peak night: Night when the most guestrooms for a group are sold.

Pickup: Actual number of guestrooms reserved for (or by) individuals. Group pickup is the number of guestrooms reserved for individuals in a group block. For example, if 200 group rooms are blocked for a specific night, and 150 represent confirmed reservations, the pickup would be 150 rooms, or 75 percent (150 ÷ 200 = 75 percent).

Similarities in the group's booking patterns may provide clues to future booking activity and demand. Recall that one of the best ways for FOMs to predict the future is to reference the past. Note also that the group's total pickup and block size has been

Year	Blocked	Picked-up	Percentage
2003			
Wed.	100	82	82.0%
Thurs.	125	101	80.1%
Fri.	150	138	92.0%
Sat.	200	175	87.5%
Total	575	496	86.3%
2004			
Wed.	100	75	75.0%
Thurs.	125	115	92.0%
Fri.	150	129	86.0%
Sat.	200	165	82.5%
Total	575	484	84.2%
2005			
Wed.	75	71	94.6%
Thurs.	100	89	89.0%
Fri.	125	121	96.8%
Sat.	175	155	88.6%
Total	475	436	91.8%

FIGURE 5.13   Group history for an organization staying at the Altoona Hotel.

declining over the last two years, despite an increase in the group's total pickup percentage. This information is important when the FOM or DOS establishes the initial size of the group's room block. Similarly, when history shows that a group's block and pickup are growing, the hotel should probably create initial group room blocks that are larger than those in prior years.

Many factors can affect a group's actual pickup in a specific year, and FOMs must consider them when evaluating the group's pickup history. For example, if the group holds its meetings in different cities, an individual group member's perception of the desirability of each city may affect his or her attendance (and hotel reservations). Seasonality, program content, local attractions and activities, perceived demand for area hotel rooms during the meeting dates, and sometimes the room rates offered by a **host hotel** may affect the total number of rooms an FOM forecasts as the group's final pickup.

FRONT OFFICE SEMANTICS

Host hotel: Property that serves as the headquarters for a group when multiple hotels must be used to house all group members.

Group Cutoffs

A blocked room is not a sold room until it is assigned to an individual guest. Often, a group's block is much larger than the number of rooms the group will actually use. For most group customers, the prospect of not having enough guestrooms available for the group is so unpleasant that meeting planners overestimate need to ensure that the hotel "holds" (blocks) more rooms than they will actually need. Generally, the number of times a group does not use all rooms in the original block exceeds the number of times that a group's actual pickup is in excess of the original estimate.

Current run date:	June 1, 200X				Total hotel rooms: 300
	Reservations				Availability
Sales date	Transient sold	Group sold	Remaining in block	Total	Rooms available
August 1	100	50	100	250	50
August 2	150	125	25	300	0
August 3	150	75	75	300	0

FIGURE 5.14   Rooms availability summary for the Altoona Hotel.

FOMs respond to this tendency by carefully monitoring the speed (pace) at which group members actually reserve rooms in the block and by extending or enforcing contractual **cutoff dates.**

FRONT OFFICE SEMANTICS

Cutoff date: Date on which unreserved rooms held in a group block are returned to the hotel's general rooms inventory.

To understand how pace and cutoff affect the FOM's forecasting, consider the decision facing Allisha Miller, the FOM at the Altoona Hotel. She has 300 rooms available to sell. One year ago, the hotel agreed to hold 150 rooms in a group block for the Southwestern Soccer Association Tournament for an event that will now (one year later) occur in two months. Individual association members were to contact the hotel to make their own reservations from the group's block. Allisha's PMS rooms availability summary for June 1 appears in Figure 5.14.

MODERN FRONT OFFICE ISSUES AND TACTICS

How Low Can You Go?

One of the FOM's major responsibilities has been to work with the sales and marketing department to monitor group cutoff dates. In most cases, a group contract written by the sales department and signed by the guest would stipulate the number of rooms to be held for the group, the price of the rooms, and the length of time the rooms were to be held. After the cutoff date, the unsold group rooms would be placed back into the hotel's rooms inventory to be sold at a rate deemed appropriate by the hotel's revenue management team. Often, the rate was highly reduced because the date for which the rooms were available was so near. Increasingly, however, clients who are responsible for negotiating their group's room rates are demanding (and getting) more control over the price at which the hotel can sell that remaining inventory.

Their rationale is based on a simple and fairly noncontroversial premise that meeting attendees should get a better room rate than the average, individual traveler who stays at the hotel during the same time period. These sophisticated negotiators cite the basic economic proposition that states as volume rises, prices should fall. In theory, a group buying 500 rooms should get a better rate than an individual buying a single room. But as hotels have increased their use of Internet discounters to sell their remaining "last minute" room inventories (more about that in Chapter 7), meeting attendees can often secure a lower rate than the contracted group rate.

In response, and to ensure that they truly get the "lowest" rate, some meeting planners insert a clause into their group contracts that states no lower rates shall be offered to other groups or to individuals, whether directly or through any third party, for any days of their event unless that rate is made available to all of their attendees. As a result, they get a lowest rate guarantee that can easily be monitored simply by reviewing the hotel's Internet pricing strategy.

Some in the hotel industry do not agree with the notion that groups should always receive the lowest rate at the hotel. They cite the factors that influence the group's negotiated room rate, including date security, complimentary meeting space, reduced food and beverage charges, and significant use of convention service personnel, as well as other customized items a meeting planner might need to make a meeting successful. These same hoteliers also think that after a group's cutoff date has passed, the hotel should be free to price its rooms at any level it feels is best for its long-term business strategy.

Regardless of which side you take, it is clear that the future holds challenges for hotels and their group clients as they openly debate the question of how low can you go.

Allisha currently has 50 rooms available to sell on August 1 but no rooms available on August 2 or 3. If all the rooms in the group's remaining block were picked up, the hotel would be in a sellout situation on August 2 and 3. If, however, soccer association members do not pick up their remaining rooms on those days, the hotel will have rooms available. For August 1, Allisha has sold 100 rooms to transient guests and 50 rooms to individuals in the group block. There are 100 rooms remaining to be sold in the group block. Therefore, 250 rooms are sold or committed and 50 rooms remain to be sold on that date. In this situation, should Allisha accept a new transient reservation request for the three nights of August 1–3?

The answer relates to the cutoff date negotiated with the group as part of its contract with the hotel. In this situation, Allisha's dilemma would be resolved if the group had been assigned a 60-day cutoff. In other words, both parties had agreed that rooms would be held in the block until 60 days prior to the group's arrival (on August 1), that is, until June 1. After June 1, the remaining rooms would be released to the hotel's general rooms inventory. The impact of the cutoff date in this case is immense, because when the soccer group's cutoff date is enforced, Allisha will have 75 additional rooms to sell for August 3. As a result, her rooms availability forecast for that date will immediately change from its current 0 percent to 25 percent (75 available rooms ÷ 300 rooms = 25 percent).

FOMs who are forecasting group room demand must pay close attention to group history, pickup patterns, and cutoff dates when much of the hotel's business is group related. In large hotels, there can be hundreds of active group contracts. Fortunately, a PMS-generated group cutoff date report that details upcoming cutoff dates is a standard feature, and FOMs should review it daily.

SECTION REVIEW AND DISCUSSION QUESTIONS

Section Objective: Explain how an FOM can use PMS data relating to transient and group guests to make room demand forecasts.

Section Summary: FOMs must use predictive data, techniques, and strategies to forecast demand for future room sales to transient and group guests. When forecasting room demand for transient guests, FOMs can examine trend lines suggested by internally generated data. They can also use information available from Smith Travel Research (STR) and TravelCLICK. STR tracks information from more than 23,000 hotels, which represents more than 20.8 million rooms. STR uses its database to provide a participating hotel with statistics applicable to its local area and its competitive set. These data allow FOMs to compare their sales performance with that of other properties, and the data provide useful input to room forecasting and price-setting decisions. TravelCLICK reports the advertised selling prices listed on nearly 100 individual and hotel company-operated Web sites on the GDS.

Reservation patterns of transient travelers must be considered separately from group patterns. The best predictive sources of room demand for groups are group history and group booking pace. Cutoff dates for guestroom blocks are also critical to ensure that rooms that will not be used are placed back into the hotel's rooms inventory.

Discussion Questions:

1. Assume that you are an FOM and are analyzing the most recent copy of the STR's monthly STAR report. You note that your occupancy rate is lower than the area average for the past three months. How can you use this information to make room forecasts and pricing decisions? What would you do with the knowledge that your hotel's booking performance is less than that of other hotels in the area?

2. How would your response to the previous question be different if your occupancy rates were lower (and decreasing) than rates of your property's competitive set?

3. What factors would influence the cutoff date for a group that is negotiating a contract for a meeting at your property?

4. What types of information about group histories would you normally expect to obtain from a group and from another hotel in your chain that has hosted the group?

MANAGING OCCUPANCY FORECAST REPORTS

FOMs track room demand with historical, current, and future data generated from internal and external predictive data sources to improve their forecasts. A professionally developed occupancy forecast is not just an estimate of the number of rooms that

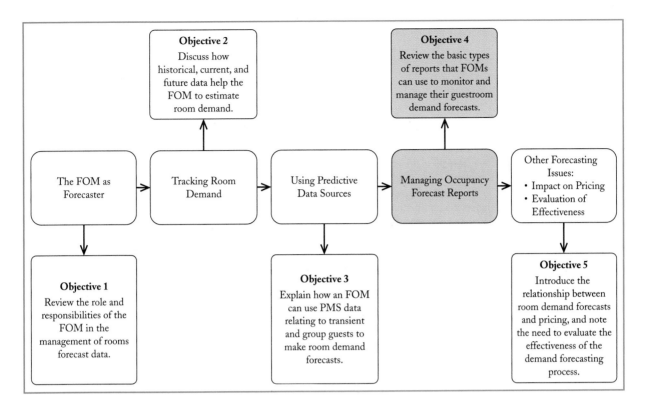

ROADMAP 5.4

can be sold. Rather, it is a multifaceted process consisting of four essential activities performed in the following order:

1. Generating the demand forecast
2. Establishing an initial rate strategy
3. Monitoring pickup reports
4. Modifying rate strategy (if necessary)

As suggested in Roadmap 5.4, several PMS reports are available to assist FOMs as they monitor and manage their forecasts and establish their rate strategies. The initial development and then management of a hotel's rate strategy is such an important part of the FOM's job that Chapter 6 of this text is devoted to it.

PMS reports related to creating initial demand forecasts vary by the system selected. However, every PMS produces reports that assist FOMs in forecasting demand for their property. Some of the most important are pickup reports and reports of 10-day forecasts, 30-day forecasts, and extended forecasts. Each will be examined to show how it can improve FOMs' forecasting abilities.

Pickup Reports

A **pickup report** summarizes reservation activity. Recall that the term, *pickup*, indicates the actual number of rooms reserved by (sold to) individual travelers. As a result, any report that summarizes this reservation activity is considered a pickup report.

Reservation, nonguaranteed: A reservation in which the hotel agrees to hold a room until a specific time (by hotel industry tradition, usually 4:00 p.m. or 6:00 p.m.) after which the hotel can sell the room to another guest. This type of reservation is sometimes erroneously called a "confirmed" reservation, which is incorrect because all reservations that result in a guest receiving a confirmation number are, in fact, confirmed reservations. Guests with a nonguaranteed reservation are not charged if the room is not used.

Reservation, guaranteed: A reservation in which the hotel agrees to hold a room until the guest arrives or until the hotel's designated check-out time the next day. Guests with a guaranteed reservation who do not actually use their room (they are no-shows) will typically be charged for the first night of their reservation period.

Reservation, advance payment deposit: A reservation in which the hotel agrees to accept a guest's reservation only upon full or partial prepayment of the established room rate charged. Guests who have made an advance payment (deposit) will typically forfeit all or part of their advance payment (deposit) if they are no-shows or stay for fewer days than covered by the reservation.

FIGURE 5.15 Most common types of hotel reservations.

FRONT OFFICE SEMANTICS

Pickup report: Any of a variety of PMS reports designed to summarize reservation activity.

Pickup reports are necessary because it is not possible for FOMs to evaluate the demand impact of individual reservations for guestrooms. Consider that small hotels will likely make dozens of transient guest reservations daily, and larger hotels may make hundreds or even thousands per day for dates that may be a year or more in the future.

Every PMS allows an FOM to review a listing of all reservations made on a specific day. That reservation information alone would not, however, be sufficient to create an effective demand forecast for any future date. To illustrate, assume an FOM in a 300-room hotel reviewed a list of daily reservations and found that 200 rooms were reserved on Monday for the upcoming Friday night. Based on that information, the FOM might forecast strong demand for Friday and set the hotel's rate strategy accordingly. If, however, on the following day, 190 of the 200 guests who made these reservations canceled them, demand for the date would not be strong. If the FOM did not monitor both the hotel's reservations *and* reservation cancellation activities, the demand forecast would not be accurate or effective in the development of the hotel's rate strategy.

Common pickup reports include reservation activity, reservation turn-aways (due to room unavailability or other factors), cancellation activity, pace summaries, and reservation summaries by arrival date, room type, rate, or any other data field (see chapter 4) that FOMs choose to predict room demand. Pickup reports are primarily designed to summarize reservation data. Therefore, FOMs must consider the three most common types of reservations encountered in most of hotels; these are presented in Figure 5.15.

FRONT OFFICE SEMANTICS

Reservation, guaranteed: Reservation in which the hotel agrees to hold the room until the guest arrives, and the guest agrees to pay for the room even if he or she does not arrive (i.e., is a no-show).

Many hotels require that guests use a bank card or other type of payment card to guarantee their reservations.

Frequently a difference exists between no-show activity and cancellation activity among the three reservation types: for example, guests with *nonguaranteed reservations* tend to be no-shows at a higher rate. Therefore, the best PMS reports allow FOMs to review reservation summary data by (1) activity (e.g., older reservations generally are canceled at a higher rate than reservations made more recently); (2) selected data field (e.g., guests staying for one or two days generally cancel at a higher rate than guests staying for longer periods of time); and (3) type (nonguaranteed reservations tend to cancel at a higher rate than those that are guaranteed or include an *advance payment deposit*).

Ten-Day Forecasts

Although there is no industry standard that indicates the best length of short- or near-term forecasts, many FOMs prepare and distribute a 10-day forecast to selected hotel staff daily. Figure 5.16 is a sample forecast. With this PMS system, the 10-day forecast is an availability forecast. (Recall that this is the inverse of an occupancy

Business Date: 6/22/200X   Shift: 1   User: DH

Date **B**	Jun 22, 0X	Jun 23, 0X	Jun 24, 0X	Jun 25, 0X	Jun 26, 0X	Jun 27, 0X	Jun 28, 0X	Jun 29, 0X	Jun 30, 0X	Jul 01, 0X
	Tue	Wed	Thu	Fri	Sat	Sun	Mon	Tue	Wed	Thu
C Room Type										
BK	5	4	2	2	7	7	7	6	6	6
BNDD	30	31	33	0	21	29	37	39	39	43
BNK	7	8	3	−1	8	14	15	14	15	16
DD	14	17	19	18	19	22	22	22	22	22
HNDD	2	2	2	2	2	2	2	2	2	2
NDD	20	19	24	10	19	30	32	32	32	33
SBDD	0	0	2	1	1	2	2	2	2	2
SBK	1	0	−1	0	1	1	1	1	1	1
SBK 1	4	4	4	4	4	4	4	4	4	4
SBNDD1	1	1	1	1	1	1	1	1	1	1
SBNK	1	1	2	1	2	1	2	2	2	2
SBNK 1	1	2	2	1	2	2	2	2	2	2
SHD	1	1	1	1	1	1	1	1	1	1
SK 2	1	1	1	1	1	1	1	1	1	1
Rooms Total:	89	91	95	41	89	117	129	129	130	136

D

E

FIGURE 5.16   Ten-day availability forecast.

forecast.) Another PMS system might generate an occupancy forecast. This PMS report reports the following details:

A. Date and time the forecast was prepared
B. Specific days included in the forecast
C. Hotel's available room types
D. Actual number of each room type remaining to be sold at the time of the report's preparation
E. Total number of rooms of all types remaining to be sold per day

FOMs commonly prepare short-term room reports of actual availability or forecasted occupancy because managers in several departments use the information. The front office must be appropriately staffed to handle anticipated guest registrations and check-outs. Housekeeping managers need to fine-tune staffing patterns and employee schedules, some of which may have been developed one or two weeks earlier. In a full-service hotel, food and beverage managers must forecast restaurant and lounge volume. In a limited-service hotel, forecasts help those responsible for managing the hotel's complimentary breakfast program to estimate food purchases and staffing requirements. Managers in the maintenance and engineering department and the security department, and even the controller's office, are affected by the number of rooms sold and the resulting house count.

Short-term forecasts are useful in all hotels, but they are of particular importance to properties that have a significant volume of group business. Assume that Allisha

Miller, the FOM at the 300-room Altoona Hotel, has—for a date eight days in the future—50 rooms currently reserved by individual guests, and that she is holding a group block of 100 rooms. The **rooming list** for the group block is due tomorrow (one week before the group's arrival). If the rooming list for the full block (100 rooms) is received by the hotel at the scheduled time, the number of actual sold rooms would change from 50 to 150 at the time the rooming list names were entered into the PMS. The impact on Allisha's 10-day forecast would be significant, because a room that is part of a block in the PMS is generally considered to be held, but not sold, until it is actually assigned to an individual guest.

Hotels with business from large groups (and, consequently, large numbers of rooming lists) will experience dramatic changes in confirmed occupancy rates when rooming lists are actually entered into the PMS. Therefore, FOMs in these properties should create and evaluate near-term forecasts on a daily basis, and sometimes even more frequently.

FRONT OFFICE SEMANTICS

Rooming list: Registry of the names of the specific individuals who are part of a group reservation. The rooming list details each guest's arrival and departure dates as well as the form of payment to be used.

Thirty-Day Forecasts

In addition to near-term forecasts, most FOMs maintain 30-day forecasts that are often outputs from the budgeting process. Hotels typically create an annual (12-month) revenue and expense budget in monthly increments, so the 30-day, or monthly, forecast is a common way to compare the hotel's budget forecast with an occupancy (or room revenue) forecast.

Recall that an FOM's best forecast uses historical data from the PMS. These data will likely include last year's occupancy and booking pace and other statistics believed to be relevant. Current data (e.g., the number of rooms on-the-books) from the PMS would then be evaluated. Figure 5.17 is an example of using current data to develop a 30-day occupancy forecast at the Sleep Well Hotel. The report tallies current PMS data on June 1 to create the monthly forecast for July (the following month). As current PMS data change, so will the forecast; an FOM evaluates the same data to prepare a forecast for any time period. In Figure 5.17, the FOM can consider the following PMS information 30 days before the start of the month for which the forecast is prepared:

A. Run date indicates when the report was prepared.

B. Date column identifies the day of the month.

C. Day column identifies the day of the week.

D. Rooms column shows the total number of rooms in the hotel (141 in this example).

E. OOO column represents the number of rooms that are estimated to be unavoidably out of order and *not* be available for sale on a specific date (see July 2).

Run Date: 6/1/200X

B Date	C Day	D Rooms	E DHS	F Stay-overs	G Arrivals	H Due Out	I Available	J Trans Ngtd	K Trans Gtd	L Group Ngtd	M Group Gtd	N Total Occupied	O Occ %	P Group Block	Q Potential %
7/1/200x	Thurs.	141	0	5	1	9	114	0	1	0	0	6	4.26%	21	19.15%
7/2/200x	Fri.	141	2	5	4	1	-1	0	3	0	1	9	6.38%	131	99.29%
7/3/200x	Sat.	141	0	9	3	0	119	0	3	0	0	12	8.51%	10	15.60%
7/4/200x	Sun.	141	0	4	0	8	127	0	0	0	0	4	2.84%	10	9.93%
7/5/200x	Mon.	141	0	3	0	1	130	0	0	0	0	3	2.13%	8	7.80%
7/6/200x	Tues.	141	0	3	0	0	53	0	0	0	0	3	2.13%	85	62.41%
7/7/200x	Wed.	141	0	3	2	0	51	0	2	0	0	5	3.55%	85	63.83%
7/8/200x	Thurs.	141	0	4	4	1	118	0	4	0	0	8	5.67%	15	16.31%
7/9/200x	Fri.	141	0	4	52	4	20	0	8	31	13	56	39.72%	65	85.82%
7/10/200x	Sat.	141	0	47	9	9	20	0	5	1	3	56	39.72%	65	85.82%
7/11/200x	Sun.	141	0	9	2	47	113	0	2	0	0	11	7.80%	17	19.86%
7/12/200x	Mon.	141	0	4	0	7	125	0	0	0	0	4	2.84%	12	11.35%
7/13/200x	Tues.	141	0	4	3	0	24	0	2	0	1	7	4.96%	110	82.98%
7/14/200x	Wed.	141	0	5	3	2	23	0	2	0	1	8	5.67%	110	83.69%
7/15/200x	Thurs.	141	0	7	7	1	10	0	6	0	1	14	9.93%	117	92.91%
7/16/200x	Fri.	141	0	12	14	2	103	0	3	0	10	26	18.44%	12	26.95%
7/17/200x	Sat.	141	0	21	31	5	50	1	3	1	26	52	36.88%	39	64.54%
7/18/200x	Sun.	141	0	21	6	31	73	0	2	0	4	27	19.15%	41	48.23%
7/19/200x	Mon.	141	0	9	28	18	70	2	10	0	16	37	26.24%	34	50.35%
7/20/200x	Tues.	141	0	35	7	2	26	0	6	0	1	42	29.79%	73	81.56%
7/21/200x	Wed.	141	0	37	2	5	20	0	1	0	1	39	27.66%	82	85.82%
7/22/200x	Thurs.	141	0	16	3	23	31	0	0	0	3	19	13.48%	91	78.01%
7/23/200x	Fri.	141	0	10	18	9	63	0	5	1	12	28	19.86%	50	55.32%
7/24/200x	Sat.	141	0	26	9	2	75	0	2	0	7	35	24.82%	31	46.81%
7/25/200x	Sun.	141	0	7	2	28	132	0	2	0	0	9	6.38%	0	6.38%
7/26/200x	Mon.	141	0	5	13	4	92	0	4	0	9	18	12.77%	31	34.75%
7/27/200x	Tues.	141	0	12	1	6	106	0	1	0	0	13	9.22%	22	24.82%
7/28/200x	Wed.	141	0	8	0	5	71	0	0	0	0	8	5.67%	62	49.65%
7/29/200x	Thurs.	141	0	4	0	4	92	0	0	0	0	4	2.84%	45	34.75%
7/30/200x	Fri.	141	0	0	16	4	83	0	4	2	10	16	11.35%	42	41.13%
7/31/200x	Sat.	141	0	12	8	4	57	0	3	0	5	20	14.18%	64	59.57%
Total		4371	2	351	248	242	2190	3	84	37	124	599	13.70%	1580	36.15%

FIGURE 5.17   Sleep Well Hotel—monthly occupancy detail for July 200X.

F. Stayovers are the number of rooms occupied by guests on the previous day who are not scheduled to check out. (Recall that this number will be *decreased* by the actual number of early departures and *increased* by the number of actual overstays experienced by the hotel on that day.)

G. Arrivals include all guests with reservations recorded in the PMS. The number in this column represents rooms, not the number of guests staying in the rooms, which is computed by adding the data in columns J, K, L, and M. Some PMS reports provide both numbers—rooms and number of guests staying in rooms.

H. Due Out (departures) estimates the number of rooms occupied by guests who indicated at the time of check-in that this was their intended departure date.

I. Available is the total number of additional rooms in the hotel that may be reserved by guests (column D, less columns E, F, G, and P), as rooms in column P are already blocked (held) for group guests.

J. Trans Ngtd is the PMS code for transient, Non guaranteed room reservations. (Recall that individuals with these confirmed reservations tend to be no-shows at a higher rate than are guests with reservations that are guaranteed.)

K. Trans Gtd is the PMS code for transient, guaranteed room reservations.

L. Group Ngtd is the PMS code for group, non guaranteed room reservations.

M. Group Gtd is the PMS code for group, guaranteed room reservations.

N. Total Occupied is the number of rooms calculated to be occupied on that date (column F plus column G).

O. Occupancy % is column N divided by column D. In some PMS reports, OOO rooms are subtracted from column D before the calculation is made. In that case, the computation would be modified: column N ÷ (column D − column E).

P. Group Block is the number of rooms currently held (usually determined by contracts) for the hotel's group guests. As these rooms are reserved by individual guests or by rooming list, they will be subtracted from this column and added to column K or L, depending on the type of reservation made.

Q. Potential % is the occupancy percentage the hotel would experience if all currently reserved rooms and currently blocked group rooms were sold on an individual date (columns F and G, plus column P).

Even though each PMS may be different, the conceptual factors affecting occupancy (availability) remain unchanged and are expressed as follows:

	Total rooms
Less	Unavailable rooms
Less	Committed rooms
Equal	Sellable (available) rooms

Perhaps the most important concept expressed in Figure 5.17 is, simply:

The data in a PMS summary represent the current status of hotel occupancy; the data are not *an estimate of how many rooms will actually be sold on any day.*

In other words, the number of rooms that will actually be sold on any given night is directly related to the actual pickup of any group blocks held and, equally as important, the rooms pricing decisions made by the FOM or other person serving as the revenue manager. These pricing decisions are always best made after reviewing the current data summaries produced by the PMS.

The occupancy reported in Figure 5.17 is rather low. The hotel will probably achieve a July occupancy percentage much in excess of that indicated. This is typically the case with current data 30 days before, or even closer to, the forecast date. Many July guests will not make reservations until closer to the date on which they will arrive. Also, many arriving guests will be walk-ins. The lead time between when guests make reservations and the time of their actual arrival has been shortening in recent years. In many hotels, 50 percent or more of reservations are made within seven days of the reserving guest's arrival date. This makes forecasting more complex. First, the value of current data is reduced, and second, the FOM must rely more on historical data and estimates of future data trends.

Extended Forecasts

FOMs often project room demand far into the future. For example, an FOM may be asked to predict room demand for a 30-day period that is six months in the future— a prediction in May about the room demand the following November. To comprehend the difficulty of this task, consider the value of the three sources of data that FOMs rely on to make their demand forecasts:

- *Historical data.* Historical data do not *change* as they age. In other words, data from one year ago remain constant six months ago, today, and six months from now. An FOM who wants to forecast November demand in May would find it easy to use last November's historical data to help with the task. However: historical data do *age*. If an **extended forecast** is for a period more than a year in advance (e.g., an 18-month projection in May of this year for room demand for November of *next* year), historical data may be two years old when the forecasted time period actually arrives. In this case, historical data are likely to be of less value than more recent historical data.

FRONT OFFICE SEMANTICS

Extended forecast: Occupancy forecast that projects room demand more than 30 days into the future.

- *Current data.* Data for time periods that have yet to occur, but for which the PMS is accepting reservations and reporting reservation-related information, can be useful for extended forecasts, but only if guests made their reservations far in advance. However, as we have seen, the advance (lead) time between booking a reservation and arrival is typically short and is becoming shorter. A hotel catering to business travelers may, for example, have few reservations on-the-books for dates that are more than four or five months in the future, even though it is likely that the hotel will secure many reservations for those periods. Therefore, as the time frame for an extended forecast is pushed forward, the amount of useful current PMS data is typically reduced. Nevertheless, a talented FOM can use the limited current data available to improve forecasting. For example, note the data about reservation booking pace for the Altoona Hotel in Figure 5.18.

Assume that, on June 1, the Altoona Hotel's FOM creates an on-the-books pace report detailing all reservations currently in the PMS for the next

Report run date: _____June 1, 200X_____

Altoona Hotel **Six-Month Pace Report**

June 200X

	1	2	3	4	5	6	7	8	9
	On-the-books Next 6 months	On-the-books Prior 6 months	PACE Variance	PACE Variance Percentage	ADR Next 6 months	ADR Prior 6 Months	ADR Variance	MONTHLY PLAN (Budget)	Percent of Budget
June 200X	$ 79,250	$ 75,466	$ 3,784	5.01%	$77.42	$70.40	$7.02	$150,450.00	53%
July 200X	$ 44,521	$ 43,703	$ 818	1.87%	$79.25	$75.74	$3.51	$142,325.00	31%
August 200X	$ 17,080	$ 18,100	($ 1,020)	−5.63%	$82.12	$80.82	$1.30	$163,650.00	10%
September 200X	$ 14,314	$ 8,752	$ 5,562	63.55%	$81.04	$78.77	$2.27	$155,475.00	9%
October 200X	$ 13,631	$ 7,741	$ 5,890	76.09%	$79.56	$77.43	$2.13	$189,315.00	7%
November 200X	$ 6,534	$ 2,369	$ 4,165	175.80%	$81.45	$82.34	($0.89)	$112,000.00	6%
Totals	$175,330	$156,131	$19,199	12.30%				$913,215.00	19%

FIGURE 5.18 Altoona Hotel six-month pace report.

six months (see column 1). Note that as the monthly reservation data are totaled further into the future, the current data related to that month are reduced. In most hotels, this occurs because of the short-term booking nature of transient guests.

Column 2 details the same information from the identical report created one year ago. Column 3 and 4 report, respectively, the dollar and percentage variances (differences) between the booking paces of the two time periods. Note that for the six-month period examined, bookings are running at a pace approximately 12.3 percent above that of last year (column 4). This information would be helpful to the FOM forecasting future room demand for the hotel.

Figure 5.18 also shows the on-the-books ADR during the two comparative periods (columns 5 and 6) and the dollars of ADR variance (column 7). ADR is important because increases in this RevPar component affect the revenue totals summed in columns 1 and 2. The report also details the hotel's monthly plan, or budget (column 8), and the percentage of the hotel's planned rooms sales that has been achieved (booked) as of the report date (column 9).

- *Future data.* As FOMs forecast demand far into the future (12 or more months), they face increasing challenges because the quality of information available is diminished. New hotels open and existing hotels close. Economic activity, legislation, and weather are hard-to-predict factors that affect demand. Consider also terrorism: No one predicted the events of September 11, 2001, and their impact on hotel occupancy in New York City and across the country.

Despite the difficulty in preparing them, accurate extended forecasts are important for several reasons: determining long-range revenue budgets, planning for human resources needs, and scheduling hotel renovations and repair. The most important reason, however, for developing extended forecasts relates to their impact on room pricing.

SECTION REVIEW AND DISCUSSION QUESTIONS

Section Objective: Review the basic types of reports that FOMs can use to monitor and manage their guestroom demand forecasts.

Section Summary: FOMs track room demand using historical, current, and future data generated from internal and external predictive data sources. Accurate estimates of occupancy rates contribute to better decisions about room pricing. FOMs typically use four types of occupancy forecast reports. Pickup reports refer to any PMS report that summarizes reservation activities. They include reports about reservations (by type) that are made and those that are turned away, cancellation activity, pace summaries, and reservation summaries by arrival date, room type, rate, or any other factor that an FOM considers important when predicting demand. A 10-day forecast is a common short-term room report that estimates room occupancy or availability and is used by managers throughout the hotel. A 30-day forecast is often tied to budget development and evaluation, even though there is a trend toward decreasing time between the booking of hotel rooms by transient guests and their arrival. An extended forecast is made from an analysis of historical, current, and future data. The number of and potential importance of unforeseen factors make it difficult to make pricing and other decisions based on these longer-term estimates.

Discussion Questions:
1. For what purposes would an FOM want information from pickup reports? How, does data in pickup reports affect decisions about room pricing?
2. For what purposes, do managers in departments throughout the hotel use information from 10-day forecasts?
3. Can you think of situations in which the less than accurate data from extended forecasts can be useful?

OTHER FORECASTING ISSUES

This chapter has emphasized that FOMs must be concerned about forecasts of the number of rooms to be occupied (available) on future dates. First, FOMs want to ensure that all guests with a reservation for a specific type of room will have the preferred room available at time of registration. Second, FOMs need room demand information when they make pricing decisions. As noted in Roadmap 5.5, the

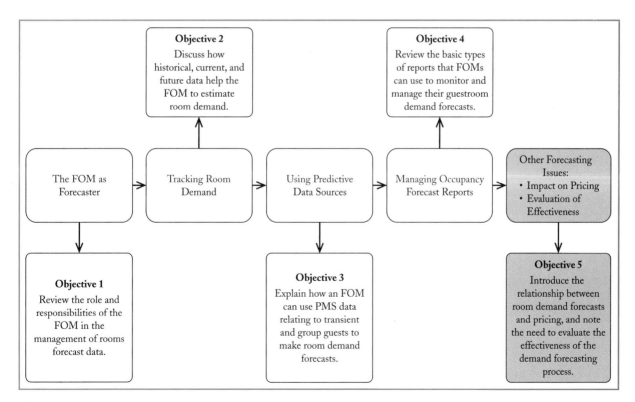

ROADMAP 5.5

chapter concludes by previewing the importance of room demand forecast on pricing—a topic treated in-depth in the next chapter—and by providing suggestions to evaluate the effectiveness of the forecasting process.

Impact on Pricing

Pricing decisions naturally follow the development of room occupancy or availability forecasts. Until recently, surprising little was written about the complexity of hotel room pricing. Most of the literature focused on the pros and cons of a variety of formulas developed to establish initial room rates. Whether based on building costs, amenities offered, operating expenses, room size, or other factors, the development of the hotel's initial (target) ADR is important. What is vastly more important, however, is the need to manage the hotel's room rate in a manner that maximizes RevPar, or **GoPar** as some hoteliers have recently advocated.

FRONT OFFICE SEMANTICS

GoPar (gross operating profit per available room): Average gross profit (revenue less management-controllable expenses) generated by each guestroom during a given time period. The GoPar formula for a given time period is

$$\text{Revenue} - \text{Management-controllable expenses} \div \text{Available rooms for that period}$$

Because this book is about professional front office management, RevPar pricing is relevant. RevPar pricing involves variables that are within the control of FOMs; that is, at least, FOMs can manage, compute, and monitor RevPar-related data. By contrast, GoPar calculations are affected by everything from the hotel's utility use to fixed costs to banquet costs. As a result, the information required to measure GoPar might not be readily available to FOMs. Even if the data were available, FOMs are less able to significantly influence these data than RevPar variables.

Whether GoPar will replace RevPar as the standard measure of a hotel's revenue management effectiveness is beyond the scope of this discussion. Although some would argue that GoPar is a better measure of expense management than of revenue-related decision making, the fact remains that room demand forecasts should affect pricing decisions made by the FOM.

Let's assume that an FOM in a 500-room property forecasts that for a Sunday two weeks away, the hotel's likely occupancy will be 25 percent or less. At one time there was little the FOM could do to directly address this situation. Changing (reducing) room prices or increasing the value of room discounts for that day was not possible, because most of a hotel's room pricing information was distributed to buyers by print media (e.g., brochures and ads in industry directories) that required a long lead time and could not be changed rapidly. The FOM might assume that a reduced price would increase the sale of rooms, but there was no effective way to inform travelers or travel buyers about the reduced rates. Only guests who contacted the hotel directly, typically by calling the front desk, could be informed about reduced rates. The number of guests who would be willing buyers at the reduced rates would likely be high but many would likely have been willing to buy at the hotel's original (nondiscounted) printed and published rates.

Today, the world of hotel sales is completely different from the sales environment at the beginning of the new millennium. An FOM can now change room rates instantaneously. In fact, with immediate (less than 60 seconds) updating of Web-based pricing and with the ability to contact past guests by e-mail, an FOM might, in only minutes, "publish" reduced room rates on literally thousands of Web sites. The FOM could also e-mail selected guests such as those who had stayed on previous Sunday nights, who might impulsively decide to take advantage of a reduced-price room. The overall result might be a significant increase in room sales. To maximize RevPar, FOMs must know when room demand is strong (or weak) enough to dictate changes in pricing strategies, and to obtain this knowledge, FOMs need accurate room forecast data.

MODERN FRONT OFFICE ISSUES AND TACTICS

The Sky Is *Not* the Limit!

What is a hotel room worth when demand for it absolutely explodes? If your answer is "the sky is the limit," then you may have a public relations problem and a legal problem! In most states, predatory pricing is illegal, and hoteliers publicly accused of it will clearly face negative publicity and potential legal action as well.

Government officials responsible for monitoring illegal pricing tactics rightly become vigilant during times of natural disasters and other emergencies. To understand why, consider the demand for hotel rooms that resulted from the 2005 hurricanes Katrina and Rita. These storms decimated hotels on the U.S. Gulf Coast, causing a decline in the number of rooms available to sell while at the same time driving demand for the remaining hotel rooms through the roof. Many in the hotel industry responded by housing refugees for little or no charge, but very few hoteliers responded to the extraordinary demand by raising rates to two or three times their normal rack rate. For these hotels, the inevitable result was the attention of local law enforcement officials.

Most states have antigouging laws that restrict the prices hoteliers can charge in emergency situations. For example, Oklahoma's price-gouging law stipulates that prices cannot jump more than 10 percent above the price normally charged, unless the spike is caused by nonemergency factors and does not result in an increase in profit. State laws vary, so all front office managers should know about their state's laws that regulate allowable room rates during times of emergencies.

Evaluation of Effectiveness

Accurate and useful forecasts are important to all hotels. The hotel business is, however, often unpredictable; as a result, forecasts that are 100 percent accurate are rare. Even in properties with consistent sales volume, with an excellent PMS that provides accurate historical and current data, and with an FOM who effectively monitors trends, forecasts are likely to be off to some degree. Forecasts that are consistently or significantly in error, however, will ultimately yield financial or operational difficulties or both. Forecasts that are unrealistically high

- cause out-of-reach expectations for hotel owners,
- increase feelings of frustration in staff when forecasted levels are not attained,
- produce budgeting and spending errors by overstating anticipated revenues,
- lead to lack of recognition of excellence in other aspects of the FOM's managerial decision making because of a focus on forecast shortfalls, and

- result in impractical and overly aggressive determinations of room rates (rates are set too high).

Alternatively, demand forecasts that are consistently and unrealistically too low can

- lead managers to believe they are performing at levels that are higher than actual performance levels,
- undermine the credibility of the forecaster because of the suspicion that actual variations in forecasts are due to **lowballing** of forecasts, and
- result in impractical and underaggressive determinations of room rates (rates are set too low).

FRONT OFFICE SEMANTICS

Lowballing (forecasts): Developing forecasts that are unrealistically conservative (low) for the express purpose of more easily achieving or exceeding them. The practice is most prevalent in hotels that emphasize achieving or exceeding previously budgeted forecasts.

Experienced FOMs can produce room demand forecasts that will be within 1 percent to 5 percent of actual sales of hotel rooms achieved by the property. To increase accuracy, many hotels produce an extended forecast of one year (or more), but then alter those forecasts monthly as new data become available. Although forecasts that are many months away may be modified only slightly each month, the hotel's 30-, 60-, and even 90-day forecasts will become increasingly accurate. Experienced FOMs use the latest historical data, the most recent current PMS data, and the most up-to-date future data to fine-tune near-term forecasts. Accurate demand forecasts enable FOMs to better establish room rates. The complex and increasingly difficult decision-making process necessary to do so is the subject of the Chapter 6.

From the Front Office: Front-Line Interview

Lori Zupin
Director of Operations
SunStream Hotels & Resorts (550 rooms companywide)
Fort Myers, Florida

No Extra Charge for the Complete Wildlife Package!

Lori graduated with a degree in hospitality business in 1995. She has stated that her education "has proven to be incredibly beneficial in opening doors of opportunity that have led me on a fast-track career. Coupled with the internships and classroom experience, my education has proven to be the springboard for my success in the hospitality industry."

1. **What are the most important responsibilities in your present position?**
    Presently, my responsibilities include leading the seven general managers of our company's resort properties. I also direct the day-to-day efforts of our corporate human resources department, which includes the management of benefits, compensation, and training for all employees. I also partner with the directors of sales and marketing and finance to ensure

effective communication among the different sectors. This results in increased revenues and improved guest and employee satisfaction.

2. **What are the biggest challenges that confront you in your day-to-day work and in the long-term operation of your property's front office?**
Our latest challenge has been that of a companywide property management system (PMS) conversion. This involved the creation and implementation of new polices and procedures and subsequent training of our staff members. Our long-term goal for our front office operations is to establish consistency between the seven different properties. Then we can transfer guest service employees seamlessly from one operation to the next as they advance in their careers.

   SunStream has always excelled in outstanding guest service to our external guests and our internal guests (employees). We recognize that guest satisfaction and employee satisfaction are essential to our long-term success in a competitive marketplace. With the PMS conversion, our two end users (employees and guests) will benefit. The success of this conversion is imperative to our future. Since the completion of the conversion just a few months ago, we have met regularly to monitor adherence to the new policies and procedures and to evaluate the new system for deficiencies.

3. **What is your most unforgettable front office moment?**
This is difficult to answer—the front office is the hub of the entire resort. Calming an irate guest is always unforgettable, and there have been several memorable moments as I have done so. One involved a guest who informed me that his entire vacation was ruined because a raccoon ventured a little too close to him on the pool deck. (We joked among ourselves that we thought he had purchased the Complete Wildlife Package!) Another unforgettable moment occurred when, as a front office manager, I had to turn the whole house of 285 rooms on one Sunday. That was a formidable effort. It involved 285 check-outs and 285 check-ins, while at the same time I had to coordinate the front office with the housekeeping and maintenance departments. Another more recent memory is the crash of our entire front office system, along with the backup. We had to rebuild more than 1,800 reservations. We managed to complete the task in one week with no interruption in service.

   The more unforgettable front office moments are those that challenge you beyond what you once thought was your limit. They are the moments that initially seem to unconquerable tasks, but at the end of the day, through the assistance of a great team, everything gets done.

4. **What advice do you have for those studying about or considering a career in front office or hotel management?**
This answer could take a while! The hospitality industry is always changing and will always challenge you. Every day will be different, with different opportunities, different successes, and different lessons. Each day you learn more about yourself and your capabilities, and you also learn more about your guests, your employees, and your competition. It is essential to your success to know them all.

   The hospitality industry is not for those that want to sit back and relax; it is for those that want to take advantage of every second of every day to make a difference. If you are looking for a career that allows you to think quickly on your feet and to lead and develop a team while challenging your own abilities, you can find success in the hospitality industry.

SECTION REVIEW AND DISCUSSION QUESTIONS

Section Objective: To introduce the relationship between room demand forecasts and pricing and note the need to evaluate the effectiveness of the demand forecasting process.

Section Summary: A current topic of discussion in the hotel industry is whether hotel pricing should maximize revenue per available room (RevPar) or gross operating profit per available room (GoPar). Both have useful attributes, but RevPar addresses issues that are more within the control of the FOM. Today, as never before, an FOM can make pricing decisions and make them known almost instantly by use of the Web and e-mail. Accurate forecasts of room demand provide the information necessary to make decisions that can be adjusted on an as-needed basis to achieve positive impacts on RevPar.

There are several disadvantages to room demand forecasts that are implausibly too high or unrealistically too low. FOMs should use PMS data along with their own experience to produce demand forecasts that are as accurate as possible. They can do so by using the latest historical data, the most recent current PMS data, and the most up-to-date future data to fine-tune near-term forecasts.

Discussion Questions:
1. What are the pros and cons of using Web-based pricing tactics frequently, say several times weekly, to change room rates?
2. Why might room occupancy (availability) forecasts be significantly incorrect on an occasional basis? On a frequent basis?
3. What would you do, as a general manager, if you believed that the FOM used lowballing tactics to underestimate room occupancy data?

The FOM in Action: A Solution

What should FOMs do when they are asked, as they commonly are, to predict the future? The answer is "their best." In many occupations an individual's ultimate success depends on his or her ability to provide a best estimate of the future (e.g., weather forecasting and selecting financial investments).

As you read in this chapter, accurate revenue forecasts provide important information, and they are critical in establishing room rates and managing RevPar. If estimated demand is unknown, yield management principles will be impossible to implement effectively. For these reasons the general manager and, in this case, regional managers regularly require FOMs to forecast room revenue and later to compare actual revenue results with that forecast.

No revenue manager can predict the future with 100 percent precision; however, basic forecast strategies can help FOMs reach high levels of accuracy. Renee, the FOM of the Santa Clara Suites, should follow the three basics of forecasting: Renee should evaluate her historical data (room revenue achieved in prior Octobers); evaluate her current data (reservations on-the-books for October); and gather data about the events, if any, that will affect future revenue estimates.

Many FOMs do a good job of retaining records about past performance. For most, however, current data will be minimal for a time period that is nine months away because many travelers do not book their room reservations that far in advance. Reports about transient booking pace, however, can give meaningful insight into short-term booking trends that may continue in the future. Often, the best predictor of what *will* happen is what *has* happened. STR reports and other data produced in the hotel or the local area may give Renee useful information about city or state trends that could affect her October forecast.

Unlike bookings for individual travelers, group bookings are frequently made months or even years in advance and will have a significant impact on Renee's forecast. Therefore, Renee needs to communicate with sales and marketing department personnel about their revenue forecasts for October so that she can improve her forecast. Outstanding record keeping and a willingness to collect and evaluate quality data from a variety of sources will help Renee excel at the important task of revenue forecasting.

FRONT OFFICE SEMANTICS LIST

Sellout
Global Distribution System
   (GDS)
Occupancy forecast
Availability forecast
Track
Historical data
Current data
Future data
Stayover
No-show
Early departure
Overstay
Cancellation number

YTD (year to date)
On-the-books
Distressed passenger
Convention and visitors bureau
   (CVB)
Package
Group
Block
Group history
Trend line
Competitive set
STR index
E-distribution channel
Feeder market

Group (reservation)
DOS (director of sales)
Peak night
Pickup
Host hotel
Cut-off date
Pick-up report
Reservation, guaranteed
Rooming list
Extended forecast
GoPar (gross operating profit
   per available room)
Low balling (forecasts)

FRONT OFFICE AND THE INTERNET

FOMs must thoroughly understand the forecasting components built into their property's PMS. Additional forecasting resources can be useful and here are some examples:

Web address	Subject area
www.vanguardsw.com/decisionpro/jforecast.htm	Forecasting software
www.claritysystems.com	Forecasting software
www.optims.com/UK/rush/optims_rms.htm	International forecasting software (English version)
www.smithtravelresearch.com	Industry data compiler
www.htrends.com	Industry trend reporter and data publisher
www.travelclick.com	E-commerce industry data compiler

REAL-WORLD ACTIVITIES

1. Check out the Smith Travel Research and TravelCLICK Web sites. Select several categories of data generated by these organizations and consider how FOMs can use this information to forecast room demand and to make pricing decisions.

2. Assume that you and a classmate are, respectively, the FOM and director of sales and marketing at a hotel. Develop an extensive list of factors that both of you would want to know as you consider the "worth" of a group that is interested in booking a meeting at your property. What information, if any, would be available from historical data about the group's past meetings? What information, if any, would likely be available even if historical data were not available?

3. If possible, make an appointment with the FOM of a local property. Ask the FOM about the types of PMS reports that are most useful to make room demand forecasts. Ask if you could see a sample report. The PMS may have a training module that permits viewing and developing a report with generic (i.e., nonproprietary) data.

4. What are the pros and cons of generating the majority of rooms business from transient guests? From group guests? What impact, if any, do Web-based and GDS pricing strategies have on attracting group business? How might these strategies affect the future of group reservations?

5. Recall the discussion about managing room rates in a manner that maximizes RevPar or GoPar. Discuss the pros and cons of both philosophies with a local hotel manager. If this is not possible, review hotel print and electronic media to obtain further information. Make a recommendation about the best approach and support your recommendation.

6

Revenue Management

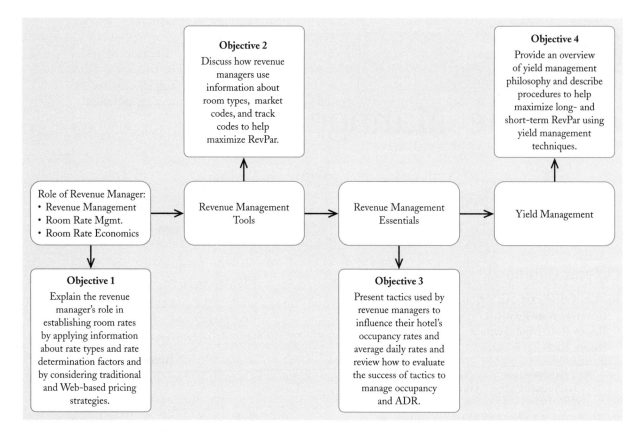

CHAPTER ROADMAP

Chapter Preview

A hotel's ability to effectively compete and financially prosper in today's lodging market is increasingly tied to the skill of its staff in pricing and selling its guestrooms. This complex process, called *revenue management*, is the topic of this chapter.

In some hotels, the FOM or a subordinate may be solely responsible for revenue management; in other properties, the duty may be shared by the FOM, other front office staff, the general manager, and the director of sales and marketing. In all cases, those responsible for revenue management must understand the economics of room rates and carefully consider the relationships between supply and demand and between determining and managing room rates. Both traditional and modern methods of room rate determination are involved.

The chapter reviews tactics to price different types of rooms and to make decisions related to market and track codes. The essential goal of a revenue manager is to maximize RevPar. Therefore, the management of occupancy levels and ADR are analyzed, as is GoPar—a new and increasingly popular method of evaluating the effectiveness of revenue management tactics.

The chapter concludes with a thorough examination of a revenue-enhancing methodology first used in the airline industry: yield management, a term whose use has expanded greatly from its original set of managerial techniques. Essentially, yield management is a RevPar-maximizing technique that incorporates many of the concepts of revenue generation discussed in this chapter. Because of its conceptual importance, the concept of managing yield is reviewed in two ways: from a philosophical perspective and in a discussion of practical principles and techniques that can be used to incorporate its best features while minimizing potentially negative outcomes.

The FOM in Action: The Challenge

Considering the events of the prior three hours, the evening was going well. The afternoon shift had started with 50 unsold rooms for that night. However, in the past few hours, the telephones were ringing incessantly, and persons with Internet reservations for the night were arriving every few minutes. Danielle Pelley, FOM at the Radisson Courtyard Hotel, looked over at Sandy, the front desk agent who was helping her on this busy Friday night.

"How many rooms do we still have vacant, Sandy?" Danielle asked.

Sandy made a few quick strokes on the keyboard of her PMS terminal, called up a "Vacant, Ready, and Unoccupied" report, and looked intently at her terminal. "Looks like 10 rooms remaining to sell and two suites. Twelve total. And the phone calls keep coming in," she said as she reached to pick up the line now ringing at her station.

It was 8:30 p.m. with 12 rooms left to sell and plenty of demand, mostly because of the snowstorm that had slowed nearby interstate traffic to a near standstill. It was always hard to predict when weather would drive demand, but Danielle thought she and her team had done a good job responding.

"Let's sell the last 10 rooms at rack rate," said Danielle, "and no reductions on the suites. This is not a night to accept discount reservations."

"Okay," replied Sandy, "that's what we'll do."

Just then the telephone rang again, and Danielle picked it up. "Thank you for calling the Raddison Courtyard. This is Danielle, how may I help you?"

"Dani," said the voice on the other line. "It's Tim Berger at the Hempsted Plaza. I'm glad I got you." Danielle knew Tim. He was a good friend and the FOM of a hotel about three miles away. "Tim," she said, "We're busy; bet you are to."

"Dani," he replied, "I need a favor. We are 15 rooms oversold and getting zero cancellations. I need to walk some folks. Can you help me out? And," he finished, "can you cut us a break and give us our walk rate?"

"I know I can sell my remaining rooms at rack rate," thought Danielle, "Now what do I do?"

ROLE OF THE REVENUE MANAGER

As indicated in Roadmap 6.1, our discussion of revenue management begins by considering the role of the revenue manager. The hotel's revenue manager is responsible for making decisions to maximize RevPar. In larger hotels, a revenue manager may be a full-time position. In mid-size to smaller hotels, the FOM or director of sales and marketing (DOSM) may serve in this role and make recommendations to the general

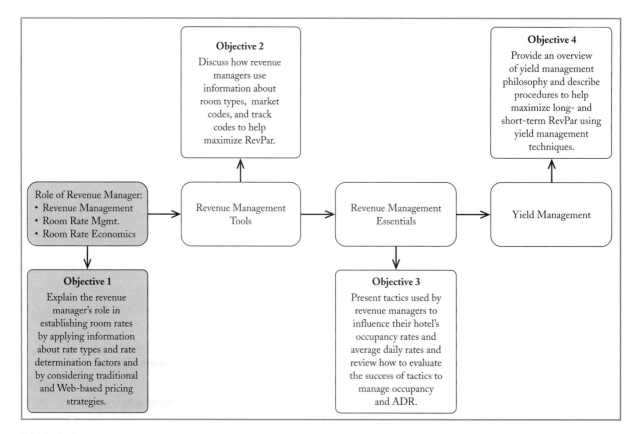

ROADMAP 6.1

manager. In very small hotels, most likely the general manager will have this responsibility. In this chapter, the term *revenue manager* refers to any individual who assumes RevPar management responsibilities.

Realistically, the task of maximizing RevPar is part of every employee's job. For example, housekeepers must clean rooms properly so these rooms can be sold at the highest possible rate. The restaurant server who addresses the needs of hotel dining guests encourages them to return. In both of these cases and in others, employees provide value to guests and encourage their return by delivering quality service. The revenue manager must, then, devise and implement pricing strategies to meet the goals of the hotel and its guests.

How important is the revenue manager to the success of a hotel? The Kimpton Hotel & Restaurant Group (www.kimptonhotels.com) operates outstanding hotels that include the Allegro (Chicago) and the Monaco (Denver). Its chairman and CEO believes that the most important person in a hotel is the revenue manager because of his or her role in managing rooms **inventory.** He states that the revenue manager "should be the highest paid (person on a hotel's staff)."[1]

[1]LaTour, T. 2004. Quoted in *Hotel and Motel Management.* July 5, p. 29.

Providing exceptionally well-cleaned rooms helps the front office to sell a hotel's rooms at the highest possible rate.

FRONT OFFICE SEMANTICS

Inventory (rooms): Rooms that are available to be sold by the hotel.

To fully understand the importance of the revenue manager, consider two hotels (250 rooms each) in the same city. Both are branded with well-known franchisors, are part of each other's competitive sets, and offer similarly priced rooms and amenities. The average ADR for the city is $100, and the average citywide occupancy for May is 65 percent. Noel is the revenue manager at one hotel; JeAnna is the revenue manager at the other.

On May 1 (current year), the city's CVB announced that the city will host next year's meeting of the State Association of Retired College Professors in the city's downtown convention center. This nonprofit association rotates its annual meeting at sites throughout the state and generates more than 5,000 room nights during its three-day meeting period. The last time the group met in this city, most area hotels achieved occupancy levels over 90 percent for the three days, and better-recognized hotel brands sold out on two or three of group's three meeting days.

| | Noel's hotel (250 rooms) | | | | JeAnna's hotel (250 rooms) | | | |
Meeting date	Rooms sold (1)	ADR (2)	Occ. percentage (3)	RevPar (4)	Rooms Sold (1)	ADR (2)	Occ. percentage (3)	RevPar (4)
Day before	205	117.21	82.0%	$ 96.11	158	99.11	63.2%	$62.64
Meeting Day 1	230	135.45	92.0%	$124.61	249	89.53	99.6%	$89.17
Meeting Day 2	226	131.25	90.4%	$118.65	230	91.14	92.0%	$83.85
Meeting Day 3	228	132.22	91.2%	$120.58	248	92.15	99.2%	$91.41
Day after	195	115.21	78.0%	$ 89.86	138	101.51	55.2%	$56.03
Five-day total								
Rooms sold	1,084	(sum of column 1)			1,023	(sum of column 1)		
ADR	$126.80	(sum of column 2 ÷ 5 days)			$93.62	(sum of column 2 ÷ 5 days)		
Occupancy	86.7%	(column 1 ÷ 250 rooms)			81.8%	(column 1 ÷ 250 rooms)		
RevPar	**$109.96**	(sum of column 4 ÷ 5 days)			**$76.62**	(sum of column 4 ÷ 5 days)		

Rev Par Difference = ($109.96 − 76.62)/ 76.62 = 43.5%

FIGURE 6.1   Two hotels: two strategies—two RevPars.

At Noel's hotel, the news about the meeting was immediately passed from the general manager to the hotel's DOSM who, without delay, routed the information to Noel, the FOM and revenue manager. She had been at the hotel for nearly 10 years and well remembered the last time the group met in town. In her role as a front desk agent, Noel had checked the association's members in and out of the property, and she recalled them as a friendly and good-natured group.

Three months after the CVB announcement, JeAnna, who also served as her hotel's FOM and revenue manager, heard about the group's selection of her city during a quarterly sales meeting with the hotel's DOSM. JeAnna had joined the hotel from another city just five months previously.

The year passed, the State Association of Retired College Professors met, and Figure 6.1 details the RevPar achievements of the two hotels. The results in Figure 6.1 are interesting for at least two reasons:

- JeAnna's hotel achieved an occupancy percentage higher than Noel's hotel's on each of the group's three meeting days.

- RevPar at Noel's hotel for the three meeting days and the day before and after the meeting was 43.5 percent higher than at JeAnna's hotel:

$$(\$109.96 - \$76.62) \div \$76.62 = 43.5\%$$

The total revenue generated by the two hotels can be computed by multiplying each property's RevPar (from Figure 6.1) times the number of rooms available to sell (250 rooms × 5 nights = 1,250) as follows:

Hotel	RevPar	Rooms	Total
Noel's	$109.96	1,250	$137,450
JeAnna's	$ 76.62	1,250	$ 95,775
		Total revenue difference	$ 41,675

This chapter will examine the strategies and tactics JeAnna should have used to achieve Noel's results. By the end of the chapter, the revenue manager's value to a successful hotel will be unquestionable.

Revenue Management

Some hotel observers believe that the terms, *room rate management* and *revenue management* are synonymous. They are not. In many cases, revenue managers establish room rates, but in many other hotels they do not. For example, the hotel's owners, the general manager, or the DOSM may dictate the rack rate to be charged at a specific time or on a specific date. The revenue manager, however, must still "manage" that rate. In a properly managed hotel, even with an established rack rate, there is no such thing as a single, inflexible rate for a guestroom. For most revenue managers, the correct reply to the common question, "How much are your rooms?" is based on responses to these questions: "Who are you? How many rooms do you want? When do you want them?"

To illustrate, assume that the FOM (who is also the revenue manager) of the 300-room Altoona Hotel desires a $100 per night ADR and sets the rack rate for the hotel's standard room type at $100 nightly. A potential guest wishes to purchase 50 rooms per night for each of the next three Sunday nights. The Altoona traditionally achieves a 20 percent to 25 percent occupancy level on Sunday nights, so the FOM wants this business. The guest, however, has a budget of only $80 per night. Should the hotel accept the business? In the overwhelming majority of cases, the answer would be yes. Why? The hotel will have the rooms available and can generate an additional $4,000 each night ($12,000 for the three nights) with the only direct costs being those required for housekeeping staff to clean the rooms.

Now assume that the Altoona has, for the past five years, experienced a sellout during the weekend that the state's girls' high school softball championships are held in the city. For that weekend, a potential guest has requested five rooms for two days (10 room nights) but has a budget of only $80 per night. Normally, the revenue manager would *not* recommend that the hotel extend a discount, even though the potential guest will go elsewhere. Why? The hotel will, based on historical data, sell these rooms to other guests who will pay the $100 rack rate (or more) for them.

Another reason that a revenue manager's job is complex is because hotels routinely offer discounts off the rack rates to a variety of entities. For example, to attract more mature leisure travelers, discounts may be offered to guests who are members of the American Association of Retired Persons (AARP). Similarly, some hotels identify other large groups and offer their members specific discounts. One group offered discounts by many hotels is the American Automobile Association (AAA), whose members merely verify their membership at time of check-in to receive the discount. AAA uses these discounts to solicit new members on its Web site. (To review current discount information, go to www.autoclubgroup.com.) As part of their overall marketing strategy, Choice Hotels executives have determined that the advantages gained from offering the AAA discount will more than offset the resulting 10 percent decline in ADR that their hotels will experience by participating in the program. Other large groups that have traditionally received significant discounts off a hotel's rack rates include local, state, and federal government employees, members of the military, and the clergy.

In addition to discounts for large groups and nonprofit entities, most hotels empower the revenue manager to approve exclusive rates for select hotel guests.

These **negotiated rates** are usually established for a specific time period (one year or more), at which time the hotel and the client can renegotiate the rate.

FRONT OFFICE SEMANTICS

Negotiated rate: Special room rate offered for a fixed period of time to a specific hotel client. Used as in, "What is the *negotiated rate* we should offer to Wal-Mart employees next year?"

In some cases, the negotiated rate may be in effect on any date the guest wishes to use it. In other cases, **blackout dates** may be identified and become part of the **negotiated rate agreement.**

FRONT OFFICE SEMANTICS

Blackout date: Any day in which the hotel will *not* honor a negotiated rate. Blackout dates should be identified at the same time the hotel and the client agree on a negotiated rate. Common blackout dates include New Year's Eve and other times the hotel believes its best interests are served by disallowing the negotiated rate.

Negotiated rate agreement: Document that details the specific contractual obligations of a hotel and client when the hotel has offered, and the client has agreed to, a negotiated rate. Typical agreement content includes start date, room rate to be charged, agreement duration, and blackout dates (if any). The agreement should be signed by a representative of the hotel and the client.

Although room rates are important to revenue managers, they are not the only factor that influences RevPar. In many hotels, revenue managers are just as concerned about **length of stay (LOS)** as they are about rate.

FRONT OFFICE SEMANTICS

Length of stay (LOS): Number of nights a hotel's individual guests use their rooms. LOS is computed on a per-stay basis. For example, in a hotel that sold 300 group room nights to 100 guests, the LOS would be computed as

$$\text{Room nights sold} \div \text{Rooms sold} = \text{LOS}$$
$$300 \quad \div \quad 100 \quad = \quad 3$$

Recall that RevPar is affected by both the rate at which rooms are sold and by the number of rooms sold. Revenue managers who devise strategies to encourage increased LOS will positively affect their property's RevPar. For example, in Figure 6.1 note that Noel's hotel achieved significantly higher occupancy levels than JeAnna's hotel on the day before and the day after the meeting. Revenue managers can encourage meeting attendees to increase their LOS by offering special discounts for arriving one day before staying one day after the meeting. This is especially true for properties located in leisure and resort areas where attendees may have a reason to extend their stay. Promotions such as "stay four nights; get the fifth night free" or "come early; stay late" are examples of programs designed to increase LOS and the property's RevPar.

The average LOS is important to any leisure or business hotel. Operationally, as LOS increases, housekeeping costs decrease, because the time and material costs

During high-demand periods, such as graduations or home football games, hotels near colleges and universities may decide to set a minimum length of stay for guests requesting reservations.

required to clean a stayover room are almost always lower than those required for a check-out. At the front desk, it is less labor intensive to reserve a room for and to check in and check out one guest for three nights than it is to complete these processes for three guests each staying one night.

Room Rate Management

Guests are becoming increasingly sophisticated about locating, comparing, and selecting their hotels. In most consumer surveys, the location of a hotel is the most important reason for its selection by a guest. The second most important consideration is price (i.e., room rate). Many guests will travel a significant distance from their desired location to secure a room with a lower room rate. The decision to select a hotel based on its location and rate is most often made without guests contacting the hotel directly. Instead, they receive their information from one or more varieties of revenue generators: the hotel's franchisor-operated or independently affiliated **central reservation system (CRS),** property-level reservation agents, the sales department, e-distribution channels, and the property's own Web site.

FRONT OFFICE SEMANTICS

Central reservation system (CRS): Entity, operated by a franchisor or independently affiliated, that offers potential guests the opportunity to make reservations at the entity's affiliated (branded) hotels by telephone, fax, or the Internet. Used as in, "What percentage of our transient business last month was generated through the *CRS*?"

Each revenue generator is managed by either the FOM (in the case of property-level reservationists) or by the DOSM (in the case of the sales department). In some circumstances, the management of one or more revenue generators may be shared.

When different departments within a hotel are responsible for managing revenue generation, difficulties can arise. Assume the DOSM of a 300-room property won a group bid for 100 room nights during a slow period for the hotel. The DOSM offered the group a rate of $100 per night ($10 below the hotel's normal ADR), and two **comp** rooms for every 50 rooms picked up by the group. Assume also that two days before the group's arrival, the demand for these rooms was still light, and that the FOM instructed reservationists to quote a rate of $75 per night to guests calling the hotel directly for the same arrival and departure dates as group members. Further instructions were to post this reduced rate on the hotel's Web site. When this strategy was implemented, group members (who can easily access the hotel's rates via the Web site) began to cancel their room reservations within the group block and rebook the lower-priced rooms on the Web site.

FRONT OFFICE SEMANTICS

Comp: Short for *complimentary* or *no charge* for a product (room) or service.

The result of this scenario is likely to be reduced RevPar for the hotel as well as an unhappy group organizer (because the reduced pickup in the group block will yield a reduced number of comp rooms). In addition, imagine the difficulties at the front desk when arriving group members begin to share information about the two different rates they are paying. Finally, it is also *very* likely that conflict will result between the FOM and the DOSM because each, in attempting to meet individual goals, has created a difficult situation.

In a very large property the positions of revenue manager, FOM, and DOSM may be at the level of department head, which may entail supervising staffs of a significant size. As shown in Figure 6.2, room rate management tasks intermingle. Let's consider how they can be coordinated.

- *Revenue Manager and FOM.* Many guests locate a hotel through key word searches on search engines. Others may first locate a hotel on an Internet travel site such as Travelocity or Expedia; then they access the hotel's proprietary

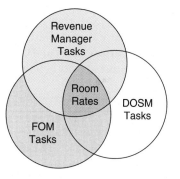

FIGURE 6.2   Shared responsibilities for room rate management.

Web site. Still others call the hotel directly to book a reservation. Regardless of the source, it is critical that the rates encountered by the guest be identical or, at least, internally consistent. Rates on a Web site and all other e-based delivery systems should be monitored (reviewed) regularly by the hotel's revenue manager. If rates are adjusted after consultation with the FOM, the information must be relayed to the hotel's in-house reservations staff. This is true of rates to be charged for dates far into the future as well as for **day of.**

FRONT OFFICE SEMANTICS

Day of: Short for *day of arrival.* Used as in, "Let's hold the rates at $100 per night for the 22nd but re-examine that decision *day of.*"

- *Revenue Manager and DOSM.* Ideally, the hotel's plan for rate positioning is developed as part of the overall business and marketing plan developed by the hotel's DOSM and approved by the general manager. The plan should consider the hotel's competitive set, group bookings history, **rate resistance** as reported by the property's in-house reservationists, and the demand forecasts that include the period of time covered by the plan.

FRONT OFFICE SEMANTICS

Rate resistance: Refusal to make a reservation because the rate quoted is perceived to be too high.

The revenue manager and the DOSM need not schedule tedious meetings, but they must be able to make decisions, coordinate their efforts, and adjust rate strategies as conditions dictate. The DOSM should recognize that the revenue manager can provide important input about the number of rooms to be sold by group sales and the number to be held for transient guests.

For example, assume that a business-oriented hotel has 300 rooms. The hotel's sales department has a client that wants all 300 rooms on a Wednesday two months in the future. If the sales department makes the sale, no rooms will be available on that Wednesday night for any other guests. Assume also that the hotel has a core of approximately 50 transient business guests who check in every Monday and stay through Friday morning. In this case, the decision to make the group sale would mean that some revenue generated from the 300-room group would merely **displace** a significant amount of revenue that the hotel would have received from its 50 transient business travelers. Each of these frequent guests would now be staying at another property, and they may be sufficiently upset to stay there again.

FRONT OFFICE SEMANTICS

Displace (revenue): To substitute one source of revenue for another.

- *Revenue Manager, FOM, and DOSM.* Every individual reservation made through the hotel's front office, as well as every group room sale made by a hotel's sales department, affects the property's revenue forecasts and, therefore, affects rate management. Methods used by the revenue manager, FOM, and

DOSM to share information and to coordinate their activities vary between properties. Nevertheless, collaboration can be achieved through periodic updates that involve all members of the revenue management team. Failure to coordinate efforts can result in presentation of an inconsistent or even incoherent rate message. In some cases, consumers may correctly perceive that a hotel that cannot manage to get its pricing structure straight may well have the same problem when it comes to serving them as guests.

Management of room rates is a critical activity. Properly coordinated within the hotel, it helps to maximize RevPar. Improperly done, it can damage a hotel's reputation, alienate guests, create unnecessary rate resistance, and actually reduce occupancies and ADRs.

Room Rate Economics

Any serious exploration of hotel room rates and their management must include detailed information about room rate economics. The study of **economics** related to room rates (1) examines the social science associated with the making, marketing and consumption of goods and services and (2) considers how the forces of **supply** and **demand** allocate scarce resources (such as hotel rooms). Revenue managers must know and use **room rate economics** to price rooms and to understand how consumers react to the pricing strategies they use.

FRONT OFFICE SEMANTICS

Economics: Social science associated with the making, marketing, and consumption of goods and services and how the forces of supply and demand allocate scarce resources.

Supply: Total amount of a good or service available for sale.

Demand: Total amount of a good or service consumers want to buy at a specific price.

Room rate economics: Process by which revenue managers price rooms while considering how consumers may react to the pricing strategies that are used.

The fundamental rules of economics of most importance to hoteliers differ based on the time frame examined. In a short-term time frame, the **law of demand** is most important.

FRONT OFFICE SEMANTICS

Law of demand: Concept of economics that recognizes when supply is held constant, an increase in demand results in an increase in selling price. Conversely, with supply held constant, a decrease in demand leads to a decreased selling price.

Understanding the law of demand is critical because, unlike managers in other industries, hoteliers cannot increase their inventory levels (supply) in response to known (or projected) increases in demand. The ability to comprehend the impact of this fundamental concept is a most critical characteristic of outstanding revenue managers.

To illustrate, assume that a city will be the site of a major annual convention to be held 12 months from now. The convention will attract enough attendees to sell all hotel rooms in the city. Despite the fact that demand will increase greatly for the several days of the convention, the number of hotel rooms available to be sold (supply) will remain constant. New hotels cannot be conceived, financed, designed, and constructed in 12 months. Hoteliers cannot add more rooms to their existing inventory, nor would it be advisable to do so if they could, because demand for these extra rooms will disappear when the convention ends. Contrast this situation to the taxicab business in the same city. Taxicab managers will likely increase the number of cabs available during the convention. They may extend the hours drivers are on duty, add more vehicles, secure additional drivers, or use a combination of these strategies.

The impact of the law of demand on hotel inventory is immense and twofold. In addition to recognizing that the short-term supply of rooms cannot be increased, outstanding revenue managers understand that their own inventory of rooms is highly perishable. In contrast, consider, the situation of a shoe store manager in the convention city. If on the Monday the convention begins, a specific pair of shoes does not sell, the manager can try to sell that pair of shoes on Tuesday. If the hotel does not sell room 101 on Monday night, it will never be able to sell that room on that night, and the potential revenue that would be generated from the sale is lost forever.

Now assume that at one minute before closing, a specific pair of shoes has not sold. Also assume that the store manager knows that at one minute after closing, these shoes will disappear forever. How should the store manager price those shoes if a customer walks into the store at one minute before closing? Understanding the shoe store manager's dilemma in this situation is the key to understanding the challenges of a hotel's revenue manager. In a hotel, unsold inventory vanishes forever!

All hoteliers must also understand the **law of supply** because of its long-term impact. The price a hotel charges for its rooms is influenced by many factors. One of the most important is the number of rooms (supply) available relative to the extent of demand for these rooms. Consider, for example, a city in which the average demand (all sources) for rooms during an entire week consists of 600 room nights. Assume also that the total number of rooms available to house these travelers is 1,000; five hotels each offer 200 rooms for sale. The citywide occupancy rate is 60 percent (600 rooms ÷ 1,000 rooms = 60 percent). If one of the hotels closed and the demand for rooms remained unchanged, the occupancy rate would increase to 75 percent (600 rooms ÷ [1,000 rooms − 200 rooms] = 75 percent). If this happened, the laws of supply and demand would likely affect the pricing strategy implemented by each hotel's revenue manager.

FRONT OFFICE SEMANTICS

Law of supply: Concept of economics that recognizes when demand is held constant, an increase in supply leads to a decreased selling price. Conversely, when demand is held constant, a decrease in supply leads to an increased selling price.

Now, assume that a new hotel with 200 rooms opened in the city. If the demand for rooms remained the same, the occupancy levels for the hotels would now be 50 percent (600 rooms ÷ [1,000 rooms + 200 rooms] = 50 percent). Again, prices for hotel rooms would likely be affected by the laws of supply and demand. In long term, new hotel openings (which create additions to supply) and hotel closings (which yield reductions in supply) affect the number of rooms available to sell. Therefore, if demand is unchanged, the pricing strategies for these rooms will likely be affected.

The supply (number) of rooms in a market area is relatively easy for revenue managers to assess. When they have determined the amount of supply and have accurately estimated room demand, effective pricing decisions can be made. If, however, revenue managers significantly overestimate or underestimate demand, critical errors can be made as room rates are established and marketed. That is why an FOM's (or revenue manager's) ability to accurately forecast demand (see Chapter 5) is so critical to a hotel's financial success. By combining knowledge of supply (which is readily known) and forecast data (which help to estimate demand) with an understanding of the various rate types used in the industry, revenue managers can best manage the relationship between guestroom supply and demand.

Rate Types

When revenue managers consider a hotel's room rates, they must generally consider multiple **rate types.** Because of the importance of room rates, revenue managers must become familiar with the common rate types used in most hotels.

FRONT OFFICE SEMANTICS

Rate type: Single (unique) rate for a specific type of room that is programmed into a hotel's PMS.

Recall from Chapter 4 that *rack rate* is the price at which a hotel sells its rooms when no discounts of any kind are offered to the guests. Rack rates, however, typically vary by the type of room. For example, the rack rate for a hotel's best, or most popular, room will be higher than that for its least popular room. Larger rooms, suites and rooms with special amenities, views, or other features typically have their own unique rack rates. Figure 6.3 lists the rack rates that might be associated with a midsize convention hotel (e.g., the Altoona Hotel) with a fairly limited number of different room types.

FRONT OFFICE SEMANTICS

Concierge level: Section of a hotel (usually with restricted access) reserved for special guests who pay a higher rate.

Note that at the Altoona Hotel rack rates vary by bed type (kings are more expensive than doubles), by amenities (executive rooms are likely to have features not found in standard rooms), by location (concierge-level rooms are more expensive than rooms not located on restricted floors), and by size (suites are more expensive than rooms). Some larger hotels may have dozens of different room types, each with

Effective 1/1/200X	
Room type	**Rack rate**
Standard double	$109
Standard king	$119
Executive double	$149
Executive king	$164
Executive double (**concierge level**)	$199
Executive king (concierge level)	$214
Double parlor suite	$269
King parlor suite	$289

FIGURE 6.3   Rack rates for the Altoona Hotel.

A hotel room with luxurious amenities typically sells at a higher rate than a room without amenities.

its own unique rack rate. Even the smallest of hotels have several room types and, therefore, multiple rack rates.

Some hotels experience strong seasonal demand. For example, hotels near mountains that are good for skiing have high occupancy during the ski season but may experience lower occupancy in the off-season and will likely respond by varying rack rates. These hotels, then, have a **seasonal rate** that is higher (or lower) than the standard rack rate.

FRONT OFFICE SEMANTICS

Rate (seasonal): Increase or decrease in rack rate based on the dates when the room is rented. For example, a beachfront hotel may have a seasonal rate offered in the summer with a lower "winter" rate offered in the off-season.

In some cases, revenue managers create **special event rates.** Sometimes referred to as *super* or *premium* rack, these rates are used when a hotel is confident of very high demand levels.

FRONT OFFICE SEMANTICS

Rate (special event): Temporary increase in rack rate based on a specific event such as a concert, sporting event, or holiday. Sometimes known as *super* or *premium* rack. Examples are rates for rooms during New Year's Eve in Manhattan and during Super Bowl weekend in the host city.

Earlier in this chapter, you saw how hotels create negotiated rates for selected guests. In most cases, the negotiated rates also vary by room type. In addition to rack and negotiated rates, hotels typically offer **corporate rates, government rates,** and **group rates.**

FRONT OFFICE SEMANTICS

Rate (corporate): Special rate offered to individual business travelers.

Rate (government): Special rate offered to the employees of local, state, or federal governments.

Rate (group): Special rate offered to a hotel's large-volume guestroom purchasers.

When a hotel creates a package, the **package rate** charged must be sufficient to ensure that all costs associated with the package have been considered.

FRONT OFFICE SEMANTICS

Rate (package): Special rate that allows a guest to pay one price for all of the features and amenities included in the package.

Some package rates are used so frequently that they have become a standard in the industry: the **American plan (AP), modified American plan (MAP),** and **all-inclusive** plan.

FRONT OFFICE SEMANTICS

American Plan (AP): Special rate that includes specifically identified guest meals (typically, breakfast, lunch, and dinner).

Modified American Plan (MAP): Special rate that includes a specifically identified guest meal (typically one per day—often breakfast).

All-inclusive (rate): Special rate that typically includes all guest meals and unlimited beverages as well as the use of specifically identified hotel amenities and services.

Although the American Plan and Modified American Plan are popular in many resort areas, most full-service American hotels continue to operate under the **European Plan (EP);** that is, they provide no meals with the room charge. In response to the complimentary breakfasts offered by most limited-service hotels, some full-service hotels have adopted a variation of the MAP and offer guests some type of partial or full complimentary breakfast.

FRONT OFFICE SEMANTICS

European Plan (EP): Room rate that does not include guest meals.

Two other common rate types are the **day rate** and the **half-day rate.**

FRONT OFFICE SEMANTICS

Day rate: Special rate that typically includes 8- to 12-hour use (but not overnight use) of a room.

Half-day rate: Special rate that typically includes 1- to 4-hour use (but not overnight use) of a room.

These two rate types can result in hotel occupancy levels in excess of 100 percent. Effective marketing of these rates, especially in areas that generate significant need for short-term room use (e.g., near airports and train stations), can contribute positively to a hotel's RevPar.

Revenue managers and FOMs can create discounts at various percentage or dollar levels for each rate type we have examined. A hotel with multiple room types and multiple rate plans may have literally hundreds of rate types programmed into its PMS. In addition, the use of one or more **fade rate** levels can create dozens more.

FRONT OFFICE SEMANTICS

Fade (rate): Reduced rate authorized for use when a guest seeking a reservation exhibits price (rate) resistance. Sometimes called *flex* rate.

A fade rate is initiated when a potential guest exhibits price resistance after being quoted a room rate. For example, a family traveling on vacation may enter a hotel lobby as a walk-in and inquire about renting a room. If the front desk agent quotes a price of $100 per night and believes these potential guests will decline the rate to seek less costly accommodations, the agent may be empowered to fade, or flex, the rate to a lower level. In this example, for instance, the agent may be authorized to fade (reduce) the original quote by $10 in an effort to sell the room.

The use of fade rates requires excellent training of front desk agents so that they know how to justify the fade, or else sophisticated travelers will wonder why they were not offered the more attractive rate originally. Fade rates can, however, be very effective. In a hotel located at the entrance/exit of a major interstate highway, large numbers of travelers may arrive at the hotel without a reservation and inquire about rates. When rate resistance is encountered, some FOMs authorize their front desk agents to fade the rate *if* it is the guest's first time visiting the hotel. Most travelers will likely be first-time visitors, so this fade approach may be effective and will likely be perceived as a logical marketing strategy to many potential guests.

Given the number of room types found in a typical hotel and the number of rate types associated with each room, you can appreciate the complexity of managing a hotel's room rates. Add to that challenge the fact that each rate type can be discounted or increased by any number of percentages and at various times of the year or in response to specific special events. Now the true intricacies of the rate management process become apparent. Despite the difficulties involved, however, initial room rates must be determined.

Rate Determination

Despite some arguments to the contrary, this old saying likely applies to the development of a hotel's rack (standard) room rate: There is nothing new under the sun. Professional hoteliers have, for centuries, been required to effectively price and market their rooms. A uniquely modern (and many times, unfortunate) belief of some contemporary hoteliers is that there are "new" ways to manage hotels (including the pricing of rooms) and that these new methods are superior to the "old" ways. Some hoteliers appear more interested in pursuing "today's" methods than in reflecting on lessons learned from history. As a result, looking backward is not considered valuable. However, contemporary hoteliers can benefit from understanding the strengths and weaknesses of traditional room pricing (and other operational) techniques. Then they can incorporate the best historical tactics into modern pricing methods, which are increasingly dependent on and must be compatible with e-distribution.

Traditional Pricing Strategies   In the past, hoteliers wanted to maximize their profits and charge the highest rate possible for their rooms. They still do. The rate cannot be so high, however, that it discourages guests from staying at the hotel. Similarly, the rate cannot be so low that it prevents the hotel from being profitable. Therefore, the room rate should not result from a mere guess about its appropriateness; ideally, it should evolve from a rational examination of guest demand and a hotel's costs of operation. Mathematically, such a rate should be easy to compute with specific and accurate assumptions.

Even the most current textbooks about hotel accounting or front office management include a description of the Hubbart room rate formula. Known by hoteliers worldwide, this formula for determining room rates was developed in the mid-1950s by two national accounting firms (Horwath & Horwath and Harris Kerr Forster). The model was named in honor of Roy Hubbart, a Chicago hotelier and a major advocate of the formula's approach.

Essentially, the formula seeks to determine what a hotel's ADR *should* be to reach the hotel owner's financial goals. To compute the Hubbart formula, specific financial and operational assumptions must be produced. These include dollar amounts for property construction (or purchase), total cost of operations, number of rooms to be sold, and the owner's desired **return on investment (ROI)** on the hotel's land, building, and **FF&E (furniture, fixtures, and equipment).**

FRONT OFFICE SEMANTICS

Return on investment (ROI): Percentage rate of return achieved on the money invested in a hotel property.

FF&E: Short for the furniture, fixtures, and equipment used by a hotel to service its guests.

The Hubbart formula continues to survive, probably less for its tangible usefulness in determining ADR than for its systematic evaluation of the factors important to those who buy and operate hotels. To illustrate the formula's use, assume an investor has decided to pay $8 million for a 200-room hotel and desires a 12 percent return on the investment. Assume that the owner will incur mortgage repayments of $750,000 per year and additional fixed costs of $250,000 per year. Assume also that, at a 60 percent occupancy level, direct operating costs related to providing rooms and food and beverage services to the hotel's guests will be $2 million annually, and indirect expenses related to operating the hotel will be $1 million annually. Finally, assume that the investor wants to generate a profit of $125,000 per year from the food and beverage department and $25,000 from telephone charges and all other non-rooms departments.

The steps required to compute the Hubbart formula in this example are as follows:

1. *Calculate the hotel's target profits.* Multiply the required ROI by the owner's investment:

$$\$8,000,000 \times .12 = \$960,000$$

2. *Calculate all fixed expenses.* Include estimates of all fixed costs including leases, depreciation, interest expense, property taxes, insurance, mortgages, and fixed management fees. In this example, the total cost of mortgage and other fixed costs is:

$$\$750,000 + \$250,000 = \$1,000,000$$

3. *Calculate all operational costs.* Include expenses directly associated with selling and cleaning rooms and providing food services. Include all costs incurred to operate the front office. Additional direct operating costs include housekeeping-related expenses for labor, guestroom supplies, laundry, and cleaning the hotel's public spaces. (Note that the expenses required to operate a food and beverage department are considered a direct expense of selling rooms.)

   In addition to direct operating expenses, indirect operating expenses that cannot readily be assigned to the front office, housekeeping, or the food and beverage department must be computed. These will include a variety of costs such as those for administrative and general tasks, data processing, human resources, marketing, property operation and maintenance, franchise fees, and energy costs. In this example, operating costs are:

$$\$2,000,000 + \$1,000,000 = \$3,000,000$$

4. *Calculate non-rooms income.* Hotels can make profits from a food and beverage department or from telephone toll charges as well as from other minor sources unique to a specific hotel. If these sources generate a loss, the Hubbart formula requires the amount of the loss to be entered into the formula. In this example, the profit from non-rooms departments would be:

$$\$125,000 + \$25,000 = \$150,000$$

5. *Determine the total room revenue required to meet the hotel's goals and obligations.* Sum the owner's desired ROI ($960,000), hotel's fixed expense ($750,000 + $250,000), direct expenses ($2,000,000), and all indirect operating costs ($1,000,000). Then *subtract* the amount of non-room revenue anticipated by the hotel ($125,000 + $25,000). If there was a loss from the non-rooms departments, this loss would be *added* to the total room revenue required to meet all of the hotel's goals and obligations. In this example, total required room revenue is $4,810,000:

$960,000	+	$1,000,000	+	$2,000,000	+	$1,000,000	−	$150,000
ROI	+	Fixed expenses	+	Direct expenses	+	Indirect expenses	−	Non-rooms revenue

6. *Forecast the number of rooms to be sold based on estimated occupancy.* Multiply the number of rooms available by the projected occupancy rate. In this example:

$$(200 \text{ rooms} \times 365 \text{ days}) \times .60 = 43,800 \text{ rooms}$$

7. *Calculate the hotel's required ADR.* Divide the required room revenue (see Step 5) by the number of rooms to be sold:

$$\$4,810,000 \div 43,800 = \$109.82$$

The seven steps required to compute the Hubbart formula are summarized in Figure 6.4.

The Hubbart formula is useful because it requires the user to consider the owner's investment goals and the costs of operating the hotel before determining the room rate. It has been criticized for relying on assumptions about the reasonableness of an owner's desired ROI (Step 1) and the need to know operating costs (Step 3) that are affected by the quality of the hotel's management. Another criticism is the formula's requirement that the room rate compensate for operating losses incurred by other areas (e.g., from food and beverage operations). The formula's primary shortcoming, however, relates to the number of rooms forecasted to be sold (Step 6).

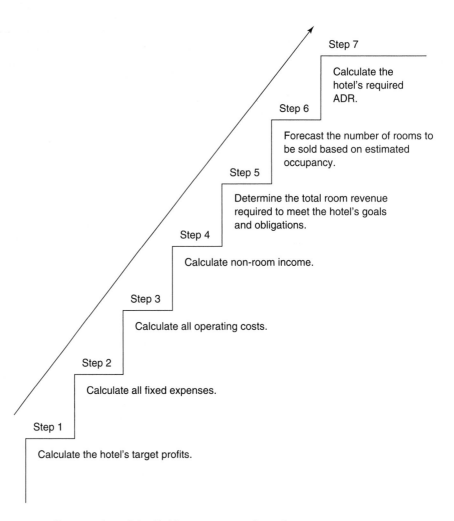

FIGURE 6.4   Computation of the Hubbart room rate formula.

The number of rooms sold usually depends on the rate charged for rooms. However, the Hubbart formula requires that the number of rooms sold be estimated *before* knowing the rate at which rooms will sell.

Despite its limitations, the Hubbart formula remains an important way to view the necessity of developing a room rate with these characteristics:

- Provides an adequate return to the hotel's owner
- Covers the hotel's fixed costs
- Considers the hotel's operating costs
- Accounts for all the hotel's non-room income (or loss)
- Results in a definite and justifiable rate goal

Hoteliers have used other methods to determine room rate. One of the most interesting applies the "$1 per $1,000 rule." Critics and proponents frequently argue the merits of this approach, which was introduced in the 1940s; however, even with its limitations, it has remained helpful. Essentially, the rule states that for every $1,000 invested in a hotel, the property should support $1 in ADR. Some proponents feel the investment amount should include FF&E; most do not. Because the rate is so closely tied to occupancy level, most proponents also believe a 70 percent occupancy assumption (and appropriate management) is required for the formula to be useful. Also, the computed rate must be *increased* proportionately if occupancy is below 70 percent and decreased proportionately if it exceeds that level.

Few would argue that the costs of items such as the land and labor required to build a hotel are the same in Manhattan and rural Georgia. However, advocates defend this rule of thumb because areas in which building or purchase costs are higher tend to be the areas where ADRs can also be higher.

To illustrate the rule's use, assume that an investor is considering the purchase of a 117-room, limited-service hotel for $6 million. The $1 per $1,000 rule would be computed as follows:

$$\$6,000,000 \quad \div \quad 117 \quad \div \quad \$1,000 = \$51.28$$

$$\text{Purchase price} \div \frac{\text{Number}}{\text{of rooms}} \div \$1,000 = \frac{\text{Rate to be}}{\text{achieved}}$$

Assume also that this buyer projects a 60 percent (not 70 percent) occupancy rate. Thus, the occupancy rate projected is 14.3 percent lower than the rule's standard ([70 percent − 60 percent] ÷ 70 = 14.3 percent), so the rate to be achieved would be *increased* by that amount as follows:

$$\$51.28 \quad \times \quad .143 \quad + \quad \$51.28 \quad = \quad \$58.61$$

$$\frac{\text{Rate to be}}{\text{achieved}} \times \text{Adjustment} + \frac{\text{Rate to be}}{\text{achieved}} = \frac{\text{Adjusted rate}}{\text{to be achieved}}$$

The rate computed using the $1 per $1,000 rule does not become the hotel's rack rate; rather, it is the hotel's ADR. In this example, the hotel's owner may establish a rack rate of, for example, $89 per night. However, the owner would seek an ADR of $58.61 after all rate discounts. Few sophisticated investors would use the $1 per $1,000 rule exclusively to evaluate the feasibility of a hotel purchase. The rule does, however, promote the tendency for hotel buyers to discuss selling prices in terms of a hotel's **cost per key,** which is a mathematical variation of the $1 per $1,000 rule.

FRONT OFFICE SEMANTICS

Cost per key: Average purchase price of a hotel's guestroom expressed in thousands of dollars. For example, a 200-room hotel offered for $12 million is selling at a cost of $60,000 per key ($12,000,000 ÷ 200 rooms = $60,000). Sometimes called *cost per room.*

Another method of rate determination involves basing rates on the square footage of guestrooms (assuming that a hotel's larger rooms should sell for more than its smaller rooms). Rates have also been determined by various "ideal" sales levels of the different hotel room types available to be sold. These rates include those derived from **bottom-up selling** (selling the hotel's least-expensive rooms first), **top-down selling** (selling the hotel's most expensive rooms first), and pricing schemes that consider an equal sale of higher- and lower-priced rooms.

FRONT OFFICE SEMANTICS

Bottom-up selling: Tactic to first sell the hotel's least expensive rooms.

Top-down selling: Tactic to first sell the hotel's most expensive rooms.

Web-Influenced Pricing Strategies   Contemporary hoteliers understand that properly pricing their rooms is critical to attracting first-time and repeat business. Close examination of many tactics used by revenue managers reveals that they often use one or more of the following nontraditional methods to establish rates:

- *Competitive pricing.* Charge what the competition charges.
- *Follow the leader pricing.* Charge what the dominant hotel in the area charges.
- *Prestige pricing.* Charge the highest rate in the area and justify it with better products, better service levels, or both.
- *Discount pricing.* Reduce rates below that of the likely competitors without considering operating costs.

All of these pricing systems appear to be seat-of-the-pants approaches, because they reflect supply, demand, and the psychological aspects of consumer behavior without considering a hotel's cost structure. Closer examination, however, reveals that they are also logical responses to a simple but vitally important observation: *The world of rate determination as known by previous generations of hoteliers is gone forever.* The best revenue managers understand this. Hotel investors continue to use traditional accounting formulas to determine whether specific hotels are a wise purchase. Determining the

Hotels that are grouped in close proximity may carefully monitor each other's room rates to best implement their competitive pricing strategies.

proper room rate to charge, however, is more complex and more important than it has ever been. The reasons for the change in rate-setting "rules" are straightforward: the consumer's use of the Internet and the competition's use of the Internet.

MODERN FRONT OFFICE ISSUES AND TACTICS

Hubbart? What Hubbart?

The events of September 11, 2001 devastated the hotel business in New York City in the short run. Not surprisingly, in the immediate aftermath of the attack that destroyed the World Trade Center, convention groups canceled their events, business and leisure travelers to the area canceled most of their trips, and occupancy rates plummeted. The rates suggested by formulas for a specific property were irrelevant; rates were affected by events, and all rates went down.

On a smaller scale, but in response to significant events in their market areas, modern hoteliers must manage rates *not* on the basis of what conditions *should be* but on what they *are*. Competitive hotels will be doing the same. If a hotel is to obtain a fair share of the market, its revenue manager must respond—quickly—to the events and circumstances that affect room rates in either a positive or negative direction.

Today, revenue managers must determine room rates based on the realities of a challenging environment unknown to previous generations of hoteliers. To better understand today's rate determination realities, visit a consumer-friendly Web site such as www.sidestep.com. Within seconds users can compare alternative room rates for all of the hotels in their desired travel area. Any traveler with access to the Web can compare the room rate offered by one revenue manager to the rates offered by all of the competitors. Users can contrast the prices of well-known hotel brands and franchises and independents. They can then book their rooms online, as rapidly increasing numbers of travelers choose to do.

Just as consumers can easily compare prices, so can a hotel's major competitors. Gone are the days when night auditors or others in the Front Office staff conducted the nightly **call-around** and used the information obtained (often of questionable accuracy) to make decisions about what the hotel's rates should be.

FRONT OFFICE SEMANTICS

Call-around: Telephone "shopping" technique in which a hotel staff member calls competitive hotels to inquire about room rates and availability. The information is used by the calling hotel to help determine room rates.

The call-around was standard practice as late as the early 2000s. Now, however, revenue managers can use one of many Web sites (e.g., www.travelaxe.com) for the following purposes:

- Select competitive hotels whose rates are to be monitored
- Obtain real-time room rates offered by these hotels on any number of travel Web sites advertising the rates
- Search the rates and Web sites as frequently as desired
- Perform rate comparisons by specific check-in and check-out dates
- Make rate comparisons based on LOS

- Assess rate comparisons based on room type
- Analyze rate comparisons based on **market code**
- Develop rate comparisons based on **track code**
- Group and print data by competitive hotel, specific travel Web sites, arrival dates, and other factors important to the revenue manager

---

FRONT OFFICE SEMANTICS

Market code: Guest types differentiated by sales source. Typical market codes include transient and group.

Track code: Guest types differentiated by traveler demographics. Typical track codes include those related to the purpose of the traveler's trip (such as business [corporate] versus leisure) and those related to LOS (transient versus long-term stay). A track code can be created for any traveler demographic determined important enough to create and monitor a reservation field in the PMS.

Revenue managers who think they are too busy to closely monitor their competitors' rate information might use the service of companies such as RateGain (www.rategain.com). These companies will create daily, weekly, or on-demand competitor reports and e-mail them to the contracting revenue manager whenever a competitor's rates rise or fall below preselected thresholds.

When guests and competitors can discover rates online, the dynamics of rate making change. Rates are often set independent of traditional operating cost considerations. Instead, the hotel's rates are more heavily influenced by the laws of supply and demand. Assume that on a given Saturday all similar hotels in a market area offer guestrooms in the range of $100 to $150 per night. It is difficult for a single hotel of the same type to command a rate of $250 per night even if its operating costs justify this rate. If the revenue manager of that hotel placed a $250 per night rate on the hotel's Web site, it is unlikely that any but perhaps the most brand-loyal consumers would select the property. The Web is now the major source of traveler information related to hotel room prices. Senior citizens, one of the last demographic groups to log on, are using the Web in ever larger numbers. Future generations of travelers will grow up without knowing anything except the Web as a source of travel-pricing information, and the impact of that fact is tremendously significant.

In the past, if a traveler called a hotel directly, obtained the rack rate, and booked the reservation, it would have been perceived by the hotel to be a successful sale. Today, after making the hotel reservation, the traveler could go online to shop for an even lower price for the same room. If the traveler finds a lower rate, he or she could recontact the hotel to secure the new, lower rate. This consumer would likely feel frustrated that the hotel did not offer its lower rate initially! As a result of this new operating paradigm, **rate integrity (parity)** across all of a hotel's varied **distribution channels** is critical. In fact, it is of such vital importance to FOMs and revenue managers that Chapter 7 is devoted to the topic.

FRONT OFFICE SEMANTICS

Rate integrity (parity): Degree to which a hotel's room rates are comparable regardless of the distribution channel on which they are found. Sometimes called *rate parity* or another term that implies rate consistency.

Distribution channel: Source of potential room reservations. Sources include the hotel's direct telephone number, its franchisor-maintained Web site, its own Web site, all third-party Web sites advertising the hotel's rates, the front desk (for walk-in guests), and the hotel's sales department.

Rate integrity implies that rates across all distribution channels are comparable, but they do not necessarily have to be identical. As we will see in Chapter 7, there are several reasons for revenue managers to determine and market different rates for different distribution channels, just as "yesterday's" revenue managers created different rates for different room types. Today's revenue managers still face the room type challenge, but they also face the challenge of managing distribution channels in an environment transparent to consumers and competitors.

Modern pricing techniques cannot involve seat-of-the-pants approaches. Instead, they must be highly sophisticated and logical reactions to real-world information and resulting supply and demand forces examined earlier in this section. Revenue managers must use PMS information along with specific pricing strategies that are adjusted (often daily) to meet the known realities of their market areas. As they do so, revenue managers can have a tremendous influence on increasing their property's RevPar.

SECTION REVIEW AND DISCUSSION QUESTIONS

Section Objective: Explain the revenue manager's role in establishing room rates by applying information about rate types and rate determination factors and by considering traditional and Web-based pricing strategies.

Section Summary: The primary role of the revenue manager is to maximize RevPar. Many complex factors must be considered in efforts to do so. Discounts from rack rate may be allowed on specific dates or as the number of room nights increases according to the laws of supply and demand. Discounts may also be offered to members of specific groups, government and military staff members, and to the clergy and selected other guests.

Large properties typically have a full-time revenue manager with a staff to do all of the work that is required. In smaller properties, revenue management duties may be assumed by the FOM or the DOSM, or both. In still smaller properties, the general manager likely assumes the role of revenue manager.

The typical hotel has many types of rooms, all of which may have different rack rates and rates that vary based on discounting structure. Some traditional approaches to determining rates still have conceptual impact. For example, the Hubbart formula seeks to determine what a hotel's ADR should be to reach financial goals, and a more simple rule of thumb suggests charging $1 in ADR for every $1,000 invested in a hotel. However, consumers and hotel competitors now have real-time web access to rates being charged by a hotel and its competitors for current and future dates. The dynamics of rate making have changed, and the laws of supply and demand tend to be more important than traditional considerations of operating costs.

Discussion Questions:

1. Assume that you are traveling to a specific area and are on a relatively tight budget. How would you determine hotels located at your destination? How would you determine room charges? How important would the room rate be in your hotel selection? What other factors would be important?

2. This section of the chapter provided examples of times when a reduction in a specific type of rack rate might be in order. It also mentioned the possibility of increasing the rate beyond the rack rate. Can you think of times when the laws of supply and demand suggest that room rates can be charged in excess of the rack rate? As a revenue manager, are there times when you would not do so, even if there was an excess demand for rooms? What, if any, legal implications might relate to room charges in excess of the rack rate?

3. Assume that you will be attending a meeting and your group's meeting planner has negotiated a specified rate with the host hotel. Would you consider doing an independent search for a lower room rate? If so, how would you conduct the search? What would you do if you found a lower room rate at a property that competes with the host hotel?

REVENUE MANAGEMENT TOOLS

Some revenue managers consistently do a better job than others (recall the example of Noel and JeAnna early in this chapter). Like any hotel staff members, revenue managers must have the proper tools to perform well, and they must learn how to skillfully use

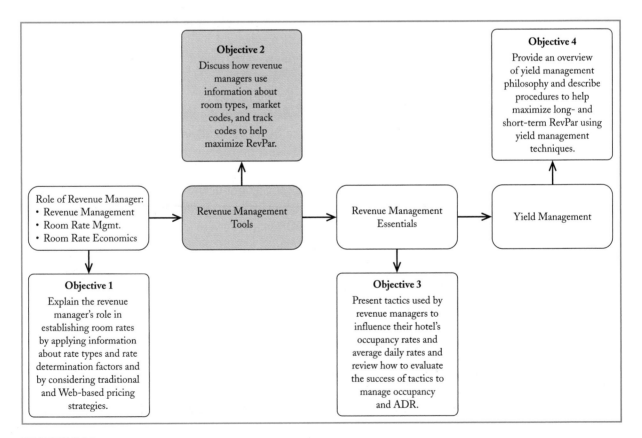

ROADMAP 6.2

these tools. Education, experience, and talent are essential personal traits, but all revenue managers can use additional RevPar maximizing tools to their hotel's advantage. As noted in Roadmap 6.2, this section of the chapter reviews the three most important tools of revenue management: room types, market codes, and track codes.

Room Types

In the revenue manager's ideal world, every guest making a reservation would want the highest-priced room available when the reservation was requested. In fact, many guests seek the lowest-cost room available, and it is a challenge for the reservations agent or front desk agent to upsell rooms to the greatest degree possible. Doing so benefits the hotel because of the increased ADR, and the guest, who will have purchased a room that, although more expensive, will better meet his or her needs.

Chapter 4 described how different room types do not necessarily sell at different ADRs. Most hotels will, for the same basic bed type, charge the same rate for a smoking-permitted room as for a nonsmoking room. Normally, however, revenue managers in hotels with legitimate and explainable multiple room types can create an effective upselling program to increase RevPar.

MODERN FRONT OFFICE ISSUES AND TACTICS

Upselling the Hard Way

Even more so than in the past, today's consumers want to know if the room rates they are paying make sense so that they can judge value. Consumers understand that a hotel's most elegant suite costs more than the same hotel's smallest room. They may not know, however, why an executive king costs more than a standard king. Hoteliers may know the fine differences in room types; most consumers do not.

When various room types are created for legitimate reasons, upselling a guest from a lower-priced to a higher-priced room type becomes the job of the front desk agent or reservations agent. Consider, however, the following all-too-real exchange that can occur when front office staff do not know the differences between the hotel's designated room types.

> *Desk agent:* Mr. Anthony, I see that you have reserved a king room for tonight; would you like to upgrade to an executive king for only $15 more?
>
> *Guest:* Well, I might be interested. What's the difference between the two rooms?
>
> *Desk agent:* As far as I know, it's $15.

All front office employees must be well trained to understand and appreciate the actual differences between the hotel's designated room types. If they do not, their upselling ability will be ineffective.

Hotel guests, like all consumers, appreciate having choices. Revenue managers can increase RevPar by working hard to promote and, in some cases, to create alternative room types. For example, assume that Loni is an FOM at a hotel constructed with 250 virtually identical rooms. The only discernible difference in room types at her hotel are bed type (king versus double), and the guest's smoking preference. The ADR for her hotel is approximately $125. In this situation, it might appear that the ability of Loni and her front office staff to upsell is limited. In fact, Loni, with the approval of her general manager, has created a special room type that is available on weekdays. Targeted toward business travelers, the program consists of selected nonsmoking

rooms with king-size beds; the rooms are outfitted with a complimentary office supply kit (e.g., pens, pencils, paper, stapler, paper clips and Post-it notes) placed on the
room's work desk. In addition, a late check-out of 5:00 p.m. is granted automatically
at time of registration, and an in-room continental breakfast is delivered between
6:00 a.m. and 9:00 a.m. as an additional complimentary amenity. These special rooms
are upsold for an additional $20 per night. Consider the conversation that might
ensue as Ms. Swanson, a guest with a reservation for a standard room on a weekday
night (Sunday through Thursday) checks into Loni's hotel.

> *Desk Agent:* Good evening Ms. Swanson, your reservation is for one room
> with a king size bed, at a rate of $125. Is that correct?
>
> *Ms. Swanson:* Yes, that's right.
>
> *Desk Agent:* Your room is ready now; however, since I see you are staying with
> us for one night, I would like to make you aware of a room special
> that I think you might really appreciate.
>
> *Ms. Swanson:* What is it?
>
> *Desk Agent:* We've selected exceptional rooms in the hotel that include all the
> office supplies you are likely to need during your trip, a compli-
> mentary in-room continental breakfast, and an automatic late
> check-out of 5:00 p.m. It's called an executive class room. It's a spe-
> cial upgrade, and the cost is only $20 more than our standard room.
>
> *Ms. Swanson:* That could be really helpful. I've got a 2:30 p.m. meeting near the
> hotel tomorrow, and the late check-out would give me a chance to
> return to the hotel after lunch and finish polishing my sales pres-
> entation. Thanks. I'll take the upgrade.

Loni's PMS will likely enable her to create an additional room type by simply
adding an "E" to the prefix (or suffix) of her existing room types. For example, the
NSK (nonsmoking, king-size bed) rooms would, under the new program, be separated into regular NSK (the standard room type) and ENSK (executive class, nonsmoking, king-size bed). Because of this change, Loni's staff will be able to upsell
selected hotel products and services.

Resourceful revenue managers know that creating room types with amenities
guests truly desire (1) allows them to offer their guests additional choices and
(2) creates an upselling potential even when the physical differences between
rooms are negligible. The key to success involves offering true value to guests.
Guests must be able to easily understand and appreciate the differences between
the room types offered if front desk agents are to successfully market these additional room types.

Actual room characteristics desired by guests vary by hotel. Figure 6.5 lists some
of the most common features that can differentiate rooms and allow the creation of
alternative room types. Some features can be helpful even when the differences in
actual room configuration are slight or nonexistent.

Market Codes

Nearly all hotels sell group or other discounted rooms; as a result, market codes can be
used to determine the proportion of total rooms sold that were allocated to these and
other market segments. Note that the term *market* actually has a variety of meanings
in the hotel industry. It can refer to the selling process, a specific target audience or,
in the case of market codes, a specific sales source or channel.

Feature	Examples
Location	Near convenient parking Beachfront Bayfront Secluded area Newly renovated area Restricted floor or area Lower floor Upper floor
View	Sunrise Sunset Beach Bay Other desirable view
Amenities	Larger square footage Unique square footage configuration Special room amenities Corner rooms All inclusive rates
Other	Special decor In-room spa Hospitality package (including robe, slippers, complimentary in-room movies, and newspaper)

FIGURE 6.5 Typical room features used to create alternative room types.

To illustrate the importance of market codes to revenue management, consider Figure 6.6. Note that the Altoona Hotel has an overall ADR of $100 ($600,000 ÷ 6,000 rooms). This ADR, however, is a combination of three distinctly different market code ADRs. The Altoona sells to transient guests and also offers discounted group rooms to large-volume purchasers. In addition, the hotel has signed a two-year agreement with an airline serving the local airport to house all the airline's flight crews and its distressed passengers who require overnight lodging. At the Altoona, airline-rented rooms are given the distinct PMS market-code of *contract*. In January, guests coded into the PMS as *transient* generated an ADR of $125. The group market-code rooms generated an ADR of $85 and the contract market-code achieved an ADR of $70.

Market code	Rooms sold	ADR	Total revenue
Transient	3,000	$125	$375,000
Group	1,000	$ 85	$ 85,000
Contract	2,000	$ 70	$140,000
Property total	**6,000**	**$100**	**$600,000**

Total rooms available = 9,300 (31 × 300)
Occupancy % = 64.5 % (6,000 rooms ÷ 9,300 rooms)
RevPar = $64.52 ($600,000 ÷ 9,300 rooms)

FIGURE 6.6 ADR by market code for the Altoona Hotel (300 rooms) for January 200X.

Recall from Chapter 4 that RevPar is computed by dividing the total number of rooms available for a selected time period *into* the total room revenue achieved during that same period. Therefore, the computation in Figure 6.6 is shown to be $600,000 ÷ 9,300 = $64.52. (Note that mathematically the same result is achieved by multiplying ADR times occupancy rate; in this example, $100 × 64.52 percent = $64.52.)

As can be seen in Figure 6.6, the proportion of rooms sold to various market codes significantly affects total RevPar. Group rooms and specially contracted rooms are typically sold at a rate lower than the hotel's overall ADR. This can be a good strategy when the additional occupancy levels gained (rooms sold) offset any negative effects of reduced overall ADR. When, however, lower-rated rooms are sold *instead* of higher-rated rooms that could have been sold, RevPar is affected negatively.

To illustrate, assume that the Altoona is located near a professional baseball stadium. The hotel typically sells out ($150 rack rate) during the professional team's Saturday night home games. A representative of a visiting baseball team inquires about renting 50 rooms at a reduced group rate to house the team during its next Saturday night game. If the Altoona agreed to do this, it would no doubt depress the ADR at a time (Saturday night) when the hotel could normally sell out at full rack rate. The revenue manager will likely decline this business based on the impact the market code ADR (group) will have on total RevPar: The sale of the lower-rated group rooms would simply displace the sale of higher-rated transient rooms.

As more rooms are sold at rates below the hotel's overall ADR, more rooms must be sold to maintain or improve total RevPar. As a result, the proper proportion of a hotel's rooms to be set aside for sale to transient guests and group guests or by special contract should be the subject of serious discussion in regular meetings between the DOSM, FOM, revenue manager, and general manager. In many cases, DOSMs are rewarded for increased group sales. Therefore, they often seek additional room allotments for groups. Conversely, FOMs are most often rewarded for their efforts in selling transient rooms, so they want as many rooms for this market code as possible. In these cases, the revenue manager must remain objective. Four principles will help revenue managers in allocation discussion of market codes:

- Maximize room sales whenever possible to the market code that will generate the greatest RevPar *not* the highest ADR or occupancy rate.
- Allocate rooms to heavily discounted groups or contract clients only when those rooms would likely go unsold.
- Consider the impact that market allocation decisions will have on all of the hotel's revenue generators.
- Consider the long- and short-term impact of market allocation decisions.

To illustrate these principles, let's return to the example of the visiting baseball team. First, make these assumptions:

- The team is seeking the hotel's $85 group rate.
- The visiting team will arrive on Friday night (the day before the game) and will depart on Monday morning (the second day after the game).
- The team will consume all meals (Friday night through Monday morning) in the hotel's banquet facilities.
- The team plays 15 games per year in the city, and only 3 of them are on weekends.

Now let's return to the four rev4enue management principles and match them with the characteristics of this potential business.

- A lower rate does not, by itself, mean that a piece of business should be refused. Remember that it is RevPar (not ADR or occupancy) that should be maximized.
- The Saturday night home games have traditionally created sellouts for the Altoona Hotel, but the occupancy data from the Friday night before and the Sunday night after these games are equally important considerations.
- The impact of the group's food purchases to the food and beverage department is a consideration.
- If, by securing the visiting team's business this first time, the Altoona could maintain it during periods that were not as busy (the 12 games that are not on Saturday night), the total value of the sale could be measured in terms of 15 stays (not just one stay), because the team will need a hotel for all of its games.

  A hotel that allocates too many group rooms, however, may displace regular transient guests, who must find alternative accommodations, at other hotels, and may not return. Few revenue managers would allocate 100 percent of a hotel's total room count to group rooms even when temporary demand for the property's group rooms is strong enough to do so.

The decision about when to accept or reject a specific piece of business is similar to that of considering when to allocate rooms to specific market codes. Each decision must be based on the unique characteristics of the sale, the dates involved, or both. Then the revenue manager must carefully consider the total revenue and long-term marketing impact before suggesting specific allocation levels.

Track Codes

Track codes, like market-codes, are used to segment travelers. Whereas market-code segments generally relate to group and transient guests, track codes make distinctions about guests within market-codes. It is possible to create any number of track codes that the hotel's management team will find useful. Figure 6.7 illustrates how a hotel could use track codes to further subdivide its market-codes. In this illustration, the Altoona Hotel's managers have created seven track codes. Each code is assigned a PMS code to be used when making guest reservations and, ultimately, for generation of summary reports.

Generally, the more information a hotel has about its current and prospective guests, the better it can serve them. Revenue managers should develop and monitor track codes that make sense for their specific hotels. These codes should be entered

Market code	Track code	PMS code
Transient	Leisure	TRL
	Corporate	TRC
	Government	TRG
Group	Leisure	GRL
	Corporate	GRC
	Government	GRG
Contract	Airline	CTA

FIGURE 6.7   Track and PMS codes for the Altoona Hotel.

Hotels can define their guests' unique characteristics by using track and market codes.

into the PMS, and the reservation fields containing them should be filled out each time a room reservation is made. This segmentation is important to revenue managers for several reasons:

- *Market size variation.* Hotels are commonly referred to being either business- or leisure-oriented. Although each hotel attracts a specific clientele, most hotels find that they actually serve multiple types of guests. For example, a large convention hotel might serve both corporate and leisure groups. Corporations may conduct employee training sessions, annual shareholder meetings, or events designed to reward the company's best performers. Leisure groups may meet for annual conventions, reunions, and social events. If a hotel has the amenities desired by corporate groups, this market segment may be most important. For hotels with extensive options for on-site leisure activities, leisure groups may represent a larger market. Some hotels market heavily to business travelers during the week and attract leisure travelers on the weekend. Only by tracking guest types can hoteliers fully understand the markets they are serving and consider tactics to attract larger and potentially more profitable market segments.

- *Variability in ADR.* Historically, room rates charged by hotels vary by track segments. For example, many hotels offer government workers a discounted room rate based on the worker's per diem. As a result, the ADR associated with government travelers typically is lower than that of other guests. For most hotels, group ADRs tend to be lower than the rate for transient travelers. Consumers expect, quite naturally, to receive a reduced room rate if they buy several guestrooms at a one time. If revenue managers are to make informed decisions about the wisdom of allocating rooms between group and transient travelers, they must know the specific ADR likely to be associated with the potential group or transient sale.

* *Variability in date demand.* Some track segments travel at different times than do others. **Shoulder dates** vary by hotel. Business travel is strongest though the week and lighter on weekends. In many hotels, leisure travelers make up the largest part of weekend and summer business.

FRONT OFFICE SEMANTICS

Shoulder date: Hotel term for a day, or even a season, between two busier time periods. For example, in a specific hotel, Thursday may be a slower shoulder date between the busy weekdays (Monday, Tuesday, and Wednesday) and the busy weekends (Friday and Saturday).

Similarly, the actual day of the year may affect who visits a hotel. Few business travelers, for example, travel overnight on the Thursday on which Americans traditionally celebrate Thanksgiving. Most national holidays result in reduced business travel. Those same holidays may, however, result in increased leisure travel as people visit their families and friends. Every hotel is unique, and the use of track codes allow revenue managers to better predict who is coming to their hotels as well as when these travelers are most likely to arrive.

* *Variation in room (bed) type demand.* For hotels with a mix of room types, track codes are important because different track segments frequently prefer different room types. Most often, these preferences relate to bed configuration. Given a choice between a king-bedded room and one with two double beds, most business travelers will select the room with the king-size bed. Many revenue managers use this information to recommend that king-bedded rooms sell for a premium over double-bedded rooms during the peak business travel nights (Monday through Thursday). On the other hand, families traveling for leisure activities typically prefer double-bedded rooms. Many revenue managers sell this type of room at a premium during weekends or at other times when leisure travelers are generating the greatest room demand.

Track code segmentation is also important to the individual responsible for the coordinating the hotel's sales and marketing efforts, because it provides information about the overall effectiveness of the hotel's sales team. Analysis of travelers' track codes can lead to decisions about where additional sales efforts should be expended and about where, if at all, current marketing efforts should be adjusted or charged.

SECTION REVIEW AND DISCUSSION QUESTIONS

Section Objective: Discuss how revenue managers use information about room types, market codes, and track codes to help maximize RevPar.

Section Summary: Some hotels naturally have rooms of different types that can be sold at different rates. Common room-type distinctions are made because of location in the hotel and guestroom features, including type of beds. Revenue managers in hotels with rooms that do not enable obvious distinctions can be creative and develop packages that allow front office personnel to upsell rooms and, in the process, to increase RevPar.

Market code distinctions relate to rooms that are used for different types of guests (e.g., transient, group, and contract). Rooms of different types typically sell for different amounts, so revenue managers must interact with other hotel managers to ensure that rooms are sold in a way that generates the greatest RevPar.

Revenue managers use track codes to further segment travelers. Transient travelers, for example, may be classified as leisure, corporate, or government guests. Market size variation, variability in ADR, date demand, and room (bed) type all affect the number and rates of rooms that can be sold and, in turn, the hotel's RevPar.

Discussion Questions:
1. The chapter provides an example of how a creative revenue manager can package amenities for business travelers and, in the process, provide opportunities for front office personnel to upsell rooms. Use your creativity to develop another package that might be of interest to business travelers. Also develop a package that could be sold to transient family guests and to adults traveling without children.
2. As suggested in the chapter, the number of hotel rooms allocated to different markets (transient, group, and contract) varies depending on the total estimated RevPar generated by the mix of rooms that are sold. Develop a scenario relating to potential hotel business that allows you to apply the four principles that are important when making market code allocations.
3. Assume that your hotel tracks a significant number of business travelers during the week. The hotel is located in a large city that is distant from the state's capitol. What are some tactics that you might use to attract government employees who travel on a per-diem rate?

REVENUE MANAGEMENT ESSENTIALS

Revenue managers maximize room revenue by managing room inventories while applying analytical and technical knowledge of hotel reservation and Front Office systems. They develop, implement, monitor, and control revenue (money) and sales (rooms) strategies and interact with the DOSM to ensure the proper mix of transient, group, and other guestroom allocations to maximize RevPar. When they understand how to best use their room types, market codes, and track codes, they can address the important tasks of managing their hotel's occupancies and ADRs. Revenue managers must also objectively evaluate their own efforts so that improvements can be implemented. Roadmap 6.3 shows that this section of the chapter focuses on essential tactics used by revenue managers.

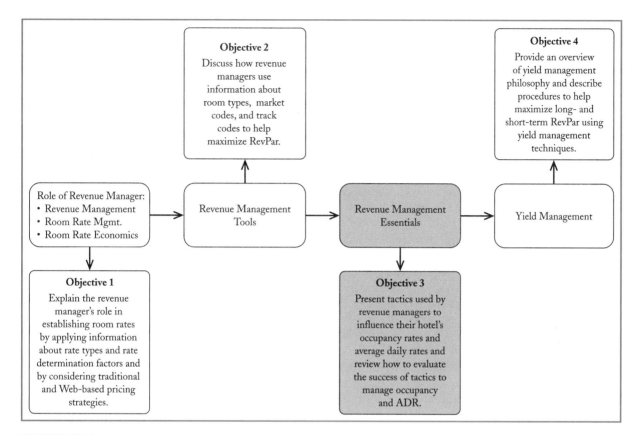

ROADMAP 6.3

Managing Occupancy

The DOSM is most often responsible for maximizing the hotel's sales efforts, but the revenue manager is responsible for maximizing the hotel's occupancy. These two tasks are related but not identical. Skillful revenue managers make decisions that improve occupancy rates based on unique demand situations experienced by their property. A few examples will demonstrate this.

Assume that the Altoona Hotel's sales team has successfully booked many guests for a specific weekend one month from now. Assume also that this 300-room hotel's revenue manager faces the situation in Figure 6.8. Demand for rooms is very strong on Saturday, weaker on Friday, and much weaker on Sunday. The revenue manager's goal is to maximize RevPar, so he or she must attempt to increase occupancy by identifying Saturday as a day that has MLOS (minimum length of stay) attached to it or, alternatively, by designating Saturday as a day that is **CTA (closed to arrival).**

	Friday	**Saturday**	**Sunday**
Rooms to sell	120	25	250

FIGURE 6.8   Sample forecasted room demand for one specific weekend at the Altoona Hotel.

FRONT OFFICE SEMANTICS

CTA (closed to arrival): Term that indicates the hotel declines reservations for guests wanting to arrive on a specific date.

The revenue manager may identify Saturday as a day that has a MLOS of two days attached to it. As a result, only reservations from guests requesting arrival on Saturday (or Friday) with the intention of staying for two (or more) days are accepted. Guests who request a one-night stay with arrival on Saturday are declined. By managing the length of stay required for a Saturday arrival, the revenue manager is attempting to maximize *total* weekend occupancy by selling potential guests a room on both Saturday and Sunday night. This MLOS strategy is illustrated in Figure 6.9

Recall that the hotel has only 25 rooms left to sell on Saturday night. Therefore, the revenue manager is making the MLOS decision based on the belief that the proportion of potential guests who want to stay two nights is significantly smaller than those who want to stay one night. However, the revenue manager also believes that the market of these guests is large enough to allow the hotel to sell all of its remaining 25 Saturday night rooms (and an additional 25 room nights on Friday or Sunday because of the two-night MLOS).

Instead of a MLOS strategy, the revenue manager may decide to use a CTA strategy. Identifying Saturday as a day that is CTA is logical if it is assumed that, based on current booking patterns, the demand for Saturday night reservations will likely exceed the number of rooms available for that night. If so, then it may be wise to deny reservations for guests requesting to arrive on Saturday in favor of guests who will arrive on Friday and request both a Friday and Saturday (or longer) stay. By denying guests the opportunity to arrive on Saturday (closing it to arrival), the revenue manager attempts to maximize total weekend occupancy by increased Friday night sales.

Some revenue managers who use a MLOS strategy rarely use a CTA strategy. They point out that the hotel (as in this example) that implements a CTA approach runs the risk of denying a reservation to a guest who may have wished to stay many days. For example, a guest who wishes to arrive on Saturday and stay for seven nights would, with a CTA strategy in place, be denied a reservation. Clearly, the

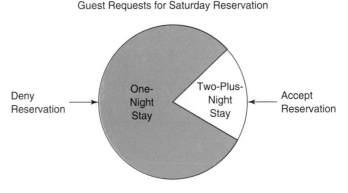

FIGURE 6.9   Two-day MLOS strategy.

hotel would want to accept such a reservation; however, a rigid CTA strategy would prevent it.

The question of when to use MLOS and CTA strategies is subject to debate. Many times the actual demand for a date (or dates) is not clearly known; instead, demand must be estimated. This is especially so when one-time or first-time events in an area strongly affect local room demand. Skillful use of MLOS and CTA strategies can make a significant impact on a hotel's overall occupancy rate. In fact, those strategies are so important that many PMS systems flag (i.e., identify) dates for which these approaches may be applicable.

MODERN FRONT OFFICE ISSUES AND TACTICS

But We Were Supposed to Be Busy!

Forecasting room demand can be complicated, especially when no historical data exist on the event driving demand. A good example are presidential nominating conventions. They are held every four years, but not in the same city.

In August 2004, the Democrats held their convention in Boston. As soon as the decision was announced, hotels in the city and suburban areas assumed increases in demand, and their telephones began to ring with reservation requests.

However, in mid-July 2004, the *Boston Globe* reported that the room demand anticipated by suburban hotels never materialized. For each night of the convention, one hotel had blocked 328 of its 367 rooms for convention guests. Hotel managers subsequently learned that convention organizers would need only 50 rooms per night, potentially costing the hotel more than $350,000 in lost revenue. Another suburban hotel had originally expected that the Secret Service would require as many as 100 of its 180 rooms. One month before the meeting, hotel managers learned that the agents would be staying at a hotel closer to the city. Even worse for some hotels, many convention attendees decided to stay in the area only three nights, rather than the five or six nights the hotels had expected. Room demand was there—or was it?

Adapted from Talcott, S. 2004. *The Boston Globe*, July 14.

In times of minimal demand, the management of occupancy is more closely tied to pricing and sales efforts than to the individual decisions made by revenue managers. In times of strong demand and potential sellouts, however, their decision making is extremely important. Many revenue managers believe that, in times of strong demand, they must oversell to maximize the chances of a sellout. This technique, perhaps the most well-known but least understood method of managing occupancy, is known as **overbooking** the hotel.

FRONT OFFICE SEMANTICS

Overbooking: Situation in which the hotel has more guest reservations for rooms than it has rooms available to lodge those guests. Sometimes referred to as *oversold*.

Any discussion on overbooking must begin with a simple truth: *No experienced hotel revenue manager would ever take a reservation for a room knowing in advance that the guest, upon arrival would, without doubt, be* **walked.** There are at least two reasons why this statement is true. First, a guest with a confirmed reservation who arrives to find there is no room available is inevitably and rightfully angry. No revenue manager wants to create angry guests. Second, from the hotel's financial point of view, the guest will be expensive to relocate. In most cases, the hotel that has walked a guest must pay at least the following costs:

- Transportation to the relocation property
- Telephone calls made by the guest to inform those who need to know about the change in lodging accommodations. With the increased use of cell telephones, this practice may someday cease; for now, however, complimentary phone calls are viewed by guests as a minimum courtesy to be offered by the hotel forcing the walk.
- Cost of the first night's room and tax charges at the relocation hotel

---

FRONT OFFICE SEMANTICS

Walk(ed): Situation in which a guest with a reservation is relocated from the reserved hotel to another hotel because no room is available at the reserved hotel. Used, as in, "We are three rooms oversold tonight, if we don't have some cancellations or no-shows, we will need to decide where we want to *walk* those guests."

Why do hotels overbook? Sometimes it is a mistake: for example, a guest reservation is made but mistakenly not recorded. Sometimes, however, an experienced revenue manager wants to maximize occupancy and intentionally accepts more reservations than it appears the hotel can accommodate. The revenue manager wants to fill the hotel and anticipates that some of the guests with room reservations will be no-shows. For example, a 100-room hotel with a 5 percent no-show rate may sell 101 rooms on a given night. Although technically overbooked, the hotel is not likely to walk a guest, because the average number of no-shows (five rooms) will exceed the size of the reservation oversell (one room).

No-shows are not unique to the hotel business. Restaurants, airlines, and rental car agencies are just a few of the businesses that must manage their reservations knowing that a certain percentage of those making reservations will not arrive to claim their product or service. If a hotel's total occupancy management plan is too conservative (e.g., it does not factor in no-shows), rooms will likely go unsold, even on "sold-out" nights. If it is too aggressive (e.g., it factors in an excessively large number of no-shows), too many guests with confirmed reservations will arrive at the hotel. The occupancy management skills of the revenue manager allow the hotel to sell the "right" number of total rooms during high demand periods.

Managing ADR

Most revenue managers understand that because of room rate economics (examined earlier in this chapter), the best way to maximize ADR is to manage room rates in conjunction with anticipated demand. When total demand is forecasted to be strong, discounting room rates is not typically necessary to ensure the sale of rooms. Similarly, when there is strong demand for a single room type, discounting that specific room type is not generally advisable, even if discounts will be offered on other, less popular types of rooms. The ADR management goal of revenue managers should be to achieve an ADR that is as close as possible to the hotel's rack rate.

Assume that a hotel has established its rack rate at $125 and now anticipates a sellout date. The revenue manager will not sell any rooms for that date at a discounted rate. The goal is to achieve an ADR for the high-demand date that is as close as possible to $125. The hotel will, of course, honor previously established negotiated or contract rates; however, the transient and group room rates offered will reflect the date's anticipated strong demand and the hotel's resulting no-discount (from rack rate) selling strategy. In fact, when demand is predicted to be exceptionally strong, revenue managers may even establish a special event rate for all the hotel's unsold rooms.

Whereas hotels can achieve success in driving the ADR up during times of high demand, reducing the ADR does *not* typically result in increased benefits to a hotel. Certainly hotels will have difficulty selling rooms if rates are too high relative to their perceived value. A significant lowering of rates, however, generally does not attract many more guests; a reduction of room rates by a single hotel when demand for rooms is slight is unlikely to significantly increase demand. The concept of reducing rate to drive demand is based on the assumption that room rate is a guest's most important consideration when selecting a hotel. This is not necessarily true. Price is important, but location, brand quality, brand loyalty, service, and frequent-guest programs all may be more important factors when guests select a hotel, and these factors are not affected by rate reductions.

The tendency to attempt to influence a hotel's overall occupancy rate by varying published room rates (and, therefore, ADR), is a tactic experienced revenue managers resist. Although revenue managers cannot significantly increase demand by reducing room rates, this does not mean rate discounts should never be offered. In all of the following situations, room discounting may be an effective managerial strategy and should be seriously considered:

- *When the guest's anticipated length of stay is long enough to offset a loss in room rate.* A corporate guest requesting a reservation for a seven-night stay may be offered a rate lower than another corporate guest requesting only a one-night stay.

- *When the dates requested by the guest include one or more days for which the hotel anticipates minimal demand.* In a hotel with minimal demand for rooms on Sunday night, a guest arriving on a Sunday night for a two-night stay may be offered a lower rate than a guest arriving on Tuesday (a high-demand day) for a two-night stay.

- *When the number of room nights to be purchased is large.* A guest who wants to reserve 50 rooms for a three-night stay (150 room nights) may receive a lower rate than a guest who wants to reserve one room for a three-night stay.

- *When the number of unique stays per year is high.* A guest who wants to reserve 50 rooms every other month for 12 months (six stays) may be offered a lower rate than a guest seeking to reserve 50 rooms for a one-time stay.

- *When the total revenue to be achieved by the hotel is high.* A guest who wants to reserve 100 rooms for three days and who will purchase three meals daily for the rooms' 100 occupants may be offered a lower rate than a guest seeking to reserve 100 rooms for the same three days without food and beverage purchases.

These examples illustrate that manipulating ADR does, in some cases, make good sense and can contribute to the achievement of a revenue manager's RevPar goals.

Evaluating Effectiveness

How do revenue managers evaluate the effectiveness of their occupancy and ADR management decisions? How are their decisions evaluated by those who supervise them? Historically, the persons responsible for rate and occupancy decisions have been evaluated based on the hotel's occupancy rate and ADR. More recently, RevPar has been the major factor used to evaluate revenue managers. Currently, some industry observers and professionals have suggested that GoPar (see Chapter 5) is a more useful measure of effectiveness. General managers and revenue managers should understand the advantages and limitations of each of the following measurement tools and know how to use them: occupancy index, ADR index, RevPar index, and GoPar.

Occupancy Index

One question frequently asked by persons with limited knowledge of the hotel industry is, "How's your occupancy?" The question implies that a high level of occupancy is good, and that a lower level of occupancy is bad. Even though that may, in fact, be true sometimes, it is a very limiting approach to occupancy management. In most, if rooms were sold for $1 per night, the hotel would achieve a sellout each day and would achieve a 100 percent occupancy rate. However, the hotel would not likely stay in business despite its good occupancy. If a hotel's rates are in-line with rates of its competitive set, the **occupancy index** is the industry's standard for measuring the management of occupancy rates.

FRONT OFFICE SEMANTICS

Occupancy index: A ratio measure computed as

$$\frac{\text{Occupancy rate of a selected hotel}}{\text{Occupancy rate of that hotel's competitive set}} = \text{Occupancy index}$$

Assume that you are a hotel owner and that your revenue manager informs you that your hotel achieved a 60 percent occupancy last month. Did managers do a good job of managing the hotel's occupancy? To make this evaluation, you must know how the hotels with which you directly compete (i.e., your competitive set) managed their occupancy levels. The occupancy index developed by Smith Travel Research is the measurement tool developed to do this.

Competitive sets and indexes were introduced in this text as means of predicting future rooms volume (see Chapter 5). They also can assist in making decisions about occupancy management. If your hotel achieved a 60 percent occupancy rate, the performance of your revenue managers would likely be considered good if the occupancy rate achieved by your hotel's competitive set was 45 percent (therefore, your occupancy index was 133 percent: $60 \div 45 = 133$ percent). If, however, the competitive set's occupancy rate for the same period was 80 percent, your occupancy index is 75 percent ($60 \div 80 = 75$ percent). This figure indicates that your managers were less effective decision makers than their direct competitors. Figure 6.10 details the evaluations routinely made when examining a hotel's occupancy index.

Occupancy index	Assessment and recommended action
Far below 100%	Management is ineffective. ADR is excessive for the market. Action: Reduce rack rate.
Below 100%	Management is less than effective. Actions: Evaluate weekday and weekend ADR index; closely examine sales efforts.
At (near) 100%	Management is effective. Action: Consider eliminating discounts for most popular room types during high-demand periods to test the hotel's ability to maintain the index.
Above 100%	Management is less than effective. Action: Immediately eliminate discounts for most popular room types during high-demand periods.
Far above 100%	Management is ineffective. ADR is too low. Action: Increase rack rates on all room types at all times.

FIGURE 6.10 Occupancy index evaluation.

For some hotels, an evaluation of monthly or even weekly occupancy indexes may be misleading, because the hotel's volume may vary greatly within a week. For example, a hotel may run a very strong occupancy index through the week and a much lower index on the weekends. In other hotels, this trend is reversed. Therefore, many revenue managers monitor their weekday and weekend occupancy indexes separately.

ADR Index

Chapter 4 described how ADR and occupancy percentages are equally weighted components of RevPar. Therefore, control of ADR is just as important for revenue managers as occupancy management. Many hoteliers believe that a hotel's occupancy rate is tied to the hotel's selling ability and that ADR is more related to the guest's perception of value. Guests who think that the room rates they paid are reasonable are likely to return. Those without this perception of value are less likely to return. Revenue managers must ensure a rate structure that maximizes their guests' feelings of value.

Earlier in the chapter we examined a variety of methods used for determining initial room (rack) rates. Recall that the development of rack rates is a starting, not ending, point in managing room rates. Revenue managers continually make decisions related to transient room discounting, establishment of negotiated rates, and granting discounts for large groups. In addition, the skillful use of special event rates and blackout dates significantly affect a hotel's ADR. If a hotel's rack rates are essentially in-line with rates of its competitive set, the **ADR index** is the industry's standard for measuring the effective management of room rates.

FRONT OFFICE SEMANTICS

ADR index: Ratio measure computed as

$$\frac{\text{ADR of selected hotel}}{\text{ADR of that hotel's competitive set}} = \text{ADR index}$$

In an evaluation of an ADR index, it is especially important that a hotel's competitive set is truly competitive. If, instead, a hotel's competitive set comprises hotels that are inferior to the hotel being evaluated, the resulting ADR index will be artificially inflated. Similarly, a hotel whose competitive set consists of properties

ADR index	Assessment and recommended action
Far below 100%	Management is ineffective. Actions: Evaluate appropriateness of the competitive set; evaluate rack rate structure; increase rack rate.
Below 100%	Management is less than effective. Actions: Evaluate weekday and/weekend ADR index, increase rates for either period if the index for that portion of the week exceeds 100%.
At (near) 100%	Management is effective. Actions: Monitor the competitive set's percentage change in ADR from prior month and prior year for evidence of competitors' increases in room rates; maintain rate parity.
Above 100%	Management is less than effective. Actions: Evaluate room rates in conjunction with the occupancy index. If the occupancy index is above 100%, increase rates. If the occupancy index is below 100%, consider increasing discounts during slower periods to maximize RevPar.
Far above 100%	Management is ineffective. Action: Evaluate competitive set for appropriate fit. (The ADR *may* be too high if occupancy index is significantly below 100%.)

FIGURE 6.11   ADR index evaluation.

that are in a significantly higher market segment (with higher average selling rates) will find that achieving an ADR index of 100 percent or higher may be very difficult or even completely unrealistic. Figure 6.11 details the evaluations typically made when examining a hotel's ADR index.

In addition to helping revenue managers evaluate the effectiveness of rate strategies, the ADR index can help them know when to modify rack rates. Consider the data from the Altoona Hotel in Figure 6.12. A review of the ADR indexes reveals that, recently, the Altoona has not increased its rates at the same pace as has its competitive set. In fact, the hotel has seen its ADR index slip from a three-month ending high of 102.52 in 200X (column G, line 14) to just 98.52 in 200Z (column G, line 16). From reading the report, it is not possible to determine precisely why the Altoona has, for only 4 of the past 13 months, been able to retain its rate premium and/or improve its ADR index (see column H, lines 1, 2, 5, and 10) The hotel's revenue manager can determine, however, that revenue managers in the competitive set hotels have been more aggressive in increasing rates. Note also that the rate decrease relative to competitive hotels has occurred despite the fact that, for the three months of August, September, and October of 200Z, the Altoona did show a positive ADR increase from the prior year (see column D, line 16). Therefore, although the Altoona has been somewhat effective in increasing its ADR from levels of prior years, it is losing ground to its competitive set. The overall trend in the Altoona's ADR index is a downward one, and this deserves management's careful attention.

RevPar Index
A hotel's **RevPar index** is the ultimate measurement of a revenue manager's skill.

FRONT OFFICE SEMANTICS

RevPar index: Ratio measure computed as

$$\frac{\text{RevPar of a selected hotel}}{\text{RevPar of that hotel's competitive set}} = \text{RevPar index}$$

Line	Year	Month	C ADR property	D Percentage Change	E Comp set	F Percentage Change	G ADR index	H Percentage Change
1	200Y	Oct.	$ 125.71	3.45	$ 124.51	3.21	100.96	2.15
2	200Y	Nov.	126.10	3.25	125.99	3.40	100.09	0.74
3	200Y	Dec.	116.89	2.45	117.50	2.10	99.48	(1.05)
4	200Z	Jan.	122.30	1.20	123.45	3.40	99.07	(2.22)
5	200Z	Feb.	127.80	0.78	126.99	2.55	100.64	0.01
6	200Z	March	115.08	1.22	117.66	1.45	97.81	(0.05)
7	200Z	April	125.65	1.40	128.95	2.66	97.44	(1.25)
8	200Z	May	122.24	0.61	124.50	5.41	98.18	(2.01)
9	200Z	June	126.13	2.20	127.11	4.51	99.23	(3.25)
10	200Z	July	125.98	2.51	128.91	2.60	97.73	1.52
11	200Z	Aug.	126.12	1.40	129.54	1.98	97.36	(3.13)
12	200Z	Sept.	126.74	0.66	128.63	2.65	98.53	(2.20)
13	200Z	Oct.	127.02	0.01	131.25	5.41	96.78	(4.15)
			Three months—ending October					
14	200X		122.41	4.50	119.40	4.10	102.52	2.30
15	200Y		126.54	3.37	125.01	4.70	101.22	(1.27)
16	200Z		126.75	0.17	128.66	2.92	98.52	(2.68)

FIGURE 6.12   ADR Indexes for 13-month period at the Altoona Hotel.

In addition to the revenue manager's decision making, a variety of other factors can cause a hotel's RevPar index to be lower than that of its competitive set:

- Inferior management of room cleanliness and facility maintenance
- Poor franchise (brand) name
- Poor exterior signage, property access, or both
- Poor **room mix** for the market
- Substandard furnishings or decor
- Sales and marketing and advertising budgets too small
- Sales and marketing staff too small
- Ineffective marketing staff

FRONT OFFICE SEMANTICS

Room mix: Ratio of a hotel's room types. For example, number of double-bedded rooms compared to king-bedded rooms, number of smoking-permitted rooms compared to nonsmoking rooms, and number of suites compared to standard rooms.

Some revenue managers dislike STR reports because they view them as objective measures (indexes) of a subjective activity (management). However, despite their limitations, STR RevPar reports are perceived as the best indicator of a hotel's operational quality and managerial proficiency.

A high occupancy index compensates for a lower ADR index (and the reverse is also true). Therefore, the interpretation of a RevPar index is more complex than that of either the occupancy index or ADR index. A RevPar index above 100 percent, however, generally implies that a hotel leads its competitive set and is making good

RevPar index	Assessment and recommended action
Far below 100%	Management is ineffective. Actions: Evaluate room rates in conjunction with occupancy index. If the occupancy index is near or above 100%, increase rates. If the ADR index is near or above 100%, consider increasing discounts during slower periods to maximize RevPar. If both indexes are substantially below 100%, reevaluate the competitive set.
Below 100%	Management is less than effective. Actions: Evaluate room rates in conjunction with the occupancy index. If the occupancy index is below 100%, reduce rates. If the ADR index is below 100%, consider raising rates or eliminating discounts during high-demand periods.
At (near) 100%	Management is effective. Action: Monitor occupancy and ADR indexes to maintain no more than a 10-point difference between these two measures.
Above 100%	Management may be effective. Actions: Evaluate room rates in conjunction with the occupancy index. If the occupancy index is above 100%, increase rates. If the ADR index is above 100%, consider increasing discounts during slower periods to further maximize RevPar. If more than 10 percentage points separate the two indexes, take corrective action to improve the lower index.
Far above 100%	Management (or ownership) is less than effective. Actions: Evaluate the competitive set for appropriateness of fit; increase rack rates; aggressively seek to increase ADR during high-demand periods; consider building additional room capacity.

FIGURE 6.13 RevPar index evaluation.

revenue management decisions. Figure 6.13 details the evaluations typically made when examining a hotel's RevPar index.

GoPar

The concept of GoPar has recently been touted as an alternative method of evaluating the effectiveness of the DOSM's sales efforts as well as the decisions of revenue managers. Chapter 5 explained that GoPar is the hotel's total revenue minus the expenses controllable by management. For example, the costs of a hotel's gardening services, utility bills, and even food and beverage expenses are assessed when computing GoPar. These same expenses, by contrast, are not considered when computing RevPar. Neither the revenue manager, the FOM, the DOSM, nor their staff control most of the costs used to compute GoPar.

If revenue managers do not directly control most of the costs involved in operating their hotels, why is GoPar (a term more familiar to hospitality accountants than revenue managers) suggested as a method to evaluate their decision making? The answer can be found in the way some hoteliers manipulate the RevPar index. To see how this manipulation can occur, assume that the revenue manager of the Altoona Hotel has achieved the RevPar index listed in Figure 6.14. Assume also that the

Hotel	Occupancy Percentage	ADR	RevPar	RevPar index
Altoona	75%	$100.00	$75.00	98.40
Competitive Set	74%	$103.00	$76.22	101.63

FIGURE 6.14 RevPar index comparison.

Hotel	Occupancy Percentage	ADR	RevPar	RevPar index
Altoona	78.33%	$98.27	$76.33	100.01
Competitive set	74.00%	$103.00	$76.22	99.86

FIGURE 6.15 New RevPar index comparison with low-priced sale (300 room nights at $40 per night).

Altoona's revenue manager is told by the hotel's owners that the FOM and the revenue manager will each receive a $1,000 bonus anytime the hotel's monthly RevPar index exceeds 100. The following month, a potential client approaches the FOM to request the purchase of 75 rooms per week (a total of 300 during the month) at a price of only $40 per night. If the sale is made and, if there are no other changes in either the Altoona's sales or those of its competitors, the following month's RevPar index would that shown in Figure 6.15.

Note that the Altoona hotel's occupancy percentage increases (because of the 300 extra rooms that were sold) while its ADR declines (the effect of 300 rooms sold at $40 per night). The result is a $1.33 increase in RevPar (from $75.00 to $76.33). The revenue manager and the FOM would have achieved their bonuses (RevPar index = 100.01), but the hotel may actually have suffered because of the sale. Why?

Remember that each time a room is sold, the hotel incurs costs to clean the room. Some would argue that any revenue above the direct costs (e.g., housekeeping labor costs for cleaning and providing guestroom supplies) for renting a room should be considered positive and, therefore, of benefit to the hotel's bottom line. Others would point out that excessive wear and tear on rooms when minimal incremental revenue is achieved actually damages the hotel in the long run. If, in this example, it cost $35 in direct expenses to clean a room, the hotel would have achieved $1,500 in incremental income from the sale (300 rooms × [$40 − $35]). This amount is actually insufficient to fund the $2,000 bonuses to be paid by the hotel's owners!

Those who advocate GoPar as the best measure of sales effectiveness will also be concerned about a sales department that spends $1,000 to advertise rooms and generates less than $1,000 in additional room revenues. In this case, RevPar will increase, and the hotel's sales department may look better when it is measured solely by RevPar. The hotel's profitability, however, will certainly suffer. The difficulty in these cases, is not that RevPar is a poor form of measurement. Rather, RevPar should not be the *only* measurement of a revenue manager's effectiveness (nor should GoPar). General managers, owners, and others should look to RevPar and its index as well as other measures of efficiency (including GoPar) when evaluating the entire hotel's sales and marketing efforts.

SECTION REVIEW AND DISCUSSION QUESTIONS

Section Objective: Present tactics used by revenue managers to influence their hotel's occupancy rates and average daily rates and review how to evaluate the success of tactics to manage occupancy and ADR.

Section Summary: Revenue managers can use several tactics to improve their hotel's occupancy rates. When, for example, demand is strong on some dates, they can impose MLOS or CTA policies. Revenue managers must also carefully review overbooking policies and, perhaps, act conservatively when estimating the number of no-shows likely for dates on which the property is oversold.

Revenue managers must also manage ADR. Increasing rates when justifiable will increase RevPar; decreasing rates to increase occupancy does not typically result in increased benefits to the hotel. However, there are times when room discounting is in order; revenue managers must know about and use these occasions to consider the need for rate reductions.

Four measures are commonly used to evaluate the effectiveness of occupancy and ADR decisions: occupancy index, ADR index, RevPar index, GoPar—all of which have advantages and shortcomings. The best approach is to use each measure to determine where corrective actions can be taken to increase RevPar.

Discussion Questions:
1. Do you agree with the observation that it is frequently difficult to increase occupancy rates by reducing the room rate? Why or why not? What additional tactics can a revenue manager use to sell rooms on dates when there will likely be many vacant rooms?
2. The chapter presents two examples of times when RevPar data can look favorable relative to past periods but have no financial benefit for the property. Can you think of other examples of ways that RevPar data can be manipulated in ways detrimental to the hotel?

YIELD MANAGEMENT

Hoteliers and consumers know that when demand for rooms is high, rates may also be high. When occupancy levels (demand for rooms) are relatively low, room rates will also likely be lower. As RevPar is a function of occupancy and ADR, any decrease (or increase) in one of these factors that is offset by an equal increase (or decrease) in the other factor will *yield* the same RevPar. Yield management is simply a set of techniques and procedures used to manipulate occupancy, ADR, or both to maximize the hotel's revenue yield. The business philosophy behind yield management, the principles involved in its proper use, and the techniques available to implement it are important concepts for revenue managers to understand, and as noted in Roadmap 6.4, yield management is the subject of this final section of the chapter.

Philosophy

Consider the following situations:

- As a typical consumer, you go to your local grocery store to buy a loaf of bread that usually costs $3. On this day, however, you find that the bread costs $6. When you inquire about the high price, you are told that the store anticipates significant demand for this type of bread on this day, and that the store will likely sell all of this type of bread that it has stocked. As a result, the price per

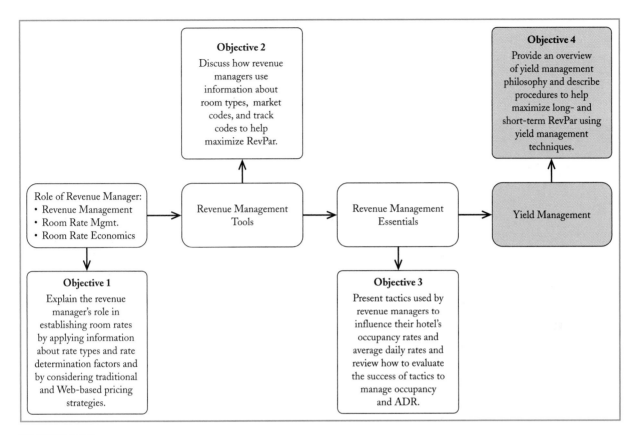

ROADMAP 6.4

loaf has been increased. Would you buy the bread? Would you return to this store in the future?

- You want to attend a concert by your favorite, internationally known musical group. You want front-row seats and are told that, because only a few remain, they will cost twice as much as a seats several rows back. Would you purchase the better seats?

- You would like to rent a guestroom near Times Square in Manhattan on New Year's Eve so that you can easily join the crowds celebrating the New Year. The reservations agent says that, because demand for these rooms is heavy, available rooms on that date have been assigned a special event rate and will cost twice as much as normal. Would you book the room?

In each of these cases, the consumer-business interaction is affected by strong demand, a supply shortage, or both. The airline industry is commonly recognized as the first business to actively manage (vary) pricing in response to strong changes in consumer demand. Airline officials have perfected techniques to increase ticket prices when demand is heavy and to maximize revenue by lowering prices when they antici-pate fewer tickets will be sold. As a result, passengers on the same flight often pay different fares. Some of the variance relates to service levels (first class, business class, or coach), some is the result of timing of ticket purchase (e.g., 21-day advance or same-day purchase), and some is due to the number of tickets purchased by whole-salers, business and leisure travelers, and others. Not surprisingly, rental car agencies also manage yield with pricing tactics. Other industries that use yield management techniques include cruise ships, railroads, condominiums, time-shares, and live theaters. The common denominator is the daily perishability of inventory—inventory, such as unsold hotel rooms, that cannot be carried over to be sold the next day.

Hotel rooms are perishable items (as are airline seats), so it makes sense for revenue managers to study how their rooms are typically rented to understand the best time to discount or to increase a room's price. For example, if a hotel is usually completely booked every October, there is little reason to offer a discount to a group that wants a block of rooms at that time, unless the group is willing to purchase enough additional services to justify the discount.

In most cases, consumers intuitively understand that businesses increase prices when there are limited product inventories. Not all industries, however, can effectively implement yield management strategies. Ethically, for example, few consumers would condone an emergency medical supply company that significantly increased its product prices immediately after a disaster caused an increase in demand. Similarly, consider the public's consistent response to the routine increases in gasoline prices before holidays when automobile use is expected to significantly increase. Public reaction typically ranges from cynicism to absolute outrage and a demand for federal investigations of and price controls for the "big oil companies." In hotels, yield management tactics that are improperly planned or implemented at a time that makes little sense to guests can generate the same negative reactions by consumers. Consider the legal implications of and harm to a property's reputation when rates for rooms are raised as citizens leave their homes because of dangers from hurricanes, forest fires, earthquakes, and other natural disasters. (Florida has laws that prohibit price gouging during emergencies, and the state took court action against at least two hotels during the aftermath of Hurricane Charley in August, 2004.)

Implementation

Yield management can be viewed as the application of tactics that predict (forecast) consumer behavior and effectively price highly perishable products to maximize RevPar. Industries that can easily carry inventory to the next day (e.g., carpet, lumber, and computer businesses) have difficulty using yield management, because customers do not accept price variation. Industries that are perceived by customers to be able to increase inventory without difficulty (e.g., bread and milk producers and restaurants) do not generally use yield management even though they may sell a perishable commodity.

The goal of yield management is to consistently generate the highest possible revenue from a given amount of inventory. The techniques of yield management are used during periods of high and low demand. Revenue managers should be implementing yield management procedures under the following conditions:

- Demand for their rooms varies by day of week, time of month, or season, or in response to local special events.
- Their demand variance is predictable.
- They have turned away a potential guest willing to pay a higher price for a room because available inventory had been previously sold to another guest at a lower price.
- Their hotel serves guests who are value conscious as well as those who spend more for reasons of convenience, status, or another motivating factor.

- They have, or can create, clearly discernible differences in service or product levels that can be easily explained to guests.
- Their property is willing to commit the resources necessary to properly train staff before implementation of yield management.
- They seek to maximize RevPar.

Techniques

Actual yield management techniques used by a revenue manager vary by property. Nevertheless, in their most simple form, these techniques perform the following actions:

- Forecast demand
- Eliminate discounts in high-demand periods
- Increase discounts during low-demand periods
- Use MLOS and CTA to maximize revenue in high-demand periods
- Implement special Event rates during periods of extremely heavy demand

Chapters 4 and 5 examined how hoteliers use the PMS to help forecast demand for rooms. This chapter focused on the importance of establishing room rates and managing those rates in response to guest demand. Many of the techniques used by modern PMS software to accomplish these tasks are mathematically advanced. However, their results must be easily understood by revenue managers; if they are not, they should not be used. In the final analysis, it is revenue managers' skill and experience in maximizing yield that is most critical to the process.

Assume that you are the revenue manager for a hotel hosting teams in a regional tournament leading to the NCAA basketball finals. Your hotel has secured the business of the team ranked number 12 in its bracket, and it is playing the team ranked number 1 on this night. The team has reserved rooms for the next three nights, but, if it loses tonight's game, it will go home in the morning. If it wins, it will stay another night (or two). In 95 percent of the cases, it will lose. How do you know? Because you understand basketball rankings and the historical frequency (almost never!) that a team ranked number 12 beats the team ranked number 1. Therefore, you predict that the team at your hotel will be an early departure. Your PMS does not "understand." The system simply knows that the team is planning to stay until the final game. Computers and sophisticated software programs are tools to be used by revenue managers, but they cannot replace experience, common sense, and human insight (plus, as many FOMs would attest, a little luck) when making revenue management decisions.

As another example of the importance of human intervention, consider the case of the corporate traveler who stays at her favorite hotel nearly every Tuesday and Wednesday night. On one Tuesday, she is told that her normal, discounted corporate rate of $99 cannot be honored because the hotel forecasts a sellout. The rate she must pay is now $149. In this case, the hotel's new revenue manager is aggressively managing yield and, perhaps appropriately, has eliminated corporate discounts on this day. When the corporate traveler complains that she is a loyal customer who has always been willing to pay the assigned corporate rate (even when the hotel was not busy), the front desk agent says, "There's nothing I can do." Should the hotel be surprised when that guest leaves and doesn't return? It should not, and she likely will

Hotel	Occupancy Rooms available	Percentage	ADR	RevPar
Low-priced competitor	300	75%	$100.00	$75.00
Altoona	300	50%	$150.00	$75.00
High-priced competitor	300	40%	$187.50	$75.00

FIGURE 6.16   RevPar comparisons for the Altoona Hotel and two competitors.

not. Recall that the goal of a revenue manager is to increase RevPar not only on a daily basis but over the long term as well. Offending loyal guests by incompetently managing yield benefits neither the guests nor the hotel.

A PMS can assist hoteliers with yield management decision making, but the system must be programmed in harmony with the yield philosophy of the revenue manager. To see the importance of different yield management strategies, consider the Altoona Hotel's data and the data of two other hotels with which it competes. Each of the hotels has 300 rooms, and the RevPar calculations for last night are shown in Figure 6.16.

Note that each hotel achieved a RevPar of $75. Recall from our earlier discussion of RevPar that each of these hotels would, therefore, have identical RevPar indexes on their respective STR trend reports. Yield management of these hotels, however, is being conducted in very different ways. The low-priced competitor (ADR = $100) obviously values occupancy rate over ADR; it has the highest occupancy rate (75 percent). This may be an effective strategy if, for example, the total revenue from all sources (including food and beverage sales, telephones charges and pay-per-view movies) generated by this large number of guests helps to offset the hotel's lower ADR. The high-priced competitor (ADR = $187.50) has the lowest occupancy rate (40 percent). This hotel will likely find operating costs reduced (fewer rooms to clean) and may be able to offer superior service levels (because the total number of guests to be served is smaller), which helps to justify the hotel's higher rate. The Altoona Hotel's strategy falls between those two extremes.

Despite individual differences in philosophic approach, most revenue managers would accept these principles:

- *Occupancy and ADR indexes should be close.* Ideally, the occupancy index and ADR index should be close; that is, percentages should be within a few percentage points of each other. If the occupancy index is well over 100 percent (110 percent or more), the hotel should attempt to increase its ADR but also be prepared to lose some occupancy index points. If the occupancy index is well below 90 percent, the hotel should consider a reduction of selected rates.

- *Rate integrity is essential.* Pricing on e-distribution channels as well as on in-house channels of distribution should be coordinated to ensure that decisions are made for the hotel's long-term benefit.

- *Revenue management is a daily activity.* Room demand should be monitored daily (or hourly). To keep current with market demand, some revenue managers monitor competitors' e-channel room rates daily. In addition, many revenue managers anonymously phone their competitors every day to inquire about walk-in rates.

- *It is necessary to gamble at times.* An aggressive revenue manager can make a significant difference in a hotel's RevPar. Overbook on high-demand nights but do so based on known no-show data for similar dates. Minimize costly walks.

SECTION REVIEW AND DISCUSSION QUESTIONS

Section Objective: Provide an overview of yield management philosophy and describe procedures to help maximize long- and short-term RevPar using yield management techniques.

Section Summary: Yield management is a manual- or PMS-driven system designed to maximize revenue by holding rates high during times of high room demand and by decreasing room rates during times of lower room demand. It is used by the airline, hotel, and other industries that sell a perishable commodity (e.g., an airline seat on a specific flight or hotel guestroom on a specific night). Revenue managers need to know when yield management should and should not be used. For example, they should not decrease selling prices when it is not necessary to do so, and they should not increase prices when there will be significant complaints, legal implications, or long-term negative impact on RevPar. Most revenue managers agree that occupancy and ADR indexes should be close. Rate integrity is essential, and revenue management is an ongoing, daily activity.

Discussion Questions:

1. In some cases revenue managers should implement yield management procedures. Provide examples of commonly occurring situations in hotels where these procedures would be appropriate.
2. In some instances room rates should not be increased for selected guests even when yield management data suggest increases. Can you think of examples of situations when the revenue manager's common sense should prevail?
3. Figure 6.15 reviews RevPar comparisons for the Altoona Hotel and two competitive hotels. In which of the three hotels would you like to be the revenue manager? Why?

The FOM in Action: A Solution

FOMs, in their role as revenue managers, must often make difficult pricing decisions. In Danielle's situation, it is likely she could sell all 12 of her remaining rooms at the hotel's rack rate because of the snowstorm. Doing so would certainly maximize RevPar on the remaining rooms and that should be her primary goal. Hoteliers work together, however, and in this case, her colleague, Tim, is asking that she honor a reduced rate for the guests he has to walk because his hotel is oversold. Tim is implying, of course, that if Danielle needs rooms in the future, his hotel will reciprocate.

The question of whether to grant Tim's request is one that actually should have been addressed ahead of time. Hotels that agree to walk rates (rates they will charge each other in the event rooms are needed) should be spelled out in writing. Allowable rates to be charged and the duration of the agreement should be clearly indicated. In most cases, walk agreements of this type are written subject to room availability. That is, one hotel is not obligated to take guests that are walked from another hotel if the FOM to receive the walked guests does not think it is in his or her best interest to do so.

Whether Danielle should accept the guests walked from Tim's hotel on this day may depend on their past history, the frequency with which walk rates are requested, and the difference between the negotiated walk rate and the rack rate Danielle would receive for her remaining rooms. Danielle's response to Tim's request may be, "Tim, I have good news and bad news. I do have the rooms, but unfortunately, because we are forecasting a sellout, I am not able to honor a discount rate."

Tim may decide to secure rooms from another hotel. Danielle will sell her rooms without the guests from Tim. As he phones other hotels, Tim is likely to find few low-cost options available, because most hotels are also likely to be full. This is truly one of those cases where Danielle, as an effective FOM, must know when to diplomatically say no to discounted rates.

From the Front Office: Front-Line Interview

Mike Mackaluso
Front Desk Associate
Candlewood Suites Hotel (128 rooms)
Lansing, Michigan

Sorry, No King-Size Beds!

Mike began taking hospitality business classes during his sophomore year of college and during his junior year he completed an internship at a local Radisson hotel. He fulfilled another internship obligation during the summer before his senior year at the Candlewood Suites Hotel and remained with the property while completing his graduation requirements. His initial career plan was to begin working in the hotel industry in an operations position. His long-term goal was to become the general manager of a large hotel.

1. **What are the most important responsibilities in your present position?**
   I think the most important responsibility for someone in my position is to ensure that every guest that comes through our front door is happy and satisfied with the level of service and the quality of product that we provide. No matter how busy we are, every guest must be treated the same way: like they are the most important person staying at the hotel. Guests are hesitant to compliment good service but will tell you very quickly about poor service. They will do the same to their family and friends: If you provide poor service to a guest more people will know about it then if you provided good service to the guest.

2. **What are the biggest challenges that confront you in your day-to-day work and in the long-term operation of your property's front office?**
   The largest challenge everyday is being polite to all of our guests. No matter how rude guests are to you, it is your responsibility to treat them with the best of manners. A person may be upset about something that is not even related to the hotel and will take it out on the front desk agent when checking in or checking out. It is important to have a "thick skin" and be able to maintain it throughout the day. The moment that you begin to take guest comments personally, you begin providing bad service. Always treat guests like they are the only concern that matters to you at that point in time.

The largest challenge in the long-term operation of the front office is communication. It is essential to communicate every day with your co-workers. On every shift change, effective communication is important so everyone knows what is going on. Communication is also important because, if a guest has a question about something that happened earlier in the day, it is much easier to respond when you know exactly what occurred. This is a challenge because it is difficult to effectively communicate everything that is important for the next shift. Having a log book is a good solution to this problem. Everyone can read it, write in it, and refer to it when needed.

3. What is your most unforgettable front office moment?

My most unforgettable front office moment occurred when a gentleman checked in to the hotel on a busy afternoon. A few moments after he checked in he came down to the front desk. There was a lobby full of people, and he began cursing and yelling loudly about his displeasure with our queen-size beds. He wanted a king-size bed.

My first goal was to get him to calm down (there were children in the lobby). Then I was able to talk to him and let him know that the hotel did not offer king-size beds, and it was just not possible for him to have one. After he realized what a scene he had made, he was embarrassed and apologized. After he walked away, everyone in the lobby applauded and told me that I handled the situation very well. I thought that was a nice gesture, and it made me appreciate my job even more.

4. What advice do you have for those studying about or considering a career in front office or hotel management?

Listen to your instructors. Most of them have been in the field for many years, and many are still active in the industry. They can provide you with real stories and issues that arise everyday, along with suggestions about how to manage them.

More advice: Always leave your personal problems at the door when you come to work. You will hear everyone else's concerns throughout the day. Leaving your issues outside of work will better allow you to effectively help your guests.

Always smile, even when talking on the phone. People can "hear" your smile through the phone. Also, do not take things that happen at the hotel personally. Some guests may seem to blame you because their plane was late or their food was cold at dinner. Front desk agents must try to help guests forget about the issues over which they (the agents) have no control and take responsibility for the ones that they can address.

Everyone in the hotel is part of one team. There are no individual teams within a property. If someone has a problem with something, never blame someone else. Take responsibility to correct the problem no matter who may be at fault.

A final thought: Have fun and enjoy your job. This is a great industry, and you can work in an awesome atmosphere. You get to meet new people every day as guests come and go, and, you may get to know many guests as they become regulars at the property.

FRONT OFFICE SEMANTICS LIST

Inventory (rooms)	Day of	Law of supply
Negotiated rate	Rate resistance	Rate type
Black-out date	Displace (revenue)	Concierge level
Negotiated rate agreement	Economics	Rate (seasonal)
Length of stay (LOS)	Supply	Rate (special event)
Central reservation system (CRS)	Demand	Rate (corporate)
	Room rate economics	Rate (government)
Comp	Law of demand	Rate (group)

Rate (package)
American Plan (AP)
Modified American Plan (MAP)
All-inclusive (rate)
European Plan (EP)
Day rate
Half-day rate
Fade (rate)
Return on investment (ROI)

FF&E (furniture, fixtures, and equipment)
Cost per key
Bottom-up selling
Top-down selling
Call-around
Market code
Track code
Rate integrity (parity)
Distribution channel

Shoulder date
CTA (closed to arrival)
Overbooking
Walk(ed)
Frequent-guest program
Occupancy index
ADR index
RevPar index
Room mix

FRONT OFFICE AND THE INTERNET

The following Web sites relate to the content of this chapter:

Web address	Subject matter
www.micros.com/products/hotels/hotel_management	Yield management software
www.innquest.com	Yield management software
www.hotellinx.com	Yield management software
www.promisehotel.com	Yield management software
www.hotel-management-software.com	Yield management software
www.mediavue.net/software/hotel_software	Yield management software
www.resortdata.com	Yield management software
www.sddsystems.com	Yield management for telephone revenue

REAL-WORLD ACTIVITIES

1. Assume that you are the general manager of a 500-room hotel and that your staff includes an FOM, revenue manager, and DOSM. To what extent, if any, do you want to be involved in decisions relating to setting rates for transient guestrooms today, in the near term, and in the long term? Do you expect to be involved in decisions relating to guestroom charges for small groups? Large groups? What other decisions related to guestroom pricing are important to you?

2. Assume that you are an FOM developing a training program for your front desk agents. Your goal is to minimize guest complaints and employee stress when the hotel is overbooked and when guests with confirmed and guaranteed reservations must be walked. Make a list of common reactions that guests will likely have in this situation. Briefly script an acceptable response to the comments for front desk

agents. Also make a list of comments that front desk agents should and should not make in these situations.

3. As the chapter noted, airline passengers typically pay different prices for the same flight. Assume that you are an FOM who is hearing a complaint from an attendee of a group meeting who "demands" the same (lower) room rate that is being paid by several other attendees. How would you respond to this attendee? List the basic points of your response and develop a script that details your response.

4. Assume that a DOSM desires to increase weekend guestroom sales in a business-oriented hotel. The DOSM develops several packages (e.g., Weekend Getaway, Shop Till You Drop, and See the Home Team Play). Each package has several (or more) amenities in addition to the guestroom. What factors will you, as the FOM, consider when discussing the charge for the guestroom component of the package?

5. If possible, talk with a general manager, FOM, or revenue manager in a local hotel. What are the most difficult challenges to maximizing RevPar? How does he or she address these challenges? What role do PMS data and reports play in assisting decision makers? How, if at all, do yield management techniques fit with other strategies used to maximize RevPar?

7

Distribution Channel Management

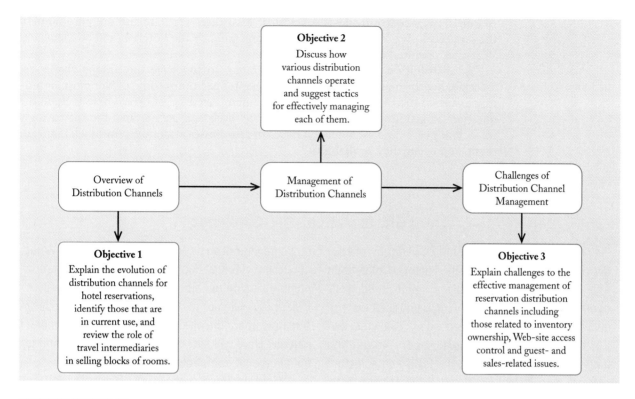

CHAPTER ROADMAP

Chapter Preview

One of the greatest challenges facing today's front office manager is that of distribution channel management. When potential guests want to make a reservation at a specific hotel, they have a variety of ways to do so. Each involves a separate reservation distribution channel. This chapter introduces the most popular distribution channels and describes how they can be managed effectively.

Most users of distribution channels have options. For example, a travel agent can make a hotel reservation for a client in a variety of ways. The agent can send an e-mail to the hotel requesting the reservation, phone the hotel's central reservation system, (CRS), use the travel agency's Global Distribution System (GDS) terminal, or make the reservation on the Internet. Each of these alternatives represents a different distribution channel, and the hotel's cost for the reservations depends on the method selected to make the reservation. Therefore, it is in the hotel's best interest to operate each distribution channel efficiently and to direct channel users to lower cost channels rather than to higher cost channels when feasible.

At one time, there were only a few ways that guests could make reservations. As a result, FOMs had few distribution channels to administer. Today, FOMs must manage reservations made by walk-in guests, telephone, traditional mail, and group sales, along with the distribution channels already noted, which are being used with increasing frequency. The Internet has radically changed management of distribution channels, because it provides users with at least three separate and unique channels: the property's own Web site, the Web site operated by the hotel's brand or chain, and Web sites operated by third parties.

As distribution channels have proliferated, so too have the unique challenges associated with their management. This chapter examines some of the most significant issues of distribution channel management faced by FOMs. These include the question of inventory ownership, control of Web site access, and the increasingly important guest- and sales-related issues of rate consciousness, group-block management, and occupancy tax liability.

The FOM in Action: The Challenge

"It's really very simple," stated Lee Lagget, executive director of the Bay City Visitors Convention and Visitors Bureau (CVB). "I just build your overnight package as you want it, and then we can sell it on our Bay City Web site." Lee was discussing the bureau's most recent marketing initiative with Teri Persanti, the FOM and assistant general manager of a 200-room, full-service hotel located in downtown Bay City. Teri's boss was attending a regional franchise conference, so Teri had been assigned to meet with Lee.

As a resident of Bay City and a member of the Bay City business community, Teri supported the CVB's marketing efforts. She was not, however, clear about Lee's latest idea. "Lee," said Teri, "I don't want to appear negative, but please help me understand your proposal. If we create the package, how will you sell it? Will you be accepting credit card payments on your Web site? How will those payments be deposited in our account? What about interfacing confirmation and cancellation numbers? With each hotel in the city using its own PMS, how will your staff know what format to use? And how about the site's policies regarding cancellations? How will site visitors know what is and is not allowed if each hotel sets its own terms?'

"Hold on Teri," replied Lee, "I'm no expert on front office mechanics. That's your area, but I'm sure we can work those issues out. After all, we all want to promote the hotel business in Bay City, and this Web site is a great way to do it! We get more and more hits on the site every month. By charging only a very small fee for every room sold on our site, we can secure additional funds to do an even better job of promoting Bay City."

"This," thought Teri, "seems like the beginning of a really bad idea. I wonder what we should do in this situation?"

OVERVIEW OF DISTRIBUTION CHANNELS

In Chapter 6, a *distribution channel* was defined as a source of potential room reservations. For example, a hotel's telephone is a distribution channel. Individuals can telephone the hotel to learn about room rates, room availability, and hotel features and amenities. To maximize room sales, the FOM wants the hotel telephone to be answered promptly by friendly, knowledgeable, and well-trained reservationists. If the FOM is managing this specific distribution channel well, a larger number of reservations will be made at higher ADRs than in a hotel with poorly trained reservationists who do not effectively represent their property.

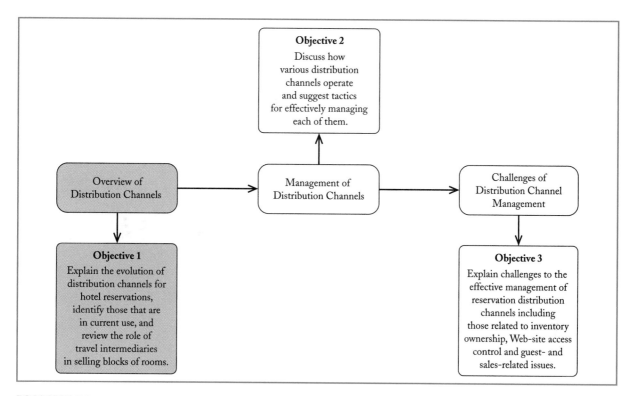

ROADMAP 7.1

Similarly, a potential guest could e-mail a hotel requesting property information or a reservation. In this case too, hotel staff must promptly and effectively reply to the guest using this distribution channel. It is critical that FOMs professionally manage *all* distribution channels that guests can use to communicate with a hotel. As Roadmap 7.1 indicates, an overview of distribution channels opens this chapter.

Not all guests make their own reservations. As shown in Figure 7.1, an **intermediary** may contact the hotel to make a guest's reservation. A guest who wants a reservation may contact a **travel agent** to serve as an intermediary with the hotel.

FRONT OFFICE SEMANTICS

Intermediary: Entity authorized by a guest to make a hotel reservation on the guest's behalf.

Travel agent: Hospitality professional who assists clients in planning travel.

Hotel staff must accurately inform the intermediary about what the guest will receive, because there will be no opportunity to discuss the reservation inquiry directly with the guest. Therefore, it is as important to properly manage distribution channels used by intermediaries as it is to manage distribution channels used directly by guests. (Travel intermediaries are discussed later in this section.)

To best understand hotel distribution channels—their emerging importance and management challenges—let's first examine them from a historical perspective. This examination can then serve as the basis for understanding the significant changes resulting from the industry's increasing reliance on e-distribution channels.

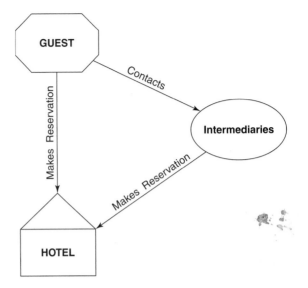

FIGURE 7.1   Role of hotel intermediaries.

Brief History of Distribution Channels

Processes used to make hotel reservations have undergone significant changes during the history of travel. In the earliest days of the hotel industry, travelers' first contact with an inn was when they physically arrived at a property. With no dependable mail service, no telephones, and no assurance about when they would arrive at a destination, early travelers were truly on their own when securing overnight accommodations.

The advent of a government-operated mail service was a milestone in the hospitality industry. Guests could use this new distribution channel (mail service) to communicate directly with hotels. In addition, intermediaries could contact hotels on behalf of their clients and maintain a written record of what they requested for the traveler and what the hotel promised to provide.

Before 1970s, the primary distribution channels used by hotels, travelers, and travel agents were the telegraph, the mail system, and the telephone. In the mid-1970s, a major transformation began. The change was initiated not by hotels but by airlines. As commercial airlines developed in the United States, they created the same traditional relationships with travel intermediaries as hotels, cruise lines, and trains had done earlier. In the early stages of the airline industry, travel agents referred to printed flight schedules distributed by the airlines. They then contacted an airline to inquire about seat availability for clients on specific flights. By the end of the 1970s, however, airlines provided travel agencies with an electronic method for verifying availability and making reservations. The Global Distribution System (GDS) provided the growing airline industry with an electronic ticket-booking system that was more efficient and cost-effective than the existing distribution channels of telephone, telegraph, and mail. Continued development of the GDS soon allowed travel agents to book car rentals and hotel room reservations on the same system.

As travel agencies increasingly found electronic booking on the GDS less costly for their own businesses, they began to insist that all of the products they reserved or purchased be available for booking through this emerging distribution channel. In

The hospitality industry transformed concurrently with the evolution of the airline industry.

the late 1970s, GDS bookings comprised less than 5 percent of all hotel reservations made. Now GDS bookings exceed 20 percent, despite fierce recent competition from the Internet (another distribution channel that would, when it emerged in the 1990s, radically change the way hotels sold rooms).

The GDS initially consisted of two main systems: Sabre (the American Airlines electronic booking system) and Apollo (used by United Airlines). Other airlines (e.g., Eastern, TWA, and Delta) also created and named their own electronic reservation systems. Unfortunately, but not surprisingly, as each of these systems was initiated by competitors, the systems were developed independently of each other and could not be interfaced (i.e., connected electronically). As a result, a travel agent using the Sabre system to book a client's outbound American Airlines flight had to use a completely different electronic system (Apollo) to book the client's return flight on United Airlines. Problems occurred when a ticket was booked, and travel agents were confused. One airline might identify its flights by letters, whereas another used numbers or a combination of numbers and letters. Some systems abbreviated a city with four letters; others used three. In addition, each airline's system required a directly connected, designated computer terminal within the travel agency.

Naturally, expansion and improvement of the GDS focused on the airline industry, because the system was developed for the airlines. The fact that travel agencies wanted to book both air travel and hotel rooms on the same system was bothersome to some airline officials. As a result, hotel companies had to interface their own reservation systems with the airline systems in the GDS. Travel agencies soon found that they could not compete effectively unless their agents knew and could use the many reservations systems that were available. To entice travel agents to book flights with them, individual airlines worked hard to constantly improve and enhance their own reservation segment of the GDS. The result was constant change within the GDS and increased confusion as hotels struggled to keep up with it.

Not surprisingly, the airlines charged hotels for access to the GDS. Large chain hotels had the financial ability to develop reservation systems that interfaced directly with the GDS. Smaller hotels had to hire specialized companies to create interfaced reservation systems. Financially, the use of the GDS altered a hotelier's traditional view of room rates. A guest who walked into a hotel and rented a room for $99 gave the hotel $99. If that same guest booked a reservation through the GDS, the hotel's owners incurred these costs:

- A commission to the travel agent (usually 10 percent)
- A fee set by the airlines for use of the GDS
- A reasonable amount to the hotel chain's or brand's centralized reservations department to help offset the cost of developing the chain's interface system

Clearly, the cost of a reservation made through this distribution channel was significantly higher than that of a walk-in guest. Traditional telephone reservation systems staffed 24/7 by hotel chains, however, were also expensive to operate, and telegraph and mail channels were too slow to be effective.

The higher costs associated with securing a GDS reservation meant that hotel chains did not want to use the system heavily. Travel agents, however rapidly embraced the GDS. To understand why, consider the case of a travel agent in St. Louis, Missouri, whose client wants to reserve a room in New York City for a weekend day two days from now. The agent's mailed inquiries to New York City hotels requesting rates and availability would not be received until after the guest's requested arrival date. In addition, the agent might have to manually identify New York hotels, place several long-distance telephone calls to hotels to verify room availability, compare quoted room rates, and make another telephone call to the selected hotel to make the client's room reservation. All of these labor-intensive, time-consuming, and expensive tasks could be accomplished in seconds and at little cost to the travel agency when the GDS was used. Centralized reservation systems developed by hotel chains helped reduce travel agents' telephone costs by providing travel-agent-only toll-free telephone numbers. Nevertheless, a travel agent phoning, for example, Hilton's toll-free number could not make a reservation at a Marriott property.

Faced with the reality of increased use of the GDS, several of the largest hotel chains banded together to share the costs of developing their own reservation interface system and then to negotiate a lower per-reservation GDS usage fee with the airlines. The organization developed to design and maintain the hotel chains' reservation interface system was called **THISCO**.

FRONT OFFICE SEMANTICS

THISCO (The Hotel Industry Switch Company): Now called Pegasus Solutions, this organization is the most frequently used "switch" to interface information from all hotel and airline systems.

Developed by Best Western, Choice, Days Inn, Hilton, Holiday Inn, Hyatt, LaQuinta, Marriott, Ramada, Sheraton, and Forte, THISCO was founded in

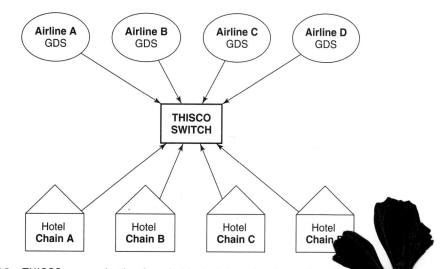

FIGURE 7.2   THISCO—organization founded by hotels to develop an interface w̶i̶t̶h̶ ̶t̶h̶e̶ industry's GDS.

1989. Its goal was to develop a "switch" that would act as a translator to interface information from all hotel and airline systems with the GDS. The result (see Figure 7.2) was to be a seamless system in which travel agents could, simultaneously, look at the availability and rates of a variety of hotels and select the one best fitting their clients' needs.

THISCO met with such great success that other organizations developed additional hotel, car rental, and other-industry switches. THISCO (now called Pegasus Solutions) remains the largest switching provider in the hospitality industry. However, Cendant, a very large hotel franchisor, also maintains a switch. In some cases, large hotel chains have found it cost-effective to build and maintain their own switches to Sabre, Galileo, Amadeus, and Worldspan (the four remaining but much advanced components of the original GDS).

The mid-1990s saw the advent of another major distribution channel. In 1994, Hyatt Hotels worked with TravelWeb, a Web site developed by THISCO, to develop an online, integrated, reservation system. Hotels whose rooms were booked on the system paid an Internet booking fee for reservations made and a separate fee for their hotels to be listed on the site. Because room availability changes so rapidly, this new system had to be interfaced with the GDS. Travel agents with access to the Internet, however, could use the new system, and many agents found it easier to work with than the GDS terminals. Simultaneously, major airline companies, who had once encouraged travel agents to book through the GDS, were cutting (or eliminating) travel agent commissions for airline bookings.

The introduction of Internet-based room reservations, the deteriorating relationship between airlines and travel agents, and the public's love of booking travel on the Internet have not meant the end of the GDS. However, the Internet has added another significant distribution channel for hoteliers to manage. In fact, all of the remaining GDS entities, which are now separated from their airline parent companies, maintain their own Web sites to make access to the GDS easier for travelers and travel agents.

Many travelers believe that using the Internet to book their reservations will give them the lowest room rates.

Use of Intermediaries

Intermediaries have a long history within the travel industry. The most common is the travel agent. Traditionally, travel agents either dealt directly with travelers or acted as **travel wholesalers.**

FRONT OFFICE SEMANTICS

Travel wholesaler: Entity that purchases blocks of hotel rooms and, in turn, sells them to travel agents.

These early intermediary relationships are important because they help explain the complex intermediary environment in which today's hotels operate. Figure 7.3 illustrates the relationship between the hotel, travel wholesaler, travel agent, and guest. When reviewing Figure 7.3, note the following four steps:

- Step 1: A hotel sells rooms to a travel wholesaler.
- Step 2: The travel wholesaler sells rooms to a travel agent.
- Step 3: The travel agent sells rooms to an individual guest (or group).
- Step 4: The guest (or group) stays at the hotel.

To understand the rationale of each entity in this process, let's examine the motivation of seller and buyer during each step.

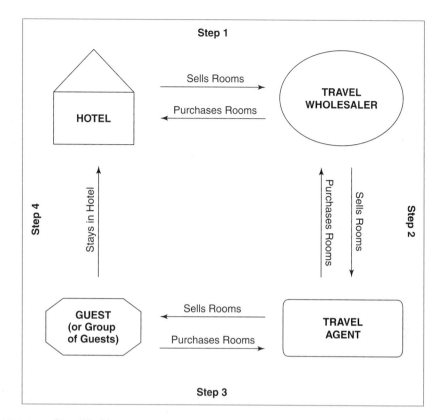

FIGURE 7.3 Simplified intermediary process.

- *Step 1: A hotel sells rooms to a travel wholesaler.*
  Seller's Motivation: When FOMs determine that there will be periods of slow demand for hotel rooms, they may discount the rooms that otherwise would likely be vacant on dates of reduced demand. For example, a ski lodge may sell rooms at a reduced rate during the summer when no skiers rent rooms, but when potential guests may be interested in other activities. If a travel wholesaler offered to purchase a substantial number of rooms during this period, the FOM would likely sell them at a significant discount. The hotel and travel wholesaler would negotiate a contract to establish the terms of the sale. At a minimum, the contract would address these items:
  - Selling price of the rooms
  - Actual number of room nights sold to the wholesaler
  - Specific dates on which the rooms could be used
  - Any hotel services and amenities that would accompany the sale of the rooms (e.g., meals and activities)
  - Payment terms
  - Penalty clauses for nonperformance by either party

  An FOM who establishes a positive relationship with a travel wholesaler can typically sell rooms that would otherwise not be sold, and the wholesaler gains the potential for profit when the rooms are resold.

Buyer's Motivation: The buyer's motivation in this transaction is very straight-forward. The travel wholesaler wants to buy rooms at a reduced rate. Then, when the rooms are resold to individual guests (or to travel agents who represent guests), the wholesaler can make a profit.

An individual guest may be able to obtain a fairly low rate for a room during the off-season by contacting the hotel directly. However, an individual guest would not purchase the large number of rooms to which a travel wholesaler will commit. Therefore, the individual traveler would not likely receive the very low rate offered to the travel wholesaler.

• *Step 2: Travel wholesaler sells rooms to a travel agent.*
Seller's Motivation: A travel wholesaler who purchases a large number of hotel rooms at a significant discount must sell the rooms before the dates for which they are reserved. The best manner for wholesalers to sell "their" rooms is to price the rooms attractively and to solicit as many individual travelers or travel agents as possible to maximize the prospects of selling the rooms. The number of individual travelers who *could* be interested in purchasing rooms is large but difficult to contact directly. Most travel wholesalers, therefore, attempt to sell the rooms directly to (or through) individual travel agents.

Buyer's Motivation: Unless a travel agency has a very large volume of business, it is unlikely that it can buy hotel rooms at a price as low as a travel wholesaler can afford. When travel agents recommend rooms to their clients, they desire to deliver real value and cost savings to those clients, while making a reasonable profit. Their profit margins improve when they can purchase rooms at the lowest-possible price.

In Europe, some of the largest national and multinational travel agents serve as their own successful tour wholesalers. In the United States, the American Automobile Association is an example of an organization that serves as both a travel agency and tour wholesaler.

• *Step 3: Travel agent sells rooms to a guest.*
Seller's Motivation: Travel agents typically secure travel services for their clients. From a legal perspective, travel agents, unlike travel wholesalers, have a **fiduciary** responsibility to their clients.

FRONT OFFICE SEMANTICS

Fiduciary: Relationship based on trust and the responsibility to act in the best interest of another when performing tasks.

Travel agents must be knowledgeable about the products they sell. They are liable for their own actions and for the service levels and behavior of the service providers (such as hotels) with whom they do business. Assume that a travel agent books a room for a client at a hotel in a large city. The agent represents the hotel as a four-star property in a safe part of the city. In fact, the agent knows that the hotel is a two-star property in a high-crime area. In this case, if the travel agent's client is injured during the hotel stay, he or she could bring legal action against the travel agent because of misrepresentation. As in the past, it is still in the best interests of travel agents to recommend only those hotels they are convinced will meet their clients' requests. Doing business only with dependable and reputable travel wholesalers helps them achieve this goal.

Travel agents buy (or recommend the purchase of) rooms or entire travel packages from travel wholesalers with the goal of making a resale profit. They want, therefore, to sell rooms they have purchased to as many of their clients as possible.

Buyer's Motivation: Travel agents have been of great value to their clients because they possess specialized knowledge about the travel industry. The quality of hotels, the ratings of restaurants, and the lowest-cost travel alternatives are examples of information they provide to clients. In return, they are paid for their services by the clients or the businesses that they recommend. Now the Internet can provide the average traveler with much of this information. Nevertheless, many travelers still rely on travel agents to help with travel purchases for reasons such as convenience, potential cost savings, and need for specialized information.

- *Step 4: Guest stays in hotel.*

Hotel's Motivation: Unlike the previous three steps, this section is not titled "Seller's Motivation." Why? In this situation, the travel wholesaler is the hotel's client, *not* the guest, staying at the property. The hotel's first legal responsibility is to fulfill its contractual obligation to its client (the travel wholesaler). Clearly, however, it is in the hotel's best interests to satisfy all hotel guests. If it does, it may be able to sell additional rooms to the travel wholesaler and, in the process, increase its RevPar.

Guest's Motivation: Hotel guests expect to receive a quality lodging experience regardless of how they arranged the room purchase. Generally, guests who have a travel package anticipate the same level of service that they would receive if they made a reservation directly with the hotel. FOMs should remember that even though these guests are only indirectly the hotel's *clients*, they are the hotel's *guests*. They should be treated the same as all other guests. This can be a challenge when front office staff are aware of (and may resent) the steep room discounts given to travel wholesalers and, as a result, to guests who purchase these heavily discounted rooms.

MODERN FRONT OFFICE ISSUES AND TACTICS

Just Who *Is* Responsible?

The lodging industry is part of the larger travel industry. As a result, rooms are often included in complete travel packages developed and marketed by tour operators and travel agents. Many travelers find it convenient to purchase a package that generally includes transportation, meals, and lodging as well as leisure activities.

If part of the travel experience goes awry, it can be challenging to determine exactly who is responsible to the traveler. Assume a wholesaler purchases 50 guestrooms from a four-star hotel at a steep discount and resells the rooms to a tour group. Who is responsible if the hotel does not actually live up to its four-star status? If a hotel does not operate in the manner promised to the travel wholesaler, the wholesaler may request compensation for poor service. Any refund is typically refunded to the hotel's client (the tour operator) who, in turn, compensates his or her clients (the hotel guests).

That logic, however sound, will be lost on the irate guest who wants to see the manager because he was "promised" a room with a king-size bed when, in fact, the FOM actually sold the tour operator other types of rooms.

Despite the large number of complex distribution channels in use today, the fundamental motivations of travel supplier and intermediary have remained essentially unchanged.

Current Distribution Channels

For hundreds of years, relatively no change occurred in the number of distribution channels. Today, FOMs must manage traditional channels, new channels, and the many variations of each that have developed. The rapidly evolving landscape of GDS modification, Internet and Web site development, and changing interface technology make predicting the future of distribution management complex. In fact, new variations of existing distribution channels seem to develop monthly. For most FOMs, however, the following distribution channels, or sources of business, and their variants will likely be of most importance: walk-in guests, telephones, fax, e-mail (or, in some cases, traditional mail), group-sales personnel, the GDS, chain or brand central reservation systems, and the Internet.

FOMs should evaluate the pros and cons, associated costs, and long-term benefits involved with accepting a reservation from each of the distribution channels and their variations. Although Internet-based booking is the wave of the foreseeable future, effective FOMs manage all possible distribution channels by understanding their unique differences.

SECTION REVIEW AND DISCUSSION QUESTIONS

Section Objective: Explain the evolution of distribution channels for hotel reservations, identify those that are in current use, and review the role of travel intermediaries in selling blocks of rooms.

Section Summary: In the earliest days of the hotel industry, guests could not make room reservations. Rather, they inquired about room availability when they arrived at their destination. Before the 1970s, hoteliers were able to use the telegraph, mail, and telephone to make advance reservations. In the mid-1970s, the airlines developed the Global Distribution System to help travel agents book airline trips for their clients. In the late 1980s, hotel organizations designed THISCO (a reservations system that could be interfaced with the GDS used by airlines), and, in the mid-1990s, online, integrated reservation systems became available. Today, most FOMs manage the following distribution channels (sources of reservations): walk-in guests, telephones, fax, e-mail, traditional mail, group-sales personnel, the GDS, a chain (brand) central reservation system, and the Internet.

Intermediaries such as travel agents and travel wholesalers often purchase guestrooms on behalf of clients or potential clients. Travel wholesalers are an excellent source of room sales for hotels during times when forecasts suggest low occupancy levels. However, hotels often give deep discounts to wholesalers to allow them to profit from the risk they take when they purchase these rooms.

Discussion Questions:

1. If you are traveling to a distant location and need a hotel room, which of today's most common distribution channels are you most likely to use? Why?
2. Assume that a guest who has a travel package including a room that was negotiated with a travel wholesaler is complaining to you, the FOM, about an amenity that was promised by the wholesaler. You know that this amenity was *not* negotiated as part of the contract. How would you handle this situation? What would you say?
3. How might hoteliers inform travel agencies around the country about their property? What would be the "ideal" relationship between a hotel and the travel agents who serve as an intermediary between guests and the property?

MANAGEMENT OF DISTRIBUTION CHANNELS

As suggested in Roadmap 7.2, management of distribution channels involves understanding how they operate and selecting tactics to manage them. Much is written in the hospitality industry press about distribution channels, probably because each channel is a source of reservations.

Because travel agents are a source of reservations (they make reservations for their clients), some in the industry believe that a hotel's travel agent relationships

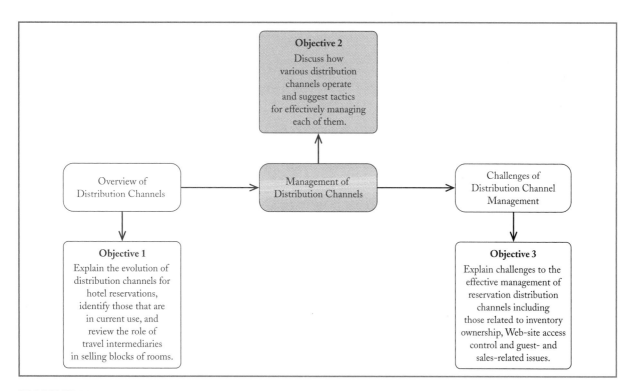

ROADMAP 7.2

should be managed as one distribution channel. The difficulty with this approach is that it confuses a buyer (user) with the method of buying (the channel). For example, a travel agent or individual guest could phone a hotel for a reservation. They also could request a reservation by e-mail or book the reservation directly on the hotel's Web site. A travel agent could use the GDS (either directly or through the Internet) to make the reservation.

Regardless of their preferred method of making a reservation, the user should find the hotel easy to communicate with, professional in its presentation, and logical in its pricing structure. FOMs must know how to manage each distribution channel, be aware of the relative costs of each channel, and know how to move potential guests from a higher-cost to lower-cost channel. Potential guests and intermediaries must use the distribution channels managed by the hotel. As users, they can choose from among a variety of distribution channels and hotels can, in many cases, influence which distribution channel a user selects.

To illustrate the concept of moving potential guests from one channel to another, consider the guest who reads the following fictional traveler-help article in a consumer magazine.

Be Thrifty!

If you usually book your hotel room online to save money, a new study suggests you should pick up the phone instead. After getting hotel prices online, our reporters received lower prices in three of every four attempts just by calling on the telephone and haggling.

We assigned a reporter to phone hotels for their lowest rates. When a hotel gave the reporter a room rate, the reporter would use a rate found on the Internet as leverage in asking for a better price. If the reservation agent could not go lower, the reporter asked for a different sort of discount, such as reduced parking or a room upgrade.

Our recommendation: Compare prices! Check the Internet travel sites before phoning the hotel's toll-free reservation number, and then call the specific hotel itself. And don't be afraid to haggle!

Some members of the hotel industry would consider this article negative because it provides travelers with "inside information" that may be helpful in receiving a lower rate. Based on their knowledge of distribution channels, however, savvy FOMs would make these conclusions:

- It is the hotel's revenue manager (not the channel) that establishes room rates.
- The costs associated with the use of each channel are different; therefore, any information that moves consumers from a higher-cost channel to a lower-cost channel benefits the property financially.
- Any business that does not offer fair and understandable pricing will not retain its customers.

FOMs who effectively manage their hotel's distribution channels provide a valuable service to their property and to their guests. When channels are well managed, the hotel will receive the maximum number of reservations from lower cost channels. When FOMs pass along some of those savings to guests, the guests will enjoy lower room rates and be more inclined to visit that hotel (or brand) more often.

Some industry observers believe that distribution channel management is actually a sales and marketing function and should be the responsibility of the hotel's DOSM rather than the FOM. (In smaller properties, these two positions may be held by the same individual.) In all cases, however, since the front office staff deal directly with reservations and with guests, the FOM must manage the hotel's distribution channels or have significant input into their management.

Walk-in Guests

In the past, FOMs expected guests to arrive with a reservation. (Those who arrived without one were viewed with some amount of suspicion!) If a hotel had vacant rooms, walk-ins were often quoted a higher rate than that given to guests who make advanced reservations. Today, walk-in guests are taken for granted, and they are considered a valuable revenue generator with no "recruitment" costs. As seen in Figure 7.4, the hotel pays no reservation fees for a walk-in guest. In contrast, the hotel pays at least three reservation-related fees (those for the Internet site, GDS, and CRS) for the reservation made on the Internet. These fees may represent from 5 percent to 30 percent of the quoted room rate. If rooms are available, the wisdom of making every effort to sell a room to each walk-in is clear.

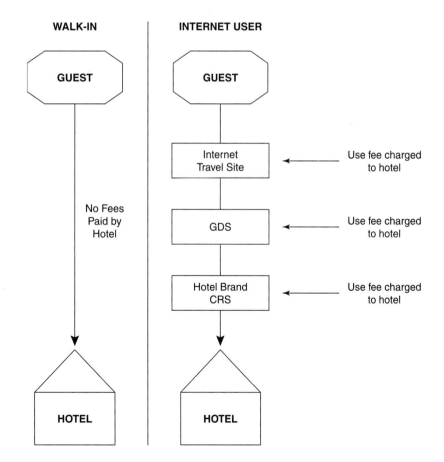

FIGURE 7.4   Walk-in guest versus guest who used the Internet to make a reservation.

To do so, FOMs should ensure that the rates quoted to walk-in guests will be acceptable. The walk-in guest may represent the hotel's last chance to sell a vacant room before its revenue potential disappears forever. Specific steps may help maximize rate acceptance by walk-ins:

- An immediate welcome and a friendly approach
- Attractive and clean lobby area
- Special discounts for last-minute travelers
- An upgraded room assignment, from a standard to a higher level room type, to increase perceived value and help ensure the room's sale
- A logical fade rate (see Chapter 6) if resistance is encountered

Telephones

Hotels still receive many reservations by telephone. Although individual circumstances vary, hotels with fewer than 200 rooms typically have no full-time reservations agent answering the telephone. Instead, front desk staff serve as the hotel's contact for telephone reservations. The manner in which reservation calls are handled can significantly affect a hotel's booking success. Compare, for example, two telephone greetings that might be used when the telephone is answered at the Altoona Hotel.

Front Desk Agent A: Altoona Hotel
Front Desk Agent B: It's a great day at the Altoona Hotel. This is Kimberly. How may I assist you?

To check the effectiveness of telephone sales efforts, some FOMs hire outside parties to "shop" the hotel for a reservation. How reservation requests and cancellation processes are handled is critiqued in detail in a written summary provided to the property's FOM and general manager. Such analyses can help to identify areas for improvement. Some hotel chains telephone-shop their franchisees and offer assistance in improving selling skills. In addition, training organizations have created tools to help FOMs ensure that their telephone distribution channel is an effective, and lower cost, option than other alternatives.

The art of selling rooms by telephone is a highly developed skill. FOMs who wish to improve the effectiveness of their staff should examine the following aspects of the selling process:

- Displaying appropriate telephone etiquette
- **Qualifying** the guest
- Describing the property
- Presenting the rate
- Overcoming price resistance
- Upselling
- Closing the sale (i.e., making the reservation)
- Recapping the sale

FRONT OFFICE SEMANTICS

Qualifying: Process of asking questions of guests to obtain answers that will better help the hotel salesperson meet the guest's reservations needs. For example, a front desk agent might ask, "Would you prefer one bed or two?"

Telephone reservations taken by the hotel's staff are free from fees, except for direct labor costs and franchise fees based on total room revenue. The telephone distribution channel, like the walk-in distribution channel, offers a cost-effective way to obtain a room sale. FOMs can take specific steps to help maximize the effectiveness of a hotel's telephone distribution channel:

- Implement an effective training program to teach telephone skills to all new front desk agents and reservations staff.
- Commit to ongoing use of a shopping program to ensure that quality standards are maintained.
- Provide adequate staffing to ensure rapid pickup (usually defined as three rings or less) by reservations personnel.
- Examine closely the experience of guests who must temporarily be placed on hold. Develop an effective and professional on-hold recording that encourages guests to stay on the line until they can be helped and find ways to minimize wait time.
- Use a logical fade rate if rate resistance is encountered.

Fax

Despite tremendous advances in computer technology, the fax remains a popular distribution channel, especially internationally, with people who do not use computers, and by with guests who want a written confirmation that a reservation has been made. At one time, a written confirmation letter was a hotel service desired by many guests, but many online booking sites do not offer this service.

Guests continue to request reservation information by fax, and the costs associated with accepting a fax for a reservation are relatively low. Therefore, FOMs are well served by careful management of this source of reservations. The following steps can help maximize the effectiveness of the fax distribution channel:

- Provide guests with a designated toll-free telephone number that is used for all incoming fax reservations.
- Train reservations staff to respond to a fax reservation request immediately upon its receipt.
- If reservations personnel have access to the Internet, consider purchasing software that allows the use of the hotel's e-mail system to reply to fax reservation requests. This method of response will enhance quality, speed, and record keeping.
- Keep adequate fax supplies (e.g., ink cartridges, paper, and cover sheets) on hand to ensure that no incoming fax (or its reply) is unnecessarily delayed.
- Ensure that fax cover and content sheets used to respond to reservations are professionally prepared, have large and easily readable type, and are recognized as selling tools that reflect positively on the hotel's quality.

E-Mail and Traditional Mail

E-mail and traditional mail distribution channels can be considered together because of their similarities. In both cases, the sender has the opportunity to ask, in detail and directly to hotel personnel, reservations-related questions. In addition, both provide a written record of the inquiry. Despite the similarities of the two channels, however, users of the two channels often have different timing expectations. The e-mail user reasonably expects a reply the same day or, at the very latest, the next day. Users of traditional mail would expect a reply to take several days or longer, depending on their own location and that of the hotel.

FOMs recognize that these channels, like some others, bypass third-party reservation fees. Although franchise fees must still be paid on the value of the reservation, the **net ADR yield** from mail sales is much higher than that from many other distribution channels. This is especially true of e-mail, where reservation costs are limited to the maintenance of a computer terminal and an e-mail address along with the direct labor needed to answer the e-mail.

FRONT OFFICE SEMANTICS

Net ADR yield: Rate (ADR) actually received by a hotel after subtracting the costs of fees and assessments associated with a room sale. The formula for net ADR yield is

$$\frac{\text{Room rate} - \text{Reservation generation fees}}{\text{Room rate paid}} = \text{Net ADR yield}$$

Typical reservation-related fees include those charged by travel agents, the GDS, a hotel's CRS, and operators of Internet booking sites.

FOMs understand that all revenue dollars are *not* created equally. A $100 room sold by channel with a high net ADR yield is more profitable than the same rate sold on a channel with a significantly lower net ADR yield.

Guests continue to request reservation information by e-mail and, to a lesser degree, traditional mail, so the management of these two channels is important. The following specific steps can be taken to help maximize the effectiveness:

- Reply to all mail inquires within 24 hours (sooner, if possible).
- For e-mail, use the hotel's name in the "from" line when responding to a message.
- For traditional mail, use professionally printed stationery and prohibit use of photocopied fill-in-the-blank letters that are not personalized for each guest.
- Use automated spell-check software on each mail reply before it is sent.
- "Sign" all mail clearly; include typed name, position, address, and direct contact information (telephone or e-mail) of the person replying to the reservation inquiry.

Group-Sales Department

A hotel's group-sales department may not seem like a separate distribution channel. When the hotel's sales and marketing personnel block rooms for a group, however, the rooms are taken out of the rooms inventory and are resold to the group's individual members. A hotel's group-sales department is, in fact, a distinct method of reservation delivery and should be viewed as a separate distribution channel.

Group rooms are usually sold at a discount off rack rate. Meeting planners and other buyers of group rooms expect to pay less per room when they book many room nights than when they purchase fewer room nights. If group rooms are sold at highly discounted rates, which may occur during a slow period, the effect on revenue is much the same as if the rooms were heavily discounted and sold to a travel wholesaler.

The decision to sell group rooms during busy times is often made in a consultation of the general manager, DOSM, revenue manager, and FOM. However, a block of rooms "sold" to a hotel's group-sales department does not entail the fees and charges associated with other channels of distribution. It is always better to discount rooms for the hotel's sales staff than to offer the same discount on rooms to be sold through a more costly distribution channel.

The discounting of unsold rooms during times when a hotel is hosting a group can be perilous. For example, consider a group sale at a specified price and group members who subsequently learn that the hotel is offering the same rooms for the same dates at a lower rate on a different distribution channel. This situation can cause the sales staff, as well as the hotel's FOM, much difficulty. Assume that the president of a state's Chess Players Association asks the sales department of a 600-room hotel to quote a group rate for its annual two-day meeting. The hotel's revenue management team quotes a rate of $99 per night. The group accepts the rate and signs a contract guaranteeing that its members will, by calling the hotel individually, purchase 200 rooms per night. One week before the meeting, however, the hotel's revenue manager, in an effort to sell the last 100 rooms remaining unsold on the two meeting days, posts a rate of $69 per night on the hotel's Web site. Members of the chess group who see the 69 rate will probably book their rooms outside the block or cancel reservations previously made within the block to purchase the less expensive rooms. They will also inform their friends who will then do the same. These actions will cause the revenue manager's estimates of group room pickup to be inaccurate and will depress ADR and RevPar during the period. Members of the association are also likely to express their displeasure to the club's president. They will logically suggest that the president did not secure a "good" rate for the association's members, because it is $30 per night higher than they themselves could secure from the Internet.

This situation will also cause the group's pickup to appear worse (lower) than it actually was and potentially (and unjustly) might trigger **attrition** clauses and penalties in the group's contract.

FRONT OFFICE SEMANTICS

Attrition: Difference between the original room request and the actual purchase of a group. For example, a group might reserve 100 rooms but use only 50 rooms. A hotel's standard contract for group rooms may stipulate that the group must pay an attrition penalty for over-reserving.

To complicate matters further, some members who did book within the group's block will, during check-in, angrily demand the lower rate advertised on the alternative distribution channel. Creating an unhappy group membership with a very unhappy president does not encourage repeat business! This increasingly complicated issue of group rooms distribution will be examined later in this chapter, along with effective strategies to counter the problem.

Global Distribution System

As described earlier in this chapter, the GDS is one of the older and more established hotel distribution channels. Some hospitality industry observers believe the GDS, once the booking choice of travel agents, is in decline. The Internet has emerged as a powerful challenge to the GDS, and many travelers no longer use a travel agent to book hotel rooms. Hoteliers who dismiss the GDS and its influence, however, may not fully understand its actual position in the industry.

The number of travel agencies and agents in the United States is declining. Those that remain serve, for the most part, clients with cruise and tour package needs, because many travelers desire the agent's skills for these bookings. Also, many travelers continue to use travel agents for airline tickets. The number of agencies using the GDS to make their clients' travel arrangements has remained relatively stable. Approximately 95 percent of all travel agencies use one of the four components (as of this writing) available in the GDS. Of the four (Galileo, Sabre, Worldspan, and Amadeus), Sabre is the most popular.

The GDS is not likely to be completely replaced by the Internet. Reservations booked by travel agencies (and, therefore, through the GDS) must be interfaced directly with a hotel's PMS to provide real-time rooms inventory, rates, and availability information. Hotels have incurred significant costs to create the switches (interfaces) that connect their hotel's PMS to the GDS. They are unlikely to abandon them in favor of creating the hundreds of switches that would be required to directly connect thousands of Internet booking sites to their hotel's PMS.

Also, recall that a travel agent using the GDS can simultaneously book airfares, hotel rooms, and car rentals. At the time of this writing, most hotel-operated Web sites do not provide this option. Most important, brand-operated Web sites do not allow travel agents or travelers to comparison shop. A visitor to the Hilton Web site will not see advertisements for Marriott hotels on the site. Travel agents have a fidu-

Travel agents use the GDS as well as the Internet to get their clients the lowest room rates.

ciary responsibility to their clients, so they are unlikely to switch from booking hotel rooms directly through the GDS to using a hotel-operated Web site that does not allow comparison shopping. Travel agents must be able to find the best-possible room rates for their clients. Even if travel agents (1) determine their clients' needs, (2) comparison shop on the GDS, and (3) use a hotel brand's Web site to book a lower room rate, all the booking information must travel back to the GDS to inform travel agents worldwide that the hotel has one fewer room to sell on a specific night. If room rate data and availability information were not centralized somewhere (and that "somewhere" is the GDS), travel agents and individual travelers would not know if rooms were available at a specific hotel. If rooms are available, the price at which these rooms can be purchased must be known. Currently, no Internet entity has challenged the GDS as the central warehouse of global information about hotel rates and availability.

GDS operations are likely to be changed, but not replaced, by the Internet. Travel agents increasingly check the Internet to compare prices hotels offer their clients through the GDS with prices these hotels post on their own and third-party Web sites. Far from disappearing, the services that the GDS offers to travel agencies and hotels are likely to expand and improve. When FOMs use this distribution channel, the following steps can help maximize its effectiveness:

- Monitor, on a regular basis, the number of hotel reservations received from each component of the GDS.
- Establish a relationship with one or more contacts from each GDS component that will yield significant sales volume to ensure the hotel's information on the GDS is accurate and to fully understand the fees charged for GDS use.
- Establish a relationship with one or more travel agents who can, on a regular basis, evaluate the accuracy of the hotel's information on the specific component of the GDS used by their agency.
- Consider travel agents as a unique and important "market" that can significantly affect reservation volume. Track the agencies that provide the most business to the hotel and maintain close contact with them in the same manner that the hotel maintains a close relationship with a high-volume transient client.
- Consider joining and becoming active in the American Society of Travel Agents (ASTA) to keep abreast of trends and changes occurring in the GDS. (To find out more about ASTA, go to www.astanet.com)

Central Reservation System

The hotel chain's or brand's CRS is an important source of reservations for a franchised hotel. In a strong brand, the reservations generated by the CRS may constitute 20 percent or more of a hotel's total monthly room revenue. Typically, a brand's CRS consists of a toll-free telephone call center, chain-operated Web site, e-mail and traditional mail reservations division, and a group-sales division. Of these, the call center and chain-operated Web site usually generate the most reservations. Also, because the hotel brand's CRS is interfaced with a switch to the GDS, in most hotels 70 percent or more of the travel agent and Internet bookings are routed through the CRS. The brand usually provides FOMs with significant details about the origination of the reservations channeled through the CRS, and FOMs should monitor the data carefully.

Hoteliers commonly complain that their CRS does not generate sufficient volume. FOMs who desire to maximize the revenue-generating potential of this distribution channel can take the following steps:

- Ensure that all hotel-related information supplied to the brand's call center is accurate and current.
- Conduct periodic shopping calls to the CRS to ensure that selling of the hotel's services and amenities is effective.
- Consider an annual visit to the brand's call center to personally meet its staff and to promote the hotel.
- Ensure that all information listed on the hotel's specifically assigned location on the brand's Web site is accurate and up-to-date.
- Supply attractive photos and creative copy for the Web site; describe the hotel's features and amenities to maximize interest.
- Follow up promptly (or coordinate follow-up with the sales and marketing department) on any group business leads provided by the CRS. Remember that potential clients' views of the entire chain will be influenced by the speed and quality of response to their inquiries.

Internet

If this book had been written five years ago, this section would have been of little or no interest to most FOMs. Today, entire books are being written on the importance of managing a hotel's Internet presence. The reason is clear: Travel is the most popular item sold on the Internet. Beginning in early 2001, the growth of room sales on the Internet became explosive. It is now estimated that by 2008 more than 50 percent of all room reservations made will be made over the Internet.

The hotel industry's relationship with other travel entities operating on the Internet did not get off to a particularly good start. In 2001, just as travelers' use of the Internet began to accelerate, the hotel industry began a multi-year slump. Some observers think the slump started with the tragic events of September 11, 2001, but others believe the occupancy decline had begun months earlier. Regardless of when the problem began, for several years hoteliers faced large numbers of unsold rooms at the same time that many travel wholesalers moved their businesses onto the Internet. Hoteliers regularly gave steep room discounts (often 30 percent or more) to travel wholesalers conducting business on the Internet. What hoteliers failed or refused to understand was that, for the first time, *all* customers could view the discounts posted by travel wholesalers on their Web sites. This was not the case in the pre-Internet hotel world. As a result, in the earliest days of room sales on the Internet sales, FOMs

- excessively discounted rooms sold to **e-wholesalers,**
- failed to appreciate the importance of rate integrity,
- gave up too much control over how their rooms were sold on the Internet, and
- were forced to take major steps to enhance their Internet presence quickly and to regain control of their pricing and business structures.

FRONT OFFICE SEMANTICS

E-wholesaler: Room reseller that obtains reduced (wholesale) room prices and inventory commitments directly from a hotel or through an agreement with the hotel's corporate brand managers. The wholesaler then publishes "retail rates" on its Web sites, usually at a mark-up of 20 percent to 40 percent. Examples are Travelocity, hotels.com, TravelWeb, and Expedia.

In 2004, at a hotel investment conference in Berlin, Germany, Hilton Hotel's chairman and chief executive officer Stephen Bollenbach was quoted as saying, "Internet intermediaries are not bad in the biblical sense. They just charge too much."[1] A hotel brand such as Hilton has its own Internet sites. Bollenbach's reference to intermediaries was directed at e-wholesalers with whom hotels collaborate to sell rooms.

Internet intermediaries are expensive. In 1995, estimated markups made by all Internet intermediaries were between 15 percent and 25 percent (or more) of the price these intermediaries actually paid for the rooms they purchased from hoteliers. Thus, despite the fact that guests are paying a higher price to the intermediary, the hotel actually achieves net ADR yields that can be significantly below those of other distribution channels. So one of the most popular distribution channels, the Internet, can also be one of the least desirable (i.e., least profitable) channels for hotels.

For today's FOMs and revenue managers, Internet sales can be good or bad. For example, if a hotel "sells" a $100 per night room on the Internet to a travel agent, the actual amount received can be $60 per night or even less. Recall that when a hotel sells a room through an online intermediary, it typically incurs Internet fees, GDS and CRS fees, and, as in this case, a 10 percent commission to the travel agent who booked the room. In addition, franchised hotels pay a fee of 2 percent to 10 percent to their franchisor on the room revenue generated by this sale. In most cases, a room sold on the Internet may originally have been discounted heavily by the hotels so it is not surprising that hoteliers monitor their e-wholesalers' Web sites carefully. Managing this distribution channel is even more critical when e-wholesalers promise the hotels working with them better placement on their Web sites in exchange for even greater room discounts.

FOMs who rely too heavily on some portions of the Internet for securing hotel revenue may be successful in building sales but not hotel profits. As Bollenbach's comment implies, a room properly sold through an Internet intermediary may be profitable and in the long-term best interests of a hotel. However, rooms that are inappropriately sold may actually cost the hotel much more money than is first apparent. Why? Because hotel rooms that are heavily discounted on a public distribution channel such as the Internet will be more difficult to sell at higher rates through other distribution channels with higher net ADR yield.

In addition to using e-wholesalers, FOMs can sell rooms on the Internet directly on their hotel's Web site, their brand's Web site that is part of the chain's CRS distribution channel, or third party Web sites (these are discussed later in this chapter). Regardless of how a hotel communicates with potential guests via the Internet, there are some basic principles that FOMs should consider for all Web sites:

- *Ensure accuracy.* Many Internet sites require that a hotel's information, rates, and room availability be updated frequently. Overwhelming amounts of data entry can create human error. When the FOM or revenue manager makes

[1]Scovick, M. "Internet Wars." *Hotels*, May 2004, 40.

MODERN FRONT OFFICE ISSUES AND TACTICS

Pricing Glitch or Bargain?

A computer glitch resulted in $61 round-trip tickets to Iceland for more than 100 people who noticed the "bargain" on www.cheaptickets.com, a travel Web site that offers travelers airline tickets, hotel rooms, rental cars, and cruises. The airline involved agreed to honor the ticket prices.

The airfare, mistakenly posted on May 25, 2004, for just over one day was less than 10 percent of the actual cost of a round trip ticket from the United States to Iceland. On the same day, competing Web sites listed round-trip tickets for approximately $787.

The Web is a powerful marketing tool that promotes FOMs' best ideas as well as their biggest mistakes. Instantaneous updating of a hotel's Web site is easy, but the double-checking for data-entry errors is critical. Legally, it would be difficult for a hotel to refuse a guaranteed reservation made via the Web if the consumer simply responded to an advertisement authorized by the hotel, even if the room rate charged in the advertisement was unrealistically low.

Let the seller—FOM—beware!

hundreds of allotment, pricing, blackout and MLOS decisions daily or weekly, data entry errors may occur. These can be eliminated through a series of checks and balances, and FOMs must do so or face the possibility of $1 (oops, $100!) room rates posted on the Internet.

- *Update regularly.* More Internet booking sites are now interfaced directly with the CRS of the hotels listed on their sites. Therefore, FOMs may not think it is necessary to communicate directly and regularly with the booking sites. Changing hotel features, amenities, renovations, specials, and in-house promotions, however, are examples of information that may need regular updating. FOMs should know the most important of their Internet reservation producers and visit those Web sites regularly to ensure that the information they contain is up-to-date.

- *Monitor placement.* In some cases, an individual using the Internet to search for a hotel room encounters only a few hotels, and a brief description of each will easily fit on the first "page" of the user's computer screen. In other situations, a search may reveal literally dozens of hotels; therefore, a specific hotel's **sell position** on the Web site may be strong or weak.

FRONT OFFICE SEMANTICS

Sell position: Specific placement order of a hotel's information on an Internet booking site. Hotels whose listings are "higher" (appear earlier) on a site are said to have a higher (better) sell position. Each Internet site determines its own listing order requirements, and FOMs should know them.

Those knowledgeable about the habits of computer users say that few users look beyond the first page or two of listings when selecting a hotel. If a hotel is listed on the third, fourth, or even later pages, the FOM should consider how the hotel can be moved up on the site's listings. If it cannot be relocated, the FOM may consider dropping the site, unless it is a proven revenue producer. The FOM should know on which sites the hotel is listed as well as where on the site the hotel is listed. Although a strong sell position on the site's first page is most desirable, the cost of securing this position should be considered carefully.

FRONT OFFICE SEMANTICS

Search engine: Web site specifically designed for the purpose of directing its visitors to other Web sites.

- *Manage search engines.* Probably the most important Internet process that FOMs must understand involves **search engines** and their role in selling rooms.

    More than 75 percent of people who log on the Internet use search engines for help in researching travel needs. Many hotel brands have had difficulty grasping the power of search engines such as Google and Excite. As a result, they have not used this important aspect of the Internet very well.

    Search engines work on a fairly simple principle. Their main goal is to direct searchers to the sites they seek. They do so by providing (listing) web addresses that the search engine believes best match the interests of the user of the search engine. For example, if a searcher enters the **keywords** *hotel*, *New York*, and *Times Square* into a search engine, hotels located in that area of New York will appear on the results screen.

FRONT OFFICE SEMANTICS

Keyword: Word or phrase used to find products, brands, services, or information via search engines.

Search engines look for and identify specified keywords contained on the Web pages of hundreds of Web sites. Then they create, for the searcher, a list of these sites in order of relevance.

It is common for hotels to buy the rights to keywords used by specific search engines.

Of course, hotel Web sites identified from a search want a favorable sell position, that is, to be listed as high as possible on the engine's results page. Search engine operators know this and typically charge hotels for a favorable listing position. These charges may take many forms; however, the most common involves selling keywords to hotels. A hotel, or hotel company, buys the right to be more favorably listed when specific keywords that have been purchased are used by searchers. A hotel near a sports arena, for example, may pay a search engine to have its Web site prominently placed to be seen by Internet users seeking information about the arena. FOMs should understand how search engines operate and ensure that the wording on all Web sites used by the hotel includes the keywords most likely to appear when the user of a search engine is a potential hotel guest.

The search engine industry is evolving constantly. FOMs need to monitor this process to achieve maximum site placement in search results. This can be done by adjusting various technical elements of a hotel's Web site. An increasingly popular relationship forged between hotels and search engine operators is the **pay-per-click** arrangement. In this creative partnership, rather than buy keywords, a hotel elects to pay more per click to obtain better placement on some sites but to pay less on other sites that are not considered as important in generating hits to the hotel's Web site.

FRONT OFFICE SEMANTICS

Pay-per-click: Arrangement in which a hotel Web site operator pays a search engine operator a fee for each hit (click) on the hotel's Web site that was initiated by the search engine's users.

- *Maintain rate integrity.* Rate integrity (parity) is a hot topic for FOMs. In relation to Internet sales, however, rate integrity simply means making logical decisions regarding the prices listed on each site advertising the hotel's room rates. This is not to imply that rates should or could be identical on all Web sites. In fact, hotel brand managers (franchisors) are now insisting that their affiliated hotels not offer—on any Internet site—room rates lower than those offered on the brand's site. The legality of such a mandate has yet to be tested. Nevertheless, it makes little sense to post widely varying room rates on various Internet sites unless there is a compelling rationale for doing so.
- *Monitor results.* A surprisingly high number of otherwise sophisticated hoteliers fail to monitor the results achieved by some of the Internet sites with which they do business. Hotel brands vary in the detail they can provide about the source of room reservations for a specific hotel. Usually however, they can provide helpful information about the relative contribution of a Web site to the brand's overall generation of reservations. Sites that charge for placement should be able to provide current **look-to-book data** to help justify their charges.

FRONT OFFICE SEMANTICS

Look-to-book data: Hotel term for the number of bookings achieved relative to the number of hits (looks) on a specific Web site. The best sites have high look-to-book ratios.

Any site that advertises room rates represents a potential sale. Effective channel distribution management, however, requires that FOMs look beyond the number of hits on a site and focus on the number of room sales that can be directly attributed to a specific site. This is especially true if the site is charging (and the hotel is paying) for an improved or enhanced sell position on the site. Although there are many ways in which hotel rooms can be sold on the Internet, FOMs commonly view Internet sales as having been produced by a property, chain, or third-party Web site.

Property Web Site

A hotel's individually developed and maintained Web site is one of the best ways to secure an Internet room sale. The reason is financial. When an Internet user buys a room directly from a hotel (as is also the case with a walk-in, telephone, e-mail, traditional mail, or fax request), the fees paid by the hotel on that sale are either eliminated or reduced. In the past, many franchised hotels resisted operating their own, independent site, because they did not have the ability to interface the site directly with their PMS. Independent hotels, however, that also needed the ability to sell online designed procedures to work through this challenge. Even now surprisingly few chain-affiliated hotels (most of the properties are located in the United States) operate their own Web site.

Most franchise or brand hotels rely on the Web sites designed and operated by their chain's CRS for their Internet presence. This is unfortunate because less than 25 percent of Internet travelers search for hotels by brand name. More than 70 percent search for hotels by using a search engine and typing in a query such as *hotels in Boston* or *Boston hotels*. In most cases, these searches produce results filled with travel wholesalers, travel agencies, and other sites selected by the search engine. The goal of a hotel's FOM, however, is to have the hotel's site appear early in search listings. The ideal situation is for a hotel's individual Web site to show up in the first 10 or 15 listing results from a relevant search. Why would an FOM want third-party sites selling rooms at much lower net ADR yields to rank ahead of the hotel's site?

If properly understood and managed, the Internet provides a hotel with an easily accessible location for it to meet and interact with its customers. This lowers the hotel's dependence on third parties to increase bookings. In the Internet age, meaningful and effective management of e-distribution channels begins with the hotel's main (and independently operated) Web site, because it can be one of the property's lowest-cost and highest-net-ADR-yield channels. The hotel's site should encourage visitors to book rooms in a quick, easy, and logical manner. Complete development of a hotel's Web site is beyond the scope of this text. From the perspective of distribution channel management, however, hoteliers should carefully consider the following factors when developing property Web sites:

- *Written content.* A site's written content should answer questions that site visitors are likely to have about the hotel (e.g., what? where? how much?) and encourage visitors to book rooms. Sources for key information about the hotel already exist. The property's current brochures, sales letters, promotional kits, and other marketing items should be designed for placement on the Web site. Other important content areas include nearby attractions, activities, and local areas of interest.

  Written content is the single most important element of any Web site, because it will be scanned by search engines responding to queries from potential guests. Therefore, it is usually helpful to seek the assistance of a search engine specialist before finalizing the site's content. When checking the content, the specialist should not change what is said but how something is said. Search engines have rules about the number of times a term can be used, how terms should be used, and where terms should appear in site documents. A search engine specialist can help the FOM to maximize the chance of having a strong sell position in search results.

- *Visual and audio content.* As more and more U.S. Internet users acquire high-speed Internet access, hoteliers will likely increase the visual and audio content of their Web sites. This content includes logos, graphics, digital photography, and all forms of streaming audio or video. Not all users will want to "waste time" with extensive streaming video or audio. Long lead-ins and excessive delays can be caused by excessive content downloads. For example, recently many hotels have added **virtual tours** to their sites.

FRONT OFFICE SEMANTICS

Virtual tour: Streaming video located on a Web site that shows sections of a hotel in a 360-degree view.

Often virtual tours are very slow to load, move too slowly, and show only one aspect of a hotel at a time (e.g., a room or lobby area). Short videoclips showing key aspects of the hotel may be more effective, and these can also be e-mailed to guests who want more information, burned onto a CDs for give-aways, and mailed to tour operators.

- *Reservation device.* Guests must have the ability to book a room directly from a hotel's proprietary Web site. Potential guests want to know immediately if their requested room is available. Therefore, a property's Web site must have a reservation device that displays real-time reservation availability. If it does not, many site visitors will browse to another hotel site in just seconds.

- *Appropriate links.* Effectively linking a Web site is a key strategy. Links from other Web sites mean your Web site is connected to a larger portion of the Web and may improve your hotel's exposure on the Internet. Links should be established with area demand generators such as local attractions, the chamber of commerce, and the convention and visitors bureau. The hotel's Web developer should contact these generators and ask for a reciprocal link.

Chain Web Site

Technically, a chain's own Web site is a part of its CRS. In 2004, chain-operated Web sites were estimated to account for 60 percent of all Internet hotel bookings.[2] At the same time, however, franchisors were frustrated to learn that travelers were booking a large numbers of rooms (40 percent) on third-party Web sites. These third-party bookings most often consisted of rooms sold by hotels to wholesalers at a significant discount; this meant reduced revenues for franchisees and reduced franchise fees to franchisors.

The reasons for the popularity of the third-party sites are twofold. First, travelers can often purchase rooms at a lower rate on these sites. Second, users have the opportunity to compare the prices of different chain hotels on one site. This is much faster than going to multiple chain-operated sites (each of which lists only its own hotels) when comparing room prices. Most consumers want the capability of shopping multiple hotel brands at the same time.

[2]Gilbert, R. A. "Distribution Madness." *Lodging*, July 2004, 40.

To respond to the challenges of third-party sites, most franchisors have instituted the **lowest-rate guarantee.**

FRONT OFFICE SEMANTICS

Lowest-rate guarantee: Program that assures travelers that the lowest available rate for a specific room type on a specific date will be found on the franchisor's Web site.

Lowest-rate guarantees are popular with travelers and have increased bookings on franchisor-operated Web sites. Franchisors have instituted another method to drive consumers to their sites: They are denying frequent-guest program points to consumers who do not make their Internet room purchase on their Web site.

Chain-operated Web sites will continue to be a strong distribution channel. Many travelers first seek third-party sites to research area hotel availability and rates. They then surf to the preferred chain-operated site to secure a hotel's guaranteed lowest rate and other benefits provided by chain sites.

Third-Party Web Sites

Third-party Web sites work in a manner similar to the way a telephone company's Yellow Pages would work if travelers had easy access to every single hotel listing. Consumers could, at one time, see the names and addresses of competing hotels located in the same geographic area. Third-party Web sites provide consumers with this benefit, and it is a powerful one. Comparison shopping tools available on third-party sites such as Expedia, hotels.com, Orbitz, and SideStep may well ensure the long-term viability of these sites, even if chain-operated sites continue their lowest-rate guarantees.

Although operators of third-party Web sites continue to improve their sites, products, and services to attract more consumers, FOMs (and all hoteliers) need to remember that these sites do not own or operate hotels, and they have no rooms to sell that have not been provided by hoteliers. The hotel industry has had mixed feelings about selling rooms to third-party sites. In the past, FOMs made a business decision that it was advantageous to sell steeply discounted rooms to travel wholesalers. The decision to sell to third-party Web sites, however, hurt hoteliers when these rates were then advertised on the Internet. For example, a hotel could not effectively promote a rate of $100 per night at the front desk or on its Web site when a third-party site offered rooms that had been sold to it at up to 50 percent off for $75. In this case, the third-party site marked up "its" rooms by 50 percent of the price it paid. When the additional costs of travel agent, GDS, and CRS fees are considered, some hotels find that their net ADR yields are less than 30 percent on rooms sold to third-party sites! Net ADR yields like these prompt industry leaders such as Stephen Bollenbach to make comments similar to the one quoted earlier in this chapter.

Not all third-party sites operate in the same manner. Two very different models are in operation: the merchant model and the opaque model. FOMs need to be aware of the fundamental differences in these two types and how they affect distribution channel management.

Merchant Model.   In the early 2000s, many hoteliers did not understand how the Internet and online distribution worked. The result was proliferation of **merchant model** sites in which operators of third-party sites bought (or reserved), at great discount, hotels' excess rooms inventory and advertised those rooms for sale online.

FRONT OFFICE SEMANTICS

Merchant model: Internet sales method in which hotels sell or commit rooms to operators of Web sites. These sites, in turn, allow consumers to enter requested location and arrival dates; consumers are presented with a choice of specific hotels and associated rates available for immediate purchase on the Web site.

At that time, the hotel industry was behind other sectors of the travel industry in adopting the entire Internet as a significant distribution channel. A weak travel environment and the results of the terrorist attacks on September 11, 2001, found many hoteliers unprepared (financially and technologically) to deal with the explosion in online bargain hunting and bookings. Online discounters exploited this naivety and desperation in the hospitality industry. Many hoteliers who were looking for a quick fix for their eroding occupancies and RevPars turned to these discounters for "free" services.

What most revenue managers did not realize (or chose to ignore) was the long-term impact on hotel brand image and the downward rate pressures that would result from publicly advertising heavily discounted rates. The new breed of "yield manager" of a 300-room hotel could, for example, sell the operator of a third-party site 100 rooms for a Sunday night when these rooms were certainly going to be vacant. As the logic went, if these rooms were sold to the site operator for $50, who then resold them on the Internet for $75, the hotel still achieved an additional $5,000 (100 rooms at $50 each = $5,000) in revenue.

Unfortunately, even in the best-case scenarios, hotels achieved acceptable occupancy rates only at the expense of much lower ADRs and permanent damage to their rack

Many travelers use third-party Internet sites to comparison shop.

rates. FOMs believed they had little expectation of maintaining occupancy, so they made their inventory available at extremely steep discounts, and third parties virtually charged whatever they wanted. In fact, operators of third-party Web sites routinely achieved net profit margins on their sales of 25 percent to 40 percent. These profit levels were much higher than the 10 percent commission travel agents traditionally had received.

Most hotel owners and managers liked the sites because of the sales they generated. Consumers liked the sites because of the savings they achieved. The operators of the third-party sites enjoyed much greater levels of profits compared with traditional travel agents. In fact, even travel agents liked the sites, because they found that these sites frequently offered room rates lower than those on the GDS, and hotels still paid travel agents their 10 percent commission regardless of the distribution channel (e.g., telephone, fax, GDS, or Internet).

Eventually, hotel franchisors and savvy operators began to realize the difficulties associated with the sites of third-party merchants. Chain managers were not happy that their own franchisees (who, in exchange for using the brand name, pay franchise fees based on total room revenue) were offering big discounts to Web sites of third parties. The chain-operated Web sites were selling rooms at significantly higher rates or, in some cases, were not selling any rooms at all because those available had already been sold to operators of merchant sites. Chain operators realized that their franchisees were simply training customers to select their brands only when they could receive a significant discount, and this diluted the brand's value. Franchisors also realized that the extensive television marketing campaigns designed by operators of third-party sites reinforced the message that the chain-operated sites were a more expensive place to shop. Individually, the chains did not have the funds needed to effectively refute these claims.

To combat the rise of third-party, merchant model sites, chains began investing more heavily in the improvement of their own Web sites. They began to guarantee and publicize that their brands' sites offered prices that were the same or lower than prices available anywhere else. The tactics worked, and more consumers began using chain-operated sites. In the future, hotel chains will likely find additional ways to move consumers away from third-party sites and onto their own sites.

Merchant model Web sites, however, will continue to flourish, because they allow for comparison shopping. Fundamentally, there is nothing wrong with an FOM using online discounters to unload excess or distressed inventory. However, it is financially unwise to turn these online services into a hotel's primary and, in many cases, only Internet distribution channel. If a hotel appears on the Internet only through discounted rates offered by the online intermediaries and merchants, Internet users will *always* encounter the hotel's discounted rates. Then, as no other rates are listed on the Internet, these discount rates will become, in the consumer's mind, the hotel's rack rate.

Opaque Model. On an **opaque model** site, buyers (consumers) do not know the name of the hotel they have chosen until after they have committed to purchasing the room.

FRONT OFFICE SEMANTICS

Opaque model: Internet sales method in which consumers "bid" an amount they are willing to pay for a room on a specific arrival date, and the operator of the third-party Web site matches that bid with a hotel willing to sell rooms at that rate.

Studies have shown that rooms sold by opaque sites that do not disclose the brand name or exact location of a hotel until after rooms are booked are 30 percent to 40 percent cheaper than the same rooms sold through merchant sites. Opaque sites appeal to travelers who are price conscious and who are not loyal to a specific hotel brand. Opaque models have been popular with hoteliers. The advantage of these sites to FOMs is that, unlike merchant sites, they do not publicly display heavily discounted rates that may make it more difficult for hoteliers to sell rooms at higher ADRs through other distribution channels.

For travelers, opaque models are typically less expensive, but they do have disadvantages. The nondisclosure of hotel names and specific locales may be annoying to shoppers who have a favorite chain and to shoppers who want to redeem frequent-guest points or to stay in a specific location. The opaque model, however, does benefit consumers who enjoy reduced prices. Opaque sites are hotel-friendly businesses because they help protect the integrity of a hotel's overall pricing structure.

An Evolving Channel

The Internet continues to evolve as an effective distribution channel. Professional FOMs must continue to monitor its development to position their hotels in a way that maximizes RevPar. At this time, FOMs can take the following steps to improve the effectiveness of the Internet:

- Seek rate parity across all distribution channels, including the Internet.
- Show the hotel on as many sites as is realistically profitable.
- Keep only current information about the hotel on Web sites.
- Promote the use of lower-cost sites (higher net ADR yield) over higher-cost sites.
- Use information found on competitors' Web sites to compare and evaluate rate management decisions.

SECTION REVIEW AND DISCUSSION QUESTIONS

Section Objective: Discuss how various distribution channels operate and suggest tactics for effectively managing each of them.

Section Summary: Distribution channels through which hotel reservations are made must be managed effectively to maximize RevPar. Alternatives include some that have been used for many years (e.g., walk-in guests, telephone, fax, and traditional mail). More recent methods are e-mail, use of the hotel's group-sales departments, the Global Distribution System, and central reservation systems. Today another distribution system—the Internet—is increasingly used by individual properties, franchise organizations, and third-party sellers to advertise rooms and by potential guests looking for rooms. The hotel industry was relatively slow at recognizing the potential of the Internet and how it could be used to its advantage. Now, however, hoteliers recognize problems that can be created when the Internet is not used properly and advantages that occur when it is used effectively.

Discussion Questions:
1. The chapter suggests that a hotel's group-sales department can be considered a distribution channel for reservations. Do you agree? Why or why not?

2. The text mentions four successful third-party Web sites: Expedia, hotels.com, Orbitz, and SideStep). Review these sites and address the following questions:

- What types of consumer information on these sites is common to all sites?
- What, if any, information is unique?
- Which site appears to be the most friendly? Why?
- Which site or sites would you use most frequently use if you were a consumer? Why?

CHALLENGES OF DISTRIBUTION CHANNEL MANAGEMENT

As indicated in Roadmap 7.3, this concluding section of the chapter addresses the challenge of managing distribution channels. First review Figure 7.5, which summarizes the various distribution channels discussed in this chapter.

FOMs can influence their sources of reservations and, therefore, profits by managing distribution channels. One way to do so is to convert repeat customers to less-expensive distribution channels. For example, consider guests who booked their first stay at a hotel via the Internet. When they are checking out, they can be asked about reserving a room for future use. This approach allows the hotel to avoid Internet,

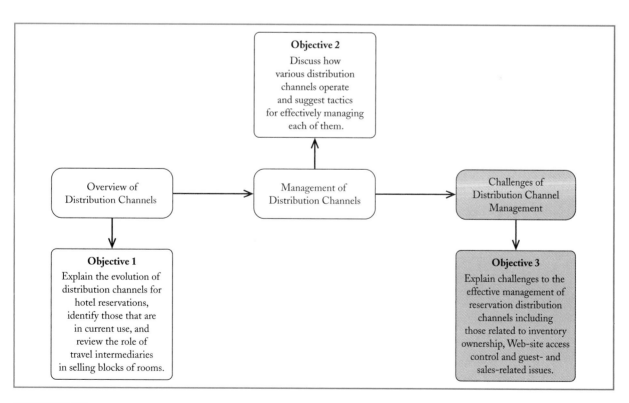

ROADMAP 7.3

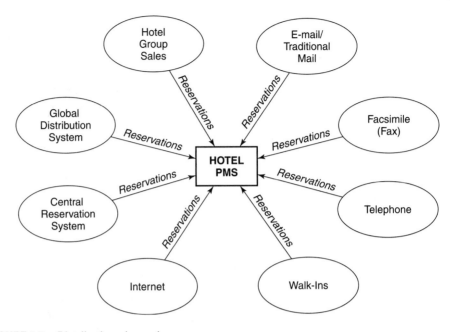

FIGURE 7.5   Distribution channel summary.

GDS, and CRS fees for that reservation, because the sale is made without any intermediaries who must be paid. The result is a higher-net ADR yield and greater profitability for the hotel. FOMs should ensure that each of their distribution channels is managed properly and functions effectively, and they must work to make the reservation process simple for guests.

Figure 7.6 displays the net ADR yields typically associated with the different distribution channels examined in this chapter. They are averages, not absolutes. These yields vary by Web site used, franchisors' policies, and the skill of hotel managers in negotiating fee structures. Nevertheless, note that the source of a reservation does have a big impact on the amount of revenue the hotel actually collects.

Distribution channels discussed will likely continue to evolve. Some will grow and others will decline; still others will cease to exist and be replaced by new alternatives. As these changes occur, the challenges faced by FOMs as they manage distribution channels will change as well. Currently, significant issues faced by FOMs relating to the channels of distribution described in this chapter involve inventory ownership, control of Web site access, and guest-and sales-related issues (rate consciousness, group-block management, occupancy tax liability). Each of these challenges is reviewed next.

Inventory Ownership

Most hotels rely on intermediaries to help fill their rooms. As a result, they typically enter into fixed-term contracts with wholesalers and large travel agencies to supply an agreed-on number of room nights at discounted rates. Allotting blocks of rooms for exclusive use by these intermediaries, however, may mean refusing

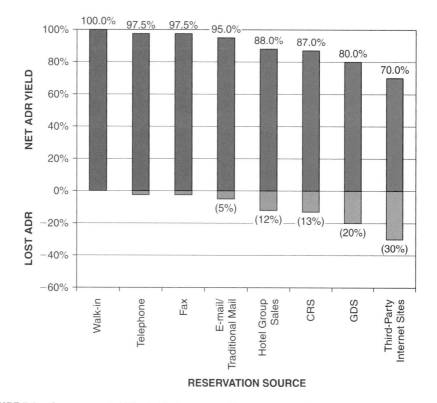

FIGURE 7.6   Average net ADR yields by reservation source.

allotment requests by smaller agents and individual consumers who would pay higher rates.

Many hoteliers have entered contracts with intermediaries (third-party Web sites) at rates they later regretted. A sold room, however, is a sold room. Every FOM, DOSM, or revenue manager who sells rooms to an intermediary must understand that the rate at which the rooms were sold

- has been agreed to by the hotel as part of its contract with the intermediary,
- may become public information,
- will likely allow the intermediary to compete for customers *directly* against the hotel, and
- can lead to very low net ADR yields (relative to other distribution channels) for the hotel.

Once a room is sold, FOMs may have little or no control over how it is resold. At the time of a sale, ownership (control) of the hotel's rooms inventory moves from the hotel to the intermediary. This concept dates back to the earliest days of the relationship between the hotel and travel wholesaler and has not been changed because of the Internet. Instead, the Internet has made it easier for an intermediary partners to compete directly against the hotel using the rooms sold to them by the hotel, unless the hotel has put restrictions on how these rooms will be resold. FOMs must carefully examine the partners to whom they sell rooms and learn how the rooms will be remarketed.

MODERN FRONT OFFICE ISSUES AND TACTICS

Industry Leadership

Operators of third-party Web sites were nothing short of stunned when International Hotel Group (IHG), the world's largest hotel company, announced it was adopting new standards for its brands selling or reselling hotel room inventories through online travel companies. IHG's portfolio includes, at the time of this writing, more than 3,500 hotels (e.g., InterContinental Hotels, Holiday Inn, Holiday Inn Express, Candlewood) representing more than 500,000 guestrooms.

In early 2004, IHG said it was committed to working only with online distributors and their affiliates who did not engage in confusing and potentially unclear marketing practices and who clearly presented taxes and fees to consumers, respected IHG's trademarks, and ensured that reservations were guaranteed through an automated (real-time) confirmation process. The immediate result of the announcement was that companies such as Travelocity, Expedia, and Hotels.com could no longer set the contractual terms for the hotels in IHG's portfolio.

Third-party Web sites grew their businesses during the most recent lean years of hotel operations (2001–2004). Some hoteliers looked at third-party sites as the solution to their occupancy problems and assigned them large amounts of heavily discounted rooms inventory. They placed few, if any, restrictions on how those rooms could be marketed for resale. In the mid- 2000s, due in large part to decisive actions such as those initiated by IHG, the balance of power began to shift back to hotels.

If and when third-party Web sites actually operate hotels, they will be able to set the terms for room sales. Until then, savvy FOMs can learn from watching industry leaders manage and influence third-party sites that partner with them to sell or resell the *hotel's* inventory of rooms.

Control of Web Site Access

A hotel's Web address is intended to direct Internet users to the specific property's Web site. A business's Web address identifies its location on the Internet in much the same way that a street address identifies its physical front door. Internet addresses (doorways), however, have unique problems. Specifically, if they are not managed properly, they can easily disappear; that is, be stolen or hijacked. As a result a hotel's potential customers may be led to inappropriate content sites or even to the hotel's competitors.

To see how easily it is to hijack clients, let's revisit the Altoona Hotel. Mike Hernandez, the property's DOSM, worked with an online Web site designer to create a site for the hotel and to secure www.altoona-hotel.com as the site's address. Mike bought the rights to the keyword *Altoona* from several prominent search engines. Thereafter, when a user typed the word *Altoona* into the search engine, the hotel's Web site appeared in a favorable sell position on the results page. The Altoona's Web site was designed to attract visitors and lead to reservations. Well-designed and user-friendly, the site soon attracted a significant numbers of hits and clients.

A technology-savvy competitor, however, contacted the same search engines and bid on a select list of keywords, each of which was sold inexpensively because there was little or no demand for them. (Recall that any hotel or hotel company can buy the right to be more favorably listed when specific keywords that have been purchased are entered by users of the search engine). Mike's competitor purchased the following keywords:

- Altona
- Altoona-Motel

- Alltona
- Altuna Hotel
- Altoona *and* Gotel
- Altoona *and* Jotel

Note that keystroke errors, misspellings, and uncommon phrasings can all lead unsuspecting searchers to a site they had not intended to visit—the competitor's site. Hoteliers who do not aggressively protect their online addresses may be left to the mercy of unscrupulous third-party operators who divert users to their own sites. A common technique used by these operators is a paid placement in which the third parties bid on brand-name keywords in the search engines and divert the customer to the site of their choice rather than to the customer's intended site.

Approximately 70 percent to 80 percent of the information searchers find on the Internet is provided by the larger search engines. Therefore, the best way to attract visitors to a Web site is to have a high ranking in the main search engines. Before submitting a site to the search engines and directories, FOMs should learn how to write the title, headings, and the first few paragraphs of each page submitted. Doing so will help maximize keyword use and obtain a better ranking. After submitting a Web site, FOMs should periodically review their ranking in the search engine listings by the key phrases they have chosen as well as by variations of their own keywords that might be used by competitors. In some cases, a professional in the field of Web site traffic generation may be needed to assist in the efforts. Also, FOMs should consider purchasing the rights to words similar to the keywords most used by a hotel (include misspellings and variations).

Guest- and Sales-Related Issues

Many management tasks and issues involving distribution channels are internal to the hotel; others, however, involve guests and their direct purchase of rooms. Some of the most important concerns relate to an increase in guests' rate consciousness, new and increasingly difficult challenges in group-block management, and the looming and unresolved issue of occupancy tax liabilities resulting from sales by third-party sites.

Rate Consciousness

The emergence of the Internet in the 1990s increased the transparency of hotel room rates. The availability of real-time rate information on the Internet allows business and group travelers to examine all rates listed by hotels and quickly revise their reservations if a hotel posts a lower rate. Therefore, business and group rates, instead of being true negotiated rates, are actually becoming negotiated *maximum* rates. It is critical that FOMs and revenue managers understand this. As a distribution channel, the Internet may allow a hotel to quickly adjust its rates downward to fill remaining inventory, but it often does so while putting intense downward rate pressure on the hotel's other distribution channels.

The Internet has also reduced search time, particularly for leisure travelers. The act of shopping around has been reduced from time-consuming telephone calls to a few mouse clicks. Approximately 75 percent of Internet reservations are made by discount seekers; that is, people using the Internet to secure the lowest-possible price for hotel reservations. The remaining 25 percent of Internet reservations are made by convenience bookers; that is, people who use the Internet to avoid speaking with a travel agent or calling a reservation center. FOMs who monitor their competitor's rates on the Internet often find that in periods of high demand, room rates posted on the Internet can be increased significantly to improve RevPar and to drive volume to lower-cost distribution channels.

Group-Block Management

Chapter 6 introduced the issue of conflict between group and transient room rates. The potential problem involves maintaining the hotel's rate integrity (consistency) when there is a significant difference between transient room rates quoted for single rooms and group room rates negotiated for (or given to) groups during the same period. For FOMs in full-service and meetings-oriented hotels, there is no greater rate issue than the management of group room rates and blocks within the context of effective yield management.

The sale of group rooms represents a significant distribution channel. Because group buyers purchase a large number of rooms, they are often offered rates below those offered to individual travelers. For example, say the Altoona Hotel's ADR is $100 and a group buyer approaches the hotel to purchase 1,000 room nights to be used in a one-week period. The hotel will likely attempt to secure the sale by quoting a room rate well below its average rate of $100. Assume now that the hotel offers, and the buyer accepts, a group room rate of $75 per night. In this case, it is unlikely that the hotel will encounter parity issues about the group-block rate. The rates offered to this group's members are likely to be well below the individual room rates that will be publicized and offered on the hotel's other distribution channels, for the same arrival and departure dates.

Sometimes, however, group rates are negotiated that are higher than the room rates offered on other distribution channels. To understand how this can occur, consider the information in Figure 7.7. This paragraph is an excerpt from a standard **RFP** issued by a group room buyer. In this instance, the buyer is the National Collegiate Athletic Association (NCAA), and it is seeking rooms for rounds one and two of the women's Division 1 basketball championship.

FRONT OFFICE SEMANTICS

RFP (request for proposal): Official request by a room buyer asking that a hotel quote its rate and contract terms in response to the buyer's specific room and meeting space requests.

NCAA First and Second Round Headquarter Hotel Agreement

If the hotel is selected as the NCAA headquarters, the hotel agrees to:

1. Provide two rooms upgraded to bedroom parlor suites for use by the NCAA Division 1 Women's Basketball Coach Representative at the contracted standard room rate.
2. Provide two rooms upgraded to bedroom parlor suites for use by the Head Coach and primary administrator at the contracted standard room rate.
3. Provide one complimentary standard room night for each 30 room nights actually occupied.

FIGURE 7.7   Excerpt from standard group contract.

Source: Clarion Hotel and Conference Center/Greater Lansing Visitor and Convention Bureau Public Record Bid Offering, May 2004.

There will be a cost to the hotel to make the special allowances shown in Figure 7.7. Other groups may ask the hotel for a variety of additional items, including complimentary meeting space, free use of audiovisual equipment, complimentary welcome receptions, and rebates or commissions to be paid to the group. In most cases, the hotel will grant these requests, but the hotel will grant them dependent on the group actually using the number of rooms requested.

In cases where the group provides a rooming list of attendees, rate comparison issues are minimal. If, however, individual group members must contact the hotel to secure their own rooms from the reserved block (see Chapter 9), rate issues can be significant. The estimated cost of group giveaways and allowances must be factored into the room rate quoted to the group. When the requests of a group buyer involve a large amount of meeting space and significant numbers of complimentary services or payments, the hotel may quote a room rate for the block that is equal to or even higher than the hotel's normal transient room rate. In addition, the hotel is likely to tie the granting of the buyer's requests to the group's actual room pickup (see Chapter 5). Thus, the potential for significant conflict exists in managing group blocks.

As travel Web sites offer more choices and become easier to use, individuals attending meetings are discovering that they can often obtain lower prices then group rates. In addition, independent travel companies have begun to aggressively target meetings and convention attendees with e-mails and faxes offering cheaper rooms at hotels other than the headquarters (host) hotels. Also, if a hotel's revenue manager lowers room rates when the group is meeting in the hotel (e.g., by posting discounted rates on Internet travel sites), group members are likely to book these rooms rather than the ones originally blocked for the group.

Of course, lower room rates are of interest to attendees, but they can become a major problem for the hotel and the meeting planner. To encourage meeting attendees to purchase rooms from within the group's reserved block, many meeting organizers ask attendees not to book cheaper rooms at competing hotels. Others have started charging two registration fees for their events: A lower fee is charged to those paying the official room rate, and a higher fee is charged to those who make other lodging arrangements. Some meeting organizers have even prohibited attendees who make other lodging arrangements from using services such as shuttle buses or from attending some sponsored events. Meeting attendees must weigh their potential savings with the inconvenience of staying at a hotel other than headquarters and the damage they can cause their association by "unofficially" staying at the official hotel which occurs when they purchase rooms from the host hotel but outside the group block of rooms.

FOMs and revenue managers want to sell as many rooms as possible within the parameters of effective yield management and rate integrity. It makes little sense for an FOM to establish, for example, a group's rate at $100 per night while posting rooms at $50 per night on an Internet travel site in the belief that any sale is better than no sale. Heavily discounting rooms during the time of a group's meeting may result in those consequences:

- Upset the group's leadership. Group leaders will seem to be poor negotiators who were outsmarted by the hotel.
- Upset the hotel's sales representative responsible for servicing the group. Rather than appearing to have given the group a good rate, the hotel sales representative will seem to have taken advantage of the group. The result is a loss of credibility on the part of the sales representative and the hotel.

- Create hard feelings and accounting difficulties as meeting planners attempt to receive the concessions promised in their contracts. In many cases, group members will have purchased the total number of room nights they had contracted to buy. However, the hotel's management of channel distribution drove attendees away from the group block (but not away from the hotel), so these attendees' room night purchases will not be counted as part of the block pickup.
- Provide lower net ADR yields for the hotel. Distribution channels that allow hoteliers to quickly reduce their rates at the last minute to sell rooms are the same channels that produce low net ADR yields. A hotel that tries, at the last minute, to **dump rates,** will almost always find any rooms that sell do so only at severely reduced profitability levels.

FRONT OFFICE SEMANTICS

Dump rate: Hotel term for significantly reducing room rates for a given date or dates. Used as in, "We need to *dump the rate* for our suites this weekend."

FOMs, hoteliers, and meeting planners need to monitor the difficult and complex issue of maximizing RevPar while maintaining block rates that are "fair" to the hotel and its group clients.

Occupancy Tax Liability

Chapter 4 explained that an occupancy tax involves special assessments collected from guests and paid by a hotel to a local taxing authority. The tax rate is set by local authorities and is assessed on the selling price of a hotel's guestrooms. Although it seems fairly straightforward to determine how much tax should be charged and collected, a question arises about the taxes due on a room sold to a third-party, e-commerce wholesaler. If a local occupancy tax rate is 5 percent, then a $100 room sold to a hotel's typical walk-in guest would generate a tax of $5. If, however, that same room were sold to an Internet wholesaler for $50 and then resold by that wholesaler for $80 should the tax be assessed on $50 or $80? The tax issue is difficult because it could mean that either the hotel or the wholesaler has paid too little tax and may have a large tax liability. In dispute is whether taxes should be paid on the amount a wholesaler pays to the hotel or on the amount paid by the guest. In this example, above the wholesaler would send the hotel $2.50 to cover the occupancy tax ($50 × 5% = $2.50). The guest, however, would be charged $4 ($80 × 5% = $4).

The issue is significant because it is estimated that as much as 30 percent of the operating profit of many third party web-site operators arises from fees and the tax savings that occur from calculating the tax rate based on the wholesale room price rather than on retail price.[3] Hotel guests buying through these sites are taxed on the retail rate they pay for their rooms, and the wholesaler keeps the difference. Wholesalers, not surprisingly, believe taxes should be paid on the wholesale price because, historically, hotel occupancy taxes did not apply to intermediaries and their services. Others disagree and believe that the retail rate is the reasonable rate on which to charge the tax. They point to the fact that the wholesalers themselves collect taxes on the retail rate. In all likelihood, the issue will be settled not by those in

[3]Eavis, P. 2004. Travel-site operator faces hotel mutiny. *The Street.com*, May 6, 2004. Retrieved May 6, 2004, from http//www.thestreet.com.

the hotel industry but by local taxing authorities. Until the issue is resolved, FOMs must understand the position of their own local taxing authority to ensure that their hotels are collecting and paying the proper occupancy taxes.

Today's FOM must be a skilled professional who truly understands how to read and interpret PMS data (see Chapter 4), who can use the data to forecast room demand (see Chapter 5), who is proficient in revenue management skills (see Chapter 6) and who understands distribution channel management (discussed in this chapter). When a reservation is made, the hotel's income-producing process begans and leads to charges incurred by a guest (even if the guest is a no-show). The FOM must consider how guest charges and records of important events that do not result in guest charges are interfaced with the hotel's PMS. This important interfacing process is discussed in the next chapter.

SECTION REVIEW AND DISCUSSION QUESTIONS

Section Objective: Explain challenges to the effective management of reservation distribution channels including those related to inventory ownership, Web site access control, and guest- and sales-related issues.

Section Summary: FOMs frequently "blame" intermediaries for purchasing discounted rooms and competing with hotels for the sale of these rooms on the basis of rates. Hoteliers themselves, however, "own" the rooms and negotiated and agreed to the rates. FOMs must carefully consider how and the rate at which discounted rooms will be sold. As FOMs become more knowledgeable about Internet sales and the practices of travel wholesalers and other intermediaries, they will be better able to consider the big picture RevPar as they make decisions.

FOMs must be alert to ways in which competitors divert sales from hotel Web sites. Hoteliers who pay a high price for the position of their property in search engine results need to ensure that these advertising dollars are not wasted.

FOMs must also recognize that the Internet has allowed rate-conscious travelers to shop around for prices that significantly impact (reduce) RevPar. Meeting attendees have opportunities to discover room rates lower than those negotiated by their meeting planners. Sometimes problems that can be avoided are, in fact, created by rate postings made by FOMs.

Another issue of concern to FOMs is occupancy tax liability. Taxing authorities must determine whether taxes should be paid based on the revenue the hotel collects from the wholesaler or the revenue that the wholesaler collects from the room buyer.

Discussion Questions:

1. What major concerns confront FOMs as they consider the need to sell heavily discounted rooms to intermediaries? How might a hotelier decide when this should be done? What basic factors should be considered as part of the decision-making process?

2. Assume that you are visiting a city and require a hotel room. Go to a specific hotel brand's Web site, select a specific property, and determine the rate for the dates you desire. Then go to a third-party Web site (see the section that follows). What, if any, differences in rates did you observe? How often would you, as an FOM, make such comparisons?

3. What issues would you, as an FOM, raise with a group-sales representative as you make pricing decisions about a proposed room block? Consider two situations: In the first instance, there will be few additional rooms to sell if the group sale is made. In the second situation, the hotel will have many remaining rooms to sell.

From the Front Office: Front-Line Interview

Winnie Yeung Man Wa
Assistant Front Desk Manager
The Peninsula Hong Kong (300 rooms)
Hong Kong, China

A Great View of the Hong Kong Harbor!

Winnie graduated from the Hong Kong Polytechnic University with a Higher Diploma in hotel and catering management. She believes it is important to serve a one-year internship to obtain cross-exposure in the hotel and to become familiar with the basic operation of and linkages between hotel departments.

1. What are the most important responsibilities in your present position?
To ensure that our guests' expectations are exceeded. We work hard to attain this goal by providing proper employee training and by consistently following the hotel's policies and procedures. Front desk staff must respond to each guest's special requests, needs, problems, issues, and concerns.

2. What are the biggest challenges that confront you in your day-to-day work and in the long-term operation of your property's front office?
There is significant competition among the many five-star hotels in Hong Kong. Therefore, constant provision of quality service becomes a main concern and challenge. Demand is increasing for a higher standard of service, and our guests tend to look for more personalized service. This requires us to pay more attention to the details in our work.

   Also, there are often personnel transfers in our hotel as staff members discover their main talents and interests in different departments. Our hotel must provide training for these staff members so that they gain the knowledge and skills necessary to successfully perform their new jobs.

3. What is your most unforgettable front office moment?
I fondly remember an elderly couple who visited the hotel to celebrate their 50th wedding anniversary. We upgraded them to a very nice harbor-view suite, and it was obvious that they appreciated it very much. They said that the view helped them to recall their memories in Hong Kong when they were young. After their visit, they sent me a card describing their warm feelings about their stay with us, and I was impressed.

4. What advice do you have for those studying about or considering a career in front office or hotel management?
You need to have a cheerful character with a strong orientation toward guest service. You also should recognize that the greatest sense of achievement and satisfaction will be felt whenever you can do something to make your guests' visits more pleasant.

The FOM in Action: A Solution

The Internet has radically changed the way hotels do business. There is, perhaps, no area in the hotel industry where that is more true than in the management of the front desk. What can today's FOMs do to ensure they are using the Internet as an effective distribution channel, especially when there are many options available to them? In most cases, the answer is a systematic and realistic examination of what a particular Web site can and cannot do.

In the case of the Bay City CVB, the intent of the Web site host, Lee Lagget is admirable. Promotion of a city's hotels on a CVB Web site is an increasingly popular method of enhancing tourism. For an FOM such as Teri Persanti, however, the practical challenges of establishing a new distribution channel can be substantial, because many questions must be answered before the channel can be used effectively.

The first questions to be asked when evaluating a new distribution channel are, simply, who is the buyer and who is the seller? In this example, the identity of the buyers is easy to understand: visitors to Bay City who select an overnight package marketed on the Bay City CVB Web site. The matter of who constitutes the seller is complicated. If the CVB actually "sells" the room, it becomes a third-party wholesaler (intermediary), and the relationship between the CVB and the hotels listed on its site must be carefully identified.

Selling hotel rooms on independent Web sites is a tricky business, as most hoteliers found in the early 2000s. When a property's rooms inventory is not directly interfaced with a seller's site, management of real-time rooms inventory is impossible—there is a real potential to sell rooms that have already been sold through other channels. Alternatively, to block rooms for a single distribution channel can easily result in loss of sales through other channels that could have sold rooms but did not because the rooms were blocked for a nonproducing channel.

In Bay City, Teri must work closely with Lee to fully understand the CVB proposal. Teri is responsible for pointing out the difficulties that must be addressed and overcome so that a beneficial Web site partnership can be established between the hotel and the CVB. The FOM is the expert who must ensure that the relationship between the hotel and the CVB will work well for both parties and for potential guests.

FRONT OFFICE SEMANTICS LIST

Intermediary	Net ADR yield	Look-to-book data
Travel agent	Attrition	Virtual Tour
Travel wholesaler	E-wholesaler	Lowest-rate guarantee
Fiduciary	Sell position	Merchant model
THISCO (The Hotel Industry Switch Company)	Search engine	Opaque model
Qualifying	Keyword	RFP (request for proposal)
	Pay-per-click	Dump rates

FRONT OFFICE AND THE INTERNET

The following Web sites relate to the content of this chapter:

Web address	Subject area
www.travelclick.net	Channel management
www.esitemarketing.com	Channel management
www.innquest.com	Channel management
www.innessystems.com	Channel management
www.hotel-online.com	Channel management news
www.ei-ahla.org	Telephone skills training material
www.businessvoice.com	Telephone skills training material
www.keynote.com	Internet site quality evaluation
www.thayerinteractive.com	Search engine marketing assistance
www.ezyield.com	Internet intermediary management assistance

REAL-WORLD ACTIVITIES

1. Meet with a hotel general manager or FOM to discuss procedures the hotel uses and suggestions the hotel gives to meeting planners to ensure that meeting attendees book rooms in the group's block at the negotiated rate. Ask the interviewees if they can provide anecdotes about this issue.
2. This chapter gives examples of ways that FOMs try to encourage reservations to be made in less-expensive distribution channels. What additional examples can you provide?
3. Meet with a travel agent to learn his or her perspective about the process of making hotel room reservations for clients. Ask what can be done to make the process better from a travel agent's perspective.
4. Review the Web sites of several hotels in your community. Can you make suggestions that would better enable the hoteliers to increase the number of reservations generated from their Web site visitors?
5. Interview an FOM about the primary sources of reservations at his or her hotel. What distribution channels does the FOM prefer to use? Why? What tactics does the FOM use to increase reservations generated through these channels?

8

Management of Data-Generating Front Office Subsystems

Chapter Outline

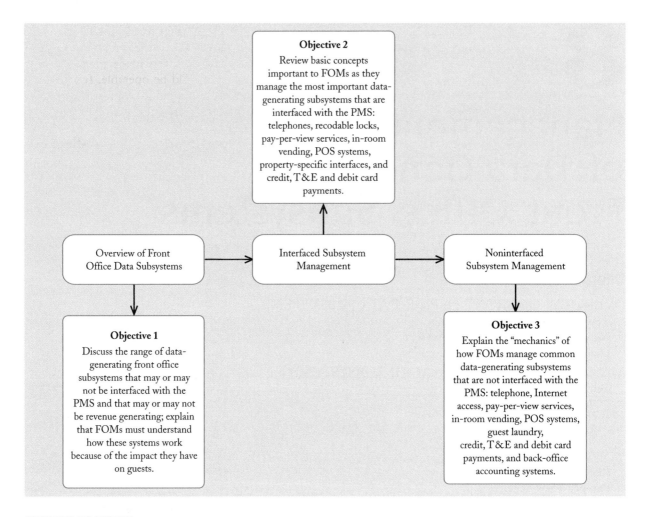

Chapter Preview

The property management system generates the data that are most important for the front office. However, there are a variety of other data-generating subsystems that FOMs must also manage. Some are directly interfaced (electronically connected) with a property's PMS; others are not. This chapter explains the role of subsystems, how they affect guests, and how FOMs can best manage them to maximize guest satisfaction and hotel profitability.

Chapter 4 described how a hotel's PMS primarily records information directly related to a guest's assigned room such as room type requested, reservation-related data, and actual room assignment and charges. Subsystems provide data about a guest's purchase of non-room-related items; these items must also be managed carefully to ensure that the hotel receives the appropriate revenue. For example, a guest enjoying a drink in the hotel's lounge may want to charge (bill) that drink to the guestroom. If the hotel allows that (and, for the guest's convenience, it should), data about the guest's drink purchase must be collected and transmitted to the hotel's PMS. Then, at check-out time, the guest's bill will be correct and up-to-date.

Some hotel subsystems generate data that are important to the hotel's operation but do not directly produce hotel revenue. A property with an electronic locking system, for example, must maintain records about which keys were made, to whom these keys were issued, and the length of time the keys should be operable. Information from the PMS (e.g., the name of the guest assigned to room 205) must be available to the employee who is replacing an electronic key for the guest who is stating that he lost his key.

Hotels with relatively new PMSs have many revenue- and non-revenue-generating subsystems interfaced directly with the PMS. However, in hotels with an older PMS, FOMs will find that some important subsystems are not directly interfaced. Data generated by these systems must be manually entered into the hotel's PMS. This chapter discusses the most common interfaced subsystems and how FOMs can effectively administer these subsystems when they are not interfaced.

The FOM in Action: The Challenge

"Here we go again," thought Belinda. As hard as she tried, it was difficult to remain upbeat, because for the fourth time this morning, she was dealing with the same guest complaint.

"I never watch in-room movies," said Mr. Qualman, "and I'm not paying the charge for it!" Mr. Qualman was checking out and Belinda, the hotel's FOM, was assisting him. Mr. Qualman—like Mr. Thompson, Ms. Delvinette, and Mr. Croft—had the same complaint: mysterious movie charges posted to their folios.

"I'm sorry, sir," said Belinda, "I'm not sure what happened, but I'll be happy to deduct the charges from your bill."

"This wouldn't be happening," thought Belinda, "if the interface was working, and if Jim (the night auditor) paid more attention to his job!"

The pay-per-view interface was, indeed, in need of repair. A manufacturer's mandatory upgrade of the PMS had improved its functionality. At the same time, however, the in-room movie interface went down. A service technician had been informed about the issue, but had not yet identified the problem or its solution. In the meantime, a list of movies and the guestrooms selecting them could still be downloaded from the movie system software. The night auditor then posted (usually about 2:00 a.m.) the movie charges to the appropriate room. Invariably, the process yielded several guests who claimed they were erroneously charged.

"This has got to stop," Belinda thought. "It may be weeks before we are back to normal." What can Belinda do to minimize the difficulties guests and the hotel will likely encounter during this time?

OVERVIEW OF FRONT OFFICE DATA SUBSYSTEMS

Although a hotel's PMS forms the nucleus of its data management system, it is not the lone provider of information about hotel guests, their activities, and their purchases. As indicated in Roadmap 8.1, supplemental systems (subsystems) also exist. They all generate and record data important to the hotel. The PMS is the hotel's central data storage unit. Data generated from many subsystems are so important that they must also be stored in the hotel's PMS.

Consider, for example, the guest who wishes to make a telephone call from her room. The hotel must have a record of the telephone call (assume it is an international, long-distance call), because the guest may want verification that the telephone

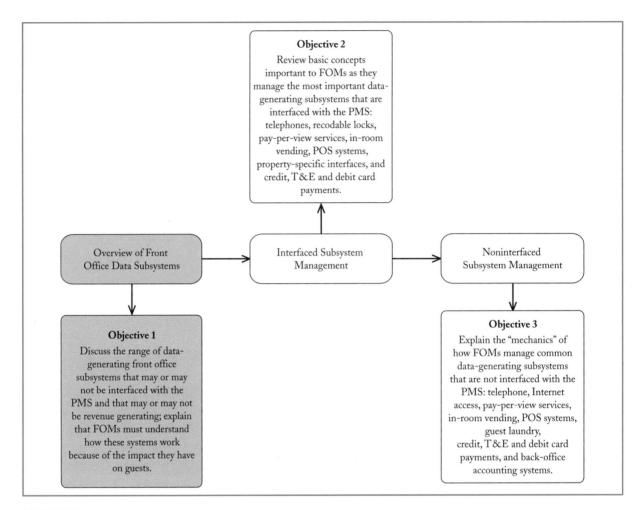

ROADMAP 8.1

charges were incurred. To enable verification, the hotel must record the following data as the call was made: date and time, origination point (typically a room number), number called, length of call, and hotel charges assessed (typically on a per-minute basis). Call-related data must be collected even if the hotel does not charge guests for telephone use. Even when calls are **free-to-guests,** the hotel will generally be charged a fee by its telephone **carrier** for each call that requires its services.

FRONT OFFICE SEMANTICS

Free-to-guests: Service provided to the hotel guest at no additional charge beyond normal room rental charges. Examples are local telephone calls, use of Internet connections, and access to the hotel's pool or workout facilities. Ultimately, the hotel must absorb the costs of providing these services to guests; therefore, the term does not mean that the services are free to the hotel.

Carrier (telephone): Company providing a hotel's telephone service. In many areas this will be a local carrier (for local calls) and a separate, designated, long-distance carrier. The telecommunications industry continues to consolidate services; thus, some hotels now use the same carrier for local and long-distance calls.

Telephones may be either a revenue-generating or non-revenue-generating subsystem of a hotel.

The only way an FOM can verify the accuracy of telephone charges is to have a record of each call made on the hotel's telephone lines. In a mega hotel with thousands of rooms and about as many managers, supervisors, and staff, tens of thousands of telephone calls may be made each day. The hotel's call accounting system is the subsystem that maintains records of and charges for telephone calls. Theoretically, one could manually track each telephone call, post charges to guests' folios for applicable calls, and allow routine calls made by managers and employees to be made without charge. Such systems, however, would be impossibly labor intensive, unwieldy, and expensive. Therefore, automated call accounting systems identify and cost chargeable telephone calls; in nearly all cases, these systems interface with the hotel's PMS to allow immediate posting of telephone tolls to the proper party.

Telephones are not the only non-room, revenue-generating center within a hotel. Others are the food and beverage department and **pay-per-view** movies and games.

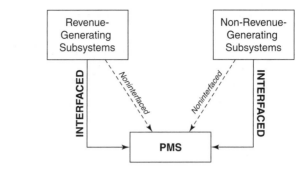

FIGURE 8.1 Subsystems of the PMS.

FRONT OFFICE SEMANTICS

Pay-per-view: Industry term for a video or audio service, usually delivered on the guestroom television, in which guests are charged for the time they actually use the service.

Some subsystems that are interfaced with the PMS are important to the hotel but do not directly generate revenue. Examples include room locking, energy management and back-office accounting systems. Although many revenue- and non-revenue-generating subsystems are, like the telephone, interfaced directly with the PMS, some subsystems may not or cannot be interfaced.

As shown in Figure 8.1, PMS subsystems may be revenue-generating or non-revenue-generating. Subsystems may or may not be directly interfaced with the PMS. The remainder of this chapter examines the most common and important subsystems of concern to FOMs. Regardless of its purpose, a subsystem interfaced with the PMS will be managed by the FOM differently than a subsystem that is not interfaced. FOMs who manage some common, but frequently noninterfaced subsystems, face unique challenges.

MODERN FRONT OFFICE ISSUES AND TACTICS

Voice-Over Internet (Telephony)

Since the earliest days of the Internet's development, those in the telecommunications industry have been interested in it as a means of sending and receiving telephone calls. As the technologies necessary to deliver clear and understandable voice signals over the Internet have improved, hoteliers' interest in voice-over Internet (also known as *telephony*) has increased.

The technology required to efficiently convert the sounds of a voice carried by a standard telephone's analog system to the digital data required by the Internet is progressing rapidly. In fact, the sophistication of telephony has advanced to the point that some hotel chains (e.g., U.S. Franchise System's Microtel) can profitably offer free-to-guest local and long-distance calling, along with complimentary Internet connections, by converting completely to a voice-over system. In most cases, hotels that convert realize significantly reduced telephone costs because their usage charges are based on the amount of Internet bandwidth purchased rather than the number and length of telephone calls routed through the telephone system. Telephony is a technology whose time has come, and FOMs must thoroughly understand its advantages and drawbacks.

Revenue-Generating Subsystems

In many cases, hotels create operating subsystems for the purpose of increasing revenues. For example, a resort hotel may sell sunglasses, lotions, and hats at a kiosk near the swimming pool. Guests making a purchase could be required to pay cash. More sales are likely, however, if guests are allowed to charge purchases to their rooms. In this case, a PMS interface would be required to

- identify the guest,
- determine the guest's room number (folio),
- post the appropriate charges to the folio, and
- create a paper or electronic document, signed by the guest, to verify the purchase if the guest disputes it.

In addition to requiring a cash payment or using a PMS interface, a third billing option is available. A guest's charges could be manually posted to his or her folio. To do so, the prices of items purchased would be totaled and tax would be added, where appropriate. The sales amount would then be physically taken or electronically sent to the front desk where the charge would be posted to the guest's folio. The potential for posting errors and lost revenue in such a manual system increases the desirability of interfaced revenue-generating subsystems. This is especially true in hotels that offer a large number of revenue-generating options to guests.

Figure 8.2 lists many (but not all) revenue-generating subsystems that may be operated by a hotel. In each subsystem, revenues from guest purchases must be (1) collected at the time of sale, (2) transferred to the front desk for manual posting, or (3) posted via an interface. Not every hotel offers each of the subsystems listed in Figure 8.2, and each hotel's ownership must decide which, services, if any, will be designated as free-to-guests. In each case, some method for determining charges and collecting payment will be in place, and the method of payment collection will directly affect the front office.

An effective interfaced or manual revenue-generating subsystem must include the following verifiable and reliable data:

- Date of purchase
- Individual (or room) authorizing the purchase

• Telephone calls	• Vending purchases (in-room)
• Internet access fees	• Gift shop purchases
• Food and beverage purchases in dining room	• Golf fees
	• Ski equipment rental and lift tickets
• Food and beverage purchases in lounge	• Water sports rentals
• Food and beverage purchases through room service	• Horseback riding and other activities charges
• Banquet food purchases	• Health club and spa charges
• Banquet beverage purchases	• Beauty salon charges
• Meeting room rental charges	• Barber shop charges
• Audiovisual equipment rental charges	• Concierge purchases on behalf of guests
• Pay-per-view movie and game services	• Federal Express, United Parcel Service, and other package shipments and mail services (including packaging materials)
• Business center charges	
• Video rentals	

FIGURE 8.2 Selected revenue-generating subsystems.

Revenue-generating subsystems should be properly interfaced with the PMS to save time and money.

- Room or group folio to be charged
- Items purchased
- Cost of items
- Applicable taxes or service charges to be added to the guest's total charge

In large hotels with many sales outlets, optional information may include the specific location of the purchase, the name of the employee providing the product or service, and if relevant, the time at which the purchase was made. In most cases, a hard copy or electronically signed document may be created to verify the guest's purchase. These documents can be of invaluable assistance if a guest disputes all or part of the folio charges at check-out time.

Non-Revenue-Generating Subsystems

Although many subsystems record guest purchases and hotel revenue, some do not. Every modern hotel has telephones in guestrooms. Many have added a voice-mail subsystem to the main telephone system. Voice mail allows callers to leave a message for a guest at the assigned room telephone. Voice mail is a convenience for guests and eliminates the need for a front desk agent to manually take telephone messages. For voice mail to work properly, however, it must be interfaced with both the telephone system and the PMS so that messages can be recorded and saved in the proper guestroom's voice mailbox. If a telephone voice message is to be left for Mr. Jones, it is the PMS (not the telephone system) that must provide the voicemail system with the information that Mr. Jones is in room 205 (and not room 502!).

Hotel managers must determine which non-revenue-producing subsystems should be provided for their guests. New non-revenue-generating and revenue-generating subsystems are developed and marketed to hoteliers regularly. In many cases, the subsystems are useful but expensive to purchase and operate and time-consuming to maintain. These subsystems are often interfaced with the PMS, so FOMs should be familiar with them. Even when they are not interfaced with the PMS, FOMs may have administrative responsibility for some or all of those that do not produce revenue. Some of the most common non-revenue-generating subsystems available are listed in Figure 8.3.

One subsystem can consist of both revenue- and non-revenue-generating elements. The best example is the telephone subsystem. Within-hotel (room-to-room) calls are free. Local calls made through the same telephone subsystem are often free to guests, especially in the limited-service hotel segment. Many (but not all) full-service hotels charge guests for local calls. Long-distance calls in nearly all hotels result in a guest charge.

Subsystem	Purpose
Form printing programs	Printing folios, registration cards, confirmations, letterhead, checks, statements, and envelopes directly from the PMS database
Telephone actuator	Turning guestroom telephones on or off at check-in or check-out; programming wake-up calls; turning message lights on or off
Voice mail	Creating in-room, remotely accessible voice mailboxes for guests
In-room check-out	Allowing folios to be viewed in guestrooms and allowing in-room check-out
Housekeeping management	Using guestroom telephones to signal room status changes (e.g., clean, dirty, and out of order); scheduling employees based on forecasted room volume
Electronic (recodable) lock system	Making guestroom keys (for guests) and master keys (for hotel staff)
Payment card processing	Allowing each front office workstation to scan bank (credit and debit) cards and receive authorizations automatically without manually entering information into a credit card terminal
Energy management	Turning guestroom heat, air-conditioning, and lights on and off at check-in and check-out
Central reservations	Linking the reservation systems of multiple hotel properties to allow for the creation of a central reservations center
Back-office accounting	Creating the hotel's financial documents directly from data held in the PMS

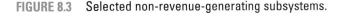

FIGURE 8.3   Selected non-revenue-generating subsystems.

Diagnosis of Subsystem Malfunctions

FOMs are often responsible for resolving the difficulties arising from malfunctions in subsystems, whether the subsystems are interfaced or not. For example, assume that a hotel has installed an energy management system to control utility costs. The system is interfaced with the PMS. A couple who has just checked in returns to the front desk and complains that the entry light in the room does not come on when they enter it. In situations such as this, FOMs or their staff must consider possible causes of the problem and make a diagnosis:

- The PMS has not communicated to the energy management system that guests have been checked into that room. Diagnosis: Problem is in the PMS.
- The PMS has properly communicated to the energy management system that guests have been checked into that room, but the energy management system is not accepting the message. Diagnosis: Problem is in the interface.
- The PMS has properly communicated to the energy management system that guests have been checked into that room; the energy management system has accepted the message, but does not instruct the light to turn on. Diagnosis: Problem is in the energy management system.
- The PMS has properly communicated to the energy management system that guests have been checked into that room; the energy management system accepts the message; and the energy management system is functioning properly. Diagnosis: Probable burned out lightbulb.

FOMs must properly diagnose subsystem malfunctions and seek appropriate assistance needed to solve the problems. To do so, FOMs must have a reasonable understanding of how interfaced and noninterfaced subsystems work. Based on this knowledge, FOMs can develop a systematic approach to troubleshooting these subsystems when necessary.

SECTION SUMMARY AND DISCUSSION QUESTIONS

Section Objective: Discuss the range of data-generating front office subsystems that may or may not be interfaced with the PMS and that may or may not be revenue generating; explain that FOMs must understand how these systems work because of the impact they have on guests.

Section Summary: There are two basic types of data-generating office subsystems: those that are, and those that are not, interfaced with the PMS. Subsystems can be further divided into those that are, and those that are not, revenue producing. Some subsystems, such as those involving telephone charges and pay-per-view movies, are available in nearly all properties. Other subsystems, such as those related to the use of a business center, may be available if the property believes that revenues beyond maintenance costs will be generated or that the amenities are necessary to remain competitive.

Discussion Questions:

1. Review the list of revenue-generating subsystems in Figure 8.2. Can you think of additional examples? Which subsystems are most likely interfaced with the PMS? How would you, as the FOM, decide whether a subsystem should be interfaced?

2. Review Figure 8.3. What additional examples of non-revenue-generating subsystems can you add to the list? Provide examples of how the FOM and front office employees must interact with guests relative to each of these subsystems.

3. The text provides an example of a hotel with an energy management system interfaced with the PMS to control use of electricity in guestrooms. What steps would you, as the FOM take if the problem regarding the room's entry light occurred frequently and most often was traced to a burned-out lightbulb?

MANAGEMENT OF INTERFACED SUBSYSTEMS

As noted in Roadmap 8.2, FOMs manage subsystems that are interfaced with the hotel's PMS. In theory, an interfaced subsystem saves time and money, because data from the subsystem are shared automatically with the PMS, and the PMS shares its data with the subsystem. When the interface works properly, real savings occur. However, software depends on hardware, and difficulties can arise with the software, hardware, or both. Even though most FOMs do not program software or repair their own computers, they should be able to identify problem areas and seek help from the proper vendor when difficulties arise.

This section of the chapter examines the most common interfaced subsystems—what they are designed to do and what indicators may suggest that they are not working properly. Many subsystems can now be connected to the PMS, so FOMs need to have a basic understanding of those that are most commonly used: telephones, recodable locks, pay-per-view services, in-room vending, point-of-sale (POS) systems, property-specific interfaces, and credit, T&E, and debit card payments.

Telephones

Technology related to telephones has changed rapidly in the past decade, and the changes have affected hotel telephone systems. Not long ago, hotels could make a profit on their telephone systems by charging guests more for telephone calls than the hotel was itself charged. Today, two major factors have combined to limit or eliminate telephones as a hotel profit center. The first is the increased popularity of 1-800 numbers that allow guests to phone sources (e.g., 1-800-DIAL ATT) to avoid what they perceive to be excessive charges for in-room telephone use. Second, the ubiquity of cell phones and the improved calling-area coverage provided by cell phone companies have virtually eliminated the telephone as a source of profit in many hotels.

Reduced telephone profit is not, however, simply a result of reduced telephone-related revenue. It is also the result of an increase in the number and complexity of subsystems connected to a hotel's primary telephone system. The purchase and

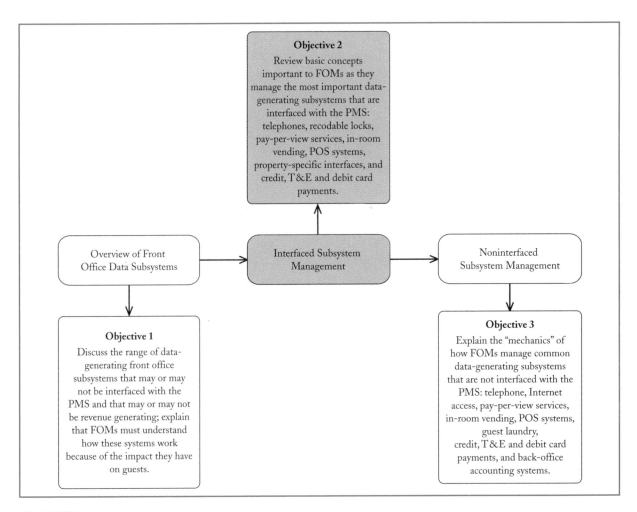

ROADMAP 8.2

maintenance of these subsystems have substantially increased operating costs. The five most common telephone subsystems, as noted in Figure 8.4, are the **auto-attendant,** voice mail, **message on hold, automated wake-up,** and call accounting systems.

FRONT OFFICE SEMANTICS

Auto-attendant: System in which incoming calls transferred from the telephone system are answered automatically as they are received. In most cases, callers are asked to select where they want the system to direct (route) their call from a list of options.

Message on hold: System that eliminates the silence that occurs when guests are required to wait (hold) for their call to be picked up by the party the caller is attempting to reach.

Automated wake-up: System in which guests (or front office staff) may use the hotel's telephone system to program a prerecorded call to be received in a guest's room at a time requested by the guest.

A variety of manufacturers offer hotel telephone systems; Panasonic, Nortel, and Mitel are among the most popular. An examination of the design, programming, and

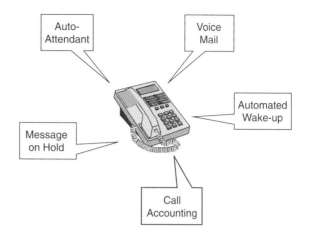

FIGURE 8.4   Common telephone subsystems.

installation of a complete telephone system is beyond the scope of this text. FOMs should know, however, that their telephone system supplies the basic PBX functions required by the hotel and most often includes one or more of the following integrated programs:

- Wireless or voice-over technology capability (or both)
- Caller ID
- Automatic call-back capability
- Conference call capability
- Telephone volume control
- Speed dialing
- Call forwarding, hold, transfer, and do not disturb
- Voice messaging

As many experienced FOMs can attest, any one of the listed components on a digital system can occasionally deprogram, malfunction, or wear out. Therefore, one of the most important features a system can have is the capacity to be remotely accessed by telephone or computer to be reprogrammed by the manufacturer or local service provider. This capacity avoids the loss of time and money required to have a service technician travel to the hotel site to perform needed diagnostic and repair activities. The remote-access service feature is available on all modern digital systems, but FOMs working with older systems may not enjoy the benefits of this service. In either case, FOMs must know who manufactured their telephone system as well as where dependable local service for the system can be obtained.

In addition to having a well-designed basic telephone system, many hoteliers add enhancements for their guests or for their own ability to manage telephone revenues and expenses. Today's FOMs will likely encounter and be responsible for maintaining one or more of the following PMS-integrated telephone subsystems.

Auto-Attendant

The auto-attendant is the electronic voice that answers each call made to the hotel's telephone system. Telephone calls can be programmed to route directly to the auto-attendant or to ring individual extensions (numbers) first and proceed to the auto-attendant if the call is not answered. Many large hotels use an auto-attendant to answer calls quickly (usually at the first or second ring) and then to route them. Some hoteliers, however, feel auto-attendant telephone answering indicates a lack of guest service orientation and still prefer to employ people as operators for this task.

Essentially, the auto-attendant uses a series of questions or instructions to route the call to the desired location (e.g., a specific guestroom, a hotel reservationist, the sales department, or an administrative staff member). Callers typically follow a menu of options that allows them to connect to a specific room, name, or department, or even to an operator. Auto-attendant systems can also be programmed to function only as an overflow option when a hotel's operators are experiencing a heavy volume of telephone calls.

When working properly, the auto-attendant can be an efficient way to handle a high volume of calls. If not working properly, the auto-attendant may *fail* to pick up calls coming into the hotel. For an FOM, the result of this situation can be disastrous. Consider the difficulties that would be encountered if an auto-attendant that has been programmed to answer *all* incoming telephone calls does not work. Family members would be unable to phone and check on the arrival of their relatives. Reservations could neither be made nor canceled. As a result, revenues would be lost, and guests who were subsequently billed as no-shows would be angry because they tried to phone the hotel to cancel but could not connect to the property. Employees would not be able to call their supervisors to let them know that they will be late in arriving for work or that they are not coming to work at all. Sales inquiries about large numbers of group rooms could not be handled by the sales staff, and family members of employees would not be able to reach them in an emergency.

Connecting an auto-attendant (or any other telephone subsystem) onto a hotel's main telephone system can be helpful when the subsystem operates as it should. Malfunctions, however, can cause many difficulties. FOMs operating in an auto-attendant environment must know whom to contact if service is needed. FOMs must also know if the system is designed so it can be disabled; in that case, they can return to a manual operator if necessary.

Voice Mail

Voice mail is commonly interfaced with the PBX but is, in fact, a separate telephone component. A properly operating voice mail system is nearly mandatory for hotels that seek to attract business travelers. In a modern telephone system interfaced with voice mail, the voice mailbox (guestroom number) for a guest is activated by the PMS at check-in and deactivated by the PMS when the guest checks out. Voice mail is also critical for managers who must have telephone contact with guests or potential guests (e.g., the sales and marketing department). When voice mail malfunctions, front office staff will likely be the first to know, because guests will be unable to receive or to retrieve messages that they think (or know) have been left for them. In such cases, rapid repair is important.

Message on Hold

A message-on-hold system allows the hotel to play a "message" on the line when a caller is placed on hold. For example, a caller attempting to make a room reservation may be placed on hold until the next reservationist is available. During this time, a recorded message may inform the caller about hotel features, provide a general apology for placing the caller on hold, and offer an assurance that the call will be answered shortly. Some message-on-hold systems simply play background music. In the best case, a message-on-hold apparatus creates an interface with the PBX by providing a combination of pleasant music and well-written marketing script. These systems can be programmed to intercept incoming calls as well as calls placed on the hotel's **house phones.**

FRONT OFFICE SEMANTICS

House phone: Publicly located telephone within the hotel that can be used to call the front desk or, in some cases, the front desk and guestrooms.

Fortunately, if message-on-hold systems malfunction, they do not typically cause an interruption in total telephone service. A system malfunction constitutes less of an emergency than failure of other telephone subsystems. Even so, FOMs need to understand and know how to arrange service for message-on-hold systems.

Automated Wake-Up

Traditionally, guests who want to wake up at a given time have called the front desk to request a wake-up call. A staff member would then personally call the guest at the requested time. Today's telephone systems can be interfaced to automate wake-up calls. Requests can be programmed into the PBX by guests in their own rooms or by front desk staff.

Call Accounting

Despite the reduced frequency of calls made on hotel telephones, a property's call accounting system is important. In most hotels, the call accounting system selected to interface with the PMS performs five important functions; it

1. Makes a record of all incoming and outgoing calls
2. Chooses the least-cost method of sending outgoing calls
3. Maintains records of who will be charged for calls
4. Maintains records of how much should be charged for calls
5. Posts appropriate telephone charges to the proper guest's folio

Even a small hotel may have hundreds of telephones that are used by guests and employees. Hotel managers need to know who is making calls and to where these calls are made. For guests, this information is necessary so that they can be charged properly (if the hotel levies fees). For employees, this information is important to ensure that telephone use is not abused and that inappropriate or nonessential telephone charges are not incurred. A call accounting system records the source, length, and destination of each call and helps the FOM ensure that concerns about guest charges and employee telephone use are properly addressed.

When guests or staff members make calls outside the hotel, the calls should be routed in a way that minimizes the property's cost. For example, if a registered guest phones a person in another state by dialing directly from her room, the hotel will be billed for the call. The FOM, of course, wants the cost of providing such calls to be as low as possible, while ensuring that guests have quality long-distance service. The federal government's 1981 actions, which resulted in deregulation of telephone services, have allowed hoteliers to consider competitors and select a company to provide access to telephone lines. In most areas, hotels can chose from one or more local carriers as well as long-distance carriers, each of which prices its services as it wishes. In most modern call accounting systems, a device called a **smart switch** can be incorporated into the call accounting system to provide **least-cost routing (LCR)** for each call made.

FRONT OFFICE SEMANTICS

Smart switch: Device that detects detailed information about the destination of a telephone call when it is made.

Least-cost routing (LCR): System using a preprogrammed, interfaced smart switch to select the telephone route that charges the least based on a call's specific destination.

Regardless of the carrier chosen for a specific call, the hotel may add a charge to the guest's folio to offset the cost of the call. Use of in-room fax machines or other telephone-related services such as **dial-up Internet** can also be charged automatically to the guest's folio when the call accounting system is interfaced with the PMS.

FRONT OFFICE SEMANTICS

Dial-up Internet: Method of Internet connection that uses a standard telephone and telephone call (usually a local or toll-free call) for connection to the World Wide Web. Typically, dial-up systems upload and download data in a slower manner than do high-speed Internet access systems.

The call accounting system should not, in most cases, be programmed to charge for every call made in a hotel. Often hotels do not charge for local calls made by guests. Most hotels charge guests for long-distance calls, but obviously a sales employee talking with a client in another state should not be personally charged for the call. Call accounting systems can be programmed to assign telephone charges to specific hotel departments. Therefore, a call accounting system can be programmed to identify the source (extension number) of a specific telephone and, based on the extension number, assess or not assess charges. Systems can also be programmed to block calls to specific numbers (e.g., those selling adult content material) that pass the charges back to the telephone caller's (hotel's) bill.

Deregulation of the telephone industry has allowed hotels the freedom to charge what they want for telephone services. Most hoteliers and hotel companies have not resisted the temptation to price telephone calls in a manner that actually discourages (some would say aggressively discourages) the use of the telephones in guestrooms. Some guests do use their in-room telephones, however, and call accounting systems must be able to record and print, for guest inspection, a record of the time, length, and telephone number of each call made from guestrooms and for calls made from administrative phones. These **call records** must be accurate so that hotels can collect fees from guests who initiate the calls.

FRONT OFFICE SEMANTICS

Call records: Listing of the source, length, and destination of each telephone call made within a hotel during a specific time period.

To understand how a call accounting system is programmed to price telephone calls, let's review a few commonly used but sometimes misunderstood definitions and concepts. Contrary to public perception, the **local call** is not "free" to the hotel. Hotels pay a usage fee each time its lines are connected to those of a carrier, regardless of whether the carrier is handling the hotel's local or long-distance service. Sometimes hotels purchase a telephone plan (much like those purchased by individual users of cell phones) that allows a predetermined number of local calls or minutes monthly at a specific price. Each local call results in a direct charge or is counted as part of the hotel's monthly plan. In most areas, the charge to a hotel for a single local call is modest, and many hotels make these calls free-to-guests.

FRONT OFFICE SEMANTICS

Local call: Telephone call typically made within a small geographic area.

Most travelers understand the concepts of **long-distance calls** and **international calls.** Hotels generally imply or state that if guests make one or the other of these calls, they will be charged. What most guests object to is arbitrary and excessive pricing for telephone service.

FRONT OFFICE SEMANTICS

Long-distance call: In general, a call made to a telephone extension located in an area code outside of the call's originating area code.

International call: Call made to a telephone extension located in a country code outside that of the call's originating country code.

A call accounting system is programmed to compute and assign *predetermined* telephone usage charges to guests' folios when calls are made. The per-minute or per-connection charge for each call made is predetermined by the hotel's management, not by the telephone company. FOMs must have a thorough understanding of their hotel's telephone service pricing philosophy and the specific pricing decisions that have been made. To illustrate why FOMs must understand how telephone calls are priced, consider the following conversations between guests looking at their telephone call charges when they are checking out and the front desk agents who assist them.

Scenario A

Guest: I see you have charged me for five long-distance calls, and each of them was $3?

Front desk agent: Yes sir. That's correct.

Guest: But I didn't make any long-distance calls.

Front desk agent: According to our system, you called 555-347-1252 five times last night.

Guest: Yes, but the calls never connected. I should know; I let it ring 10 times, and no one was there!

Front desk agent: There is an access charge that is initiated after eight rings.

In this case, the hotel's management elected to charge a flat $3 access fee anytime a long-distance call was made and allowed to ring eight times.

Scenario B

Guest: I see you have charged me for a local call. Your advertisements say they are free.

Front desk agent: Yes ma'am. They are free, but only for the first 10 minutes. After that, we charge a one-time per call fee of $1. Your local call lasted 85 minutes.

Guest: I dialed into the Internet to check my e-mail.

In this case, the hotel's management elected to make local calls free but only to a maximum of 10 minutes on the line.

Scenario C

Guest: What are these telephone charges for? I only phoned using my calling card.

Front desk agent: The hotel assesses a line usage fee for all 800 calls. That's because we are charged for providing the long-distance lines to you.

In this case, the hotel's management elected to charge guests an access fee to use a toll-free number.

In each of these scenarios, the front desk agent must know and understand the hotel's policies about telephone usage charges. The hotel policies described in these scenarios should not be considered good or bad. It is not possible to generalize about

A hotel may decide to charge guests based on the length of time they are connected during their telephone calls.

appropriate telephone rates in a specific hotel any more than it is to generalize about appropriate ADRs. Each situation is unique.

Few general managers expect FOMs to be able to program charges on a hotel's automated call accounting system. FOMs must, however, have a thorough understanding of the system. In addition, they must be able to train front office agents so that they understand the following aspects of the telephone service pricing structure:

- Definition of a local call
- Definition of a long-distance call
- Conditions under which charges for local or long-distance calls, or both, will begin
- Number of minutes for which a local call is "free" (subject to normal pricing), and the length of time after which additional charges, if any, for local call use are assessed
- The hotel's pricing policy about toll-free calls made by guests if these charges are imposed
- The hotel's policy for waiving toll charges in cases involving guest disputes

Telephone revenue as a percentage of total hotel revenue has been declining in recent years. Nevertheless, a properly managed and functioning call accounting system is still a vital part of any effective front office operation, because uncollected telephone revenue that results from an improperly managed system damages the hotel's profitability. Also, a malfunctioning system resulting in charges that guests believe are inaccurate or unfair certainly does not add to the hotel's reputation in a positive manner.

At least annually, FOMs should seek the advice and counsel of a specialist in telephone systems. A specialist can provide ongoing recommendations to reduce costs, optimize the hotel's telephone networks and systems, and improve the quality of the services provided to guests. **IT (information technology)** specialists can usually, for a reasonable cost, assist in the management and control of telephone technology, including placing orders, tracking and following up on all **move/add/change** requests, and troubleshooting; they also can resolve billing issues with service providers.

FRONT OFFICE SEMANTICS

IT (information technology): Broad term used to identify areas of management related to the design and administration of computer-related hardware and software programs.

Move/add/change: Process of reconfiguring or reprogramming a call accounting system to, for example, move an extension from one location to another, add an additional extension, or change a line from one that posts charges for use to one that does not.

Recodable Locks

At one time, a hotel's purchase and use of a **recodable locking system** was a significant event that allowed it to market its use of these locks to potential guests.

FRONT OFFICE SEMANTICS

Recodable locking system: Hotel locking system designed so that when a guest inserts a key card into a lock for the first time, the lock is immediately recoded and entry authorization for the previous guest is canceled.

Recodable locks have become the standard in the hotel industry.

Today, recodable locks are the industry standard, and no hotel should operate without them. TESSA, Saflok, and VingCard are among the most common systems used. In the earliest days of electronic locking systems, many hoteliers could not interface the new subsystems with their PMS. Now, hoteliers' interface options are greater, and they may or may not choose to have these systems interfaced. When they are interfaced, FOMs must know whom to contact when problems occur that cannot be solved by the hotel's maintenance and engineering staff.

Essentially, a recodable locking system, regardless of manufacturer, consists of electronic door locks that "stand alone." There is no need to wire the locks back to a central computer, although that can be done. Except in life-threatening emergencies, only a magnetic-stripe card issued at the front desk opens the door lock. The hotel's entire guestroom security system is controlled by software contained in the locks themselves and activated by cards coded on a keycard-issuing computer.

Each lock contains a card reader and an electronic control module connected to a motor-actuated lock mechanism. Standard alkaline batteries (double A) power the entire lock. A warning light visible only to staff warns when batteries are within three months of needing to be replaced. When a guest inserts the keycard into the lock for the first time, the lock is immediately recoded and entry authorization for the previous guest is canceled. In a high-quality system, multiple keycards can be issued to the same guest. In addition to their use for guestrooms and exterior doors, recodable locks can be used to limit guest access to designated hotel areas such as elevators for special floors, swimming pools, spas, exercise rooms, and reserved breakfast or bar areas. Recodable locks can also limit employee access to specified storage areas or other locations in the hotel. Because guestrooms must be regularly cleaned and maintained, master keycards are issued to staff who need them.

When an electronic locking system or system interface goes down, front desk agents are no longer able to create and issue keys for a guestroom. What if a 500-room hotel experiences a total power outage and loses the ability to operate its key-making equipment? FOMs should have previously made emergency keys available. Each manufacturer of a lock system has a set of recovery procedures to be used when their locking system malfunctions. Experienced FOMs make themselves *very* familiar with those procedures.

Pay-per-View Services

Pay-per-view services originated when companies other than hotels began offering systems that allowed guests to watch popular movies in their rooms. Charges were added to guests' hotel bill. In today's environment, a provider (e.g., OnCommand or LodgeNet) creates a partnership with a hotel. The property supplies guests and the pay-per-view service provider offers services or activities delivered to guestroom televisions. Revenues from sales are split according to contract terms between the two parties.

These systems began by offering movies but now guests have access to pay-per-use video games, music, high-speed Internet access, and special features such as live broadcasts of sporting events and concerts, as well as free-to-guest channels. An additional feature allows hotels to use one or more channels to provide guest information about the hotel and current activities. Hotels can also sell time on these channels for exhibitors to advertise products or services to guests attending trade shows. Some properties have started to show videos of a wedding reception or other celebration that can be played for guests after the event.

The content of many pay-per-view systems is delivered to the hotel by satellite, so reception quality can be affected by the weather, the hotel's location, and even the building's wiring system. The quality of the picture received on a guestroom television is typically a matter addressed by the hotel's maintenance department. Guest charges (and complaints) for pay-per-view services, however, are addressed at the front desk during check-out. Therefore, the FOM must understand the features offered by the pay-per-view provider and the appropriate charges for their use. If the pay-per-view service is interfaced with the PMS, the FOM must ensure that the system is working properly and that the proper charges are posted to the proper guestroom.

In-Room Vending

The in-room vending of products to hotel guests began when hotels offered alcoholic beverages, soft drinks, and sometimes dry snacks to guests who liked the convenience of purchasing these items in their rooms. Minibars, as they were termed by guests, quickly became popular. Today the vended products offered by hotels may include bottled waters, healthful snacks, and even toiletry items such as combs, razors, and brushes. In customer satisfaction surveys, female business travelers in particular have expressed an interest in having reasonably priced and popular items available in minibars.[1]

Today, instead of equipping guestrooms with a small refrigerator for in-room vending, most hotels use some variation of an **e-fridge.**

---

[1] Wyndham International. 2004. Wyndham unleashes another hotel industry first: Affordable minibars. Wyndham press release, April 28. Retrieved April 28, 2004, from http://www.wyndham.com.

FRONT OFFICE SEMANTICS

E-fridge: Cabinet, usually including both refrigerated and nonrefrigerated sections, designed with an electronic processing unit that allows a direct interface with the PMS.

When guests check in to their rooms, the PMS activates (unlocks) the in-room e-fridge. Sensors located in the units are preprogrammed to know the type and cost of the items stocked. As vended items are removed by guests, the electronic sensors detect the missing items and post their cost to the guest's folio. The data can be transmitted to the PMS through direct wiring or by a **Wi-Fi certified** product and **hot spot.**

FRONT OFFICE SEMANTICS

Wi-Fi certified: Short for wireless fidelity certified. More technically, the term refers to any products tested and approved as Wi-Fi Certified (a registered trademark) by the Wi-Fi Alliance and certified as interoperable with each other, even if they are from different manufacturers (e.g., e-fridge and PMS manufacturers).

Hot spot: Wi-Fi area that allows for high-speed wireless Internet access or other data transmission. An analogy is a reception zone for a cell phone.

Unlike older minibars, e-fridges can be deactivated at check-in if requested by guests. For example, a family with young travelers may want the e-fridge deactivated. Employee theft is virtually eliminated because the units remain locked when a room is vacant. Also, any item removed by an employee in a room that does not have a registered guest is recorded by time and date, because recodable locking systems

Some hotels purchase e-fridges to store and display their in-room minibar items.

indicate which employee key was used to enter a room and when it was used. Restocking units is simple because the processor reports, by room number, the identity and quantity of items to be delivered to the room to replenish the unit.

The advantages of minibars designed to interface directly (or even indirectly through a hand-held portable processing unit) with the PMS are many. Like all other interfaced devices, however, malfunctions can occur and cause disruptions. Experienced FOMs identify competent technicians who are ready to repair minibar interfaces when necessary.

Point-of-Sale (POS) Systems

In many hotels, guests can make purchases from hotel-operated restaurants, lounges, gift shops, business centers, and other revenue-generating sources. Guests can pay for their purchases when they are made, or they may be able to charge purchases to their room. Guest purchases can be electronically charged to the guest's room if the **POS (point of sale)** is interfaced with the PMS as shown in Figure 8.5.

FRONT OFFICE SEMANTICS

POS (point of sale): A location in the hotel (excluding the front desk) at which hotel goods and services are purchased. In many hotels, a POS is interfaced with the PMS.

When the POS is interfaced with the PMS, a **POS terminal** is used by a cashier to record the following data:

- Name of the item or items purchased
- Quantity of items purchased
- Price of each item purchased

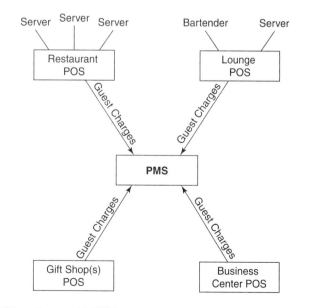

FIGURE 8.5   POS interfaces with PMS.

- Total cost of all items purchased
- Amount of applicable taxes
- Total to be entered into the folio and to be collected from the guest at check-out

---

FRONT OFFICE SEMANTICS

POS terminal: Computer system containing its own input and output components and, perhaps, some memory capacity, but without a central processing unit. A large restaurant, lounge, or gift shop may have several POS terminals so that servers and cashiers have rapid access to a unit when the operation is busy.

In most cases, information sent to the PMS from a POS terminal is the same that guests would expect on their guest check (for restaurant or lounge charges) or their purchase receipts (for items other than food and beverages). The form of payment (e.g., cash, credit card, or debit card) used by a guest at check-out does not affect the information relayed to the PMS. The critical issue for the hotel is to ensure that guest charges are accurately routed to their folios *before* the guests check out of the hotel. In an interfaced system that is working properly, the process is virtually instantaneous. Guests cannot make a purchase and check out of the hotel before the amount charged has been hand-carried or transmitted to the front desk for posting to their folios as can occur in a POS system that is not interfaced.

Property-Specific Interfaces

Unique hotels have unique interface opportunities and issues. FOMs need to understand the capabilities of these interfaces so that they can to detect malfunctions. Some of the more popular and most common property-specific interfaces are listed here:

- *Ski lift tickets.* Many hotels in ski areas allow guests to charge lift tickets, equipment rentals, and other ski-related items from ski shops to their rooms. Fundamentally there is no difference between these purchases and those made at any other POS terminal.
- *Greens fees.* Golf resorts typically allow guests to charge greens fees, cart rentals, and pro-shop purchases to their rooms. Interfaced systems can share information both ways (from property to guest and vice versa), so a hotel's interface with its golf pro shop allows guests to schedule tee times, lessons, and meal reservations from the hotel's front desk or concierge areas.
- *Other service fees.* Additional common interfaces include posting of charges related to the hotel's Internet access fee, health club, spa, beauty shop, barber shop, and florist.

Because interfaced POS systems are revenue-producing subsystems, FOMs must ensure that they are well understood, well maintained, and when necessary, repaired or restored rapidly.

Credit, T&E, and Debit Card Payments

Since the 1960s, **credit cards** and **T&E cards (travel and entertainment cards)** have been a common form of guest payment at most hotels. Now **debit cards** are being used by an increasing number of guests to pay bills.

FRONT OFFICE SEMANTICS

Credit card: System by which banks loan money with interest to consumers as purchases are made. Also known as *bank cards*. Merchants accepting the cards for payment are charged a fee by the banks for the charges made by their customers. Examples of credit cards are Visa and MasterCard.

T&E card (travel and entertainment card): Payment system by which the card issuer collects full payment from the card user each month. Card companies do not typically assess interest charges to consumers; instead, they rely on fees collected from merchants accepting the cards. Examples of T&E cards are American Express and Diners Club.

Debit card: Payment system in which money collected by a merchant (e.g., hotel) is automatically (electronically) deposited into the merchant's local bank account. As with credit and T&E cards, merchants accepting the cards are assessed a fee for the right to do so.

For the FOM, payment cards of these types (as well as the new **smart cards**) are helpful, because when they are interfaced with the PMS, they can speed guest payment and check-out.

FRONT OFFICE SEMANTICS

Smart card: Payment card in which user information such as demographics, purchase history, and product preferences is contained within a computerized chip embedded in the card.

In many hotels, payment cards rather than currency are commonly used by guests to settle accounts. A full examination of payment card use and accounting is presented in Chapter 11. Managing the interface between issuers of payment cards and the hotel involves managing the link between the hotel's PMS and its **merchant service provider**.

FRONT OFFICE SEMANTICS

Merchant service provider (MSP): Entity that, for a fee, manages payment card acceptance and collection of funds for businesses such as hotels.

Payment card issuers and merchant service providers charge a fee for their services. The card issuer charges a **discount fee**. The merchant service provider charges for a variety of services; fees include those for system setup and individual transactions, programming, statement development, and other tasks related to managing the PMS (e.g., equipment rental and connectivity).

FRONT OFFICE SEMANTICS

Discount fee: Amount (percentage) payment card issuers charge merchants for the right to accept their cards. Discount fees may range from 1 percent to 5 percent of a consumer's total purchase.

In most cases, hotels have little option but to accept the most popular payment cards. There are options, however, when considering the MSP. Experienced FOMs select their MSP after careful discussion of the following items that affect the price the hotel will pay for the services it receives:

- Average bill (folio) paid by the hotel's guests
- Total number of payment card transactions processed by the hotel annually
- Hotel's own creditworthiness
- How the hotel will connect its point-of-sale systems (PMS, restaurant, lounge, retail, and any other system) to the MSP

The technology chosen for the interface (manual, dial-up or high-speed, dedicated, leased line) has a significant impact on the hotel's assigned discount rate as well as on other service fees the hotel will be charged. An MSP may encourage a hotel to use its proprietary interface in exchange for assessing lower processing fees. However, this decision can lock the hotel into a poor business relationship by making it difficult to switch MSPs. Instead, the FOM should insist on a universal interface that allows the hotel to switch MSPs if it wishes to do so.

Maintaining the quality of the interface between the MSP and the hotel's revenue-generating subsystems is just as important as maintaining adequate control over the money handled by the hotel's cashiers. A hotel that accepts payment cards does not actually receive cash from its card sales. Instead, it will be credited the money due via **electronic funds transfer (EFT)**. If the interface between the PMS and MSP is faulty, the results may be slow processing, errors, omissions, and even disappearing revenues.

FRONT OFFICE SEMANTICS

Electronic funds transfer (EFT): Electronic movement of money from one bank account to another; commonly called *EFT*.

SECTION REVIEW AND DISCUSSION QUESTIONS

Section Objective: Review basic concepts important to FOMs as they manage the most important data-generating subsystems that are interfaced with the PMS: telephones, recodable locks, pay-per-view services, in-room vending, POS systems, property-specific interfaces, and credit, T&E, and debit card payments.

Section Summary: Interfaced subsystems save time and money and can reduce errors because data are automatically shared between the PMS and the subsystems. FOMs must (1) know the basics about the subsystems used at their property, (2) identify problems as they arise, and (3) seek assistance from suppliers to provide prompt corrective action.

Common telephone subsystems include those related to auto-attendant, voice mail, message-on-hold, automated wake-up, and call accounting systems. Recodable locks provide a degree of guest safety that has become a recognized standard in the industry. Pay-per-view services have moved beyond the traditional offering of movies to the availability of games, music, high-speed Internet access, and other amenities. Improvements in in-room vending systems have reduced the incidence of disagreements between guests and hotels about use of items and about employee theft. POS systems allow guests to make purchases throughout the property with immediate posting of charges to their folio. Depending on the property, other interfaces (e.g., those for the purchase of ski lift tickets or greens fees) can be electronically transferred to a guest folio using a POS system. More guests now pay hotel charges with credit, T&E, and debit cards. Interfaces with the PMS system are of obvious importance to ensure that check-outs can be done quickly and accurately and to ensure that hotel revenues are appropriately accounted for and received.

Discussion Questions:

1. If you were a guest in a hotel that charged access fees for guests to be connected to 1-800 numbers, would you be upset? Why do you think some FOMs continue to assess these charges? Do you think offering complimentary Internet access is a competitive edge for hotels today? Will it be tomorrow?
2. Many guests use pay-per-view services and purchase in-room vending products. Some guests then disclaim use and purchase at the time of check-out. How would you, as the FOM, instruct your front desk agents to deal with guests who claim incorrect billing?
3. What factors would be important to you, as an FOM, when considering which credit, T&E, and debit cards should be accepted at the property? How would you determine which merchant service provider should be used?

MANAGEMENT OF NONINTERFACED SUBSYSTEMS

FOMs are also involved with the management of noninterfaced subsystems, as noted in Roadmap 8.3. FOMs may be responsible for managing one or more subsystems that are not interfaced with the PMS on either a temporary or permanent basis. Let's begin by considering a hotel's electronic voice-mail system that is interfaced but becomes inoperative because of a hardware malfunction. It may be days or longer before a replacement part is shipped, programmed with information necessary to reestablish the interface between the voice mail system, the phone system, and the PMS, and then properly installed. During this time the FOM's staff must take telephone messages manually, and the FOM must immediately implement procedures to ensure accurate and timely message recording and delivery to guests and hotel employees. The FOM must be able to quickly convert from an interfaced to a noninterfaced (backup) system when necessary.

In other situations, hotel owners may determine that the expense related to purchasing an interface for a specific subsystem cannot be justified. For example, interfacing the sale of in-room vended products from minibars may, in some hotels, require the complete and costly replacement of perfectly well-functioning in-room refrigerators that were not manufactured with interface capability. In such a situation, the costs may simply be too high to justify replacement of the refrigerators with modern units that could be easily interfaced.

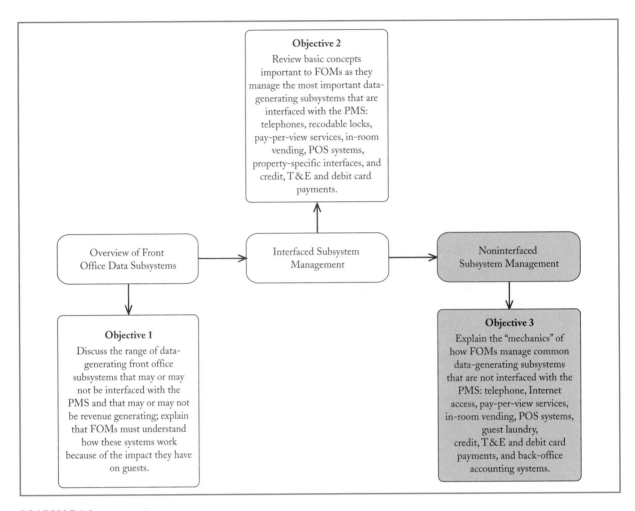

ROADMAP 8.3

Interfaces are expensive to buy and difficult to maintain, and they are also disruptive to operations when they malfunction. Therefore, most hoteliers are selective when deciding which interfaces to use. This section describes some of the common issues that FOMs encounter and the techniques they use to manage selected noninterfaced subsystems.

Telephones

Alexander Graham Bell invented the telephone in 1876. The first commercial switchboard serving 21 extensions on eight incoming lines began operating in 1878. Until the early 1920s, telephones lacked dials, and all callers had to connect with an operator who placed their calls. Operator assistance was required for long-distance calls until the early 1950s. By the 1960s, most businesses and homes in the industrialized world had telephones, and currently the telephone is the most often used technology for business communication. Therefore, it *is* possible (but inconvenient) to design a system to manually transfer calls and deliver telephone messages. The same is true for recording requests for and making guest wake-up calls.

Before electronic voice mail, guestroom telephones had message lights to indicate that a message had been received. The light was activated and deactivated manually at the front desk. Today's in-room telephones have the same capabilities, so FOMs can use (temporarily or permanently) a manual message and wake-up system if their system is properly designed.

Messages

Accurate recordings of voice messages can be critically important to hotel guests and staff. Consider the reaction of a guest if a telephone message describing a family member's emergency medical situation is "lost." Similarly, think of the reaction of a hotel salesperson who has worked hard to secure a large-volume client's potential business and does not receive—until the next morning—a telephone message that the client will be in town tonight and should be given the **VIP** treatment.

FRONT OFFICE SEMANTICS

VIP (very important person): Term used to identify guests who should receive special treatment or attention during their visit.

In most cases, taking telephone messages manually involves entering information into a computer located near the telephone (an excellent system because it allows for immediate e-mailing of the message to hotel staff) or writing the message on a two-copy (carbon copy) message pad similar to that shown in Figure 8.6. If a message is taken for a guest, the message light on the guest's room is activated, and when the guest phones the front desk, the message is orally repeated by the front office agent. The guest may also pick up the message at the front desk. A hotel that uses a carbon copy system retains a record of the call.

Front office staff answering the telephone must be ready to take notes. One of the problems with oral communication in general is that messages may be quickly forgotten. A properly functioning, noninterfaced message subsystem requires staff to be prepared to record these essentials of telephone calls:

- Name and organization of the person calling
- Phone number (including the country and area code if different from that of the hotel) and the extension of the person calling
- Day and time of the call (noting any differences in time zones)
- Subject of the message
- Specific agreements about responsibility for subsequent phone calls (e.g., will the caller contact the guest again or should the guest contact the caller?)

For critical information such as return telephone numbers, monetary amounts, spellings of names, and specific courses of action, staff members should repeat or rephrase what the caller has said to be sure the message is correct.

Wake-Up Calls

Nearly all hotel rooms today have alarm clocks for guests who wish to use them. Many guests do not trust them, however, or are not certain about their ability to program the alarm function on these clocks. Most automated telephone systems have a feature that allows guests to program their own wake-up calls. Many older systems (and some less expensive newer ones), however, do not have this feature.

Timely wake-up calls are so important to guests that at least one hotel chain (Crowne Plaza Hotels & Resorts) offers a guaranteed wake-up call program to ease guest anxiety associated with oversleeping. The guarantee: Guests will receive their

Message Record

TO_____   DATE_____

TIME_____

WHILE YOU WERE OUT

M_____

of_____

Phone_____

MESSAGE_____
_____
_____
_____
_____

___Telephoned   ___Please call
___Was in to see you   ___Will call again
___Wants to see you   ___Urgent
___Returned your call

Message Taken By _____

FIGURE 8.6   Manually recorded telephone message.

wake-up call within five minutes of the their specified time or their stay is free. Imagine the challenges confronting an FOM with that or any other well-managed hotel's guarantee about operational effectiveness!

Most FOMs can design an effective manual wake-up call system. Such systems simply require the recording of the guest's name, room number, and preferred wake-up time. Experienced FOMs know, however, that maintaining an accurate **wake-up log** can be as challenging as it is important.

FRONT OFFICE SEMANTICS

Wake-up log: Written record of wake-up call requests made by hotel guests.

In smaller hotels, or as time allows in larger hotels, FOMs may prefer that their staff personally make wake-up calls rather than using automated systems. The reason: Guests may perceive the personal call as an extra-special service.

Internet Access

Providing guests with in-room Internet service, especially high-speed access, is a relatively new feature for hotels, but it is fast becoming a standard room and property amenity. Currently, some hotels attempt to recover some of the costs of providing the service with guest charges. If guests are charged, a system is needed to identify users and to post those charges to the PMS. At this time, only a few Internet delivery systems (and virtually no wireless delivery systems) are directly interfaced with the products marketed by the major PMS manufacturers.

Pay-per-View Services

A variety of pay-per-view services are available in hotels, for example, movies, Internet access, and video games. The challenges for an FOM operating a noninterfaced system are similar to those encountered by FOMs who manage interfaced systems.

Essentially, a noninterfaced pay-per view system uses a designated printer to record and report guest use based on the parameters authorized by the hotel's management. Recording and reporting take the form of a printed or on-screen record of use by guestroom and time, but typically not by movie title or Web sites viewed. Charges are incurred whenever a guest exceeds the grace period for viewing established by management. For example, assume that pay-per view movies are delivered to guestrooms by a videotape-based system. Managers must determine how long the tape is to run before a charge is to be initiated. From the perspective of the company providing the pay-per-view movies, this grace period should be short (usually less than one minute).

The service provider will likely go to great lengths to ensure that guests can avoid any "accidental" usage charges by requiring a series of specific guest actions. The hotel, however, likely wants to avoid the difficulties encountered from guests who claim they "accidentally" activated a movie and, therefore, were charged inappropriately. The grace period chosen by the FOM should be long enough to avoid most of such guest claims, yet not so long as to incur charges by the service provider. In most cases, appropriate grace periods are the result of negotiations between the pay-per-view service provider and the hotel.

Pay-per-view companies reasonably expect to charge hotels for their guests' actual use of the system. Although estimates vary, some industry experts believe that as many as 10 percent of the guests who view movies on a pay-per-view system dispute one or more of their charges at check-out time. Therefore, when a manual posting system is in use, the FOM must maintain a documentation procedure that allows the hotel to note the date and time of guests' movie or other programming selections. In the case of movies, the front desk staff is not typically supplied with specific information about the exact movie selected because, in many hotels, a large percentage of the movies offered and viewed are adult oriented. It serves little purpose and can be detrimental to maintain a pay-per-view system that permits front desk agents access to information not actually required for the verification of charges.

MODERN FRONT OFFICE ISSUES AND TACTICS

Pay-per-Play: Gambling Arrives at Non-Casino Hotels

As the Internet continues to expand, FOMs can expect new challenges. One example involves the meeting of online gambling services and hotel guests' in-room capacity to access the Internet.

In 2004, the OnCommand Corporation, one of the two largest providers of in-room pay-per-view services, signed a multiyear contract with BettingCorp, a wholly owned subsidiary of OpenTV, one of the world's leading interactive television companies. The contract provides that BettingCorp will develop interactive games for OnCommand. As a result, OnCommand will be able to offer hotels in-room gaming and betting services across the Internet and via Wi-Fi platforms.

Regardless of their personal views about gaming, savvy FOMs should monitor this development with great interest. The potential for "interesting" guest relations issues is quite evident:

> *Guest:* But I thought I bet a dollar not ten thousand dollars!
> *Front desk agent:* Never draw to an inside straight!

In-Room Vending

Many hotels still offer in-room vending with a system not interfaced to the PMS. In these cases, usually a housekeeping employee services the in-room units and records the items consumed by the guests. The units are then restocked and product usage data are transferred to the front office for posting to the guest's folio. The sum of the numbers of each product used is simply multiplied by the single-item purchase price to arrive at the total amount of the charge. In some cases, charges may be posted manually using a POS system in the food and beverage department.

Not surprisingly, questions arise about charges. Consider the case in which Ms. Abbott, staying in room 269 at the Altoona Hotel, checks out at 9:00 a.m. Later that afternoon, the hotel's in-room vending attendant discovers that several items were removed from the room's minibar during the previous 24 hours. The attendant transfers these charges to the front desk after the guest has checked out, or even worse, the charges are accidentally posted to the folio of the new guest in room 269! The real problem, of course, is that Ms. Abbott is no longer in the hotel, her folio has already been marked paid in full, and she presumably owes money to the hotel. As a result, a **late charge** will be posted to her folio.

FRONT OFFICE SEMANTICS

Late charge: Departmental charges, such as those for food and beverage or in-room vending purchases, that were entered into the billing system late and which are posted to a guest's folio even though that guest has checked out.

Small late charges are typically written off (absorbed) by the hotel. Of particular difficulty is the guest who, after being contacted about significant late charges, claims not to have made the purchase. If a guest has paid the hotel bill by credit or debit card, attempts by the hotel to change the totals sent in for collection may be met by the guest's refusal to pay the higher amount and by an unwillingness by the card companies to process such charges. Collection, especially for small amounts, is difficult and can easily result in guest unhappiness and ill will.

Despite the difficulties, FOMs working with noninterfaced in-room vending systems must develop procedures to help ensure the timely posting of charges to the proper folio. They must also maintain written backup documentation of the charges for inspection by the many guests likely to dispute them. Efforts must be made to minimize late charges by promptly posting submitted charges. In keeping with a hotel's policies, legitimate and significantly large late charges should be pursued for payment in a reasonable manner.

Point-of-Sale (POS) Systems

Virtually every noninterfaced POS system in a hotel presents the same challenges regarding late charges as those created by noninterfaced in-room vending. If legitimate charges do not arrive at the front desk to be posted to a guest's folio before that guest departs, payment collection problems increase significantly. Another problem with noninterfaced POS systems is the potential for human error. Consider the employee responsible for manually posting hundreds of charges to dozens of different guest folios. It is reasonable to assume that errors will be made. The correct amounts will be charged but to the wrong folios; or the proper folio will be charged with an incorrect amount. In both cases, guests typically dispute the charges at time of check-out, especially if the error is not in their favor. The results are delays in check-out times, increased guest dissatisfaction, and the real potential for creating ill will.

MODERN FRONT OFFICE ISSUES AND TACTICS

Subsystems Inside Subsystems

As technology advances, specialized interfaces of subsystems within subsystems are becoming more common. For example, it is typical to interface a hotel restaurant's POS system with the hotel's PMS, but some providers of POS kitchen management software interface their own program with accounting programs such as QuickBooks from Intuit. QuickBooks is a leading business accounting program that facilitates transaction recording, posting to ledgers, writing checks, preparing invoices, performing reconciliation, and preparing monthly financial statements.

When a hotel's kitchen management program is interfaced with an accounting program such as QuickBooks, food and beverage (F&B) managers can easily obtain more detailed information about the individual menu items sold, inventory items on hand, vendor pricing, and food costs than is available with a general accounting system. This is especially true for the F&B managers at smaller hotels that do not have fully integrated accounting systems. In these situations, F&B managers must create their own cost-control tools. By establishing a subsystem interface between their POS and a simplified accounting system, F&B managers can get the best from both systems while eliminating double data entry. Look for more hotel-related examples of inter- and intra-departmental interfaces in the future, including those that directly affect the front office.

Guest Laundry

Most hotels do not operate an in-house guest laundry service; instead, they contract with a local laundry and dry cleaning company to provide these services. Typically, the hotel's housekeeping department supplies guestrooms with disposable laundry bags and laundry tickets identified by tracking numbers. A sample of a three-copy laundry ticket is shown in Figure 8.7:

- Copy 1 is retained by the laundry service provider.
- Copy 2 is retained by the front desk to post charges.
- Copy 3 is returned to the guest with the cleaned items.

Guests use these numbered tickets to indicate the items to be cleaned. Prices for cleaning services are preprinted on the tickets so guests know the amount they will

81595

Kent

VALET SERVICE | **DELUXE CLEANERS**
2911 S. WASHINGTON

FOR PICK-UP CONTACT BELL STAND

NAME:

ROOM#:   DATE:

CLEANING				LAUNDRY		
M. SUITS	pc.	10.25		STARCH: NO L M H		
JACKETS		8.75		FOLD	HANGER	
TROUSERS		6.50		SHIRTS		2.25
OVERCOAT		11.75		POLO SHIRTS		3.50
SWEATERS		6.25		UNDERSHIRTS		2.00
TIES		4.25		UNDERSHORTS		2.00
				SOCKS		.65
L. SUITS	pc.	10.25		HANDKERCHIEFS		.35
DRESSES		10.50		PAJAMAS		3.50
SLACKS		6.50		ROBE		10.00
SKIRTS	pleats	6.25				
BLOUSES		6.25		BLOUSES		6.25
				SKIRTS		6.25
SP. COAT		6.50		DRESS		8.75
				UNDERPANTS		2.00
VEST		4.75		SLIPS		2.00
				BRAS		1.00
COVERALLS		7.75		GOWNS / PJ'S		6.25
				ROBE		10.00
SILK SHIRTS		6.25		SHORTS		4.25
				SHIRTS (TUX)		3.50
SHOP COATS		6.25		JEANS		6.25
D. C. TOTAL				LDRY. TOTAL		

31607   A53, 814

FIGURE 8.7   Sample laundry ticket.

be charged. Laundry bags are either taken to the front desk by the guest or picked up from the guest's room by a staff member, depending on hotel policy. The numbered laundry bags with the guest's items are picked up by (or delivered to) the off-site laundry company. Cleaned items are returned to the hotel, and charges for cleaning are manually posted to the appropriate guest folios.

For FOMs, challenges related to providing laundry services include ensuring that laundry items are picked up promptly, that they are returned to the proper guest or guestroom, and that the proper charges are posted to the correct guest folio. Hotels usually operate a computerized or manual laundry log system that records the following information:

- Name of guest using the laundry service
- Guest's room number
- Laundry ticket number used by guest
- Date laundry was sent out
- Date laundry was returned to hotel
- Date laundry was returned to (or picked up by) guest
- Amount charged to guest's folio
- Name of person posting laundry charge to folio

Experienced FOMs know that if the preceding information is maintained accurately; problems with guest laundry service can be minimized, and guest satisfaction with the service can be maximized, even though charges for laundry service are not interfaced directly with the hotel's PMS.

Credit, T&E, and Debit Card Payments

When payment cards are not directly interfaced with a PMS, FOMs face two distinct challenges. The first is the challenge of accurately placing a **hold** on the card.

FRONT OFFICE SEMANTICS

Hold: Action taken by a hotel notifying a payment card administrator or issuer that a cardholder will likely be charged for a specific dollar amount. In response, if the card has sufficient credit available (or, in the case of debit cards, sufficient funds on deposit), this amount will be "held" until the charge is either initiated or until the hold is released. Sometimes referred to as placing a *block* or *authorization* on a card. Used as in, "Put an additional $500 *hold* on Mr. Lacey's Visa card because he has decided to stay three more nights."

When payment card systems are not interfaced with the PMS, a front office agent can record the wrong authorization to the wrong room. Consider Mr. Haley in room 228 who had his Visa card authorized for $1,000. If the information about the hold is posted to Mr. Hansen in room 288, it will appear that Mr. Haley does not have credit established when, in fact, he does. In addition, Mr. Hansen could, theoretically, leave without paying for his room. If the hotel did not establish a payment card hold for Mr. Hansen, it could have difficulty collecting from him because no authorized form of payment is on file.

A second challenge faced by FOMs without interfaced payment card systems involves the manual recording of payment card authorization numbers and payments. When a hotel requests a payment card hold, it is assigned a specific authorization tracking number. These multidigit numbers (sometimes a combination of numbers and letters) can easily be transposed by employees working in a manual system. This makes reverification of hold request activity difficult.

The specific procedures FOMs should use to settle accounts of guests who use payment cards and the manner in which funds are actually transferred to the hotel's bank account are detailed in Chapter 11. The need for front desk agents to be accurate as they implement procedures in a noninterfaced system is critical.

Back-Office Accounting

FOMs often find that their back-office accounting system, which is used to create financial summaries and reports needed by the hotel's owners and managers (see Chapter 4), is not directly interfaced with the hotel's PMS. The reasons for not interfacing the accounting system with the PMS are varied:

- *Multibrand ownership.* Hotel franchisors require franchisees to use a specific PMS. When a franchisee owns multiple properties, difficulties can arise. For example, a franchisee who owns a Holiday Inn Express (InterContinental Hotels Group), a Comfort Suites (Choice Hotels), and a Ramada Plaza (Cendant Hotels) may be required to use three different PMSs. The franchisee, however, may want to create consolidated financial statements for all three of the properties he or she owns. It simply may not be possible to find a company that manufactures an accounting software package to interface with all three mandated PMSs.

- *Financial confidentiality from entities external to the hotel.* In today's environment, a hotel's PMS is typically interfaced directly with a hotel franchisor's central reservation system. This allows the franchisor to have access to the franchisee's financial information held in the PMS (e.g., ADR, occupancy rate, and food and beverage sales posted through the PMS). However, the hotel's owner may prefer that the franchisor not have access to the hotel's non-PMS financial records (e.g., payroll, accounts payable, operating expenses, and taxes). Therefore, the hotel's financial summary records may have to be kept separate from the financial data held in the PMS.

- *Financial confidentiality from entities internal to the hotel.* Some hotel owners and management companies prefer that financial summaries prepared for a hotel not be available to those working at the hotel. For other reasons, they may not want to generate a property's financial statements on-site. Therefore, they use a **centralized accounting system** rather than a **decentralized accounting system.**

FRONT OFFICE SEMANTICS

Centralized accounting system: Financial management system that collects accounting data from one or more hotels and combines and analyzes the data at a different (central) site.

Decentralized accounting system: Financial management system that collects accounting data from an individual hotel site and combines and analyzes that data at that same site.

In a centralized accounting system, the financial data from the hotel are transmitted by computer (e.g., by e-mail, network, intranet, or Web page) to a central location. These data may be recorded and then analyzed by management or combined with other hotel properties for analysis. To illustrate why some hotels operate under a centralized system, assume that an owner operates five full-service hotels in the Southeastern United States and that the owner's office is in the Midwest. Assume also that each day the owner wants to know the combined revenue generated by the five hotels on the previous day. To do so, each hotel's controller reports the previous day's revenue to the owner's office where the owner sums the revenues to yield the previous day's total sales. If the five hotels operated with different PMSs, the report likely could not be produced using a single interface. Centralized accounting is most prevalent in chain-operated or multiproperty hotel companies. When a centralized accounting system is selected, it is less likely that the PMS will be interfaced with the back-office system.

Even though some improvements have been made recently, the hotel industry and its suppliers have not, on the whole, done an especially good job of ensuring that all subsystems are well integrated with the PMS. FOMs should be aware that there are four principal goals of integration:

- Integration should be based on guests' needs so that they enjoy a seamless experience.
- Integration should address the needs of other customer groups such as corporate account executives, meeting planners, travel wholesalers, travel agents, third-party Internet sites, and other appropriate distribution channels.
- Integration should encompass all hotel operations to improve customer service, to reduce costs, or to do both.
- Integration should assist hoteliers in their decision-making tasks.

Interface systems often focus only on revenue-generating subsystems. Most income-producing interfaces perform only the basic functions of authorizing and posting room charges (although recodable locks, central reservations, and Web-booking interfaces are exceptions). Historically, and with some justification, most full-service hotels spend roughly similar amounts of money on the PMS (the main system) as they do on the following four major subsystems: POS systems, telephone-related services, guest-room entertainment (primarily on-demand video and free-to-guest television), and recodable locks. For the most part, the PMS and the four subsystems each evolved independently; each developed its own technology, manufacturers, and vendors. Today, there is less rationale for the continued existence of these distinct systems. Technology will likely permit each separate system to be replaced by a single hotel management system (the super PMS?). As that happens, the new system will inevitably be more capable of meeting a hotel's core business needs and of achieving the four primary goals of subsystem integration.

SECTION REVIEW AND DISCUSSION QUESTIONS

Section Objective: Explain the "mechanics" of how FOMs manage common data-generating subsystems that are not interfaced with PMS: telephone, Internet access, pay-per-view services, in-room vending, POS systems, guest laundry, credit, T&E and debit card payments, and back-office accounting systems.

Section Summary: There are many front office subsystems that may not be interfaced with the PMS either on a temporary basis or on a permanent basis. Interfaced systems may malfunction, and some interfaces may be considered cost prohibitive for a specific hotel. In both of these instances, FOMs must know about and monitor manual systems.

For years, hotels provided messages for guests and employees and wake-up calls to guestrooms with noninterfaced telephone systems, and some properties still do. Other common systems that may not be interfaced are pay-per-view services, in-room vending, POS systems, and guest laundry. The manual systems that are in place must be accurate, must provide written backup to confirm that guest purchases were actually made, and must be timely so that charges are posted to folios before the guests check out. Credit, T&E, and debit card payments can also be processed manually. However, the potential for human error is significant, and revenue collection may suffer as a consequence.

In the past, PMS information has not been interfaced with back-office systems. Some hoteliers, especially franchisees, prefer this; technology suppliers, however, are now developing an interface for hoteliers who desire it.

Discussion Questions:

1. What specific topics would you, as an FOM, include in a program to train new front desk agents about procedures for taking messages and providing wake-up calls if a noninterfaced telephone subsystem is in use?

2. How might an FOM define a "significant" late charge, the payment of which should be pursued from a guest? What tactics could be used in efforts to collect this late charge?

3. What financial data would you, as a franchisee, want to provide freely to your franchisor? What data might you not prefer to share? Why?

From the Front Office: Front-Line Interview

Ada Tung Yan Yan
Assistant Front Desk Manager
The Peninsula Hong Kong (300 rooms)
Hong Kong, China

Getting What You *Really* Want!

Ada graduated from The Chinese University of Hong Kong; her major was Japanese studies. She began working in The Peninsula Hong Kong as a receptionist.

1. **What are the most important responsibilities in your present position?**
   This is an easy question to answer: facilitating the work of our staff members.

2. **What are the biggest challenges that confront you in your day-to-day work and in the long-term operation of your property's front office?**
   To meet the hotel's standards with available labor resources during times of high occupancy. We are currently making a special effort to manage the overtime incurred by our front office staff.

3. **What is your most unforgettable front office moment?**
   When we turned a complaining guest into a satisfied guest! I recall a gentleman who was upset at check-in because the room he was assigned was not what he requested. After we talked with him to better discover his needs, we were able to provide the appropriate room. Now he had what he *really* wanted, and he was very pleased with our services.

4. **What advice do you have for those studying about or considering a career in front office or hotel management?**
   Be aware of the often difficult work environment and be prepared for it! A career in front office is rewarding but challenging. Work experience is essential to achieve success.

The FOM in Action: A Solution

FOMs with subsystems that are not interfaced with their PMS learn to adapt to the situation. Similarly, FOMs with interfaced subsystems soon take the interface for granted. The challenge for FOMs arises when a normally interfaced system is, for whatever reason, temporarily inoperable. FOMs confronted with such a situation can best deal with it by asking and then answering a series of questions:

1. What is the impact on the guest's experience?

   In Belinda's case, guests are primarily affected when there is a posting error. The quality of the in-room viewing product is not affected, but some features such as video check-out might be. Belinda can systematically determine the guest experiences that will likely be affected by the interface failure and take necessary steps to minimize the negative impact on guests.

2. What is the likely impact on employees?

   In this specific situation, Jim, the night auditor, has likely been placed in a position with which he is unfamiliar. He needs to be informed about the importance of accurate manual posting and taught a process designed to ensure that it can be achieved. Unless Belinda trains Jim well, posting errors will probably continue. Front desk agents will also be affected as they interact with guests who discover posting errors. These employees should be empowered to make folio adjustments and take other steps to satisfy affected guests.

3. What is the impact on the hotel's financial situation?

   Some interfaces that become inoperable (e.g., as telephone call accounting) can cause revenue loss. Others, such as failure of a recodable locking system interface, may not result in direct revenue loss but may require additional labor expenditures. Failure of the recodable locking system also may involve significant legal liability. Generally, the greater the negative impact on a hotel's revenue, the more critical it is to design and properly implement a manual backup system.

4. What is the effect on records and data management?

   The PMS is the hotel's primary record-keeping system, so whenever an interface is lost, the data generated by the interfaced subsystem may be lost. In many cases, the FOM must devise a system of data collection and maintenance that ensures adequate record keeping. In Belinda's case, the in-room movie vendor bills the hotel on the basis of the number of movies viewed per month. To ensure accurate billing, and until the interface is repaired, Belinda must be concerned about the individual posting of movie charges and the total number of movies viewed. An accurate manual record-keeping system is critical to maintaining that information.

FRONT OFFICE SEMANTICS LIST

Free-to-guests	Dial-up Internet	Wi-Fi certified
Carrier (telephone)	Call records	Hot spot
Pay-per-view	Local call	POS (point of sale)
Auto-attendant	Long-distance call	POS terminal
Message on hold	International call	Credit card
Automated wake-up	IT (information technology)	T&E card
House phone	Move/add/change	Debit card
Smart switch	Recodable locking system	Smart card
Least-cost routing	E-fridge	Merchant service provider (MSP)

Discount fee	Wake-up log	Centralized accounting system
Electronic funds transfer (EFT)	Late charge	Decentralized accounting system
VIP (very important person)	Hold	

FRONT OFFICE AND THE INTERNET

The following Web sites relate to the content of this chapter:

Web address	Subject area
www.lodgenet.com	In-room, pay-per-view services
www.oncommand.com	In-room, pay-per-view services
www.panasonic.com/business/hospitality	Telephone systems
www.nortelnetworks.com	Telephone systems
www.mitel.com	Telephone systems
www.isi-info.com	Call accounting systems
www.metropolis.com	Call accounting systems
www.tesalocks.com	Recodable locks
www.saflok.com	Recodable locks
www.vingcard.com	Recodable locks
www.bartech.fr/	Minibars
www.microfridge.com	Minibars
www.panasonic.com	POS systems
www.micros.com	POS systems
www.squirrelsystems.com	POS systems
www.peachtree.com	Back-office accounting software

REAL-WORLD ACTIVITIES

1. Review the Web sites of several providers of recodable locks (see the Front Office and the Internet section). What advantages to these systems, as quoted by the manufacturers, appear to be common? What advantages seem to be unique? Which system appears to have the most advantages? What factors would you, as an FOM, consider when giving an opinion about a recodable lock system?

2. How would you, as an FOM, determine the type of services to be offered on your guest telephone system? Review the Web sites of the providers of telephone systems (see the Front Office and the Internet section). What factors do these suppliers suggest are most important in the selection decision?

3. Review the Web sites for the minibar manufacturers (see the Front Office and the Internet section). What features are noted that would help a hotel manager determine the total charges due from a guest? What features make it easy to determine the value of purchases made during a time that a specific guest occupied the room?

4. Which of the data-generating front office subsystems discussed in this chapter are of most importance to guests? Why? Which systems do you think cause the most trouble for guests? Why? If you were an FOM developing a training session for your front desk agents, what would you tell them to help prevent problems from occurring in the subsystems you just suggested?

5. Do you think that POS subsystem interfaces increase the revenue generated from hotel outlets that provide this service to guests? How would you, as a hotel manager, determine which outlets, if any, should provide this service? How would you determine whether you should continue with a noninterfaced subsystem?

9

Reservation, Reception, and Room Assignment Management

Chapter Outline

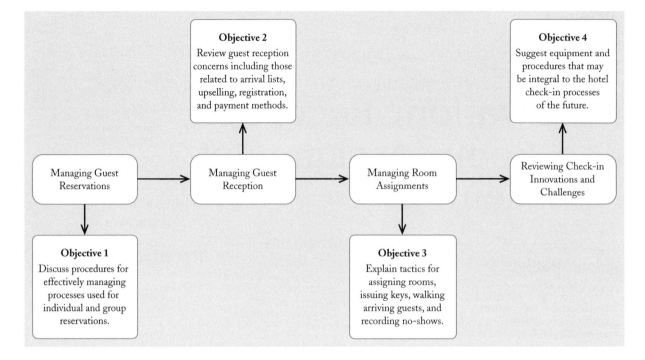

Chapter Preview

Systems must be in place to manage guest reservations, provide guests with friendly and efficient reception when they arrive at the hotel, and promptly assign guests to rooms. This chapter focuses on three critical responsibilities: reservation management, reception procedures, and room assignments.

In most hotels, there are two basic types of reservations: individual and group. There are significant differences in how each type is managed. Consider, for example, the special challenges of monitoring the group reservation block, tracking reservations submitted in a rooming list, and properly recording reservation cancellations.

After arriving at the hotel, a guest is checked into the room that best meets his or her needs. This is done, in part, by the upselling process described in Chapter 6. FOMs must ensure that the reception process results in accurate recording of all important information about the guest's stay and about the guest's ability to pay for anticipated purchases. Procedural techniques are outlined in this chapter.

After being greeted properly, a guest should be promptly assigned a specific room and be issued keys for that room. In some cases, a guest cannot be accommodated and must be walked to another hotel. This chapter describes the proper procedures for recording this action. The chapter also explains what to do if guests cannot immediately receive room keys because the room is not yet available. Procedures for handling no-show guests are also discussed.

Many FOMs are now investigating the pros and cons of automating the guest check-in process to allow guests to check in without assistance. Some innovations are examined in relation to fundamental principles required of all guest registration processes.

The FOM in Action: The Challenge

"But this is the bride's grandmother," said the young man standing at the front desk.

"I'm sorry sir," replied Shalaya, the front desk agent on duty, "but our rates for tonight are $199 for a single."

"That's what I'm trying to tell you," said the man, "she's with the Alexander wedding party that received a group rate of $119. I know because that's what I'm paying. I'm the bride's brother, and she is my dad's mother. I know she didn't reserve ahead of time, but she has been ill, and we just found out last night that she could attend the wedding. I picked her up at the airport an hour ago. I don't understand why you can't give her the wedding rate. We have more than 175 guests in your hotel."

"I'm truly sorry sir," replied Shalaya, "it is a busy night in the hotel, and the rate my manager authorized me to quote walk-in guests is $199 per night."

"Fine," replied the young man, "I'll wait until my dad arrives to check in, and then we want to talk to the front office manager. My father is paying for this event, and he is going to have a fit when he hears about this!"

If you were the FOM, how would you act when you meet the brother and the father of the bride?

MANAGING GUEST RESERVATIONS

As shown in Roadmap 9.1, this chapter begins with a discussion of managing the process of guest reservations. In most hotels, a potential guest can make a room reservation for almost any future date. Until that date, the reservation may be modified, extended, or, with some restrictions, canceled as the guest wishes. The reservation changes to an

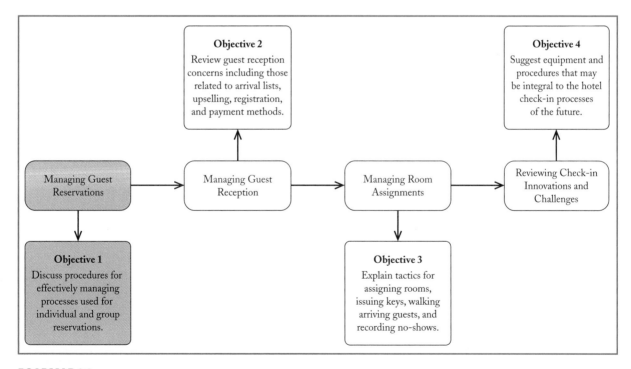

ROADMAP 9.1

"arriving" reservation, or **arrival,** on the date the guest is to begin occupying the reserved room. A guest may modify a reservation up until the time he or she arrives at the hotel and is actually assigned to a room. However, it may become more difficult to accommodate requests for changes as the arrival date draws nearer. In most hotels, FOMs and their staff manage future reservations, changes to reservations, and arrivals.

FRONT OFFICE SEMANTICS

Arrival: An arriving guest. Arrivals are typically counted by the number of individuals. Used as in, "There will be 300 *arrivals* tonight, including 150 children."

FOMs must manage two basic types of reservations: individual and group. Each type has unique characteristics that must be well understood to be managed professionally. Each type of reservation, if canceled, must be properly recorded.

Individual Reservations

Individual reservations make up the vast majority of business for many properties, especially small, limited-service hotels without meeting space. In these, as well as many other properties, individual reservations are taken by a **reservations agent.**

FRONT OFFICE SEMANTICS

Reservations agent: Front office employee whose job consists primarily of taking and entering individual and group reservations into the hotel's property management system.

Chapter 4 detailed the information recorded in the property management system (PMS) when a typical reservation is made. Now let's consider how different types of individual and group reservations (see Chapter 5) are processed at the front desk when a guest arrives. Recall that when guests make a reservation, they may actually pay for the room by providing an advance deposit **(prepaid reservation),** guarantee the reservation with a payment card (guaranteed reservation), or request a reservation without providing payment to guarantee the reservation. **Nonguaranteed reservations** are typically honored until 4:00 p.m. or 6:00 p.m. on the day of arrival. To ensure consistency in the brand, some franchisors mandate the time of release after which the reserved room can be sold to another guest, and the guest with the original reservation will not be charged for the room. FOMs should ensure that their procedures for releasing nonguaranteed reservations are consistent with their franchisor's recommended policies.

FRONT OFFICE SEMANTICS

Prepaid reservation: Room reservation in which guests, prior to their arrival, provide payment for their rooms. Sometimes referred to as an *advanced deposit reservation*.

Nonguaranteed reservation: Room reservation for which guests do not provide payment at the time the reservation is made.

In nearly all hotels, some guests arrive without a reservation. The "reservation" that is made seconds before room assignment for these walk-in guests is also important, because front office staff must still provide an appropriate guest reception and implement an efficient process of room assignment.

In some hotels, the reservation system and the front office may be combined into the same department.

Prepaid Reservations

When guest reservations are prepaid, the FOM must deal with two distinct challenges: proper posting and refund payments.

- *Proper posting.* When a hotel accepts funds from guests in advance of their arrival, the guests expect the funds to be applied to their eventual folio balance. However, no folios exist when the advance payments are received because the guests have not checked in to the hotel. At check-in, guests are assigned a room number, which allows **credit posting** on guests' folios. Therefore, an **advance deposit account** must be established to indicate the names of prepaid guests and the amounts of money they have prepaid.

FRONT OFFICE SEMANTICS

Credit posting: Entry on a guest's folio that either applies a payment toward the guest's balance that is due or that effectively reduces the total amount due.

Advance deposit account: Account used by a hotel to record prepayments by guests.

When prepaid guests check into the hotel, the amount of their prepayment will be deducted from the advance deposit account and will be credited (added) to their individual folio balances. This process of recording payments and crediting payments to individual folios calls for close cooperation between the controller's office and the FOM. Written procedures for documenting and posting prepayments and credits are critical.

• *Refund payments.* Refunds due to guests who prepay their reservations and then require a refund can be challenging. Consider, for example, Doug Stone who planned to stay at the Altoona Hotel for 10 nights at a rate of $100 per night. He prepaid in full by check 30 days in advance. On the second day of his stay, however, a family medical emergency caused him to check out of the hotel eight days early. In this case, an $800 refund is due. Assume, however, that the front desk agent does not have that much cash available to immediately pay Mr. Stone. Assume, as well, that Mr. Stone rightfully believes the hotel should promptly refund the overpayment, either by cash or hotel-issued check at the time of check-out.

Consider the following situation: A guest prepays for a stay of several days by personal check at the time of check-in. The next day the guest seeks a partial refund claiming that a personal emergency requires an early check-out. The FOM must protect the hotel against a guest who attempts to defraud the property by writing a worthless check and then seeking a "refund" before the bank notifies the property about the **returned check.**

Many hotels process prepayment refunds in excess of a specified amount (e.g., $50) only by hotel-issued check with approval of the controller. Individual hotel policies about refund payments vary, but hotels recognize the importance of protecting the property while limiting the time that prepayment funds due to guests are held in hotel accounts. Front desk agents should understand the prepayment refund policy of their hotel and clearly articulate that policy to guests. The best practice is to ensure that guests understand the hotel's refund policies when funds are received, at time of check-in, or when prepayments are actually posted to their accounts.

FRONT OFFICE SEMANTICS

Returned check: Check deposited by a hotel into its bank account that, for some reason, is not honored. Checks of this type are "returned" to the hotel. Sometimes referred to as a *bad, bounced,* or *hot* check.

Guaranteed Reservations

As described Chapter 5, a guaranteed reservation allows the hotel to hold the guest's room until arrival or the hotel's designated check-out time the next day. A guest with a guaranteed reservation will be charged as a no-show for nonuse of the room. To ensure that the payment will be received and to reduce the instances of no-shows, a form of payment is frequently required when the reservation is made. Typically, this consists of accepting a payment card i.e., travel and entertainment (T&E) card, credit card, or a debit card. When the hotel's reservation system is interfaced with its payment card processing system, it is possible to **authorize payment card** when the reservation is made. If there is no interface, unscrupulous but sophisticated guests can defraud the hotel by supplying an invalid account number for the payment card.

FRONT OFFICE SEMANTICS

Authorize payment card: To ensure a card's validity and payment ability and capacity.

For example, this can be done by reversing one or more numbers on a valid payment card. If the error is detected, the guest can claim that the card was misread. If the error is not detected, the guest may be a no-show for the reservation without fear of being billed. FOMs with PMS systems that are not directly interfaced with their credit card processor should implement a procedure to confirm and authorize payment card numbers within 24 hours of being used to guarantee a reservation.

At the time a reservation is made, a credit card is merely authorized, not charged. Within the cancellation policies established by the hotel, therefore, guests can cancel their reservation without having their payment card actually billed. (The payment card authorization and billing process is explained fully in Chapter 11.) If a prospective guest provides a card number that cannot be authorized, the hotel must contact the guest to obtain an account number. This will help to reduce losses from no-shows and ensure that guaranteed reservations taken by the hotel are, in fact, secured with a valid form of payment.

Nonguaranteed Reservations

Many hotels accept nonguaranteed reservations that hold a room until a specific time, after which the hotel can sell the room. If the guest does not claim the reservation, the hotel does not have the right to bill the guest as a no-show. From the hotel's perspective, a nonguaranteed reservation is never as desirable as one that is guaranteed.

Why then do hotels accept nonguaranteed reservations? Consider Otis Pennycuff who is 80 years old, has never had a credit card and never will have one. A survivor of the Great Depression of the 1930s, he is a cash-only guest, and many hotels find such guests desirable. For a variety of reasons, some guests prefer that there be no credit card record of their hotel stay. If FOMs decide to accept nonguaranteed reservations, they must recognize that the hotel's no-show rate on these reservations will be higher than that on guaranteed reservations. It may be in the hotel's best interest to accept nonguaranteed reservations, especially during slow periods. Note also that the hotel that accepts nonguaranteed reservations will likely require that guests produce a credit or debit card, or prepay with cash at check-in, to reduce the chances of the guests leaving the hotel with an unpaid folio balance.

Walk-In Guests

From a record-keeping perspective, a walk-in guest is one whose reservation was made on the day of arrival. Other than recording the time the reservation was made and noting that the guest was a walk-in, the PMS will make no distinction between walk-in guests and their counterparts who arrive with a reservation. The reservation data maintained about the guest, including room preference and rate paid, will be identical to the data for a reservation made days earlier by another guest.

Walk-ins make up a large percentage of the guests in some hotels, especially those located near an interstate highway or other high-volume traffic area. FOMs must establish the rates to be quoted to walk-in guests on a daily basis as well as the fade rates that employees working after 4:00 p.m. can use to sell rooms to these guests. If properly managed, walk-ins can be an important source of revenue. In some hotels, FOMs provide

Walk-in reservations often generate large revenues for some hotels.

extra sales training to front desk agents to maximize their ability to encourage walk-in guests to accept the quoted room rate and, in turn, increase occupancy and RevPar rates.

Group Reservations

Neither the front office nor the reservations department typically manages group reservations. Instead, group reservations are generated by the sales and marketing department. For example, a travel agent can readily book a reservation for a transient guest through the Global Distribution System (GDS), but the agent cannot usually book a room for a group member in that manner. This is logical, because a hotel wants to minimize its distribution channel costs for group sales. As a result, a member of the hotel's sales team interacts with front office or reservations staff, or both, to enter and modify group reservations made by the sales department. Figure 9.1 illustrates the shared responsibilities for group reservations.

Group business is critical to the success of many hotels; however, there is no universally accepted definition of *group* business. In mid-size to larger hotels, personnel from the sales and marketing department typically accept the responsibility for selling group rooms. Groups may consist of tour groups, sports teams, conventions, trade shows, corporate training meetings, wedding blocks, special travel packages marketed by the hotel's sales department, and other users of multiple rooms. Reservations for very small groups may be managed by the front office reservation system. The FOM and the director of sales and marketing (DOSM) must coordinate efforts to best serve the hotel's guests. Communication about group room management should be ongoing; when it is not, difficulties can occur, and mistakes can be made.

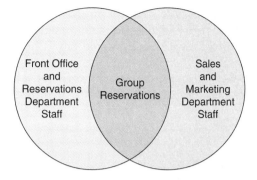

FIGURE 9.1   Shared responsibilities for group reservations.

Consider the case of Rival State University and the Altoona Hotel. Rival State University competes in the same athletic conference as does the university in the Altoona's community. On alternating years, when Rival State plays football against the local university, the Altoona Hotel sells out because the Rival State team, coaches, and fans stay at the hotel. This business is profitable, and the Altoona's DOSM works hard to maintain it.

One afternoon, a front desk agent receives a call from the coach of the women's swimming team at Rival State. Because of the excellent recommendation from her colleague (the coach of her school's football team), she wants to reserve five rooms for two days for the upcoming women's swimming championship scheduled for the local campus. Assume that the front desk agent makes the reservation under the coach's name but does not record any information about the stay of the Rival State team. Several situations can occur that will create problems for the group and the Altoona Hotel:

- In an overbooked situation, the entire group may be walked to a competing hotel.
- In an overbooked situation, guests in several of the five rooms may be walked to a competing hotel.
- The group may not be welcomed by the hotel in a manner consistent with the group's importance to the hotel's overall business (e.g., in-room welcome baskets, complimentary amenities, personal attention to room selection, or other perks offered to VIPs).
- Room assignments may be made arbitrarily, so the team members may not be located in close proximity.
- Bed-type requests made for the swimmers may not be honored; for example, the rooms assigned by the front desk agent when the team arrives may have only one king bed rather than the two double beds requested.
- The coach may not be offered a complimentary room upgrade, which is an **SOP (standard operating procedure)** at the Altoona.
- The DOSM, who is not aware that the group is in the hotel, misses an opportunity to further solidify the Altoona's relationship with Rival State.

FRONT OFFICE SEMANTICS

SOP (standard operating procedure): Policy or procedure that is so routine it should be readily known and followed by all affected employees.

Regardless of property size, group business in a convention hotel often represents the majority of annual room nights sold. By contrast, group business in a small, limited-service hotel located near a highway may comprise a small fraction of total rooms sold. For most full-service hotels and limited-service properties with meeting space, the guestroom revenue generated by group business is significant. Group reservations are handled differently than reservations for transient guests. Let's see how group folios, group blocks, and the reservation recording process for group rooms are managed.

Group Folios

Perhaps the most important difference between an individual reservation and a group reservation is that a group folio **(master bill)** will usually be established for the group.

FRONT OFFICE SEMANTICS

Master bill: Single folio (bill) established for a group that includes specifically agreed-upon group charges. Sometimes called a *group folio* or *group bill.* Used as in, "our group will pay for room and tax on the *master bill*, but any room service charges are the responsibility of individual group members."

Master bills are helpful when one member of the group is responsible for paying all hotel charges. If a company sponsors a training session for 75 employees, it is likely to be most convenient for that company's accountant to pay one invoice for hotel rooms rather than to reimburse 75 individuals for the cost of individual rooms. Similarly, a coach traveling with a sports team will probably find a master bill to be the best way to as pay for the team's rooms. The management of a master bill is basically the same as management of a regular folio with one major difference: The names of those in the group authorized to make purchases charged to the master bill must be obtained during check-in.

Identifying the person or persons with **signature authority** for a group folio is important for several reasons. During the group's stay, a front office staff member must know who can authorize purchases charged to the master bill to ensure that all other hotel staff members act appropriately.

FRONT OFFICE SEMANTICS

Signature authority: Right to authorize and incur expenditures on behalf of a group.

Consider this typical scenario: A group with 50 individuals checks into a hotel for a sales seminar. During the meeting, a call is received by the front desk requesting that the food and beverage department replenish the coffee that was served during the afternoon break. In most hotels, guests can purchase coffee by selecting a fixed quantity (typically sold by the gallon or liter) or by purchasing unlimited coffee at a price-per-person amount. *If* the front desk instructs the food and beverage department to supply the additional coffee, *if* the food and beverage department does so, *if* the coffee was originally sold by the gallon and not at a price-per-person amount, and *if* the group member with signature authority for the master bill was *not* the person who made the coffee request, the food and beverage department is likely to add the cost of the coffee to the master bill. This charge will, in all probability, later be disputed by the individual with signature authority for the account. ("I did not order the coffee, and my group is not going to pay for it.")

This relatively uncomplicated example demonstrates how easy it is for hotel staff members (even in their efforts to effectively serve guests) to create billing difficulties on group folios. In this example, the front desk agent should inform the food and beverage department about the request and instruct the department to obtain a signed authorization for the additional purchase from the group member with signature authority for the master bill. If an adjustment to a group's bill is required, the person with signature authority must agree that the adjustment is acceptable. Before a group leaves the hotel, the individual responsible for the bill will probably want to review it with either the FOM or a member of the hotel's sales staff. Therefore, identification of the individual with signature authority for the group folio is critical.

Room-Block Management

When a group reserves hotel rooms, the rooms are placed in a group block, and the rooms are held for the exclusive use of the group that reserved them. When the contract terms between a hotel and a group are established, the cutoff date when the rooms will be released from the block should be promptly communicated to the FOM who must then monitor those cutoff dates. If a group's pickup is less than anticipated, the FOM returns the nonreserved rooms to the rooms inventory. Alternatively, if the group's pickup is very strong (it exceeds original estimates), the group's agent may request that more rooms be added to the block as the cutoff date approaches. The FOM may or may not agree to do so. Group members can select rooms from a block in two ways: Individuals can contact the hotel directly, or the group can submit a single reservation list—a rooming list—with the names and arrival and departure dates of the group members. Each of these two reservation methods must be understood and managed by the front office staff.

Individual Call-In Reservations

Recall that the hotel sales department is typically responsible for the overall management of a group's reservations. Nevertheless, most of the contacts with individual group members involve front desk or reservations staff when the group members have been told to contact the hotel directly for reservations. As a result, the FOM's staff is involved in making these individual reservations. In an **individual call-in reservation,** group members contact the hotel and reserve a room from the block the hotel is holding for that group.

FRONT OFFICE SEMANTICS

Individual call-in reservation: Type of reservation in which guests who are part of a group contact a hotel and reserve their own rooms from within that block.

The room types held within the block should reflect the needs of the individual call-ins. A group block held for a corporate training meeting could, in most cases, consist of rooms with one bed. A block held for a group of bowling team members competing in a local tournament should, generally, contain rooms with two or more beds.

Also, some group members may want to spend more than others to reserve the hotel's best rooms; those on a budget may seek less expensive rooms. FOMs who are carefully monitoring group blocks will know which rooms are more popular with the group so that more can be added, if needed and which room types are less desirable so that they can be removed from the block. FOMs must make these changes while maintaining the total number of committed rooms. FOMs must also ensure that all group members who select the same room type receive the rate promised in the group contract.

Sometimes, individuals calling the hotel for individual room reservations within the group's block may present specific challenges or require special information. Front office personnel handling individual call-ins for a group block must be well informed about these items:

- Block cutoff dates
- Designated rates for special room types (upgraded rooms) not originally blocked by the hotel
- Extra charges, if any, for additional room occupants
- Special cancellation policies, if applicable
- Any special features or amenities offered by the sales department and included in the rate quoted to the individual call-in guests. (Examples are baggage handling, complimentary receptions, and special discounts on meals).

Rooming List Reservations

Many groups staying at a hotel will know the individual names and arrival and departure dates of their members. Consider, for example, a college swim team attending a swim meet. The team's coach knows, before the group arrives, the names of the swimmers, coaches, and trainers attending the meet along with their arrival and departure dates. In these cases, it is common for the coach to submit a rooming list (see Chapter 5) to the hotel before the group's arrival. Rooming lists can be submitted by the group that is actually staying at the hotel or, in some cases, by the local area convention and visitors bureau (CVB). FOMs must understand how to manage both methods of submitting rooming lists.

Group-Submitted Rooming List   When group members make reservations on their own rooming list, the group contract negotiated by the hotel's sales department includes a date for submitting the list to the hotel. The reservation process with this type of rooming list is relatively straightforward. Rooming lists furnished to the hotel should include the following information:

- Group's name
- Individual group member's name
- Arrival date
- Departure date
- **Shared room assignment** (if applicable)
- Special requests and features required

FRONT OFFICE SEMANTICS

Shared room assignment: Placement of two or more unrelated individual guests into the same sleeping room.

Front office staff must promptly enter the reservation information from the rooming list into the PMS and immediately identify any potential difficulties in housing the group. Typically, if problems occur, they are related to special requests. For example, the rooming list may request a large number of nonsmoking rooms, but an insufficient number of these rooms may have been blocked for the group. Whenever possible, requests made should be honored. Sometimes, however, requests cannot be accommodated. Consider, for example, a request that all the reserved rooms be on the same floor and include smoking and nonsmoking rooms. In many hotels, these rooms are separated by floor, so this request could not be accommodated. Additional requests may include the number and location of **roll-away beds** to be provided, contractual upgrades required, and early check-in or later than normal check-out times.

FRONT OFFICE SEMANTICS

Roll-away bed: Type of bed, usually designed for use by a single guest, that can easily be transported from one guestroom to another. Typically referred to as *roll-aways*.

CVB-Submitted Rooming List   In some cases, a local CVB assumes (or is assigned) the responsibility of providing hotels with a group's rooming list. This service is increasingly offered by CVBs and is popular with very large groups that require more than one property to fulfill their lodging needs. For example, assume a group such as the National Restaurant Association (NRA) attracts several thousand attendees to its annual convention. The group requires multiple hotels. Members attending the convention will likely be asked to select a first, second, and third choice for their pre-

A local CVB may provide hotels in the surrounding area with a rooming list for large groups.

ferred lodging. These requests will be compiled by the housing division or segment of the local CVB (or even by a professional meeting planning company) to make the required room assignments. Participating hotels will receive, over a period of several days or weeks, a series of individual reservations that will, collectively, form that hotel's portion of the group's total rooming list.

Even if a CVB was not originally asked to assist with a group's rooming list, it may help with housing if the group requires the use of one or more overflow hotels. Assume that the sales department of the 300-room Altoona Hotel successfully negotiated a contract with the State Association of High School Principals. The group traditionally requires 200 rooms for the weekend of its annual conference and, as requested, the Altoona blocked that number of rooms. As negotiated in the group's contract, the group committed to submitting a single rooming list to the hotel two weeks before the event. Meanwhile, because of strong demand in the area, the Altoona sold its remaining 100 rooms and has no excess rooms inventory available for the weekend of the meeting.

As the deadline for submitting the rooming list approaches, the group's contact person informs the Altoona that 300 (not 200) sleeping rooms will be needed. The Altoona cannot accommodate the extra room requirements, so the group may contact the local CVB to identify one or more overflow properties of similar quality and with reasonable proximity to the Altoona. The overflow hotels will probably be asked by the CVB to match the Altoona's room rates, but each hotel is free to agree or not to agree to any terms of the contract between the Altoona and the group. Many revenue managers consider selection of their property as an overflow hotel to be an opportunity to maximize ADR, because the rooms requested are needed and will likely be sold. On the other hand, some hotels, especially those near larger convention-type properties, want to be regularly selected as an overflow option and routinely match the rates and amenities offered by host hotels.

Regardless of the reaction of the overflow properties to the proposed new business, the CVB may, if requested, help find all needed sleeping rooms. If supplemental rooming lists are required by the overflow hotels, the CVB may assist the group in preparing them.

Reservation Cancellations

Cancellations are an inevitable part of the reservation management process. For many reasons, guests with a transient reservation or guests who made a reservation in a designated block or were included on a rooming list will need to cancel their reservations.

In some resort and specialty hotels, and during selected time periods in nearly all hotels, a reservation cannot be canceled. Some properties require that the full amount of room charges for the reservation be paid when the reservation is made. This may occur, for instance, in a period of high demand when the revenue management team determines that this policy is necessary. That fact that the reservation cannot be canceled must be clearly communicated to the guest when the reservation is made. In fact, when a no-cancellation policy is in effect, it is an industry **best practice** to e-mail (or, if time permits, to send by regular mail) a written confirmation that a reservation has been made, and that the hotel will not accept its cancellation. If this is *not* done and, if a guest challenges the charges to a payment card, some card companies (e.g., Visa) will not allow cardholders to be charged. An exception: when guests were given a 72-hour prior-to-arrival cancellation period or were notified in writing about the no-cancellation policy. FOMs must know the policies of the payment cards their hotels accept relative to cancellation charges and the billing of no-shows.

FRONT OFFICE SEMANTICS

Best practice: Process or practice unofficially considered to be an industry standard that is used by professionally operated properties.

When a guest must cancel a reservation, the front office employee accepting the cancellation should always follow this procedure:

- Note (in a permanent record) the date and time the reservation was canceled.
- Identify, by first and last name, the individual (guest) who canceled the reservation.
- Identify, by first and last name, the hotel staff member who canceled the reservation.
- Attempt to determine the reason for the cancellation.
- Provide the guest with a reservation cancellation number and record that number in the PMS. (Names of hotel staff members are never an acceptable substitute for a **unique cancellation number.**)
- Thank the guest for making the original reservation and note the hotel's interest in being considered for a reservation at another time.

FRONT OFFICE SEMANTICS

Unique cancellation number: Number or series of numbers and letters used to identify the cancellation of a single reservation. A unique cancellation number is used only one time to identify the cancellation of only one reservation.

FOMs or a member of their staff should monitor the hotel's cancellation activity as reported by the PMS on a daily basis. This is the only way that FOMs can detect cancellation trends that may significantly affect the hotel's occupancy forecasts and decisions about room rates.

SECTION REVIEW AND DISCUSSION QUESTIONS

Section Objective: Discuss procedures for effectively managing processes used for individual and group reservations.

Section Summary: FOMs deal with two basic types of reservations: individual and group. Individual reservations are made with a hotel representative before the day of arrival. They may be prepaid (payment is made before arrival), guaranteed (a payment card is used to ensure that the room will be held until arrival), or nonguaranteed (a room will be held for a specified time after which it can be sold to another guest). Walk-in guests basically make a reservation at the time they enter the property.

Group reservations are handled differently from typical transient reservations. Group reservations are generated by the sales and marketing department, so coordination between sales and marketing and front office personnel is needed to manage reservations before the day of arrival. A group folio (master bill) is typically established that allows the person or persons with signature authority to authorize purchases for the group. Management of group room blocks can be a challenge, especially when a cutoff date is approaching, and there seem to be too few or too many rooms reserved. Group reservations can be made by individuals within the group or by rooming lists. The group can submit a rooming list that it has generated or the group can involve the local CVB in preparing the list. CVB involvement is important when more than one hotel must handle a very large group.

Reservation cancellations are inevitable. Hotel policies range from full payment required when the reservation is made to no obligation if a guest cancels within a specified time period (sometimes a few hours before scheduled arrival time).

Discussion Questions:

1. Pretend that you are developing a training program on managing guest reservations for front desk agents. How would you explain the difference between prepaid, guaranteed, and nonguaranteed reservations? Pretend that you are a front desk agent talking with a guest who has just arrived with a nonguaranteed reservation, but there is no room available. How *exactly* would you explain the situation to the guest?

2. The text describes a walk-in guest as a hotel guest whose reservation is made at the time of arrival at the property. Do you think this is a good analogy? What factors would you consider when traveling to help determine whether you will guarantee a reservation, obtain a nonguaranteed reservation, or assume that rooms will be available for walk-in guests?

3. Assume that you are in charge of a relatively large group staying at a hotel for a convention. Develop a list of policies concerning your group's master account. (Who can charge to the account? What types of purchases are permitted? How will the account be "audited" by the group before the bill is paid?)

MANAGING GUEST RECEPTION

As you would expect, and as Roadmap 9.2 shows, managing guest reception follows managing guest reservations. The first person that many guests encounter when they arrive at a hotel is a front desk agent. In a large property, a valet parking, door attendant, or a bell services staff member may provide the initial greeting. However, in nearly all small or mid-size properties (those with fewer than 300 rooms), the guest will approach the front desk area to check in and will encounter, for the first time, a hotel staff member.

FOMs must develop a variety of managerial systems and strategies to greet and identify arriving guests, to obtain and properly record information about their stay, and to ensure that an appropriate form of payment is secured or documented.

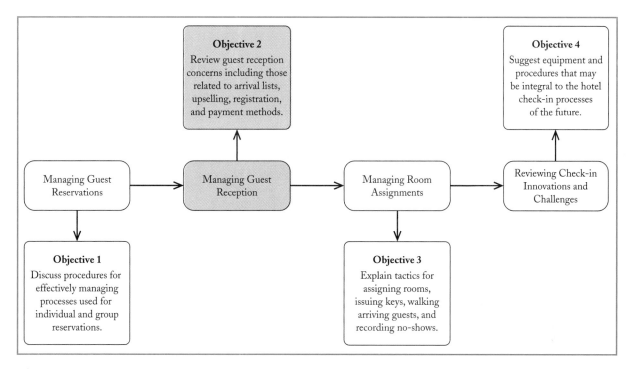

ROADMAP 9.2

Additionally, some guests may need to be walked in a professional manner if they have a reservation but cannot be accommodated. This section describes how FOMs manage these tasks.

Arrival List

FOMs should know the number and names of the guests with reservations who are expected to arrive each day. Although a significant number of walk-in guests arrive at limited-service properties with airport or highway access, most guests have made either a guaranteed or nonguaranteed reservation. The most critical information about guests with reservations has already been collected and is in the PMS. By printing (or examining on a computer screen) a daily **arrival list,** front desk agents can be prepared for the guests due to check in that day.

FRONT OFFICE SEMANTICS

Arrival list: PMS report that details the number and names of guests arriving at the hotel during the report period. The arrival list often contains additional information such as each guest's departure date, room type request, and room rate.

An arrival list indicates guests with reservations who are due to check in during the report period. An arrival list could cover one, two, or more days, but the FOM is generally interested in arrivals for one 24-hour period. For example, on a Tuesday morning FOMs may want to learn about arrivals for that day as well as the next day (Wednesday). In this case, an arrival list would be printed for each of the two days

Arrival List			Altoona Hotel						
A Business Date: 10/05/200X				B Shift: 1	C User: LN				
D Room	E Guest Name	F Account	G Arrive	H Depart	I PPL	J Type	K Rate	L GTD
608	Barth, Steven	145324	10/05/200X	10/06/200X	2	Suite 1	$149.99	DIS
	Bauer, Trisha	145323	10/05/200X	10/07/200X	2	K	$ 79.99	6 P
	Bolenbach, David	145350	10/05/200X	10/06/200X	4	DD	$ 89.99	MC
	Bolenbach, David	145200	10/05/200X	10/07/200X	4	DD	$ 89.99	MC
615	Brown, Latoya	144863	10/05/200X	10/06/200X	2	Suite 1	$ —	Comp
805	Dadis, Carol	145272	10/05/200X	10/06/200X	2	Suite 2	$179.99	MC
	Kerry, Johnathan	144944	10/05/200X	10/10/200X	1	NK	$ 85.99	VI
	Kline, Mike	144877	10/05/200X	10/06/200X	1	K	$119.99	AMEX
	Larson, Scott	144525	10/05/200X	10/06/200X	1	NDD	$ 85.99	MC
	Monteagudo, Gene	145326	10/05/200X	10/07/200X	1	NK	$ 89.99	DB
	Richardson, Kassandra	143890	10/05/200X	10/09/200X	1	NK	$ 89.99	VI
	Rodgers, Michele	145256	10/05/200X	10/07/200X	1	K	$119.99	AX
	Saunders, Allichia	145370	10/05/200X	10/07/200X	2	K	$ 85.99	6 P

M Total Arrivals = 13

N Print Date/ Time 10/01/200X 10:15 a.m.

FIGURE 9.2   Arrival list for the Altoona Hotel.

(24-hour periods). FOMs may be interested in arrival lists for dates that are very near or for dates that are still quite distant.

In a very large hotel, an arrival list could contain information about hundreds or even thousands of guest reservations. The principles of managing these reservations and arrivals, however, are the same regardless of the size of the arrival list. Figure 9.2 is an abbreviated example of an arrival list. It contains information about 13 reservations.

Although specific information on an arrival list may vary based on the PMS, all arrival lists are likely to contain the following information in addition to the report's name and hotel name:

A. *Business date:* The 24-hour period for which the arrival information is requested. In this example, the date requested is October 5, 200X.

B. *Shift:* When the arrival list was requested. This report was requested during the first shift (typically between 7:00 a.m. and 3:00 p.m.).

C. *User:* Initials or name of the staff member requesting the report. This report was requested by an employee with the initials "LN."

D. *Room:* A specific room requested by a guest. The guest may have previously stayed in the room and enjoyed it. In other cases, a room is **preblocked** for a guest because it represents a specifically requested type of room. A specific room number must then be assigned to the arriving guest by the FOM to ensure that the guest receives the room type or room location requested. In this example, 3 of the 13 arriving guests asked that a specific room be preblocked.

FRONT OFFICE SEMANTICS

Preblocked room: Specific room number that has been assigned to an arriving guest before arrival. FOMs ensure that needed rooms are preblocked to meet guests' requests for a specific location or to ensure that guests receive the room type they have reserved.

E. *Guest name:* Name under which the guest's reservation was made. In most cases, names can be sorted in alphabetical order by reservation (account number), or by any other data field in the arrival list. Great care must be taken when making reservations because any spelling errors introduced at that time can translate into real difficulty when a guest arrives. First, the front desk agent may not be able to locate an arriving guest's reservation information. For example, if the reservation says "Launders, Allichia" and, the guest attempting to check in is "Saunders, Allichia," this guest will likely think that the entire reservation was mishandled. Second, if Ms. Saunders is processed as a walk-in (because her reservation did not appear on the arrival list), it is likely that "Ms. Launders" will be billed by the hotel as a no-show. No guest wants to learn that his or her name was misspelled. Experienced FOMs train their staff to search for logical spelling variations on arrival lists and to ask a guest to supply a first name when the guest's reservation cannot be found. They also train front desk agents to use their computer terminal to sort arrival lists by reservation number or by account number as well as by guest name.

F. *Account:* Confirmation number (account number) assigned to the arriving guest by the PMS when the reservation was made. The account number can be helpful when the spelling or pronunciation of a guest's name makes finding arrival information difficult.

G. *Arrive:* Date the guest is to arrive.

H. *Depart:* Date the guest is to depart. This important date is one of the two pieces of information that must be reverified at check-in (the other is rate).

I. *PPL:* Number of people (PPL) arriving with each individual reservation. In addition to forming the database required to generate a house count (see Chapter 4), this information is useful when the number of sold rooms of a particular type exceeds the number actually available. For example, assume the Altoona Hotel has 300 rooms: half with two double beds and half with a single king-size bed. If the hotel is oversold on rooms with double beds, a guest such as Scott Larson (see Figure 9.2), may be asked to switch to a king-size bed at no additional charge, rather than be assigned to the originally reserved room with two double beds. This strategy may allow the Altoona to meet the needs of its guests who reserved a room with two double beds, even though that room type was oversold. Clearly, however, David Bolenbach's arrival is not one where the suggestion of moving from a double-bedded to a king-bedded room would be appropriate, because there are four guests arriving for each of the two reservations.

J. *Type:* Originally requested room type. Proper management of room types is important to guests and the hotel. Knowledge of a guest's originally requested room type is critical especially when preblocking rooms or making actual room assignments.

K. *Rate:* Charge for room. If the appropriate room rate is not confirmed with the guest at check-in, difficulties and hard feelings will likely arise during check-out. Therefore, guests in most hotels are asked to physically verify the room rate they have agreed to pay, usually by initialing the relevant section of the **registration card.**

FRONT OFFICE SEMANTICS

Registration card: Physical document a guest signs during check-in. Information contained on the registration card varies based on the specific PMS but always includes the guest's name, room assignment, room rate, and departure date. Often called the *reg card*.

L. *GTD (guaranteed):* This column identifies the payment arrangement associated with each reservation. Guests could, for example, guarantee their reservations by the use of payment cards which are (identified by initials), for example, VI for Visa, MC for MasterCard and AMEX for American Express. In the case of Gene Monteagudo's reservation, a **direct bill** (DB) arrangement was used to guarantee the room reservation.

FRONT OFFICE SEMANTICS

Direct bill: Special arrangement that allows a guest to purchase hotel services and products on credit terms because the guest's creditworthiness has been preapproved by the hotel.

Note in Figure 9.2 that both the Bauer and Saunders reservations are identified in the GTD column as 6 P. This refers to a confirmed, but nonguaranteed, room reservation that will be held by the hotel until 6:00 p.m. on the guest's scheduled day of arrival. Note also that in the case of the complimentary (Comp) room for Latoya Brown, no additional form of payment will be requested at the time a reservation is made. In some cases, only the cost of the room and the taxes associated with it are complimentary from the hotel. Then, a guest may be asked to present a form of payment to cover any **incidentals** associated with the stay.

FRONT OFFICE SEMANTICS

Incidentals: Non-room charges that may include items such as telephone charges, food and beverage purchases, pay-per-view movie rentals, and minibar purchases.

M. *Total arrivals:* Number of guests arriving. This number is useful for employee scheduling as well as for matching available room types with guests who have yet to arrive. Each time a guest is actually checked into the hotel, that guest's name and reservation is removed (transferred) from the arrival list and added to the **in-house list.**

FRONT OFFICE SEMANTICS

In-house list: Record of all guests, by name and room number, who are checked in to the hotel when the list is printed.

N. *Print date/time:* Date and time the arrival list was printed. FOMs might print one arrival list for the day. When the hotel is very busy or when room-type matching is challenging, the arrival list may be printed several times hourly because of the constant change. The arrival list in Figure 9.2 was printed on October 1, 200X, at 10:15 a.m., four days before the actual arrival of these guests.

Upselling

The arrival list should give the front desk staff the information needed to complete an arriving guest's check-in and to assign that guest to a specific room. However, a guest's arrival also creates an additional upselling opportunity for the property. Some FOMs do not upsell because they consider it a high-pressure sales tactic. Guests should not feel pressured to upgrade their room, nor should hotel staff suggest the room type originally reserved is substandard. Guests can be informed, however, about other room types that are available during check-in, the reasons why the room types may be a good choice for that guest, and the price differences of the alternatives.

FOMs should use an upselling program that is appropriate for their property, guest profiles, and inventory of room types. Properly implemented, an upselling program can increase ADRs from 1 percent to 10 percent (or more) above those of similar hotels that do not implement such programs.

Registration

Professional FOMs understand the significance of guest registration. Most countries and all U.S. states require, by law, that a record be kept of all guests who have rented rooms in a hotel. Record keeping is accomplished through the physical process of registering guests during check-in when a guest physically (or electronically) signs a registration document. The registration information required may vary but must always include the guest's name and room assignment. This information is important in case a disaster such as a fire makes evacuation of the hotel a necessity: rooms known to be occupied would be checked.

Additional information about guests may include home address, telephone number, e-mail address, automobile data (e.g., make, model, and license plate number), form of room payment, and anything else considered relevant and freely provided by the guest. Front office staff should verify the accuracy of the guest's stay information at check-in and confirm the guest's departure date, the room rate to be paid, and the method (form) of payment to be used.

Information Accuracy

Guest information gathered for the PMS when a reservation is made (refer to the reservations screen in Figure 4.8) is the same as that used to create the guest's registration card. The actual check-in process, however, allows guests to physically review information on the registration card to correct mistakes such as misspelled names and erroneous street addresses and update data such as a change in telephone number. After an appropriate greeting by the staff, guests arriving at the front desk should be asked to verify the accuracy of the hotel's registration card information. Any significant changes should be noted in the PMS, and a new registration card should be printed for the guest's inspection and acceptance.

Departure Date Confirmation

The departure date should be reconfirmed at check-in for several reasons:

- Accuracy of the rooms sales forecast
- Matching of available room types to the needs of future arriving guests
- Impact of stayovers and check-outs on the scheduling of hotel housekeepers. In most hotels, stayover rooms can be cleaned in less time than can check-out rooms.

All arriving guests should initial the check-out date preprinted on their registration card and identify any errors.

Rate Agreement

Unless there is agreement about room rate when guests check in, significant issues can occur when guests check out. Confirmation of a guest's room rate at check-in may seem relatively straightforward and uncomplicated. As experienced FOMs will attest, however, often it is not. Misunderstandings about the room rate can be created by guests and hotel staff.

Guest-Initiated Difficulties　Sometimes guests do not understand their room rates. Assume that Mr. Sharp arrives at the Altoona Hotel four weeks after his administrative assistant made his telephone reservation through the hotel's central reservation system. He honestly, but erroneously, believes that his assistant was quoted a room rate of $85 per night. In fact, Mr. Sharp's assistant was quoted a rate of $95 per night but made an honest mistake when transmitting that information to Mr. Sharp. At check-in, Mr. Sharp protests that the rate printed on his registration card is higher than the rate he was originally quoted.

Now, consider Ms. Cahill. She was quoted a rate of $95 per night when she made her reservation but the quoted rate did not include a mandatory 5 percent state sales tax and an 8 percent local occupancy tax. The addition of these taxes brings her actual total room bill to $107.35 ($95 × 1.13 = $107.35). She protests that if the true cost of the room was to be $107.35, she should have been quoted that rate.

Finally, assume that the Altoona Hotel was contacted by Mr. and Mrs. Westmont to arrange a block of rooms for guests attending their daughter's wedding reception. The hotel agreed to an $85 per night rate and to hold 20 rooms in the block until two weeks before the wedding date. Two weeks before the wedding the block pickup was 18 rooms and, as a result, the two remaining rooms were returned to the hotel's general rooms inventory. One week before the wedding, Mr. Lansgton, Mrs. Westmont's brother, called and booked a room at the $95 nightly rate then being quoted. At check-in, however, Mr. Langston states that he is attending the wedding, and his rate should be adjusted to $85 rather than the $95 he was quoted.

In these three examples, the FOMs did not error when establishing room rates; however, rate-related challenges developed. FOMs must train staff about the hotel's desired response to the types of guest-initiated difficulties typically encountered in their property.

Property-Initiated Difficulties　Hotel staff can misunderstand or make honest rate-related mistakes. Assume that Mrs. Cooper made a four-night reservation at the Altoona Hotel and plans to check in on a Thursday evening. The demand for rooms is only moderate that particular night, and the property revenue manager has authorized room rate quotes of $95 nightly for rooms on that date. By Saturday of that same week, however, a sellout is forecasted, and Saturday night room rates of $159 per night have been set for the room type reserved by Mrs. Cooper. Upon arrival (but not at the time the reservation was made), Mrs. Cooper is informed of the **split rate,** and she states, correctly, that she was not told about the rate changes when she made her reservation.

FRONT OFFICE SEMANTICS

Split rate: Room rate that changes during a guest's stay based on room demand.

Split rates are commonly used when a guest's stay extends from a period of low demand into a period of high demand. It is legal and ethical to use split rates, but guests *must* be informed when the hotel plans to do so at the time the reservation is made. If the hotel does not inform guests about split rates, problems will occur during check-in or, in an even worse scenario from an accounting perspective, after the guest's folio has been billed, and the guest is checking out.

Just as guests can misunderstand the room rates that have been quoted, reservation agents can misstate rates, especially when reservations are made by telephone. Assume that Ms. Davis calls a chain's centralized reservations call center. The staff member answering the telephone may make hundreds of reservations per day. On this extremely busy day, the agent quotes a rate of $85 per night when, in fact, the number appearing on the reservation screen is $95 nightly. In this case, Ms. Davis received an oral quote that will be different from the rate in the hotel's PMS, which is what she will see when she checks her registration card.

Some hoteliers, faced with rising costs, attempt to modify quoted room rates by assessing guests mandatory charges for items that the guest may or may not want and may or may not use. Examples are energy surcharges and assessments for hotel telephone, room safe, and "resort" fees. This practice continues in some hotels despite the clear illegality of the approach. Guests may be assessed charges for items they agree to purchase. The courts have clearly ruled, however, that mandatory surcharges and usage fees must be disclosed to guests when they contract (make a reservation) with a hotel. Not doing so constitutes fraud on the part of the hotel and will usually lead to difficulties during check-in or check-out.

MODERN FRONT OFFICE ISSUES AND TACTICS

Surcharges and Lawsuits Go Hand in Hand

Lawyers routinely turn the tables on hotels that surprise guests with hidden surcharges for everything from use of swimming pools to electricity. Some chains are settling class-action lawsuits that allege the extra fees were not fair because customers were not told about them in advance. Consider the proposed settlement involving the nine-hotel Station Casinos in Las Vegas. The class-action notice calls for $5.50 in coupons good for room discounts to 940,000 eligible former guests who stayed in the hotels between April 1, 2001, and April 4, 2004. Why? The hotels added $1 a day for room telephones (regardless of whether they were used) and a $3.50-a-day energy surcharge to room bills.

Los Angeles attorney Mitch Kalcheim, whose firm initiated the action, says that a room rate quoted to people should include all mandatory charges. Kalcheim's organization stands to earn $550,000 if the settlement against Station Casinos is approved, and the organization has filed similar surcharge lawsuits against the Stardust, Tropicana, and Circus Circus hotels in Las Vegas. Other hotel companies are facing lawsuits for similar pricing tactics, for example, Starwood Hotels & Resorts with its Westin and Sheraton brands. Starwood has settled one energy-surcharge lawsuit and has two resort-fee lawsuits pending according to spokeswoman K. C. Kavanagh. Hilton is offering coupons to settle an energy-surcharge case. "We thought we did notify people," said Hilton spokeswoman Kathy Shepard. "We had signs on the reservations desk. We told them online. But there's always somebody who didn't get informed."

The best practice for professional FOMs is to include *all* mandatory charges in the room rate that is initialed during a guest's check-in. Hotels that want to assess one rate for the room they sell, and add mandatory usage fees (regardless of a guest's use of the item) will be forced to return the money collected if there is a lawsuit. This is not to state that hotels cannot charge guests for guest-initiated use of items such as movies and spas. When guests initial a room rate, however, a legal agreement has been made regarding the rate. To change that contract without the guest's expressed consent is ethically questionable and, in today's judicial system, legally indefensible.

Adapted from Woodyard, C. 2004. *Money.* September 27, p. 1b.

The potential for guest- and property-initiated difficulties about room rates means that an FOM's staff must be well trained about the hotel's policies and procedures. Guest registration should not be considered properly concluded until there is complete agreement between the hotel and the guest about the room rate that will be charged during the entire period of the guest's stay.

Methods of Payment

In most hotels, guests must demonstrate their ability during check-in to properly settle their account at check-out. The basic forms, or methods, of payment acceptable to most hotels are payment card, direct bill, cash and prepaid deposit. In some instances, a room or a stay may be complimentary.

Payment Card   The acceptance of valid payment cards by hotels is nearly universal. The physical existence of a bank card, however, does not ensure that it is a valid card. Credit, T&E, and debit cards can be stolen, expired, or used fraudulently. Sometimes the amount that can be charged to such cards is insufficient to settle the guest's account. When an arriving guest indicates an intent to settle the account at check-out

At check-in, the front office agent and the guest should be in agreement about the room rate and any applicable fees and taxes to be paid at the time of departure.

by payment card, the front desk agent should always complete the following payment card processing steps:

- Physically accept the payment card from the guest.
- Swipe the card through the hotel's interface to the merchant service provider.
- Obtain an authorization for an amount in keeping with the hotel's credit policies. (Some FOMs require that a card be authorized for an amount equal to one night's stay; others insist on authorization equal to two or even more nights' stay.)
- Obtain the guest's signature on a registration card, which clearly indicates the specific payment card charged to settle the account at check-out.

Failure to complete any of these four key steps can result in the hotel forfeiting the right to charge the guest's card, even for legitimate purchases. Why? Technically the banks and financial institutions that issue payment cards view the hotels, not the guests, as their primary customers, because the hotels (not the cardholders) pay the financial institutions a fee for the card's use. However, most card issuers will, if called on, support their cardholder's refusal to pay a bill unless the hotel has carefully followed each of the four processing steps reviewed in Figure 9.3.

Direct Bill   In some cases, all or part of a guest's charges will be billed directly to an entity preapproved for on-credit purchases. For example, a hotel may create a direct bill account for a local business that allows selected individuals associated with that business to charge hotel services directly to it. Typically, these accounts are preapproved by a member of the hotel's management after the organization requesting credit submits an application for direct billing. A sample direct bill application is shown in Figure 9.4.

To appreciate the reasons why a hotel might extend credit to a guest organization, consider Rae Dopson, president of Dopson Construction, a mid-size road construction firm. Rae's company has been awarded a state contract to construct two miles of new highway near the Altoona Hotel. The job is a big one and will last many months. It will involve dozens of workers, each of whom will require Monday through Thursday night lodging near the work site. Lodging of its workers will be an expense of Dopson Construction, so the company's managers face two alternatives: (1) allowing workers to stay at a hotel of their choosing and then reimbursing each individual worker for the lodging, or (2) negotiating with a single hotel to place all of the company's business at that property and requesting the hotel to charge the company directly for all lodging expenses.

It is in the best interests of Dopson Construction to select the second alternative. The company's bookkeeping operation will be simplified if the company is awarded direct bill status. The company will also likely be able to negotiate a better nightly rate, because it can guarantee a predetermined number of room nights on a regular basis. The selected hotel benefits from simplified billing as well, because only one invoice must be prepared for payment. Hotels that desire business from Dopson Construction will likely compete for that business, in part, by granting the company direct bill status.

When one or more rooms are to be direct billed to an account, proper identification must be made of the individuals who incure charges and of the direct bill account number. This information is programmed into the hotel's PMS when a direct billing account is approved.

Cash   Often confusion exists among guests about their ability to pay for their hotel stay with cash. Cash must, by federal law, always be an acceptable form of payment

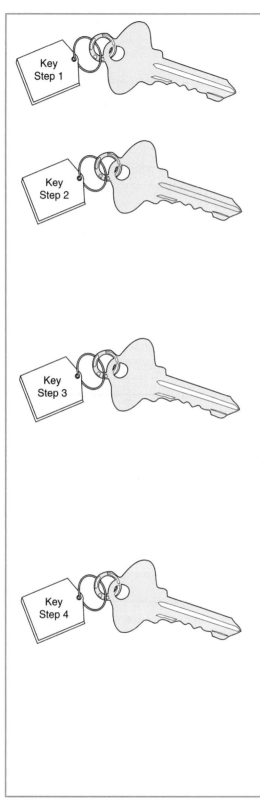

Be in physical possession of the payment card.

Rationale: Unless the hotel has had physical possession of a bank card (or a equivalent online proof of possession), an unscrupulous cardholder may, after the fact, maintain that the card was erroneously charged because the cardholder never authorized its use, nor was it actually presented for payment to the hotel.

Swipe the card through the hotel's interface to its merchant service provider.

Rationale: In addition to establishing proof that the hotel had physical possession of the card, one of the services provided by all hotel merchant service providers is verification that the card presented has not been stolen and has not expired. If the hotel ignores this step and later attempts to collect through its own merchant service provider funds due from the holder of a stolen or expired card, the service provider will refuse to pursue the funds. Why? The provider will not use its own resources to assist in reimbursing the hotel for losses caused by fraudulent guests when the hotel did not use the card verification services offered by the provider.

Obtain an appropriate authorization.

Rationale: The physical existence of a valid (nonstolen, nonexpired) card does not ensure that it can, in the future, be charged for the total amount of a hotel guest's purchases. Therefore, FOMs should insist that staff members authorize the card for a reasonable amount (predetermined by hotel policy) before allowing the guest to check in. If a card does not authorize for the amount required by the FOM, an alternative form of payment should be secured from the guest. If not, the hotel will likely find at time of check-out that it is unable to process charges on the guest's card for the total amount due. It is important that the hotel's credit policies are uniformly applied to all guests. Any variation (increase or decrease) in the dollar amount of a credit card authorization sought by the hotel as a result of a guest's race, gender, national origin, or other factor unrelated to his or her ability to pay must be strictly prohibited.

Obtain the guest's signature.

Rationale: An original signature is the universally accepted definition of agreement to pay legitimate hotel charges. It is also an opportunity for the hotel to limit fraudulent card use by comparing the signature on the valid and preauthorized card with the signature supplied by the guest. FOMs cannot expect their staff to be experts in handwriting analysis, but obvious misuse of cards (e.g., a card issued in a man's name but signed for by a female guest) can be detected. Without a physical signature, in nearly all cases a cardholder will be supported by the card issuer as well as the hotel's merchant service provider if the guest elects to dispute payment, even if the hotel limits its charges to legitimate purchases. Failure to obtain a guest's signature at check-in is not merely poor payment card management. It is also, in most jurisdictions, a violation of the laws requiring that a record be kept of all guests staying in a hotel. For guests who pay by bank card, the best practice is always to secure an original signature during check-in.

FIGURE 9.3   Four key payment card processing steps for hoteliers.

Altoona Hotel
Application for Direct Billing

Date: _____   *Federal ID #* _____

Company/Organization: _____

Division/Department: _____

Mailing Address: _____
                  Street Address   *Suite #*

                  _____
                  City   *State*   *Zip Code*

                  _____
                  (Area Code)   Phone Number   *(Area Code) Fax Number*

BILLING ADDRESS: _____
(if different from above)   *(Name of Invoice Recipient–Attention to)*

                  _____
                  Street (PO Box #)   *Suite #*

                  _____
                  City   *State*   *Zip Code*

List of those persons entitled to authorize (call-in reservation):

1. _____   _____
        Full Name   *Title*

2. _____   _____
        Full Name   *Title*

3. _____   _____
        Full Name   *Title*

Please circle the charges employees are authorized to bill. Circle all that apply:

Room and Tax Only   *Phone*   *Restaurant Bills*

Dry Cleaning   *Movies*   *Banquet and Meeting Charges*

Spa Services   *All Charges*

Credit References:

1. _____
   Hotel Name

   _____
   Phone Number

2. _____
   Hotel Name

   _____
   Phone Number

3. _____
   Other

   _____
   Phone Number

Figure 9.4 continues

FIGURE 9.4   Direct bill application form.

Company Bank:

Bank Name: _____ Account Type: _____

Account Number: _____

At least three credit references and at least one company bank are **required** to complete this application. At least two of the credit references must be hotel references; the third may be a company with which you have a billing history.

If for some reason the application cannot be completed with the requested information, please contact the Accounts Receivable Department of the Altoona Hotel.

Please allow at least 15 days for proper processing and approvals.
*Applications must be approved **before** any direct billing may take place. You will be contacted by mail about your approval status.*

By signing this document, I allow the creditors and bank listed above to release to the Altoona Hotel all necessary information for the proper processing and approval of this application. I understand that all accumulated charges are submitted to the accounting department upon the completion of each authorized function/stay. I also understand that payment is due within 30 days from the date of the invoice. I further understand that it is my company's responsibility to keep the list of authorized personnel updated and current to avoid improper or unauthorized use of this direct bill account, and may do so by requesting an authorization/status change form from the Accounts Receivable Department of the Altoona Hotel.

Signature of Applicant: _____ *Date:* _____

For Company Use Only:

Recommendation of Controller: _____
_____
_____
_____
_____

Approved By:

Signature: _____ *Date:* _____

FIGURE 9.4 (*continued*)

for any debt incurred in the United States including debts related to the purchase of hotel goods and services. That is *not*, however, the same as considering cash as an acceptable method of establishing credit when checking into a hotel. Therefore, many hotels require that guests preestablish their creditworthiness during check-in by use of a valid bank card or other payment form, even if they indicate that the account will be settled by using cash. It is always legal (and, in most cases, advisable) for hotels to have policies requiring that guests establish credit at check-in with a form of payment other than cash. One reason for this requirement is that the hotel has limited ability to compel a guest to pay cash in the event he or she refuses to pay a legitimate hotel bill.

Some hotels do agree to rent rooms to guests who do not offer any other credit or payment form besides cash at check-in. FOMs may allow simple payment for rooms in advance or may require room payment plus a damage deposit that will be refunded at departure. In such cases, these properties will probably not allow charges such as room service, purchase of in-room movies, or even telephone toll calls to be billed to these cash-paying rooms. In other cases, hotels make no requirements of a cashpaying guest other than requesting that the guest agree to pay cash at check-out. Each hotel must determine its own policies for accepting cash as a preapproved method of credit and payment. The hotel's policies, when fully instituted, must be uniformly and fairly applied to all guests.

Prepaid Deposit Although it might seem that guests who have prepaid for their stay do not need to establish credit at check-in, this is not the case. For a variety of reasons—including purchase of incidentals, room damages, and the possibility of extending a stay—many FOMs require prepaid guests to establish some level of creditworthiness when they check in. In most cases, the level of credit to be established by these guests is less than that for their counterparts who have not prepaid their visit.

Complimentary When guests are treated to a complimentary (comp) stay at a hotel, it is still routine to ask them about the form of payment they will use for incidental purchases. The FOM must determine the amount of credit to be established by these guests; the amount typically varies based on the hotel and the level of services it provides. Sometimes a complimentary guest may have all charges waived and will not be required to establish any creditworthiness. In these situations, the FOM should require that staff clearly note, in the guest's record, the name of the hotel owner or manager who authorized this complimentary status. Then, in the event that guest complications arise or room damages occur, the proper person in the hotel can be notified.

SECTION REVIEW AND DISCUSSION QUESTIONS

Section Objective: Review guest reception concerns including those related to arrival lists, upselling, registration, and payment methods.

Section Summary: Arrival lists indicate the number and names of guests with reservations expected to arrive each day. They provide a wide variety of information: arrival date, shift during with which the report was generated, who requested the report, guestroom (if a specific room is requested), guest name, confirmation (account) number, dates of arrival and departure, number of persons arriving with each reservation, room type and rate, guarantee (if any), total arrivals, and the date and time the report was printed.

Many FOMs implement upselling tactics to increase occupancy rates and RevPar levels and to provide an opportunity for guests to have a more complete enjoyment of their lodging experience.

Information required at time of registration includes guest name and room assignment. Sometimes information is also recorded about home address, telephone number, e-mail address, automobile (if applicable), form of room payment, and anything else considered relevant. Registration information must be accurate, departure date must be confirmed, and guests must verify the room rate to be charged.

The forms of payment acceptable to most hotels are payment card, direct bill, cash, and prepaid deposit. Some guests receive complimentary rooms for which no payments for rooms, taxes, and, perhaps, incidentals are to be collected. Other comp guests must pay for all non-room and tax charges.

Discussion Questions:

1. Assume you are an FOM and that many times there are long registration lines. What are some tactics you can implement to manage the length of time that guests must wait to check in? Consider how the processes used for check-in can be modified and what can be done to make waits more "enjoyable" for guests.

2. A guest has verified a specific departure date, but on the morning of that day, the guest notifies the front desk that the stay must be extended by several days. Unfortunately, the hotel is overbooked for these nights. How should the situation be explained to the guest? What, if anything, can be done if the guest refuses to check out of the room?

3. The text discusses some advantages to a direct bill agreement between a business organization and a property. Can you think of additional benefits that might accrue to the business or the property?

MANAGING ROOM ASSIGNMENTS

Roadmap 9.3 indicates that managing assignment of rooms to guests involves several tactics. At the time of arrival, guests confirm their requested room type with the front desk agent, review and approve their registration information, and provide the hotel with proof of their ability to pay. Front desk agents then assign guests to a room and issue room keys. When an appropriate room is readily available (clean and vacant), this process is relatively uncomplicated and proceeds smoothly. At times, however, the task of room assignment is difficult because of these reasons:

- Hotel cannot accommodate the guest's request for a specific room type or location
- Hotel can accommodate the guest's request but not at the time the guest wants to check in
- Hotel cannot accommodate the guest's room request on the day the guest is to arrive
- Hotel can accommodate the guest, but the guest does not arrive

Experienced FOMs know that their staff must be prepared for each eventuality related to room selection and the issuance of keys. This section describes what a front desk agent must know and do to properly complete the guest registration process.

Room Selection

Room selection is the process of selecting a *specific* guestroom from the hotel's inventory of available rooms when the guest checks in. Available rooms are noted on the PMS list of clean and vacant, or available to assign, rooms on the **room status report.**

FRONT OFFICE SEMANTICS

Room status report: Listing of the current housekeeping status of each available room.

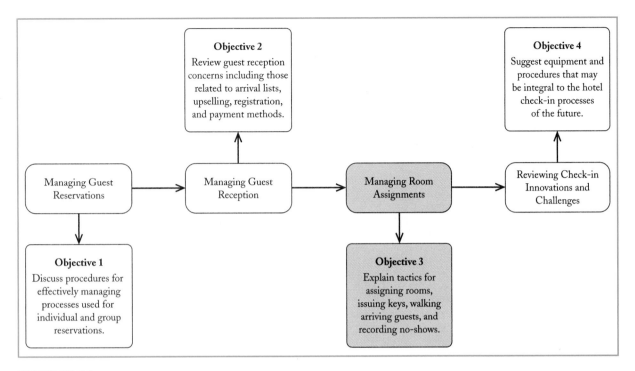

ROADMAP 9.3

This report, which is updated throughout the day by the housekeeping department as rooms are cleaned and inspected, comprises the existing room assignment options available to front desk staff.

Some guests will have very specific requests regarding room selection, and they should be accommodated whenever reasonably possible. Even in hotels with only a few room types, room selection is an important part of the guest registration process. Consider Mr. and Mrs. Seastone and their reservation at the Altoona Hotel for a non-smoking room with a king-size bed. When they check in, they request a room on a lower floor. If, at the time of their check-in, the Altoona's clean and vacant list shows only double-bedded, smoking-permitted rooms on lower floors, the couple will not be pleased.

Unfortunately, many guests do not make their specific room requests known until they check in. Sometimes these requests can easily be accommodated, but at other times it is impossible. Consider two couples traveling together: One couple prefers a smoking-permitted room; the other wants a nonsmoking room. Additionally, one couple prefers a double-bedded room, and the other requests a king-bedded room. Most hotels do not offer smoking and nonsmoking rooms in the same section of the property. Similarly, room types are frequently grouped together; that is, most king-bedded (or double-double) rooms are likely to be near each other. As a result, guests who request dissimilar rooms in close proximity may learn that it is impossible for their requests to be accommodated. Other common guest-initiated requests include connecting rooms, rooms on upper or lower floors, and rooms near ice machines or other property amenities such as a swimming pool, exercise room, or specific meeting rooms.

FOMs must ensure that a guest's room assignment is recorded properly in the PMS. It is equally important for FOMs to ensure that proper records are kept of guests who are moved during their stay, and the PMS will maintain this information if it is entered correctly. Reasons for guest moves during a stay are varied but can

Sometimes guests may request a room in a very specific location in the hotel.

include dissatisfaction with a specific room location or room type, maintenance-related issues such as leaky plumbing or malfunctioning **HVAC** systems, or even hotel-initiated upgrades for preferred guests.

FRONT OFFICE SEMANTICS

HVAC system: Heating, ventilating, and air-conditioning system.

Arrival lists (see Figure 9.2) include information about a guest's requested room type, and all reasonable efforts should made to match arriving guest's reservations with their requests. After a specific room type and location have been selected and approved by the guest, the front desk agent's next task is to create and issue room keys.

Issuance of Room Keys

FOMs are responsible for proper procedures for issuing room keys. Two procedures require special employee training—timing and security.

Timing Concerns

When a guest arrives at a hotel and the assigned room is listed in the PMS as clean and vacant, it is simple for a front desk agent to create the guest's room key in a recodable locking system and issue it to the guest. Some hotels, but very few, still maintain **hard key** systems for their rooms, but such keys are not considered an industry standard and should not be used.

FRONT OFFICE SEMANTICS

Hard key: Usually a metal key that is not remade each time it is issued. The potential for unscrupulous duplication of such keys makes their use for guestrooms unacceptable in nearly all cases.

Variations in key issuing procedures occur when a guest requests an **early check-in.**

FRONT OFFICE SEMANTICS

Early check-in: Request by a guest to take possession of a room before the hotel's normally established check-in time.

Early check-ins create no unusual problems for a hotel's front office. If the chosen room is listed in the PMS as clean and vacant, and an early check-in is granted, the PMS records the guest to be checked into the room. Unless the guest is to be assessed additional charges for the early occupancy (a policy not typically practiced in the United States), the time of check-in is recorded by the PMS, and the room status is changed to "occupied" in the PMS.

A **delayed check-in** occurs when a guest is assigned to a specific room that is not ready for occupancy. Delayed check-ins may be implemented in these circumstances: (1) a guest's specifically assigned room has not been vacated by the previous guest, (2) the room is vacant but has not yet been cleaned, or (3) needed but not completed maintenance prevents the immediate issuing of keys to the guest.

FRONT OFFICE SEMANTICS

Delayed check-in: Procedure in which guests are assigned a room, but the issuing of a key is delayed.

Most hotels allow guests to check into their rooms at 3:00 p.m. or later on the day of arrival. Because check-out times are typically 11:00 a.m. or noon, the housekeeping staff may not have finished their required work in a guest's specifically assigned room when the guest is ready to occupy it. Experienced FOMs implement procedures for accommodating delayed check-in. These may include storing luggage, providing complimentary beverages in the hotel's restaurant or lounge, and describing available hotel amenities for guest use until the room has been properly prepared.

When a hotel is experiencing delayed check-ins, efficient and rapid communication is necessary between housekeeping and front desk staff. For example, if housekeeping staff are promptly notified of the need for specific rooms, the amount of time guests must wait can be significantly reduced. In most hotels, the practice of issuing guests a key for a room that has not been cleaned and inspected is prohibited. Despite the wait that guests may encounter, experienced FOMs insist that keys only be issued when the status of the assigned room is shown on the room status report to be clean and vacant.

Security-Related Concerns

It is difficult to overstate the magnitude of the error in the following brief, seemingly innocent exchange between a front desk agent and a guest overheard during a hotel's busy check-in period with many guests waiting in line to be registered:

> *Front desk agent:* Ms. Jackson, your room number is 205. Just follow the hallway to the elevator. Your room is on the second floor.
> *Guest:* Thank you.

When keys are issued to guests, room numbers should not be announced in a manner that can be overheard by others. The best practice is to train front desk agents *never* to announce room numbers aloud. Instead, the number should be written on the guest's **key packet**.

FRONT OFFICE SEMANTICS

Key packet: Envelope or wrapper designed for holding guestroom keys.

In addition, it is never advisable to announce a guest's name in conjunction with a room number. The risks to guest security that can result from such a comment are too great.

Walking Arriving Guests

The responsibilities of a hotel toward its arriving guests who are walked are described in Chapter 6. When a hotel has guaranteed reservations for more arriving guests than it has available rooms, walking of some guests will be unavoidable. One of the most challenging aspects of an FOM's job involves the development of reservation management, reception, and room assignment policies related to when and how individual arrivals are to be walked when property occupancy is below 100 percent. (Rooms are available, but they are not of the type requested by a guest when the reservation was made.) These policies must be well thought out and clearly communicated to staff and guests, because the number of decisions that must be made to walk (or not to walk) a guest can be significant and complex.

Assume that the Altoona Hotel has a reservation for Mr. Taylor who has reserved a no-smoking-permitted room with a king size bed. When he arrives at the hotel, the only room type listed in the PMS as clean and vacant is a no-smoking-permitted room with two double beds. Even though there will be a variety of room types available that evening, Mr. Taylor's specific request cannot be met at this time. Few FOMs would decide that Mr. Taylor should be walked to another hotel and that the Altoona should bear the associated costs to do so. It is reasonable to assume that a double-bedded room, although not the guest's requested type, is a reasonable substitute for his original request. Few guests will have major objections to this substitution.

Now assume that Ms. Alverez is the coach of a girls' basketball team visiting the Altoona for a basketball tournament. The team consists of 10 players and the coach. Ms. Alverez has reserved three no-smoking-permitted, double-bedded rooms. Her plan is for two girls to share each bed with one bed remaining for her. Upon arrival, only three rooms with king-size beds are available; all double-bedded rooms are occupied. In this situation, the proposed substitution of room types is likely to be a significant and unacceptable substitution. In fact, the proposed change may result in the coach and her team refusing to check into the hotel.

FOMs must develop policies and communicate them to front desk staff and prospective guests about whether the hotel is guaranteeing a room type or merely a room when a reservation is accepted. This distinction is critically important. Sometimes policies may be influenced or dictated by the hotel brand, the management company operating the hotel, or the ownership or management. Many FOMs take the position that a room can be guaranteed by reservation but a room type cannot. For them, room type requests made by guests at the time of reservation are to be honored whenever possible, but they are not guaranteed. This policy may, depending on the unique characteristics of the hotel, make good sense. If that is the hotel's policy, guests should be informed of it when they are making reservations.

Other FOMs implement policies that *do* generally guarantee room type. In some cases, this includes reservations for no-smoking-permitted rooms. If no-smoking-permitted rooms are available at the time of check-in, they will be assigned. In some hotels, guests who refuse smoking-permitted rooms when they are the only ones available at check-in will not be walked at the hotel's expense nor be offered refunds on prepaid rooms.

Still other FOMs implement policies that guarantee the number of beds in the room. In these hotels, a reservation request for a room with two double beds may be filled by a room with a king-size bed and a roll-away bed or a king-bedded room that includes a **pull-out** (i.e., a sofa sleeper).

FRONT OFFICE SEMANTICS

Pull-out: Industry term for an in-room sofa that converts to a bed. Also called a *sofa sleeper*.

FOMs know that sometimes they must walk guests who have requested specific room types that are unavailable, despite the fact that alternative room types are available. Factors to consider include the extent to which guests are upset, the cost to the hotel of walking, and the possibility of lost goodwill in the case of frequent guests.

Recording No-Shows

Recall from Chapter 5 that a no-show is a guest who makes a room reservation but fails to cancel the reservation as required or to arrive at the hotel on the date of the reservation. As a result, although such guests will be included on the hotel's arrival list, they will not occupy a room on the day of their reservation.

No-shows can create significant forecasting problems for hotels, and efforts should be made to minimize them. Many FOMs site the following reasons for no-shows:

- A guest making duplicate room reservations under the same account number
- A guest checking into the right brand but the wrong property (e.g., making a reservation at a Marriott Residence Inn but ariving at a Marriott Courtyard)
- Staff canceling the wrong reservation because a guest was not given a confirmation number at the time the reservation was made
- Staff canceling the wrong reservation due to misreading or mishearing the confirmation number
- Administrative mix-ups (e.g., wrong spelling of name or incorrect arrival date)
- A guest canceling after the hotel-established deadline has passed

Regardless of the reason for the no-show, these guests should be recorded in the PMS as a no-show to cancel their reservation for their day of arrival. In most PMSs, this action will also (1) cancel that specific room reservation for all future nights if it included nights beyond the original arrival date, (2) remove the guest from the occupancy forecast for any future reserved nights associated with that reservation, and (3) identify the reservation as a *potential* no-show for billing purposes.

Some FOMs instruct night auditors to actually check no-shows into the PMS (as if they were arriving guests) at the time the night audit is completed. This practice may be used when FOMs want to maximize their occupancy percentage rates that would otherwise be reduced. Most PMSs do not include no-shows in sold rooms totals; therefore, these rooms are not included in the daily occupancy percentage computations. When bonuses or other performance incentives are tied to sellout nights, there is a temptation to check no-shows into vacant rooms (in some cases even out-of-order rooms!) to maximize reported occupancy. The better procedure is to identify the no-shows, cancel any room nights remaining on their reservations, and reforecast occupancy based on the impact of the no-shows. Actually billing these guests as no-shows is a topic that can be more complex than it might appear and will be examined in Chapter 11.

SECTION REVIEW AND DISCUSSION QUESTIONS

Section Objective: Explain tactics for assigning rooms, issuing keys, walking arriving guests, and recording no-shows.

Section Summary: The room assignment process is relatively uncomplicated when the guest's preferred room is available (clean and vacant).

Policies about whether a reservation includes a room or a specific type of room must be in place, must be consistently applied, must be known and practiced by all front desk agents, and must be clearly communicated to the guest when the reservation is made.

Room keys are not issued until a guest accepts an available room. In the case of delayed check-in, the room is assigned but is not yet available because of further housekeeping tasks. The FOM should implement practical procedures for accommodating guests while they wait for a room. A front desk agent should never announce a guestroom number in a way that information can be overheard by others.

The room assignment process becomes more difficult when guest requests cannot be accommodated for any number of reasons. If the preferred room type is not available, the front desk agent may need to assign an alternative type. The guest may or may not be happy about this change, and a hotel may or may not (but probably will not) walk a guest at its expense.

Discussion Questions:
1. What are some tactics that you, as an FOM, might use to better ensure that the room type preferred by a guest who has made a reservation is likely to be available at check-in?
2. Consult the Web sites of major hotel chains. Review policies, if any, related to the guarantee of room type and what these organizations will do if the room type is not available at check-in.
3. Why is it a breach of the hotel's security when front desk agents publicly announce the name or room number of a guest? What would you do if you were a guest checking into a property and your name or room number could be overheard by others?

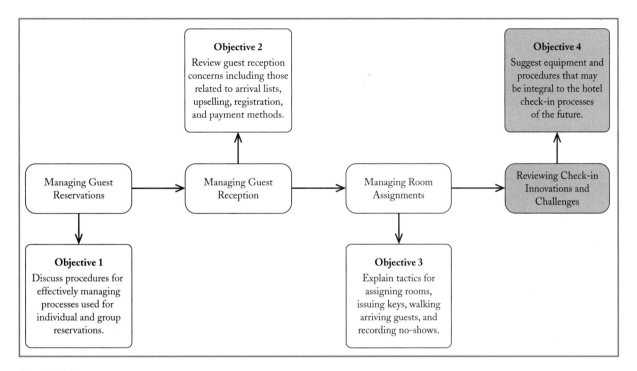

ROADMAP 9.4

REVIEWING CHECK-IN INNOVATIONS AND CHALLENGES

As indicated in Roadmap 9.4, this chapter concludes with a discussion of check-in innovations and challenges. Hotel companies are experimenting with methods to speed up guest check-in and check-out processes. Improvements in PMSs and the increased technological sophistication of guests have driven advances. Though relatively new to hotels, the implementation of expedited check-in is well underway with airlines and car-rental companies. For example, many major airlines allow passengers to check in over the Internet or at kiosks in airport terminals to shorten airport waits. Some car-rental agencies have developed advanced self-check-in procedures that allow their customers to immediately go to their cars and avoid the rental counter.

In theory, highly advanced hotel self-check kiosks should be fairly easy to develop, construct, and operate. Information technology staff tout the advantages of guest-operated kiosks. FOMs who understand reservation, reception, and room assignment processes, however, recognize difficulties associated with the use of self-check kiosks.

Of major concern is the interface issue so frequently encountered by FOMs. Companies selling self-check-in systems to hoteliers must create and maintain interfaces to the PMS of hotels, and there are many PMS alternatives because each hotel chain maintains its own system and upgrades it frequently. The provider of kiosk software must keep up with these changes or face immediate product obsolescence.

Some manufacturers want to provide only the physical kiosk structure or only the hardware required for the physical kiosk. The amount and complexity of this hardware is significant and typically includes these elements:

- Credit card reader for guest identification
- Physical, real-time interface to the hotel's merchant service provider to confirm payment card validity and to establish appropriate guest credit

- Printer to give the guest a written record of rate to be charged, date of departure, and a map with room directions
- Blank key dispenser and key encoder to make the guest's keys
- Networking equipment required to interface to the hotel's PMS

Think of the hardware-related difficulties that could be associated with kiosks. In addition, other challenges must be overcome. Recall that payment cards are merely one way of establishing identification and creditworthiness. Guests who are direct billed, are paying cash, have prepaid, or are enjoying a complimentary stay may not be able to use the kiosk. What if the guest's room will be available but not at the precise time that the guest wishes to check in? The kiosk will not be able to issue the guest's room keys nor inform the guest about precisely when the room will be ready. Guests who must be walked will find that their attempted use of a kiosk was a waste of time, which adds more friction to the situation. Despite these limitations, the hotel industry will continue to explore methods of speeding guest reception and check-out through the use of advanced technology.

MODERN FRONT OFFICE ISSUES AND TACTICS

Log On and Check In

Radisson Hotels & Resorts, a division of Carlson Hotels Worldwide, has more than 435 locations in 61 countries. Radisson's "Express Yourself" program allows guests at most properties to check themselves into their rooms via the Internet. At select properties, guests can check in before arrival by using an online check-in process. Guests can log on to the Web at their convenience and provide room-related preferences in advance of their arrival to virtually eliminate the traditional check-in process.

The process is straightforward. First, guests reserve a room through any distribution channel (e.g., Web site, call center, hotel or travel agent). Then, seven days before their visit, they receive an e-mail inviting them to "express" themselves by checking in at the Radisson Web site (www.radisson.com). Guests can indicate personal preferences such as a specific room location, high-speed Internet access, or special services. When they arrive, guests simply identify themselves at the front desk and pick up the key to their preblocked room. The system allows guests to "express themselves" until 6:00 p.m. on the day of arrival and at least two hours before check-in.

The long-term popularity of Radisson's program is yet to be determined. However, expect to see more innovations as progressive hoteliers improve the check-in process with advanced technological applications. The goal is to allow staff to concentrate on welcoming the guests and allowing guests to be quickly checked in to their rooms. Of course, the process will be faster if guests do not have to wait for front desk agents to complete the required, but time-consuming, information gathering and confirmation procedures that have traditionally been necessary.

Adapted from Schurr, T. 2004. Business Wire (press release). New York, October 4.

With or without the use of advanced technology, hotels must greet their guests properly. Each hotel, depending on its guest base, prices, and amenities, greets guests in the manner considered appropriate for the property. Regardless of hotel type or system of processing information, however, the guest registration process should include the actions identified in Figure 9.5. FOMs who want to evaluate and

☑ 1. Appropriate greeting
☑ 2. Confirmation or revision of registration card information
☑ 3. Confirmation of departure date (by initial)
☑ 4. Confirmation of room rate to be paid (by initial)
☑ 5. Payment and credit information (obtained)
☑ 6. Guest signature above or near printed name (obtained)
☑ 7. Room assigned
☑ 8. Room keys issued

FIGURE 9.5   Front office guest reservation, reception, and room assignment checklist.

improve their guest reservation, reception, and room assignment procedures can use the checklist to ensure that their procedures best serve the hotel guests. Just as importantly, FOMs who follow the checklist will help ensure that the hotel obtains the information needed to record guest charges and to collect guest payment at check-out. The specific processes required to properly post charges to guests' folios and, at check-out, to settle guest accounts are the topics of the next chapter.

SECTION REVIEW AND DISCUSSION QUESTIONS

Section Objective: Suggest equipment and procedures that may be integral to the hotel check-in process of the future.

Section Summary: Innovative hoteliers will continue to develop technological applications that make reception and check-out processes easier and faster for their guests. To do so requires creative applications that involve interfacing systems with the hotel's PMS. Other aspects of guest check-in such as verifying credit and issuing room keys must be integrated into the system. Regardless of whether manual or automated systems are used, hoteliers must ensure that their reception processes provide for an appropriate greeting, collection of registration card information, confirmation of departure date and room rate, verification of payment method, guest signature, room assignment, and issuance of room keys.

Discussion Questions:
1. What are the advantages and disadvantages of the use of an automated reception system from a guest's perspective?
2. Assume that you are an FOM considering the implementation of an automated reception system. What factors would you consider in making this decision? What tactics would you use as the automated system was implemented to acquaint guests and front desk staff with the new system?
3. Do you think that implementation of an automated reception system has, in part, an objective of eliminating or reducing front office labor costs? Defend your response.

The FOM in Action: A Solution

What should FOMs do when called on by guests to make exceptions to established selling policy? In all but the smallest of hotels, selling guestrooms is a team effort. FOMs and their staffs work with sales and marketing personnel, and often the general manager, to make sales decisions that are in the long-term best interest of the hotel. In some cases, this means that the FOM and DOSM must agree on an approach that requires compromise on both sides.

In the case of the Alexander wedding it is understandable that guests attending the same event may be confused about variances in rates for rooms. Confusion can often turn to anger. Experienced FOMs, like Shalaya's boss, will quickly identify the situation:

- The sales department established a group rate for the wedding.
- The group picked up the number of rooms it needed
- As the wedding date approached, the block "dropped," unsold rooms were removed from the block and placed back into the general rooms inventory.

Unsold rooms are typically released 30 days or more before the group's arrival date. These available rooms are then sold subject to normal revenue management decisions. Decisions are made in response to anticipated room demand and are communicated to the front office staff responsible for selling the rooms.

FOMs must be flexible and exhibit common sense. In this case, the hotel is hosting an event for which a great deal of money is being spent for sleeping rooms, a wedding reception, and other services. Although it may not be "normal" to extend a group rate to walk-ins on the date of arrival, in this case that is exactly what should be done. Remember that policies and procedures should usually be followed; however, exceptions that are in the best interest of the guest are often exceptions that are in the best interest of the hotel. When that is true, FOMs should not hesitate to make exceptions.

The failure to accommodate the grandmother of the bride is likely to result in further unpleasant meetings with the salesperson who sold the wedding. The salesperson will likely bear the brunt of the guest's complaint and will not be pleased with the front desk agent's refusal to honor the group rate. And the DOSM, and perhaps even the general manager, will not be happy to learn that the bride's father became an unhappy guest immediately upon arrival at the hotel!

From the Front Office: Front-Line Interview

Rick Lai
Front Desk Manager
The Peninsula Hong Kong (300 rooms)
Hong Kong, China

Team Work Got the Job Done!

Rick graduated from Hong Kong Polytechnic University with a Higher Diploma in hotel management. He notes that a formal education can be very helpful and provide basic knowledge about the front office and hotel operations. However, he realizes that there are significant and immediate interactions with guests, and hotels operate differently. Therefore, on-the-job experience is important to succeed in front office positions.

1. **What are the most important responsibilities in your present position?**
   I must interact with the reservation manager and the revenue manager to control our rooms inventory, to manage the business demand, and to ensure that our guests' preferences are addressed. I must also ensure that we consistently maintain the quality of service that our staff members provide to our guests.

2. **What are the biggest challenges that confront you in your day-to-day work and in the long-term operation of your property's front office?**
   The increasing business volume! A major challenge of our front desk department is to cope with today's business volumes that are the highest in the history of our hotel. At the same time, we must provide the quality services that our guests require with existing labor resources.

   The travel practices and expectations of our guests are changing, and the concept of *service* is in everyone's mind. Therefore, the traditional idea of service provider is not realistic. Today, we must think and manage "out of the box," and this is crucial to our department's and to our hotel's success.

3. **What is your most unforgettable front office moment?**
   A situation in which all of our front office staff members needed to work as a team. It happened when a party requiring more than 100 rooms wanted to check in at the same time. All front desk agents, concierge staff, and front office managers assisted with check-in and the delivery of luggage to the guests' rooms. We completed the entire process within 45 minutes! The group's organizer was obviously surprised at our accomplishment, which couldn't have occurred without the involvement and cooperation of our entire team.

4. **What advice do you have for those studying about or considering a career in front office or hotel management?**
   Have a passion for your work! It is very important for anyone who works in the hotel industry to have passion for the work and passion to please guests.

FRONT OFFICE SEMANTICS LIST

Arrival
Reservations agent
Prepaid reservation
Nonguaranteed reservation
Credit posting
Advance deposit account
Returned check
Authorize payment card
SOP (standard operating procedure)
Master bill

Signature authority
Individual call-in reservation
Shared room assignment
Roll-away bed
Best practice
Unique cancellation number
Arrival list
Preblocked room
Registration card
Direct bill
Incidentals

In-house list
Split rate
Room status report
HVAC system
Hard key
Early check-in
Delayed check-in
Key packet
Pull-out

FRONT OFFICE AND THE INTERNET

The following Web sites relate to the content of this chapter:

Web address	Subject area or product
www.mastercard.com	Rules regarding cancellation and no-show billings
www.visa.com	Rules regarding cancellation and no-show billings
www.discovercard.com	Rules regarding cancellation and no-show billings
www.americanexpress.com	Rules regarding cancellation and no-show billings
www.dinersclub.com	Rules regarding cancellation and no-show billings
www.pmskiosk.com	Self-check-in/check-out kiosks
www.galaxyhotelsystems.com	Galaxy hotel software
www.micros.com/products/hotels/	MICROS-Fidelio PMS software
www.msisolutions.com	Multi-Systems PMS software
www.innsystems.net	INNSystems PMS software
www.hotel-online.com	Electronic, technology-related publication
www.hotelbusiness.com	Electronic, technology-related publication

REAL WORLD ACTIVITIES

1. Despite the explanatory attempts of the hotel industry, some guests (and prospective guests) do not understand the difference between the terms *reservation, confirmed reservation, nonguaranteed reservation* and *guaranteed reservation*. As a top-level executive in a hotel chain, what would you do to ensure that guests understand these differences when they call the chain's reservation center, contact the hotel directly, or make a reservation on the organization's Web site?

2. Assume that you are an FOM interacting with a DOSM monitoring a reservation for a group that meets at your hotel annually. Assume also that the group has historically had difficulty in accurately estimating the number of people who will attend their meeting. What suggestions can you make that will help the meeting coordinator, the DOSM, and you to minimize the possibility of extensive underbooking or overbooking of rooms?

3. Assume that you are an FOM of a large property that markets to business travelers during the week and to persons traveling for personal reasons on the weekends. Develop a policy relating to walking guests at the hotel's expense when the rooms requested at the time of reservation are not available at the time of reception. Consider the need, if any, for different policies relating to the two market types.

4. As an FOM, what policies might you develop relating to payment methods for guests who will be staying at your hotel for several weeks (or more) and who wish to pay by credit card and by cash?

5. Why have "modern" guestroom locking systems become the industry norm instead of hard keys? What are your thoughts about systems to control guestroom access in the future?

10

Front Office and the Guests: Delivering Quality Service

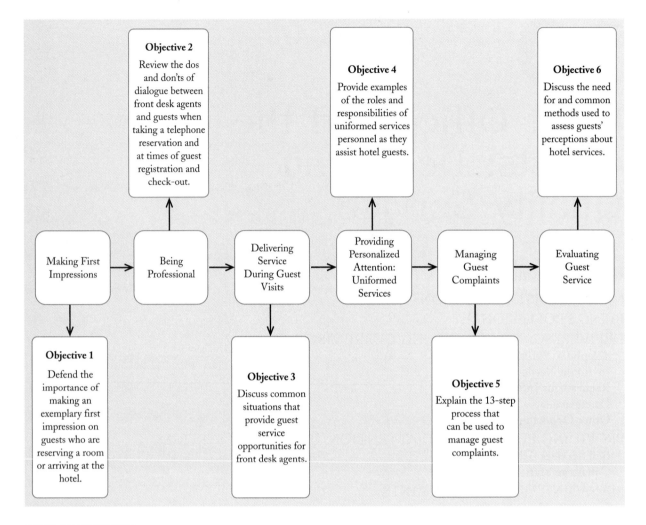

CHAPTER ROADMAP

Chapter Preview

The front office is correctly referred to as the communication hub of the hotel. This chapter focuses on how personnel in the department communicate with the guests. Later, in Chapter 14, you will discover how front office personnel communicate with their peers in other departments.

FOMs and other hotel managers are responsible for identifying what their guests want and developing processes to deliver those services to them. The planning and development activities occur before the guests arrive at the hotel, and they are applicable to most guests. However, defects in processes occur, and some guests have unique needs or desires that are not addressed by the processes. These are times when front office personnel must be empowered to deliver out-of-the-ordinary guest service.

This chapter describes the types of human relations skills that effective front office personnel use to consistently satisfy their guests. They must, for example, demonstrate basic telephone skills as reservations are taken and as guests contact the front office during their stay. Front office personnel and their peers who transport guests to the hotel or greet them as they enter the front door and lobby areas are the first hotel representatives to welcome most guests. The impressions they make set the scene for the guests' visit. It takes no additional effort to make a positive impression rather than a negative impression.

The need for responding to guest requests after they check in also requires front office personnel to know and practice basic human relations and communication skills. This chapter reviews appropriate responses to guest requests for service, to emergencies, and to other situations in which guests rely on front desk personnel to address problems. Front desk employees are not the only front office staff who deliver guest service. Two of the most important uniformed services positions are the bell services attendant and the concierge.

Even in the best-run properties that employ staff members who desire and have been trained to deliver quality service, problems occur that affect guests. This chapter explores a process for managing guest complaints. A service recovery model is presented to help ensure that problems (let's call them opportunities!) are (1) resolved to guests' satisfaction and (2) become learning experiences that move the property along on its service journey.

How do FOMs and other managers learn about guest experiences and the ways that guest stays can be made more enjoyable? Processes must be in place to solicit guest input, to analyze responses and take corrective actions, and to ensure that hotel staff are doing all that is reasonably possible to make guest visits pleasurable.

The FOM in Action: The Challenge

Manfred is the FOM in a 500-room convention hotel. During a busy morning of check-outs, two of his front desk agents became ill and needed to go home. "This will be a good chance," thought Manfred, "to fill in at the front desk and obtain an updated view of what my staff encounters on a routine shift."

During the three-hour period he worked, Manfred was surprised that three guests who were checking out remarked about the problem of no luggage carts. In fact, Manfred had scheduled two uniformed services attendants to work the shift and the hotel had five luggage carts available for guest use. Manfred believed that at least 10 carts would have been appropriate based on the use and waiting times he observed. Unfortunately, the shortage meant guests who did not want the assistance of a uniformed services attendant struggled to get their luggage down the elevator and out to their cars or taxis.

"No real problem," thought Manfred, "I'll talk with the general manager and put in a request for additional carts. There's plenty of room in the lobby area for them. I wish I would have known or thought about this a long time ago. I wonder if there are other easy-to-resolve issues my employees know about? How can I find out?"

MAKING FIRST IMPRESSIONS

The need for all front office employees to provide exemplary guest service is a major theme of this book. Chapter 2 introduced tactics that FOMs can use to identify guest needs and to design processes for addressing them. Chapter 3 showed that job descriptions for front office personnel include tasks relevant to delivering guest service.

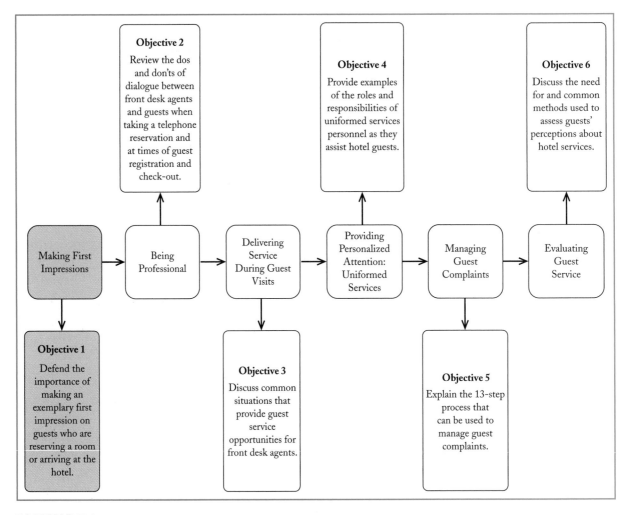

ROADMAP 10.1

Chapter 9 described procedures that should be implemented to allow front office personnel to meet guests' needs during their initial experiences at the property.

This chapter focuses on how front office personnel deliver service to guests during their visit at the property. However, it is unlikely that any interaction can create more of an impression than the initial contact between front office personnel and guests. As indicated in Roadmap 10.1, first impressions are the topic of this section of the chapter. Figure 10.1 reviews situations that provide opportunities to make *positive* first impressions.

As shown in Figure 10.1, some first-time guests form a first impression when they contact the hotel for reservation information. A reservations agent at a large property or a front desk agent at a smaller property make an impression when helping guests to determine if they want a room and to learn what they should expect when visiting the hotel. First-time walk-in guests may form first impressions as they arrive at the hotel location, enter the lobby, and are greeted by uniformed services staff and the front desk agent. For repeat guests, employees provide positive impressions as guests make a reservation or arrive at the property by assuring them that the service that encouraged their return will be continued during this visit.

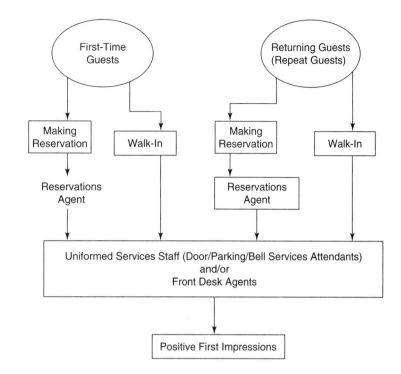

FIGURE 10.1   Who is responsible for the guest's first impression?

In some properties planning for first impressions is nonexistent; in others, planning may involve little more than the uniformed services manager or FOM suggesting, "Be sure to say hello and be sure to smile." In fact, proper dialogue is important, and so is a genuine smile. However, the sequence of events after this initial greeting is also part of forming the first impression, and this is where process planning (see Chapter 2) is important.

Some in the industry say that guest service has its own personality represented by the sum of staff members' attitudes and the processes used to deliver service. In fact, employees' concerns about guests represent the glue that holds service delivery together. At the hotel's front door and at its front desk, staff members have their first opportunities to begin saying and doing the "little extras" that set the stage for the guests' total experience at the property.

Many hotels enjoy a significant repeat business; in fact, it is more accurate to say, "Many hotel's have *earned* a significant repeat business." Managers of these properties know that guest service does not mean doing a couple of nice things for guests. They know that the level of service required to bring guests back involves more than just a "hello" at the time of registration, a clean room with a working television and alarm clock, and a "thank you" as the guest departs. Instead, guest service is a seamless connection of processes designed to please the guests. It requires empowered staff who can make decisions as circumstances require to ensure an overall pleasing experience for guests. These two factors—guest-friendly processes and guest-friendly employees—give properties a competitive edge over counterparts who do not effectively plan for and deliver service. FOMs know that guests can find a safe and clean hotel room at a competitive price elsewhere. They also understand that guests most appreciate a hotel where they are made to feel comfortable, where their wants and needs are anticipated and addressed, and where they perceive that the staff consider them special.

A good first impression at check-in will help create a pleasant guest experience.

Some hoteliers believe that good service relates to speed, for example, quick registration or problem resolution. Others think that good service will occur if they just talk about it or adopt a motto such as, "We're in business to serve our guests!". Still other managers believe that pricing is the key. All hoteliers can achieve service-related goals when they follow these steps:

- Understand what service is from guests' perspectives.
- Develop processes to deliver the service guests want.
- Provide the necessary equipment, tools, and training to help staff members consistently deliver the service guests want.
- Establish a benchmark to indicate where you are as you begin your journey toward consistent delivery of desired service.
- Monitor service improvements and guest satisfaction levels.

One goal of providing the appropriate level of guest service is to make guests glad that they checked into the hotel. If this occurs, repeat business is more likely at the property and within the brand, and positive word-of-mouth advertising will encourage others to visit the property or another in the chain. In a much broader sense, a service goal of the travel and tourism industry is to make travel pleasurable. Hoteliers are more likely to "win" when their guests' first impressions are positive, when the experiences during their visit are enjoyable, and when the check-out and departure process reaffirms the positive impressions that were initially made and reinforced during the visit.

Figure 10.2 lists basic tactics that front desk agents can use to help ensure that their guests will have a positive first impression. Note that these tactics appear obvious. For example, who would argue with the first tactic: Provide a genuine welcome.

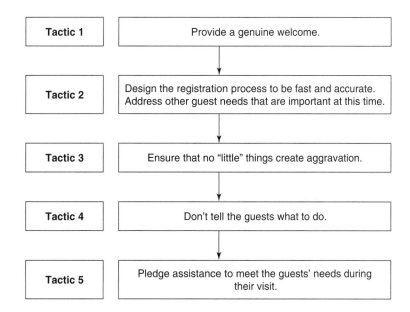

Tactic 1	Provide a genuine welcome.
Tactic 2	Design the registration process to be fast and accurate. Address other guest needs that are important at this time.
Tactic 3	Ensure that no "little" things create aggravation.
Tactic 4	Don't tell the guests what to do.
Tactic 5	Pledge assistance to meet the guests' needs during their visit.

FIGURE 10.2   Tactics to help ensure a positive first impression on guests.

Even so, in some hotels, the first comment by an employee may be, "Next!", "Checking in?", or "What is your name?". Each tactic suggests basic common sense. Consider the second tactic—Isn't it obvious that the registration process should be fast and accurate, and that it should address other needs of the guest at the same time? Often this tactic is overlooked when, for example, the front desk is understaffed (long check-in lines result), and when employees are not empowered to make decisions in response to guests' needs.

Of course, as the third tactic suggests, there should be no "little" things to create aggravation. However, this tactic is often violated, for example when a new front desk agent is trained at the "expense" of the guests and when some front desk agents appear to dislike having personal conversations interrupted by a guest's arrival. One need not be a psychologist to comprehend the fourth tactic; that a hotel employee should not tell guests what to do. This happens all too frequently; for example, a front desk agent may issue one of these directives: "You need to take the elevator to the third floor." "You have to get to the restaurant within 10 minutes because it is closing," "You must check out by noon." Finally, pledging assistance to meet guests' needs during their visit (the fifth tactic) is vastly different from the comment, "Hope you'll enjoy your stay," which seems to be more of a wish than a pledge!

In this book service is defined as the consistent delivery of products and services. The issue of consistency is important because every opportunity to provide service during a visit will be evaluated by the guests. Wise FOMs recognize that service is the experience that the hotel provides to its guests. Opportunities to provide this service occur at planned and unanticipated times. Properly trained and empowered front office employees recognize that service requests provide opportunities to improve the relationship between the property and its guests. Service is important at all times, but it is never more important than when the relationship between the guest and the property is being initially established.

SECTION REVIEW AND DISCUSSION QUESTIONS

Section Objective: Defend the importance of making an exemplary first impression on guests who are reserving a room or arriving at the hotel.

Section Summary: Opportunities for guest service begin when guests contact the property to make reservations, when guests arrive at the hotel property and enter the lobby, and when repeat guests return for a subsequent visit. In each instance, the first impressions made by uniformed services staff or front desk agents should establish the foundation for the level of service that will be provided during the entire stay.

Front desk agents should provide guests with a genuine welcome, use a registration process that is fast and recognizes guest needs, and ensure that there are no distractions to aggravate guests. In addition, front desk agents should remember *not* to tell guests what to do but to pledge assistance in meeting the needs of guests.

Discussion Questions:

1. Think about some of the good and bad experiences you have had as you entered a hotel lobby or registered for a room. What are some of your best and worst experiences? What could you do, as an FOM, to help ensure that good experiences are replicated? What could you do to ensure that bad experiences are not repeated?
2. Assume that you are an FOM, and you are confident that the guest registration process meets the needs of most your guests. What tactics would you use at time of staff recruitment, selection, orientation, and training to make sure that your front desk agents will consistently exhibit the proper guest service attitude (which is the most important factor in making a positive first impression)?

BEING PROFESSIONAL

The consistent delivery of quality guest service represents a paradox. Hotels might be able to "defend" less-than-desirable approaches to guest service if a significant amount of money could be saved in the process. However, as noted earlier in this chapter, service delivery begins with an attitude that guest service is important, and employee attitudes are not "purchased." Therefore, it costs no more to be hospitable to guests than it does to be inhospitable to them. FOMs must select the best job applicants and then train them to follow standard work processes that incorporate a can-do approach to service.

FOMs can use two additional tactics to help ensure that guest service is delivered consistently. First, they can **role-model,** through their words and actions, consistent concerns about pleasing guests. Second, they can provide basic **dialogue training** to prepare personnel for common interactions they will have with guests. FOMs who recognize and respond to common guest situations in a way that shows guests

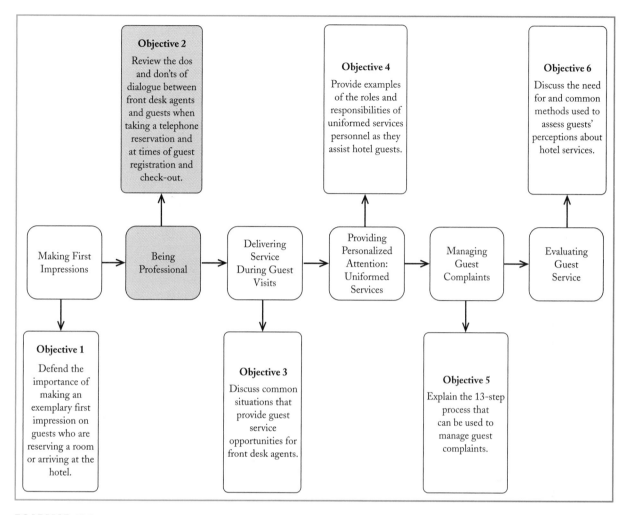

ROADMAP 10.2

their importance demonstrate no-cost ways to deliver guest service. Wise FOMs practice the art and science of hospitality because they recognize the innumerable benefits—and no disadvantages—of doing so.

FRONT OFFICE SEMANTICS

Role-model: Act of behaving in a manner that is consistent with the behavior desired of others.

Dialogue training: Teaching employees what to say in conversations and how to respond to common situations that occur on the job.

Roadmap 10.2 summarizes the topic of this section: Front office personnel must think and act like professionals. Being professional involves recognizing the subtle distinction between the terms *efficient* and *effective.* A front desk agent can be efficient, that is, do the right things; but an agent may not be effective, that is, may not do the right things in the right way. Hotel guests want to be treated with respect and

MODERN FRONT OFFICE ISSUES AND TACTICS

Kiosks Back in the News

Travelers have always disliked long lines at the front desk for check-in. Many hotel observers think that the time is right for paperless check-in, self-service kiosks, and even a Web check-in system that allows guests to register at a hotel before they arrive.

Starwood Hotels & Resorts uses paperless check-in at some properties. The process takes less than one minute at a kiosk and less than three minutes at the front desk (excluding wait times).

Hilton Hotels are partnering with two major airlines to offer their guests the option to print boarding passes from the hotel lobby. In Hilton's view, kiosks do not save labor, but they influence customer loyalty so they are an important customer service initiative. Both Hilton and Starwood station front desk agents at the kiosks to assist guests with room selections or to provide other services.

Guests in Radisson hotels will be able to use the Internet from seven days until two hours in advance of arrival to check into a property. This system will reduce no-shows, because it physically connects each guest to a room and charges the guest's credit card. When arriving at the property, all the guest needs to do is show the hotel pass that was printed earlier and obtain a room key.

Hoteliers like the new systems because they allow hotels to serve guests better without significant capital investments, and they make hotel operations more efficient. As long as guests like them, these self-service systems will be used and other self-service processes will be forthcoming.

Adapted from Giannak, K. 2004. The great kiosk comeback. *Hotel Interactive*, July 27. Retrieved July 27, 2004, from http://www.hotelinteractive.com/news.

---

dignity in addition to receiving efficient service. Most guests like to be referred to by name and most like to be thanked for their business. What front desk agents say and do—and do not say and do—can have a significant impact on the guest experience and, therefore, on the extent to which guest service goals are attained. There are few, if any, time or financial costs involved in interacting with guests in professional and courteous ways that meet or exceed the intent of being hospitable. Figures 10.3 through 10.5 review, respectively, conversations that can occur between a front desk agent and a guest when a reservation is made, while the guest is being registered, and during the check-out process. For each activity, possible dialogues are presented for a front desk agent who is "just following procedures" and for a front desk agent who is performing like a hospitality professional. Which would you most appreciate if you were the guest? Which would you want staff members to use if you were the FOM?

As you review the scenarios in Figures 10.3 through 10.5, think about how much additional time and expense were incurred to provide a professional, respectful, and cordial response as the guest made a reservation, registered, and departed from the hotel. There were, of course, none! Also, think about how much better the guest likely felt when staff delivered professional guest service. Common sense suggests that the service attitude and dialogue of the hospitality professional was much better than that of an untrained or noncaring peer. Many travelers, however, more frequently identify with the guest "served" by the front desk agent who "just follows procedures."

FOMs should not require front office staff to memorize the proper dialogue for these or situations involving guest interaction. Rather, FOMs can encourage staff to

Text continues on page 425.

Reservation activity	Just following procedures	Performing like a hospitality professional
Provide telephone greeting.	"Hello, this is the Hilotown Hotel; how can I help you?"	"Good afternoon, this is Lani from the Hilotown Hotel. How may I help you?"
Determine arrival and departure dates.	"What are your arrival and departure dates?"	"I certainly hope that we will have rooms available to meet your needs. On what date do you intend to arrive? Thank you, and what date will you be leaving?"
Ask for number of guests in room.	"How many people will be in the room?"	"Great news! We do have rooms available during the time you will need one. How many adults and children will be in your party?"
Determine preferred room type.	"What kind of room do you want?"	"We have several types of rooms that will accommodate your needs. Let me tell you about them."
Use upselling tactics (if applicable).	"If you want to spend just a couple of dollars more, I can upgrade you to a room with an ocean view."	"Now that you have decided on a room with a king-size bed, I hope you will let me tell you about an excellent room with an ocean view. It is only $15 a night more than our mountain view room, but it has a million dollar view of the ocean, and you will really be able to enjoy the sunset and the trade winds. We have one available during the time that you will be with us. I will be pleased to reserve it for you."
Quote room price.	"The price of the room will be $79 dollars plus about 15% in taxes."	"It is really great that you will be staying with us. The cost of the room will be $90.85 and that includes all taxes. I know you will enjoy your stay and that the room will be a great value for you."
Explain room guarantee.	"If you are going to arrive after 6:00 p.m. and want us to hold the room, you have to give me a credit card number so we can charge for the room if you don't arrive."	"I know that travel plans can change. To protect you against any arrival delays, we can guarantee that your room will be available regardless of when you arrive. All we will need is a credit card number. If you later decide to cancel the room, there will be no charge if you just let us know before 6:00 p.m. on your arrival date. If we don't hear from you, you will know that your room will be available for you whenever you arrive."
Inquire about special requests.	"Is there anything else you will need during your stay?"	"You will really enjoy the room, Mr. Perez. (The guest name is now known because of the credit card authorization.) Is there anything else that we can provide that will make your stay more enjoyable?"

Figure 10.3 continues

FIGURE 10.3   Professional dialogue when taking a guest reservation.

Reservation activity	Just following procedures	Performing like a hospitality professional
Assess whether transportation is needed.	"When you arrive at the airport, just call us, and we will come and get you."	"We offer complimentary shuttle service from the airport. You will find a courtesy phone in the bag claim area. Just give us a call, and we can usually be there within 15 minutes."
Review (confirm) reservation details.	"Okay, we're holding a room with a king-size bed arriving on 11/10 and departing on 11/12."	"Mr. Perez, I would just like to take one moment to be sure that I have recorded all this information." (Reservation information is then repeated and confirmed.)
Provide confirmation number.	"Your confirmation number is 10101."	"May I please give you your confirmation number, Mr. Perez? It will save you time if you want to contact us before you arrive, and it might be useful when you check in."
Conclude telephone conversation.	"Thanks for calling the Hilotown Hotel. Have a great day."	"Mr. Perez, thank you very much for calling us. We are going to do all we can to make your visit enjoyable. If there is anything we can do before you arrive, please give us a call. Otherwise, we look forward to you being our guest at the Hilotown Hotel."

Note: In this example, the staff member has been trained to quote the room price including taxes. Those opposing the inclusion of tax in the quoted rate point to advertisements in other industries such as retail; these businesses quote prices excluding tax. They also note that rates quoted without tax appear lower and may encourage room rental. Proponents of room rates that include taxes believe that guests want to know the total price. Most, but not all, franchisors quote rates without taxes if one calls their central reservation system or makes a reservation on their Web site.

FIGURE 10.3   (*continued*)

Registration activity	Just following procedures	Performing like a hospitality professional
Provide personal greeting.	"Next in line, please."	"May I please help you, ma'am?"
Determine if guest has a reservation.	"Do you have a reservation?"	"Good afternoon. Welcome to the Hilotown Hotel. Do you have a reservation with us for this evening, ma'am?"
Confirm reservation information.	"What is your confirmation number?"	"Great; all I need is your name or reservation confirmation number, and we can complete this registration process quickly."
Use upselling tactics (if applicable).	"I can upgrade you to a room with an ocean view if you prefer."	"I have all of your reservation information here, Ms. Smith. I note that you have reserved a room with a king-size bed and a mountain view. If you would prefer to sit on the balcony and enjoy the ocean waves, I can check you into an ocean view room for only $15 more."

FIGURE 10.4   Professional dialogue when registering a guest.

Registration activity	Just following procedures	Performing like a hospitality professional
Check for messages and packages.	"Are you expecting any messages or packages?"	"Ms. Smith, I will be happy to check for any messages or packages that may have arrived for you."
Determine method of payment.	"The reservation says you will pay by American Express. May I please have the card?"	"Do you still wish to pay for your room and other charges with your American Express card, Ms. Smith?"
Provide general hotel information.	"Our restaurant is open until 10:00 p.m. this evening, and our pool and exercise room are open until 11:00 p.m. Is there anything else you would like to know about the hotel?"	"Our restaurant is open until 10:00 p.m. this evening, Ms. Smith. We have a great menu, and there are always daily specials. We have a copy of the menu here at the front desk if you would like to see it. Otherwise, the telephone number of the restaurant is in your guestroom directory. Our restaurant host can answer any questions you might have. Also, both our swimming pool and exercise room are open until 11:00 tonight. I am giving you a brochure with your room key that provides other information about the hotel. There is also a directory of services in your room, and you can call the hotel switchboard or front desk at any time for any other information."
Assess whether assistance is needed.	"Do you have any questions?"	"If you have any other questions, Ms. Smith, or if there is anything that you need right now, I would be happy to arrange it for you."
Present room key.	"Here is your room key. The room number is written on the keyholder. You need to take the elevator over there to the third floor."	"Here is your room key, Ms. Smith, and here is the room number." (The front desk clerk shows the number to Ms. Smith without saying it aloud.)
Call for bell services assistance.	"Would you like help getting your luggage to the room?"	"I would like to welcome you once again, Ms. Smith, to the Hilotown Hotel. Please contact us at any time if you need anything. You can call us from your room or from any house phone, or just stop by the front desk. Would you like Bill, our bell services attendant, to show you to your room and explain some of its features?"
OR	OR	OR
Provide parking information and explain guestroom location.	"Here is a map of the property; here is where you are and here is where your room is. You should park somewhere around here."	"It is pretty easy to find your way around our property, Ms. Smith; however, for your reference, I have a map and will be happy to show you the best place to park and the easiest way to get to your room." *Figure 10.4 continues*

FIGURE 10.4   (*continued*)

Registration activity	Just following procedures	Performing like a hospitality professional
Follow through on special requests, if any.	The front desk agent decides to arrange later for the 6:00 a.m. wake-up call that the guest requested, because there is another guest in line.	The front desk agent immediately takes care of Ms. Smith's wake-up call request and then turns to the next guest.
Place follow-up call to guestroom.	The FOM suggested follow-up calls be made to the guestroom "when it is not too busy." However, any time there is a guest in line, it is too busy!	Ms. Smith's name and room number are entered onto a log sheet with the time of registration, along with similar information from other guests who have checked in. The front desk agent calls these guests as soon as he or she has time to do so. If the guest is not in the room, a message is left with a request to call the front desk if anything is needed.

FIGURE 10.4   (*continued*)

Check-out activity	Just following procedures	Performing like a hospitality professional
Provide personal greeting.	"Are you checking out?"	"Good morning, sir, how may I help you?"
Present copy of folio for guest review.	"Okay, here is a copy of your bill. If you want, you can look it over to see if it is okay."	"Mr. Walbert, how was your stay with us? We hope that everything met your expectations, and we would certainly like to know if it did not. I have a copy of your bill for you to review."
Resolve any disputed amounts.	"Well, this statement says that you watched an in-room movie, and the charge is $9.95 plus tax. Please wait a minute; I will get my supervisor."	"I am sorry, Mr. Walbert; there is obviously an error somewhere. I am glad that you found this overcharge; I will remove it from the bill right now." (The front desk agent has been empowered to make these decisions because the FOM knows that a quick resolution will enable the guest to complete the check-out process more quickly.)
Make sure that the guest has received all mail and packages.	"Were you expecting any mail or packages that did not arrive?"	"Before you depart, Mr. Walbert, I would be happy to check if you have any undelivered mail or packages."
Inquire about room key.	"Do you have your room key?"	"If you have your room key, Mr. Walbert, I will be happy to take it. Otherwise, if you are going back to your room, you can just leave it there, or you can drop it by the front desk on your way out. You can even give it to our van driver on your way to the airport."

FIGURE 10.5   Professional dialogue when checking out a guest.

Check-out activity	Just following procedures	Performing like a hospitality professional
Receive payment for final folio balance.	"Do you want to leave the total room charge on your American Express card?"	"This is the total amount of the room and other charges, Mr. Walbert. If you would like to leave it on your American Express card, that is fine. If you would like to arrange payment another way, that is acceptable also."
Give guest a copy of the payment receipt.	"Here is your copy of the bill; should I staple your credit card slip to it?"	"If you approve, I will staple the credit card slip to the room charge sheet and put both of them in this envelope for you."
Provide additional assistance to guest.	"Is there anything else I can do for you, sir?"	"Mr. Walbert, would you like any assistance removing your luggage from your room? Also, the van will be going to the airport in about 15 minutes. Is that convenient or would you like to arrange a later shuttle?"
Call for bell service assistance, if needed.	"I will get a bellman for you."	"Okay, Mr. Walbert, I'll ask a bell services attendant to bring a luggage cart up to your room in about 15 minutes."
Provide cordial farewell.	"Thanks for staying at the Hilotown Hotel. Come back soon."	"Mr. Walbert, I am very glad that you were able to stay with us on this trip. We do hope you will return when you are in our area again. If there is anything else we can do as you are preparing to leave, please let us know. I hope you have a safe flight and an excellent day." (On a routine but random basis, the FOM and the general manager are at the front desk during times of guest departure to personally thank the guests and accompany them to the shuttle bus or auto.)

FIGURE 10.5   (*continued*)

empathize with the guest: "If I were a guest, how would I like to be treated, and what would I like the hotel employee to say or do for me?" Words and actions let guests know their business is appreciated and that hotel staff will work hard to make their visit enjoyable.

SECTION REVIEW AND DISCUSSION QUESTIONS

Section Objective: Review the dos and don'ts of dialogue between front desk agent and guests when taking a telephone reservation and at times of guest registration and check-out.

Section Summary: It takes no additional time, nor does it cost any more, for front desk agents to be professional and respectful when interacting with guests. When being professional, front desk agents will be effective (i.e., do the correct things in the correct way) rather than just be efficient (i.e., do the correct things). FOMs and their staff should consider how they would like to be treated as a guest during interactions with hotel employees. This exercise may help FOMs to determine training needs for front desk agents and may help guide front office staff as they deliver service before, during, and at the conclusion of a guest's visit.

Discussion Questions:

1. Do you recall any instances when front office personnel treated you disrespectfully or unprofessionally when you made a reservation, registered, or checked out of a hotel? What happened? How did you feel? What could the front desk agent have done to prevent the problem from occurring?
2. Have you ever experienced a front desk agent who delivered the quality of service that you expected and appreciated? If so, what were some of the best moments of your experience? How could you ensure that your own staff repeated these desirable service tactics?
3. Assume that you are a FOM. What are some elements in dialogue training that you would use to help front desk agents prepare to interact with guests in routine situations?

A traveler will respond better to a front office agent who displays a professional attitude and is respectful than to one who is merely "processing a guest."

DELIVERING SERVICE DURING GUEST VISITS

Most front desk agents experience times during their work shifts when they are incredibly busy. At other times they are concerned about issues in their personal lives that are of equal or greater importance to them than their work activities. There will be instances when they experience unique situations not addressed in standard operating procedures. Real or imagined emergencies may result from malfunctioning equipment or even temperamental guests. These and related examples make the point that the work of the front office is never boring.

In all circumstances, however, front desk agents need to recognize their primary work responsibility: to provide a level of service that meets or exceeds their guests' expectations. As they do so, they can set the scene for innumerable positive moments of truth during their guests' visits. Roadmap 10.3 indicates that this section describes ways that front office personnel can deliver exemplary service while guests are staying at the property. This section explores common situations in which front desk agents must make a judgment about the best course of action. The factor of "what's best for

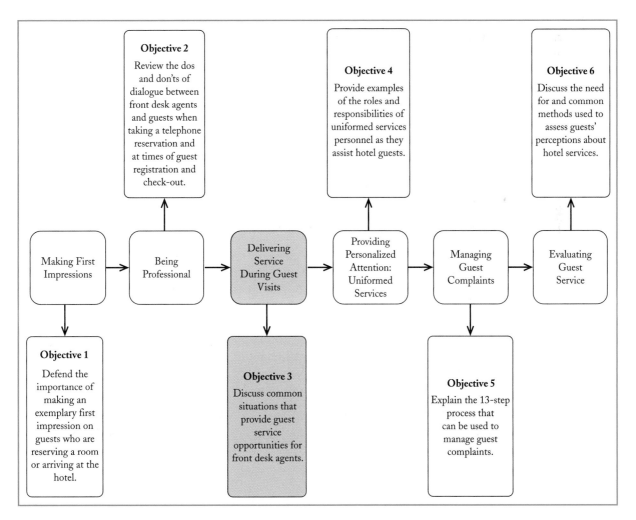

ROADMAP 10.3

the guest" will be of greatest concern to staff members who work in an environment where the FOM has created a guest service emphasis. If, however, the FOM does not manage with a guest focus, the reaction to a service opportunity might lead to questions such as these: "What is fastest?" "What is easiest?" "What is least expensive?" "What approach is closest to what we have always done before?"

As we review common situations, think about what you would like the front desk agent to do if you were the guest. Think also about what you, as an FOM, would want your staff member to do. Finally, think about what you could do to ensure that your employees respond with a guest service emphasis.

Telephone Skills

Training new front desk agents and other staff about the proper use of the telephone system should be an integral part of the front office's induction process and the training that follows it. Staff members must learn both the mechanics of the system (e.g., how to put a caller on hold or transfer a call) and proper **telephone etiquette.**

FRONT OFFICE SEMANTICS

Telephone etiquette: Procedures for using the telephone in a professional manner that are respectful of the person to whom one is speaking.

Many of the basics of telephone etiquette are just common sense. Therefore, one might argue that they need not be discussed in employee training. In fact, probably every reader of this book has participated in a business-related telephone call in which one or more of these "commonsense" tactics were omitted or abused. An unsatisfactory experience may have yielded a negative impression of the business. Because the telephone is a primary vehicle of communication between front desk agents and guests, procedures for its proper use must be an integral part of the front office training program.

Let's consider some of the basics:

- Answer telephone calls promptly; some hotels establish a standard of, for example, within three rings or fewer. Many telephone trainers suggest that a person "smile" as he or she picks up the phone to begin speaking. The telephone voice should incorporate the proper volume and speed of speaking, and tone of voice should be professional, enthusiastic, attentive, and respectful.

- Greet callers with a statement that identifies you as the front desk agent and seeks to determine the subject of call: "Good afternoon, this is Dennis at the front desk. How may I help you?" Modern hotel telephone systems frequently identify the room number and name of guest. If such a system is in use, the front desk agent can learn the name of the guest and begin using it: "We will certainly extend your check-out time, Mr. Tejada, if it is at all possible to do so. I think it will be possible to do so, but may I please call you back within five minutes to let you know for sure?"

- During the conversation, focus full attention on the caller. (This is not the time for **multitasking!**)

FRONT OFFICE SEMANTICS

Multitasking: Productivity improvement tactic in which an employee does more than one thing at the same time. For example, an employee may read a letter while on hold, awaiting the beginning of a conference call.

- Speak clearly, use simple English, and avoid unnecessary jargon. The guest's name should be used whenever appropriate during the conversation.
- Apply listening skills during a telephone call. Give full attention to the caller and the conversation and use an active listening approach. "Yes, Mr. Tejada, we do recommend that guests depart the hotel at least two hours before their flight. I would be happy to alert our van driver about the time you prefer to leave."
- Avoid phrases such as these: "I don't know." "I can't do that." "You have to." "Hold on a second." Use appropriate dialogue instead: "Please allow me to find out." "There are several things I can do." "Here is how I can help you." "It will take me a few moments to find out; if you prefer I will call you right back." "I would like to help and can make the following suggestion."
- Transfer calls only when it is necessary to do so. If necessary, the front desk agent should tell the caller that he or she will obtain the information and call the guest back or request that an appropriate staff member return the guest's call. If a transfer must be made, the employee might say, "Julie is the person who can best answer your question, Mr. Tejada. May I please ask her or someone in her department to help you?" The front desk agent should then explain to Julie why the call is being transferred and should give her the caller's name and direct number. Finally, an excellent protocol is to stay on the line and introduce the caller: "Mr. Tejada, Julie is on the line; I briefly explained the situation, and she will be able to assist you further."
- If it is necessary to take a message for someone who is unavailable, indicate when the person will be available. For example, "Mr. Tejada, I just learned that Julie will be out of the office until 3:00 p.m.; may she call you then?" Record all necessary information such as caller's name (ask for spelling, if necessary) and caller's telephone number and message (ask for clarification, if necessary). Then read back the message to the caller. Inform the caller that the message will be promptly delivered: "Thank you, Mr. Tejada; I will place this message on Julie's desk right now." A final step in the telephone message process is to inquire about any other assistance that the guest desires. For example, "Is there anything else that I may assist you with, Mr. Tejada?" End the conversation in a friendly, professional manner: "Thank you for calling, Mr. Tejada; please phone whenever we can assist you."

A range of guest service requests typically occur during hotel visits, including those that are emergencies. In an emergency, a guest's health and safety may hinge on a telephone call to the front desk. In these instances, a trained employee can assist in efforts to protect the guest who requires emergency aid, but an untrained staff member may actually hinder efforts.

In-Room Needs

Delivering effective service in the guestroom begins as the room is cleaned and made ready after the previous occupant. The guestroom sleeping and bath areas are carefully and properly cleaned, and the room is stocked with the proper inventory of bed and bath linens, toiletries, and other supplies. The housekeeper or room inspector, or both, confirm that heating, ventilating, and air-conditioning (HVAC) controls, televisions (including remote controls), radios, and all other electrical appliances are in working order. (A nice touch is to be sure the clock radio's alarm has not been set by a previous guest.) Most hotels use a detailed guestroom inspection checklist, and every detail is evaluated before the room is made available for the next guest. This final check of the housekeeping process will minimize the need for guests to make service requests about guestroom deficiencies that should have been corrected before the room was occupied.

Some guests may need assistance in learning how to use electronic keycards to gain access to the guestroom. Even more guests, however, may need assistance locating and using HVAC controls, computer data ports, and related upgraded room amenities. If a uniformed services employee accompanies the guest to the room, these and related items can be explained or demonstrated. Otherwise, the hotel should provide clear instructions in an easy-to-discover location within the room to minimize guest inconvenience and subsequent calls for assistance to the front desk.

Today's in-room televisions often do a lot more than provide guest entertainment. They may allow guests to order food and beverage items through room service, to review their guest folio during their stay, to evaluate their stay (see a later section in this chapter), and to check out. FOMs should not assume that guests will be aware of and know how to use these systems. And if they do not, how can they be expected to take advantage of these amenities that have been made available for their use? The frustration and stress that can be created for a guest because of unfamiliarity with a specific room's technology should be anticipated and addressed by hotel managers at the time the decision is made to acquire the technology. Then FOMs and their staff can decide the best way to anticipate and resolve guest service problems before they arise.

A wide range of in-room service requests occur routinely. These should be anticipated, and response tactics should be incorporated into standard operating procedures. Who should be trained and empowered to respond to these requests? The answer is simple: whomever is likely to receive them. In a large property, it will likely be the PBX operator and front desk agents. In a smaller property, it probably will be front desk agents and the FOM. In a very small property, it may be any staff member who answers a call at the front desk, including the general manager, front desk agent, or even a van driver. Here are examples of common in-room service requests:

- *Guest requests for in-room service that require the front desk agent's immediate attention.* The appropriate department should be called immediately (e.g., housekeeping for additional bath linens and engineering and maintenance for television service). The front desk agent should obtain an estimate of the amount of time before service can be rendered and should call the guest to relay this information. For example, "Good evening, Mrs. Albert. Someone from the maintenance department will be up to work on the television within the next 30 minutes. I know about the big game tonight. If the television cannot be repaired quickly, we can certainly replace it with another television so you can watch the event."

- *Personal toiletries.* Some hotels have signage in guest bath areas noting that complimentary personal toiletries including razors, lotions, toothpaste and toothbrushes, and sewing kits are available at the front desk. All other properties need to have such items available for guests who have forgotten theirs or require additional supplies. Can they be delivered to the guestroom? If so, by whom? Alternatively, must a guest personally retrieve them at the front desk or in the hotel's gift shop or "convenience store"?

- *Dry cleaning.* Hotel managers can reduce the number of service requests about dry cleaning by ensuring that adequate information is available in the guestroom. Still, many guests want to confirm pickup and return times and, perhaps charges.

- *Wake-up calls.* Many hotels have clock radios available in the rooms that guests can use for this purpose. Are clear, easy-to-read instructions available about how to set the time and to test the clock's wake-up setting for accuracy? Many guests request a wake-up call from the front desk regardless of the availability of an in-room clock radio. The front office employee who receives such a call should repeat the room number and requested call time and conclude with a statement such as, "Thank you very much for calling, Mrs. Albert; please let us know if we can assist you in any other way."

- *Restaurant reservations.* Many guests call the PBX operator or front desk agent for restaurant reservations or related information, even though the in-room telephone information may note a dedicated extension number. The front office employee who receives such a call should thank the guest for the call and route it to the restaurant, concierge, or other applicable site.

- *Business-related requests.* Many hotels catering to business travelers provide a dedicated business center. Business centers can range in size from very large areas with one or more receptionists to a very small area in the lobby with, perhaps, a computer, printer, and office supplies. Business travelers are likely to ask about copy services, computer hardware servicing and repair, locations of businesses selling office-related supplies, and sometimes services for translation, transcription, or word processing. Front office staff who receive these requests should recognize that their guests' businesses depend on correct information. The availability of an on-site business center (or at least access to business services) is an important factor in the hotel selection decision of many guests.

MODERN FRONT OFFICE ISSUES AND TACTICS

Hotels Increasingly Cater to Business Travelers

More hoteliers now recognize the need for businesspersons to have access to the latest technology as they conduct their business while traveling. Hilton Hotels & Resorts has developed the "Hilton Integrated Business Solution," which offers a flexible and convenient collection of business amenities and services that will be available at all properties in the United States. Several features suggest the basics that business travelers increasingly expect:

- High-speed Internet access in guestrooms and meeting rooms (wired or wireless format)
- Wireless high-speed Internet service in public areas such as lobbies, lounges, and restaurants
- Availability of 24-hour, self-service business centers with individual workstations, document printing, and copying services. Business guests appreciate the availability of essential office supplies and personal computers equipped with the most popular business productivity software, high-speed Internet access, and compact disc (CD) burners.
- Secure remote printing services. Guests may want to connect their notebook computer or supported mobile or wireless devices to the hotel's high-speed Internet service to send documents, spreadsheets, and presentations securely to the property's self-service business center.
- Mail and shipping services. Guests using the self-service business center can pack, weigh, label, and ship packages anywhere in the United States anytime. An inventory of packing supplies and materials will be available.

- Comfortable work spaces in guestrooms. Properly equipped guestrooms will have work desks, comfortable chairs, task lighting, and power and communication outlets at desk height to help ensure that business guests are as productive as possible when they need to be.

    Charges incurred for business center services can be charged to a credit card or can be posted to the guest folio through the PMS.

    Adapted from Hilton Hotels new standard for business technology in hotels aims to be consistent, integrated and seamless. Hotel Online Special Report. Retrieved July 22, 2004, from http://www.hotel-online.com/News/PR2004_3rd/Jul04_HiltonTech.html.

- *In-room service problems.* In spite of careful inspections before rooms are rented, guests may encounter problems with dripping faucets, running water in toilets, burned out lightbulbs, and related inconveniences that disrupt their stay. Procedures are needed to alert maintenance personnel and to follow up to ensure that corrective actions are taken on a timely basis.

- *Requests to speak with other hotel staff.* Guests who are awaiting a package may want to talk with a representative from the hotel's receiving department. Guests may be at the hotel to plan a meeting and want to talk with someone in the marketing and sales department or convention services department. Guests may wish to be connected to the concierge desk or make a reservation for shuttle service to the airport. These and related calls are important to guests; therefore, they must be important to front office personnel. If the requested staff member is not immediately available, the best tactic is for the person taking the call to leave a message with the affected staff member that includes the guest's name, room number, and time of call. The guest should be informed that a staff member will return the call. A follow-up call to the department will help ensure that the guest's request for service was properly routed. (Isn't this approach better than the front desk agent saying, "I am sorry, the person you want to speak with isn't there. The office hours are 8:00 a.m. to 5:00 p.m. Can you please call during these times?")

Requests for Information

For most hotels that do not have concierge staff, front desk agents will likely be the guest's source of information about local attractions, shopping, restaurants, churches, driving instructions, and a wide range of other concerns of travelers who do not have knowledge of the area. Many hotels offer large-scale maps. Some, but fewer, provide a nice touch: Driving directions to and from the most frequently requested sites are preprinted and are provided to guests who desire them. How should front desk agents respond to this common question: "Where is the best place to eat in town?" A great response follows: "There are many nice restaurants in town. One of them is right here in the hotel! Lots of locals enjoy our nightly seafood specials because our chef uses only the best, fresh seafood that is available."

Emergencies

The general manager and all department heads, including the FOM, must give considerable attention to preventive measures to reduce the occurrence of emergencies. They also must have plans in place should emergencies arise. These plans must consider, first and foremost, the safety of hotel employees and guests. The role of front office employees in alerting and assisting guests during emergencies is examined in depth in Chapter 14. The subject is briefly introduced in this chapter emphasizing service, because there is no better service that front office staff members can provide than to protect the health and safety of the hotel's guests and employees.

All front desk agents in every hotel should be trained in and knowledgeable about the proper response to these signals of emergency:

- A fire alarm
- Observable smoke or fire in any area of the hotel
- A call from a guestroom about a guest who has become seriously ill or may have had a heart attack
- A notification that a hotel employee or guest has been injured from a fall, puncture wound, or accident
- Natural emergencies such as earthquakes, cyclones, hurricanes, tornadoes, blizzards, forest or brush fires, tsunamis, floods, or other potentially life-threatening emergencies in the area where the hotel is located
- Bomb threats or other alerts regarding possible terrorist actions

WHAT ABOUT 911 EMERGENCY TELEPHONE CALLS?

The ability of a person to go almost anywhere in the United States and phone 911 to report an emergency makes many travelers feel that they know what to do when an emergency arises. However, today's enhanced 911 services only provide electronic information about a hotel's name and street address. If the property has hundreds of guestrooms and thousands of square feet of public spaces, emergency responders need much more specific information to provide timely assistance.

Technology companies address this potential problem with a number of solutions. Some systems use an attendant notification process to alert the hotel's PBX operators that a guest has placed a 911 call. Previously identified persons on-site can be brought into a conference call, and the guest's name and room number will be displayed on their telephone console units. Another application allows the PBX operator or other designated employee who receives a 911 call to dial a specified number to connect wireless and stationary phones throughout the property. Different codes can be used for medical, security, and maintenance emergencies. Hotel operators may not always know who is on duty, so a systemwide notification of the 911 call to all persons on a predetermined list is possible.

To reduce the number of false 911 calls, some hotels have all such calls routed to hotel security personnel to check the validity of the call before sending it out. A representative of the hotel's security department equipped with a wireless phone can respond more quickly to an on-site emergency than can external emergency services. Then, only security personnel can call 911.

Software can also notify the hotel's PBX operator, front desk agent, or both, about a 911 call by providing an audible alarm with distinctive ring and a printout to the front office. Included in this information is the room location from which the call originated. Trained hotel employees then can begin to handle the situation, and prepare for emergency responders. Although many systems are available, most properties route 911 calls through the front desk to be sure that emergency responders will know where to go when they reach the property.

Adapted from APCO International (Association of Public-Safety Communications Officials). June 3, 2002. Retrieved from http://www.apcointl.org/about/pbx/hotel_mgt_mag.html.

Other Opportunities for Service

There are many other types of guest requests that are difficult to classify. Some arise more frequently than others. Some are very unique and may be beyond the limits of what a hotel and its employees can do to satisfy its guests. Let's first consider a service request that, unfortunately, arises more often than hoteliers desire:

- *Concerns about excessive noise.* A guest may notify front desk personnel about a loud party in an adjacent or nearby guestroom, noises in a corridor outside the guestroom, noises from an elevator, or even noises external to the building. In properties with on-duty security personnel, the front desk agent can quickly notify the security department and request that a representative investigate and resolve the problem. ("I'm sorry about the noise problem that you are experiencing, Mrs. Lee. We have security staff on duty, and I will ask someone to come to the area of the disturbance immediately.") If no security staff are available, the front desk agent may need to call the room or go to the area where noise has been reported.

  Some noise-related problems such as elevator sounds, running water, or street noise may not be resolvable without relocation of the guest. ("I am sorry, Mrs. Lee, I certainly understand how noise from the elevator can be disruptive. We have another guestroom available; I would be pleased to send a bell services attendant to help you relocate to the other room. Would that be acceptable?" Consider also: "We are sorry, Mrs. Lee, I know that noise from the elevator can be disturbing. Unfortunately, we do not have another room available in the hotel this evening. If it is acceptable, we will not charge you for your guestroom this evening, and we will help you to relocate to another room tomorrow morning. Will that be satisfactory?")

  Excessive elevator noise is probably a well-known issue to the hotel's managers, including the FOM. Perhaps, for example, it is hotel policy that the room be assigned only when there is no other room available. Perhaps the maintenance and engineering department manager has budgeted for a solution, or perhaps a project to resolve the problem has been judged too costly. It is also costly, however, to ignore the problem and hope that guests assigned to the room will not care about the noise (or will not complain about it). In fact, many dissatisfied guests probably will not complain; instead they will not return to the property. It is important, therefore, that decisions be made about how to manage this room and that front desk agents know how to respond to complaints when they are made.

Other service requests occasionally occur in many properties:

- *Assistance with in-room, pay-per-view movie systems.* First, providers make every attempt to influence guests to purchase in-room movies and, second, to make them as accessible as possible. Still, some guests, especially those who do not travel frequently and those who are less technologically savvy, have difficulty accessing preview information for movies, making selection decisions, and understanding what charges will be incurred. Others may need assistance in blocking movie access for children and others. Instructions may be provided by bell services attendants who assist guests to their rooms. Still, a call to the front desk is likely if a guest is having trouble with this amenity.

- *Connecting to high-speed Internet systems.* Many hotels contract with an external company to provide 24/7 assistance through an 800 number at no charge to the

Instructing guests about high-speed Internet connectivity is one form of guest service that is becoming more important.

guest who requires assistance with Internet access. Unlike in-room movies, access procedures for this amenity may differ significantly between hotels, and even frequent travelers may encounter difficulty. Uniformed services personnel and front desk agents must know and understand required procedures. They must be able to make a suggestion about what to do if a guest is having difficulty even when the guest is following procedures.

• *Assistance with guestroom telephone connections.* Sometimes instructions for charges to and use of guestroom phones are difficult to locate or are incomplete and cause guest frustration. Frequent calls to the front desk about telephone operation should be investigated to determine whether improved instructions are needed. Questions about how to access a number required for using a prepaid telephone card and for international dialing are examples of guest service requests.

Some service requests are relatively unique and, perhaps, beyond some hoteliers' definition of *service*. Nevertheless, these requests can be addressed by hotel personnel (recall that the guest is always right!):

• Multiple (hourly) wake-up calls (e.g., between 6:00 a.m. and 11:00 a.m.)
• Special use of the hotel vehicle beyond the vicinity to which the hotel normally provides complimentary transportation
• Shipping boxes of an exact size, which may require personnel to make a special trip to an office supply store

- Warming a baby bottle or food for a child (or an adult guest) during a time when the kitchen of a full-service property or lobby foodservices of a limited-service hotel is not in operation
- Flowers, champagne, candy, or other items to be placed in a room before a guest's arrival
- Provision of a can of sanitizing or air-freshener spray for use in the room (Some hotels make this provision at time of check-in *before* the guest is assigned a room.)

Another issue that sometimes arises involves a guest who requests that a hotel employee provide a shopping service or other service after work-hours in return for an agreed-on fee or a gratuity. The employee may desire to be hospitable but needs time for a personal life. Most FOMs discourage employees from conceding to after-work-hour requests. As an alternative, the employee might check with the supervisor to determine if an on-duty staff member could provide the service.

This section concludes with examples of actual service requests that add credibility to this book's premise that a front desk agent's job is seldom boring, and that the job is usually very interesting. These requests must typically be declined, but the front desk agent must do so in a courteous and professional manner.

- "Can you please call someone in housekeeping to iron my shirt?"
- "Can the hotel van take me to the airport?" (The airport is 75 miles away!)
- "Can I have a room with a different color wallpaper?"
- "I need more closet space. Please bring three luggage carts to my room. I'll need to keep them throughout my four-day stay."
- "I have invited a few friends over. I'll need three roll-away beds brought to my room." (The room already has two double beds!)
- "Can you check on my dog during the day? Fido gets lonely and never bites!" (This occurred in a property with a no-pet policy!)

MODERN FRONT OFFICE ISSUES AND TACTICS

Sell the Guests What They Want!

Some high-end hotels have turned their guestrooms into virtual retail showrooms and offer nearly everything in the room for sale. Sale of furniture and amenities provides additional revenue and may help to prevent theft.

The Westin Tabor Center in Denver, Colorado, provides guests with brochures advertising the sale of $130 dual shower heads, $2,990 king-size down featherbeds, and $165 bed trays just like those in the rooms. The Broadmoor Hotel in Colorado Springs sells $42 bone-shaped dog dishes and $142 pet beds with the Broadmoor logo. Guests can even buy the dinner plates used for room service for $22 or a coffee cup and saucer for $16. The Ritz-Carlton Hotel in Beaver Creek sells imported sheets, duvet covers, feather pillows, and king-size beds. (Some guests have paid $4,000 for the complete package.) The Ritz-Carlton Hotel chain sells hundreds of thousands of dollars worth of bedding in addition to guestroom furniture.

What will hotels sell? The answer seems to be "almost anything"—mattresses, box springs, nightstands, and pearl wastebaskets. Some customers have spent $20,000 to $25,000 to replicate an entire hotel room in their home. At least one property (St. Regis Resort & Spa in Monarch Beach California) has an online catalog of its room furnishings.

Some guests purchase items because they want to remember a great vacation. Others feel a sense of status that is tied to luxury hotel rooms. Still others just like the look and feel of high-quality furnishings that are available at some of the nation's best hotels.

Adapted from Alsever, J. 2004. Hotels first ventured into retail amenity sales offering robes for sale; now guests are laying out $4,000 for a complete Ritz-Carlton bed set; the Broadmoor generates $500,000 a year selling room amenities. *The Denver Post*. Retrieved May 23, 2004, from http://www.hotel-online. com/News/PR2004_2nd/May04_HotelProducts.html. See also, Luxury hotels transforming into mini-department stores; hotel guests clamor to buy furniture, sheets, pillows, china. *The Orange County Register*. Retrieved July 6, 2004, from http://www.hotel-online.com/News/PR2004_3rd/Jul04_SheetSale.html.

SECTION REVIEW AND DISCUSSION QUESTIONS

Section Objective: Discuss common situations that provide guest service opportunities for front desk agents.

Section Summary: Telephone service is probably the most common way front office staff provide guest service. Four situations are also guest service opportunities for front desk agents: in-room needs, information requests, emergencies, and other types of requests. Service requests that are common and occur frequently should be anticipated. Front desk agents should be trained in and know about tactics to address the requests. Other service requests are unique. For these, front desk agents must be empowered to make decisions based on the primary goal of consistently providing exemplary service. They must also be delegated the responsibility to assess which service requests are reasonable and which should be referred to the FOM or other manager for consideration.

Discussion Questions:
1. Assume that you are a FOM and that your staff members have been receiving an increasing number of requests for room amenities (e.g., personal toiletries and bath linens). Likewise, your employees are receiving an increased number of complaints about inoperative guestroom equipment. These problems seem to relate to responsibilities of the executive housekeeper and housekeeping staff. What would you say to this department head and what, if any, assistance could you offer to help resolve the problem?
2. What sources of information would you, as a FOM, use to help develop the appropriate response for a front desk agent to use when alerted about a guest experiencing a health-related emergency? Describe the training about the desired response that you would provide for new front desk agents.
3. You are the FOM of a large hotel close to an airport. One of your guests was scheduled for an out-bound flight that is now canceled because of the delayed arrival of an in-bound flight. The guest is requesting that the hotel van transport him to another airport that is approximately 125 miles away. You consider this to be an unreasonable request. (The hotel has two vans, and they are in constant use transporting guests between the local airport and the hotel.) What would you say to this guest? Would your response differ if you were dealing with a frequent guest?

PROVIDING PERSONALIZED ATTENTION: UNIFORMED SERVICES

The uniformed services department provides a wide variety of services to guests (see Chapter 3). In a large property, the department will likely have specialized positions: bell, door, and parking attendants, as well as concierge staff and van drivers. In a small property, the tasks of all these positions may be collapsed into one: bell services attendant. As Roadmap 10.4 suggests, all those in uniformed services positions provide personalized attention to hotel guests.

Bell Services Attendants

Figure 10.6 shows the job description for bell services attendants, which was introduced in Chapter 3. As you review Figure 10.6, note the heavy emphasis on delivering guest service.

In all of their job descriptions, many hotels add a final job task: Performs additional job tasks as assigned. FOMs expect their staff members to be part of the team

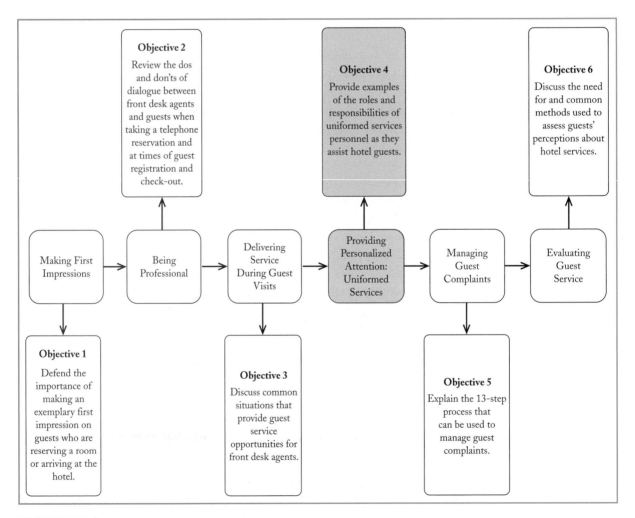

ROADMAP 10.4

Bell Services Attendant

Responsible to assist guests with luggage and parcels. May also serve as door or parking attendant and van driver.

- Helps guests by transporting luggage to their rooms.
- Shows guests around their rooms; explains equipment such as television, lighting, air-conditioning, and Internet access hookups.
- Describes hotel facilities such as the restaurant, swimming pool, and exercise facilities; shows guests to these locations if requested.
- Parks guests' cars and helps guests to secure taxis.
- Runs errands for guests including taking and picking up dry cleaning.
- Posts letters and messages.
- Provides directions.
- Answers questions (e.g., about local attractions and shopping).
- Assists guests with luggage needs at check-out.
- Delivers items such as flowers, parcels, and messages.
- Knows about and can assist with emergency guest evacuation.

FIGURE 10.6   Job description for bell services attendant.

The bell service attendant has many duties, including handling luggage and escorting guests to their rooms.

and to help where needed. Recall that cross-training allows staff members in one position to become competent in performing some of the work responsibilities of their peers in other positions.

An all-inclusive statement suggesting a variety of work tasks is most appropriate for the position of bell services attendant. The primary responsibility of employees in this position is to assist guests. It is difficult to develop a comprehensive list of specific tasks that would be in the job descriptions of all bell services attendants. In addition to having the responsibilities listed in Figure 10.6, in many hotels these employees also perform the following tasks:

- Transport passengers in a hotel vehicle to and from the airport, area attractions, shopping sites, and other destinations
- Drive a hotel vehicle to run errands for hotel managers such as to make **petty cash** purchases

---

FRONT OFFICE SEMANTICS

Petty cash: Small amount of cash available on-site that is not commingled with cash banks for revenue centers and is used to make small, miscellaneous purchases. Funds are usually managed so that the sum of the cash plus invoices for purchases always equals a preestablished amount.

- Maintain the safety and cleanliness of the hotel's primary entrance and lobby areas. (e.g., clean lobby door, windows, and door handles; place slip-resistant mats and "wet floor" warning signs during inclement weather; update the property's **daily function board**)

FRONT OFFICE SEMANTICS

Daily function board: Place in the lobby and other locations used to post information such as name of function, time, and room number for applicable events scheduled in the hotel on a specific date.

- Deliver statements of charges during the early morning hours to the rooms of guests scheduled to check-out that day
- Deliver newspapers and, when applicable, copies of convention- or conference-related materials to guestrooms so they will be available before guests leave their room in the morning
- Assist guests having problems with their autos (e.g., dead or weak batteries during very cold weather)
- Transport packages to and from guestrooms and within-hotel meeting areas
- Deliver room service orders to guestrooms (in small properties that do not have room service attendants)

As you can see, bell services attendants may perform a wide variety of tasks. This is usually a **tipped position,** so actual compensation may be significantly greater than the wage paid by the hotel. It is an excellent entry-level position for persons considering a career in the hospitality industry because of its primary emphasis on guest service and the opportunity to interact with peers in many departments.

FRONT OFFICE SEMANTICS

Tipped position: Position in which the incumbent routinely receives a gratuity from a guest based on, at least in part, the quality of service that was rendered. The word *tip* is an acronym for "to insure promptness."

Concierge Staff

The term *concierge* is French and means "keeper of the keys." It has evolved from the era when a gatekeeper held the keys to the castle at its front gate. The gatekeeper greeted travelers and local guests, attended to their needs, and provided services to household members living within the castle. In more modern times, many European hotels adopted this tradition of hospitality by employing a concierge to assist their guests. Today, professionals serve in this capacity in lodging properties throughout the world. The job description for this position, which was introduced in Chapter 3, is shown in Figure 10.7. Note the range of services that a concierge provides to hotel guests. Services can be provided by a single concierge or by a staff of several trained persons working in this position.

Concierge staff provide services to accommodate very ordinary to very unusual guest requests. Traditionally, concierge staff assisted guests after they checked into the hotel. Today, however, many upscale hotels also offer a "virtual concierge" on their Web site. This allows guests who have made a reservation and who would like assistance in making arrangements before their arrival to request information

---

Concierge

Responsible to provide individualized and requested special services to guests.

- Provides world-class service for and is responsive to every guest request in a professional manner.
- Provides accurate and current information to guests about the hotel and city.
- Assists guests in the purchase of tickets for entertainment, athletic, and other events.
- Provides detailed services and assists individuals designated as preregistered and VIP guests.
- Maintains a house bank of a predetermined amount and posts charges to guests' accounts; balances house bank each shift.
- Maintains accurate log of mail, packages, parcels, and miscellaneous items for delivery or pickup.
- Takes reservations for all food and beverage outlets and inputs data into the computerized restaurant reservations system.
- Maintains proper telephone etiquette and displays a professional attitude at all times.
- Coordinates, maintains, and disseminates information to managers of specific outlets regarding food and beverage functions and events (e.g., birthdays, anniversaries, and dinner parties) that require special preparations.
- Provides information about, reserves, and obtains services of babysitters.
- Performs special services for VIPs: ensures that they receive a note from the concierge department, inspects rooms before arrival, places special gifts, and escorts VIPs to their rooms.
- Handles guest complaints.
- Assists with guests' special business-related needs.

Note: Some hotels have VIP or concierge floors that provide private registration, lobby (reading), meeting and refreshment areas for those paying a higher room rate. This area may be supervised by a concierge staff member.

FIGURE 10.7 Job description for concierge.

Your Request*: _____

Service Date: _____   Preferred Time: _____

Name of Party: _____   Number in Party: _____

Comments:

Your Information

First Name: _____   Last Name: _____

E-mail: _____   Telephone: _____

Preferred Contact Method: _____

Arrival Date: _____

SUBMIT

*Services that can be requested may include:

- City Restaurant Reservations
- Hotel Brunch Reservations
- City Tours/Sightseeing
- River Cruises
- Local Attractions
- Golf Tee Times
- Babysitting
- Car Rentals

- Floral Arrangements
- Limousine Services
- Personal Care/Massage Therapy
- Medical/Dental Arrangements
- Newspaper Requests
- Recreational Activities
- Secretarial Services
- Other Services

FIGURE 10.8   Sample online form for requesting information from a virtual concierge.

through an online form. The type of information that can be requested from the virtual concierge is shown in Figure 10.8.

CODE OF ETHICS AND PROFESSIONAL STANDARDS FOR A CONCIERGE

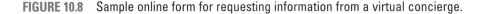

- Always conduct oneself in a professional manner. Remember that you represent the hotel to your guests.
- Never show impatience in front of guests. Use the proper, professional language and do not appear frustrated. Always remain calm.
- Never practice or permit discrimination of any kind.
- Never assist guests with illegal activities.
- Do not demand goods or services from businesses, restaurants, or others for whom you make recommendations to guests.
- When visiting a restaurant at its expense, do not bring a guest unless the restaurant's representative proactively suggests it is proper to do so. Do not order the most expensive items on the menu. Always leave a generous gratuity. Thank the host before you depart and send a follow-up note of thanks.
- Dress appropriately for all functions and drink moderately, if at all.
- Do not give invitations intended for concierge personnel to others.

Adapted from New Orleans Concierge Association. Retrieved from http://www.angelfire.com/home/noca1.

Technology also helps concierge personnel as they deliver face-to-face services to guests. Web-based systems are common and can be accessed by several users in real time. Hotels, for example, may use a customized database of restaurants, airlines, and the other types of businesses from which guests frequently desire information. Concierge staff no longer need hardcopies of telephone or log books. In some cases, restaurant reservations can be made online.

Computerized systems can also generate personalized confirmation letters, schedules, and directions and maps, which can be printed or e-mailed to best meet guests' needs. These high-tech systems can also track packages, amenities, and faxes from the time they reach the concierge desk to the time they are delivered to guests. Some systems allow a guest reservation history to be developed. Then, repeat guests who want to dine where they did the last time or want to try something new can be easily accommodated. Systems can also be used to determine currency exchange rates and to check on upcoming events in the hotel and the community.

Reports generated by an electronic system tally individual requests and produce productivity and performance reports for individual concierge staff and for the department as a whole. An electronic system can be used by separate concierge desks (stations) located throughout a large hotel or property. Front desk personnel can also have access to the system at times when a concierge is not available to assist a guest.

SECTION REVIEW AND DISCUSSION QUESTIONS

Section Objective: Provide examples of the roles and responsibilities of uniformed services personnel as they assist hotel guests.

Section Summary: Much, if not all, of the work performed by uniformed services staff relates directly to providing guest service. As is true with other positions in the front office, uniformed services positions become specialized in large properties (e.g., bell services attendants, door and parking attendants, concierge personnel, and van drivers). In contrast, in small properties the roles and responsibilities for all of these positions might be merged into one or two positions. Many guests require a wide variety of services and assistance during their hotel stay. All hotel staff members may provide assistance to guests, but no staff members do so with greater frequency than those in the front office department. In that department, uniformed services personnel are at the forefront of helping to ensure that each guest's stay is as hospitable as it can be.

Discussion Questions:
1. Given the wide variety of tasks that a bell services attendant might be called on to do, how can an FOM plan a training program to prepare new employees?
2. Hotels in gateway cities such as New York City, Miami, and Los Angeles attract guests from around the world, some of whom who are not likely to be fluent in the English language. What tactics can FOMs use when recruiting and training uniformed services personnel to ensure that these staff members can effectively communicate with the largest possible number of guests?
3. What are some of the pros and cons to beginning a hotel career as a bell services attendant or a concierge staff member in the uniformed services department? In which position (if either) would you like to work? Why?

MANAGING GUEST COMPLAINTS

In spite of the best efforts of the FOM and staff, guest-related problems will likely arise. As Roadmap 10.5 shows, management of guest complaints is the topic of this section. Complaints should be infrequent if process planning and service delivery procedures are being used consistently. Ideally, isolated instances of complaints will be identified before guests check out so that problems can be quickly corrected. As this occurs, the guests will become more aware of staff members' genuine concerns for them. As the **service recovery** process evolves, guests will observe staff acting on the hotel's philosophy that "our first responsibility is to serve guests."

FRONT OFFICE SEMANTICS

Service recovery: Sequence of steps used by hotel staff to address guest complaints and problems in a manner that yields a win–win situation for both the guest and the property.

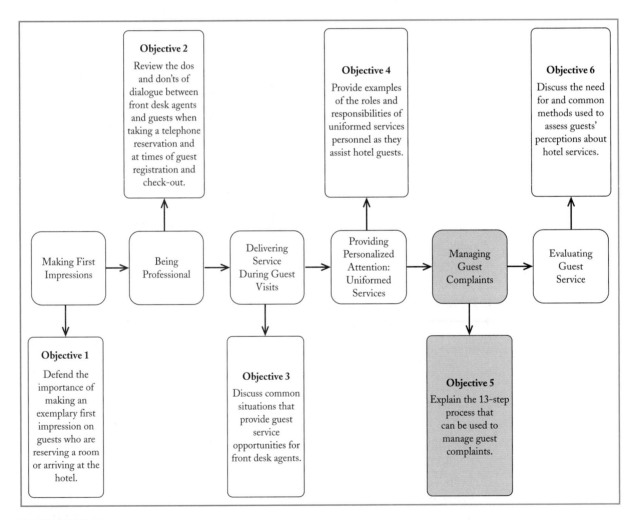

ROADMAP 10.5

Service Problems Do Occur

Guests are likely to contact front desk agents about *any* type of problem that arises *anywhere* in the hotel involving *any* department. The exception may be service-related problems that occur in à la carte dining or banquet rooms. Service and product concerns in public dining areas are frequently discussed and resolved with dining room or banquet staff and the restaurant or banquet manager. Still, guests frequently express concerns about food- and beverage-related problems at time of check-out (or earlier) to front desk agents.

Why do guests complain? Perhaps, they are just having a bad day, perhaps there have been transportation delays or related problems enroute to the hotel. Personal problems may be creating stress and frustration. Some guests may seek perfection; because they are purchasing the hotel's products and services, they may think they are entitled to identify the smallest imperfection and have it resolved. Still other guests may believe that complaints will yield reduced charges as compensation for their problems. The 100% satisfaction guarantee promoted by some hotel chains in their advertising campaigns may contribute to this perception. As an extreme example, consider the guest who rented several guestrooms for several days and, at time of check-out (but not before), complained about a faucet that dripped water and made it difficult to sleep. The guest's demand was that the several rooms rented should be complimentary because of the 100% satisfaction guarantee advertised by the hotel and its franchisor.

WHAT HAPPENS WHEN A GUEST COMPLAINS AFTER CHECK-OUT?

Some hotel chains use a systemwide guest feedback system. In some systems, guests are encouraged to contact executives at the highest level of the organization. What happens when a guest calls a 1-800 complaint line, e-mails a complaint, or sends a postage-paid, self-addressed evaluation form to a franchisor's corporate headquarters alleging a problem applicable to the 100% satisfaction guarantee of the organization?

Most franchisors do not mandate when a guest should receive a 100 percent refund, and they are not concerned about whether a complaint was raised with hotel staff during the visit or whether the concern is first being raised in a communication after check-out. Franchisors want a record of the hotel's response to the guest. Hotel managers actually make the decision about complaint resolution and are given a significant amount of discretion in doing so. However, if the franchisor feels the hotel is completely out of line (e.g., a guest's room had no water and the property refused to compensate the guest in some way), the franchisor may decide to compensate the guest and charge the cost of the compensation to the hotel through an add-on to its franchise fees.

In most cases, a franchisor tallies the number of complaints per month or per 1,000 rooms, and that score is reviewed regularly with the hotel's general manager or owner. An average score might be one or two complaints per 100 rooms. However, individual properties may have many more or fewer, and franchisors are very concerned about the former.

Guests may complain to front desk agents about problems that are beyond the control of front office personnel. Problems with the condition of the property's interior and exterior and with the performance of the hotel's employees may be the responsibility of all hotel managers. However, front office personnel are the guests' focal point of communication with the property, so they are notified of all issues.

Guests may also complain about guestroom or service shortcomings that distract from the their experience at the property.

Although it is important for front office employees to properly manage and resolve all guest complaints, those caused by defects in work processes provide significant opportunities for a property to take one additional step on its quality journey. The first concern, of course, should be to satisfy the guest. Nevertheless, it is also important for staff members to identify the root cause or causes of defects. By doing so, they can provide input to the analyses used in revising the processes, thereby helping to ensure that no other guests will be inconvenienced by the defects.

Experienced hoteliers likely have many anecdotes to dispel the statement that "the guest is always right." Still, this philosophy is useful as a foundation for developing and implementing a service recovery model. It is likely that front desk agents and others can manage the problem resolution process in a way that satisfies most, but certainly not all, of guest concerns. The time for front desk agents to learn about and practice service recovery tactics is during a risk-free training session *not* when the guest phones or approaches the front desk with a problem. The tactics suggested in the next section can be used by front desk agents and by the FOM in situations where an employee is not empowered to address a specific situation and must, therefore, pass the responsibility to the FOM.

Service Recovery Model

Figure 10.9 outlines tactics that can be used to help manage a guest complaint. As suggested below in the third tactic, it may be necessary to isolate an irate guest who is complaining loudly as an early step in the service recovery process. A request such as the following one may help to ensure that other guests are not disturbed by the situation: "Do you mind if we move out of the registration line so I can give you the undivided attention that you deserve?" Then a series of simple questions may help calm the guest while, at the same time, provide assurance that the front desk agent wants to help (e.g., "When did this happen?" "What exactly caused the problem?"). At this point, use of the remaining service recovery tactics in Figure 10.9 will usually help to satisfactorily address the problem.

This discussion about service recovery would not be complete without noting that an empowered front desk agent can much more easily resolve guest complaints than an agent without authority to suggest resolution alternatives. Some front desk agents may be authorized to "comp" a guest bill of, for example, several hundred dollars or more. Even agents with little experience should be able to make decisions about charges for in-room incidentals such as minibar and pay-per-view movies that were or were not incurred by a guest. Front desk agents and their peers are on the firing line and have the most immediate, direct, and extensive interactions with guests. Service recovery is slowed, and the guest is made to feel that the FOM does not trust or view employees's professionals when the response to a guest problem is, "Excuse me, but it is necessary for my supervisor to help you."

Are there situations in which even the most highly motivated and most experienced front desk agent should not be empowered but should be instructed to involve the FOM in the service recovery process? Yes, there are. Situations involving significant sums of money are likely on a referral list, as well as others involving potential liability, theft, injury, or the improper behavior of hotel employees.

Tactic	Tactic in action
1. Acknowledge the guest.	This service recovery example involves Mr. Elroy, who has just completed the registration process at the front desk. Mr. Elroy has arrived after 2:00 p.m., the time that the hotel states rooms will normally be available. Because of many late check-outs from the preceding evening, however, rooms are not ready for guest occupancy.
2. Carefully listen to the guest's problem.	Mr. Elroy has explained that he must have access to his guestroom immediately to prepare for a business meeting that evening.
3. Isolate the guest, if necessary.	Mr. Elroy is not angry, abusive, or loud. He is not disturbing other guests, so the front desk agent determines that the conversation can continue at the front desk.
4. Remain calm; give undivided attention.	The front desk agent who is speaking with Mr. Elroy and giving him complete attention knows that no room of the type Mr. Elroy requested will be available for at least 45 minutes.
5. Ask questions; take notes if necessary.	"Mr. Elroy, I'm sorry that our business center is closed today; it is being recarpeted. Do you just need a quiet place with a desk and a hookup for your computer?"
6. Empathize with the guest.	"It must be very frustrating to have first had the transportation problems you told me about and to now be at your hotel and be unable to check into your guestroom. I realize that you have a serious problem, and I would feel exactly the same way that you do."
7. Apologize for the problem and accept responsibility to resolve it.	"I am very sorry, Mr. Elroy, that the room will not be ready for about 45 minutes."
8. Do not justify or place blame.	The front desk agent does not tell Mr. Elroy about cleaning delays caused by the large number of late check-outs or about the several housekeepers who did not arrive for work this day. He also does not tell Mr. Elroy that hotel managers are now helping to clean guestrooms as quickly as they can.
9. Provide problem resolution options (if possible). Emphasize what can (not what cannot) be done.	"Mr. Elroy, there must be somewhere here that you can do your work while the room is being readied. Please let me see if our conference room is available or if there is a manager's office not currently in use. We may even be able to set up a table for you in a banquet room that will not be used for a function this evening. Then we can put your luggage into our storage area, and you'll be able to do some work."
10. Provide time frame for remedial action.	"It will take just a few minutes, Mr. Elroy, for me to find out about these and, perhaps, other options. I hope we will have a quiet place for you in just a few minutes."
11. Monitor problem resolution progress.	"A 10-person conference room was scheduled for the entire day, Mr. Elroy. However, I have good news: The meeting ended early and the guests have left. There are a few scattered pieces of paper left on the table, and the floor has not been vacuumed. However, the room has a very large desk and comfortable leather chairs, and it is very quiet. Would that be satisfactory? I will ask James, our bell services attendant, to check your luggage into our bag room and to escort you to the meeting room."
12. Follow up with the guest.	The front desk agent calls Mr. Elroy in the conference room, inquires if he needs anything, and asks Mr. Elroy if he would like a complimentary cup of coffee while he is working.
13. Learn from the experience.	When repeating this story to his peers, the front desk agent learns that there is also a small training room close to the human resources department that might be available for similar purposes in the future. The FOM may suggest that future renovations to the business center be done late at night when there is less chance that the area will be needed.

FIGURE 10.9 Service recovery model.

When dealing with a guest complaint, the front office agent should implement a well-planned recovery system to satisfy the guest.

SECTION REVIEW AND DISCUSSION QUESTIONS

Section Objective: Explain the 13-step process that can be used to manage guest complaints.

Section Summary: Guests may complain about hotel products or services for many reasons. Front desk agents must be trained in a process that will resolve these problems and enhance the relationship between the hotel and the guest. A 13-step service recovery model suggests the importance of acknowledging the guest, carefully listening to the problem, isolating the guest if necessary, and remaining calm and providing undivided attention to the guest. Service recovery tactics also include asking questions and taking notes, empathizing with the guest, apologizing for the problem, and accepting responsibility to resolve the problem. Concluding tactics are also important: Do not justify the problem or place blame for it; provide resolution options, suggest a time frame for remedial actions, monitor progress, follow up with the guest, and learn from the experience.

Discussion Questions:

1. Have you ever experienced a product or service problem when you were a guest at a hotel? If so, what was the problem, what did you do about it, and how was it resolved?
2. If you were an FOM, how would you want front desk agents to respond to a guest complaints that were, from the hotel's perspective, totally unreasonable?
3. Would the service recovery process differ for a guest who was a first-time visitor and for a guest who was a repeat visitor? Would the process differ for a travel arranger of a large group and for a member of that group?

EVALUATING GUEST SERVICE

"How are we doing?" is a question that all hotel managers generally and FOMs more specifically must ask often. Experienced hotel managers know that guests, not hotel managers, are the only people who can reliably answer this question. To remain competitive, hotels must continually improve. This can happen only when managers identify potential areas of improvement, prioritize them, and work with staff members to plan and implement improvements. Roadmap 10.6 indicates that evaluation of guest service concludes this chapter's discussion of delivering quality service. How can hotels' products and services be improved? This question is best answered by asking the guests, by assessing the hotel experience from the perspectives of guests, or by doing both.

Guest Comment Cards

Hoteliers have traditionally used a simple comment card system to learn about their guests' service-related and other experiences at the property. Comment card systems can address concerns of current guests with the goal of identifying problems and resolving them, perhaps even while guests are still at the property.

Guest comment cards can be designed by a specific property (e.g., an independently owned or managed hotel), by a franchisor, or by a management company. Many large management companies develop their own comment cards because they operate several brands of properties and want to measure their managers against each other using common factors. This might be more difficult to do if input came from different types of comment cards used by the various franchisors. A sample comment card is shown in Figure 10.10. Note that the comment card requests that hotel staff be notified about problems so they can be corrected before the guest departs. The general manager wants guests to know about the staff's sincere interest in addressing problems to the guests' satisfaction. As this occurs, the likelihood of repeat business increases dramatically.

Careful analysis of information on comment cards helps to identify problems. Perhaps resolution will involve a new policy, training, purchase of tools or equipment, or changes in operating procedures. Perhaps the general manager alone, or all department heads, or other managers working together should decide what to do. Other persons on the hotel's team may or may not be asked for advice. Will a cross-functional team be needed for careful study and analysis? An effective hotelier will know the best approaches to address problems after they are identified.

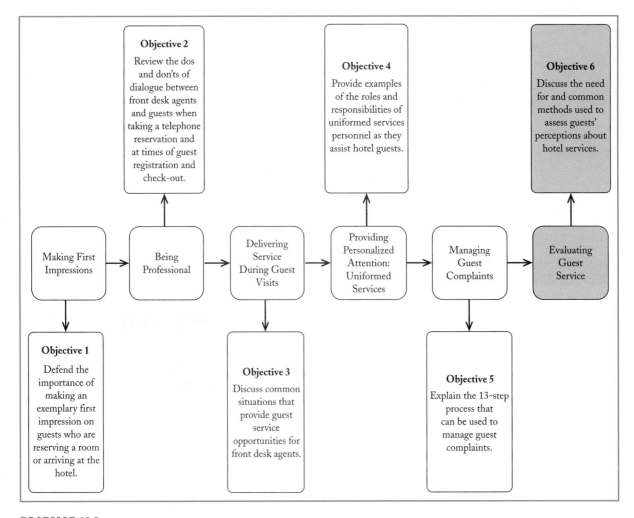

ROADMAP 10.6

As with so many areas of front office management, technology can assist FOMs with service evaluation. Electronic versions of comment card surveys are now available for guest completion through in-room televisions. These systems permit fast and accurate tallies of survey results, provide data for specific time periods, and provide data for comparisons between time periods as well as for between-hotel property analysis, if applicable.

Advantages of a guest comment card system do not accrue to the hotel unless the data are used. This may seem obvious, but managers in some hotels collect data "because we have to." Some rationalize that guests with negative input are wrong; others quickly implement "solutions" to perceived problems before they have even been accurately defined. Still other managers use an approach called "10 percent means a problem." They believe a problem has been identified and should be addressed only if 10 percent or more of guest comments identify the problem. In fact, many guests do not complete and submit comment cards, so managers have little idea about the actual number of guests experiencing any service defect. A better philosophy is one of zero defects; that is, problems identified by one or more guests should be addressed. No hotel, or any other business, can be successful when 1 of every 10 guests (customers) leaves unhappy. First, the unhappy guest is unlikely to return and, second, this guest is likely to discuss negative

Comment cards are a common way of evaluating a hotel's performance.

experiences with family members and friends so still more people are dissuaded from visiting the property.

A better approach is to recognize every complaint as an opportunity to improve. Make it easy for guests to provide feedback. Quickly address and resolve any issues that are identified. Thank guests for their input and encourage staff members who are closest to the source of the problem to recommend resolution alternatives. Then closely monitor the areas of identified concern to ensure that the same or similar problems do not recur.

Mystery Shoppers

Some hotels use **mystery shopper services** to help evaluate services and operations from their guests' perspectives.

FRONT OFFICE SEMANTICS

Mystery shopper service: Method of product and service evaluation in which a person poses as a guest, experiences the products and services provided, and reports on the perceived quality of products and services received during the visit.

Where do hoteliers find mystery shoppers? For-profit businesses provide this service in many parts of the country. Others retained for this purpose may be peers in hospitality associations, friends, family members, neighbors of managers, and even students in hospitality management or related classes. In many instances, the mystery shopper meets with members of the hotel management team before the visit. This provides an opportunity for the shopper to learn about areas that should be

---

What Do You Think About Our Hotel?

Your time is very important and so are your thoughts about your stay at ____(name of hotel)____ . We would sincerely like to learn about your experiences during your visit. Will you please complete this survey and place it in the Guest Comments Box at the front desk or mail it to us?

While You Are Here

We want you to be 100 percent satisfied about every experience you have during your visit. If there is anything we can do, please let us know. If you encounter any problem, we *guarantee* to correct it. Please call the hotel operator to let us know what we can do to make your stay with us more enjoyable.

We are committed to making your visit enjoyable and free of hassles; please tell us how we are doing.

Thank You!

_____(general manager's personal signature)_____

FIGURE 10.10   Guest comment card (front side).

emphasized during the evaluation, including those where there may be special concerns or where training activities were conducted recently.

Professional mystery shopping services often provide comprehensive and detailed reports about visit. Figure 10.11 presents sections of one report applicable to the front office. The entire report is 10 pages long and can be viewed on the Web site noted in the figure. After the mystery shopper's evaluation is completed and the report is developed, often the mystery shopper meets with affected hotel managers to provide additional information as necessary.

Some hotels use a mystery shopping service only when there are special concerns, such as a significant decrease in guest comment scores or a concern about theft by a specific employee. Other properties use these services on a routine but random basis as an integral element in their service and product evaluation efforts.

Franchisor Report Cards

FOMs and general managers in most franchised hotels have an additional source of guest evaluations of hotel stays. A monthly report summarizing property defects and service is compiled and sent to the franchised properties. A typical system involves data submitted

	Exceeded Expectations	Met Expectations	Missed Expectations
Front Desk Staff	❑	❑	❑
Housekeeping Staff	❑	❑	❑
Restaurant and Lounge Staff	❑	❑	❑
Your Guestroom	❑	❑	❑
Restaurant and Lounges	❑	❑	❑
Lobby and Other Public Areas	❑	❑	❑

1. During your visit, did you have any problems?
   ❑ Yes   ❑ No
   If so, please tell us what happened.
   _____
   _____

   Was the problem reported?
   ❑ Yes   ❑ No
   If yes, to whom? _____
   _____

   Was it resolved to your complete satisfaction?
   ❑ Yes   ❑ No
   If not, what could we have done differently to satisfy you?
   _____
   _____

2. Overall, did we exceed your expectations?
   ❑ Yes   ❑ No
   If not, what could we have done better?
   _____
   _____

3. If you visited this area again, would you select our hotel?
   ❑ Yes   ❑ No   ❑ Undecided

4. How many times have you stayed at our hotel during the last year? _____
   Date of this stay? _____
   Your room number: _____
   Name: _____
   Address: _____
   _____
   City: _____
   State: _____ Zip: _____
   Telephone: _____
   E-mail: _____

5. Would you like to be contacted about promotional offers?   ❑ Yes   ❑ No
   Other comments:
   _____
   _____
   _____

   Was any specific employee especially helpful to you?
   ❑ Yes   ❑ No
   If so, who: _____

   Thank you for helping us to serve you better.

FIGURE 10.10 Guest comment card (reverse side).

to the franchisor through guest complaints during the month preceding the time period analyzed. A year-end report tallies totals for the 12-month period. Discussion of report card "scores" is part of the semiannual inspection that representatives of the franchisor conduct at the property. Figure 10.12 shows a sample report. Note that tallies are made of eight different types of complaints. The total number of complaints is determined (column A) and the total number of guests quoting these complaints is reported (column B). Similarly, the number of complaints per 1,000 occupied rooms is reported (column C).

As you review the types of complaints listed, note that several (marketing programs, staff performance, reservations and billing, and miscellaneous) may be directly applicable to the front office department. Most of the remaining complaint categories involve peripheral issues that will likely affect the front desk, because complaints may be lodged with front office personnel in addition to being reported to the franchise organization.

Another Tactic: Ask Employees and Guests

FOMs spend a significant amount of time interacting with employees. In most cases, time will also be spent talking with guests—learning about their experiences with the hotel in general and the front office department in particular.

Satisfaction Services, Inc.
focusing on the formula for success in your business

Client	Hotel Client
From	11/21/200X To 11/22/200X
Location	Location 1
	321 West St.
	Anytown, UA 12345

Visit Information

Question	Response	Points Available	Points Awarded
1. Check-In Date (e.g., 11/14/03)	11/22/03		
2. Check-Out Date (e.g., 11/15/03)	11/23/03		
3. Day of Check-In (e.g., Friday)	Saturday		
4. Day of Check-Out (e.g., Saturday)	Sunday		
5. Time of Check-In: (e.g., 1 p.m.)	4:05 p.m.		
6. Time of Check-Out: (e.g., 11 a.m.)	11:45 a.m.		
7. Total Amount for Room (don't use dollar signs, e.g., 109.95)	187.00		

Reservations

Question	Response	Points Available	Points Awarded
1. Name of reservationist (if not offered, you must ask their name)	Corey		
2. Was the telephone answered in a prompt and professional manner?	YES	2	2
3. Was the staff member friendly and enthusiastic?	YES	2	2
4. Was the reservationist genuinely accommodating to your arrival time, date, and room size?	YES	2	2
5. Were you given a confirmation number along with a repeat of the arrival/departure date and rate?	YES	2	2

Reservation Summary

I called the hotel on Monday, November 17, 2003 at 2:50 p.m., and it was pleasantly answered after two rings by a male who said "Hello, Hotel Client. How can I help you?" I asked for reservations and was told "One minute. I'll connect you." After one ring, Corey answered the phone. I advised I was looking for a room for Saturday, November 22. He asked me to wait while he checked availability. He asked if I wanted smoking or nonsmoking, and if I wanted a king or double. I informed him I was looking for a nonsmoking king. He said he had rooms available for $179. A few seconds later he said he also had a nonsmoking king room for $159. The $179 rooms were ocean views. I booked the $159 room. He asked if I was a Hotel client preferred guest, and I advised I was not. He said they usually automatically enroll all customers and asked if I was interested. I said yes and he enrolled me at that time. He asked how I would like to guarantee the room, and I gave him my credit card information. Corey then repeated all of the reservation information, advising there would be a 5% and 6% tax on the room, and provided me with a confirmation number. I asked Corey if there were any restaurants located in the hotel. He said "One moment, I'll check." A few seconds later, he informed me that Shula's on the Beach was located in the hotel. He asked if there was anything else he could do for me, thanked me, and said to enjoy my trip. Corey's demeanor was professional, and he was helpful in making the reservation.

Courtesy of Satisfaction Services, Inc. (see http://www.satisfactionservicesinc.com).

FIGURE 10.11   Sample mystery shopper report.

Valet/Bellperson

Question	Response	Points Available	Points Awarded
1. Names of valet and bellpersons (if no name available please provide a DETAILED description)	Carlos, Randy, Henni		
2. Did either the valet or bellperson greet you promptly?	YES	2	2
3. Were you given a proper welcoming greeting? (such as "Welcome to The Hotel Client")	YES	2	2
4. Were the valet and bellpersons courteous and efficient during your stay?	YES	2	2
5. When asked, did the valet or bellpersons inform you about the hotel and amenities?	YES	2	2
6. Were the valet and bellpersons genuinely friendly and did they make good eye contact?	YES	2	2
7. Was the bellperson quick to retrieve your bags?	YES	1	1
8. Was the valet quick to retrieve your vehicle?	YES	1	1

Valet/Bellperson Summary

We arrived at the Hotel Client on Saturday, November 22, 200X at 4:05 p.m. We were promptly greeted by Carlos, the valet/bellperson. He asked if we were returning, and I advised we were checking in. He said he would take my car keys, asked if we needed help with our luggage, and said to check back with him after checking in and directed me to the front desk. I then went back outside to meet Carlos. He asked if the three bags in the backseat should be brought to the room. I informed him they should, and he advised he would be behind us. My companion and I then proceeded to the elevator, and Carlos arrived as the elevator opened. Carlos showed us to our room, initiating conversation along the way. He opened the door for us and proceeded to bring in our luggage and set it up. As we entered the room, it was odor free, which includes no strong air fresheners or perfumes in the air, but a fresh, clean smell. Carlos asked if we had ever stayed with them before, and when we advised no, he gave us information about the hotel, hours the restaurant and pool were open, ice location, and emergency exits. Carlos had an excellent knowledge of the hotel. He had a very friendly, enthusiastic demeanor, and presented a nice first impression of the hotel. I tipped him $5 because he valeted the car as well as handled our luggage. At no time did he make me feel as though it was expected. VALET CHECK OUT: We went out the front door to the valet. Randy immediately took our valet ticket and gave it to Henni who returned with our car in three minutes. Randy immediately placed our luggage in the backseat and Henni met me at the driver side door. I tipped each $2.

Reception: Check-In/Check-Out

Question	Response	Points Available	Points Awarded
1. Name (or detailed description) of check-in clerk	Rick		
2. Name (or detailed description) of check-out clerk	Maureen		
3. Were you greeted in a prompt and efficient manner?	YES	2	2
4. Were you given a proper welcoming greeting? (such as "good afternoon")	YES	2	2
5. Were you greeted in a friendly manner and did the clerk maintain good eye contact?	YES	2	2
6. Were you checked in and out in an efficient manner?	YES	2	2
7. Were you given directions to your room and provided with the hotel amenities as a courtesy?	YES	2	2
8. Were you thanked for staying and did the front desk inquire about your visit?	YES	2	2
9. Were you provided with a detailed and accurate bill at check-out?	YES	2	2

FIGURE 10.11   *(continued)*

Reception: Check-In/Check-Out Summary

We proceeded through the lobby which was very inviting and beautifully decorated for Christmas. We approached the front desk and were greeted immediately by Rick. Rick asked if he could help me, and I advised I had a reservation. He asked my name and immediately pulled it up in the computer. He confirmed that we were staying one night in a king, nonsmoking room. He asked for my credit card, ran it, and returned it to me. He then presented me with a parking pass, phone information, and two keys to the room and showed me where my room number was marked. He also informed me that he had upgraded me to an ocean front. Rick then asked if we needed help with our luggage, and I informed him that it was already being taken care of, and he directed us to the elevators. Rick had a professional, matter-of-fact demeanor. CHECK OUT: As we approached the front desk at 11:45 a.m. on Sunday, November 23, 200X, we were immediately greeted by Maureen. She said good morning and asked if she could help. I told her I was checking out, and she asked me my room number. She asked if I had enjoyed my stay and if everything was satisfactory. I advised it was very nice. Maureen brought up our invoice on the computer and asked if I would like to leave it on my credit card. She never asked me to review my final invoice before presenting me with my final copy. Maureen had a pleasant and professional demeanor.

Returns and Recommendations

Question	Response	Points Available	Points Awarded
1. Do you feel you received a good value?	YES	3	3
2. Based solely on this visit, would you return to this hotel?	YES	5	5
3. Based solely on this visit, would you recommend this hotel to others?	YES	5	5

Additional Comments and Observations

CONCIERGE: We approached the concierge at 10:50 a.m. on Sunday, November 23, and we were pleasantly greeted by Jan. He was nicely dressed in a suit and asked if there was anything he could do to help us. I asked him if there was anywhere close by for jet ski or boat rentals. He gave us directions and prices on several possibilities. He was very helpful and informative. SUMMARY: The people we encountered at the front desk, as well as the valets and bellpersons, were friendly, helpful, and had pleasant demeanors. We had a very enjoyable stay at the hotel. The upgraded ocean front was spectacular from the 11th floor. The employees at the hotel were very customer oriented. All the uniforms of employees were neat and clean and looked professional. While up in the room, which overlooked the pool, we noticed a number of employees routinely checking the area and cleaning debris. It was kept neat and orderly. As I checked out, I asked Maureen for restaurant receipts. She did not really seem to understand what I was looking for and advised there was a recap of all expenditures on my final bill. I would have liked to have been presented duplicate copies of all of my restaurant receipts charged to the room with detailed expenditures. Our entire visit, which consisted of only about 20 hours, kept us quite busy during the evaluation in order to cover all areas that needed to be reviewed, write up complete evaluations, and complete the report within the deadlines. This might be better served by a second night in the hotel to more appropriately space the assignments.

FIGURE 10.11 *(continued)*

Front desk agents and other entry-level employees typically spend more time in direct interactions with guests than do other front office personnel, including managers. They can, therefore, provide current and useful information about service processes and the extent to which they are judged friendly by guests. Effective FOMs can learn useful information just by talking with staff members. These opportunities can occur informally during one-on-one conversations at workstations or more formally during staff meetings. Questions that FOMs can pose to yield useful evaluation information include these:

- What are some things that we require our guests to do that they do not like to do?
- What types of comments do you most frequently receive from our guests?
- What can we in the front office do to more effectively serve our guests?

Property: _____   Report Period: _____

Type and Number of Complaints*

1	2	3	4	5	6	7	8	Total Complaints (A)	Total Guests (B)	Complaints per 1,000 Occupied Rooms (C)

*Type of Complaint	**Examples**
1. Housekeeping	Inefficient service, bathroom mold, old or soiled linens, dirty pool or hot tub, dirty carpet
2. Maintenance	Dripping faucets, broken toilet, peeling wallpaper, plumbing problems, broke locks
3. Marketing programs	Complaints related to American Automobile Association,* family plan, complimentary breakfast
4. Staff performance	Language barrier, rude, uncooperative, inefficient
5. Reservations and billing	Walk policy not honored, reservation missing, corporate rate or other discount not honored
6. Insurance and legal	Accident, police called to property, discrimination, Americans with Disabilities Act issues
7. Unresponsive hotel	Failure to respond to guest complaint when requested to do so by corporate
8. Miscellaneous	Shuttle service erratic, external noise, inadequate lighting, insufficient parki space

*Note: AAA receives complaints and forwards them to the hotel.

FIGURE 10.12   Sample franchisor report card.

- How can I as the FOM better help you to better serve our guests?
- What was the last guest complaint that you received? How did you handle it?
- What can I do to better help you as you deal with guest complaints?
- During the past several months, do you think our service to guests has improved, remained the same, or become more troublesome?

Many other questions can be asked, but the main point is that FOMs have access to a great source of information about the status of guest service: All they must do is ask their employees.

MODERN FRONT OFFICE ISSUES AND TACTICS

Hoteliers Aren't the Only Ones Who Evaluate Hotels!

The global hotel industry is dominated by a relatively few international chains. Most have developed brands that fit into categories that correspond roughly to star ratings: Accor Hotels has a one-star chain (Motel 6) and a five-star chain (Sofitel). Marriott has a three-star brand (Courtyard) and a five-star chain (Ritz-Carlton).

Corporate travel reimbursement policies often dictate the price level and even brands that an employee may use. Therefore, frequent business travelers can usually determine the rank of a domestic hotel. However, some ranking systems claim to be more discriminating. In the United States, there are two major ranking systems: Mobil Travel Guides (which ranks with stars) and Triple A Travel Guides (which ranks with diamonds). In 2005, Mobil gave five stars to only 31 of the estimated 50,000 hotels in the United States; Triple A awarded five diamonds to only 85 lodging properties in the United States.

Travelers abroad are often confused by hotel ratings. In some countries, hotels are rated by government-affiliated tourist agencies that rely on simple physical evaluations. In other countries, a rating may represent a government designation that indicates, for tax reasons, what a hotel is charging.

Some hotels provide amenities and services that go beyond what some observers believe to be the "standard" for the highest ratings. Consider, for example, the Burj Al Arab Hotel. Its least expensive room is for $666 per night; a standard two-bedroom suite costs $2,231. This hotel, and a very few others maintain a "champion" status with exquisite personal service, unparalleled location, often personal chefs, and, in general, "genteel exclusivity."

Room price may not be the defining factor for hotel ratings. Nevertheless, guests who pay $700 to $800 per night (or more) will expect their hotel to be highly ranked.

Adapted from Sharkey, J. 2004. In a galaxy of hotel ratings, are 5 stars enough? *New York Times*, July 4. Retrieved from http://www.nytimes.com.

Many FOMs enjoy opportunities to talk with their guests and, in the process, learn much from them. Being available at the front desk and in the lobby area during the most popular times of registration and check-out is a popular tactic. To obtain useful information, FOMs must go beyond the typical greeting (i.e., "Hello, how are you? Did you enjoy your visit with us?"). Instead, they can learn more by asking open-ended questions: "Hello, I am David Jack, the front office manager here. How well did we meet your service expectations, sir? What would you have liked us to have done that we did not do?" What if, during this conversation, the FOM was walking the guest to the front door and helping him with his luggage? What if the FOM placed the luggage on the hotel shuttle bus and opened the door of the taxi for the guest? Almost certainly the guest would be impressed, and hotel staff would notice that providing service is the job of *every* hotel employee.

SECTION REVIEW AND DISCUSSION QUESTIONS

Section Objective: Discuss the need for and common methods used to assess guests' perceptions about hotel services.

Section Summary: FOMs must be alert to guests' perceptions about service to identify where service processes can be revised to better meet guests' needs. The FOM and other hotel managers should have a fairly comprehensive overview of guests' perceptions about the property and their experiences with it. Common methods to obtain this information include the use of guest comment cards and mystery shoppers. Franchised hotels typically receive a report from the franchisor that indicates the number and type of service-related and other complaints that were sent directly to the organization's headquarters. FOMs can also gather data about the need for service improvements simply by asking front office personnel and by speaking directly to guests.

Discussion Questions:

1. Think about a hotel you visited that provided guest comment cards. What kind of information did the comment cards solicit? What types of information seemed to be emphasized? Would sincere responses adequately identify problems? Were any incentives provided for you as a guest to provide input? Can you make any suggestions from a guest's perspective to improve the guest comment card system in the hotel?

2. Assume you were asked by an FOM to provide mystery shopping services to help evaluate the front office department. Develop a list of factors that you think should be evaluated. How would you evaluate each of the factors?

3. Have you ever worked for a supervisor in the hospitality industry or another industry who asked you how guest service could be improved? If so, what thoughts did you have about the manager who asked this question? Do you think that entry-level employees would like to provide such information to their supervisor? Why or why not?

The FOM in Action: A Solution

FOMs and other managers should not be surprised that their employees often have great ideas about how to better please guests. In fact, entry-level employees have significantly more guest contact than do many managers, and these interactions can suggest ways to identify unmet needs.

Manfred, the FOM at the convention hotel, learned about the need for additional baggage carts by listening to guests. When asked, several front desk agents volunteered that they had heard the same remarks from other guests, but they hadn't passed the suggestion on to Manfred because they thought the idea was "no big deal."

Manfred normally scheduled meetings with the front office staff once a month. At the next meeting, he set aside the last 15 minutes of the session to address one question: "What remarks do you commonly hear from our guests that suggest opportunities for us to improve and provide a more ideal lodging experience?"

Manfred was amazed that in less than 10 minutes employees raised these issues:

- Guests who parked in specific areas of the parking lot had to carry their luggage up steps: Wouldn't a sloping pathway next to the steps make this task easier?
- Guests were often confused about the location of the main ballroom: Signage could be improved.
- Guests frequently commented favorably about the complimentary newspaper delivered to their room; however, many did not know about it until they opened the guestroom door to leave and saw the newspaper. They would have enjoyed reading it with their in-room coffee.
- Several guests had commented that the operating hours for the à la carte dining room as stated in their in-room directory of services were different than the actual hours of

operation. Manfred recalled that dining room hours had been revised recently and was reminded that these changes had not been reflected in the guestroom services directory.

Manfred learned several significant things in the short session with his staff. First, guests note significant concerns on guest comment cards, but they are less likely to note relatively minor issues. Second, employees typically have good ideas about process improvements. Third, he needs to obtain ideas from his front-line employees on a regular basis, because they often know better than he how guest services can be improved.

From the Front Office: Front-Line Interview

Kehaulani Bushnell
Concierge
Marriott Waiohai Beach Club (231 rooms)
Koloa, Kauai, Hawaii

A Vacation Turned From Sour to Sweet!

Kehaulani received her degree in marketing from Loyola Marymount University in Los Angeles, California, in 1996, and has worked in customer service ever since. She began in retail and was promoted to a management position that she held for six years. Kehaulani moved from Honolulu to Kauai when the Marriott Waiohai Beach Club opened, and she was offered a front desk position. She has since transferred to the concierge desk and has been with the property for approximately two years.

1. **What are the most important responsibilities in your present position?**
   The most important responsibility for any employee who is part of the front line is guest service and guest satisfaction. This means making sure you have the tools needed to satisfy your guests' needs. Our manager depends on us to take care of the desk to the best of our abilities, and I believe that our concierge staff does an excellent job. Our staff is unique in that we not only book dinner reservations and activities for guests, but we are also involved in all the activities offered by our resort, including lei making, hula lessons, and other arts and crafts.

   It breaks down to this: Make sure guests are informed about what is offered, listen to what the guests are asking for, correctly book the activities, follow through, and be sure that the guests are satisfied with the services that are provided. Our motto is to provide a memorable vacation experience, and we take this very seriously. Of course, making money for the resort is another top responsibility and, by following the steps I just mentioned, our desk has been successful in doing so. Our resort has one of the highest customer service ratings in the Marriott chain.

2. **What are the biggest challenges that confront you in your day-to-day work and in the long-term operation of your property's front office?**
   I think one of the biggest challenges at the concierge desk is trying to satisfy everyone. This is difficult to do every day, but just making the effort takes you a long way. If you can please 9 out of 10 people, I think you have succeeded.

   As part of a company, one needs to work as a team member to reach overall goals, and that can sometimes be a challenge. I am fortunate that all my co-workers are easy to get along with, but I have been in circumstances where different opinions have caused problems. Everyone needs to communicate openly and arrive at a consensus that will work for everyone.

Long-term challenges include keeping the desk profitable by coming up with new ideas so that guests are excited and come back. You also must keep yourself and your employees motivated if you are in a management position.

3. What is your most unforgettable front office moment?

My most unforgettable moment involves a family. When they first approached my desk, they were in a terrible mood. Their plane had been delayed for more then a day, and the original hotel in which they were booked had given up their room. Our front desk staff was able to get them a room, and I wanted to make sure that the rest of their vacation was as enjoyable as possible. We explored a wide range of possible activities, and they decided what they wanted to do. I set up their entire itinerary for the week, including dinner reservations, so that they wouldn't have to worry about anything.

At the end of their stay they came up to the desk, gave me a hug, and thanked me for turning their vacation from sour to sweet. They had a great time and actually decided to purchase an ownership week so I would see them again the following year. Their little girl also gave me a picture that she had drawn of her family on one of the outings. The scene showed them all smiling and having fun. I still have that picture up on my refrigerator door to remind me that what I do every day at work is appreciated.

4. What advice do you have for those studying about or considering a career in front office or hotel management?

A career in front office or hotel management may not be for everyone, but if you have the motivation and the personality then it can be very rewarding. There are a lot of opportunities to move up in the industry as well as within the hotel. Keep in mind, though, that you may need to move to a different property or even to a different state for a preferred management position.

FRONT OFFICE SEMANTICS LIST

Role-model	Multi-tasking	Tipped position
Dialogue training	Petty cash	Service recovery
Telephone etiquette	Daily function board	Mystery shopper service

FRONT OFFICE AND THE INTERNET

- Want to learn more about how technology helps concierge personnel? If so, check out www.goconcierge.com to view the site of a company that develops popular concierge-related software.

- Using your favorite search engine, type in *virtual concierge* and review the Web sites of several hotels that provide guests with this service.

- To learn more about mystery shopping services for hotels and other organizations within the hospitality industry, go to www.satisfactionservicesinc.com. At that site, you will learn much about the company, and you can view sample reports of mystery shoppers for hotels, restaurants, and other hospitality businesses.

- Want to learn about software that helps to identify, track, and eliminate problems that cause significant concerns for many guests? Check out www.guestware.com

- To see actual job descriptions for bell services attendants, type that position title into your favorite search engine.

REAL–WORLD ACTIVITIES

1. Assume that you are an FOM talking with a new front desk agent during induction to the department. What points would you make about the role of persons in that position in (1) providing positive first impressions for hotel guests, (2) making guest service a priority, and (3) making decisions as part of the service recovery process?

2. Some FOMs ask friends, family members, or others to telephone the hotel to assess the quality of service provided by PBX operators, reservation clerks, front desk agents, and other entry-level staff who answer the phone. What are the pros and cons of this practice? Would you ask others to make these evaluation calls? Why or why not?

3. What type of training would you, as an FOM, provide to new bell service attendants and concierge personnel? If you were an FOM in a large hotel with a human resources department, what part of the training would you expect staff members in that department to do? Can you think of training topics for which someone in the front office would be responsible?

4. During service recovery training, what advice would you give to a front desk agent for the following situation: It becomes obvious that the purpose of a guest's complaint is to receive a reduction in the hotel bill? Should a modest discount be given? Why or why not?

5. Assume that, as an FOM, you retained the services of a mystery shopper. During the visit, the shopper experienced and reported on an unpleasant exchange with a front desk agent. The mystery shopper noted the name of the staff member. You know that the employee has been with the hotel for three months, and you have not received any other complaints about this staff member. What would you do if anything, now that you have knowledge of this incident?

11

Guest Charges, Payment, and Check-Out

Chapter Outline

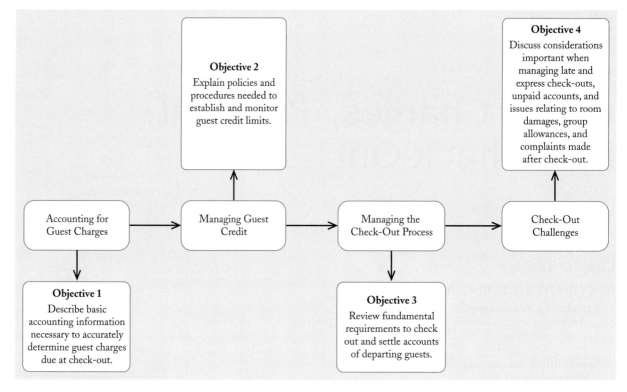

CHAPTER ROADMAP

Chapter Preview

FOMs do not need the same set of skills as do hotel controllers (i.e., accountants). They must, however, understand the purposes and rules of accounting, because they are responsible for maintaining a key part of a hotel's total financial management and reporting activities. This chapter begins with a brief overview of the accounting process and includes a detailed examination of the FOM's role in and responsibilities for bookkeeping, accounting, and financial management.

Most hotel guests make room, products, and service purchases on credit. FOMs must be familiar with their hotel's procedures used to establish and monitor credit limits. If necessary, FOMs may have to remove guests for nonpayment. In this chapter, the issues of establishing and monitoring credit limits are examined.

The chapter concludes with a study of the check-out process. The following 10 steps required for proper guest check-out are discussed and special attention is paid to guests' actual payment (i.e., settlement) of their accounts:

• Creation of departure list
• Confirmation of guest identity
• Stay inquiry

- Property exchange
- Final data entry and posting of charges
- Production of folio for guest inspection
- Processing of guest payment
- Future reservation inquiry
- Filing of documentation
- Revision of room status

The processes used for most guest check-outs are routine. However, variations such as late check-outs and unpaid accounts do occur, and FOMs must be prepared for them. Also, hotels are increasingly using nonconventional methods of guest check-out. Some of these processes are interfaced with the hotel's PMS; others may not be. Challenges confront FOMs when unusual occurrences adversely affect the check-out process. These challenges include assessments of room damage, strategies for group allowances, and adjustments for complaints made after check-out. Many check-out situations can test the experience and professionalism of FOMs; as savvy hoteliers; they and their staff must be ready to meet the challenges.

The FOM in Action: The Challenge

"It's like I told you; they aren't going to pay," said Karla, the accounts receivable and credit manager at the 250-room Lenox Hotel. Karla was talking to Trisha, her friend and the FOM at the busy hotel located in the downtown center of a large city.

"But I don't understand," said Trisha "I looked it up after you called me this morning. Mr. Keefer stayed with us last month. He checked into room 240 and stayed three nights. When he checked out, he signed his folio because his company had been preapproved for a direct bill. It's on the list of authorized direct bill accounts."

"That's right," replied Karla, "Greenfield Financial, the company Keefer works for, does have a direct bill established with us. But it specifically says the company will only pay room and tax but not incidentals. Keefer had almost $200 of non-room charges when he checked out, and those are the charges Greenfield is refusing to pay. Room service, movies, telephone calls—a little bit of everything. I talked to their accounts payable person myself. They are adamant that these are not allowable charges."

"But," protested Trish, "how was our front desk agent to know what they would and wouldn't pay for? We have dozens of direct bill accounts!"

"All I know," replied Karla, "is that I either need to make a bunch of revenue adjustments that will be charged to your department, or you need to get in touch with Keefer. What do you want me to do?"

ACCOUNTING FOR GUEST CHARGES

In addition to greeting guests, assigning them to rooms, and attending to their needs during their stay, FOMs must ensure that all guest charges are processed according to proper **accounting** standards. As shown in Roadmap 11.1, this section of the chapter describes how to account for guest charges.

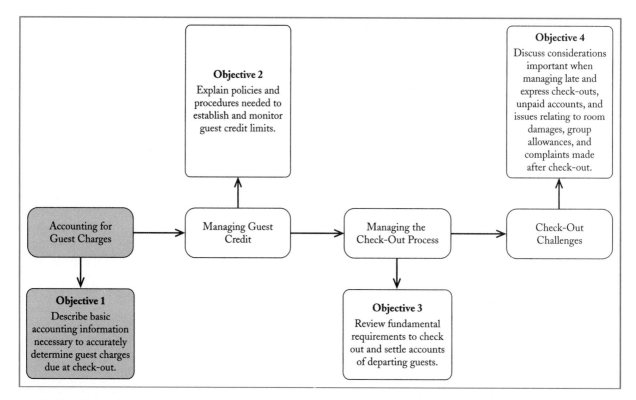

ROADMAP 11.1

FRONT OFFICE SEMANTICS

Accounting: Process of summarizing and reporting financial transactions.

In smaller hotels, nearly 100 percent of all guest charges (and, therefore, hotel revenue) is processed through the front office. In larger hotels, this percentage may be smaller, but guest charges always include these items:

- Guestroom charges
- Taxes related to the sale of guestrooms
- Guest-initiated room telephone charges
- Food and beverages and other product and services purchases charged to the guest's room
- Charges for any other goods and services directly interfaced with the PMS

These items account for the majority of sales in most hotels. In the hotel industry, the accounting processes performed at the front desk are so important that hoteliers make a distinction between **front-office accounting system** and **back-office accounting.**

FRONT OFFICE SEMANTICS

Front-office accounting system: Automated (or manual) system of data collection and reporting that summarizes and documents the financial activities of the front office.

Back-office accounting: Process of summarizing and documenting the financial activities and condition of the entire hotel.

Although FOMs need not be **certified public accountants (CPAs)** to do their jobs well, they must understand basic accounting principles, major tasks related to front office accounting, and how that information supports the efforts of the hotel's **controller.**

FRONT OFFICE SEMANTICS

Certified public accountant (CPA): Designation given to an individual who has passed a national qualifying examination related to accounting practices and principles. CPA designations are granted and administered by state boards of accountancy.

Controller: Individual (or department) in a hotel responsible for maintaining the back-office accounting system.

Accounting Fundamentals

If the hotel managers who read their property's financial statements are to have faith in the information, they must know and understand the principles and practices used to collect and report the data. If they do not, or if those reporting the information

The FOM and controller work closely to ensure accurate financial management.

intentionally or unintentionally mislead readers, the result will likely be inaccurate information leading to inadequate decision making. Therefore, financial information reported by FOMs and controllers should follow **generally accepted accounting principles.**

FRONT OFFICE SEMANTICS

Generally accepted accounting principles (GAAPs): Standards and procedures that have been adopted by those responsible for preparing business financial statements for the purpose of ensuring uniformity.

FOMs do not need in-depth knowledge of hotel accounting procedures, but FOMs should understand these fundamentals of hotel accounting: differences between bookkeeping and accounting, purposes of debits and credits, and front office posting responsibilities.

Bookkeeping and Accounting

Accounting is the process of summarizing and reporting financial transactions. Most of the financial reporting tasks completed at the front desk, however, involve **bookkeeping** rather than accounting. Bookkeeping involves the initial recording of financial transactions.

FRONT OFFICE SEMANTICS

Bookkeeping: Process of initially recording financial transactions.

Bookkeeping output yields data used by accountants. For example, the recording of an individual financial transaction such as an in-room movie sale is a bookkeeping task. The FOM tallies the total revenue generated from movie sales during the month, and this information is incorporated into the hotel's monthly financial statements, which are analyzed by the controller, general manager, and others. If improper bookkeeping is done (e.g., movie sales are not recorded properly), the resulting financial data will be inaccurate. Then decisions made based on the "numbers" supplied by the FOM may be flawed. As seen in Figure 11.1, bookkeeping forms the foundation of

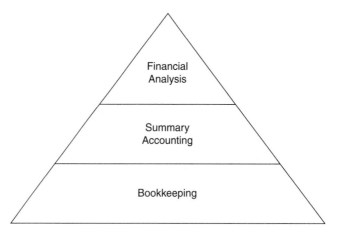

FIGURE 11.1   Financial management begins with bookkeeping.

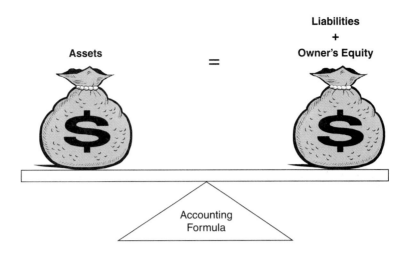

FIGURE 11.2   Fundamental accounting formula.

financial management. It is not possible to effectively analyze a hotel's financial standing if the data summarized are erroneously or carelessly generated by those performing bookkeeping tasks.

The accounting process is based on the fundamental accounting formula shown in Figure 11.2. **Assets** refer to everything owned by the hotel.

FRONT OFFICE SEMANTICS

Asset: Item owned by a business, for example, cash on hand, money in checking or other accounts, money owed to the business, inventories, property, equipment, and furnishings.

Liabilities refer to what the hotel owes to others.

FRONT OFFICE SEMANTICS

Liability: Debt owed by a business.

Owner's equity refers to the hotel's actual financial worth. It is the amount of money left to the hotel's owners if the hotel's assets were used to pay all of the outstanding debt (liabilities) owed to nonowners; thus, some consider owner's equity to be the amount owed to owners. In some cases, a hotel may actually owe more money to creditors than the total value of its assets. The hotel would then have a negative net worth; however, the same accounting formula is used to gain an accurate picture of its financial standing.

FRONT OFFICE SEMANTICS

Owner's equity: What remains after subtracting what the business owes others (its liabilities) from what the business owns (its assets).

Under accepted accounting rules, dollars on the "left" side of the accounting formula's equal sign must always equal the value on the "right" side.

In general, hotel owners or accountants are not legally required to follow any specific procedures when recording financial transactions. There are, however, laws requiring owners to properly account for, report, and pay taxes when due, to file certain documents with the government, and to supply accurate business data. Therefore, many hotel companies require their managers to use a system of accounting procedures created specifically for hotels. These have been developed by hospitality accountants in conjunction with the Educational Institute (EI) of the American Hotel & Lodging Association and are called the **Uniform System of Accounts for the Lodging Industry.**

FRONT OFFICE SEMANTICS

Uniform System of Accounts for the Lodging Industry (USALI): Standard set of accounting procedures used to record a hotel's financial transactions and condition.

The USALI provides a consistent and easily understood roadmap to record revenues and expenses and to report the hotel's overall financial condition. (A copy can be purchased at www.ei-ahla.org)

Hotel owners and managers want accurate financial data to help ensure good decision making; however, they are not the only ones interested in consistent and accurate reports of a hotel's financial activity. There are others who want to know about the financial health of the business. The following individuals and business entities review the financial data of a hotel and count on the data to be collected and reported in a way that yields accurate information about the hotel's financial position:

- *Owners.* A hotel's owners want to monitor the business's financial condition. They may be large or small corporations, partnerships of one or more individuals, or even the hotel's managers.
- *Investors.* Savvy investors want to put their money in businesses that will grow their wealth. To determine whether a hotel is doing (or can do) that, these individuals and organizations need accurate financial information.
- *Creditors.* Those who lend money or extend credit require accurate, timely information about a hotel's financial condition. Then they can evaluate the likelihood that debt can be repaid according to the terms of the loan or the credit extended.
- *Hotel operators.* In many cases, one hotelier reports financial data directly to another hotelier. For example, the general manager of a single hotel in a multiunit organization may report financial data to an area manager who is responsible for several hotels in a specific geographic area. The area manager may, in turn, summarize areawide information in a report to the regional manager.

The FOM, as much as any other hotel manager, benefits from the consistent use of accurate bookkeeping and standard accounting procedures in the front office.

Debits and Credits

The accounting formula presented in Figure 11.2 forms the foundation for understanding other important accounting concepts, including the purpose of an **account.**

FRONT OFFICE SEMANTICS

Account: Device used to show increases or decreases in the asset, liability, or owner's equity sections of the fundamental accounting equation. Because of the visual appearance of accounts, accountants refer to them as *T accounts* (refer to Figure 11.4).

Accounts are created to provide details helpful for financial reporting. Assume that the Altoona Hotel has $50,000 in its bank account and that it owns a $5,000 printer used in its front office. Both of these items are hotel assets, and both must be accounted for separately. Similarly, assume the Altoona pays $25,000 per month on its 20-year mortgage (a liability). This expense is a different type of liability than the taxes owed by the hotel and should, for clarity, be recorded in a separate account.

Within each of the three major components of the accounting formula, accountants create individual accounts to clarify the financial standing of a hotel. Some of the most important accounts are identified in Figure 11.3.

FRONT OFFICE SEMANTICS

Accounts receivable (A/R): Money owed to a hotel.

Accounts payable (A/P): Money owed by a hotel.

Retained earnings: Profits earned but not paid (disbursed) to the business owners.

Every account can experience increases or decreases. For example, funds in bank accounts (an asset) can increase or decrease, money owed for refunds to guests (a liability) may go up or down, and profits maintained by the hotel's owners (owner's equity) may become larger or smaller. To record changes to the hotel's accounts, a technique called **double entry accounting** is used.

FRONT OFFICE SEMANTICS

Double entry accounting: System of recording financial transactions in a way that maintains the equality of the fundamental accounting equation: assets = liabilities + owner's equity.

Figure 11.4 illustrates an account. Note its T shape, which explains how the name *T account* originated. Each account has its own name and a space for both **debit** and **credit** entries (adjustments).

Asset accounts	Liability accounts	Owner's equity accounts
Cash on hand	**Accounts payable**	Stock
Funds in bank accounts	Taxes payable	**Retained earnings**
Accounts receivable	Short-term debts (notes) payable	Revenue accounts
Inventories	Long-term debts payable	Expense accounts
Land		
Buildings		
Equipment		
Furniture		

FIGURE 11.3 Example of asset, liability and owner's equity accounts.

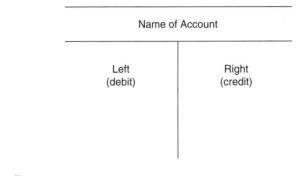

FIGURE 11.4   T account.

FRONT OFFICE SEMANTICS

Debit (accounting): Accounting transaction that records a change on the left side of a T account in an asset, liability, or owner's equity account.

Credit (accounting): Accounting transaction that records a change on the right side of a T account in an asset, liability, or owner's equity account.

When double entry accounting is used, the total of the debits (changes made to the left side of one or more accounts) always equals the credits (changes made to the right side of one or more accounts). This ensures that the fundamental accounting formula stays in balance. Figure 11.5 summarizes the impact of each kind of entry— debit and credit—on each of the three major components of the fundamental accounting formula.

Let's see how the use of debits, credits, and double entry accounting affects individual accounts. Assume that the Altoona Hotel has an account titled "Uniforms" and another called "Cash on Hand." When the FOM purchases uniforms for front office staff, this transaction involves debiting Uniforms (an asset) and crediting Cash on Hand. As seen in Figure 11.5, this increases the value of the Uniforms account and decreases the amount of money in the Cash on Hand account.

To see how credits, debits, and double entry accounting affect the fundamental accounting formula, assume that the Altoona's financial condition is as follows:

$$\$13,000,000 = \$10,000,000 + \$3,000,000$$

$$(\text{Assets}) = (\text{Liabilities}) + (\text{Owner's equity})$$

Accounting formula component	Entry (adjustment)	Result
Asset	Debit	Increase
	Credit	Decrease
Liability	Debit	Decrease
	Credit	Increase
Owner's equity	Debit	Decrease
	Credit	Increase

FIGURE 11.5   Impact of debit and credit entries on the accounting formula.

Controllers record credits and debits in their revenue and expense accounts.

The owners are considering purchasing a vacant lot adjacent to the hotel for $50,000. If they agree to pay $50,000 for the lot and secure a bank loan to finance the purchase, the following account changes affect the accounting formula:

- A debit (increase) in an asset account (Land) to reflect ownership of the $50,000 lot
- A credit (increase) in a liabilities account (Notes Payable) by $50,000 to reflect the loan

The accounting formula for the Altoona would be revised to read:

$$(\$13,000,000 + \$50,000 \text{ lot}) = (\$10,000,000 + \$50,000 \text{ loan}) + \$3,000,000$$

$$(\text{Assets}) = (\text{Liabities}) + (\text{Owner's equity})$$

or

$$\$13,050,000 = \$13,050,000$$

After the land is purchased, both sides of the equation would still be equal (i.e., in balance with) each other.

Various revenue and expense accounts are used by FOMs. They are part of the owner's equity portion of the accounting equation and are summarized at the end of each accounting period in an income (profit and loss) statement. Figure 11.6 demonstrates the impact of debit and credit entries on revenue and expense accounts.

An FOMs' primary accounting responsibility is to manage guest folios, which can be considered individual accounts for each guest. Therefore, debit and credit entries for these accounts should follow the same rules as those used for all other hotel accounts. Assume a guest stays at the Altoona Hotel and owes the hotel (has a folio balance of) $100. Two accounting entries will properly record the guest's payment.

Sub account	Entry (adjustment)	Result
Revenue	Debit	Decrease
	Credit	Increase
Expense	Debit	Increase
	Credit	Decrease

FIGURE 11.6   Impact of debit and credit entries on revenue and expense accounts.

One entry (a decrease in accounts receivable) of $100 reduces the account that the guest owes to the hotel. The second entry (a $100 increase in the cash account) is used to account for the transaction.

For some FOMs, the principles of recording financial transactions are easy to understand; others may have more difficulty comprehending the hows and whys of accounting procedures. All FOMs, however, can learn and manage the specific posting (recording) procedures mandated by their property.

Posting Responsibilities

Chapter 4 explained that *posting* is the process of entering financial data (including guest charges) into the PMS to create a permanent record of the transaction. Careful posting of guest purchases and payments is required so the hotel can balance its books (i.e., its financial records) and meet requirements of the accounting formula. Interfaced revenue-producing subsystems (e.g., call accounting and pay-per-view movies) allow automatic posting to a guest's folio (see Chapter 8). When these subsystems are used, the FOM's responsibility is to ensure that the interface is working properly and that accurate prices are charged to guests.

When revenue-producing subsystems are not interfaced, the posting process is more complex and requires at least one additional control device. Consider this hypothetical situation: Bob is a member of the front office team at the Altoona Hotel. At this property, pay-per-view movies are not interfaced directly with the PMS. Jessie, a frequent guest, has colluded with Bob to watch pay-per-view movies at no charge during Bob's shift. Bob does not post charges to the folio maintained for Jessie, who has agreed to pay Bob a discounted amount of cash for each movie watched. This fraudulent activity could be eliminated or significantly curtailed if the FOM implements a system to ensure that each pay-per-view movie purchased is recorded, posted to a folio, and reviewed to ensure 100 percent compliance with posting procedures.

Each noninterfaced subsystem that generates revenue must have its own unique control device to help ensure that charges are posted to the proper folio. Otherwise, (1) employees may defraud the hotel, (2) assessments of income and expenses related to that subsystem's revenue-producing ability will be flawed, and (3) ultimately the hotel will experience significant loss of revenues.

Front-Office Accounting

In addition to maintaining important statistical information about hotel revenues, ADR, RevPar, and related statistics, FOMs must manage the hotel's front-office accounting system. Regardless of a hotel's size, FOMs usually have these responsibilities:

- Creating registered guest accounts (folios) and maintaining accounts used by nonregistered guests

- Posting debits and credits to the appropriate accounts as needed to maintain their accuracy
- Recording payment information
- Implementing procedures to help ensure the accuracy and completeness of the accounting system

Hotels sell products and services to guests who have rented sleeping rooms and to those who have not. FOMs must maintain a **guest ledger** and, in addition, will likely have some responsibility for front-office accounting tasks related to **city ledger** accounts. Together, the guest ledger and city ledger record all of a hotel's sales and payment transactions, and information from them is regularly transferred to the hotel's **general ledger.**

FRONT OFFICE SEMANTICS

Guest ledger: Set of accounts used to record charges to and payments from a hotel's registered guests. Sometimes called the *front office ledger* or *rooms ledger*.

City ledger: Set of accounts used to record charges to and payments from a hotel's nonregistered guests. Examples include persons not staying in the hotel who purchase the hotel's meeting space, food, or beverages.

General ledger: Primary ledger that contains all of a hotel's accounts used to create its income (profit and loss) statement.

An overview of the relationship between these ledgers is shown in Figure 11.7. FOMs must thoroughly understand the impact of posting charges to the guest and

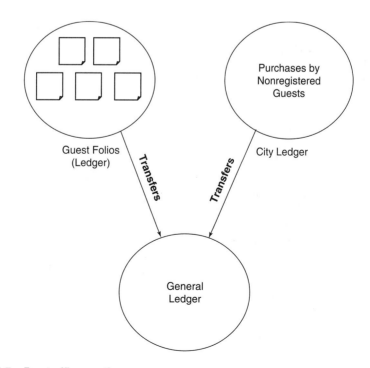

FIGURE 11.7   Front office postings.

city ledgers. They must also develop procedures that allow their staff to make authorized adjustments to the accounts in these ledgers when necessary.

Posting to Guest Ledger

Most guests purchase the hotel's goods and services on credit using a debit or credit card during check-in to establish their creditworthiness. Other methods include cash deposits or direct bill arrangements. In all cases, however, each guest's folio (the record of charges and payments) must be accurate and current. FOMs do not typically know exactly when a guest will check out; therefore, systems must be in place to ensure the timely posting of guest charges so folios can be up-to-date regardless of when the guest chooses to check out.

As noted earlier, when revenue-producing accounts are interfaced with the PMS, the posting of guest charges (i.e., folio updating) is automatic. The FOM's role in such a case is to ensure the proper functioning of the interfaces and the accuracy of charges that are posted. When revenue-producing accounts are posted manually, FOMs must devise systems to help minimize the time that elapses between the guest's purchase and posting of the charge.

For most guests, the room charge with applicable taxes is the single largest posting recorded in their folio. For many guests, this is the only prepayment posting recorded in the folio, and it is automatically performed by the PMS during the night audit. Additional postings to a guest's folio can include these items:

- Food and beverage purchases
- Gift shop purchases
- Telephone toll charges

Purchases in the hotel's gift shop may be charged to a hotel guest's folio.

- Parking fees
- Business related charges (e.g., copy and fax fees, postage, and Internet access charges)
- In-room movie and entertainment charges
- Hotel-specific service charges (e.g., golf greens fees, spa use fees, and the like)
- Gratuities

Guests expect their folios to be accurately maintained. In an increasing number of hotels, guests can review their folios in their rooms before checking out by using their in-room television system.

In some cases, the room rate charged is not shown on the guest's copy of the folio. Instead, it is **suppressed.**

FRONT OFFICE SEMANTICS

Suppressed rate: Term used to indicate that a guest's room rate is not to be displayed on the guest's copy of the folio. Used as in, "*Suppress* the rate on all the folios created for the tour group arriving this Friday."

Suppressed rates are used, for example, when a travel wholesaler buys hotel rooms for resale to individual travelers. In these cases, the FOM may, at the request of the client (the wholesaler), suppress the room rates of the individual travelers while still maintaining accurate and viewable records of these guests' other purchases at the hotel.

As discussed in Chapter 9, a single folio (master bill) may be established for a group to which charges from each registered guest's folio are posted. Master bills are common, especially in full-service hotels. Regardless of whether guest charges are posted to individual folios or master bills, FOMs must establish and enforce procedures to ensure that all appropriate charges are posted properly.

Posting to City Ledger

As shown in Figure 11.7, postings to the city ledger, like those to the guest ledger, are ultimately transferred to the hotel's general ledger. FOMs who maintain all or part of the city ledger postings are concerned about commonly recorded financial transactions such as these:

- Deposits for meeting room rental
- Refunds of meeting room deposits
- Charges for meeting room services and rentals (e.g. audiovisual or computer equipment)
- Payments for meeting room services and rentals
- Charges for food and beverage purchases
- Payment of food and beverage charges
- Parking charges and payments

Some postings to the city ledger may be done automatically; some noninterfaced charges must be entered manually.

Adjusting Accounts

Although posting charges and payments to guest accounts might seem straightforward (especially with a computerized PMS), there are a variety of "unusual" postings that must be made regularly. Consider, for example, the guest who announces that she wishes to check out two days early:

> *This hotel is just too noisy. I couldn't sleep last night because of the music coming from the room next door. I want to get some sleep tonight, and I don't think I can do that here.*

In this case, most FOMs would compensate the guest for her inconvenience. Normally, this would involve an adjustment to her bill. In many hotels, FOMs and their staff have significant latitude to determine when to post an adjustment. Figure 11.8 illustrates a document to record folio adjustments or billing allowances. From an accounting perspective, the vouchers are important. They help to balance actual monies collected with funds that have been previously billed (posted) to guest accounts. They are also important because they identify operational shortcomings.

Note these numbered elements in the voucher form shown as Figure 11.8:

1. Sequence number for control purposes
2. Space for the date when the voucher is used
3. Space for the name of the guest for whom the adjustment was made
4. Space for the guest's identifying room or account number
5. Space to explain the event or circumstances to justify issuing an adjustment
6. Space for the initials or signature of the employee initiating the adjustment
7. Identification number for reordering purposes

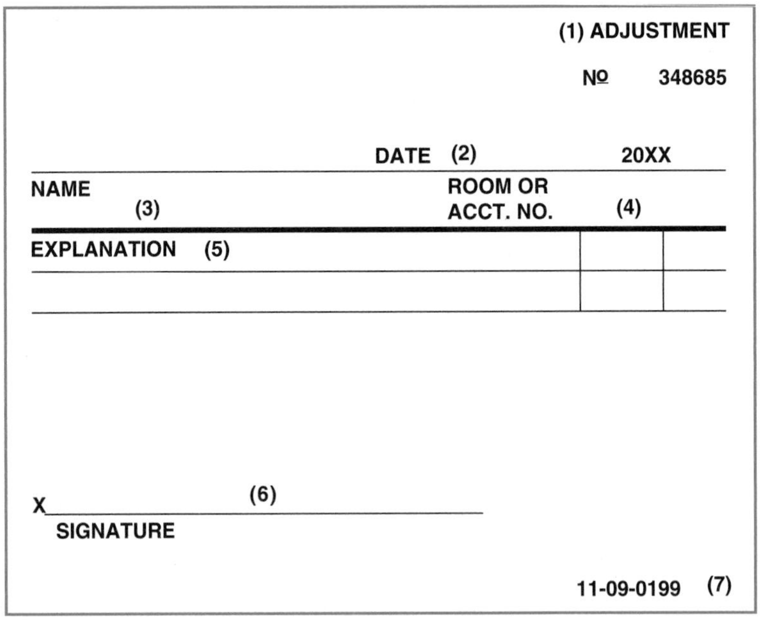

(1) ADJUSTMENT
NO 348685
DATE (2) 20XX
NAME (3)
ROOM OR ACCT. NO. (4)
EXPLANATION (5)
X (6)
SIGNATURE
11-09-0199 (7)

FIGURE 11.8 Adjustment voucher.

In a smaller property, each voucher would be tabulated and personally reviewed for accuracy by the FOM before, probably, being given to the general manager. In a larger property, the data from a number of vouchers might be summarized before review by the FOM and other department heads.

Daily analysis of guest accounts by the FOM is important because of three situations that can result in the need for an allowance or adjustment voucher:

- *Posting errors.* Despite appropriate training, employees sometimes make errors in the amounts charged guests. This problem can range from charging guests the wrong room rate to charging one guest for services used by another guest.

    When an error is discovered, it must be adjusted to reflect the correct charge if an incorrect charge had been posted to a guest's account. Assume that Mr. and Mrs. Guild, who were staying in room 417, had appetizers in the hotel lounge and signed a guest check charging this purchase to their room. However, the bartender mistakenly charged the appetizers to room 471. The Guilds checked out on Sunday morning and paid only the amount in the room 417 folio. On the following Monday, the guest in room 471 is checking out, reviews the bill, and refuses to pay the incorrect charge. An allowance and adjustment voucher to remove the charge for appetizers must be prepared for this guest. It may be impossible to collect on the charges originally incurred by the Guilds.

- *Hotel-related problems.* Despite the best efforts of the hotel's managers and staff, some guests experience problems during their stay. For example, an ice machine stopped working; before it could be repaired, a guest who wanted ice was inconvenienced. In another situation, a hotel employee offended a guest. In both cases (and many others) a guest may, during check-out or before, request or demand a reduction in charges. To make an allowance or adjustment requires the completion of a voucher such as the one shown in Figure 11.8. The FOM must review these vouchers to determine where training or other tactics are needed to correct recurring problems.

- *Guest-related problems.* In some cases, guests cause problems for other guests. Complaints ranging from excessive noise in adjacent rooms to rowdy guest behavior in public spaces can cause guests to request compensation for an unpleasant experience. The FOM or other front office staff member must decide if an allowance or adjustment to the guest's bill is justified; if so, the adjustment voucher is filled out.

The total cost of allowances and adjustments compared to total overall room revenue can be tracked monthly using the following formula:

$$\frac{\text{Total monthly allowances and adjustments}}{\text{Total room revenue}}$$

$$= \text{Room allowance and adjustment percentage}$$

This percentage will likely vary based on the age of the hotel, the quality of staff and training programs, and even the type of guest typically served. Industry averages typically range from 1 percent to 3 percent of room revenue. FOMs should monitor the average monthly room allowance and adjustment percentage and work to keep this percentage as low as possible.

Back-Office Accounting

The back-office accounting system includes all of a hotel's accounts, including those in the guest ledger and city ledger. Recall that guest folios and city ledger accounts are records of charges and payments. Collectively, these two types of accounts comprise the hotel's accounts receivable: the sum of what registered and unregistered guests owe the hotel. Accounts receivable are assets; as soon as a guest incurs a charge to be posted to a folio or city ledger account, the hotel's accounts receivable increase. By contrast, payments made by cash or payment card decrease accounts receivable. A guest's folio is updated whenever a charge is incurred or a payment is made. At the time of guest check-out or account settlement (for city ledger accounts), the total amount of accounts receivable to be collected must be brought to zero in a process called account **settlement.**

FRONT OFFICE SEMANTICS

Settlement (account): Collection of a payment for an outstanding account balance. Settlement may involve the guest paying cash or charging the account balance to a valid payment card or another hotel-approved account.

If a departing guest pays the full amount owed by cash or check, the folio balance is reduced to zero. The cash amount is subtracted from accounts receivable (A/R account) and is *added* to the cash account (also an asset account) to keep the accounting formula in balance. Payments made by a payment card are somewhat different and are discussed in the next section. When a guest does not pay the full amount owed, settlement is still necessary. This is done by moving (transferring) the remaining guest folio (accounts receivable) balance to a different receivable account or by transferring the remaining balance owed to a **house account.**

FRONT OFFICE SEMANTICS

House account: Account whose entries are assessed to another hotel entity such as the sales and marketing department, the general manager, or the FOM.

Transfers to Hotel Receivable Accounts

In many hotels, use of a payment card is the most common way guests settle their accounts. Guests may make partial payments to their accounts at any time during their stay. At check-out, their account balances, if not paid in cash, must be transferred from the guest ledger to the city ledger. Assume that Ms. Grayson has been a guest at the Altoona Hotel. During her stay, her account balance has been maintained in the guest ledger. Now that Ms. Grayson is checking out, her account balance must be removed from the guest ledger, which is reserved for registered guests. Any amount that Ms. Grayson owes after check-out must be transferred to a city ledger account. The two most common methods of noncash guest settlement involve transfer of outstanding balances to a payment card or to a direct bill account.

Payment Cards   When it issues a payment card, a financial institution agrees to pay debts owed by the cardholder if the card has been legitimately issued to and used only by the designated cardholder. When the card is used during check-out, the folio account balance is transferred from the guest (to bring the guest's account balance to

More guests now use debit cards as a method of payment.

zero) *to* the payment card. If Ms. Grayson uses an American Express card, the amount she owes (an A/R account) will be reduced. An equal amount will be added to the total that American Express (also an A/R account) owes the hotel. The management of transfers from guest ledger funds to payment card accounts is an important part of the FOM's job.

As shown in Figure 11.9, four steps are required to receive money from a payment card company:

- *Initiation.* In this first step, a front office staff member verifies that the guest's payment card is active and that the amount of the proposed purchase is within the card's approved spending limit. When a financial institution issues a payment card, it generally does so with restrictions on the amount it will pay on a cardholder's behalf (popularly called the card's *limit*). Each card issuer has its own set of rules regarding if, and by how much, the cardholder can exceed the preapproved limit.

  Initiating a card typically involves one of two methods. When the guest is present in the hotel, restaurant, or another outlet, the card is physically available. To initiate the transaction, the hotel employee swipes the card through a card reader or manually keys the card number through a POS terminal. Alternatively, if a telephone or fax is used to make a payment, the card is not physically present at the hotel. Then the staff member manually enters the information, including the payment card number, expiration date, and card verification or validation codes (usually three or four digits on the back of the card).

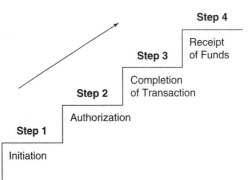

FIGURE 11.9   Payment card processing.

Additional information required to initiate a card for a holder who is not physically present includes name and street (billing) address. An **address verification service (AVS)** can help verify street numbers in the United States. FOMs who do not have an AVS available should arrange with their merchant service provider (see Chapter 8) to add this fraud-prevention service.

FRONT OFFICE SEMANTICS

Address verification service (AVS): Company that, for a fee, allows access to its database of current addresses.

- *Authorization.* The second step to ensure that a hotel receives payment involves real-time authorization to reduce **chargebacks** and to identify card-entry errors.

FRONT OFFICE SEMANTICS

Chargeback: Payment card charges disallowed (reversed) when a cardholder successfully protests the legitimacy of the charge or because the hotel made an error in processing a charge. When a charge-back request is initiated by a cardholder, the hotel must respond promptly, or else the request will usually be granted.

Authorization occurs when the guest's payment card number is entered in the processing terminal. Software transmits the credit card number, its expiration date, and the sales total to the hotel's merchant service provider (MSP). The MSP transmits the data to the guest's bank or other financial institution that issued the card, which will approve or decline the transaction.

- *Completion of transaction.* A transaction is completed when the total number of individual credit card transactions (called a *batch*) completed in a shift (or day) are summarized and transmitted to the hotel's MSP. Information about the batch may be transmitted manually, but more typically it is done electronically. The MSP forwards the pertinent information about each individual transaction to the proper payment card company (e.g., MasterCard, Visa, American Express). The payment card company forwards information about the transaction to the appropriate card-issuing bank that, in turn, debits the guest's (cardholder's account) and credits the account of the MSP (not the account of the hotel).

- *Receipt of funds.* The final processing step is the actual receipt of the money due to the hotel. After all previous steps have been completed, the MSP credits (makes a deposit to) the hotel's account (usually within two to four business days). During this time, the MSP may contact the hotel to clarify any questionable sale. It is important to note that initiation, authorization, and even completion of a transaction do not guarantee a hotel's payment. These steps only mean that payment has been approved at the time of the transaction.

The monies owed to a hotel are issued by electronic funds transfer (EFT). All charges and fees imposed on the hotel by the card issuer or the hotel's MSP are deducted before the hotel receives its payment. EFTs are safe, fast, and reliable, and leave an identifiable accounting trail that can be reviewed by the FOM or controller. EFTs of all kinds are issued through the Automated Clearing House (ACH) network, a highly reliable, nationwide, batch-oriented EFT system governed by the operating rules of the National Automated Clearing House Association (NACHA). The NACHA represents more than 12,000 financial institutions and 650 organizations. It develops operating rules and business practices for electronic payments in the areas of Internet commerce, electronic bill and invoice presentment, e-checks, and international currency payments.

Direct Bills   If a guest's folio balance is not settled with cash or a payment card, the account balance may be transferred from the guest ledger to the portion of the city ledger that records direct bills (see Chapter 9). Recall that direct bills are used when an entity preapproved for credit agrees to pay the charges incurred by a guest. This transfer reduces the guest's portion of accounts receivable and adds the same amount to the direct bill section of the city ledger.

Transfers to House Accounts

Sometimes a guest's account balance is transferred to one or more house accounts. Assume that Donna Berger is checking out. She says that, although her hotel stay was fine, the meal she charged to her room was substandard because of poor service. She says she will continue to stay at the hotel because she likes it and often recommends it to others, and she wants the FOM to know about her experience. Most FOMs in this situation would agree that some form of compensation is appropriate. From an accounting perspective, Ms. Berger has a "balance due" in the food and beverage portion of the hotel's accounts receivable. To eliminate this amount but to balance the hotel's overall accounts, Ms. Berger's accounts receivable balance for the meal would be transferred to the manager's house account to eliminate (move) her charge. At the end of the accounting period, the balance in the manager's house account will be reduced to zero, and the amounts in it are transferred to a guest relations or guest comps expense account.

House accounts serve many purposes. Managers use them to compensate guests for difficulties encountered during their stays. Sales and marketing staff use them to promote the hotel by providing complimentary food, beverages, or rooms to potential guests. Telephone and fax charges, postage, laundry, and taxicab charges are among other house accounts that may be established for staff use. Any guest account balance to be transferred to a house account should be recorded along with the name of the individual authorizing the transfer to reduce the chance for fraud by employees or managers. (Recall the example earlier in the chapter that involved collusion between a front desk agent and a guest who abused in-room movie accounting procedures.)

SECTION REVIEW AND DISCUSSION QUESTIONS

Section Objective: Describe basic accounting information necessary to accurately determine guest charges due at check-out.

Section Summary: FOMs do not need to be trained accountants, but they must have a basic understanding of accounting principles as they relate to guest charges and payments. In other words, they must be knowledgeable about front-office accounting techniques.

Most of the work done by front office personnel involves bookkeeping, the recording of financial transactions. Use of accepted rules of accounting ensures that the fundamental accounting formula (assets = liabilities + owner's equity) is always maintained. In addition, use of an appropriate system to generate accounting information helps users of the data (e.g., owners, investors, creditors, and hotel operators) to understand the hotel's financial position.

FOMs are accountable for many financial management tasks such as creating registered guest accounts, maintaining accounts used by nonregistered guests, posting debits and credits to the appropriate accounts, recording payment information, and implementing procedures to help ensure the accuracy and completeness of the front-office accounting system. Information must be recorded properly in the guest ledger or city ledger before being transferred to the hotel's general ledger. Modern PMSs make this task relatively easy for routine transactions. Nevertheless, it is important to ensure that information entered into guest folios is current and accurate. Most likely adjustment vouchers will be necessary in some instances to compensate guests for operational shortcomings, posting errors, or other problems.

When guests check out, their account balance must be reduced to zero, which can be done easily if the payment is made by cash or check. The process becomes more complicated when payment cards are used. Then the amount owed is transferred from a guest receivables account to a credit or debit card receivables account. Alternatively, payment folio balance can be transferred to a direct bill section of the city ledger or to a house account that will transfer charges to a hotel entity such as the sales and marketing department.

Discussion Questions:
1. What roles should the FOM and the hotel's controller play in establishing policies and procedures applicable to front-office accounting?

2. What are the main differences in bookkeeping procedures required to reduce to zero a folio balance when it is paid by cash or payment card (credit or debit) or when it is charged to a house account?
3. Can you think of examples of guest folio charges that might be transferred to a hotel's house account?

MANAGING GUEST CREDIT

The FOM serves an important role as a credit manager, because most guests purchase the hotel's goods and services on credit. Each hotel has policies about who may establish a line of credit and how large each guest's accounts receivable balance may become before some payment is required. Roadmap 11.2 indicates that tactics to manage guest credit will now be discussed, and these tactics are important because each affected front office staff member must be thoroughly familiar with the hotel's credit policies and procedures to enforce them equally and fairly for all guests.

At most hotels, payment cards are the most common method used to ensure payment. At check-in, the card is initiated and authorized for a predetermined amount; the guest may then charge room rental and product and services purchases up to this

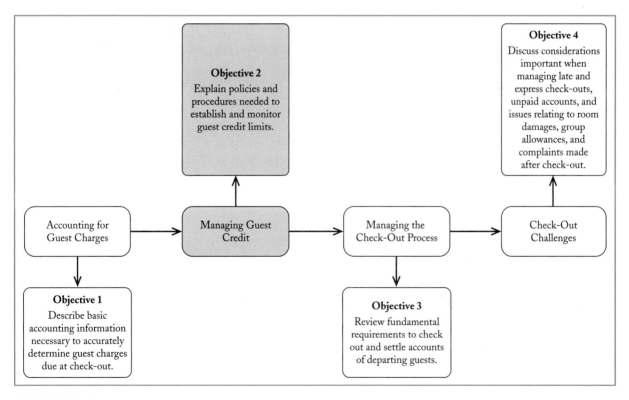

ROADMAP 11.2

1. Resubmit all authorization information to ensure that the decline is not the result of a hotel staff member's entry error.
2. To the extent possible, discuss the difficulty with the guest in a private setting.
3. Use care when explaining the problem. Avoid insulting the guest about his or her ability to pay.
4. Suggest that the guest offer an alternative card for authorization. Promptly seek authorization on the alternative card.
5. Provide a private setting and telephone access (when appropriate) for the guest to contact the payment card company.

FIGURE 11.10   Procedures to follow when guest payment cards are declined.

amount. When the process of approval of the payment card goes smoothly, little attention is paid to it. When it does not, difficulties can arise. Figure 11.10 details the procedures to be followed when a hotel's MSP declines an authorization for a payment card. When a payment card is authorized for a preestablished amount in a noninterfaced system, the front desk agent should record the authorization number in the hotel's PMS. In an interfaced system, the number is automatically recorded in the PMS.

Sometimes guests use alternative methods to establish credit. Direct bill accounts, prepaid deposits, cash prepayment of estimated charges, and deposits of cash at check-in can all establish a guest's creditworthiness and credit limit. The FOM's two most important activities in managing credit limits are to establish and to monitor credit limits.

Establishing Credit Limits

FOMs must understand the initiation and authorization process for credit and debit cards to effectively develop policies about credit limits. Credit and debit cards are not the same, and different issues can be encountered.

When a guest's payment card is initiated and authorized, a fund **block,** or hold, is established. The guest's available credit (if a credit card) or the balance in the bank account (if a debit card) is reduced by the amount of the authorization. Assume a guest checks into the Altoona Hotel for five nights. The guest's room is $100 per night and, by hotel policy, the entire amount of the stay ($500) is blocked. When determining the size of the hold, some hotels add charges for taxes and estimated incidentals such as food and beverage purchases.

FRONT OFFICE SEMANTICS

Block (funds): Amount by which a card's available credit (if a credit card) or balance (if a debit card) is reduced. Also called a *hold*.

If the guest uses the same card authorized at check-in when he or she checks out, the final charge (credit card) or final amount (debit card) will replace the block in a day or two. However, if the guest pays with a different card or with cash or a check, the card-issuing company might maintain the block for up to 15 days after check-out. The reason for this is that the company was not notified about the final payment (recall that the guest did not use the card to settle the account); therefore, the hold is continued. The hotel could contact the card issuer in such a case, but this is not practical in a larger hotel and is typically done only at the guest's request.

Credit cards are generally authorized for more than the estimated amount for a guestroom's charges to ensure that the guest's available credit will be sufficient for payment of all charges.

Blocking ensures payment. If a guest is not near the credit limit (or has sufficient funds in the bank account), blocking is not a problem. If, however, the authorized account reaches the card's limit or bank account balance, the guest may be embarrassed to have a card declined when attempting to use it elsewhere. It also can be inconvenient, especially if an emergency purchase is required, and insufficient credit or bank account funds remain after the block is established. Even worse, blocking a debit card can lead to charges for insufficient funds if the guest uses the card elsewhere while the block remains in place. FOMs must ensure that their staff understand and their guests are informed about the hotel's blocking policies and about their impact on the guests' credit and debit card accounts.

MODERN FRONT OFFICE ISSUES AND TACTICS

Debit Cards or "Where's My Cash?"

More and more Americans prefer to make purchases using debit cards rather than credit cards. In fact, some payment card companies now report that the number of their cardholders using debit cards exceeds the number using credit cards.

Debit cards now rival cash and credit cards as the preferred payment form of travelers, including those staying in hotels. Debit card advocates cite significant benefits, including security and the fact that the cards help them maintain their budgets. Unfortunately, however, an additional characteristic of the cards is the fact that blocked funds are not available for spending. In some cases, it may take 3 to 10 days for blocked funds to again become available for the cardholder's use.

Prepaid cards are also gaining in popularity. With these cards, consumers "buy" a fixed amount of money and then make purchases that are charged against the prepurchased funds.

FOMs must reexamine their preauthorization and blocking procedures for debit and prepaid card transactions. Hotels need to be protected against possible fraud while not needlessly withholding funds from guests. What would you do if you thought you had money in a debit account and then learned that a hotel's blocking procedures "took" your money (even temporarily)? The FOM or another staff member of the hotel would probably hear from you!

Monitoring Credit Limits

FOMs must monitor guest purchases and credit limits daily, because guests can quickly spend up to and exceed their authorized credit limits. Consider a guest staying one night in a $100 per night room; this guest's payment card was blocked for $200 at check-in. Unless controls are in place, the guest can spend several hundred dollars in the hotel's restaurant hosting a large group of friends and request that these charges be billed to the room. In this case, the guest will have quickly exceeded the authorized credit limit. If the guest's card is reauthorized by front office staff to include this larger amount, no difficulty ensues. Assume, however, that the guest significantly exceeds the credit limit, which is not reauthorized to increase the blocked funds. At check-out, there may be insufficient funds available to completely settle the guest's account. Therefore, FOMs must devise systems to ensure that all guest accounts are monitored daily to confirm that credit limits are not exceeded.

Tactfully dealing with guests who are approaching or exceeding their credit limit is a skill that FOMs must learn quickly. Extending additional credit is one way to avoid the situation of guests exceeding their credit limits; accepting partial (or full) payment is another way. However, FOMs are under no legal obligation to extend additional credit to guests.

When guests check in, it is reasonable to assume they will pay their bills. Hoteliers may or may not extend credit, as long as the methods for doing so do not unlawfully discriminate among guests. Assume a guest exceeds his credit limit and refuses to pay or to offer an alternative method of establishing credit. He can be removed from the hotel for nonpayment because, subject to local laws, a transient guest can be removed from a room for nonpayment of charges.

Should the hotel remove a guest who has exceeded his or her payment card limit and, therefore, is unable to pay? This is a judgment call to be made by the FOM. In cases of lost cards or travelers checks, blocked funds from other merchants, or for a variety of other circumstances, a guest's inability to pay may only be temporary. FOMs must protect the financial interests of their hotel while attempting to accommodate the guest. When it is clearly apparent, however, that the guest either will not or cannot pay and also refuses to vacate the room, it is a standard hotel industry procedure to contact local law enforcement officials to assist in the guest's removal.

Often, the mere arrival of a law enforcement official encourages the guest to pay the bill. Generally, however, police will not arrest a guest for nonpayment. Efforts to collect money must be pursued according to the hotel's policy and applicable state and local laws. (The topic of guest removal is discussed further in Chapter 13.) In most cases, the cost of collecting money due from these guests is high in terms of time and money. Therefore, it is best to avoid the situation by carefully monitoring guest credit limits before they are exceeded. A PMS can usually produce, on demand, a list of guests who are at or near their credit limits (see Chapter 12). FOMs should then make arrangements to monitor and act on these reports.

SECTION REVIEW AND DISCUSSION QUESTIONS

Section Objective: Explain policies and procedures needed to establish and monitor guest credit limits.

Section Summary: In many hotels payment cards are the most common method used to pay guest charges. The best tactic to ensure that no problems arise during check-out is to conduct proper authorization during check-in. This involves blocking the amount of the estimated guest charge. If the amount is not approved, the card's limit has probably been reached, and the front desk agent must determine creditworthiness in another way.

It is equally important to monitor a guest's credit limit during his or her stay. If the amount initially authorized is exceeded, or soon will be, by charges to the guest folio, the front desk agent will have to reauthorize the card for a larger amount. If additional credit cannot be established, it may be necessary to remove the guest from the hotel for nonpayment.

Discussion Questions:
1. What roles should the FOM and the hotel's controller play in establishing and monitoring credit limits for guests using payment cards to settle hotel charges?
2. Do procedures for establishing credit limits of a single, transient guest who wants to pay hotel charges by use of a payment card differ from procedures used to establish credit limits for a person who wants to use a payment card for group charges to a master bill?
3. A guest has checked into the hotel and has presented a credit card that has subsequently been authorized for a credit limit estimated to approximate charges. During the next several days, however, extensive food and beverage bills are charged to the guest folio. Each day the guest credit card has been reauthorized for a larger amount. Now, several days later, no additional funds can be blocked on the guest's preferred payment card. What should the FOM do?

MANAGING THE CHECK-OUT PROCESS

Managing details of the check-out process is just as important as managing check-in procedures, and as indicated in Roadmap 11.3, check-out procedures are the focus of this section of the chapter. The check-out process is made easier because a hotel's PMS can generate a **departure list** daily or as frequently as the FOM requires.

FRONT OFFICE SEMANTICS

Departure list: Report, by name and room number, of all guests scheduled to leave the hotel on a specific date.

Although each hotel's policies vary, many properties establish a check-out time of 11:00 a.m. or noon. Guests are given until that time to settle (bring to a zero balance) their accounts and depart, ask to extend their stay, or request a **late check-out.**

FRONT OFFICE SEMANTICS

Late check-out: Arrangement that allows a guest scheduled to leave the hotel to maintain access to his or her room after the standard check-out time.

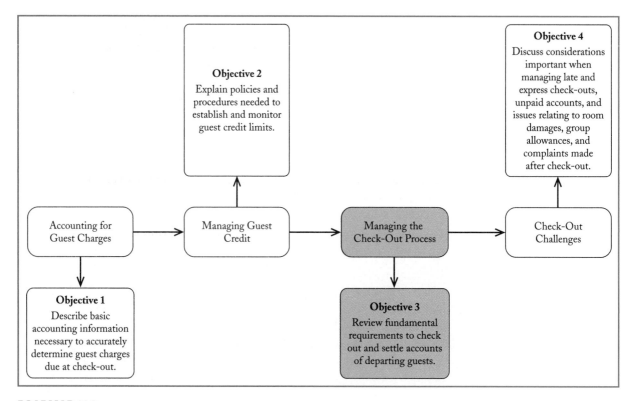

ROADMAP 11.3

Traditionally and subject to availability, a late check-out of one or several hours may be granted. Policies for when and by whom late check-outs are granted must be established by the FOM. The goal of the policies should be to accommodate registered guests while recognizing that housekeeping staff must clean late check-out rooms without incoming guests encountering long waits for their rooms.

Guest check-out is typically straightforward, especially if the guest's form of payment was confirmed at check-in, if credit monitoring has taken place regularly, and if ongoing and thorough **bucket checks** have verified guest information.

FRONT OFFICE SEMANTICS

Bucket check: Industry term for a systematic examination of guests' folios to ensure the accuracy of information. Bucket checks typically include rate verification, credit monitoring, and confirmation of departure date and guestroom assignment.

A well-designed check-out system includes completion of fundamental tasks associated with guest departure and account settlement and requires the skill and flexibility of front desk agents to deal with challenges that occur.

Check-Out Fundamentals

FOMs must establish a check-out process that meets their property's needs. These procedures typically include the activities noted in Figure 11.11. Let's consider each of these check-out fundamentals:

- *Creation of departure list.* The departure list may be generated manually or by the PMS. Because it indicates the number of check-outs likely for a specific day, it is helpful in developing work schedules for front desk agents. It also helps front office staff to ensure that all guests scheduled to check out have departed, extended their stay, or been granted a late check-out.

- *Confirmation of guest identity.* When guests check out, staff members must identify them by name and room number. "Good morning. How may I help you?" is a much better method for achieving this task than a curt, "Checking out?" Obviously, guests must be given information about *their* stay and not that of other guests. Most guest-related data are stored in the PMS, so identification by room number is generally preferred. Room number is important when common names (e.g., Mr. Jones or Ms. Smith) could result in folio confusion or when one guest is paying for multiple room charges.

- *Quality of stay inquiry.* Check-out is a time to determine if a guest's stay was a good one. If problems remain unresolved, guest satisfaction suffers, and the likelihood that the guest will return or recommend the hotel to others is diminished. In most cases, guests will comment that their visit was enjoyable. If guests encountered difficulties (excessive noise, defective plumbing, or poor service, for example), front desk agents must be responsible to take corrective action, yet be aware of their limits in making rate reductions and allowances. The FOM should empower responsible staff to make folio adjustments up to a predetermined amount, and assign a supervisor or manager to authorize adjustments in excess of that amount. Similarly, the FOM may be authorized to make adjustments subject to the authority delegated by the general manager.

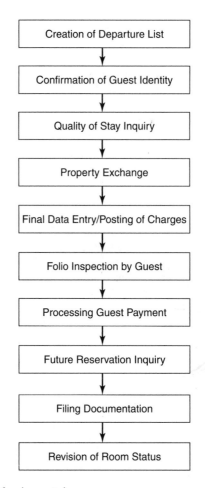

FIGURE 11.11   Check-out fundamentals.

Front desk agents must also understand their responsibility to report room-related problems to the proper department so corrective actions may be taken. Assume the front desk agent talks with the guest checking out of room 301. She states that the air-conditioning system was noisy. This information must be related to the maintenance department so that equipment can be repaired. When front desk agents are trained to seek guest comments about the guest visit, they help ensure guest satisfaction and improve the experiences of future guests.

• *Property exchange.* Some guests who are checking out may have property in the hotel's safe-deposit boxes, may have received late-arriving faxes, or in the case of a hotel without an automated voice mail system, may have telephone messages not yet received. These items should be returned or delivered to guests at check-out. Hotels that still use hard keys for guestroom door locks, which is not rec-ommended, or that have issued keys for minibars or in-room safes, should request these items from guests during check-out. Additional items such as resort or swimming pool passes that were provided to guests at check-in should also be requested.

• *Final data entry and posting of charges.* After a guest has indicated the intention of checking out, any final charges should be posted. Some FOMs instruct their staff to confirm that a guest's frequent-traveler program numbers or credits are entered at this time. Mileage points and frequent-guest program credits are important to many travelers; taking the time to ensure these are recorded for a guest increases guest satisfaction.

* *Folio inspection by guest.* Most guests review their charges before payment. The presentation of a hard (paper) copy of the folio, or the opportunity to view charges on an in-room computer or television screen, is an important feature of a good check-out system. Folio copies should be produced in a type size large enough to be read easily. The folio should be designed so that individual charges and total amount owed are easily determined. In many hotels, guests are asked to sign a copy of the folio. The signed folio serves as both the list of guest charges and the document filed to verify guest acceptance of the charges.

* *Processing guest payment.* This task can be complex and is discussed in the next section of the chapter.

* *Future reservation inquiry.* Many hotels depend on return guests for their success. For hotels serving a corporate market, opportunities to make future reservations for guests when they check out can significantly increase business. Front desk agents should ask *every* departing guest the following question: *"May I make a future reservation for you?"* When guests have had an enjoyable stay, the answer to this question is often yes if the guest requires a room in the area or at another location (if the property is part of a chain). As described in Chapter 7, the hotel's cost to book a reservation directly through the front desk is among the lowest of all distribution channels available and, therefore, results in one of the highest net ADR yields.

* *Filing documentation.* Signed copies of guest folios must be kept for two main reasons. First, they provide a **paper trail** for management.

FRONT OFFICE SEMANTICS

Paper trail: Accounting term for trackable, physical evidence that a financial transaction has occurred.

MODERN FRONT OFFICE ISSUES AND TACTICS

Do You Get What You Pay For?

D. K. Shifflet & Associates analyzed Internet reservations for hotel chains and found that guests who booked through the chain's own Web site rated their experience higher in service and value than did guests who booked through third-party merchant sites such as Expedia, Orbitz, and Travelocity.[1] This finding suggests that room assignments may be made based on the reservation distribution channel. The result, it appears, is that guests who reserve rooms through merchant model sites (see Chapter 7) receive substandard rooms and reduced service. Of course, all of a hotel's rooms should be in good condition. It should come as no surprise to third-party site operators, however, that a hotelier wants to place guests who pay the highest rate in the best rooms. Certainly this is more likely than is a practice of placing the lowest-paying guests in the best rooms. The significance to front desk agents as they check out guests is this: Anticipate lower levels of satisfaction (increased complaints) from guests assigned rooms based on reservation distribution channel.

[1]Third party websites deliver potential trouble for hotels. Press release retrieved May 2, 2004, from http://www.hotel-online.com.

Second, if a guest questions the amount he or she agreed to pay after check-out, the signed folio provides evidence that the guest understood the hotel's charges. Additional paperwork may include signatures on safe-deposit box returns, check approval codes, or **currency conversion** computations.

FRONT OFFICE SEMANTICS

Currency conversion: Process of accepting payment for charges computed in one currency but paid in the currency of another. A European traveler visiting New York City, for example, who wished to pay a bill in Euro dollars rather than in U.S. dollars, would require a *currency conversion* if the hotel provided this type of service.

MODERN FRONT OFFICE ISSUES AND TACTICS

Currency Conversion Made Easy

Experienced FOMs know that many guests and some front desk agents become confused when dealing with an unfamiliar currency. The mathematical computations required to accurately convert one form of currency to another can be complicated. Hotels located in cities that attract international travelers find that their guests often carry their own currencies and prefer to pay their bills with that currency. As a result, forms and formulas that make currency conversions easy for front desk agents and for guests to understand are extremely helpful. Fortunately, software programs that provide instant currency conversion computations are available and inexpensive. To see one of the best, consult this Web site: http://www.aquariussoft.com/pc-currency-calculator/.

---

* *Revision of room status.* After a guest has checked out, the status of the guest-room must be changed in the PMS. This generally means changing the room status from "occupied" to "vacant and dirty." If, during check-out, the guest has indicated a significant problem with the room, the room status may be changed to "out of order" until problems are corrected. In either case, changing the room status notifies the housekeeping department of the guest's departure and is the first step in the room being cleaned.

  In hotels where housekeeping staff do not have direct access to PMS data, front office personnel may notify the housekeeping department when each guest checks out. Alternatively, check-out data can be reported on a regular (hourly or half-hourly) basis to ensure that housekeepers have timely information.

When all of the 10 steps just discussed are successfully completed, the guest check-out process is finished. The process becomes routine when front desk agents are well trained in account settlement methods.

Account Settlement Methods

The proper settlement of guest accounts is critical in ensuring that the hotel receives proper payment for each guest charge. Basic methods used to settle guest accounts depend on the type of payment: cash and check, payment card, direct bill, combined settlement, and no-show billing. Let's look at each of these alternatives.

Cash and Check

Some guests prefer to pay their bills with cash, and some hotels accept checks. The collection of cash for guest account settlement is generally straightforward and simple if FOMs have developed appropriate systems and procedures. The front desk agent verifies the charges due, collects the proper amount of cash, enters the payment in the PMS, and provides a receipt and copy of the folio to the guest.

Unfortunately, some guests knowingly or unknowingly pass counterfeit bills. Suggestions about ways to detect counterfeit money are offered by the U.S. Secret Service (www.secretservice.gov), the federal agency charged with policing counterfeiters in the United States:

- A suspect note should be compared with a genuine one of the same denomination and series. Look for differences, not similarities.
- The portrait on a genuine bill appears lifelike and stands out distinctly from its background. Counterfeit currency is usually lifeless and flat.
- The sawtooth points of the Federal Reserve and Treasury seals on a genuine bill are clear, distinct, and sharp, not uneven, unclear, or broken as on counterfeit seals.
- Border lines on a genuine bill are clear and unbroken. On counterfeit bills the lines in the outer margins and scroll work are frequently blurred and indistinct.
- Genuine serial numbers have a distinctive style, are evenly spaced, and are printed in the same color ink as the Treasury seal. On a counterfeit bill, the serial numbers may be a different color or shade from the seal, and the numbers may not be uniformly spaced or aligned.
- Genuine currency paper has tiny red and blue fibers (security threads) embedded throughout. Counterfeit bills may have tiny red and blue lines printed on the paper's surface.

Equipment is available to detect counterfeit currency. Tabletop and portable (handheld) units use both ultraviolet and incandescent light technology. When bills are placed under these lights, printing and features of a genuine bill can be seen that are invisible under conventional lighting. Other equipment scans bills to detect printed text that cannot be seen without magnification. Front desk agents can use handheld currency validator pens to mark currency. If the ink disappears, the bill is good; if the bill it turns color, the bill is suspect.

Paper used for U.S. currency is almost impossible to duplicate because it really is a cloth material. Recently these changes have been introduced to U.S. currency: color-shifting inks that change color when tilted, and watermarks embedded in bills. If these bills are held up to light, these features are visible.

The Secret Service also has suggestions about what to do if a counterfeit bill is received:

- Do not return it to the passer; delay him or her if possible.
- Observe the passer's description as well as that of any companions and, if applicable, the license plate number of any vehicle.
- Contact the local police department or U.S. Secret Service field office.
- Write your initials and the date in the white border areas of the suspect note.
- Limit handling of the note; carefully place the note in an envelope or other protective covering.
- Surrender the note only to a police officer or U.S Secret Service special agent.

1. Confirm, by picture identification, that the name preprinted on the check is the same name as the person presenting the check.
2. Note the form of identification (e.g., passport or driver's license) used to verify the check writer's identity on the back of the check.
3. Ensure that the check
   - is written out to the hotel,
   - has the correct date,
   - is written for the correct amount,
   - has an identical numerical and written dollar amount,
   - includes the address of the bank issuing the check, and
   - is signed by the same person whose name is preprinted on the check.
4. Require that all checks include a telephone number of the check writer.
5. Develop specific policies for the acceptance of personal checks issued by out-of-town banks because of difficulty of collection.
6. Establish a maximum amount for which a check can be written without preauthorization from the check-issuing bank.
7. Use a check verification service.
8. Require the front office agent to initial the check to verify that all required procedures have been followed.
9. Deposit all checks on a daily basis.
10. If checks are returned for nonsufficient funds and reasonable collection efforts are ineffective, enlist the help of local law enforcement agencies.

FIGURE 11.12   Procedures for minimizing fraud involving personal checks.

The potential for check fraud occurs when a hotel accepts personal checks. Although it may be impossible to prevent all check fraud, Figure 11.12 lists actions to minimize the acceptance of a worthless check. In many cases of check fraud, the criminal has committed identity theft and is forging a check using the victim's ID. Modern prevention of check fraud usually focuses on techniques to reduce the criminal's ability to falsify or provide the victim's personal information, including Social Security or driver's license numbers. Although such fraud is difficult to detect, use of a **check verification service** or **check guarantee service** can help protect a hotel.

FRONT OFFICE SEMANTICS

Check verification service: Process of matching check writers with databases of acceptable and unacceptable accounts to minimize the acceptance of bad checks.

Check guarantee service: Service that ensures checks accepted by a merchant (e.g., hotel) that follows specific procedures will be collectible.

A check verification service screens checks and check writers against databases of open and closed checking accounts and writers of bad checks. When a guest presents a personal check, the front desk agent typically uses a POS terminal (or real-time Internet process) to check the service provider's databases. Generally, if the guest has a history of writing bad checks or has closed the account, the transaction will be declined. If not, the check is approved. Approval does not ensure that the hotel will collect on the check, but a check guarantee service ensures collection. The service provider charges the hotel a fee on all checks accepted (typically about 2 percent of the check amount) and agrees to pay for all returned checks if the hotel has followed the service provider's methods and procedures for personal check acceptance.

Payment Card

The process used to settle folios and accounts of guests using payment cards was described earlier in this chapter. From an accounting perspective, a guest's use of a payment card for account settlement results in a transfer of debt from the guest to the card company. The amount owed to the hotel is moved from the guest ledger to an accounts receivable section of the city ledger to bring the guest's account balance to zero. The card user (guest) promises to pay the card company, and the card company promises to pay the hotel.

In most cases, this transfer of responsibility is routine. Difficulties can arise, however, when departing guests who had payment card funds blocked for payment at check-out refuse to sign their final bill. Assume that Mr. Rios checked into the Altoona Hotel for two nights. The front desk agent authorized his American Express card for use as payment at check-out and, at check-in, Mr. Rios signed his registration card. The next morning, however, Mr. Rios wants to check out because his room's air conditioner was too noisy. When he phoned the front desk at midnight to complain, he says he was told there was no one available to fix the unit, but he could move to another room. Mr. Rios did not want to change rooms at that late hour, and now he does not want to stay because of the inadequate level of service. He refuses to sign his bill stating that, because of the noisy unit, he could not rest and should not have to pay for the room.

In this situation, and others involving guest complaints, it would be ideal if the guest could be accommodated in a way that is fair to the guest and to the hotel. If this is not possible, and the guest refuses to sign the folio statement, the guest's card can still be charged based on the signature secured at check-in. The guest must then file a protest with the payment card company stating why the forced payment was unjust.

Normally the payment card company will support the hotel in these disputes *if* the hotel followed the payment card company's established card-handling policies and procedures. Therefore, FOMs should be very familiar with the processing procedures required by each payment card company with which the hotel does business.

Direct Bill

Guest charges can be settled by transferring them from the guest ledger to a direct bill account in the accounts receivable portion of the city ledger. This transfer should be done only if the hotel's accounting manager (i.e., controller) has preapproved an application for a direct bill account (see Chapter 9). Unlike a cash sale, a direct bill settlement will not result in an immediate deposit of funds in a hotel's bank. As shown in Figure 11.13, a direct bill creates an accounts receivable that must be collected before funds can be deposited. The responsibility to invoice and collect a direct billing lies with the hotel's credit manager. To complete a direct billing at check-out, guests must sign their folios approving the posted charges. Only guests authorized to make charges to a direct bill account should be allowed to do, and their names will be listed on the application for a direct bill account.

MODERN FRONT OFFICE ISSUES AND TACTICS

Payment Card Security

Safe handling of payment card information is important to guests and to the hotels where they stay. The financial and emotional damage to a guest whose confidential payment card information is unlawfully given by a hotel employee to an unauthorized user is significant. Additionally, if the situation involves negligence, a hotel can be held responsible for damages that result from an employee's theft or sharing of confidential information.

To avoid potential liability and guest inconvenience, payment card companies advise FOMs to take these steps:

- Store all permanent records related to guests' payment cards in an area inaccessible to unauthorized personnel.
- *Never* store the three-digit number printed on the signature panel of a MasterCard, Visa, Discover, or Diners Club card or the four-digit code printed on the front of an American Express card.
- Store only critical information such as guest name, account number, and expiration date in the accounting system.
- Destroy (shred or delete) account records when they are no longer needed for the hotel's database.

For additional and specific information about guest payment card security procedures, FOMs should consult with their merchant service provider and with payment card companies.

Combined Settlement

In some cases, a guest's account is settled by a combination of accounting transactions. Consider Marc Gitmore, the keynote speaker for a convention at the Altoona Hotel. The host arranged for his room and taxes to be charged to the master bill (see Chapter 9). At check-in, Mr. Gitmore presented his American Express card to establish credit for any personal incidentals he might charge to the room. At checkout, his folio shows charges for two in-room movies. Based on the arrangements with the convention host, these charges must be paid by Mr. Gitmore. He states that

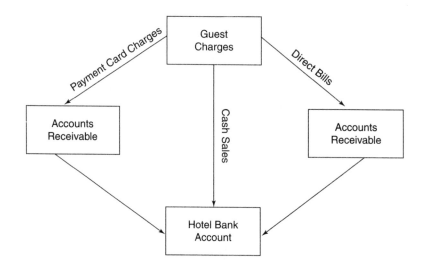

FIGURE 11.13 Guest settlement options.

two movie purchases were made because the picture quality on the first movie was unacceptable. He had called the front desk to request that someone adjust the television, a maintenance employee corrected the situation, and he repurchased the same movie. The front desk agent checks the **maintenance log** at the front desk, which confirms Mr. Gitmore's description of events. So the first movie charge is removed from Mr. Gitmore's bill.

FRONT OFFICE SEMANTICS

Maintenance log: Written record of guest-initiated maintenance repair or service requests received by the front desk and monitored to ensure their prompt completion.

In this case, the following combination of actions would be used to settle Mr. Gitmore's bill:

Item	Action
1. Room and tax charges	Transferred to a direct bill account to be settled on the group's departure
2. Movie charge 1	Adjusted by a transfer to a designated house account
3. Movie charge 2	Billed to guest's American Express payment card

Mr. Gitmore could have paid his movie charge with cash rather than with his American Express card, or he could have paid by a combination of cash and payment card. Regardless, the purpose of account settlement is to bring the amount due in the guest's folio to a zero balance even when a combination of financial transactions is required to do so.

No-Show Billing

No-show billings are special cases of account settlement. Technically they involve "guests" who have never checked in and cannot, therefore, be checked out. In some hotels, FOMs actually check no-shows into rooms and then immediately or, during the night audit, settle the guest accounts.

Regardless of how no-shows are recorded, guests with guaranteed reservations who do not check in on their arrival date are included in a hotel's total count of guest reservations. Each hotel has a no-show billing policy, and the FOM must enforce it. Usually this involves charging no-show guests a one night's room charge if the charge is justified. Each potential no-show charge should be evaluated to determine if the charge should be assessed. Sometimes the decision is not clear-cut. Consider the following no-shows with guaranteed reservations researched by the Altoona Hotel's FOM after a busy night:

- Jerry Marshall arrived one day early. As he was already in the hotel, he did not cancel his original reservation. The PMS listed Mr. Marshall as a no-show the following night.
- Thomas Ryan arrived at the hotel claiming he had a reservation, but he had no confirmation number. No reservation was found under his name. The front desk agent checked him in as a walk-in. That evening, the PMS identified the reservation of "Ryan Thomas" as a no-show.

- Doris Gaston had guaranteed her reservation and said she would be arriving very late. In fact, her flight was delayed and rerouted, and she could not arrive at the hotel at all. She was not permitted to use her cell phone while in the air, so she could not notify the hotel. The PMS identifies her reservation as a billable no-show. Doris called to cancel her previous night's reservation the next morning at 9:00 a.m. Her company is the hotel's largest corporate client.

- For the past 10 years, the Scotts family of Tennessee has held its annual reunion at the Altoona. This year, 18 rooms were guaranteed with Mr. Scotts' credit card. When the Scotts checked in, there were 17 (not 18) different parties. When asked about the 18th room, Mr. Scotts indicated that a death in the family reduced their need to 17 rooms. He apologized for not contacting the hotel earlier. That night, the PMS identifies one room for Mr. Scotts as a no-show.

As you can see, the decision to bill a no-show guest or a guest making a late reservation cancellation must be made only after carefully considering the facts. FOMs know that, of all charges posted to a guest's folio, the ones most frequently subject to a chargeback challenge relate to no-shows. If a no-show billing is undertaken, sending the guest a letter similar to the one shown in Figure 11.14 is recommended.

Altoona Hotel

Guest Name
Guest Address

Dear _____,

We missed serving you! We held a room at our hotel for you on *(date)* and we're sorry that you did not arrive as planned.

Our records show you made your reservation on _____. We confirmed the reservation by issuing confirmation number _____. The room was guaranteed with a *(card name)* payment card with the last four digits of _____.

Since, as we promised, we held your room all night, and because we do not have a record of your reservation being canceled, we have charged the payment card used to reserve your room for the amount of one night's room rate. If we have overlooked any relevant information or you have a cancellation number, please contact me.

We are sorry you were unable to stay with us. We hope that when your travels again bring you to our area, we will have another opportunity to serve you.

Best Regards,

(Signature)

(Printed name)
Front Office Manager *(Telephone number and e-mail address)*

FIGURE 11.14   No-show billing letter.

SECTION REVIEW AND DISCUSSION QUESTIONS

Section Objective: Review fundamental requirements to check out and settle accounts of departing guests.

Section Summary: Several processes must be completed accurately to best ensure smooth-flowing check-out and account settlement processes: creation of a departure list, confirmation of guest identity, inquiry about the quality of the guest stay and property exchange (if necessary). Additional activities include final data entry and posting of charges, folio inspection by guest, processing the guest payment, and a question about the guest's interest in a future reservation. After the guest departs, documentation must be completed, and the status of the room must be revised in the hotel's PMS and housekeeping records.

Guests may settle their folio at time of check-out by paying with cash or check, payment card, direct bill, or a combined settlement using one or more of these methods. FOMs must have procedures in place to address no-show billings. Proper management of each of these payment methods helps ensure that the hotel will receive all payments due from guests.

Discussion Questions:
1. How would you, as an FOM, determine the amount that a front desk agent would be allowed to deduct from a guest folio for problems alleged by the guest at time of check-out?
2. The chapter presents examples of situations that may suggest a need to make an adjustment to a guest folio to be fair to the affected guest. Can you think of situations that might prompt an adjustment? What allegations made by guests might be considered unreasonable and not likely yield a folio adjustment?
3. Comment on the following statement: When a no-show is billed for a room charge because he or she had a guaranteed reservation, the hotel will make a larger profit on the room sale because no housekeeping labor, operating expenses, utility charges, or other costs will be incurred. Therefore, it is to the hotel's advantage to have as many no-show guests as possible.

CHECK-OUT CHALLENGES

The check-out process is generally uncomplicated. However, as suggested in Roadmap 11.4, there are exceptions that FOMs and their staff must be prepared to address. Although they cannot anticipate every unusual check-out situation, staff must be able to manage the following variations: late check-out charges, express check-outs, unpaid accounts, and other challenges involving individual guests and groups.

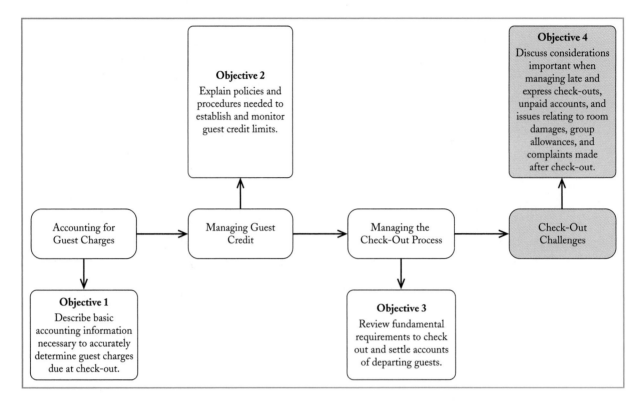

ROADMAP 11.4

Late Check-Out Charges

Check-out time is established by hotel policy, and guests can be informed about the time in a number of ways: information printed on registration cards signed at check-in, statements made by front office staff to guests during check-in, and printed notices in guestrooms. When guests know the check-out time and when the time is reasonable, most guests will vacate their room accordingly. In some cases, guests may request and be granted a check-out extension (late check-out).

Sometimes, guests simply do not vacate their room by the stated check-out time. If the delay is a matter of minutes, there is usually no problem. However, if guests delay departure for an extended period of time, significant difficulties can occur. Consider the Alexanders and the Jacksons. The Alexanders had reserved the bridal suite at the Altoona Hotel for Friday night—the night their wedding reception was held at the hotel. The wedding festivities ended late on Friday. Now it is noon (the Altoona's established check-out time) on Saturday; the Alexanders have not checked out, and they have not requested a late check-out. The hotel's normal check-in time for arriving guests is 3:00 p.m. The Jacksons have the bridal suite reserved for Saturday night and their wedding reception is also being held at the hotel. The Altoona has only one bridal suite, so housekeeping personnel will have difficulty cleaning the suite in time for the Jacksons' 3:00 p.m. check-in if the suite is not vacated in a timely manner.

Hotels do not arbitrarily establish check-out times. Rather, times are set to ensure that housekeepers have sufficient time to clean rooms for arriving guests. Check-out extensions may be granted. However, in some instances guests who check out several hours beyond the established check-out time will incur a late check-out charge, which may range from a few dollars to another full night's room charge depending on the check-out time. If possible, guests should be informed about these charges before they are posted to the folio. Otherwise, some guests will protest the charges at check-out.

Front office staff must carefully monitor departure lists to ensure that, at the hotel's check-out time, guests have (1) checked-out of the hotel, (2) extended their stay, (3) been granted a late check-out, or (4) been reminded of the check-out time and informed about the hotel's late check-out charges. If a guest has not checked out by the posted time, has not requested a late check-out, and cannot be reached by phoning the room, arrangements should be made to physically visit the room. Hotel personnel can then determine if the guest has left or has encountered a difficulty such as illness or other medical problem. If a guest overstays the hotel's check-out time by a significant amount of time (which may vary by room type, special events, or the hotel's anticipated occupancy level), a late check-out charge should be posted to the guest's folio.

Express Check-Out

Advances in technology have allowed hotels to offer their guests a variety of **express check-out** options.

FRONT OFFICE SEMANTICS

Express check-out: Any number of methods of guest-initiated check-out that do not require guests to be physically present at the hotel's front desk for folio payment.

Express check-out systems typically permit guests to review their folios before checking out. Folios may be delivered to guestrooms early on the check-out morning, or guests may use check-out kiosks or view real-time copies of folios on in-room television channels or by Internet connection. In all cases, the systems allow guests to review their bills and check out of the hotel without standing in line at the front desk.

Express check-out systems are likely to be interfaced with the PMS. If so, front office staff will know about a guest's check-out intentions. In contrast, when folios are delivered to a guest's room or when other noninterfaced options for express check-out are used, front office personnel may not be aware that the guest has checked out until a housekeeper or other employee visits the room and reports that it is vacant. If a guest uses a noninterfaced express check-out option and the guest's credit was established with a payment card, the guest's check-in signature verifies the acceptance of final charges. Front office staff should always settle a guest's account immediately on discovery that an express check-out option was used.

Unpaid Accounts

Despite the best efforts of FOMs and their staff, guests may leave a hotel without settling their accounts. In some cases, this may simply be an oversight caused by a guest in a hurry. If the guest has established credit by payment card or direct bill account, standard industry procedure is to settle the guest's account using his or her **SOF (signature on file).**

FRONT OFFICE SEMANTICS

SOF (signature on file): Signature obtained from a guest at check-in. If a guest has been properly checked in, the SOF will be on the guest's registration card.

Sometimes guests leave the hotel unwilling or unable to pay their charge. A previous section of the chapter described the procedures required to settle the accounts of guests using payment cards who refuse to sign their final bills. Occasionally, a guest's payment card cannot be charged the total amount owed because the card is not authorized for the full amount due. FOMs must ensure that their guests maintain adequate creditworthiness. Credit limits may be exceeded because of errors in credit management, a guest overstaying, or significant purchases made by the guest. If these situations are not addressed promptly, the result may be unpaid and, perhaps, even uncollectable charges on the folio. Doubtful accounts can also occur when hotels allow guests to pay with cash; no creditworthiness has been established beyond the cash received at check-in. If these guests overstay or make purchases beyond the funds already paid, collection of money owed may be difficult.

FOMs who cannot use standard methods of collecting money owed by guests who cannot or will not pay, and whose job responsibilities make them accountable for settlement of these accounts have several options:

- *Settle the account to a direct bill.* Even though the guest may not have previously established a direct bill account, the postdeparture creation of and charge to a direct bill account in the city ledger will zero out the guest's account. The hotel's normal efforts in direct bill collection could then be used to secure payment.

- *Settle the account to doubtful accounts.* When an FOM believes that the hotel is not likely to collect charges owed, identifying the debt as one whose collection is doubtful will move the balance from the guest ledger to the doubtful accounts section of the city ledger. Collection efforts may still be made on guest charges transferred to a doubtful account. However, most often these accounts are designated as doubtful because the departed guest's address or other contact information is missing, is in error, or is fraudulent. As a result, the collection rate on these accounts is typically very low.

- *Settle the account with an adjustment voucher.* Especially when the amounts owed to the hotel are relatively small, some FOMs use an adjustment voucher to immediately **write off** unpaid accounts.

FRONT OFFICE SEMANTICS

Write off: Act of declaring a legitimate debt uncollectible. A write-off can also be the result of a decision that the amount owed is too small to justify significant collection efforts. Used as in, "Tom, we have a $1 late charge from the gift shop that should have been posted to room 231. The couple in that room has already checked out, so fill out a voucher and we'll just *write off* the $1.

An allowance or adjustment voucher records the reversal of a guest's charges. This option might be used, for example, when a guest departs with unposted movie charges or minor food and beverage purchases because the POS used to record these charges is not interfaced with the PMS. When the cost of debt collection exceeds the cost of the allowance, many FOMs recognize the wisdom of not spending a large number of dollars trying to collect a small number of pennies!

All unpaid guest accounts must be settled. Recall that only currently registered guests can have balances due on the guest ledger. All other accounts must be reversed or transferred to one or more parts of the hotel's city ledger. Experienced FOMs realize the difficulties associated with collecting on unpaid accounts, and they strictly enforce preventive policies such as obtaining credit information and complete addresses and guest signatures at check-in. In addition, they manage guest credit accounts carefully (see Chapter 12) to minimize the chances that a guest's debt will ultimately become uncollectible.

Other Check-Out Challenges

Challenges in three areas demand the FOM's special efforts to develop property-specific policies and procedures: assessments of room damage, strategies for group allowances, and adjustments for complaints made after check-out.

Room Damage Assessments

Hotel rooms and their furnishings do not last forever, and hoteliers expect the normal wear and tear that comes from renting rooms. Most guests do not intentionally damage their rooms, but some do. Guest theft may exceed routine items like soap, towels, and pillows and may involve artwork, furniture, bedding, or televisions. Theft of in-room items or excessive room damage is not generally discovered until the guest has checked out. The resulting dilemma is twofold:

- Should the guest be charged?
- If so, how can payment be collected?

Each case of significant theft or room damage must be assessed individually. However, FOMs should follow written procedures approved by the general manager to ensure proper accounting for the transaction when they believe that charging a departed guest is appropriate.

Collecting money from cash-paying guests who have departed will be difficult or impossible. Guests who established credit by payment card or direct bill account, however, may have their accounts charged. For example, when Mr. and Mrs. Clark checked into the Altoona Hotel, they called the front desk to request a portable crib. The request was recorded in the maintenance log, and a crib was delivered to their room. The next morning, after they had checked out and paid by credit card, the crib was missing. Hotel managers must decide if the crib's value ($200) justifies collection efforts if they believe the crib was taken by the guests. This decision must be made very carefully. If the hotel wants to recover the cost of the crib, the Clarks' credit card could be authorized and charged an additional $200. On receiving their credit card statement, the Clarks will likely contact the hotel, dispute the charge, and initiate a chargeback request with their credit card company. When they do, the hotel will need proper backup for its actions.

Hotels must be prepared for potential collection disputes. For example, employees may take color photos when charges are to be assessed for excessive room damage. Another backup tactic is to keep signed employee statements describing the room damage or theft. A clearly identifiable paper trail should document the damage assessment and collection steps that were taken. In cases of severe damage or significant theft, police reports supplied by local law enforcement may be part of the backup file.

Group Allowances Strategies

Just as individual guests may experience difficulties that affect check-out, members of groups may encounter problems, and FOMs must carefully instruct staff about how to resolve them. Consider the Early Birds, a social club whose senior citizen members gather twice annually for bird-watching. They travel as a group (20 couples) in a chartered bus. The group arrived at the Altoona Hotel on Saturday afternoon at 3:00 p.m. (the normal check-in time) for a one night stay. Because the group had requested rooms to be assigned close together, the rooms were not ready. Some group members were assigned their rooms about 4:00 p.m., but it was nearly 6:00 p.m. before all group members were accommodated.

The next morning, most of the group checked out without incident. Mr. and Mrs. Lundquist, however, complained about the inconvenience of their late check-in (around 5:45 p.m.). To appease them and to continue checking out additional guests, the front desk agent agreed to reduce their room rate from $125 per night to $75. The front desk agent recorded the allowance, Mr. and Mrs. Lundquist expressed their satisfaction, and their check-out was completed. Ten minutes later, the Larsons, members of the Early Birds who had checked out before the Lundquists, approached the front desk and stated that they just finished having coffee with their friends. They politely requested that they be given the "Lundquist rate" because they were also inconvenienced by their late check-in (at 5:15 p.m.). Not surprisingly, the lobby was soon filled with 20 Early Bird couples, including some who had already checked out and some of whom had not. If each couple, regardless of check-in time, was granted the rate reduction, the lost revenue would be $1,000 (20 couples with a $50 discount).

This example is not presented to question whether rate reductions are proper to compensate guests who must wait for their rooms. Rather, the example illustrates what can happen when, even with the best intentions, an allowance is made for one group member without considering its impact on the entire group. FOMs must ensure that staff members follow predetermined and written procedures for group room allowances and adjustments during the group's stay and at check-out.

Adjustments for Complaints Made After Check-Out

Some guests who are dissatisfied with their lodging experience do not inform the hotel about their problems until after departure. Guests may wish to avoid what they perceive as face-to-face conflict with a front desk agent. Others may believe that a written complaint is a more powerful statement of dissatisfaction. In other cases, guests who were reasonably satisfied when they checked out will, after further consideration, conclude that they had a legitimate complaint and decide to inform the hotel. FOMs should deal with such guests in the same professional and guest service-oriented manner that they would use if the guests were still registered.

From an accounting perspective, guests who complain after check-out represent special cases. Consider Marion Pennycuff, a business traveler and frequent guest who stayed at the Altoona Hotel on a Tuesday night. When he departed the next morning, he waited for 10 minutes to check out because the front desk agent was involved in a personal telephone call. Marion waited until the call was finished, checked out, and paid the bill with his credit card. Later, Marion wrote the FOM (i.e., Allisha Miller) complaining that he missed his airline flight because it took so long to check out. If the FOM believes that this guest deserves a room rate adjustment, she should follow preestablished procedures for recording the refund.

To avoid complaints after check-out, guests should be asked to review their charges before they leave the property.

In this example, the guest has checked out, so the folio has been settled. Any credits or allowances made now will require adjustment to a segment of the city ledger (in this example, a credit card receivable account) or to the general ledger, and to the PMS to accurately record the rate actually paid, the resulting new daily ADR, and other room statistics that are affected. FOMs and their controllers should jointly establish the procedures to properly record all adjustments made after check-out to ensure that they are accounted for correctly.

From the Front Office: Front-Line Interview

Aaron Ide
Director of Front Office
Hilton New York (2,000 rooms)
New York, NY

Guests in a Large-Volume Hotel Need Attention Too!

Aaron received an undergraduate degree in hospitality business in 1998 but has worked in the industry since he was 15 years old. He spent six years at the Waldorf-Astoria in a variety of rooms division management positions and left that hotel as the front office manager. Currently, Aaron is the director of front office operations at the Hilton in New York City. His responsibilities include front office, guest service hotline, prearrivals, executive level, front services, concierge, and theater and tour desks.

1. **What are the most important responsibilities in your present position?**
   Motivating others and effectively managing and creating change within the work environment. Keeping the staff "nonrobotic" and flexible to the ever-changing needs of the hotel and its guests.

2. **What are the biggest challenges that you confront in your day-to-day work and in the long-term operation of your property's front office?**
   The biggest challenge on a day-to-day basis is the sheer volume of business that we do. We are a large operation and struggle each day to not only be efficient, but to spend enough time with our guests to give them the same warm feeling that they would have in many smaller properties. The long-term challenge continues to be the need for us to alter our approach in an ever-changing environment. The expectations of our guests are constantly changing and, to be competitive, we must always stay ahead of this. Special challenges are meeting their service and technology expectations.

3. **What is your most unforgettable front office moment?**
   September 11, 2001. A crazy time in New York City and an unbelievable show of teamwork by my staff.

4. **What advice do you have for those studying about or considering a career in front office or hotel management?**
   Obtain work experience. When beginning your job search, decide first which company is the best fit for you. Start with a company that has a comprehensive training program that will best fit your needs. Be patient; success takes time, and don't be afraid to work hard!

SECTION REVIEW AND DISCUSSION QUESTIONS

Section Objective: Discuss considerations important when managing late and express check-outs, unpaid accounts, and issues relating to room damages, group allowances, and complaints made after check-out.

Section Summary: FOMs and their staff must consistently and correctly manage common check-out challenges. Policies and procedures for late check-out times and charges must be in place. Front office staff must consider the guest occupying the room and those who are to follow, as well as the housekeeping staff who must prepare the room for the next occupants.

Modern technology allows guests to check out of their room without contacting a front desk agent. This can be done by kiosk, in-room television, Internet connection, or by review of a folio brought to the room during the night preceding check-out. Some guests may leave the hotel without settling their account. To avoid problems, the creditworthiness of guests should be determined during check-in. If payment cards are properly authorized during check-in and, if credit limits are monitored during guest stay, payment cards can be charged for the amount due even if the guests do not sign their final bill. FOMs have several other options to deal with an unpaid account. They can settle the account to a direct bill, to a doubtful account, or with an adjustment voucher to write off the account.

FOMs must implement policies and procedures to address room damage assessments, group allowances strategies, and complaints made after check-out. The best procedures are those that compensate guests without taking advantage of the property.

Discussion Questions:

1. Harvey Jones is a frequent guest with a problem. His flight, the last of the day, has been canceled and he is phoning the hotel about an hour after his late check-out. He wants to return for another night and then catch an early morning flight. The hotel, however, is overbooked, and the room rate has gone up by $40 because of expected high occupancy. What should the front desk agent do?

2. A guest who is authorized to sign a master bill for a group is upset with several minor issues and desires a significant discount on the group's bill. You are the FOM. What factors would be important as group allowances are considered?

3. Ms. Barrick has been at the hotel two nights and was checked in with a payment card that was correctly authorized. On the second night of her stay, she entertained 15 business associates and charged the expenses to her room. It is now about midnight, and she wants to check out because of an emergency at home. Her payment card cannot be authorized for the amount due, and she says she has no other card or sufficient cash to pay the bill. Ms. Barrick has offered a personal check, but it was declined by the check guarantee service used by the hotel. What should the FOM who is the manager on duty do?

The FOM in Action: A Solution

What can FOMs do to ensure that there are minimal disputes about the payment of direct bill accounts? The necessary activities vary based on the number of open direct bill accounts that the hotel has. In a large property that primarily serves corporate clients, the guests whose charges will be settled by direct bill can represent more than 50 percent of the hotel's total rooms revenue. In a smaller hotel serving the leisure market, direct bills may be only occasional. In both cases, however, FOMs must be concerned about who is authorized to charge and what can be charged.

In the example of the Lenox Hotel, the dispute has not arisen based on *who* has charged but rather on *what* that individual has charged. The company responsible for the direct bill, Greenfield Financial,

has disputed a portion of it, and it has a legitimate complaint. Trisha, the FOM, has failed to monitor the property's credit policy properly, and the result is inappropriate charges to the corporate account.

If the FOM requires that a payment card be presented by all guests at check-in, it may be relatively easy to charge the card presented by Mr. Keefer, the guest with nonauthorized direct bill charges. The signature he provided at check-in will authorize payment for his incidentals. If no payment card was required, it may be possible to collect by contacting Mr. Keefer directly either at the address recorded on his registration card or through his employer.

The responsibility to invoice for and collect on direct billing lies with the hotel's credit manager.

However, the responsibility to ensure that specific direct bill charges are valid rests primarily with FOMs and their staff. When the number of direct bill accounts is small enough that each front desk agent knows the restrictions on each account, few problems arise. Likewise, when the hotel's PMS can identify and differentiate between direct bill accounts that only permit charges for room and tax and accounts that permit incidentals and other expenses, then the problem experienced at the Lenox Hotel can be avoided. Even if neither of these options is available, FOMs must ensure that guests checking in under a direct bill account are subject to applicable credit policies to protect the party responsible for the direct bill and the hotel. If proper credit policies are not enforced, direct bill chargebacks and write-offs can be extensive and costly. Too many of them can result in some pointed discussions between the FOM and the general manager!

FRONT OFFICE SEMANTICS LIST

Accounting
Front-office accounting system
Back-office accounting
Certified public accountant (CPA)
Controller
Generally accepted accounting principles (GAAPs)
Bookkeeping
Asset
Liability
Owner's equity
Uniform System of Accounts for the Lodging Industry (USALI)

Account
Accounts receivable (A/R)
Accounts payable (A/P)
Retained earnings
Double entry accounting
Debit accounting
Credit accounting
Guest ledger
City ledger
General ledger
Suppressed rate
Settlement (account)
House account
Address verification service (AVS)

Chargeback
Block (funds)
Departure list
Late check-out
Bucket check
Paper trail
Currency conversion
Check verification service
Check guarantee service
Maintenance log
Express check-out
SOF (signature on file)
Write off

FRONT OFFICE AND THE INTERNET

The following Web sites relate to the content of this chapter:

Web address	Subject area
www.qas.com	Payment card address verification service
www.paybycheck.com	Check address verification service
www.globaladdress.net	International address verification service
www.nacha.org	National Automated Clearing House Association rules and information about electronic funds transfer
www.telecheck.com	Check verification service
www.npsglobal.com	Check verification service
www.mastercard.com	Rules regarding chargeback procedures
www.visa.com	Rules regarding chargeback procedures
www.discovercard.com	Rules regarding chargeback procedures
www.americanexpress.com	Rules regarding chargeback procedures
www.dinersclub.com	Rules regarding chargeback procedures

REAL-WORLD ACTIVITIES

1. Explain the difference between front-office accounting and back-office accounting. What is the FOM's role in planning policies and procedures applicable to both? What is the role of the controller? What types of information about front-office accounting should be taught to front desk agents as part of their initial training program?

2. The chapter describes a wide range of bookkeeping responsibilities of the front office. Give some examples of accounting procedures that must be undertaken by front office personnel.

3. Assume that a guest with a guaranteed reservation is a no-show. Develop a complete list of PMS data and statistics that will be affected if the no-show guest is charged for the room night. What data are affected by a no-show guest who is not charged for the room night?

4. A housekeeper discovers significant damage to a room's furniture and furnishings after a guest has checked out. In accord with the hotel's procedures, the guest's credit card is charged several thousand dollars for the damage. The guest calls the hotel's general manager and profusely denies any knowledge about the damage. What should the general manager do? What role, if any, should the FOM have in the process of deciding what to do? Assume that the total amount of damages could not be authorized on the guest's payment card. What should the general manager and FOM do in this instance?

5. A business traveler stays at the hotel at least once weekly and, because of this frequency, has received a very competitive rate. On almost every stay, the guest complains at time of check-out about a relatively minor problem and requests an adjustment to the bill. What, if anything, should the FOM do?

12

Night Audit and Report Management

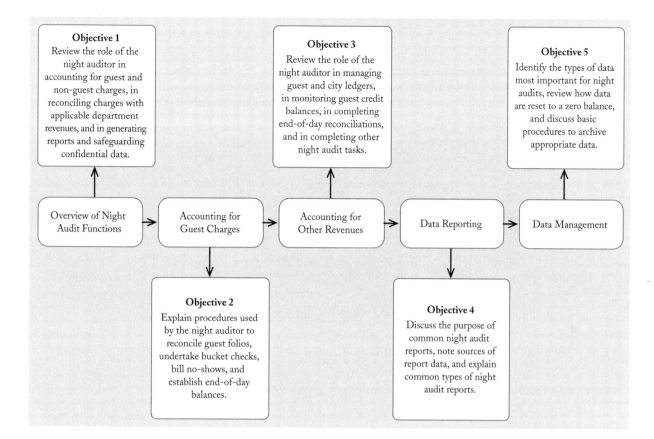

Objective 1
Review the role of the night auditor in accounting for guest and non-guest charges, in reconciling charges with applicable department revenues, and in generating reports and safeguarding confidential data.

Objective 3
Review the role of the night auditor in managing guest and city ledgers, in monitoring guest credit balances, in completing end-of-day reconciliations, and in completing other night audit tasks.

Objective 5
Identify the types of data most important for night audits, review how data are reset to a zero balance, and discuss basic procedures to archive appropriate data.

Overview of Night Audit Functions → Accounting for Guest Charges → Accounting for Other Revenues → Data Reporting → Data Management

Objective 2
Explain procedures used by the night auditor to reconcile guest folios, undertake bucket checks, bill no-shows, and establish end-of-day balances.

Objective 4
Discuss the purpose of common night audit reports, note sources of report data, and explain common types of night audit reports.

CHAPTER ROADMAP

Chapter Preview

The number of financial transactions that occur every day in a hotel can be substantial. In addition, the amount of nonfinancial information produced daily can be sizable, for example, when guests make reservations and arrive or depart. Because of the complexity of these financial and operational records, and because of the potential for errors when posting charges or recording data, hoteliers need to review and summarize information daily. This review process is called the *night audit*. Traditionally, the process occurs during the night when activity in most hotels is slowest and, therefore, when the reviewer (night auditor) experiences the fewest interruptions.

This chapter focuses on the major functions of the night audit. These include a thorough review and summary of the day's financial transactions made by in-house guests and others who used the hotel's services. Financial records are reviewed for accuracy and completeness. In the process, important information is summarized and distributed to those who need it.

Additional night audit functions include the summarization, distribution, and safe storage of nonfinancial operating reports and data that can help the FOM and other hotel managers. Most hotels now have automated systems for completing the night audit. When properly understood, designed, and managed, the night audit can be carried out quickly and efficiently.

Understanding the night audit and related data-reporting functions is important to FOMs, because in many small to mid-size hotels, the FOM directly supervises the individual responsible for it. In larger hotels, the night audit may be the responsibility of the controller. Even then, however, the daily activities of the front office make up a substantial portion of the work reviewed during the audit. As a result, FOMs must recognize the importance of their own efforts to ensure the completion of a successful night audit.

The FOM in Action: The Challenge

Felicia Henderson was the newly appointed FOM of the 105-room Harley Hills Hotel and Suites. She had studied hospitality management in college, worked hard, and graduated at the top of her class. Of course, she was delighted with her new job. She had worked as a front desk agent in high school and was a night auditor during college. She was talented, service oriented, and seldom made errors. Business was good, and the management team assembled by the general manager was excellent. Young, aggressive, and talented, the hotel's staff achieved sales levels and RevPar numbers that made the hotel's ownership happy. The meeting Felicia was now having with the hotel's general manager, however, was not making anyone happy.

"I just can't believe it!" said Gil, the hotel's general manager as he reviewed the report.

"Believe it," replied Felicia.

It was 9:30 a.m. on Monday, and Felicia had printed a reservation activity report for the previous 24 hours. Felicia discovered that Karl, a part-time night auditor, had sold 85 of the hotel's 105 rooms to one guest on a Saturday night date nine months in the future. The telephone call had come in about 11:30 p.m. and, because the guest wanted to buy so many rooms, Karl had offered a 20 percent discount on each room. The reservation was guaranteed by a single credit card.

"That's the day State University holds its graduation this year. What was he thinking?" asked Gil.

"I don't know," replied Felicia, "we've sold every room during graduation for the past four years for a rate $30 or $40 higher than our normal ADR because we can eliminate all discounts. This year, Karl has basically sold out the hotel, and our ADR compared to last year will be awful!"

"Why didn't he realize what he was doing?" asked Gil, "and who's responsible for making sure this kind of thing can't happen again?"

"Those are the right questions," thought Felicia, "and I need to find the right answers."

OVERVIEW OF NIGHT AUDIT FUNCTIONS

As shown in Roadmap 12.1, this chapter begins with an overview of night audit functions. Most hotels operate around the clock; they never close. Although this is very convenient for guests, it makes accounting for the hotel's financial transactions challenging. Even routine business questions such as "what were our total revenues yesterday?" or "how many rooms were sold today?" can be difficult to answer, because the traditional system of "advancing" the calendar at midnight to the next day does not work well in the lodging industry. In hotels, even the terms *yesterday* and *today* can be difficult to determine. Consider a guest who checks in at 4:00 p.m. on Friday and checks out the next day at 9:00 a.m. Another guest checks in at 2:00 a.m. on Saturday and checks out at 9:00 a.m. on the same day. In most hotels, both of these guests' rooms would be considered sold on Friday.

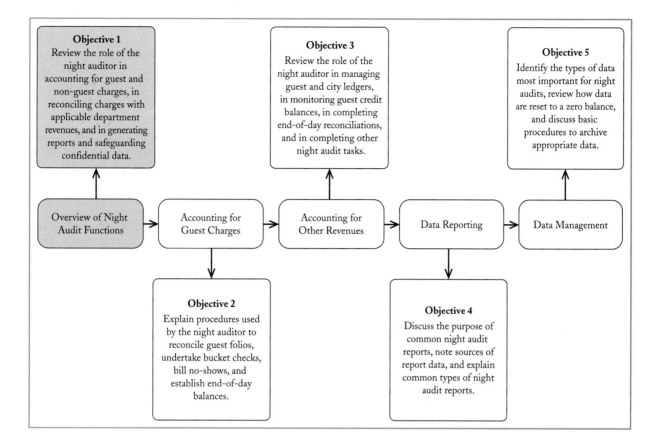

ROADMAP 12.1

To help maintain records, hoteliers select a time (usually in the middle of the night) to summarize the sales of the current day and to begin recording new sales for the next day. For many hotels, the end of one day and the beginning of another is not a fixed time at all. Rather, one day ends and a new day begins with the completion of a review and summary of the hotel's daily operating activities. This review and summarization process in a business is commonly called an **audit.** In the lodging industry, it is called the *night audit,* because traditionally the process is conducted during the night.

FRONT OFFICE SEMANTICS

Audit: Process of verifying records for correctness and completeness.

The night audit is the systematic process of reviewing for accuracy and complete-ness the accounting transactions from one hotel "day" to summarize that day's sales information. The night audit also prepares for posting the accounting transactions of the next day. In addition, the night audit records and reports important operating informa-tion. At the Altoona Hotel, for example, the person who performs the night audit (i.e., the night auditor) ensures that guests were charged the proper amount for their rooms (a review of accounting-related transactions) and prepares reports such as guest arrival lists (operating information) needed by managers for decision making the next day.

In some hotels the night auditor reports directly to the FOM. In others, the night auditor reports to the controller. In still others, especially in smaller properties, the night audit may be performed by the FOM or the controller. In all cases, however, two tasks are part of night audit activities: a series of accounting reviews and summarization and reporting of operating data.

Accounting Review Functions

Most hoteliers recognize the importance of compiling, balancing, and reviewing their financial accounts daily, and they do so with a night audit that is usually completed between 2:00 a.m. and 5:00 a.m. The time can easily vary by several hours in the same property. What is critical is that the time the night audit is completed be recorded, so that the audit can be considered 100 percent complete to that point in time. In a modern hotel, the PMS is programmed to complete almost instantaneously much of the night audit. When it is complete, the previous day is considered ended; any additional transactions are then recorded as part of the "new" day. Because manual completion of the night audit generally takes several hours, by hotel tradition any transactions that occur during the night audit process are considered to have occurred during the new day.

In a large hotel, literally thousands of financial transactions occur daily. Some such as room charges, in-room movie and minibar purchases, telephone toll charges, and overnight parking fees apply to registered guests. Other charges, such as for meeting rooms, audiovisual equipment rental, and food and beverage purchases, may be initiated by registered guests or others who are not guests. Additional accounting transactions that do not relate directly to a single day's hotel sales are managed at the front desk. These include computing travel agent commissions, posting advanced deposits received from guests for future reservations, and debiting or crediting various receivables accounts. In most hotels the accounting process performed as part of the night audit is divided into two main parts: (1) review of guest charges and (2) review of non-guest charges and property accounting.

Review of Guest Charges

Each room with a registered guest is considered a separate account and is reviewed daily. If Noel Richards is registered in room 212 at the Altoona Hotel, the night auditor reviews the status of her account. In a completely nonautomated hotel, the auditor would begin the manual account review by starting with the amount the guest owed on the previous day, then *adding* to that amount any new charges incurred during the current day and *subtracting* from that total any amounts the guest had paid toward her bill. If this is done successfully, Noel's account will be current and in balance. Figure 12.1 illustrates, from a guest's perspective and an accounting perspective, the process of auditing a single guest's account.

> **Guest's perspective:**
>
> Amount owed + Purchases − Payments = New amount owed
>
> **Accounting perspective:**
>
> Previous day's balance + Debits − Credits = New balance

FIGURE 12.1   Verification of guest account balance.

It is important that the guest and hotel agree on the amount owed, so there should be appropriate backup information if a guest requests proof of or details about specific charges. Therefore, the night auditor must ensure that each guest's account meets the following conditions:

- *Current.* The account has an accurate balance to begin the new day.
- *Complete.* All appropriate credits and debits from the previous day have been posted to the account.
- *Correct.* All credits and debits have been verified for accuracy.
- *Confirmable.* If they request, guests should be allowed to view the **source document** that initiated the charges posted to their folios. Night auditors must assemble and safeguard these documents if they are turned in to the front desk.

FRONT OFFICE SEMANTICS

Source document: Written record that initiates an account debit or credit. Examples of source documents for debits include signed guest checks (for food and beverage charges) and detailed telephone logs (for telephone toll charges). Credit card confirmations for payment produce account credits.

Review of Non-Guest Charges and Property Accounting

In addition to reviewing and verifying the accounts of in-house guests, night auditors must also authenticate the accuracy of billings and payments for accounts in the city ledger (see Chapter 11). They also review and balance daily hotel accounts that affect revenue-generating departments. To illustrate, assume that the night auditor at the Altoona Hotel must post and verify charges for the following revenue-generating hotel departments:

- Rooms
- Restaurant
- Lounge
- Telephone
- Gift shop
- Laundry
- Parking

Figure 12.2 illustrates how charges to each department are combined to create the hotel's total revenue. If payments for goods and services have been received, they are recorded. If charges are to be applied to the accounts of registered guests, the auditor must identify the appropriate room number and post the proper charge. The totals of each individual department's charges and payments should equal the total amount of charges and payments recorded for the entire hotel.

In addition to posting charges, night auditors are typically responsible for counting the cash, checks, and money orders the hotel has generated during the time of the night audit. The auditor may also be responsible for counting and safeguarding money collected by other revenue-generating departments and given to the night auditor for inclusion in the next bank deposit.

A night audit is complete when the totals for guest, non-guest, and property accounts are in balance. If the totals are not in balance, the audit is incomplete. When

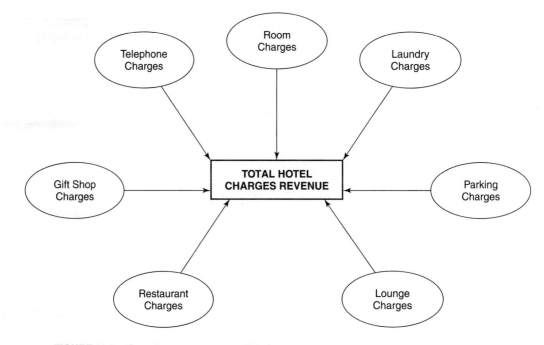

FIGURE 12.2   Sample account consolidation.

the audit is finalized, the total of credits and debits posted to guest and non-guest accounts must exactly match the total credits and debits posted to the hotel's department accounts. For example, if the hotel's call accounting system indicates that chargeable telephone tolls of $1,000 were generated since the last night audit, the total amount of toll charges to be assigned to the various guest and non-guest accounts should also equal $1,000. If accounts are out of balance, the auditor must review individual folios, account statements, source documents, and department records to discover and remedy the errors and complete the audit.

Reporting and Data Management Functions

In addition to reviewing financial accounts, the night auditor summarizes and reports other important operating statistics. These data are stored or distributed to managers who use the information to complete their own work.

Data Reports

Even the most basic PMS can create a large number of management reports, because virtually all the data required to operate the hotel is stored in the PMS. The manner in which that information can be used varies greatly. For example, all PMSs record reservations that have been made, so the night auditor can create reports that list all room reservations since the last night audit. A separate report can list the number of reservations made during each shift or by each reservationist. Additional reservation reports could list the number of reservations made for a specific room type, the ADR of the reservations made, the source (distribution channel) used for the reservations, the geographic area from which those reserving rooms will arrive, and a host of other characteristics applicable to the reservations.

One of the night auditor's duties is the creation of management reports.

The ability of a PMS to produce a massive number of potentially valuable reports is both an asset and a potential liability. Managers benefit because they can retrieve important information easily. However, massive amounts of data can, if not properly managed, lead to creation of so many reports that managers do not pay proper attention to them.

FOMs must inform other managers about their department's ability to provide useful reports. For example, virtually all PMSs can record guestrooms that are out of order (OOO). A daily report created during the night audit could list this information:

- Date the report was created
- Number of OOO rooms on that date
- Room numbers of each OOO room
- Date each room was placed on OOO list
- Name of the person placing the room on OOO list
- Reason for the OOO status
- Estimated date the room will go off OOO status

This report would be important to the hotel's maintenance staff and to others in the housekeeping, reservations, and front office departments. Professional FOMs use the night audit process to gather and disseminate key operational information. The specific reports generated and then distributed vary by a hotel's size, the amenities it offers, and the specific needs of the hotel's managers.

Data Management

The amount of data that must be stored by a hotel is significant. Consider the simple case of a guest who calls the hotel to ask if a pair of shoes left in the room at check-out was found. In this case, the FOM needs a record of the check-in date and the room to which the guest was assigned. Sales information, reservation data, room records, and statistics related to taxes collected, travel agent commissions, specific guest charges, and telephone activity are just a few more examples of the hundreds of records that must be maintained. In some cases, local or state laws dictate records to be maintained and how long they should be kept. In other cases, it is the hotel's owners or managers who decide to **archive** selected data.

FRONT OFFICE SEMANTICS

Archive: Process of preserving records or documents (when used as a verb). Records or documents that have been preserved (when used as a noun).

The night auditor has historically been responsible for creating and caring for the hotel's records. Much of the information about guests, such as their credit card numbers and home telephone numbers is confidential; therefore, it is important to protect selected records.

Position of Night Auditor

Few areas within the hotel industry have changed more in the past decade than has the night audit. Until then, the audit was the result of hours of manual postings and calculations. Today's auditor, however, is more likely to allow the preprogrammed PMS to perform most audit functions. Nevertheless, FOMs must understand the fundamentals of the night audit process, because they realize that the night auditor's position is one of the most important in any hotel.

Many skills are required to be an effective night auditor. Because the audit is always performed in the early morning hours, it takes a special type of person to complete it day after day. Before an individual is selected for the position, each segment of the job should be reviewed carefully with potential candidates. Figure 12.3 presents a detailed job description for night auditor. Although a specific document must be developed by each hotel, this description suggests the most important job tasks. As such, it provides a preview of the remainder of this chapter. The amount of variability in the work of night auditors is significant. There are some basic activities, however, and the following functions will be discussed in depth: accounting for guest charges, other night audit accounting procedures, data reporting, and data management.

Night Auditor

- Completes postings of all charges to guest folios
- Receives and records guest payments
- Prepares revenue report, including day rates posted by other shifts
- Posts daily room, tax, and other noninterfaced charges (Total room revenue should balance with the PMS room revenue report.)
- Completes resetting of data to show any adjustments for errors and gives full explanation; records last consecutive number and resets number where appropriate
- Completes high-balance credit report to identify guest ledger folios of cash-paying customers with debit balances and identifies folios with balances in excess of preestablished credit limits
- Prepares Manager's Daily report to be given to the FOM and general manager for review
- Prepares and distributes required emergency, revenue generation, reservation activity, exception, and management reports as instructed by the FOM
- Prepares and has ready by 7:00 a.m. each day the housekeeper's report, which identifies status of check-outs, stayovers, and vacant and OOO rooms for the previous night
- Prepares maintenance log report for distribution to chief engineer
- Assigns rooms in a courteous and efficient manner to late arrival guests; performs check-out procedures for early departure guests
- Records and makes all requested wake-up calls properly
- Provides information to guests in a courteous manner
- Prints and distributes folios for express check-out
- Follows appropriate policies and procedures in emergency situations
- Completes the night audit by change of shift at 7:00 a.m. Relays information to department heads (especially data pertaining to the morning's breakfast business and meeting set-ups)
- Ensures that all historical and managerial data are recorded and archived as instructed

---

FIGURE 12.3   Sample job description for night auditor.

SECTION REVIEW AND DISCUSSION QUESTIONS

Section Objective: Review the role of the night auditor in accounting for guests and non-guest charges, in reconciling charges with applicable department revenues, and in generating reports and safeguarding confidential data.

Section Summary: Night auditors may be responsible to the FOM in small properties or to the controller in larger hotels. Regardless, their work involves the same major responsibilities: to compile, balance, and review a hotel's financial accounts on a daily basis. Modern PMSs are programmed to complete much of the night audit, and this is very helpful because in large hotels thousands of financial transactions occur daily.

The night audit is divided into two main parts. First, guest charges must be reviewed to determine the new balance after the amount previously owed is adjusted by any purchases and payments. A similar type of reconciliation is required for financial transactions conducted by individuals who are not registered guests. It is important to confirm that revenues generated by hotel departments are accounted for by posting charges to guest folios or city ledgers. Second, night auditors are responsible for disseminating reports required by the FOM and other hotel managers and for archiving and safeguarding information as requested by hotel managers.

Tasks performed by night auditors vary according to the needs of the employer; however, common tasks should be identified in a job description.

Discussion Questions:

1. How can reports routinely generated by the PMS help a general manager ensure that there is no collusion between the FOM and the night auditor? For example, what if occupied rooms could be shown as unsold and, therefore, no revenue was collected?
2. Some information generated by the hotel is collected during the night audit and is confidential. In addition to the examples given in the text, what financial or personal information processed during the night audit might be confidential?
3. Night auditors may handle cash banks, and they may hold cash and currency collected by revenue-producing departments for subsequent bank deposits. What types of procedures would you, as an FOM, require to be in place to help ensure that dishonest night auditors do not abuse these funds?

ACCOUNTING FOR GUEST CHARGES

Roadmap 12.2 indicates that this section focuses on the processes used to account for guest charges. The night auditor has primary responsibility for posting charges to guest folios; however, the night auditor is not the only staff member who does this. Consider, for example, the guest at the Altoona Hotel who calls the front desk agent and states that she understands the hotel's posted check-out time is noon, but she would like to check out at 5:00 p.m. The front desk agent approves the request but informs the guest that a day rate (see Chapter 6) will be charged to her folio. The guest agrees, and she pays the extra charge when checking out. Clearly, this charge was not posted to the guest's folio by the night auditor who does not begin working until many hours later.

When guests check in very early or check out very late, partial day rates will likely be assessed and posted to the guest's folio by someone other than the night auditor. If a guest checks in after the night audit shift ends (typically at 7:00 a.m.) and checks out before the next night audit shift begins (typically 11:00 p.m.), none of the guest's folio postings will be the night auditor's responsibility.

In addition to posting folio charges and crediting guest payments to their accounts, the night auditor must verify the accuracy of all charges, complete billings for no-shows, and verify end-of-day balances. FOMs need to understand the reason for each of these accounting tasks and know how they are completed.

Folio Accounting

When all guest charges are manually posted to folios, the night auditor is responsible for making accurate postings. In most hotels today, interfaced and computerized

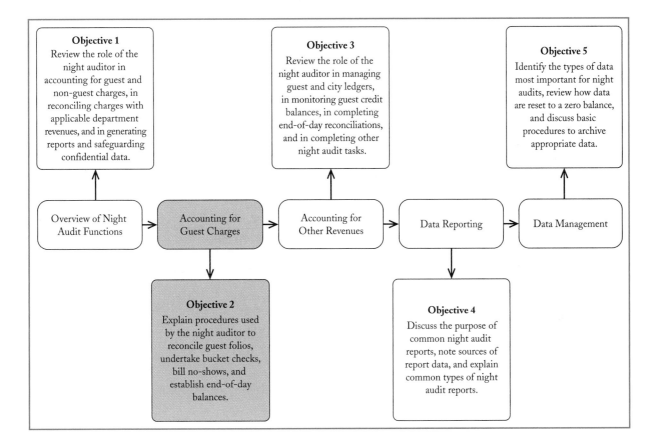

ROADMAP 12.2

PMSs credit and debit postings automatically as they occur, and guest folios are updated constantly.

In manual, noninterfaced systems, some charges are posted by the night auditor. In addition, charges (debits) and payments (credits) made during the night auditor's shift will also be recorded. This can occur, for example, when a guest checks in after 11:00 p.m., pays cash, and checks out before 7:00 a.m. As it is not possible to know when guests may check out, up-to-date folios must be ready for their inspection at any time. It is the night auditor's job to ensure that these folios are available.

A properly designed guest folio should clearly indicate the sources and amount of all guest charges and the date and amount of any payments. A sample guest folio produced by a modern PMS system is shown in Figure 12.4. Each manufacturer's PMS has its own characteristics and folio layout, and the system usually allow for some customization of content. In Figure 12.4, the Altoona Hotel's FOM has included the following data in the guest folio:

A. Space for the hotel's mailing address and telephone number to make it easy for guests to contact the hotel if, after departure, they wish to discuss details of their folio billing with a hotel representative.

B. Account number assigned to the guest's folio at check-in. In some PMSs, this will be the guest's original reservation confirmation number. In all cases, however, an identification number is assigned to each guest's folio.

Altoona Hotel A		
123 Anytown Avenue		
City, State 12345		
517-505-1212		

Account:	146583	B
Date:	10/27/XX	C
Room:	188 SFGM	D
Arrival Date:	10/26/XX 16:17	E
Departure Date:	10/27/XX 08:14	F
Frequent Traveler ID:	None	G

You were checked out by: AM   H
You were checked in by: JRG   I

ERIC MILLER   J
1234 MAIN ST
MAINTOWN, MI 12345

Post Date K	Description L		Comment M	N Amount
10/26/XX	ROOM CHARGE		#188 MILLER, ERIC	65.00
10/26/XX	STATE TAX		STATE TAX	3.90
10/26/XX	CITY/COUNTY ASSESSMENT		CITY/COUNTY ASSESSMENT	3.25
10/26/XX	MOVIE POSTING		PAY MOVIE	12.99
10/26/XX	PHONE TAXABLE		1-313-213-4567: 1min:45sec	3.90
10/26/XX	RESTAURANT CHARGE		ROOM SERVICE (REST)	25.95
10/27/XX	DIRECT BILL DUE	O	DIRECT BILL DUE	−72.15
10/27/XX	CASH PAYMENT	P	CASH PAYMENT	−42.84
10/27/XX			Balance Due:	0.00
				Q

If payment by credit card, I agree to pay the above total charge amount according to the card issuer agreement.

X ____R_____

FIGURE 12.4   Sample guest folio.

C. Date the folio was printed

D. Room number and, in this example, a track code (SFGM)

E. Date and **military time** of guest's arrival

F. Date and military time of guest's departure

G. Frequent-traveler or mileage-member number. In this example, the guest is not a member of the clubs in which the hotel participates.

H. Initials of the staff member checking in the guest.

I. Initials of the staff member checking out the guest.

J. Guest's name and address

K. Date of any credit or debit postings

L. Description of charges and payments

M. Comment section to further explain charges and payments

N. Amount of charge or payment

O. In this example, a transfer of charges to a direct bill account (room and tax charges)

P. In this example, a cash payment for incidentals

Q. Total owed by the guest (balance due) after check-out

R. Signature line for use if a payment card is used to settle the guest's bill

---

FRONT OFFICE SEMANTICS

Military time: System of time keeping that does not use the designations a.m. and p.m. to differentiate hours but, rather, identifies hours of the day by the sequence of their occurrence (1–24). For example,

Traditional time	Military time
6:00 a.m.	06:00
6:30 a.m.	06:30
10:00 p.m.	22:00
10:45 p.m.	22:45

If guests are consistently unhappy with the detail provided on their folios, the FOM should work closely with the PMS vendor, the controller's office, and the night auditor to ensure that the information guests require, and that the hotel wishes to provide, is clear and easy to understand.

Bucket Check

As an important and initial part of posting room charges to guests' folios, the night auditor must verify data accuracy. This is done through a process called the bucket check, which, as described in Chapter 11, is simply a procedure to ensure that all folio postings are correct. Buckets, the traditional name used for the place where folios were stored, are no longer used by most hotels to hold guest folios. Instead, folios exist in the hotel's PMS. Nevertheless, it is important for night auditors to verify that the room rate charged a guest is, in fact, the correct rate. This is also true in the case of **share with** room rates.

FRONT OFFICE SEMANTICS

Share with (room rate): Room rate that is split between (shared with) more than one room occupant.

The rate shown in the PMS for a room charge may be incorrect for a variety of reasons. Consider the case of Tony Spader who reserved a standard, king-bedded room at $125 per night for one night. He arrived at the Altoona Hotel at 10:30 p.m. He was greeted, initialed his room rate and departure date on the registration card, was checked in, and was assigned to room 202. On entering the room, he immediately called the front desk to report that the faucet in the tub area would not shut off completely. It was late, so no maintenance person was available to correct the problem. Therefore, Mr. Spader was moved to another room. Because the guest was inconvenienced by the move, the front desk agent decided to upgrade Mr. Spader to a suite selling for $175 per night.

The PMS will automatically display the rate for the new and more expensive room. Unless the front desk agent makes the correction to override the displayed rate and charge Mr. Spader for the cost of the room he reserved, the folio will show the cost of the higher-priced room. The night auditor, when checking to ensure that each guest is paying the proper room rate, would post a charge to Mr. Spader's folio of $175, because that is the rate programmed in the PMS for the room type he occupies. If the problem is not discovered and corrected, Mr. Spader will likely think that the hotel is attempting to overcharge him for the room.

Doing a bucket check during the night audit shift reduces errors on guest folios.

In addition to comparing registration card rates initialed by guests with the rates programmed for posting by the PMS (or posted manually), night auditors compare the housekeeper's report of occupied and vacant rooms against the in-house list (see Chapter 9) created by the PMS. The purpose is to look for rooms identified by housekeeping as occupied but not so listed in the PMS, and to discover rooms that appear from PMS data to be occupied but that are listed as vacant according to housekeeping reports. In both cases, unless these rooms are identified, there will be errors when reporting the day's revenue. If occupied rooms are not charged, hotel revenues are lost. If room rental charges are posted to folios associated with unoccupied rooms, actual room revenue will be overstated because these dollars cannot be collected.

If done properly, a thorough bucket check allows the night auditor to improve the accuracy of hotel room charges, reduces guest-initiated disputes about room rate at check-out, and minimizes the potential for the fraudulent use of rooms by housekeeping employees or other individuals.

No-Show Billings

In addition to verifying the charges incurred by registered guests, night auditors typically bill no-shows. Chapter 11 gave several reasons why guests with a guaranteed reservation might appear to be a no-show when, in fact, they did stay at the hotel. A no-show billing is appropriate when it is clear that a guest has

- made a confirmed reservation,
- guaranteed the reservation with a valid payment card (or preauthorized direct bill account),
- not arrived to take possession of the room being held (as obligated to do), and

- not provided a rationale worthy of waiving no-show charges. Documentation in these instances is very important because, in many cases, guests will dispute no-show charges when the charges appear on their payment card statement.

Night auditors should follow the no-show billing procedures developed by issuers of the payment card used to guarantee the reservation; this will help minimize successful guest challenges to the billings. In most cases, card issuers limit the amount a hotel is allowed to bill a no-show. Typically, only the cost of room and applicable taxes for the first (arriving) night may be charged. Therefore, for example, no-show guests with a reservation for a three-night stay may only be billed for one night, not three. FOMs who field guest inquires about no-show billings should support the policies developed by the hotel and the actions of the night auditors who prepare them.

End-of-Day Balances

Hotel guests generate charges at all times of the day and night. A hotel usually balances all charges made by its customers with those recorded in the PMS or elsewhere at least daily. Sub-balances (also called *shift balances*) may be undertaken throughout the day, but ultimately the night auditor must balance each revenue center's revenue with the totals to be posted on the **Manager's Daily** revenue report.

FRONT OFFICE SEMANTICS

Manager's Daily: Summary of a hotel's daily revenue generation that can include additional operating data as requested by the manager.

A detailed Manager's Daily room revenue report that is typically produced directly from the PMS should contain, at minimum, the following information:

- Total room revenue
- Rooms available to sell
- Total rooms occupied
- Occupancy percentage
- Total ADR
- Total RevPar

Any additional revenue centers should be balanced, and applicable information should be included on the Manager's Daily. For example, if a hotel charges for telephone calls, all of the daily revenue generated by this department would be manually or automatically collected from the call accounting system and posted to each appropriate folio. The result would be a balancing of telephone revenues and guest folio postings. The postings for each revenue-producing center in the hotel must be in balance with guest folios and the city ledger before the night auditor can run the audit. A successful audit brings to an end the recording of one day's sales and starts the recording of the next day's sales.

SECTION SUMMARY AND DISCUSSION QUESTIONS

Section Objective: Explain procedures used by the night auditor to reconcile guest folios, undertake bucket checks, bill no-shows, and establish end-of-day balances.

Section Summary: The night auditor has the primary responsibility for posting charges to guest folios. However, other staff such as the front desk agent can also post charges. Today's interfaced and computerized PMSs credit and debit postings automatically as they occur. A properly designed guest folio accurately indicates the source and amounts of all guest charges and the date amounts of all payments.

The night auditor uses a bucket check process to ensure that all folio postings are correct. The process serves several purposes: (1) makes sure that each guest pays the proper room rate; (2) ensures that rooms identified by housekeeping as occupied are, in fact, entered in the PMS; and (3) identifies rooms that are vacant according to housekeepers but shown as occupied by the PMS.

Night auditors are responsible for no-show billings, and these must be done carefully to minimize successful guest challenges to the billings. The night auditor must also balance the revenue of each department in the hotel and post totals for the Manager's Daily report. These postings must be in balance with guest folios before the night auditor can run the audit.

Discussion Questions:
1. This section gives one example of how a room rate shown in the PMS may not be correct. Can you think of additional examples?
2. What activities might result in a room being shown as vacant by housekeepers but as occupied in the PMS?
3. Comment on the following statement: The importance of the night auditor's role has been significantly lessened since most of the information generated by this staff member can now be generated automatically and accurately by a modern PMS.

ACCOUNTING FOR OTHER REVENUES

As you can see from Roadmap 12.3, accounting for revenues other than guest charges is also part of the night audit. For example, in addition to balancing the guest ledger every day, the night auditor updates and confirms the general ledger balances. Recall that a hotel's financial records include those related to guests (the guest ledger), to persons who are not guests but who use the hotel's products and services (city ledger), and to the series of accounts summarizing the hotel's overall financial position (general ledger). This section describes how the night auditor manages guest and city ledger accounts and how that process affects the general ledger. In addition, the section presents details of credit management, end-of-day reconciliations, and other tasks of the night auditor.

Ledger Management

The hotel's ledgers must be brought into balance each day. Each hotel or PMS may have its own format for balancing the night audit; however, each uses the same basic process. Consider Charles Lohr, the night auditor for the Altoona Hotel. Each day, Charles uses the proper financial procedures to balance the night audit.

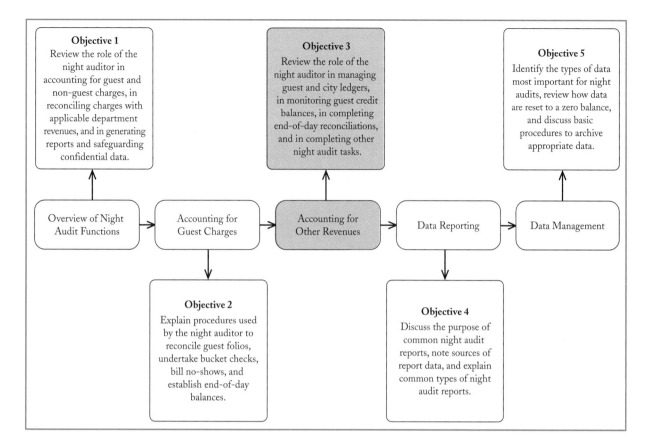

ROADMAP 12.3

Guest Ledger

To balance the guest ledger portion of the hotel's accounts, Charles uses the formula in Figure 12.5.

FRONT OFFICE SEMANTICS

Paid-outs: Payments made by the front desk for legitimate hotel expenses. Examples include the purchase of minor office supplies, guest refunds, or other expenses authorized by the hotel's FOM and recorded by the appropriate staff member.

To Balance:	
Start with	Total end-of-day departmental revenue recorded
Less	**Paid-outs**
Equals	Net revenue
Less	*Total cash received*
Equals	Amount to transfer to accounts receivable
Less	*Accounts receivable transfers*
Equals	0

FIGURE 12.5   Guest ledger balancing formula.

Night auditors balance financial records such as guest ledgers and city ledgers.

Consider a day in which departmental reports from the PMS show the following:

Room revenue	$5,000.00
Food revenue	2,000.00
Lounge revenue	500.00
Room service revenue	500.00
Telephone revenue	300.00
Total departmental revenue recorded	$8,300.00

Returning to the formula in Figure 12.5, Charles has now determined his total end-of-day revenue balance ($8,300). From that he will deduct any paid-outs. In the night audit **cashier's drawer,** Charles finds one receipt for a special power cord purchased by a member of the sales department for use in a guest meeting room. The member of the sales department who purchased the cord was reimbursed from the petty cash fund. Typically, the receipt for the power cord purchase would be attached to a petty cash paid-out voucher used to document the $10 purchase.

Total departmental revenue recorded		$ 8,300.00
Less	*Paid-outs*	− 10.00
Equals	Net revenue	$ 8,290.00
Less	*Total cash received*	−1,500.00
Equals	Amount to transfer to accounts receivable	$ 6,790.00
Less	*Today's accounts receivable transfers*	−6,790.00
Equals	0	0.00

FIGURE 12.6   Altoona Hotel guest ledger balancing formula.

FRONT OFFICE SEMANTICS

Cashier's drawer: Cash, checks, payment card copies, and other financial records for which an employee (cashier) is responsible.

Charles next records the cash received by the hotel during the day. Assume that the amount of currency and checks totals $1,500. This amount is subtracted from net revenue to yield the total resulting balance to be transferred to various accounts receivable (e.g., specific credit and debit cards and direct bill accounts). Recall that accounts receivable (A/R) represent the amounts owed to but not yet received by the hotel. Figure 12.6 reviews the flow of revenue through the guest ledger balancing process. The specific methods and procedures used to balance a hotel's guest ledger can vary. However, each night auditor must record, and each hotel's FOM and controller must monitor, the daily balancing of this ledger.

City Ledger

To balance the city ledger portion of the hotel's accounts, Charles uses the formula presented in Figure 12.7.

The city ledger is simply an A/R file maintained at the front desk. Charles checks his records, which indicate that the A/R account balance from the prior day was $70,000. To that he adds today's A/R transfers of $6,790, which yields a total A/R balance of $76,790. Next Charles *subtracts* $10,000: payments received by the hotel today that must be applied to A/R balances. This includes receipts from payment card companies, checks, and cash received that should be applied to direct bill accounts receivable. Sometimes advance deposits or prepayments are received that result in a **credit balance** for some accounts. In this example, the results of the completed account balance for the city ledger are shown in Figure 12.8.

Start with	Yesterday's accounts receivable balance
Plus	*Today's accounts receivable transfers*
Equals	Total accounts receivable
Less	*Payments received on accounts receivable*
Equals	Today's accounts receivable balance

FIGURE 12.7   City ledger balancing formula.

Start with	Yesterday's accounts receivable balance	$ 70,000.00
Plus	*Today's accounts receivable transfers*	+ 6,790.00
Equals	Total accounts receivable	$ 76,790.00
Less	Payments received on accounts receivable	− 10,000.00
Equals	Today's accounts receivable balance	$ 66,790.00

FIGURE 12.8 City ledger balancing formula.

FRONT OFFICE SEMANTICS

Credit balance: Amount owed to guests by the hotel. Used as in, "We just got a check to hold the ballroom for next year's Blondstone wedding. When we apply the check to their account, they will have a *credit balance* of $3,000."

Night auditors must balance the guest and city ledgers daily. However, they are not typically responsible for balancing the hotel's general ledger. This is done by the controller, who must work closely with the night auditor.

Credit Balance Management

One of the most important tasks of the night auditor is to monitor guests' credit balances. When guests check into a hotel they are usually extended credit immediately. Creditworthiness may be established by presenting a valid payment card, by the presence of a direct bill account, or by a cash deposit. With the extension of credit, however, comes the risks that are associated with guests who ultimately cannot, or will not, pay their legitimate bills. Night auditors help FOMs to identify and properly control those risks.

To illustrate, Katie Bardello checks in to the Altoona Hotel and, at registration, she presents a valid Visa card to establish credit. Ms. Bardello's room costs $100 per night and she plans to stay one night. In keeping with the hotel's credit policy, her card is authorized (see Chapter 11) at check-in for $200, which is two times her estimated expenditures ($2 \times 100 = 200).

The next morning, Ms. Bardello tells the front desk agent that she wants to stay two more nights. Usually, assuming the hotel has rooms available, her request would be welcome. In other cases, however, significant difficulties could now be encountered. FOMs must carefully monitor all account balances and properly react to potential problems. Night auditors play a critical role in this process and alert FOMs about potentially sensitive issues brought on by requests such as the one made by Ms. Bardello. They do so by generating a daily credit limit report.

Credit Limit Reports

Later in this chapter we will investigate many of the financial and nonfinancial reports prepared by the night auditor. One of the most important is the **credit limit report,** which compares each guest's current folio balance with the credit line established by the guest during check-in.

FRONT OFFICE SEMANTICS

Credit limit report: Comparison of a guest's folio balance to the amount of credit established for that guest. Sometimes referred to as a *high-balance report.*

Night auditors are responsible for posting guest charges. Therefore, they must evaluate the possibility that the guest for whom a charge is posted will not, or cannot, eventually pay. In the case of Ms. Bardello, the $200 hold placed on her card at check-in was sufficient to establish an appropriate initial level of creditworthiness. With her request to extend her stay, however, and in keeping with the hotel's policy, the credit limit that now must be established is $600 ($200 per night × 3 nights = $600). If the night auditor can increase the hold on Ms. Bardello's card by authorizing an additional $400, the guest's credit limit will not have been exceeded. If the card cannot be authorized for the additional amount, Ms. Bardello would have exceeded the hotels' allowable credit limit. Then Ms. Bardello's name, room number, and folio balance will appear on the hotel's credit limit report.

Credit limit reports identify guests who are near, at, or over the allowable credit limit established for them. These reports are sometimes called *high-balance reports* because they can, if the FOM desires, include information about guests from whom payment *should* be received even if they have not actually exceeded their allowable credit limit. For example, guests in an extended-stay property may occupy a room for months or longer. They may owe the hotel significant amounts of money, and payment at agreed-on intervals is a typical policy.

There are other reasons why a guest may have a high outstanding balance. Sometimes the guest has made significant food and beverage or other purchases

For transient travelers, payment cards are the most common method used to establish hotel credit.

without settling his or her account. Even though accounts are generally not settled until check-out, high-balance amounts may require close examination and, perhaps, specific management. This could be the case, for example, with a guest who has been permitted to exceed a previously established credit limit.

Credit Limit Strategies

When a guest's name appears on the night auditor's credit limit report the FOM must have a plan to address the potential problem. Usually, a decision is made to increase the credit limits or to require immediate full or partial payment. Either of these strategies will place the guest within the proper credit limit.

Many guests establish credit at check-in with a payment card; their account balance shortfalls can be easily addressed by increasing the authorization amount on the card. In the example of Ms. Bardello, the night auditor would follow the policies established by the hotel's **credit manager,** and attempt to authorize Ms. Bardello's card for the proper amount.

FRONT OFFICE SEMANTICS

Credit manager: Person responsible for establishing and enforcing the hotel's credit policies. In smaller properties, this role may be filled by the general manager, controller, or FOM. In larger hotels, credit management policy may be the result of the joint efforts of several individuals.

Alternatively, the card could be charged to reduce Ms. Bardello's folio balance. Additional holds could then, if appropriate, be placed on the card.

When a card cannot be authorized for additional funds, the FOM faces a dilemma. The extension of additional, nonsecured credit for guests who have exceeded their preestablished limits increases the risk that the hotel will not collect all the money it is owned. Denying credit to those who legitimately can pay, however, puts the hotel at a significant risk of losing sales. There is no "best" credit limit policy. Each credit manager must determine specific strategies for his or her hotel based on the characteristics of the guests who exceed their credit limits.

When approaching these guests for payment, the FOM must be tactful. Extending credit lines avoids potentially difficult situations but places the hotel at risk from those who will not ultimately pay their bills. Cases differ and, in many situations, the credit limit strategies used should vary based on the guest about whom the credit extension or denial decision will be made. The following factors are considered by FOMs who must make decisions about credit extension:

- *Credit extension amount.* When guests exceed their credit limits by small amounts, often the best action is none at all. The actual dollar amount required to be considered significant will vary by hotel, and it is only these folio or city ledger accounts that need the night auditor's and FOM's attention.

- *Potential cost.* Not all hotel products and services are equally profitable. For sleeping rooms, the actual cost to the hotel of lost revenue may represent only 20 percent to 25 percent of the hotel's posted revenue. However, for food and beverage purchases these same costs may be 80 percent to 90 percent of posted revenue because of the higher costs to the hotel for supplying the products and services. Credit extension terms often can be more liberal on products and services of higher profit margins than on their less profitable counterparts.

- *Occupancy levels.* Most FOMs apply more liberal credit policies during times of reduced occupancies and use more stringent policies during times of high demand for rooms.

- *Guest's history.* Some credit managers treat first-time guests differently than repeat guests. Guest histories are maintained in the PMS and can be reviewed easily. Frequent guests are often less of a credit risk than guests who have not stayed at the hotel.

- *Guest affiliation.* If the guest is a business traveler, the creditworthiness of the guest's employer might be considered. For example, if the guest is associated with a government agency or well-known nonprofit group or association, the financial strength of those organizations may be known and may affect the credit extension decision.

FOMs may not make credit extension or denial decisions based only on a guest's gender, race, disability, ethnic background, religion, or any other factor deemed discriminatory by federal or, in some cases, local laws. Regardless of the hotel's specific policies, the night auditor must identify guests who are at or over their credit limits, take the appropriate action, and report results to the FOM.

End-of-Day Reconciliations

Most night auditors find that it is easiest to balance their accounts when they first prepare a daily **trial balance.** This method, which varies in complexity by hotel, uses a series of procedures to identify areas where accounts may be out of balance. Night auditors can then concentrate their time on finding and reconciling problem areas instead of spending unnecessary time examining in-balance accounts.

FRONT OFFICE SEMANTICS

Trial balance: First effort to determine whether a set of debits was posted with a corresponding and equal set of credit postings.

In addition to balancing the guest and city ledgers, night auditors may reconcile a variety of different accounts used by their hotel. In a small property, the number of revenue-generating departments may be small. In addition to room charges, telephone charges may be one of the few additional revenue sources to be balanced. In larger properties, there may be many revenue-generating departments. Essentially, the night auditor ensures that all appropriate charges generated by the hotel have been posted to the proper accounts and that these postings balance to each revenue-producing department's internally generated **X reports** and **Z reports.**

FRONT OFFICE SEMANTICS

X report: Term commonly used to indicate the total revenue generated by a revenue-producing department during one part of a specific time period—typically one shift. The term is used when referring to a point-of-sale or other electronic register or system that keeps a continuous running total of revenues generated. Sometimes called a *shift report.*

Z report: Term commonly used to indicate the total revenue generated during an entire time period—typically one day. Producing a Z report includes resetting the continuous total feature of a point-of-sale or other electronic register system to zero to begin recording the next period's revenues.

In addition to reconciling revenue accounts, night auditors may complete a variety of other tasks: balancing their own cash drawer, matching housekeeping and PMS reports concerning room status, conducting bucket checks, and manually posting information from noninterfaced systems (see Chapter 8). Bank deposit slips may be balanced to check and cash revenue receipts at this time, and credit and debit card charges are typically batched during the night audit and submitted to the hotel's merchant service provider for payment.

MODERN FRONT OFFICE ISSUES AND TACTICS

Several Numbers to Remember

Credit and debit cards have generally replaced cash and traveler's checks as Americans' preferred method of payment for travel services such as airline tickets, car rentals, hotel rooms, and restaurant meals. FOMs realize the importance of regular monitoring of significant changes in the payment card industry, and they assign the daily summing and submitting of the hotel's payment card receivables to the night auditor.

One of the standardized and yet unchanging features of payment card issuers is the numeric sequences associated with their cards. Several numbers are worth learning, remembering, and teaching all front office personal who submit, accept, and process payment cards. Each card issuer maintains its own standards for card processing; therefore, it is helpful to know the type of card being processed.

Card issuer	Card number begins with
American Express	3
Visa	4
MasterCard	5
Discover	6

Other Night Audit Tasks

Individual FOMs may require specific steps to complete the night audit. Typically, these include automated components within the PMS related to the guest ledger:

- Automatic transfer of advance deposits *to* the guest ledger *from* the advanced deposits portion of the general ledger when guests check-in
- Summary, by individual account, of all debit and credit postings to those accounts since the last audit
- Creation of selected financial reports for use in the back-office accounting system

In addition to their accounting-related activities, night auditors help to produce and maintain hotel reports. These two tasks are critical to the effective operations of the front office department and the entire hotel, and they will be examined in detail in the remainder of this chapter.

SECTION REVIEW AND DISCUSSION QUESTIONS

Section Objective: Review the role of the night auditor in managing guest and city ledgers, in monitoring guest credit balances, in completing end-of-day reconciliations, and in completing other night audit tasks.

Section Summary: The night auditor updates and confirms balances in the guest and city ledgers. To balance each guest ledger, the following formula is used: end-of-day department revenue recorded − paid-outs = net revenue; net revenue − total cash received = amount to transfer to accounts receivable; accounts receivable − accounts receivable transfers = 0.

To balance the city ledger portion of the hotel's accounts, the following formula is used; yesterday's accounts receivable balance + today's accounts receivable transfers = total accounts receivable; total accounts receivable − payments received on accounts receivable = today's accounts receivable balance.

Night auditors must complete credit limit reports to compare guests' folio balances with the amount of credit established for them. When a guest's balance exceeds the credit limit, an additional amount should be authorized on the guest's payment card. If this cannot be done, it may be necessary to ask the guest to make at least a partial payment on the account. Decisions about extending credit limits relate to factors such as the extension amount, potential cost to the hotel if not paid, hotel occupancy level, the guest's history with the hotel, and the guest's affiliation, with a specific organization if the guest is a business traveler.

Trial balances are typically run to establish that the debits that were posted equal the credits that were posted. If not, the trial process helps to identify where potential errors might be located.

In addition to reconciling revenue accounts, night auditors may be responsible to balance their own cash drawers, match housekeeping and PMS reports about room status, conduct bucket checks, and manually post information from noninterfaced systems. Bank deposit slips may also be balanced to verify cash and check revenue receipts, and credit and debit card charges are typically batched for submission to the hotel's merchant service providers.

Discussion Questions:
1. What types of policies and procedures would you, as an FOM, implement to regulate your department's petty cash fund?
2. Assume that you, as the FOM, note an ever-increasing amount in the accounts receivable balance due to the hotel. What could be the reasons for this increasing balance? What would you do relative to each of the reasons you identified?
3. Assume that the balance of a guest's folio has exceeded the amount authorized by the payment card used at check-in. The guest indicates that she has no other payment card and no cash to pay the additional amount now due. As the FOM, what would you do in this situation?

DATA REPORTING

Although a hotel's controller may view the night auditor's primary task as one of assisting in the accounting effort, many hotel managers consider creation of reports to be the night auditor's critical task. The night audit closes one day's records and opens

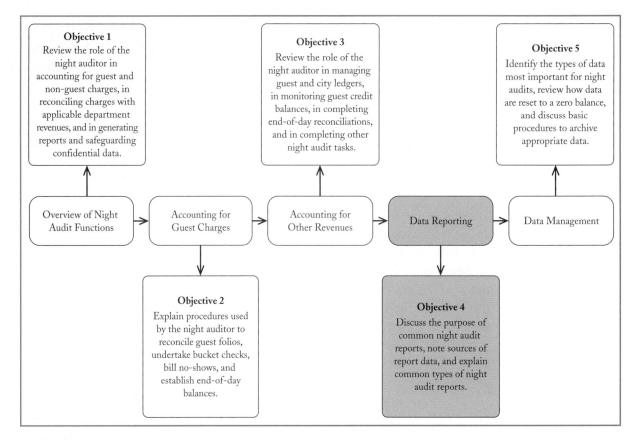

ROADMAP 12.4

records for the next day, and this process allows the summary and distribution of information to those who require it. As indicated in Roadmap 12.4, this section describes the purpose of night audit reports and examines some of the major reports typically distributed to the FOM and other managers.

Purpose of Night Audit Reports

Night audit reports help hoteliers in many ways. If the reports include forecasts of room sales, managers use them in preparing employee work schedules. For example, if a forecast calls for a sold-out hotel in two weeks, the executive housekeeper can schedule staff accordingly. If there will be low occupancy, the executive housekeeper may reduce staff or assign special cleaning tasks to staff. In either case, awareness of forecasted business volume allows managers to manage staff better and cost-effectively.

Some reports are created with the hope that they are never used. **Emergency reports** are produced to assist staff if there is a disaster such as a fire, power outage, or bomb scare. In such an event, staff would require immediate access to up-to-date property information, including occupied rooms, folio balances, and accounts receivable. For example, in case of fire, an accurate and recently created in-house guest report detailing the numbers of occupied rooms would alert firefighters about locations to be checked to ensure that all guests have been evacuated. Similarly, if a power outage caused the PMS to malfunction, an in-house guest list could help ensure that guests could be located, and that telephone calls could be manually transferred to their rooms. Despite design advance in computer hardware and software, the PMS can still go down (i.e., crash). Data stored on hard drives can become irretrievable, and guest- or room-related information could be lost. Also, backup batteries or generators used to operate the PMS during power failures can stop working.

FRONT OFFICE SEMANTICS

Emergency report: Information and lists that would be critical in the event of a disaster or a PMS crash. Sometimes referred to as a *down time report* because it is most often used when the PMS is down (i.e., crashed).

Other reports produced by the night auditor summarize information of use to specific departments. For example, a report listing the hotel's top-10 revenue-producing travel agencies may be of interest to the sales department, and a list of guestrooms designated as out of order during the past 24 hours will be important to maintenance department managers. Credit limit reports are important to the controller and FOM, and daily occupancy statistics may be required by the general manager. The number of reports created during the night audit and their specific purpose vary based on the size of hotel, the services it offers, and the desires of the FOM and other managers.

Sources of Data

For most hotels, the PMS is the major source of information for night audit reports. Some PMSs can produce literally hundreds of reports, and even the simplest PMS can produce dozens of distinctive management reports. Recall from earlier chapters, however, that not all subsystems may be interfaced with the PMS in some properties. In these cases, the required data from noninterfaced POS systems must be manually entered into selected reports. Assume that the Altoona Hotel operates a small gift shop. The Altoona's general manager has determined that the cost of interfacing the small cash register in the gift shop to the hotel's PMS is not cost-effective. Before any summary of the day's total revenue can be prepared by the night auditor, the gift shop revenue must be manually entered so the total revenue report can be created.

Types of Reports

The kinds of information needed to make management decisions may vary by hotel department. The following reports are representative of those that are in common use and that are created and distributed daily, weekly, or monthly by the night auditor: emergency, revenue generation, reservation activity, exception, and management-oriented.

Emergency Reports

Emergency reports, also called *downtime reports,* are reports that the night auditor and FOM hope will never be needed. They act as insurance against the difficulties that would be result if the PMS severely malfunctioned or if an emergency such as a fire or explosion caused an immediate need for critical information. Following are some examples of emergency reports.

- *In-house lists:* One or more complete and current listing of all guests registered in the hotel. The list may be prepared alphabetically (by guest's last name) or numerically in the sequence of occupied rooms (e.g., room 101, 102, and 103).
- *Room status reports:* Identification of rooms by their current status; for example, occupied, vacant and ready, vacant and dirty, or any other room status classification
- *Account balance reports:* Open folios and current balances; used if the PMS system is not available when guests check out

Revenue Generation Reports

Most night audits include several revenue generation reports to detail daily and month to-date or budgeted statistics or both. Comparisons to prior year or to budgeted figures, or to both, may be provided. Figure 12.9 shows a single day's ADR report for the Altoona Hotel. Note that current (today's) ADR data are compared with month-to-date ADR data, forecasted ADR data, last year's same-date ADR data, and last year's month-to-date ADR data. The comparisons are made in variance dollars and variance percentages. Figure 12.9 illustrates just one type of revenue analysis report available to managers who need more information about the hotel's revenue sources than can be learned by reviewing a single day's Manager's Daily revenue report.

Revenue generation reports are one of the most commonly used types of PMS reports, because an analysis of revenue inevitably leads to an analysis of guests and their purchase decisions. As managers learn more about their guests, they are better able to serve them. Knowledge of past behavior of guests helps to better predict future behavior. Revenue analysis reports can help FOMs learn about guest behavior as they create reports such as "Revenue by Room Type." These reports typically detail the amount of revenue generated from each of the property's room configurations (e.g., standard king, king suite, and double-double). These can help FOMs understand demand for each room type and can lead to better demand forecasting and improved pricing strategies.

The FOM is not the only manager interested in revenue reports. For example, David Berger is the food and beverage director at the Altoona. On Monday, his fine-dining restaurant reported revenues of $2,000, and on Tuesday revenues were $4,000. These numbers will mean more to David if he knows the number of guestrooms sold on these two nights. Customized "Restaurant Revenue per Occupied Room" or "Restaurant Revenue per In-House Guest" reports can help him learn the reasons for

			Altoona Hotel		
		ADR Report for:	_01/05/xx_		
Date				**Variance amount**	**Variance percentage**
1/05/XX	**Actual ADR today**		$ 97.83		
	Month-to-date ADR		$ 96.34	$ 1.49	1.55%
	Forecasted ADR		$101.23	$(3.40)	−3.36%
	Last year, same-date ADR		$ 96.11	$ 1.72	1.79%
	Last Year, month-to-date ADR		$ 95.31	$ 2.52	2.64%

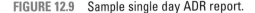

FIGURE 12.9   Sample single day ADR report.

variance between the two nights. As he does so, David will be better able to schedule staff based on forecasts of room sales.

Literally hundreds of potentially useful revenue-related reports can be generated; therefore, FOMs must be careful to create, generate, and distribute only those that will be beneficial. For many properties, the following revenue generation reports are typically most useful:

- Revenue by source of business (distribution channel)
- Revenue by room number
- Revenue by room type
- Revenue by rate code
- Revenue by guest type
- Revenue by state
- Revenue by zip code
- Revenue by telephone area code
- Revenue by individual travel agency
- Advanced deposits received
- Department sales per occupied room
- Department sales per in-house guest
- Revenue by guest arrival date
- Revenue by guest departure date
- Revenue forecasts for 10 days
- Revenue forecasts for 30 days
- Monthly revenue by source
- Yearly revenue by source

The challenge for FOMs is to determine, create, and distribute revenue analysis reports that will be the most helpful.

Reservation Activity Reports

FOMs can learn much from reports of anticipated future revenue represented by hotel reservations that have been made. Reservation activity reports can generally be sorted by the PMS according to any item of information obtained during the reservation process. This includes data about the individual making the reservation and information about the distribution channel or method used to make the reservation. Some of the most frequently generated reservation reports are listed here:

- Total reservations made today
- Total reservations canceled today
- Total reservations changed today
- Complimentary reservations made and authorized
- Group reservations made today
- Reservations by package offered
- Reservations by rate plan
- Reservations by market type (e.g., transient, corporate, and group)

- Reservations by franchisor's central reservation system
- Reservations by Internet site
- Reservations through the Global Distribution System
- Reservations pace versus prior month
- Reservations pace versus prior year
- Reservations by arrival date
- Reservations by telephone area code
- Reservations by zip code
- Share-with reservations (for separately paying guests who share the same room)
- Occupancy forecasts for 10 days
- Occupancy forecasts for 30 days

Reservation activity reports provide critical information to FOMs who must review them daily if they are to effectively manage their department and make the reservations-related decisions necessary to maximize RevPar.

Exception Reports

Exception reports identify unusual situations. They have great value because they alert staff to circumstances that require their attention without the tedious and time-consuming review of data that are *not* out of the ordinary. For example, guests do not generally exceed the credit limits for which they are authorized at check-in. If some guests do exceed their limit, the FOM must know about the situation and, when appropriate, take corrective action. Another example of an exception report is one that shows guestrooms listed as empty in the PMS and as occupied rooms in house-keeping reports. Similarly, significant variances in the amounts that cashier drawers should contain and do contain at the end of employee shifts alert supervisors to the need for analysis.

The following exception reports are common to many hotels:

- Guest over credit limit report
- Checked out with balance due report
- Cashiers' drawers with excess overs and shorts
- Complimentary rooms list with authorizing manager
- Adjustments and allowances report
- Write-off reports (all departments)

Exception reports may include very little or detailed information. For example, a complimentary rooms report could be created that simply lists the room number and occupant name for any room made a comp on a specific day. Alternatively, an FOM could design a report that includes these data:

- Room number
- Guest's name
- Number of persons in room
- Arrival date
- Departure date
- Name of the authorizing manager

Night auditors print exception reports that often require the immediate attention of department managers.

- Value of the comp
- Reason for the comp

The number of exception reports and the number of recipients vary by hotel. In all cases, exception reports are important management tools when effectively used by FOMs and others.

Management-Oriented Reports

Technically, every report created during the night audit is a management report because, if it contains important information, one or more managers will be interested in its contents. A separate category of reports is included here, however, to explain that some reports are only of interest to specific managers. For example, a no-show report that identifies guests with guaranteed reservations who failed to check in on the proper date is important for night auditors (who must bill these rooms), FOMs (who are likely to receive telephone calls or e-mails challenging the charges), and the controller (who may have to respond to chargeback efforts initiated by the guest). The food and beverage director, however, will have virtually no interest in this report, just as the FOM will not be interested in a food and beverage department report about breakfasts served per 100 rooms sold.

Each hotel manager needs different and department-specific information. FOMs must meet with their peers regularly to answer the following questions:

- What reports are currently being prepared?
- How useful are these reports?

Report	Of interest to
Arrival list	FOM
Departure list	FOM
No-show guests	FOM
In-house VIPs	FOM, general manager
Manager's Daily revenue	General manager
Complimentary rooms	General manager
Occupancy statistics	General manager
House count	General manager, food and beverage director, Executive housekeeper
Group master Pickups	Director of sales and marketing
Group master Cutoffs	Director of sales and marketing
Accounts receivables past due	Controller, general manager

FIGURE 12. 10   Selected night audit reports and managers interested in them.

- Should specific reports be eliminated or produced more or less frequently?
- What information available to night auditors would be helpful if it were provided daily?
- Are there others in the department who could benefit by receiving copies of the reports?

Figure 12.10 is a brief list of reports and the managers to whom the reports would be of most interest. Among the most popular types of management reports are those with these characteristics:

- *Credit related.* A variety of reports related to guest credit are used by the FOM, controller, credit managers, and others who need to know that specific guests are at or near their credit limit.

- *Group sales related.* In hotels with significant group, convention, and meeting business, reports related to group activities are especially useful to directors of sales and marketing, group sales managers, selected catering and food and beverage managers, and general managers. These reports can include room pickup, food and beverage activities, credit levels, and cumulative purchases.

- *Housekeeping related.* Maintaining accurate room status (e.g., occupied, clean and vacant) is always a challenge. Management reports that assist the front desk in its communications with housekeeping are indispensable.

- *Maintenance related.* Rooms that (1) need immediate maintenance-related attention, (2) are placed out of order, or (3) are scheduled to be taken out of service for maintenance affect revenue and an FOM's ability to forecast occupancy. Reports that allow front desk staff to communicate guest-initiated maintenance concerns to maintenance personnel are essential in the daily transfer of information between these two departments.

- *Accounts receivable related.* Guest folios consist of detailed lists of what the hotel is owed and records of what guests have already paid. When money is owed to a hotel at the conclusion of the night audit (i.e., a guest has an outstanding balance due), that amount is considered an account receivable. Many managers are interested in what guests owe; therefore, they value reports related to accounts receivable. Specific reports can indicate who owes what amount and provide data about **aging accounts receivable.** Other reports present information about city ledger transfers, payment card use, department revenue (cash and noncash sales), and total accounts receivable.

FRONT OFFICE SEMANTICS

Aging accounts receivable report: Detailed list of accounts receivable based on the length of time the receivable has been owed. Often these reports group accounts receivable into categories of less than 30 days, 30 to 60 days, 60 to 90 days, and more than 90 days.

- *Special coverage.* Hotels with unique features or services may require special reports. For example, if golf tee times are booked at a resort's front desk, a night audit report may be prepared daily that lists tee times for the coming day. This report would be delivered early in the morning to those managing the golf course. If a hotel operates an indoor water park, in-house guest lists designating the number of adults and children may be helpful for the manager of water park operations.

FOMs should review the reports generation section of their PMS manuals and identify the standard reports and **template reports** available and then learn how to customize these reports.

FRONT OFFICE SEMANTICS

Template report: Standard formatted report from the PMS that may be modified by the end user.

Because of the great number of reports available, FOMs may find it difficult to determine which should and which should *not* be created and distributed. An excessive number of reports wastes paper and the night auditor's time in making copies or sending e-mails. Too many reports also waste the readers' time by taking them away from more productive tasks or by providing less time to study data in critical reports. In most PMSs, the selection of reports to be run is as simple as choosing the report and then selecting *print* on the computer monitor. Almost all PMS manufacturers use a Microsoft Windows-based operating system as the platform for their software. The Windows system is an improvement over older operating systems because of the ease with which new users can learn to navigate it. Figure 12.11 shows an actual screen night auditors working with a Windows-based system would use to select the reports they are assigned to run. The terminology used to identify specific night audit reports varies by PMS manufacturer. The total number of reports available is usually limited only by the imagination of the night auditor and FOM.

PMS-generated reports may provide or seek information. Figure 12.12 shows a room discrepancy report run by the night auditor. It must be completed by the morning shift's housekeeping supervisor before being routed to the FOM. Note that instructions for completing the report are included on the form.

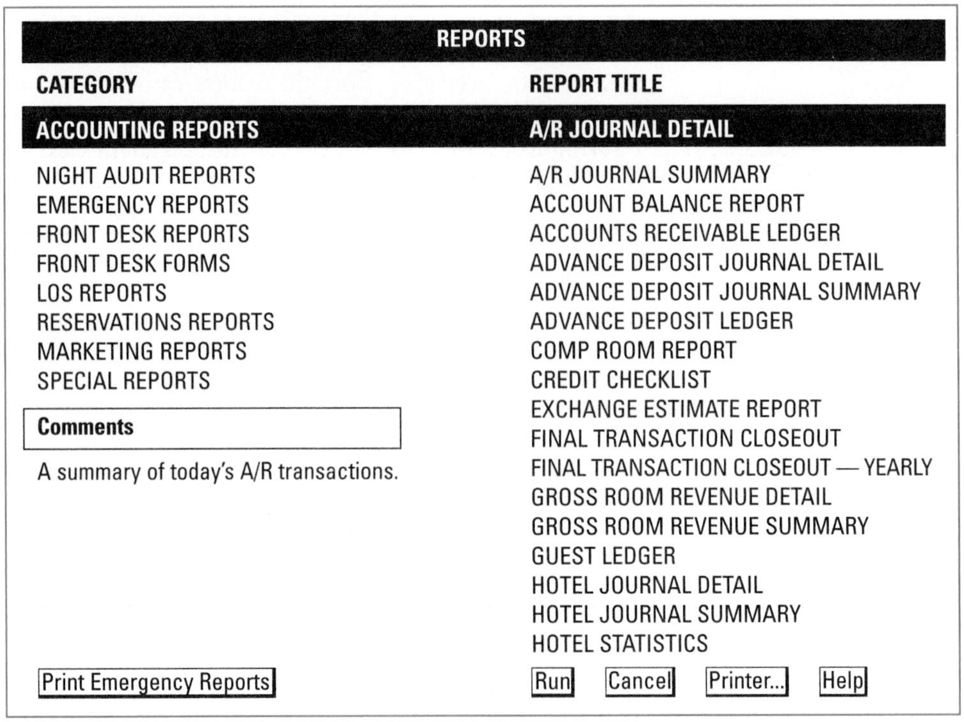

REPORTS	
CATEGORY	**REPORT TITLE**
ACCOUNTING REPORTS	**A/R JOURNAL DETAIL**
NIGHT AUDIT REPORTS	A/R JOURNAL SUMMARY
EMERGENCY REPORTS	ACCOUNT BALANCE REPORT
FRONT DESK REPORTS	ACCOUNTS RECEIVABLE LEDGER
FRONT DESK FORMS	ADVANCE DEPOSIT JOURNAL DETAIL
LOS REPORTS	ADVANCE DEPOSIT JOURNAL SUMMARY
RESERVATIONS REPORTS	ADVANCE DEPOSIT LEDGER
MARKETING REPORTS	COMP ROOM REPORT
SPECIAL REPORTS	CREDIT CHECKLIST
	EXCHANGE ESTIMATE REPORT
Comments	FINAL TRANSACTION CLOSEOUT
	FINAL TRANSACTION CLOSEOUT — YEARLY
A summary of today's A/R transactions.	GROSS ROOM REVENUE DETAIL
	GROSS ROOM REVENUE SUMMARY
	GUEST LEDGER
	HOTEL JOURNAL DETAIL
	HOTEL JOURNAL SUMMARY
	HOTEL STATISTICS
Print Emergency Reports	Run Cancel Printer... Help

FIGURE 12.11 Sample windows-based computer screen used by night auditors.

Although many reports are created and distributed daily, others may have more value if they are developed weekly or even monthly. A report of in-house VIPs must be created daily. In contrast, a listing of top-producing travel agencies may be created weekly or monthly and still provide the timely information needed to appropriately recognize the travel agents who most benefit the hotel. The best night audit programs generate a combination of daily, weekly, and monthly reports—each produced in a timely manner and each shared with the appropriate individuals.

Report Distribution

As recently as 10 years ago, the method used by nearly all night auditors to distribute reports was a fairly simple three-step process:

1. Create the report
2. Make paper copies on the front office department's copy machine
3. Physically distribute copies to the appropriate manager's office or mailbox

Today, many managers have their own PMS terminals and can select, view, and print copies of the reports that are of interest to them. Many PMS manufacturers use Microsoft office products (Word, Excel, and Access) to create their reports, so night auditors in properties using these systems can e-mail reports or send them via the hotel's intranet system. Regardless of the distribution system used, the night auditor must ensure the availability of relevant information so hotel owners, managers, and others have access to the information they need.

ALTOONA HOTEL ROOM DISCREPANCY REPORT

DATE: _____

ROOM DISCREPANCY			
ROOM NUMBER	**AUDIT STATUS**	**A.M. HSKP STATUS**	**EXPLANATION**

INSTRUCTIONS:

1. NIGHT AUDITORS MUST RUN A "ROOM STATUS REPORT" AFTER CLOSING THE AUDIT AND INCLUDE THE REPORT IN THE DAILY WORK.
2. HOUSEKEEPING WILL INSPECT THE STATUS OF EACH ROOM AND RECORD IT ON THE "A.M. REPORT".
3. THE FOM WILL COMPARE THE "NIGHT AUDIT STATUS REPORT" AND "HOUSEKEEPING A.M. REPORT" FOR ANY DISCREPANCIES IN THE STATUS REPORTED AND RECORD THEM IN THE FORM ABOVE. SEE EXAMPLE BELOW:

ROOM #	AUDIT STATUS	HSKP STATUS	
225	VC	OD	
301	OD	VC	
415	VD	VC	
416	V	OOO	
502	VC	VD	

LEGEND:

VC: VACANT CLEAN
NCI: NEW CHECK IN
OD: OCCUPIED DIRTY
OOO: OUT OF ORDER
VD: VACANT DIRTY

4. AFTER DISCREPANCIES HAVE BEEN EXPLAINED, FOM WILL APPROVE AT BOTTOM AND FORWARD TO GENERAL MANAGER FOR FINAL APPROVAL.
5. THE COMPLETED FORM WILL BE KEPT ON FILE WITH THE FOM (COPIES TO GENERAL MANAGER)

_____
DATE

_____   _____
FRONT DESK/DATE   GENERAL MANAGER/DATE

FIGURE 12.12 Room discrepancy report.

SECTION REVIEW AND DISCUSSION QUESTIONS

Section Objective: Discuss the purpose of common night audit reports, note sources of report data, and explain common types of night audit reports.

Section Summary: Night auditors must develop and distribute reports at the request of the FOM and other managers. A seemingly innumerable variety of reports can be generated from data in the PMS. These data can be supplemented, as necessary, with information entered manually from noninterfaced systems. Night audit reports can be classified as follows:

- Emergency reports provide contact information about registered guests that may be needed in the event of an emergency and other information required for guest check-out if the PMS system is not available.
- Revenue generation reports provide daily, monthly and year-to-date information—often compared with data from the previous year—that is of interest to the rooms and other departments.
- Reservation activity reports provide useful information for FOMs as they work to maximize RevPar.
- Exception reports alert managers to potential problems such as guests with outstanding balances that exceed their authorized credit limit, differences between PMS and housekeeper reports related to room occupancy, and cashier banks that are over or short.
- Management-oriented reports provide specific information to managers as they make decisions about credit, group sales, housekeeping, maintenance, or accounts receivable. Hotels with unique features or services generate special reports.

Microsoft Windows-based operating systems allow reports to be circulated by e-mail or a hotel's intranet. Managers can select and generate their own reports if they have access to these systems.

Discussion Questions:
1. The text provides examples of selected night audit reports that are useful to *all* department heads in a hotel. Can you think of additional examples of such reports? What factors should a department head consider in evaluating the worth of reports generated by the night auditor?
2. How would you, as an FOM, determine which department heads should have intranet access to all or part of the PMS database to enable them to generate desired reports without manual completion and distribution by the night auditor?
3. What practical things would you do as an FOM to help minimize the possibility that the PMS will crash and be unavailable at time of guest check-in and check-out and at the time night audit reports must be developed?

DATA MANAGEMENT

In addition to the tasks of accounting and information reporting, the night auditor is often responsible for maintaining a significant portion of the hotel's **database.** Roadmap 12.5 shows that this chapter concludes with a discussion of how data important to the night audit are managed.

FRONT OFFICE SEMANTICS

Database Collection of facts and statistics that provide useful information.

The record keeping required to maintain an accurate database is important for a variety of reasons. Hotel owners want to regularly know about their property's financial performance. This means that the FOM must supply cumulative data about rooms sold, ADRs achieved, and total departmental revenue volume. Most of the data are maintained in the front-office accounting system and are shared with the back-office accounting system. Franchisors have an interest in their franchisees' records because franchise fees are largely based on the revenue levels achieved by the franchisees. Lenders require supporting data to justify initiating or continuing loans. Governmental entities want to ensure that proper records are

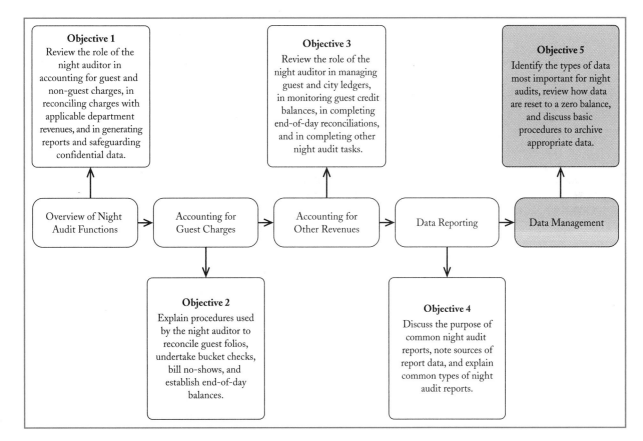

ROADMAP 12.5

maintained because sales and occupancy taxes are assessed based on the property's revenues. Hotel managers want to know what the hotel's records reveal about the property's past financial and operational performance and what current data suggest about future performance.

Types of Data

The FOM and night auditor must know about two basic types of data that must be maintained and how to do so. Technically, any items of information or fact collected by the hotel could qualify as data. FOMs, however, find it useful to designate data as either historical or managerial.

- *Historical data.* Data classified as historical represent events that occurred in the past; for example, last night's ADR, last month's room sales, and the number of times that room 101 sold last year.
- *Managerial data.* Data classified as managerial reflect information about future events; for example, reservations for future dates, room revenue forecasts, and other information that helps predict what will occur in the future.

Night auditors must determine what to do with historical or managerial data as they do their audits. Generally, the FOM and night auditor can decide to reset or archive the information.

Data Resetting

Sometimes data generated by a hotel should be collected and reported on a daily basis and then be reset to zero for the beginning of the next day. For example, the general manager and others want to know about *daily* revenues. So revenues are recorded for Monday and when the Monday night audit is run (early Tuesday morning), Monday revenues are be tallied and recorded. The daily revenue figure is then reset to zero to begin recording Tuesday revenues. Similarly, each day's revenue is reported and recorded independently. Data generated from these daily records can be used by managers in achieving the property's goals.

Resetting data is important, because many of a hotel's revenue-generating systems are based on a 24-hour billing system. For example, if a hotel charges for telephone calls, the call accounting system records the telephone calls made each day. Then the guest charges associated with these calls are posted to the appropriate folios. The next day the process begins anew: the telephone calls "balance yet to be posted" is reset to zero. If this were not done, the night auditor would have to sift through considerable data to separate today's calls (that have yet to be posted) from yesterday's calls (that were already posted). Generally, data generated from revenue-producing departments are reset to zero daily. In addition, some non-revenue-generating information such as reservations made per day, comp rooms issued per day, and other operational data may be reset to zero daily.

Data Archiving

In the past, hotels maintained paper records of their reservations and other financial transactions. These records, when aged, were boxed and stored. If records were needed, the appropriate box was located, and the documents sought were reviewed. Today, the amount of information a hotel maintains about future reservations (managerial data) and past reservations (historical data) as well as other financial information is massive. Most of this information is held in electronic (not paper) form, and data archiving is an important concern for FOMs.

Consider, for example, the PMS information of a 1,000-room conference center that allows room bookings 12 months into the future. Literally tens of thousands of reservations are held at any time in the PMS memory, with virtually no hard copy backup. In addition, the hotel maintains records of previous guests, because they might contact the hotel to request duplicate copies of their room payment receipts or to initiate chargeback requests that would require information about their stay. The FOM wants guest histories to record each guest's frequency of stay and stay preferences.

A night auditor is typically instructed to back up (duplicate) daily the data held in the hotel's PMS. This is usually done by copying the data onto a tape drive, compact disc, or other data storage device. Hotels want to minimize any data loss resulting from a complete crash or disintegration of existing records. By archiving data daily and by holding the storage device in a separate location and format, hotels protect themselves against the possibility of complete loss of data. Therefore, archiving is a critical part of the night auditor's job. FOMs, working with the controller and general manager, must determine which data files to be maintain and when (or if) these files should eventually be purged from the system to clear storage space.

SECTION REVIEW AND DISCUSSION QUESTIONS

Section Objective: Identify the types of data most important for night audits, review how data are reset to a zero balance, and discuss basic procedures to archive appropriate data.

Section Summary: The night auditor must maintain a significant portion of the hotel's information database that is, in turn, used by hotel owners, franchisors, lenders, governmental entities, and hotel managers. There are two basic types of data: historical and managerial. Decisions must be made about both types to determine whether data should be reset or archived. Data resetting involves collecting and reporting information on a daily basis and then resetting the balance to zero for the beginning of the next day. Information to be archived is generally held in electronic (not paper) form to use on an as-needed basis. Archived data are typically held in a separate location and format to minimize the possibility of complete data loss.

Discussion Questions:
1. The text provides examples of the uses that hotel owners, franchisors, lenders, governmental entities, and hotel managers have for information in the hotel's database. Can you think of additional examples?
2. What factors would be most important in determining whether database information should be reset to zero at the end of the night audit or should be archived?
3. At times, archived data must be accessed by the FOM and others. In what situations might hotel managers consult archived data?

From the Front Office: Front-Line Interview

Claudio Andrade
Front Office Manager
Waikoloa Beach Marriott (546 rooms)
Waikoloa, Hawaii

A Special Effort Located the Package!

Claudio studied biology and pathology before beginning work in the hospitality industry in 1985. He worked two years in food and beverage and one year in a front office position before joining Marriott in 1988 in Hong Kong. He has worked as a bell services attendant, concierge, front desk agent and supervisor, assistant manager, restaurant manager, chief concierge, front office manager, and director of services. Claudio has opened hotels in Recife (Brazil), Hong Kong, Australia, Singapore, and Rio de Janeiro and has worked in San Juan (Puerto Rico) as a front office manager and as director of services. He was transferred to Hawaii for his present position in late 2004. Claudio has the honor of being the first certified trainer for the rooms division for Marriott in Asia. He has attended many seminars and training sessions with Marriott that addressed technical and leadership skills.

1. **What are the most important responsibilities in your present position?**
   The front office manager must ensure that his or her team has the necessary skills, tools, and guidance to achieve our goals of profitability, guest satisfaction, and associates' satisfaction.

2. **What are the biggest challenges that confront you in your day-to-day work and in the long-term operation of your property's front office?**
   Several significant challenges are balancing rooms inventory based on guests' preferences, reducing the occurrence of problems, and improving problem resolution tactics when issues do occur. It is always important that all guests receive the utmost attention and service that is warm and courteous. This creates lasting memories so they keep returning. In the long term, developing future leaders is my main challenge. Finding talent amid a scarce labor pool increases that challenge.

3. **What is your most unforgettable front office moment?**
   At the Marriott in Hong Kong, a guest told the concierge that he had forgotten a shopping bag containing gifts and a camera under the seat of a public bus he had ridden on his return from Stanley Beach. The young concierge (Joe), who had just been promoted from bell staff, told the guest that he was sorry and said he would see if the package could be located. The guest politely told Joe not to worry. Joe called the bus company, provided the route and time, and asked if anything had been found. When the answer was no, Joe asked for the bus number and its location. After completing his shift, Joe went to the bus garage, explained the situation to the security guard, and climbed into the bus. There he found the bag under the seat. I do not have to tell you how the guest reacted when Joe later handed him the bag.

4. **What advice do you have for those studying about or considering a career in front office or hotel management?**
   First of all, if you are considering this career just for the compensation, forget it! This is a profession that requires a huge amount of dedication and commitment. Whenever you work with people, you have to be able to enjoy the contact if you want to be successful. The rewards of this profession are not solely financial—and most of the time are not financial at all! If you are genuinely interested in helping people achieve their goals (career goals in the case of your associates and travel goals in the case of your guests) and can make your own goals secondary, then you have what it takes. A great thing about this business is that what we do requires human labor. Showing genuine concern for someone's problems, sincere appreciation for someone's efforts, or gratitude is something that cannot be done by a machine; therefore, our future is bright!

The FOM in Action: A Solution

How do FOMs prevent selling mistakes such as the one made by the part-time night auditor at the Harley Hills who offered discounts on rooms for one of the busiest weekends of the year? In a large hotel, the night audit staff consists of a senior auditor and several assistants. Front desk agents, telephone operators, and cashiers may also be scheduled during the late shift to allow night auditors to concentrate on their main job. In smaller properties, however, the night auditor is typically one person, often working alone, whose primary job is the audit but who also fills the role of hotel security, emergency maintenance person, cashier, telephone operator, night manager and, as in this case, even a sales representative.

It is too late for Felicia, the new FOM, to do now what should have been done earlier. As soon as the FOM or revenue manager becomes aware that specific future dates will be in high demand, room rates for that date should be communicated to those who sell. In addition, during a high-demand date, normal room discounts should be eliminated or reduced.

The Harley Hills is legally required to honor the guests' reservations, and the cost of the mistake will be high. As Felicia is learning, one of an FOM's greatest challenges involves managing room rates. Everyone who sells rooms must be aware of the sales strategy established for each future reservation date. In a hotel with a sophisticated PMS, restrictions can usually be programmed into the system. In a manual system or in a hotel with a less sophisticated PMS, "hot dates" that will involve special selling tactics and strategies must be identified. Then special restrictions on these dates must be communicated to all staff who sell rooms. Failure to do so can result in the type of problem facing Felicia and Gil.

In the future, Felicia must ensure that her PMS is programmed properly for any date on which a reservation can be made. (Most PMSs allow selling from 50 to 52 weeks into the future.) In addition, she must ensure that her front desk staff, including each of the night auditors, are well trained in all of their varied roles, but especially in the role of hotel salesperson.

FRONT OFFICE SEMANTICS LIST

Audit	Paid-outs	X report
Source document	Cashier's drawer	Z report
Archive	Credit balance	Emergency report
Military time	Credit limit report	Aging accounts receivable report
Share with (room rate)	Credit manager	Template report
Manager's Daily	Trial balance	Database

FRONT OFFICE AND THE INTERNET

Processing of payment cards is one of an FOM's and night auditor's most important areas of responsibility. Each card issuer manages its own business; thus, the policies and procedures they enforce vary. To see how several of the major card issuers provide processing information, including how to tactfully inform a card holder that he or she has exceeded the credit limit, go to these resources:

Web address	Subject area
www.americanexpress.com	Payment card issuer
www.mastercard.com	Payment card company
www.visa.com	Payment card company

One good way to understand how different hotels structure the roles of their night auditors is to examine job postings for the position. The following Web sites contain current listings of vacant hospitality positions. Simply go to the sites and enter *night auditor* to examine the characteristics FOMs and controllers consider most important in night auditors.

Web address	Subject area
www.hcareers.com	Hospitality job vacancies
www.hospitalityonline.com	Hospitality job vacancies
www.hoteljobs.com	Hospitality job vacancies
www.hoteljobsnetwork.com	Hospitality job vacancies
www.cooljobscanada.com	Hospitality job vacancies

REAL-WORLD ACTIVITIES

1. As you have read, much of the night audit process is automated; the PMS does much of the work that, until relatively recently, had to be done manually by the night auditor. Talk with a general manager, FOM, or night auditor and ask these questions: In what ways could automation further enhance and simplify the night audit process? Have any disadvantages arisen from increased automation of this activity? What is the future of automation in the night audit process?
2. Many hotels have one or more revenue-producing departments that are not interfaced with the PMS. Talk with an FOM and review the factors to be considered as an interface decision is made. Discuss the steps that would be required to implement an interface with the PMS.
3. Talk with a night auditor about the biggest challenges that arise as the night audit is completed. If possible, meet with several night auditors at different types of properties and compare and contrast the information you gather.
4. Ask several FOMs about the tactics they use when talking with registered guests who have exceeded their payment card authorization levels. Do they have suggestions about how to make this task comfortable for the hotel representative and inoffensive to the guests?
5. Talk with one or more general managers and FOMs about the policies used at their properties related to the development and distribution of night audit reports. Is there an approval and authorization process required for new reports? Can department heads generate reports themselves using the property's intranet? What are the biggest challenges to generating and distributing night audit reports?

13

Front Office Manager and the Law

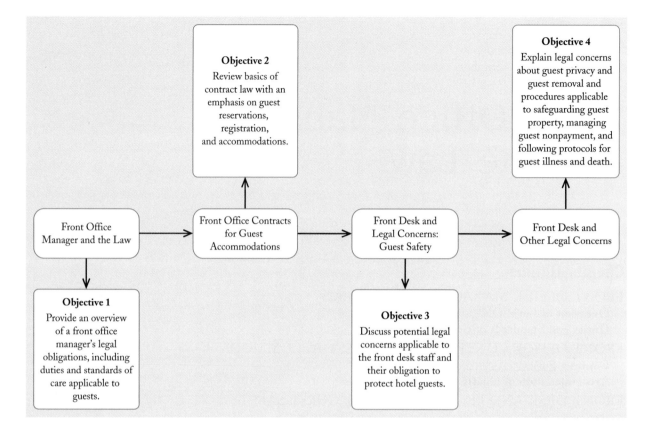

CHAPTER ROADMAP

Chapter Preview

Front office managers and their staff must know a great deal about a diverse range of topics. The topic of legal issues is important but sometimes complex. FOMs must identify concerns that are most likely to prompt litigation if front office personnel do not correctly perform their jobs. FOMs must also develop policies, procedures, and training programs to address the concerns.

FOMs are not attorneys trained to deal with the legal issues that can affect their decision making. Therefore, policies and procedures to manage legal issues must be reviewed with an attorney who is familiar with state and local laws and regulations. Management tools can then be developed in concert with legal recommendations, and a final legal review will ensure that the hotel has the basic legal foundation in place to protect its guests, employees, and owners. Even so, nonrecurring challenges may arise; FOMs should review ad hoc issues with their supervisor, who may request additional organizational assistance, legal advice, or both.

This chapter begins with an overview of how the law affects FOMs and their staff. Duties and standards of care are explained, because they establish the foundation of the expectations that guests and society have about what hotel personnel should and should not do.

Hotels establish contracts with guests when reservations are made or during the registration process. A brief overview of what does, and does not, constitute a contract is presented. The importance of hotels fulfilling their contractual obligations is emphasized, particularly in relation to guest safety. Common laws that have evolved over hundreds of years have established a foundation for many obligations that hotels have for guests. Common laws continue to create the parameters within which hotels must accommodate and protect guests.

Other legal issues are of concern to all FOMs: privacy of guests in their rooms, reasons for removing guests from their rooms, protection of guest property, procedures to minimize guest skips (i.e., departures without payment), management of illness, and death in guestrooms.

It is critical that hoteliers consult with and follow the advice of competent attorneys who are knowledgeable about the laws and regulations that apply to a specific hotel. The time to learn about legal obligations and to develop procedures to comply with them is before a problem arises. Sufficient time will then more likely be available to properly plan and implement appropriate actions to protect guests and employees and to minimize the hotel's liability. Employee training is essential to translate plans into appropriate actions so that laws designed to protect guests and the property are followed consistently.

The FOM in Action: The Challenge

Jacob is the FOM of a 350-room, full-service hotel in the suburbs of a large city. The location is great because, among other nearby attractions, there is a large arena that draws crowds from a wide geographic area for sporting events and concerts. Last July, the property was fully booked for the "Battle of the Bands"—a three-day event.

Jacob volunteered to serve as manager on duty for the entire weekend. Another department head who lives nearby was assigned to be on-call in anticipation of any problems that might arise because of the full house of concert attendees.

On the first evening of the three-day event, concertgoers began returning to the property about midnight. The hotel normally employs one security guard to make scheduled patrols of the property. A second had been retained for the concert weekend to be visible in the lobby area and to assist wherever needed throughout the property.

The problem started about 2:00 a.m. Occupants in several rooms on the second floor gathered in the elevator lobby area to play music on instruments they had brought from home. Upon hearing the noise, one security guard quickly went to the site and saw about 15 persons; he could not be certain if they were all registered guests. He asked everyone to return to their rooms or leave the property. Most people did so, but several who appeared to be intoxicated became upset and stated their intention to continue the impromptu jam session.

The security guard called the FOM and asked, "What should I do now?"

FRONT OFFICE MANAGER AND THE LAW

As you are discovering in each chapter of this book, the duties and responsibilities of FOMs are extensive. They do far more than supervise staff members who take guest reservations, register and check out guests, and resolve guest problems during their

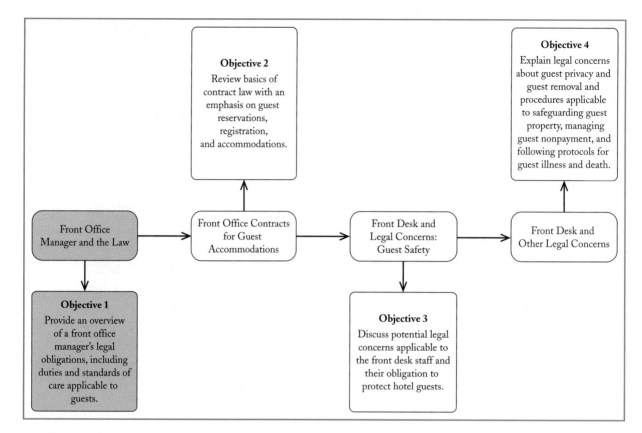

ROADMAP 13.1

stay. In fact, FOMs must know a significant amount about human resources management, technology, marketing, psychology, financial management, and so on. This chapter discusses another dimension of the FOM's job: compliance with the law. As Roadmap 13.1 shows, the discussion begins with an overview of the FOM's legal obligations.

Overview of Legal Obligations

A wide range of laws and regulations apply to all business organizations, including hotels. Think of the many legal requirements related to labor, building construction and remodeling, and tax obligations. This chapter focuses on the laws relating to the lodging property and its legal relationship with hotel guests and visitors that affect hospitality managers in general and FOMs more specifically.

Few FOMs or other hotel managers are **attorneys.** Nevertheless, they must have a general working knowledge about legal aspects of their position. What an FOM and staff say (or don't say) and do (or don't do) can have a significant impact on the hotel.

FRONT OFFICE SEMANTICS

Attorney: Trained and licensed person who represents others in issues related to laws.

Many laws that apply to hoteliers are derived from English common laws of the Middle Ages that apply to hotels of that era.

Many laws that affect hoteliers are derived from English **common laws** that evolved during the Middle Ages to address general societal concerns. For example, innkeepers were responsible for providing a safe place of rest to all those who were willing to pay for it, and innkeepers were responsible for protecting the property of travelers who sought their accommodations.

FRONT OFFICE SEMANTICS

Common laws: Laws (rules) that evolved from customs in the Middle Ages in England and that form the foundation for many contemporary laws in the United States.

In addition to common laws, FOMs must also understand the **civil laws** that address the rights and remedies of private persons in noncriminal matters.

FRONT OFFICE SEMANTICS

Civil laws: Laws (rules) that are primarily established by governmental edict or legislation. Many civil laws evolved from the time of the Roman Empire.

Government agencies create codes, statutes, or other mandates that affect the relationship between the hotel and its guests. For example, consider a guest who is injured from a fall on a wet floor in the hotel lobby. The guest may claim that the hotel is liable for the injury and could file a **lawsuit** seeking damages incurred by alleged wrongful acts of the hotel.

FRONT OFFICE SEMANTICS

Lawsuit: Legal action in a court of law based on a complaint that a person or company failed to perform a required duty, and that failure resulted in harm to the person filing the complaint.

Litigation follows a lawsuit. In this example, the injured guest's attorney will allege that the accident was preventable, and that it was primarily caused by the actions or inactions of the hotel. The attorney will ask that the injured party be awarded **damages** by the property to compensate for the incident.

FRONT OFFICE SEMANTICS

Litigation: Process of suing someone for damages caused by a wrongful act.

Damages: Amount of losses or costs assessed to the individual or company that was found to be liable for a wrongful act.

Could the FOM and staff have prevented this accident? For example, would it be their fault that the material of which the floor is constructed, while beautiful and perfect for the aesthetics of the environment, is very slippery (and, therefore, unsafe) when it is wet? The court's answer will probably be yes, if the hotel's owners or managers made the decision about the flooring material or retained the services of someone who did. If there had never been a problem before, the court may order the hotel to pay **compensatory damages.** However, if accidents had occurred previously, and the hotel ignored the obvious potential safety hazard, additional **punitive damages** might be awarded to the injured guest.

FRONT OFFICE SEMANTICS

Compensatory damages: Monetary amount intended to compensate injured parties for actual losses or damage they incurred (e.g., medical bills and lost wages). Also known as *actual damages.*

Punitive damages: Monetary amount assessed to punish liable parties and serve as an example to the liable party as well as others not to commit the wrongful act in the future.

Could the FOM and staff have done something to alert guests to the slippery floor, for example, by installing nonslip mats, posting signs, or by requiring that oral warnings be given by parking, door or bell services attendants? The judicial system makes decisions about such questions; however, many times lawsuits are settled before they reach the court system. FOMs and other managers must have a clear understanding of their duties and standards of care, and they must use this understanding to guide their actions.

Duties and Standards of Care

FOMs and all other members of the hotel's team have legal duties, that is, obligations, to guests and to others. For example, they owe a **duty of care** to those who enter the hotel or its property.

FRONT OFFICE SEMANTICS

Duty of care: Obligation imposed by law that requires a specific standard of conduct.

The hotel owes a duty of care to provide safe walking conditions on the lobby floor and for other safety concerns that can be reasonably foreseen. Consider, for example, a guest's safety while occupying a guestroom. The hotel has a duty of care to provide working door locks to prevent unauthorized opening of the room's corridor door, glass patio door, or other possible entry doors. In contrast, it may not be reasonable to expect the hotel to prevent unauthorized entry by an intruder who forcibly breaks the glass in a window or on the patio door to gain entry to the guestroom.

Hoteliers' reasonable duties of care include the following actions:

- Providing reasonably safe buildings and grounds
- Serving **wholesome** food and beverages

FRONT OFFICE SEMANTICS

Wholesome: Fit for human consumption.

- Ensuring that alcoholic beverages are served responsibly
- Selecting and training employees in a way that helps to reasonably protect guests and others against acts of **negligence** caused by staff members

FRONT OFFICE SEMANTICS

Negligence: Doing something that a reasonable person would not do, or failing to do something that a reasonable person would have done, in the same situation.

- Warning about anything that does or may pose a threat to safety
- Protecting guest property
- Registering guests properly
- Using reasonable care to prevent injury to a guest or others

In addition to meeting their duties of care, hotel employees must meet **standards of care.**

FRONT OFFICE SEMANTICS

Standard of care: Level of performance that is determined to be reasonably acceptable by the industry to fulfill a duty of care.

FOMs, for example, must provide a reasonably safe environment for the hotel's employees, guests, and visitors, but what is *reasonable?* The term is defined in the legal sense of **reasonable care.**

FRONT OFFICE SEMANTICS

Reasonable care: Legal concept that identifies the amount of care a reasonably prudent person would exercise in a specific situation.

FOMs and all other members of the hotel's management team must consistently operate the hotel with a degree of care equal to that which would be provided by their peers, that is, other reasonable FOMs and hotel managers. For example, if an FOM knows about a threat to guest safety such as a fire, it is reasonable to assume that he or she will either immediately eliminate the threat or clearly inform the guests of it. To not do so would likely mean that the FOM did not exercise the proper degree of reasonable care for the safety of guests, visitors, and employees in the hotel. If there was a threat to safety that resulted in a loss, injury, or death, and if it was determined that hotel staff did not exercise reasonable care about that threat, the hotel could be held wholly or partially liable for the loss, injury, or death that resulted from the threat.

Let's consider fire emergencies. When hotels are constructed, they must meet many strict requirements about building design, safety, signage, and other elements related to fire safety before an occupancy permit is granted by the local governing authority. Let's assume, however, that within the first several months after a certain hotel opened, a series of false alarms occurred that were immediately traced to problems with the fire alarm system and the way it was wired. Let's also assume that only several days after the system was repaired, tested, and confirmed to be functional, the fire alarm sounded again. Would a reasonably prudent FOM assume that it was another false alarm that could be ignored and that there was no need to inform guests and other building occupants? Alternatively, would a reasonably prudent FOM assume that there could be a serious potential emergency and immediately respond to the situation according to the hotel's established operating procedures for proper response to alarms? A reasonably prudent FOM or other hotel manager would consider the alarm to be real, because to do otherwise might result in serious injury or even loss of life to the hotel's guests, employees, and visitors.

MODERN FRONT OFFICE ISSUES AND TACTICS

No Price Gouging During Hurricanes in Florida

During Fall 2004, Florida was ravaged by three deadly hurricanes. Most hoteliers went out of their way to assist fleeing residents by offering reduced room rates, eliminating no-pet policies, and providing free meals or reduced-priced meals. Hotel employees in some properties without foodservices shopped at retail grocery stores to buy food for their guests. Others slept in hotel offices so more guestrooms would be available. Many hotels exhibited the spirit of hospitality and professionalism of which the industry can be proud.

At least two hotels, however, tried to take advantage of the situation by increasing advertised room rates. The attorney general's office of Florida sued one property (Days Inn Airport in West Palm Beach), which agreed to pay $70,000 to settle price-gouging allegations from customers after Hurricane Charley. In spite of a billboard near the hotel advertising all rooms for $49.99, the hotel charged two evacuees $109 for a room and a third evacuee paid $119.

Florida's price-gouging law requires that prices of necessities remain at the average price of the 30-day period before a storm. The attorney general's office filed 13 price-gouging lawsuits statewide following the hurricanes of 2004.

Adapted from Barancik, S. 2004. Florida attorney general suing two hotels for alleged price-gouging during Charley; most hotels very charitable to evacuees. Retrieved August 3, 2004, from http://www.hotel-online.com/News/PR2004_3rd/Aug04_FloridaAG.html and Days Inn hit with $70,000 price-gouging fine. *Palm Beach Post*, October 6, 2004.

SECTION REVIEW AND DISCUSSION QUESTIONS

Section Objective: Provide an overview of a front office manager's legal obligations, including duties and standards of care applicable to guests.

Section Summary: Many laws with specific applications to hotels are derived from English common laws that evolved during the Middle Ages. Examples: the innkeeper's responsibility to provide a safe place of rest for those who pay for it and the innkeeper's need to protect travelers' property. Many civil laws make hoteliers liable for wrongful acts that harm guests, visitors, or employees.

Hoteliers owe duties of care to their on-site constituencies related to the provision of reasonably safe buildings and grounds and the selection and training of employees who act in ways to protect guests and others from negligent acts. Other duties of care involve the protection of guest property and the exercise of reasonable care to prevent injuries to guests, visitors, and employees.

Hoteliers must also provide a standard of reasonable care: that which a reasonably prudent person would exercise in a specific situation. In the lodging industry, standards relate to the level of performance determined to be reasonably acceptable for professionals working in the industry.

Discussion Questions:
1. Why do you think that English common laws that are several hundred years old still influence modern laws that affect hoteliers specifically and society more generally?
2. Can you think of examples of negligent acts by front desk agents for which the hotel might be found legally responsible?
3. This section provided examples of hoteliers' reasonable duties of care. What additional examples can you suggest?

FRONT OFFICE CONTRACTS FOR GUEST ACCOMMODATIONS

Roadmap 13.2 indicates that FOMs must know the basics of contract law that are applicable to guest reservations, registrations, and accommodations. FOMs enter into **contracts** when they make a room reservation for a guest or when they sign an agreement to purchase or lease front office equipment from a supplier. They may confront potential legal issues as contracts are managed, and these issues are the topics of this section.

FRONT OFFICE SEMANTICS

Contract: Legally enforceable agreement or promise involving two or more parties.

Contract Basics

Express contracts can involve oral or written words, and contracts of both types are legal and binding if they are enforceable. To be a **legal contract,** the parties to the agreement

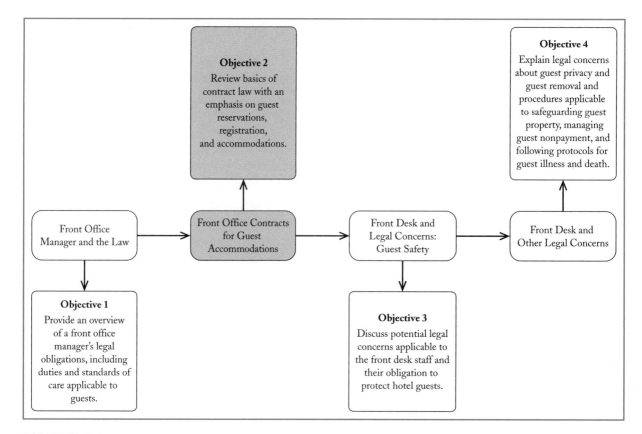

ROADMAP 13.2

must be of a specified minimum age, the parties must be mentally competent to under-stand the contract's terms, and the purpose of the contract must not violate the law.

FRONT OFFICE SEMANTICS

Contract (express): Contract that involves oral or written words.

Legal contract: Contract in which the parties to the agreement are of a specified minimum age, parties are mentally competent to understand the contract's terms, and the purpose of the contract does not violate the law.

Many contracts are expressed. Assume that a guest makes a guaranteed reserva-tion for a specific night. The reservations agent explains that the guest's credit card will be charged for the one night's stay if the guest does not cancel the reservation before 6:00 p.m. on the date of arrival. The guest agrees, and an express contract has been made. The hotel could charge the guest if the individual is a no-show on the arrival date. Detailed information about alternative types of reservations and exam-ples of times when a guest may not be charged for a guaranteed reservation (even if the hotel is legally able to do so) are presented in Chapter 11.

Implied contracts do not involve words; instead, they are inferred by the actions of one or both of the parties. For example, a guest may call the front desk agent to ask about a one-night rental cost for a roll-away bed. On learning the cost, the guest says, "Please deliver the bed to my room before 8:00 p.m." Although there was no written or oral agreement such as, "Okay, I wish to rent a bed," the guest implies acceptance, and an implied contract has been entered into when the delivery request is made.

FRONT OFFICE SEMANTICS

Contract (implied): Agreement that is not in writing but that is created by the behavior of both parties who suggest that they are acting under an agreement.

Both express and implied contracts have the following elements: offer, consideration, and acceptance.

- *Offer.* An **offer** indicates what one entity is willing to do and what that entity expects in return. For example, a hotel's registration card is a contract between the property and a guest. When a prospective guest reads a hotel's registration card, such as the one illustrated in Figure 13.1, he or she is learning about the hotel's offer to supply a specified type of room for a specified length of time at a specified price.

FRONT OFFICE SEMANTICS

Offer (contract): Element in a legal contract that indicates what one entity is willing to do and what that entity expects in return.

- *Consideration.* **Consideration** relates to money, property, or a promise exchanged for the promise made in a contract. In the example of the guest registration contract, the consideration is a room rental for a stated rental rate.

FRONT OFFICE SEMANTICS

Consideration (contract): Element in a legal contract that relates to money, property, or a promise exchanged for the promise made in a contract.

- *Acceptance.* An **acceptance** is an agreement by the second party in a contract to the terms and conditions of the offer. Agreement to a contract's terms can be made by fax, mail, express delivery service, or even e-mail; however, in today's business world, many contracts are written. If contracts concern a normally recurring issue such as guestroom rental, standardized documents are used. If necessary, they are modified by agreement of both contractual parties.

FRONT OFFICE SEMANTICS

Acceptance (contract): Agreement by the second party in a contract to the terms and conditions of the offer.

BULGA, JARAN
Arrive: 01/03/XX
Depart: 01/04/XX
Room Type: BNDD

Room: _____179_____
Account Number: 149439
Adults: 1
Children: 0

Your rate(s) are as follows

From	To	Rate
1/3/XX	1/4/XX	104.99

*Additional rate changes apply.

Rate Acceptance: _____JG_____

Departure Date Acceptance: _____JG_____

GTD/Payment: _____4P_____

Frequent Traveler ID: _____

Address: _____1234 Main Street_____

_____Anytown, CA   12345_____

E-mail: _____

Guest ID: ____1234567_____

License Plate: __B71201_____   State: ___CA___

If payment is by credit card, you are authorized to charge my account for the total amount due. The undersigned guest acknowledges all charges are personal indebtedness. I have requested weekday delivery of USA TODAY. If refused, a credit of $0.50 will be applied to my account.

I agree that my liability for this bill is not waived and agree to be held personally liable in the event that the indicated person, company, or association fails to pay the full amount of these charges.

Guest Signature: _____*J Bulga*_____

Imprint Credit Card Below

Clarion®

MY CHOICE HOTELS

Your Room Number is: _____179_____

Our telephone number is: (xxx) xxx-xxxx
Our guest fax number is: (xxx) xxx-xxxx

Check out time is: 12:00 P.M.

Our mailing address is: 3600 Hometown Drive
                           Hilotown, HI 88888

Our e-mail address is: info@hilotownhotel

If you do not find everything to your satisfaction or need additional assistance, please contact the front desk immediately. Our staff will be glad to assist you.

For reservations at this hotel please call (xxx) xxx-xxxx or to make reservations at other Clarion hotels, please call (800) 4-CHOICE.

FIGURE 13.1   Sample registration card.

Offers can be accepted orally: "Yes, I will pay $75 to rent the guestroom for one more day." Offers can also be accepted in writing: for example, the guest who signs the registration card illustrated in Figure 13.1 is providing written acceptance of the agreement. Additionally, acceptance can be made with money. This occurs when, for example, a guest makes a deposit to reserve a room or when a partial or full payment is made when meeting space is reserved.

What happens if a contract for a room is broken by a hotel that cannot honor a guest's reservation, for example, because it is overbooked? Legally, the guest could formally seek damages in a court of law. However, the amount of harm caused to the guest would typically be small; therefore, many times a lawsuit is not worth the time or effort of the guest or the courts. Instead, it is common industry practice for the hotel to compensate the inconvenienced guest by paying for the lodging and incidental expenses incurred when the guest is relocated to another hotel.

HOTEL RESERVATIONS ARE CONTRACTS

When a guest makes a hotel reservation, that guest enters into a contract with the hotel to occupy a room at a specific time for an agreed-on time. (Details about alternative types of reservations are discussed in Chapter 5.) If the reservation is confirmed but not guaranteed, the hotel agrees to hold the room for the guest only until a specified time. The contract is no longer in effect after the agreed-on time. When a guaranteed reservation is made, the guest making the reservation agrees to pay a room rental rate for at least the first night, regardless of when (or if) he or she arrives. The hotel agrees to hold the room for the guest during this time period and to provide the appropriate accommodations to the guest at arrival. The contract also allows the hotel to charge the guest if the guest does not comply with the hotel's terms, such as notification that the room is no longer needed by an agreed-on time or a failure to arrive on the agreed-on date.

In a legally binding contract, both parties must willingly accept the agreed-on terms.

Accommodation of Guests

Issues of potential legal consequence can arise before a prospective guest checks in to the hotel. Recall that common law has historically required that a hotel accept persons who desire and are able to pay for a guestroom. This judicial code, which is hundreds of years old, has been strengthened by many statutes and by state and federal government civil rights laws that prohibit places of public accommodations from discriminating against any persons because of their race, color, religion, or national origin. There are special situations, however, in which hotels have a right to refuse room rental by potential guests or in which hotels may be found negligent if they *do* allow rental:

- Persons who are under age (and, therefore, cannot be a legal party to a contract)
- Persons who are drunk or disorderly or who are suffering from a contagious disease
- Persons carrying property such as explosives or guns that may harm others
- Persons desiring to bring in pets that are not accepted by hotel policy
- Persons who cannot or will not pay for the hotel's products and services
- The hotel has no rooms available for rent (The issue of a hotel needing to refuse potential guests who arrive with an appropriate reservation is discussed in detail in Chapter 6.)

Since passage of the Americans with Disabilities Act (ADA) in the early 1990s, there have been legal requirements in the United States that mandate hoteliers to accommodate disabled guests. The ADA also requires hoteliers to accommodate disabled employees; however, that discussion is beyond the scope of this chapter.

ADA requirements pertain to the hotel building, parking lots, grounds, and public areas, in addition to the guestrooms. The requirements are designed to ensure that the hotel, as a public facility, is accessible to those with physical disabilities, and they apply to lodging operations with more than five guestrooms if they are not occupied by or are the residence of the proprietor. Thus, a small B&B operation would likely not be covered by ADA requirements.

ADA requirements are extensive and begin with the number of **accessible** guestrooms that are required. For example, a hotel with 1 to 25 rooms must have 1 accessible room; a hotel with 301 to 400 rooms must have 8 accessible rooms, including 4 with roll-in showers. In addition, accommodations must be available for persons with hearing impairments (e.g., visual alarms, notification devices, and appropriate telephones).

FRONT OFFICE SEMANTICS

Accessible (guestroom): Guestroom that is designed to accommodate persons with disabilities by removing barriers that otherwise limit or prevent them from obtaining the services that are offered.

ADA regulations require that accessible sleeping rooms and suites be dispersed among the types of rooms available to other guests based on, for example, room size, cost, amenities, and number of beds. The regulations do allow construction of accessible rooms to be limited to rooms used for multiple occupancy, if they are rented to individuals with disabilities at the cost of a single-occupancy room when requested. Rooms must be located in an area of the hotel that is accessible to guests with disabilities. ADA requirements provide many details about maneuvering spaces within the guestroom; widths of doors and doorways; accessibility of cabinets, shelves, closets, and drawers; and special requirements for bathroom facilities. Complete details about ADA standards for accessible transient lodging facilities can be found at www.usdoj.gov/crt/ada/reg3a.html#anchor-54325.

Many persons with disabilities covered by the ADA are aware of the federal requirements relating to accommodations. Those that do will likely make advance reservations to ensure that an accessible room will be available for their use when they arrive at the property. FOMs must develop policies about holding these rooms for guests who have made a reservation for them and about renting these accessible rooms to walk-in guests who are not in need of them. Front desk agents must be trained to consistently comply with these policies so that eligible guests are not denied equal access to the property.

MODERN FRONT OFFICE ISSUES AND TACTICS

Poor Pet and Service-Animal Policies Can Lead to Lawsuits from Disabled Guests

What should a front desk agent do when an allegedly disabled guest brings a seeing-eye dog or other service animal to a no-pets hotel? Must the guest be accommodated? Should questions be asked about the disability in efforts to determine its legitimacy? Should some type of "proof" be requested to verify that the animal is, in fact, a service animal? What if the guest is given a room and the service animal creates a disturbance?

According to the Americans with Disabilities Act, service animals are not pets; therefore, policies pertaining to pets do not apply. Service animals are specifically trained to protect and to help provide owners with assistance and independence. (Note that service animals are not necessarily dogs.)

Hoteliers are not permitted to discriminate against disabled guests with service animals. These guests with their service animals must be provided the same services and access to all areas of the property to which other guests are entitled, including pool areas, restaurants, and business centers. If a guest says that he or she is disabled and states that the animal is a service animal, most hoteliers would consider the appropriate procedure to be to check in the guest without further inquiry.

If other guests complain about the presence of the animal, they should be informed about the law. If the service animal becomes disruptive, the owner must control it. Most service animals are specifically trained to be comfortable around people, are not dangerous, and will not create a disturbance.

Hoteliers are not required to provide special services for the animal (food or leashes, for example). They cannot impose a separate charge or cleaning deposit for service animals even if they do so for pets.

Adapted from Orlick, M. 2004. Adopting pets and service animal policies to avoid lawsuits from disabled hotel guests. Retrieved September 2004, from http://www.hotel-online.com/News/PR2004_3rd/Sept04_PetPolicy.html.

SECTION REVIEW AND DISCUSSION QUESTIONS

Section Objective: Review basics of contract law with an emphasis on guest reservations, registration, and accommodations.

Section Summary: Guests enter into contract with hotels when they make a room reservation in advance or sign a registration card when they arrive at the property.

There are three parts to a contract: offer, consideration, and acceptance. Parties to a contract must be of a specified minimum age and must be mentally competent to understand the contract's terms and the contract must not violate the law.

Hoteliers must not discriminate against any persons because of their race, color, religion, or national origin. In some situations FOMs can refuse room rental, for example, if persons are under age, drunk, disorderly, suffering from a contagious disease, or carrying property that may harm others. Likewise, FOMs do not have to accept guests who violate no-pet policies or who cannot or will not pay for the hotel's products and services. The Americans with Disabilities Act imposes legal requirements on hoteliers to accommodate disabled guests. These requirements are extensive and address, among many concerns, the number of and requirements for accessible guestrooms.

Discussion Questions:

1. Assume that you are a front desk agent and a person who appears to be intoxicated approaches you to rent a room without a reservation. What special policies and procedures are appropriate for you to follow? Now assume that an intoxicated guest with a guaranteed reservation arrives at the hotel. Are different policies and procedures applicable?

2. What, if any, special policies and procedures would you, as an FOM, require in this situation: A sports team comprised of 20 to 30 minors and with just a few adult chaperones arrives at the hotel and requests information about room availability and rates?

3. Assume that you are an FOM whose hotel is in compliance with the requirements of the Americans with Disabilities Act. What, if any, special policies should front desk agents follow when assigning rooms to walk-in guests who do not appear to be disabled? Who indicate that they are disabled?

FRONT DESK AND LEGAL CONCERNS: GUEST SAFETY

As indicated in Roadmap 13.3, this section of the chapter focuses on legal concerns related to guest safety. All hoteliers, including those working in front office positions, have personal, professional, and societal obligations to protect their guests' safety. They also have a legal obligation to do so. We have already discussed two duties of care: the provision of reasonably safe buildings and grounds and the responsibility to warn persons about anything that does or may pose a safety threat. It would be difficult to develop an exhaustive list of potential safety problems for guests that could arise if front office employees do not provide duties of care that meet industry standards. However, three things are certain. First, FOMs must determine the types of guest safety-related situations that are most likely to occur and develop policies and procedures to address them. Second, training efforts to ensure that staff members know what they should and should not do if safety-related problems occur should be planned and implemented. Third, if the duties and standards of care applicable to

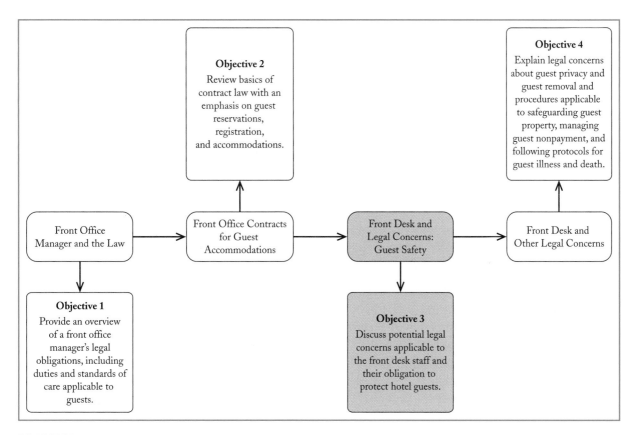

ROADMAP 13.3

safety and security are not consistently maintained by employees who act responsibly, overt legal and financial implications are likely.

Here is a list of examples based on situations that have actually arisen in lodging properties. Most, if not all, of these situations could occur almost anywhere. This list suggests the types of situations and issues that should be included in policies and procedures that are used in training programs for front office staff.

- The front desk agent, night auditor, or the owner of a small property working alone during a slow shift falls asleep or is absent when one or more individuals who are not registered guests enter the property through the lobby. These persons gain access to guestroom corridors and then into guestrooms where they harm guests. What should an employee do if he or she believes that an unregistered guest is in public areas of the hotel when there are no registered guests present?

- A security guard patrols the hotel on a schedule that includes periodic visits to the lobby or front desk area. This employee (or staff member of a contracted service) fails to appear at one or more scheduled times. What, should the front desk agent do?

- A person claiming to be a guest locked out of his room approaches the front desk to request another room key. He provides the appropriate name and room number of the guest occupying the room when asked by the front desk agent.

The "guest" obtains the key, enters the room, and harms the registered guest. What should the front desk agent have done to further confirm the person's identification?

• The front desk agent working on the night shift at a small property without a security guard receives a telephone call from a frantic guest pleading for help. She alleges that an unknown person just entered her room. What should the front desk agent do?

• A guest checking into a hotel inquires about the safety of the property's parking lot. He is concerned about personal safety and potential damage to his vehicle. He also wonders whether all personal contents should be removed from his vehicle before he retires for the evening. What should the front desk agent say if there has been significant, some, or no previous criminal activity in the parking lot?

• A front desk agent in a hotel regularly sees some visitors walking through the lobby during a period when there are criminal acts occurring at the hotel. Perhaps these visitors seem to be dressed inappropriately or otherwise stand out from most guests at and visitors to the hotel. What should the front desk agent do?

• A roadside motel uses a walk-up window for guest registration purposes during late night and early morning hours. A person expresses apprehension about completing the registration process outside in cold weather and asks to enter the building. In another scenario, a person appearing to have a weapon approaches the guest who is outside registering for a room. What should the front desk agent do in each of these situations?

• A guest who is present in the front desk area during an armed robbery is injured. The front desk agent had received no training about what to do in the event of a robbery. What should the agent have done?

• It is New Year's Eve, or the night of the season's biggest sporting event in the community, or another occasion when it is reasonable to anticipate that many hotel guests and visitors will be celebrating. What should a front desk agent be told to expect during the evening shift? What additional security precautions should be taken? Should revisions be made to work tasks that are the responsibility of the agent?

• A front desk agent observes an obviously, visibly intoxicated guest or visitor walking through the lobby area. In another scenario, the front desk agent notices an obviously, visibly intoxicated female guest being helped through the lobby and on to a guestroom elevator by two men who are not hotel guests (or are not occupants of the woman's guestroom). What should the front desk agent do?

• A guest inquires about a suggested jogging route to try the next morning. The hotel is located near areas known for relatively high crime rates or is in a high-traffic area with limited sidewalks and road shoulders. What should the front desk agent say?

• A front desk agent receives several phone calls from guests about noise in a specific guestroom. When the front desk agent or security employee go to the room, there is no noise coming from it. What, if anything, should the staff member do?

• A front desk agent notices a 911 (emergency) call from a specific guestroom. What should the agent do?

A common concern in each of these scenarios is the potential for negligence on the part of the front desk agent and, therefore, on the part of the hotel, if the employee's behavior is not judged to be reasonable in a court of law. The safety, legal, and financial problems that can arise when FOMs fail to address such concerns during training can be significant. Professional FOMs use experience gained from one situation to develop policies and procedures that could be helpful in similar situations, and they consistently assign the highest priority to protecting the safety of guests staying at their property.

SECTION REVIEW AND DISCUSSION QUESTIONS

Section Objective: Discuss potential legal concerns applicable to the front desk staff and their obligation to protect hotel guests.

Section Summary: A wide range of safety-related situations can arise that have a direct affect on guest safety. FOMs must consider those that are most likely to occur and develop policies and procedures to address them. Front desk agents and other staff members must be trained so they will know what to do should these or similar situations arise.

Discussion Questions:

1. Select one or more of the guest safety-related situations noted in this section. What do you think a reasonable front desk agent would do in the situation? Why? What major points applicable to this situation would you, as an FOM, include in a training program for front desk agents?
2. What other situations, if not handled properly, could create concerns about guest safety? How might a reasonable front desk agent handle them? How should the situations be addressed in training for these staff members?
3. Assume that you are an FOM for a hotel located in an area with relatively high crime rates. What concerns would you have about the safety of front desk agents themselves? How would you address these concerns?

FRONT DESK AND OTHER LEGAL CONCERNS

As you can see from Roadmap 13.4, front desk personnel must be familiar with a variety of legal concerns in addition to guest safety. Many concerns arise after the guest arrives at and is checked in to the hotel. Among the most important are those relating to guest privacy, guest removal, guest property, nonpayment for services, and guest illness or death.

Guest Privacy

One of a hotelier's most important duties of care is to allow lawfully registered guests the private and peaceful possession of their guestrooms. To do so requires the implementation of effective policies and procedures to prevent unregistered and unauthorized persons from entering guestrooms. Besides guests and their authorized visitors, only a few persons should have access to the room. Housekeeping personnel

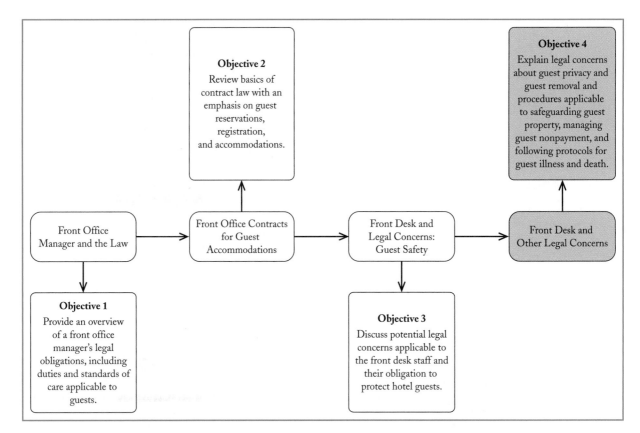

ROADMAP 13.4

must clean and foodservice employees must restock a food and beverage minibar—at times convenient to the guest. Maintenance personnel may require room access for a significant concern such as an overflowing toilet or even for routinely scheduled maintenance tasks. Hotel security or management personnel and local medical, police and fire, or other persons may need to enter a guestroom in the event of an emergency. Guests may, at their discretion, permit other hotel employees to enter their room, for example, a maintenance person performing routine work at the guest's request or a foodservice employee delivering room service.

The hotel's obligation to ensure guest privacy begins at the time of registration. Front desk agents should never announce aloud the room number of a registered guest. Likewise, neither agents, PBX operators, or others should ever provide guestroom numbers to persons inquiring at or phoning the front desk. A better response is this: "I am not permitted to release the guest's room number, but I will certainly be very pleased to put your call through to the room." Front desk agents should never give room keys to anyone but registered guests who have provided appropriate identification. Consider, for example, Mr. Tuskey, who approaches the front desk and says, "Hello, I am Don Tuskey. My wife, Lisa, is registered in room 232. She asked me to meet her there. I was just at the room, but she must have stepped out. May I please have a room key, so I can wait for her in the room?" A well-trained front desk agent will politely explain the hotel's policy and the reason for it (to protect guests) and will request that the guest wait in the lobby or another public area. This should

To ensure safety for all hotel guests, only staff members and authorized visitors should have access to a guest's room.

be the procedure even if the guest has appropriate identification to confirm that he is, in fact, Mr. Tuskey.

Guests' reasonable expectations about privacy also generally extend to registration and other records pertaining to their stay. Without a **court order** or **subpoena,** the FOM and front desk agents should not release any records pertaining to a guest's visit, and professional hoteliers have traditionally taken this obligation very seriously. However, the Anti-Terrorism Act passed in response to the September 11, 2001, attacks now provides authorized law enforcement personnel faster access to records (i.e., no court documentation is needed) and absolves hoteliers from legal remedies for doing so. (For more information about the Anti-Terrorism Act of 2001, go to: www.epic.org/privacy/terrorism/ata_analysis.html)

FRONT OFFICE SEMANTICS

Court order: Legal decision made by a court that requires that something be done or not be done.

Subpoena: Command by a court that a witness appear and testify before it.

The law is generally clear about front desk agents or other hotel employees allowing police to enter a guestroom. Assume that local law enforcement officials have **reasonable cause** to believe that a registered guest may have committed a crime. They approach the front desk to request admittance to the guest's room to obtain evidence. Typically, this cannot be done without a **search warrant** because of the U.S. Constitution's protection against unreasonable search and seizure. Therefore, hotel managers or employees generally have no authority to permit a guestroom search, and law enforcement officers have no authority to demand it without a search warrant.

FRONT OFFICE SEMANTICS

Reasonable cause: Knowledge of facts that, although not the same as direct knowledge, would cause a reasonable person knowing the same facts to reasonably conclude the same thing.

Search warrant: Written order issued by a judge that directs a law enforcement officer to search a specified place for one or more specified items of evidence.

Now let's assume that a housekeeper is cleaning a registered guest's room and notes what appears to be drug-making paraphernalia. The housekeeper advises the executive housekeeper about the discovery. Is it appropriate for this manager to double-check the housekeeper's report, to contact the police or to confront the guest? In most cases, reasonable hotel managers would agree that it is unsafe and illegal for hotel rooms to be used to manufacture or sell drugs. Such activity should be reported to the hotel's general manager and then to the local police for appropriate action. Consider also that a hotel has a duty of care to its employees. To ask a housekeeper to clean a room that is unsafe for them places the hotel at legal risk should an injury occur. For example, what if complications occur as a result of an employee's skin being pierced by a hypodermic needle hidden under a blanket or mattress by the drug user?

As with other areas of the law, sometimes special circumstances must be considered such as events that require immediate action. Police would not likely require, nor would FOMs request, a search warrant for a room into which a criminal fleeing from a crime has just entered or in which a person appears to be committing a crime against another person.

When a guestroom is no longer occupied, that is, when the guest has just checked out, an FOM may allow enforcement officials to search the room. Also, a guest can no longer expect privacy in a room for which rental payment is overdue; hotel staff can typically enter such a room to remove personnel belongings and to change the lock. Actual removal of a guest for not paying is addressed in the following section.

Guest Removal

Hoteliers who manage transient properties can normally evict transient guests from guestrooms without first going to court. A critical issue, however, is whether the room occupant is a **guest** or a **tenant.**

FRONT OFFICE SEMANTICS

Guest (hotel): Person who rents a guestroom for a short time period with no intention of becoming a permanent resident. Also called a *transient guest.*

Tenant (hotel): Person who rents a hotel guestroom for an extended time period with the intent of establishing a permanent residency.

In many locations there are residential hotels in which most, if not all, rooms are occupied by permanent guests. In some situations, there are leases, not registration contracts; and sometimes room occupancy taxes are not levied against these permanent residents. In other locations, some or many rooms in a property are occupied by permanent guests who, by definition, reside in the room for a much longer period (often years) than do transient guests.

The amount of time a hotel guest must occupy a room before he or she is considered a tenant varies by local law, but that time is often established as 30 consecutive days. A person who is legally considered a tenant can be required to vacate the guestroom only if the hotel initiates and is successful in a court proceeding. There is considerable potential for distinction in the legal definitions of the terms *tenant* and *guest* in different jurisdictions. Therefore, FOMs who are not certain if a person they want to remove from the guestroom is legally a guest or a tenant should be conservative, consult an attorney, and, if necessary, obtain the proper court orders needed to authorize the eviction.

For what reasons might the FOM want to remove a guest or a tenant? Appropriate reasons include these:

- *Nonpayment of hotel bill.* Unless a hotel receives payment in advance for a guestroom rental, the guest (recall the distinction between the terms *guest* and *tenant*) is expected to pay for the room by the hotel's posted time of check-out

If hotel guests fail to pay their bills, the hotel may have a right to evict them.

using a method of payment that is acceptable to the hotel. When a hotel guest does not or cannot pay a rightfully due bill, the term *eviction* is often used to denote the guest's involuntary removal. Legally, however, a hotel rarely files the type of lawsuit actually required in an official eviction proceeding. Rather, the guest is politely "asked" to vacate the premises. In advance of such situations, experienced FOMs may meet with local law enforcement officers and should meet with members of their own security staff to clearly define the procedures to be used for a forced removal. Doing so helps to protect the hotel in the event that the guest claims the hotel used excessive force for the removal. Note that police assistance is generally limited to removing the guest from the property; it does not include an arrest for failure to pay a bill. Bill collection tactics typically require the hotel to file a lawsuit in a small-claims court. (More information about nonpayment of hotel bills is presented later in this chapter.)

- *Violation of hotel conduct policies.* Hoteliers develop policies to protect the safety, privacy, and comfort of all guests as well as employees. Guests who are loud, threatening, disruptive, drunk, or disorderly or who destroy hotel property and its furnishings are examples of those who will be considered in breech (violation) of their room rental agreement. They should be asked to leave. If they do not leave in a reasonable amount of time, hotel managers, security officers, and, often, local law enforcement officers may be needed to remove the guests and their belongings.

MODERN FRONT OFFICE ISSUES AND TACTICS

Underage Hotel Guests

FOMs and their staff must be aware of the laws that govern guests who have not reached adulthood. Generally, because hotels have a duty of care to admit all persons seeking accommodations, underage guests must be accepted unless there is just cause to refuse accommodations. Just causes may include lack of rooms, failure of guests to pay charges, and a reasonable belief that guests may harm employees, other guests, or the property. In some locations, local laws permit hotels to refuse registration status to those younger than 18. When in doubt, what should hoteliers do?

- Determine their legal rights and obligations in consultation with a competent attorney.
- Implement clear and reasonable policies and rules as a precondition to accepting underage guests; be consistent with implementation and enforcement efforts so as to not discriminate against anyone.
- Determine the history of any types of youth-related events at the hotel and nearby properties. Contact local schools and colleges to learn about dates for which special occasions are scheduled.
- Train front desk staff about proper procedures for full identification and be concerned about underage drinking. Front desk personnel should not provide keys for in-room minibars and, if applicable, all alcohol should be removed from rooms rented by underage guests. Make sure that alcohol is not delivered by room service or as a guest amenity.
- Confirm that fire codes are followed regarding the number of occupants in guestrooms at one time. Add additional security (perhaps, at the expense of the group renting the rooms). Provide reduced room rates to parents to encourage them to chaperone the event. Let guests know that security has been increased for their protection.

- Request that payment be made in advance with cash or a payment card. Verify authorization immediately along with card ownership and the right of the underage guest to use it. Tactfully remind underage guests that disturbing noise, illegal drugs, and drinking will not be permitted.
- When they check in, ask underage guests to provide parental contact information. Alternatively, request parents to register underage guests so that they are aware of the rules and accept responsibility for damage or injury.
- Require underage guests to sign a form when checking in to verify that they are familiar with the house rules and regulations and that they agree to comply with them.
- Train all employees to consistently follow policies and regulations applicable to hotel guests who are underage.

Adapted from Barber, D. 2004. Accepting minor guests in your hotel; a checklist for handling the challenges of underage guests. Retrieved on May 4, 2004, from http://www.hotel-online.com/News/PR2004_2nd/May04_MinorGuest.html

- *Illnesses or other health conditions.* Guests who become ill with a contagious disease and those who otherwise become seriously ill, attempt suicide, or experience drug overdoses, create emergency situations for hoteliers. In such situations, local law enforcement or health authorities should be contacted and requested to assist. (This topic will be examined in more detail later in this chapter.)
- *Overstaying.* Guests who desire to occupy their room beyond the time of the original reservation and registration agreements may be asked to vacate the room, unless this is forbidden by local law. It is important to ensure that no communication problems exist between the hotel and its guests regarding the length of the room rental period. To this end, many hotels require that guests verify arrival and departure by initialing these dates on the guest registration card. Procedures useful to manage guests who overstay include obtaining legal clarifications from an attorney, providing reasonable notice to the affected guests, and perhaps, seeking the assistance of local law enforcement officials. Another tactic frequently used today is recoding electronic locking systems on the guestroom doors.

Guest Property

Early common laws placed responsibility for the safety of a traveler's property with those who owned the inn. At the time common law developed, people rarely traveled for purposes of pleasure. Instead, they traveled for trade or business, church-related purposes, or other nonpersonal reasons. Travel was difficult and frequently unsafe. For these reasons, hoteliers of the day were required to maintain an environment that protected the safety of guests who sought food, rest, and safety from them for the night.

In the past, issues regarding the safekeeping of guest property typically related to theft. This is still an important part of law today, but damage to a guest's vehicle by a parking lot attendant is another example of a property issue addressed by applicable laws. Anything that can damage a guestroom and its contents—floods, fires, damage from fire sprinklers or other water sources in the guestroom or in another guestroom or area of the hotel—can also damage guest property in the room. This, in turn, can create an event that may make the hotel liable for the damage. Exceptions to a hotelier's liability for guest property generally include damages that are beyond the hotelier's ability to control. These include "acts of God," such as storms, hurricanes, and naturally occurring flooding, as well as civil unrest and negligence caused by the guest.

Laws mandated by the jurisdiction in which the hotel is located typically place a liability limit on guest property losses unless the hotel is shown to be negligent. Such laws and other applicable statutes are included in a state's innkeeper laws, and a copy must be posted in one or more conspicuous locations where it will be seen by guests. Figure 13.2 shows the type of information that must be posted in Ohio hotels, based on the laws of that state.

In addition to placing a limit on guest property liability in the absence of negligence, other actions are routinely required by law (and common sense) to ensure that the state's limits on the hotel's liability will apply. For example, in most states hoteliers must post a notice in the guestroom that explains the availability of a safe or safe-deposit boxes and that provides information about state laws relating to an innkeeper's liability. A notice may also be placed at a front desk or other location that is conspicuous during registration; in some jurisdictions, this is a requirement.

A properly constructed safe or safe-deposit boxes for guests' valuables should be available in a secure section of the hotel's front office or in another area to which guests have reasonably ready access. Many hotels, especially those considered upscale

---

Section 4721.01 Liability for Loss of Property (GC Section 5981)
An innkeeper, whether a person, partnership, or corporation, having in his inn a metal safe or vault in good order suitable for the custody of money, bank notes, jewelry, articles of gold and silver manufacture, precious stones, personal ornaments, railroad mileage books or tickets, negotiable or valuable papers, and bullion, and keeping on the doors of the sleeping rooms used by his guests suitable locks or bolts, and on the transoms and windows of such rooms, suitable fastenings, and keeping a copy of this section printed in distinct type conspicuously suspended in the office, ladies parlor or sitting room, bar room, washroom, and five other conspicuous places in such inn, or not less than 10 conspicuous places in all, shall not be liable for loss or injury suffered by a guest, unless such guest has offered to deliver such property to such innkeeper for custody in such metal safe or vault and the innkeeper has omitted or refused to take and deposit it in the safe or vault for custody and give the guest a receipt therefore.

Section 4721.02 Extent of Liability agreement (GC Section 5982)
An innkeeper should not be obliged to receive from a guest for deposit in the safe or vault property described in section 4721.01 of the Revised Code exceeding a total value of five hundred dollars, and shall not be liable for such property exceeding such value whether received or not. Such innkeeper, by special arrangement with a guest may receive for deposit in such safe or vault property upon such written terms as may be agreed upon. An innkeeper shall be liable for a loss of any of such property of a guest in his inn caused by the theft or negligence of the innkeeper or his servant.

Section 4721.03 Limit of Liability for as to certain property (GC Section 5983)
The liability of an innkeeper whether person, partnership, or corporation, for loss of or injury to personal property placed in his care by his guests other than that described in section 4721.01 and 4721.02 of the Revised Code shall be that of a depositary for hire. Liability shall not exceed one hundred and fifty dollars for each trunk and it's contents, fifty dollars for each valise and it's contents, and ten dollars for each box, bundle or package and contents, so placed in his care, unless he has consented in writing with such guests to assume a greater liability.

FIGURE 13.2 Limitations on innkeeper liability—state of Ohio.

Safe-deposit boxes help safeguard guests' property.

properties, feature in-guestroom safes. Hoteliers must ensure that these safes are properly constructed and installed, and they may want to post a notice on these units to indicate that a hotel safe is also available. Front desk personnel should be able to provide information to guests who inquire about alternatives for safekeeping their valuables.

Front desk personnel must consistently follow appropriate procedures when guests use hotel safes or safe-deposit boxes. For example, carefully complete a deposit slip: show date, guest name, room number; give a brief description of contents and, if applicable, include a statement about the content's approximate value. Limits on the amount of money or value of jewelry that a hotelier is required to accept from a guest for safekeeping are typically imposed by state law. After the guest signs the deposit slip, one copy should be given to the guest, and another copy should be retained by the hotel. Figure 13.3 is a sample of a deposit slip. Guests are expected to make use of the hotel's facilities for safe storage of their belongings. If guests fail to take proper precautions, the hotel will not generally be held liable for any loss, unless negligence can be proved.

Secure locks on all guestroom doors and guestroom windows (if needed) are important to limit access of those who might attempt to harm a guest or to steal a guest's property. Limits on the replacement value of a guest's luggage and its contents are typically stated and will apply, unless acts of the hotel employees are negligent. The intent of state-imposed legislation to limit a hotelier's liability for guest property is based on the premise that hotel employees will be reasonably prudent in their care of the property, and that they will not be negligent while doing so. However, if negligence is proved in a lawsuit brought by a guest whose property is stolen or damaged, limits on the hotelier's liability will not usually be applicable.

SAFE-DEPOSIT BOX
TERMS AND CONDITIONS

BOX NO.	DATE ISSUED	ISSUED BY	ROOM NO.

1. Access to box shall be only by signature below, together with presentation of key in person.

2. If key is lost or is not returned when guest checks out, the box may be forcibly opened after 60 days and contents retained will be sold to pay cost of opening and replacing key, and other charges that may be due.

3. Custodian shall not be liable for acts of co-depositors and any one of them may sign Box Surrender and remove contents.

4. In consideration of the furnishing of a safe deposit box to the undersigned guest, the undersigned agrees that the innkeeper shall not be liable in case of loss or injury to such valuables for an amount in excess of that set by law, regardless of the cause of such loss or injury, and that negligence shall not be presumed or inferred from any loss of or injury to the contents of the safe deposit box.

5. Depositor agrees to notify custodian immediately of loss of key. The $_____ deposit will be refunded if key is returned when checking out.

Signature _____

Address _____

SURRENDER OF BOX

The undersigned hereby surrenders above numbered box and certifies that all property placed therein has been lawfully withdrawn and is now in the possession of the owner(s): all claims and liability of the custodian is hereby released and discharged.

Signature _____ Date _____ Clerk _____

I have opened my safe-deposit box this day.   BOX NO. _____

DATE	TIME	CLERK	GUEST

FIGURE 13.3 Deposit slip for safe-deposit box.

MORE ABOUT SAFES AND SAFE-DEPOSIT BOXES

In many hotels, only the hotel manager, FOM, and front desk agents have access to the property's safe or safe-deposit boxes. This practice is generally required to limit a property's liability for loss of a guest's personal effects under the relevant state's statutory requirements. Insurance companies may require the hotel's representative to inventory valuables before they are placed in a safe or safe-deposit box. A signed guest statement about the value of property being delivered for safekeeping is crucial. Hotels can be found negligent if, for example, front desk agents or other employees with access to the safe or safe-deposit box fraudulently remove contents or physically remove the entire safe or safe-deposit box from the hotel (and this has occurred!).

Limitations for guest property liability extend beyond the hotel's safe and the guestroom. Consider the opportunities for theft as a guest arrives and goes to the registration area, leaving baggage to be handled by a bell services attendant. Guests who check in before their room is available may wish to leave their luggage in the hotel's luggage room. This service may also be requested by guests who check out of their room but who have meetings in the property until later in the day. Hoteliers must consistently use procedures to control access to luggage storage areas to safeguard property that has been left in their care.

Guests may have luggage in their personal control stolen while they are waiting in the hotel's check-in line. What about opportunities for theft when a departing guest enters a taxi, hotel van, personal auto, or tour bus while a door attendant places luggage in the vehicle's trunk? Consider also situations that can occur when hotels offer attended coatroom and valet parking amenities. In all of these situations, limitations on the hotel's liability are generally in place, unless the hotel is proved to be negligent.

Laws typically consider that the guests assume reasonable responsibility for their property. For example, is it reasonable to think that a guest would leave luggage containing $50,000 worth of jewelry with a bell services attendant while checking in or would place a fur coat valued at several thousand dollars in an unattended coatroom? The details of specific situations make it difficult to generalize about what does and does not need to occur for a hotel to be found negligent. The FOM—working with other hotel managers, property security and risk management personnel, and others—should develop policies and procedures that reflect reasonable precautions necessary to reduce the possibility of a successful negligence claim. Then, the proposed actions should be reviewed and revised by a competent attorney, implemented, and consistently followed.

Many other situations involving guest property may have legal implications:

- *Detained property.* Guests may have unpaid bills for lawful purchases of products or services for which they refuse to pay or for which payment is past due. In some instances, hoteliers may lock a guest out of the guestroom or refuse to release a guest's auto from the parking garage until payment is made. The right of a hotel to **detain property** for nonpayment of legally owed charges stems from laws that allow the hotel to place a **lien** on property until charges have been paid.

FRONT OFFICE SEMANTICS:

Detained property: Personal property of a guest that is held by a hotel until payment is made for the purchase of lawful products or services.

Lien: Legal right of one party to retain or sell the property of another as security for or payment of a lawful claim of charges.

- *Mislaid and lost property.* Hotel policy should require that employees who find **mislaid property** or **lost property** while working must give that property to the applicable hotel manager, even if the property was found in a public place such as the lobby. The property should then be safeguarded by the hotel for a pre-determined length of time. If it is then still unclaimed, it can be given to the staff member who turned it in, to the local police, or to a charitable organization, as dictated by hotel policy.

FRONT OFFICE SEMANTICS:

Mislaid property: Personal property that has been purposefully placed somewhere but is then forgotten about by the rightful owner.

Lost property: Personal property that has been unintentionally placed somewhere and is then forgotten about by the rightful owner.

- *Abandoned property.* **Abandoned property** is given up by someone who does not intend to reclaim it. Hoteliers holding an item of real property often do not know whether it has been misplaced, lost, or abandoned. Magazines, newspapers, and personal toiletries (e.g., razors, combs, and toothpaste tubes) are typically abandoned in hotel guestrooms. A good rule of thumb is that the greater the value of a found item, the more likely that it is not abandoned. All items with value should be retained by the hotel according to preestablished policies and procedures for mislaid or lost property.

FRONT OFFICE SEMANTICS

Abandoned property: Property that is given up by someone who does not intend to reclaim it.

- *Other concerns.* A list of all situations that can involve front office employees and guest property would be lengthy. For example, property is unclaimed: a guest checks luggage into the baggage storeroom but does not return for it. Property is lost by guests or visitors in a meeting room or public area, and they contact the front desk agent. Property is left in guestrooms by departing guests who later request its return. Another property management responsibility of front desk agents is the receipt of mail, packages, or faxes for guests before, during, or after their stay at the property.

State laws vary, so FOMs and other managers must seek clarification about procedures to safeguard guest property. They must then develop policies and procedures that are in concert with the laws and train front desk agents to know and follow them. Managers should also clearly inform guests about state laws and hotel policies and procedures when guests make requests about their property. Standards of reasonable care should always be applied to duties of care.

Although the tactics discussed in this section will help to protect the hotel against claims of property loss or damage, they will not prevent such claims. Failure to follow these tactics will not ensure lawsuits but will certainly encourage them.

Guest Nonpayment

Some guests accept the hotel's products and services but then attempt to avoid paying for them. Perhaps a guest is dissatisfied with all or part of the experience at the property; perhaps a guest registered at the hotel with no intention to pay. Sometimes guests pay their bill before leaving, but do so fraudulently; that is, with an unauthorized payment card, bad check, or counterfeit funds. (Procedures to control payment fraud are discussed in Chapter 11.) Employees at the front desk who handle cash must be trained to properly process payment cards and to recognize counterfeit bills. Payments made by check should be accepted only by carefully following the hotel's established policies and procedures relating to this form of payment.

Guests who leave the hotel without paying their bill are often called **skips** because they have *skipped* (avoided) the bill payment step in the check-in and check-out process.

FRONT OFFICE SEMANTICS:

Skip (nonpaying guest): Term used to refer to a hotel guest who vacates a guestroom without paying the bill incurred for its rental and for other charges made to the room.

A property's design often makes it relatively easy for guests to leave without paying. Consider motels with outside entrances from parking lots directly to guestrooms and large, multistoried properties with large lobby areas and many exits, which are designed for guest safety and convenience rather than for revenue control.

How can FOMs and front desk agents minimize hotel skips? The most effective control procedures take place when the guest initially checks in to the property. The guest registration process (see Chapter 9), if effectively done, yields information about how the guest intends to pay. If a payment card will be used, it should be authorized for the full amount a guest is estimated to owe during the stay. Recall that one of the night auditor's duties is to verify that the amount owed by guests who indicated they will settle their folio by payment card has not exceeded the amount authorized during registration. If the amount owed is approaching this limit, the FOM usually requests partial payment from the guest or reauthorizes the payment card for an additional amount.

More and more hotels are not accepting personal checks. Availability of automatic teller machines (ATMs) makes this guest "convenience" less necessary, because guests have more convenient access to cash. Many hotels that do accept checks require that checks be preauthorized by a check approval service, or they require that the guest provide a payment card number that can be preauthorized for the estimated amount during check-in.

If a guest who is registering indicates the intent to pay with cash, the amount equal to the total number of nights for which the guest is registering should be collected in advance, and no charges to the guestroom should be allowed. An additional deposit may be required for use of the telephone to protect against toll charges made from it. Likewise, some hotels require an additional deposit as a protection against possible room damage that could occur but for which collection would be difficult.

In some cases guests do not leave the hotel but continue to occupy a guestroom and refuse to pay. They may be guilty of **trespass** and the sanctions of law that are associated with it in a specific jurisdiction. Guests such as these can generally be removed from the property.

FRONT OFFICE SEMANTICS

Trespass: Unlawful entry into or possession of another party's property.

Illness and Death in Guestrooms

Front desk agents must be capable of quickly and correctly responding to any guestroom emergency. If a guest phones the front desk to report a serious illness, the front desk agent or other staff member taking the call should immediately call 911 or another designated emergency care responder.

Hotel staff may refer ill guests to local physicians or outpatient services. Large properties may have medical personnel on-call. Front desk agents must be thoroughly familiar with the options available to their ill guests and must know how guests, or they, can quickly contact health care providers. They must also know how and when to place 911 or other emergency calls on behalf of guests and be aware of the appropriate procedures to do so. Staff must also know what to do when emergency care arrives. Who should meet the emergency responder and at what hotel entrance? The answer for this question is important at all properties and is critical in large hotel complexes. What, if any, type of care should be provided to the guest before medical personnel arrive? What care is required of the guest's property while he or she is away from the room? These and related issues (e.g., contacting family members) must be addressed by the FOM *before* emergencies, not during them.

What if a hotel employee enters a guestroom (1) for routine cleaning, (2) because the hotel received a phone call from a worried friend, relative, or business associate, or (3) because the guest has overstayed and discovers a very ill, unconscious, or apparently deceased individual? The staff member should immediately call the manager on duty, who should phone emergency personnel. If it appears that a crime has been committed, the local police should be informed. If there is a possibility that other guests are in danger, they should be notified. A hotel employee should remain outside the open guestroom door to secure the area until emergency assistance arrives. If the guest is deceased, the body should be removed by a professional who has been authorized by relatives, if the hotel was able to contact them. If a physician is not present to complete reports required by health authorities, police or local health officials will arrange for transfer of the body to a hospital or morgue.

The personal property in the room should not be removed and must be protected until local authorities indicate that the room can be cleaned. The room should be kept locked until the appropriate authorities provide further instructions. Before the guest's property is delivered to anyone, including relatives, the hotel should be sure that all applicable legal requirements have been met. If information about property removal will not be forthcoming to the hotel for several days, the hotel may receive consent from an authorized official to remove the property to another secure area. An inventory of property removed from the guestroom should be taken with a witness present who can certify by signature that the inventory list is accurate. If any property is removed by a coroner, police, or other authorized official, the hotel should receive a receipt identifying the specific property that is removed.

SECTION REVIEW AND DISCUSSION QUESTIONS

Section Objective: Explain legal concerns about guest privacy and guest removal and discuss procedures applicable to safeguarding guest property, managing guest nonpayments, and following protocols for guest illness and death.

Section Summary: A hotel's obligation to ensure guest privacy begins at the time of registration. Guestroom numbers should not be publicly announced or provided to those inquiring at or phoning the front desk for this information. Guestroom keys should never be given to persons without appropriate identification to confirm that they are, in fact, registered guests requesting the applicable guestroom key. Hoteliers have a duty of care to allow lawfully registered guests privacy and the peaceful possession of their guestroom. With relatively few exceptions, search warrants are required before police can view registration information or records or enter a guestroom.

Hoteliers can legally evict room occupants who are classified as guests (not tenants) according to laws of the local jurisdiction in situations such as these: nonpayment of hotel bills, violation of hotel conduct policies, illness or certain health conditions and overstaying beyond the time agreed to at reservation and registration.

Guest property must be reasonably protected against theft or anything that could damage it, except for legal exclusions such as "acts of God," civil unrest, and guest negligence. Protection tactics include securing access to guestrooms; providing safes, safe-deposit boxes, or in-room safes; and using a variety of procedures to notify guests about the availability of these safeguards and procedures. FOMs must also develop and use policies related to detained, mislaid, lost, and abandoned property.

Unfortunately, some guests do not pay for their guestroom or products and services charged to it. Some are skips who leave without paying. Registration procedures to properly secure guest identification, to correctly authorize a payment card, or to collect cash are good first lines of defense. Other guests may not leave the hotel but also refuse to pay. In many jurisdictions, trespass laws are in place to address these situations.

Unfortunately, an occupant may become seriously ill or die in a guestroom. Procedures for quickly notifying the appropriate authorities, protecting valuables of the guest, and complying with other requirements of the legal jurisdiction must be carefully followed.

Discussion Questions:

1. A front desk agent notices an unaccompanied item of luggage in the front desk or lobby area that has been in the same location for some time. There is no identification or marking of any kind on the luggage. If you were the FOM, what would you tell the front desk agent to do with this bag? Why?

2. The guest in room 203 was due to check out yesterday. The housekeeper reports that the guest's personal belongings are still in the room. The front desk agent has left several telephone messages on the guestroom phone, and the bell services attendant has delivered two messages in envelopes requesting that the guest contact the front office. What would you as the FOM do now?

3. A guest is checking into the hotel wearing what appears to be expensive jewelry, but the guest does not inquire about the availability of a safe or safe-deposit box at the hotel. The guestrooms do not have in-room safes. What would you as the hotel's FOM suggest that the front desk agent do in this situation?

The FOM in Action: A Solution

What should an FOM such as Jacob do when loud and disruptive guests gather in a public area of the hotel late at night to play music and then ignore a security guard's request to disperse? The contract with the hotel (i.e., the guest registration card) allows individuals access to their guestroom for a specified period of time if they follow the hotel's rules of conduct. It does not allow them to do whatever they want, at any time they want to do it, at any place on the property. These guests are, therefore, in breach of their contract with the hotel, and the FOM has the authority to remove them.

What if some persons in the group are visitors to and not guests at the property? As long as the hotel does not discriminate, it is not required to allow these persons access to the property at any time, and clearly not when all public retail outlets are closed, and when they are creating a disturbance for registered guests.

Jacob must use his judgment about whether to personally go to the public area to request that the disruptive guests return to their rooms or leave the property and to announce that local law enforcement officials will be called if they do not. If there is any concern about danger to any persons—security guards, guests, visitors, or the FOM himself—a phone call to the police is in order.

When police officers arrive, Jacob should explain the situation and direct the officers to the area of the disturbance. Just as FOMs have a responsibility to reasonably deal with guests who have paid to stay in the hotel, they are also responsible to protect other guests and employees from possible harm caused by disruptive guests and visitors. In this situation, the police should be asked to escort the disruptive individuals from the property. Police will likely accompany those who are guests to their rooms while they retrieve their property and then escort them out of the hotel. Visitors will be removed immediately. Police might also be asked to stay a reasonable amount of time to ensure that these individuals do not return. If the disruptive individuals return, this time the police will likely arrest them as trespassers.

Because these guests have not met the terms of their contract, they are not due a refund. However, some managers may do so if the guests had just occupied a room but had not used it. A deciding factor is whether housekeepers must clean the room to prepare it for the next guest.

Situations such as these illustrate why hotels and their FOMs should get to personally know and maintain a positive working relationship with their local law enforcement officials.

From the Front Office: Front-Line Drug Bust

Authors' note: The format of "From the Front Office" is different in this chapter. Instead of an interview, this chapter presents a composite of experiences from several hotel general managers and FOMs about a problem that can occur in almost any hotel at any time: interacting with local police about drug-related problems. As you read the following case study, recall the chapter's basic information about the roles and responsibilities of front office managers as they consider their obligation to protect guest privacy while, at the same time, they fulfill societal and personal obligations to notify police when there is a reasonable suspicion that laws are being broken.

The local police have contacted the front office manager because they believe that a hotel guest has or is currently violating laws. The police indicate there will be a forthcoming raid on the guest's room. What should the general manager and FOM do?

Step 1: The hotel's management team and police officials have an ongoing professional relationship and have interacted on previous occasions. The two groups have met during community service functions, and hotel managers have requested assistance from police officials to ensure the hotel's ongoing security procedures are the best they can be. This general relationship is built on trust and helps the hotel's management team know that police will take no action that could reasonably be expected to endanger other guests. Police officials know that the hotel managers will not alert a guest who is under suspicion. The police also know that hotel managers will alert them if the guest under suspicion is staying at the hotel for an extended period of time, is spending significant amounts of money, and has developed a personal or business relationship with any of the hotel's managers. Note that hotel managers can be arrested on charges that include obstruction of justice if they inform the guest that hotel management has been contacted by the police about a potential raid or about examining the guest's telephone records.

Step 2: The FOM must identify the guestroom used by the suspect to ensure that the guest has not checked out and that the guest has not been moved to another room.

Step 3: The timing for the police raid is determined and coordinated.

Step 4: Rooms adjacent to the affected room are declared out of order to prevent their sale. These rooms may eventually be occupied during the raid by backup police officers who might be needed during the arrest portion of the operation.

Step 5: One or more undercover police officers check into the hotel and show their search warrant as they do.

Step 6: Some undercover officers may take positions in the parking lot in unmarked cars or at building exits in the event that the suspect attempts to flee by car or by foot.

Step 7: The drug bust raid is initiated, and the suspect is arrested.

Step 8: The suspect is lead out of the property through a discreet, prearranged exit point. Hotel managers can reasonably insist that this be done as inconspicuously as possible. Lobby areas, of course, should be avoided if it is at all possible to do so.

Step 9: Police officers check out of their guestrooms and pay for the rooms as they do so. If the suspect is arrested, it is not likely that the room occupied by the suspect will be vacated of all personal items. These items should be removed carefully after the police have concluded any searches and have indicated that this can be done. Items should be stored according to the hotel's standard policies. In most cases, the hotel will treat the room status as a check-out. It is good practice, however, for front office staff to notify the housekeeping department that the room should be cleaned and carefully inspected. This will help to ensure that the next guest who occupies the room will not experience any difficulty resulting from illegal activity or the raid itself, such as odors and room damage.

In most cases, hotel managers have no obligation to participate in or assist police with a drug raid. Nevertheless, cooperation with local police helps to prevent illegal activities on the property, enhances the long-term safety of all guests and employees, and is, from a societal point of view, the right thing to do. Of course, all hotel personnel hope that no violent physical actions that can cause personal injury and physical damage occur during the raid. It is easy to imagine, however, that some hotel guests may become excited when they hear the police in close proximity to their room. In addition to being concerned about their own safety, they may be upset because illegal activities were going on close to them and that, whatever the problem, it was serious enough to need the police.

Unfortunately, drug dealers do use hotels to conduct business, because they can move from hotel to hotel, and because hotels usually provide easy access for them and their customers. Experienced FOMs work closely with police in their community, know and follow the law, and contact their hotel attorney whenever they are in doubt about their rights and those of their guests.

FRONT OFFICE SEMANTICS LIST

Attorney	Reasonable care	Search warrant
Common laws	Contract	Guest (hotel)
Civil laws	Contract (express)	Tenant (hotel)
Lawsuit	Legal contract	Detained property
Litigation	Contract (implied)	Lien
Damages	Offer (contract)	Mislaid property
Compensatory damages	Consideration (contract)	Lost property
Punitive damages	Acceptance (contract)	Abandoned property
Duty of care	Accessible (guestroom)	Skip (nonpaying guest)
Wholesome	Court order	Trespass
Negligence	Subpoena	
Standard of care	Reasonable cause	

FRONT OFFICE AND THE INTERNET

- To review general information about safety and legal issues applicable to hotels, go to www.hospitalitylawyer.com
- For more information about the Anti-Terrorism Act of 2001, go to www.epic.org/privacy/terrorism/ata_analysis.html
- For details about ADA standards for accessible transient lodging facilities, go to www.usdoj.gov/crt/ada/reg3a.html#anchor-54325
- To read articles related to hotel law topics, go to www.lodge-law.com. When you arrive at the site, click on "articles."

REAL-WORLD ACTIVITIES

1. A guest with several children has checked into room 766. On the second day of her stay, she phones the front desk agent to report that several of her children's expensive computer games are missing from the room. She says that the games were present when she and the children left the room to allow the housekeeper to clean it and that, when they, promptly returned to the room, the games were missing. The games are valued at several hundred dollars, and she is requesting compensation for them. How should the front desk agent respond to this guest? Why?

2. A parent calls to a reserve a room for his teenage child and several of her peers for use during the activities before and after the local high school's prom. He indicates that there will be no adults present, but that he will assume all liability for anything that happens during the time the room is rented. Many times during the conversation he states that he trusts his daughter and that nothing out of the ordinary will happen. Should the front desk agent rent this room to this parent? Why or why not?

3. A person known to the front desk agent approaches the desk and asks for a room key for another individual also known to the front desk agent. The purpose: to

bring a birthday cake and some gifts for a surprise birthday party for the room occupant. What should the front desk agent say and do? Why?

4. A couple approaches the front desk to inquire about the cost to rent a room for the night. They are en route to a new home and have two vehicles: a large rental truck and an auto with a trailer. These vehicles contain all of their household goods and other possessions. While checking in, they inquire about the safety of the hotel's parking lot. The front desk agent has been at the hotel for several years and knows that there have been at least three instances of burglary from an unoccupied auto. How should the front desk agent respond to the couple's inquiry?

5. A guest calls the front desk complaining that she is very ill and needs some medication that she has left at home. It is 3:00 a.m., and the front desk agent knows that there are no drugstores or other retail stores with a pharmacy that are open within a 30-mile radius. While explaining to the guest, the agent hears a sigh or groan and the sound of the phone being dropped. There is no other sound from the room. What should the front desk agent do?

14

Front Office: Hub of the Hotel

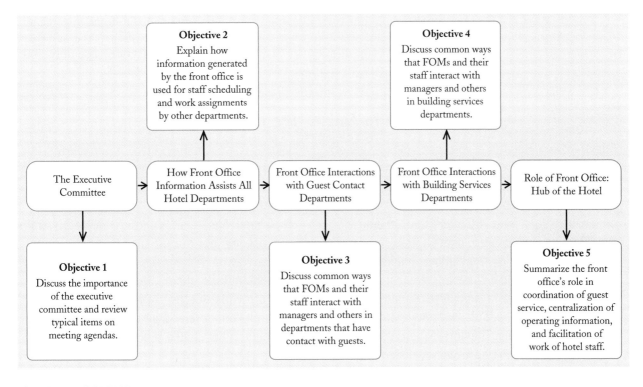

CHAPTER ROADMAP

Chapter Preview

As you approach the end of this book, recall its emphasis on the role of FOMs and other managers in determining and providing the products and services their guests desire. Recall also that technology provides FOMs and other decision makers with information required for effective planning and decision making. A primary responsibility of the front office is to coordinate the provision of guest services with development and dissemination of information to all hotel departments. This chapter focuses on how front office staff members interact with their peers in other departments as we consider the front office as the hub of the hotel.

The chapter begins with the hotel's executive committee—the hotel's top-level managers. After explaining the purpose of the committee and describing the topics of its meetings, the chapter discusses what the FOM brings to the committee's discussions.

Information provided by the front office affects every hotel department. The business volume forecasts of the front office drive the development of employee schedules and personnel assignments.

FOMs and their staff interact with all hotel departments, and this chapter looks closely at relationships in seven departments. In three departments—general manager, marketing and sales, and food and beverage—staff members have significant guest contact. In four departments—accounting, housekeeping, security, and maintenance and engineering—staff members have less guest contact but have significant influence on guest services and, ultimately, the hotel's success.

The front office is not the most important department in the hotel. Clearly, all departments and all staff are important. Nevertheless, the front office is the hub that coordinates the provision of guest services; centralizes the collection, assembly, and distribution of information; and facilitates the work of the hotel staff.

The FOM In Action: The Challenge

The Hilotown Hotel is a 75-room, limited-service property that generates a significant amount of business from persons attending meetings at a nearby convention hotel who do not want to pay its high room rates. Bino is the assistant manager of the Hilotown, and because of the hotel's small size, he is responsible for front office, housekeeping, and engineering and maintenance activities.

The hotel has always enjoyed a good relationship with its housekeepers, but now a bittersweet situation is occurring. The hotel is booked solid for every night during the next two weeks—that's the good news. Unfortunately, there is a shortage of housekeepers to work many of the shifts for various reasons: maternity leave, an auto accident, illnesses, and some turnover.

The hotel has been aggressively recruiting new employees, but the process has been slow. Even when new staff members are hired, time will be needed to train them. Shifts staffed with a reduced crew are not the most appropriate occasion for staff members or their supervisors to conduct training. What should Bino do?

THE EXECUTIVE COMMITTEE

The hotel business is first and foremost a people business. This may seem obvious, but some observers might define hotel business as renting rooms, selling services, and providing meeting space. Such a definition incorrectly places the emphasis on outputs (the purposes for which space is used) rather than on inputs (the human resources needed to produce the products and services). Hoteliers are in the *people* business—guests and employees. Earlier chapters in this book emphasized the guest; this chapter emphasizes the hotel team. The executive committee is the hotel's top management team, and as noted in Roadmap 14.1, this chapter begins with an in-depth look at its functions.

Role of the Executive Committee

As hotels become larger, more persons in more specialized positions are needed. The general manager facilitates the work of department heads who, in turn, manage the major functions in the property.

The executive committee, also called *executive operating committee*, consists of members of the management team, generally division and department heads, responsible for department leadership and overall property administration. The FOM is a member of and plays an integral role in the committee. Meeting weekly or at other intervals judged appropriate by the general manager, these top-level managers plan for and coordinate a wide range of concerns, many with between-department implications.

Concerns of the Executive Committee

Figure 14.1 lists typical items on the agenda for an executive committee meeting. Not all of the topics noted in Figure 14.1 will be discussed at every executive committee

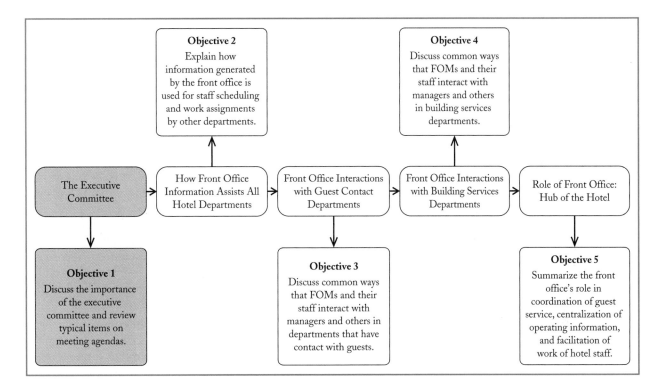

ROADMAP 14.1

meeting. In addition, other topics unique to a specific hotel or business event may suggest other items for the agenda. Nevertheless, the topics listed in Figure 14.1 indicate the scope of the meeting agenda and identify issues that can be influenced by the top-level managers who meet for analysis, discussion, and decision making.

FRONT OFFICE SEMANTICS

Deep cleaning: Intensive cleaning of a guestroom, usually including thorough cleaning of drapes, lamp shades, carpets, walls, and other room fixtures and furnishings.

- Comment card review, analysis, and corrective action
- Group business for the upcoming week
- Budget versus actual financial information
- Status of business plan and marketing plan tasks
- Policy revisions and additions
- Human resources issues
- Safety and security concerns
- Factors such as **deep cleaning** and routine maintenance that will affect short-term room status

FIGURE 14.1 Typical agenda items for executive committee meetings.

Let's consider some examples of executive committee topics in relation to concerns of the FOM:

- *Guest service input.* Chapter 10 provides detailed information about the evaluation of guest services. Issues specific to a department such as improper telephone skills of front desk agents (front office department) or food quality in a hotel restaurant (food and beverage department) would likely be discussed in a private meeting of the general manager and the appropriate department head. Many issues, however, involve more than one department and represent general concerns that are addressed in an executive committee meeting. For example, excessive delays in gaining access to guestrooms involve the front office (registration) and housekeeping (cleaning). Guest complaints about room maintenance concern housekeeping personnel (why weren't problems noticed as rooms were inspected?) and engineering and maintenance staff (who repaired or failed to repair the fixtures and systems in question). Did an inaccurate food and beverage charge on the guest folio result from incorrect information transmitted by food and beverage personnel or from incorrect posting procedures by front office staff? Executive committee discussions about guest complaints are frequently a prerequisite to their resolution.

- *Long-term group business.* Some issues are best managed by discussions between representatives of the departments that must coordinate services, for example, opportunities to provide early registration and late check-outs for group attendees, the presence of many disabled guests, and the need for special baggage handling or meeting setup requirements. If, for example, the director of sales and marketing circulates a **group resume** specifying foodservice requirements, meeting rooms needed, and scheduling concerns for a planned meeting, there is less chance for miscommunication as the event evolves.

FRONT OFFICE SEMANTICS

Group resume: Overview of important points about and needs of a group meeting, many of which require interdepartmental coordination.

- *Financial variances (budget forecasts and actual operating results).* It is one thing to plan a budget; it is another thing to achieve it. Knowledge of the current financial situation and discussions about tactics for corrective action can be synergistic, because committee members can build on each other's ideas. Department heads will likely appreciate the participative approach to decision making that is being used.

- *Policy matters.* **Policies** that affect the conduct of hotel staff members are generally discussed at executive committee meetings before they are adopted or modified. Many policies must be applicable to the entire property. For example, human resources policies relating to vacation eligibility, acceptance of suppliers' gifts, and prevention of employee harassment should affect all staff members in all departments the same way. The executive committee provides an ideal venue for discussions.

FRONT OFFICE SEMANTICS

Policy: Administrative tool or guideline that establishes parameters to be used when decisions are made.

Prior review of group requests will reduce miscommunication when the group is staying at the hotel.

Earlier in this book (see Chapter 2), cross-functional teams were introduced. The executive committee is the hotel's ultimate cross-functional team, because it focuses the combined knowledge and experiences of the hotel's most senior leaders on issues brought before it.

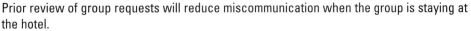

SECTION REVIEW AND DISCUSSION QUESTIONS

Section Objective: Discuss the importance of the executive committee and review typical items on meeting agendas.

Section Summary: The executive committee serves as the hotel's most senior cross-functional team. Executive committee members routinely address topics such as improvements in guest service, challenges likely from upcoming group business, variances between budget and actual financial planning tools, and policy additions or changes.

Discussion Questions:

1. Assume that a specific department head is overbudget for the month and year-to-date for expenses chargeable to his or her department. When, if at all, would conversation about this matter be appropriate during an executive committee meeting?

2. What concerns might a seasoned FOM express at an executive committee meeting?

3. Can you think of examples of discussions relative to business plans and budgets that might be on the agenda of an executive committee meeting?

HOW FRONT OFFICE INFORMATION ASSISTS ALL DEPARTMENTS

Throughout this book you have encountered examples of the information collected and generated by the front office department. Although this information is critical for the FOM's work, it is likewise necessary for all department managers. As shown in Roadmap 14.2, this section will review information that is required by all departments but that is provided by the front office.

Scheduling Staff

Many hotel employees are scheduled based on the forecasted volume of business. Whereas there is only one FOM and, in a large hotel, only a few assistant FOMs, there are likely to be many front desk agents. Many will be scheduled according to the volume of the forecasted business, that is, guest arrivals, departures and stayovers. Figure 14.2 lists other hotel departments and indicates whether front office information has a direct or indirect impact on employee scheduling in that department.

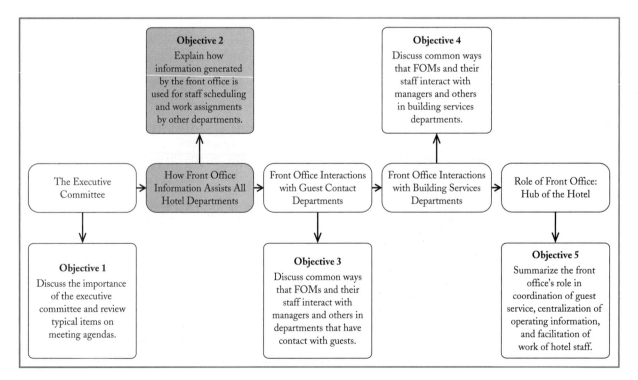

ROADMAP 14.2

| Department | Front Office Information Drives Scheduling | | Comment |
	Directly	Indirectly	
General manager		✓	Managers with propertywide responsibility are on-site during times of high business volume.
Marketing and sales		✓	Managers and account representatives must be available to assist groups.
Food and beverage	✓		Front office forecasts drive operations planning.
Accounting		✓	Managers with propertywide responsibility are on-site during times of high business volume.
Housekeeping	✓		Front office forecasts drive operations planning.
Security	✓		Front office forecasts drive operations planning.
Maintenance and engineering	✓		Front office forecasts drive operations planning.

FIGURE 14.2   Front office information affects scheduling in other departments.

All or most managers in all departments are likely to be on-site during times of high business volume. These times are known because of information from front office reports. The general manager and his or her staff, and the controller and accounting department, can assist with control and coordination activities. Marketing and sales managers will want to be available when there is significant within-hotel business, especially when it is from groups that they have attracted to the property and that require their personal services to "deliver" what the contract specifies.

Managers in the food and beverage, housekeeping, security, and maintenance and engineering departments will likely see their work volume directly affected by the occupancy rates forecasted by the front office. Because labor and labor-related expenses are their largest category of **operating costs,** these departments need accurate forecasts of business volume so that labor can be scheduled at a level allowing service standards to be met cost-effectively.

FRONT OFFICE SEMANTICS

Operating costs: Costs directly incurred to generate revenue; these costs vary by the amount of revenue (business volume) and are usually within control of the department manager.

Planning Work Volumes and Personnel Assignments

As shown in Figure 14.3, information generated and disseminated by the front office is used by department managers for purposes other than to schedule employees. The examples shown in Figure 14.3 are far from complete, and additional uses of front office information by each department are noted throughout the chapter. Managers must have timely and accurate information to determine

Department	Examples
General manager	Data used for daily, weekly, and longer-term decision making.
Marketing and sales	Data used to determine whether group business for specific dates is profitable and to set rates for transient guests.
Food and beverage	Data used to plan business volume for à la carte dining, room service, and banquet operations.
Accounting	Accounts receivable data generated as guest folios are closed, revenue data used to generate financial reports, and direct billing activities result from front office sales.
Housekeeping	Data used to plan business volume for meeting space setup, guestroom cleaning, and guest service requests.
Security	Data used to plan for special security needs because of increased or special business volume.
Maintenance and engineering	Data used to plan when extensive maintenance can be done and when additional assistance may be needed to minimize out-of-order rooms.

FIGURE 14.3   Front office information used by all departments for purposes other than scheduling.

where problems ("challenges") exist before they can implement corrective actions to address them.

General managers need front office information for short-term (i.e., daily and weekly) and longer-term decision making as they consider questions such as these: How effective is the sales and marketing department in selling guestrooms to group members? Is revenue from forecasted room sales in line with budget estimates? Have tactics in this year's business plan applicable to the sale of guestrooms been successful in attracting business?

Marketing and sales staff use information about future room availability to determine whether more aggressive tactics are needed to sell rooms and to work with the FOM to manage rate structures. Food and beverage and housekeeping managers know that business volume will affect more than employee scheduling procedures. Food and beverage products must be purchased, and housekeeping managers must plan for additional requests for guest service. Housekeeping managers plan deep-cleaning assignments during times of low occupancy when some rooms will not be sold.

Accounting managers are affected by front office information as they manage the collection of revenues due to the hotel, and as they prepare financial statements. Front office information alerts the security director to special security issues such as these: the need to interact with contracted security services retained for in-hotel conferences and the need to provide special security coverage when VIPs are scheduled to visit the property. Maintenance and engineering managers must schedule rooms for maintenance and repair during times of low occupancy, and they must maximize the number of rooms available during periods of high occupancy.

The remainder of this chapter provides details about how all department managers rely on front office information to make critical decisions that have an impact on their effectiveness.

SECTION REVIEW AND DISCUSSION QUESTIONS

Section Objective: Explain how information generated by the front office is used for staff scheduling and work assignments by other departments.

Section Summary: Managers in all departments use front office information to schedule employees based on forecasted room occupancy. Even managers whose job presence is less influenced by business volume will want or need to be on-site during periods of high occupancy. Anticipated business volume affects many additional planning tasks and activities that depend on the accuracy of front office information.

Discussion Questions:
1. The text notes that managers with property-wide responsibilities are typically on-site during times of high business volume. Why is this the case? What atypical activities are they likely to perform?
2. What are examples of unusual work tasks that the FOM and other front office staff are likely to perform during times of high occupancy?
3. What tactics can managers in the maintenance and engineering department use to help ensure that the number of out-of-order guestrooms is minimized during times of forecasted high occupancy?

FRONT OFFICE INTERACTIONS WITH GUEST CONTACT DEPARTMENTS

FOMs interact with managers in three guest contact departments: general manager, marketing and sales, and food and beverage. Managers in these departments make financial and operating decisions based on information from the front office. As you can see in Roadmap 14.3, details of the front office's interactions with these three departments are discussed in this section of the chapter.

General Manager

Technically, the general manager (GM) might not be considered a guest contact *department*. However, the FOM does have important ongoing contact with this official who, in turn, has significant guest contact. Contacts between the FOM and GM generally concern four issues: guestroom reports, financial concerns, service recommendations, and day-to-day operations.

Guestroom Reports

Chapter 4 describes the wide range of PMS reports that help the FOM develop strategies and rates for selling guestrooms. It is unlikely that a FOM makes these decisions unilaterally. In many hotels, the FOM meets with the director of sales and marketing to review occupancy forecasts and to consider room rates for future transient reservations based on forecasts. Discussions about room rates for group sales, although the responsibility of the director of sales and marketing, also may occur. A subsequent meeting with the GM will then yield pricing decisions.

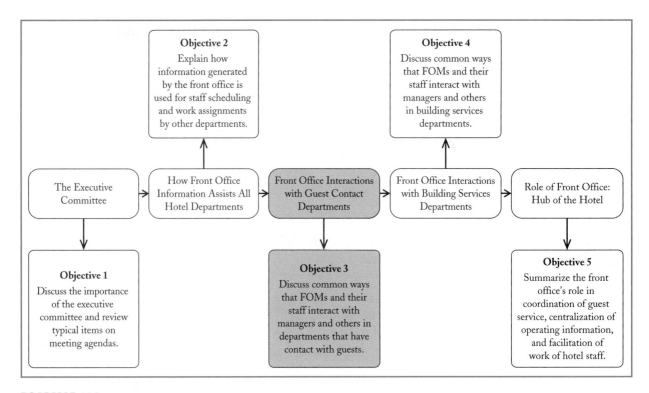

ROADMAP 14.3

Data in PMS reports help the GM evaluate the effectiveness of the marketing and sales department's efforts. Are sales for specified periods on track with the forecasts? How do sales compare with the number of rooms sold for this time period last year? When there are concerns about future room sales, the GM may place this topic on the executive committee's agenda.

One of the most important responsibilities of the FOM is to produce a daily **flash report** that gives the GM a quick snapshot of important financial information necessary to make decisions.

FRONT OFFICE SEMANTICS

Flash report: Daily information provided to the general manager that reports key financial information from the previous day and, often, accumulated data for the month and/or year to date a compared with actual data from previous years. Flash report information is used to determine where, if at all, management attention is most immediately required. Also called *Manager's Daily.*

Figure 14.4 is a sample of a hotel's daily flash report. Among other information, it provides financial highlights—today and month to date (MTD)—relative to the hotel's occupancy percentage, ADR, and RevPar. Details about revenue from room sales, food and beverage, and other sources are shown, as is information about room statistics (stats), deposits, and the number and ADR of rooms generated by the franchisor's central reservation system. The GM can also learn specifics about the sources of room sales by market mix.

	TODAY	MTD			DATE DAILY FOR TODAY	11/01/XX 10/31/XX MTD
OCCUPANCY	16.31%	57.40%				
ADR	$ 59.42	$ 71.44				
REV PAR	$ 9.69	$ 41.01		**ROOM STATS:**		
ROOM REVENUE				Available Rooms	$ 141	$ 4,371
Trans Corporate	0.00	4,553.91		Sold Rooms	23	2,464
Trans Leisure	662.94	61,627.79		Comp Rooms	1	45
Trans Government	130.00	16,995.47		Comp Bkft	2	1,117
Group Corporate	0.00	14,688.48		Out of order rooms	76	786
Group Leisure	468.02	59,102.02		**DEPOSITS:**		
Group Government	0.00	7,110.49		Cash	992.98	124,642.79
Web Reservations	0.00	1,176.91		Visa/Mastercard	13,431.75	139.001.85
Tax Exempt	78.00	2,652.00		American Express	1,863.45	31,637.29
Discount Rate	248.71	14,339.65		Diners	7.37	585.14
Allowance Room Rev	(161.71)	(2,982.50)		Discover	185.38	6,072.16
TOTAL	**1,425.96**	**179,244.22**		TOTAL	16,480.93	301,939.23
	0.00	0.00		**OVER/SHORT**		49.44
	0.00	0.00		− / +		
Banquet Bkft	0.00	3,510.50		Tax Exempt Room Rev.	78.00	18,386.09
Banquet Lunch	0.00	13,242.35		Tax Exempt Bqt. Food	0.00	8,769.00
Banquet Dinner	0.00	16,483.45		Tax Exempt Bqt. Room	0.00	300.00
Coffee Breaks	0.00	5,779.75		Tax Exempt A/V	0.00	1,330.00
Meeting Room Rev	0.00	2,633.02			**Beg. Bal.**	**End. Bal.**
A/V Rental	0.00	3,285.00		**LEDGER RECONCIL.:**		
Banquet Service Chg	0.00	7,232.39		Guest Ledger	18,169.20	3,622.88
				Direct Bill	62,253.00	60.221.51
Banquet Fees	0.00	9,400.00		Advance Deposits	(13,374.01)	(5,780.00)
Bqt. Bar Revenue	0.00	3,546.75		LEDGER TOTALS	67,048.19	58,064.39
TOTAL	0.00	65,113.21		**RESTAURANT REVENUE**		
				Restaurant Food	315.25	11,180.23
TELEPHONE REVENUE				Room Service	7.37	1,685.67
Local Calls	0.00	0.00		Bar Sales	0.00	8,373.73
Long Distance	(11.13)	543.12		Room Service Reversal	(7.37)	(1,685.67)
Pay Phone Commision	0.00	0.00		Restaurant over− & short +	(7.37)	53.26
Ph Allowances	0.00	0.00		TOTAL	307.88	19,553.96
TOTAL	**(11.13)**	**543.12**				
DAILY				**OTHER INCOME**		
TOTAL REVENUE	**1,748.69**	**269,167.92**		Guest Valet	0.00	0.00
				Movie Sales	25.98	2,126.47
SALES TAX	156.67	21,375.29		No Show Revenue	0.00	1,324.69
SALES TAX ADJ.	0.00	0.00		Vending Commisions	0.00	502.66
				Other Income	0.00	759.68
				All Other Income Adj.	0.00	0.00
				TOTAL	25.98	4,713.40

FIGURE 14.4   Sample daily flash report.

	TODAY	MTD
OCCUPIED ROOMS		
Trans Corporate	0	60
Trans Leisure	6	678
Trans Government	2	255
Group Corporate	0	203
Group Leisure	7	771
Group Government	0	109
Web	0	12
Tax Exempt	2	68
Discount Rate	6	308
Comp Rooms	1	45
TOTAL	24	2,509
ADR:		
Trans Corporate	$0.00	$75.90
Trans Leisure	$110.49	$90.90
Trans Government	$65.00	$66.65
Group Corporate	$0.00	$72.26
Group Leisure	$66.86	$76.66
Group Government	$0.00	$65.23
Web	$0.00	$98.08
Tax Exempt	$39.00	$39.00
Discount Rate	$41.45	$46.56
Comp Rooms		
TOTAL	$59.42	$71.44
MARKET MIX		
Trans Corporate	0.00%	2.39%
Trans Leisure	25.00%	27.02%
Trans Government	8.33%	10.16%
Group Corporate	0.00%	8.09%
Group Leisure	29.17%	30.73%
Group Government	0.00%	4.34%
Web	0.00%	0.48%
Tax Exempt	8.33%	2.71%
Discount Rate	25.00%	12.28%
Comp Rooms	4.17%	1.79%
TOTAL	100.00%	100.00%

# OF ROOMS	
TOTAL TRANS	8
TOTAL GROUP	7
TOTAL EXEMPT & DISCOUNT	8
COMP	1
TOTAL	24

TOTAL REVENUE	
TOTAL TRANS	$ 631.23
TOTAL GROUP	$ 468.02
TOTAL EXEMPT & DISCOUNT	$ 326.71
TOTAL	$ 1,425.96

FIGURE 14.4   *(continued)*

Reservation Contribution			
Date: 10/31/XX		Month of October	
	Today	MTD	
Room Available	**141**		
Total Rooms Sold	23		4,371
Franchisor Rooms Sold	3		2,464
Franchisor % of Total Rooms	2.13%	6.50%	
Total Room Revenue	$ 1,425.96		$179,244.22
Franchisor Contribution	$ 195.00		24,719.00
Franchisor % of Total Revenue	13.67%	13.79%	
Total ADR	$ 62.00	$	72.75
Franchisor ADR	$ 65.00	$	87.04
Difference	$ 3.00	$	14.29

FIGURE 14.4   *(continued)*

There is no universal requirement about the summary information to be included in a daily flash report. Needs are assessed by each organization; in chain properties, some GMs may request that additional information be included. Generally, flash report data are developed by the night auditor as the night audit is generated; this staff member has access to all rooms-related data. In many hotels, revenue data and sales receipts from food and beverage operations are deposited at the front desk. In these instances, the night auditor will then be able to provide the needed data about food and beverage-operations. In other hotels, especially larger ones, food and beverage data for the flash report may be generated by the food and beverage controller in the accounting department.

The GM has access to all reports that are available to the FOM. Some of the daily PMS reports, however, are of more interest to the GM:

- VIPs in-house list
- In-house groups list
- Twenty-four hour reservation activity report
- Short-term occupancy forecast (10 days)
- Thirty-day occupancy forecast
- Out-of-order room report
- Rate discrepancy report
- Comp room report

Financial Concerns

The GM and FOM typically meet monthly, or more frequently, to discuss the front office operating budget and business plan activities. Front office revenues (room sales) are likely to be a discussion topic at executive committee meetings. Front office expenses are not normally discussed in these meetings; rather, they are discussed in meetings between the GM and FOM. Likewise, tactics identified in the front office business plan will likely be discussed in a GM and FOM meeting as progress toward objectives is evaluated.

Service Recommendations

The FOM is directly responsible for many functions that have an impact on guest service. Concerns about service improvements may be identified as guest complaints are registered; however, many guest concerns can be anticipated when the FOM works proactively to improve service. Front office personnel initiate a wide range of opportunities for interaction with guests during reservation, registration, and checkout. Services provided by other staff members—uniformed services, door and parking attendants, guest transportation, and the concierge—also are evaluated by guests.

FOMs need to ask their staff members this question: "How can we improve guest service?" Most likely they will receive a variety of responses. An employee of a hotel located close to a **gateway** airport might suggest providing better information about customs, immigration, exchange rates, and related international travel concerns. Employees at another hotel might suggest improvements to a business center or to luggage storage areas. Recommendations developed by the FOM and his or her staff are typically brought to the GM with the details required to make a **business case.** Discussions of staff recommendations, whether conducted in executive committee or in one-on-one meetings, are examples of guest service being the primary focus of interactions between the GM and FOM.

FRONT OFFICE SEMANTICS

Gateway: Term relating to a location (e.g., airport or hotel) where there is significant activity involving international travelers.

Business case: Advantages that are objectively presented whenever possible in support of a proposal to improve business.

Day-to-Day Operations

An ever-changing array of issues arises daily that requires planned or unplanned, formal or informal, interactions between the FOM and the GM. Some examples follow:

- The impact of weather or other events on the need to revise room rate structures
- Special problems that are slowing guestroom assignments
- Computer hardware, software, or front office equipment problems
- Overbooking or no-show problems
- Problems about guest property or guest removal and related problems with legal implications.
- Payment card chargeback appeals
- PMS maintenance and programming issues
- Telephone call accounting and pricing issues

Marketing and Sales Department

The FOM and director of sales and marketing interact in many ways. For example, these two department heads meet to discuss room rates for transient guests. Another common interaction occurs as the director of sales and marketing considers the worth of potential group business. Assume that a sales associate receives an inquiry from a price-sensitive meeting planner who is scheduling a meeting in eight months that would require about 50 percent of the hotel's guestrooms for three nights. The planner

The FOM and the director of sales and marketing should meet regularly to discuss potential business opportunities.

states that the organization of health care administrators is looking for a property with meeting facilities that will charge attendees no more than $55 per night, which is about $25 less than the hotel's ADR for that time of year. The call is routed to the director of sales and marketing, whose first task is to determine the availability of rooms for the nights they are needed. Let's assume that the meeting planner's required rate is non-negotiable, and that there are comparable hotels in the area with the meeting space to accommodate the meeting planner's needs. Should the hotel accept this business?

While meeting with the FOM, the director of sales and marketing learns that there are a large number of rooms—more than enough to accommodate the group—that remain unsold. The room rate during this period has been reduced once already, and the number of unsold rooms is still far more than the number remaining to be sold at this time last year. Based on these data, the director of sales and marketing can make a good business case to the GM to accept this business.

By contrast, let's assume that the PMS report indicates that there are not a sufficient number of rooms available to meet the group's needs, or that rooms are available, but there are many fewer than there were at this time last year. The experience and common sense of the FOM, director of sales and marketing, and GM must be used to determine whether the proposed business should be accepted.

Now let's bring the "real world" into our analysis. Many times the decision-making process is clouded by variables that are unknown or will not be known on a timely basis. The director of the local convention and visitors bureau just announced that the community is one of two finalists for hosting a convention that will take place at the same time of the health care administrators' meeting. The convention will bring enough delegates into the community to fill every hotel room. The host community will be selected in about two weeks. Rooms can be sold to the convention delegates at a much higher rate than that offered by the meeting planner.

Now what should the hotel's management team say to the meeting planner? An obvious tactic is to ask the meeting planner for a two-week delay in making a final decision. If, the planner agrees, in two weeks the hotel team will better know what to do. If the planner wants a more immediate response, the hotel's decision becomes less objective and more difficult. Regardless, however, PMS information maintained and generated by the FOM provides the background information that is essential in making these business decisions.

IT'S MORE THAN JUST THE OCCUPANCY RATE!

It takes more than a high occupancy rate (i.e., number of rooms sold divided by total rooms available) to make a hotel successful. For example, hotel managers should factor RevPar into their definition of financial success. Recall that RevPar means revenue per available room or occupancy percentage multiplied by average daily rate. Selling many rooms at a low rate or just a few rooms at a very high rate can yield financial disaster!

Is the group that provides a full-service hotel with the highest RevPar always the "best?" Maybe, but maybe not. Some groups, but not all, require extensive banquet services that can be very profitable. Histories of groups that do not hold banquets may indicate that they generate smaller revenues in the hotel's à la carte dining and beverage operations than do groups that hold banquets. Revenues from all sources—restaurant sales, beverage sales in the lounge, parking fees, in-room movie sales, telephone tolls, and so forth—must be considered when room rates are negotiated with groups, and as the financial worth of a proposed meeting or group contract is evaluated.

In the example just discussed, the director of sales and marketing used PMS reports related to rooms forecasts. Other PMS reports frequently used by this manager include these:

- Group pickup report
- VIPs in house
- In-house groups list
- Group revenue-generated summary
- Thirty-day occupancy forecast
- Cutoff date review
- Comp room reports

Staff members of the front office and marketing and sales departments also interact frequently. They may discuss room assignments for VIPs and arrangements for special amenities for guestrooms. Additional areas of interaction may include the in-house marketing of special promotional packages sold from the front desk, the placement and total room pickup of guests who have established negotiated rates, and long-term occupancy forecasts.

Another interaction of front office and marketing and sales personnel involves groups that are **pre-keyed.** For example, consider tour groups and sports teams that have tour guides, chaperones, or coaches escorting them. Rooms for these guests may be prepaid and, at the group leader's request, access to outgoing telephone calls, pay-per-view television channels, and minibar purchases may be restricted or eliminated. When these guests arrive, they can be escorted to a meeting or lobby area away from the front desk where room assignments can be made. Keys can be distributed (e.g., to the responsible adult), and a rooming list can be developed for use by the adults and hotel staff in case of an emergency.

FRONT OFFICE SEMANTICS

Pre-key (guestroom): Making an electronic key for a guestroom before the actual arrival of the guest who will be assigned to that room.

In some hotels, rooming lists for pre-keyed groups are entered into the PMS system by marketing and sales staff; in other properties, this task is the responsibility of front office personnel.

Front office and marketing and sales personnel may also interact to determine if it is possible for members of large groups to check in early or to check out late. These decisions are influenced by a hotel's occupancy level the night before (for early check-in) and the night of check-out (for late check-out). Managers of these two departments also meet regularly to set transient room rates. For example, the rack rate for the same room might differ on the same night because of discounts for corporate travelers, members of the American Automobile Association and the American Association of Retired Persons, members of the hotel brand's frequent-traveler program, and government and military guests. **Consortia rates** may be granted to guests booked by selected travel agencies recognized by the hotel.

FRONT OFFICE SEMANTICS

Consortia rate: Room rate given to a guest whose room is booked by selected travel agencies.

Food and Beverage Department

The volume of business experienced by the hotel's food and beverage department can be affected dramatically by the number and type of guests staying at the property. When guests are not affiliated with a group offering banquet alternatives, as the number of guests increases, so typically does the volume of business for à la carte dining operations, bars and lounges, and room service. This is especially true for breakfast which, historically, is the meal most frequently purchased in the hotel by its overnight guests. As the number of guests increases, more food and beverage production and service employees are needed, and then the volume of production in employee dining operations increases. Experienced food and beverage directors estimate correlations between the hotel's occupancy rate and volume of business from hotel guests. Note that visitors who are not guests may also use the hotel's à la carte dining options and bars and lounges. However, business volume forecasts from the PMS are used to estimate guest business, and the food and beverage director develops a separate estimate for visitor business. The sum of guest and visitor business estimates drives production and service planning for these revenue centers.

Food and beverage directors are also interested in PMS information related to guests affiliated with groups meeting at the property. Many groups will have negotiated a **guarantee** for banquet events, which helps determine the number of meals to be produced. This makes it relatively easy to forecast production needs. However, the number of guests attending these meetings must be deducted from the estimated total number of hotel guests to determine requirements for à la carte dining. Also, the forecasted number of room service breakfasts (usually the busiest meal for room service) will be affected if a large number of guests will be attending a group breakfast function.

FRONT OFFICE SEMANTICS

Guarantee (banquet): Contractual agreement about the number of meals to be provided at a banquet. A guarantee must be made several days in advance of the event; at that time, the banquet host agrees to pay for the larger of the actual number of guests served or the number of guests guaranteed.

In addition to PMS reports about guestroom occupancy, the food and beverage director will likely be interested in and request these reports:

- In-house guest count (house count)
- Guest arrival summary
- Guest departure summary
- In-house groups list
- Short-term occupancy forecast (10-day)
- Thirty-day occupancy forecast

Although it may seem surprising, front office personnel also play an important role in a property's liability in regard to **dram shop law.** The FOM and food and beverage director must work together to develop and implement training programs on this topic for their staffs.

FRONT OFFICE SEMANTICS

Dram shop law: Provision in the U.S. legal code that allows an injured party to seek damages from an intoxicated person who caused the injury and from the person who provided the alcoholic beverages to the intoxicated person.

Bartenders, food and beverage servers, hosts, and other staff in the hotel's restaurants and lounges need training in responsible service of alcoholic beverages. They will then know when such beverages should no longer be served to specific guests. They will also know *how* to properly curtail service and to advise guests about the hotel's concerns for the safety of guests and others.

A potentially serious problem occurs when a guest becomes intoxicated and then decides to drive. What should front desk agents do when they see an obviously and visibly intoxicated guest walking or stumbling through the lobby on the way to the front door? What should door attendants and parking lot attendants do as these guests walk toward their auto or ask for retrieval of their auto? The food and beverage director, working with the FOM, must ensure that front office personnel know how to recognize guests who may cause harm to themselves or to others and are able to deal with these guests once identified. Persons cannot be physically restrained from entering their auto. They can, however, be advised that it does not appear safe for them to drive, and that the local police will be phoned if the person drives away. If a property does not have a door or parking lot attendant, the front desk agent may need to quickly call security, the manager on duty, or another responsible hotel staff member to intervene.

What about intoxicated guests who will not be driving but are just going to their room? They can fall, become disoriented, or be taken advantage of by dishonest persons in elevators or hallways or by those who may even enter their room. These

Bartenders and other staff members must take their responsibilities seriously when serving alcohol to their guests.

examples point to the need for the FOM to ensure that staff receive appropriate training about procedures to be followed when such situations arise.

There are other times when front office and food and beverage staff interact. In small hotels, dining room and bar receipts, along with cashier banks, are brought to the front desk after reconciliation and balancing. In some properties, this is done at the end of every meal period or shift; in other hotels, it is done once daily. The receipts (cash, checks, and payment card copies) and cash banks are given to the night auditor when the operations close. Certain information about the day's food and beverage activities is required for the daily flash report for the GM, along with room sales and other data.

Some hotels provide hot or cold beverages and snacks or other refreshments to guests in lobby areas as they wait to check in or to check out. Food and beverage personnel may prepare and transport these products to and from food preparation areas. Front desk personnel may invite guests to enjoy the refreshments, inform food and beverage staff when items should be replenished, and help to keep the service equipment and areas tidy. Many limited-service hotels offer a complimentary breakfast. The availability of **lobby foodservices** is an important factor that influences many guests' selection of a property.

FRONT OFFICE SEMANTICS

Lobby foodservices: Term describing the foodservices offered by many limited-service hotels in their lobby area.

In many of these properties, the foodservices attendant is a staff member of the front office department. This person is responsible for setting up, maintaining and cleaning up after the breakfast period. In some properties front desk agents may assist in setting up lobby foodservices, may help replenish items during especially busy times, and may fill in if the foodservices attendant must be away from the work area.

Another opportunity for interaction between front office and food and beverage staff occurs when a guest disputes a food and beverage charge made to the room. Perhaps a simple posting error occurred; for example, the lounge charge for room 313 was entered into the folio for room 331. In another case, a guest may say there is an error in the amount charged. In either instance, a front desk agent may need to contact food and beverage personnel to solve these problems.

SECTION REVIEW AND DISCUSSION QUESTIONS

Section Objective: Discuss common ways that FOMs and their staff interact with managers and others in departments that have contact with guests.

Section Summary: The night auditor—a staff member in the front office—typically prepares a daily flash report for the general manager that provides important operating information about the previous day. The FOM prepares many reports for the general manager's use and meets with the manager about issues relating to transient room rates for future dates, the front office's expense budget and business plan, service improvement recommendations, and day-to-day operating concerns.

The FOM works with the director of sales and marketing to make guestroom pricing decisions for meeting attendees. These managers may also interact to assign rooms for meeting attendees, to coordinate group check-in and check-out times, and to discuss recommendations to be made to the general manager about room rates for transient guests.

The FOM and his or her staff also interact with food and beverage personnel. Front office staff provide information that helps the food and beverage director plan work requirements and develop training for the responsible service of alcoholic beverages. Additional opportunities for interaction arise if food and beverage products and services are available in lobby areas, and if questions arise about food and beverage charges made to guestrooms.

Discussion Questions:
1. What factors other than guestroom charges would be of interest to the director of sales and marketing as decisions are being made about the economic worth of a meeting? How can the FOM provide assistance to marketing staff as these decisions are made?
2. How can an FOM assist when a hotel's business plan is focusing on an increase in transient guest business? In meeting attendee business? In the sale of rooms to business travelers? In sale of rooms to family travelers?
3. Assume that a guest disputes a food and beverage bill. Documentation is available indicating that these charges were, in fact, incurred by the guest alleging the error. What should the front desk agent do?

FRONT OFFICE INTERACTIONS WITH BUILDING SERVICES DEPARTMENTS

As noted in Roadmap 14.4, this section highlights interactions between the front office and other departments referred to as building services departments. Staff members in these departments generally have fewer contacts with guests than do staff in the departments discussed in the previous section. Four hotel units are important providers of business services: accounting, housekeeping, security, and maintenance.

Accounting Department

Managers in the accounting department including the controller develop record-keeping systems and generate information and report it in income (profit and loss) statements, balance sheets, and statements of changes in cash position (cash flow statements). They are keenly aware of the financial impact on the property's bottom line of decisions that affect occupancy rates, room pricing, and group meetings. There are several additional ways in which accounting personnel interact with front office staff:

- *Night auditor training.* In most properties, accounting managers work with the FOM and others to train the night auditor. Accounting personnel have significant input into the methods used to reconcile each day's room revenues with the number of rooms occupied. They have likely helped to design PMS reports that address financial concerns, and they are involved in the manual and automated methods used to interface the PMS and its reports with back-office accounting systems.

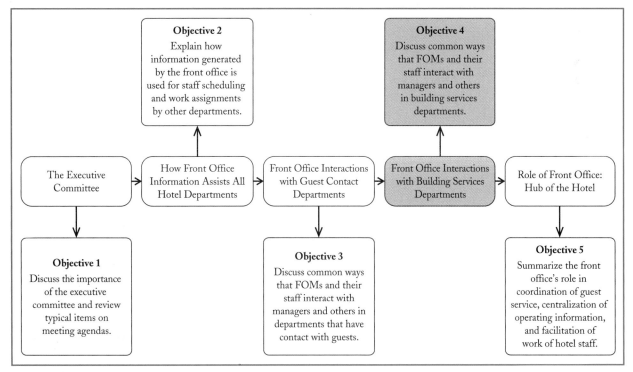

ROADMAP 14.4

MODERN FRONT OFFICE ISSUES AND TACTICS

Hotel Revenues from Guestroom Telephone Use Decrease

Many hotel guests now use their cell phones rather than guestroom phones because the cost to do so is often much less. This change yields bad news for the accounting department: Telephone revenues per available room dropped to approximately $530 per room in 2003, about 20 percent less than revenues the previous year. Front desk agents, however, may experience an advantage from decreased in-room phone use: a reduction in complaints about telephone charges erroneously posted to guest folios.

Some companies such as Marriott offer electronic packages. For example, Marriott's "Wired for Business" program charges guests $9.95 per day (24 hours) for high-speed Internet access and unlimited domestic and long-distance phone calls. In 2005, the Microtel chain (part of U.S. Franchise System), began offering complimentary high-speed Internet access and unlimited domestic and long-distance calls to all guests.

Adapted from Taylor, A. 2004. Travelers increasing use of cell phones pinches hotel's profit. Retrieved March 1, 2004, from http://www.hotel-online.com/News/PR2004_1st/Mar04_CellHotel.html

- *Guest billing problems.* Many problems related to guest charges are addressed before or at check-out. Guests are typically given the opportunity to review their bill at the front desk, on an in-room television, or at lobby kiosk as part of the check-out process. However, problems arise with guests who have never visited the hotel. Persons who have guaranteed their reservation with a payment card but who no-show in violation of the property's cancellation policies will generally be charged for, at least, the first night's stay. Some of these guests may protest and contact their payment card company directly; others may first contact the hotel. Regardless of the source of the inquiry (i.e., the merchant services provider or the guest), the accounting department becomes involved to determine whether the reservation cancellation was properly made. If it was, there should be a cancellation number for that reservation in the PMS system. Although accounting personnel have access to PMS data, they frequently interact with the front office staff about extenuating circumstances or other issues to resolve the disputed charge.

- *Policy development and change.* A wide range of financial concerns are addressed by policies in every hotel, for example, processing payment cards, reconciling guestroom revenues, requiring advanced deposits for lodging services, accommodating cash-paying guests, and managing petty cash funds. Interactions between the FOM and accounting manager suggest recommendations to the general manager as policies and procedures are established.

- *Cash bank replenishment.* At the beginning of each shift, cashier banks at the front desk must have a specified amount of currency in specific denominations (e.g., $1, $5, and $10 bills) to expedite the change-making process for guests who pay in cash. The currency in these beginning banks is obtained by cashiers from the accounting department in small properties, or cash banks are assembled by accounting department staff in larger properties.

- *Currency exchange.* Hotels that serve a large number of international travelers frequently provide currency exchange services for guests. It is the responsibility of accounting department personnel to provide front office agents with current exchange rates and to maintain cash banks for required currencies at the front desk. Some countries require persons to pay a departure tax when they leave the country and allow hotels to collect this tax and issue a receipt for it at the front desk. The accounting department is responsible for forwarding the funds collected with supporting documentation to the appropriate governmental authority.

The following PMS reports are of most interest to accounting department managers:

- Night audit reconciliation
- Payments received by shift
- Cashier over and short report
- Guests over credit limit
- Advanced deposit recap
- Guest ledger activity summary

Housekeeping Department

Guestrooms cannot be sold until they have been cleaned and made ready for the next guest. The executive housekeeper typically receives a PMS-generated report specifying the rooms that were occupied the previous evening. Information about room status is provided, for example, rooms that are clean or dirty, vacant or occupied. Chapter 4 introduced the terms commonly used to designate room status. Although formats of reports may vary by property, all housekeepers depend on the PMS and the FOM to produce accurate room status updates when they are needed.

On days when checked-out rooms are required for arriving guests, the rooms should be cleaned as soon as possible, before rooms for stayover guests are freshened. A first step is for front desk agents to notify the housekeeping department as soon as a check-out occurs. Conversely, housekeepers inform the front office about rooms that were occupied by guests who checked out without notifying the front desk. As you can see, ongoing and effective communication between these two departments is critical. The situation is complicated by the various types of rooms—smoking and nonsmoking, double-bedded, ocean view, and so on. Matching the needs of incoming guests with the sequence of rooms to be cleaned requires an executive housekeeper with a significant amount of skill, experience, and judgment.

Traditionally, after rooms are cleaned and inspected, they are ready to sell, and the front desk is notified. In some properties, housekeepers hand-carry room status reports to the front desk or phone the front desk from the executive housekeeper's office or a guestroom to inform the front desk of status changes. When telephones are interfaced with the PMS, updates can be made from the guestroom's telephone, and wireless technology even permits instant communication between the room inspector and front office personnel.

One method of interaction between the front office and housekeeping department involves room checks. In many properties, two regular room checks are made daily: one in the morning and one in the afternoon.

Morning Room Check

Each housekeeper is responsible for assessing the occupancy of all rooms assigned to him or her. The *assumed* status is shown on the room status report provided by the front office, and physical entry into the room verifies the information. At this time, the housekeeper should make these observations:

- Whether the room is vacant and ready, ready to be cleaned, or occupied (i.e., luggage is in the room)
- If the room is a **sleep out** (i.e., the room's bed was not used)
- Whether immediate maintenance, room repair, or furniture or fixture replacement is necessary
- Other relevant assessments

FRONT OFFICE SEMANTICS

Sleep out: Industry term for a room that was paid for and is listed in the PMS as occupied, but in which the bed was not used.

The morning housekeeper's report is based on a physical inventory of all guestrooms. The report serves several purposes:

- Corrects any errors made by front office staff relating to check-ins and check-outs
- Detects **sleepers**—rooms for which revenues are being posted but which are actually unoccupied
- Determines the number of guests in each room to check against the number for which charges are posted
- Reports cots and cribs in room for which charges are assessed
- Enables the night auditor to cross-check the room revenue report to ensure that every occupied room is accounted for

---

FRONT OFFICE SEMANTICS

Sleeper: Industry term for a room identified in PMS records as occupied (charges are accruing) but that is actually unoccupied.

Discrepancies between the morning housekeeper's report and PMS information are noted on the report. After any necessary corrections and modification of PMS information, a copy of the report is sent from the front office to the accounting department.

Afternoon Room Check

An afternoon housekeeping report is usually completed shortly before the day-shift housekeepers finish their work. A room check is done to verify the rooms that are (1) vacant and ready for rental, (2) on-change status (guests have checked out but rooms are not ready for rental), and (3) questionable because the housekeeper has been unable to enter. This report is delivered to the front office. There, a list of the rooms that are vacant but not ready for rental and rooms that were not inspected during the day will be developed for use by housekeeping staff on the night shift.

Other Coordinating Activities

Front office staff must keep the housekeeping department advised about the volume of late check-outs so that the cleaning of these rooms can be scheduled. Generally, most rooms are made up during the day by day-shift housekeepers and tidied up after

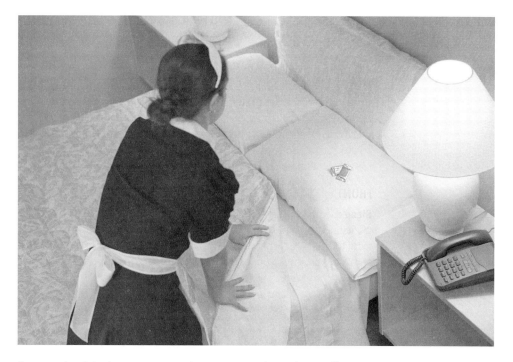

A room check is done to ensure the guestroom is ready to sell.

check-out, if necessary, by a night-shift housekeeper. The need for night staff is generally dictated by the size of the property and occupancy trends.

Sometimes guests decide to extend their departure date but do not, or forget, to inform the front desk. Such situations are noticed when a housekeeper enters a room designated as a check-out and sees that the room still contains the guest's luggage or other personal property. The housekeeper returns to the room after the hotel's check-out time has lapsed. If it still appears that the room has not been vacated, the housekeeper notifies executive housekeeper, who contacts the front desk to determine whether an extended check-out time has been requested and granted. In a well-run hotel, this situation is not likely to occur, because the front desk agent would have already relayed this information to the housekeeping department. In most cases, the guestroom that has not been vacated will be classified as a stayover. The room will be cleaned, and a message will be left for the guest to contact the front desk about a new departure date. If the guest has paid cash for the room, and no payment card is on file, the room will be locked. The guest will be denied access to the room until payment for the additional night or nights has been made or an alternative form of credit has been established.

Staff in the housekeeping department are often responsible for cleaning the hotel's lobby and other public spaces. Front desk agents and others may need to report cleaning problems that require immediate attention. In addition, *all* employees of the property work together to identify potential safety problems that need immediate attention from the housekeeping or maintenance department personnel. For example, a common problem in some locations is slippery floors as a result of inclement weather.

As you read in Chapter 13, lost and found procedures are important and often have legal implications. Lost and found activities are usually managed in the housekeeping department because many items are left in guestrooms by guests and are found by housekeepers. Lost items may also be found by employees, guests, or visitors in the hotel's public areas. Many of these items are turned in to front desk agents who, in turn, must comply with applicable hotel policies.

Not surprisingly, front desk agents receive telephone calls from guests requesting additional bed and bath linens; personal items such as toothbrushes, razors, and combs; and, if not available in the room, hair dryers, irons and ironing boards, and other in-room amenities. In many hotels, these requests are recorded by front office personnel; they then notify the housekeeping staff who bring the requested items to guestrooms.

Many lodging properties do not have housekeeping personnel available on-site throughout the night. In these instances, there may be a linen storage area such as a closet, closed shelving unit, or other space in or behind the front desk area to store items. When a request is made, a front desk agent or a uniformed services attendant may take the requested item to the guestroom. If a property has only one front desk person (e.g., a night auditor) working during the early morning hours, the guest may be asked to pick up a desired item at the front desk because the area cannot be left unattended. In some hotels, the front office employee on duty is allowed to take the item to the guestroom, and the employee places a sign at the front desk to indicate that the area will be serviced shortly.

WHEN ARE GUESTROOMS CLEANED? WHEN DO GUESTS CHECK IN?

Many people hold this stereotype: Hotel guests check out of their rooms during early morning to mid-morning; rooms are then cleaned; and by early afternoon to mid-afternoon, rooms are ready for new guests to check in. In many properties, this pattern is, in fact, typical.

Think, though, of Las Vegas. Guests check in and check out at all hours of the day and night in some properties. Front desk agents and housekeepers may be registering guests and cleaning rooms at hours when their counterparts in other locations are not even on the job.

In some parts of the world, international flights arrive at midnight or later and depart at 6:00 a.m. or earlier. Hotels serving these airports may process most of their check-outs late at night and most of their check-ins very early in the morning. Most rooms may be cleaned between 10:00 p.m. and 4:00 a.m.

Hoteliers must plan their work activities and employee schedules around the convenience of the guests, even if arrival and departure schedules are different from those experienced in other hotels.

In addition to various room status reports, PMS reports of interest to the executive housekeeper include these:

- Guest arrival summary
- Guest check-out summary
- Stayover list
- In-house groups list
- Out-of-order rooms list
- Short-term occupancy forecast (10-day)
- Thirty-day occupancy forecast

Security Department

Every guest staying at a hotel desires a safe experience while there. However, relatively few inquire about a hotel's safety precautions when making a reservation. Instead, most guests assume that procedures are in place to adequately protect them during their visit.

In the past, this lack of proactive concern may have been acceptable or, at least, explainable. In today's world, however, hoteliers and guests must be aware of potential problems, know how to avoid them, and be able to address them if they occur.

Directors of security know that their staff must always stay alert to potential problems and resolve them as they arise. They will be very interested in short-term occupancy information generated by the PMS, because additional security personnel are usually scheduled as the number of rooms sold increases. PMS reports useful to security department personnel typically include these:

- Occupied rooms listing
- In-house groups list
- VIPs in house
- Departures list
- Thirty-day occupancy forecast
- Out-of-order room report
- Comp room reports

Security Precautions

Even small hotels should form a safety committee to develop, review, and modify, if necessary, policies and procedures related to potential safety and security problems. One or more representatives from each hotel department should serve on this cross-functional committee. Front office personnel are necessary because of the critical role they play in alerting guests to emergencies and in telling them about precautions to be taken.

Personnel from the hotel's security department are involved in planning, conducting, and selecting security training programs. Such programs instruct hotel staff, including personnel in the front office, about what to do if and when a security or safety issue arises. Representatives of the local fire department, and governmental agencies may be helpful in providing information. Departments of emergency preparedness are important in areas with the potential for natural disasters such as hurricanes and earthquakes. Also, representatives of the hotel's insurance carrier can often provide resources and other input to the development of the hotel's safety training programs and operating procedures.

EVERY PROPERTY NEEDS A CRISIS PLAN

Every hotel's highest priority during a fire, bomb threat, natural disaster, or other emergency is to protect the safety of the guests and staff. A second priority is to protect the hotel's assets and its reputation. The key to managing a crisis is preparation.

All hotels need to consider the types of crises that can occur and develop plans and train staff to address them. Plans should include step-by-step procedures to follow in an emergency, including phone calls to fire and police agencies and details about when and how to evacuate the property. Keeping the hotel premises safe is an important first step, and this can help in defending the property against allegations of negligence if a disaster occurs. The alarm and emergency communications systems should be tested regularly so that, if an emergency occurs, it will be possible to alert guests, inform employees, and quickly contact emergency personnel.

The crisis plan must be kept current. Evacuation guides posted on the back of guestroom doors do *not* constitute an emergency plan. Plans should ensure that guests receive adequate warning about emergencies, including effective directions for evacuation.

Managers should provide ongoing training and conduct drills to ensure that all staff members know what to do if there is an emergency.

If a disaster occurs, guests need to be warned immediately. It may not be possible to physically accompany all guests out of the building. However, hoteliers have a professional and legal liability to ensure that there are no blocked exits or inadequate lighting that can hinder evacuation.

Front desk personnel must know how to address the specific or unique concerns of hotel guests. They must be aware of guests who have physical disabilities or who are sight- or hearing-impaired. Also, issues concerning guests who do not understand English or other predominant languages of hotel staff members must be addressed.

Security and safety involves every hotel employee; therefore, training and education must begin at the time of new employee orientation. Newly recruited front office employees and their peers should learn details about the property's safety and prevention procedures. The information presented to them should include what to do in the case of fire, storms, power outages, or other emergencies and how to report injuries, intoxicated persons, and individuals who look suspicious. Front office staff may participate in security and safety audits such as regular inspection of the locking systems of guestroom doors. They may have suggestions about ways to update safety and security procedures, and they can evaluate security training that is provided.

Security personnel typically make security rounds that require them to regularly walk through specific areas of the hotel such as public spaces, hallways, parking lots, and back-of-house areas. The lobby and front desk areas are a primary focal point of these routine inspections. Front desk agents can normally be in immediate contact with security staff by telephone or by wireless communication; however, face-to-face conversations between security and front desk personnel are important.

Security and Safety Incidents

Effective security and safety training before problems occur helps to ensure that these situations will be properly managed if they do arise. This section considers potential problems and the role of front office personnel in addressing them.

Guests who experience noise or other disturbances from adjoining or nearby guestrooms or hallways, parking lots, or other locations often notify the front desk. If the disturbance is from a guestroom, in most hotels the front desk agent or another front office employee will phone the guestroom to notify the occupants that other guests are being inconvenienced and to request that the disturbance end. A follow-up call to the complaining guest is then made: "We have contacted the guest in the room causing your complaint and have asked that the disturbance end." If there is a subsequent complaint, in some hotels a second call is made from the front desk; in other properties, a security representative is sent to the room. Of course, care must be taken in these situations. Consider, for example, the difficulty that would arise if a guest phoned the front desk to complain about excessive noise in an adjacent room and, in fact, the noise was *not* coming from that room. In this case, a call to the supposedly noisy room would likely result in *another* unhappy guest. Front desk or security personnel should always verify the source of excessive noise before acting on a complaint. If there are complaints about noise or other disturbances occurring in public areas, including hallways and parking lots, the front office employee receiving the call typically requests that a security department employee visit the location. Again, a follow-up call to the complaining guest can reassure him or her that the concern is being addressed.

Front desk personnel may receive calls from guestrooms about health emergencies. The telephone systems in many hotels route emergency (911) calls to the front desk. In potentially life-threatening situations, front desk personnel must quickly and carefully follow the hotel's procedures for alerting the 911 operator, designated physician, or other emergency service provider. Guests may call the front desk directly to request emergency assistance, and front desk agents must respond appropriately. They should never fail to comply with a guest's request even if, for example, the guest appears irrational or has made similar calls that day or during the visit. A growing number of hotels require that every security staff member be trained in cardiopulmonary resuscitation (CPR), first aid, and the use of an on-site **defibrillator.**

FRONT OFFICE SEMANTICS

Defibrillator: Machine used to deliver an electrical shock to the heart in case of cardiac arrest (i.e., a heart attack) in efforts to reestablish a normal heartbeat.

THE FRONT OFFICE AND MEDICAL EMERGENCIES

If you are a member of the front office staff and you are notified about a medical emergency, obtain the following information:

- Person's name
- Person's location
- Nature of the emergency

Notify the proper emergency responder identified on the property's list of emergency phone numbers and provide the following information:

- Hotel's name
- Address
- Nearest cross street
- Nature of the emergency
- Person's general condition and location
- Hotel entrance nearest the site of the person's location (if not the main entrance)
- Hotel's call-back number

Do not hang up until the responder's operator hangs up.
Then perform other activities:

- Alert security personnel so that they can secure the largest elevator in the lobby or other area for use by emergency personnel.
- Assign someone to go to the person's floor to assist.
- Assign someone to meet emergency personnel at the appropriate hotel entrance, to give them all relevant information, and to escort them to the person's location.
- Do not release information about medical emergencies to anyone other than management and emergency personnel.
- Cooperate fully with emergency personnel. Do not offer further help when asked to remain out of the way.
- In the event of a death, secure the area around the body until police arrive. Do not allow others in the area. Seek assistance from other employees, if necessary.

Never refuse to phone for emergency help for anyone who requests it. Call emergency personnel even if the person requesting emergency attention does not seem like a responsible person, if he or she appears to be in good health, or if he or she does not appear to need emergency assistance. Never, under any circumstances, make the decision that someone does not need emergency assistance if the person has requested it.

Guest Notification in Emergencies

Front desk personnel will likely need to alert persons in guestrooms about the presence of a fire or a potentially life-threatening storm or other natural disaster. They may also need to issue instructions about precautions to take when there is a power outage, a bomb threat, or other need for an emergency evacuation. Specific evacuation procedures must be developed for each property, but the following general procedures are integral to most plans:

- Phone 911 and state the nature of the emergency; be specific. Set off the fire alarm.
- Update and print, if time permits, a list of all occupied rooms; attach a room layout to the evacuation plan. An occupied rooms list should be among the front office emergency records prepared at least daily as an integral part of the department's standard operating procedures.
- If an emergency such as a fire pertains to a specific area of the hotel, first call the rooms occupied next to the emergency area on both sides and any rooms above or below that area. For instance, as seen in Figure 14.5, assume a two-story hotel has rooms that are numbered in a normal pattern. If room 246 is on fire, call rooms 244, 248, 146, 144 and 148, because rooms immediately next to, below, and above the fire area should be evacuated as quickly as possible.
- Do not panic guests; remain calm and direct guests outside. Calmly state:

We must request that you please vacate your room at this time. Use the nearest exit. Take your room key. Do not use the elevator. Use the stairs. Once outside, stay away from the building. If you are remaining on the property, go to the (name of area), our designated safety area.

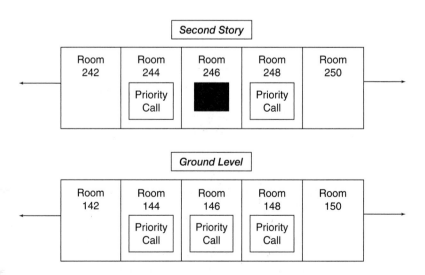

FIGURE 14.5   Fire in room 246 of a two-story hotel.

- Note rooms where you could not contact the guests. If practical, have employees start knocking on doors to evacuate these rooms. If there is a fire, do not attempt to fight it unless someone's life is in danger or the fire is very small, and staff are trained to extinguish it.
- If they are not already present, phone the general manager and maintenance engineer and advise them to go to the hotel immediately.
- Do not leave the front desk area unless that location is affected by the emergency. Front desk staff will need to handle calls from guests. In multibuilding properties, if guests call from the affected building, ask them to evacuate rooms until they are instructed to return.
- After all guests have been phoned, call their rooms a second time to ensure that everyone is out of the affected building.
- In the case of a tornado, phone guests and instruct them to go into the room's bathroom. Front desk staff should go into the office bathroom or storage room closet.

When evacuating the hotel, keep these tactics in mind:

- Do not evacuate unless told to do so because danger is imminent.
- Follow instructions given by emergency personnel.
- Walk, don't run, and keep noise to minimum.
- Do not use elevators.
- Do not push or crowd. Use handrails in stairwells and move to the right if emergency personnel are working in the area.
- Remove shoes that might cause tripping (e.g., high heels, flip-flops).
- Move to the designated evacuation area unless otherwise instructed. Check doors for heat before opening.
- Assist any nonambulatory and visually- or hearing-impaired persons.

Front office personnel should maintain the following supplies and inspect them weekly to ensure an adequate supply and proper working condition:

- Well-stocked first-aid kit
- Flashlights and spare batteries
- Weather-band radio and transistor radio with spare batteries
- Camera and film
- Chalk to mark doors of evacuated rooms
- Scissors or sharp knives, or both
- Incident reports and security log

COMMUNICATION WITH GUESTS IS INTEGRAL TO SECURITY

Residents of New Orleans, the Gulf Coast region, and the entire United States will never forget the catastrophe caused by Hurricane Katrina in early Fall 2005. The disaster will directly affect the lives of hundreds of thousands of residents in the area for years to come. For a few days, it also threatened the lives of thousands of guests staying at hotels in New Orleans during and immediately after the storm and flooding that followed.

In "normal" times, many vacationers search for value, amenities, and a hotel environment to shape an out-of-the-ordinary experience when they travel away from their homes. All guests, at every moment, are most concerned about one thing: their security. Hoteliers, including front office staff who most frequently and directly communicate with guests during their hotel visits, must remember this concern and must consider guest security a priority.

The following case study is true, and it highlights what can happen when hoteliers are concerned about their guests and staff but have not sufficiently planned for a disaster.

Arrival in New Orleans

Marilyn and her friend, Chandra, arrived in New Orleans several days before Katrina struck on August 29, 2005. They were looking forward to their stay in a prominent four-star property in the French Quarter. However, soon weather forecasters were talking about the increasing possibility that Hurricane Katrina would do the seemingly impossible: strike the below-sea-level New Orleans area with Category 5 winds followed by a storm surge that could destroy or topple levees and put the city under many feet of flood waters.

During the days preceding Katrina's landfall, Marilyn, Chandra, and other guests received no advice from hotel managers to end their visit early and leave the area because of the storm threat. After mandatory evacuation of the city was declared on August 27, guests staying at the property were basically on their own. Those staying in rooms on the third floor or below were relocated to rooms on higher levels. During this time, guests had the impression that the hotel staff wanted to help them but had no plan or current information that would enable them to do so.

Day Before the Storm

On the day before the hurricane struck, an announcement was made over hotel loud-speakers that a general meeting would be held at two different times in a public function room. The announcements were made only in public areas of the property. There were no calls to guestrooms, no notes placed under guestroom doors, and no other tactics used for notification. Fortunately, many guests were in the public areas waiting for information and heard the announcement.

The meeting was facilitated by the general manager and several department heads. No roll call of guests' names was made during the meeting. The purpose of the meeting was two-fold: (1) to emphasize the hotel's concern for guests ("You are our priority; we will do whatever is necessary to keep you safe and comfortable") and (2) to answer general questions about the storm and what to expect from it. The general manager suggested that guests stay in their rooms when the storm struck. He also indicated that, if guests checked out of the hotel, they would not be able to check back in. There was no other formal communication between guests and hotel staff—no telephone messages, no lobby bulletin-board notices, no memos distributed to guestrooms. Some guests asked concierge staff to help them obtain airline tickets, but no seats were available.

The property had no formal evacuation plan. For example, during the general meeting, guests were told that if problems arose as they stayed in their guestrooms when the storm struck, they should go to an open-air inner courtyard during the storm. Later, they were told that there would likely be greater protection under open stairwells in the hotel. Guests were also informed that the hotel would be able to generate electricity, but only for selected function rooms, the lobby, and related public areas. Guestrooms and the corridors to them would not have electricity. The hotel did not have or provide flashlights for guests. One employee indicated (perhaps in jest) that the hotel could not provide life jackets.

On the day before the storm struck, hotel managers informed their employees that they would be released from work or they could bring their families (including pets) to stay at the property; many did. Guests and employees were invited for complimentary meals in a public function room. The service plan was "first come, first served." After guests were served, the same meal was provided for employees and their families. (The first meals served after the storm were brown-bag cold meals made from food items available at the hotel. By the next day, hot meals were prepared on gas grills and served on paper plates.)

When asked (but only then), front desk staff told guests that they would be charged only a "minimal" amount for their rooms. Staff suggested the charge would be about $75 per day, which was substantially less then the daily rate of several hundred dollars in effect before the storm.

During the Storm

Although hotel employees had not suggested that they do so, Marilyn and Chandra purchased bottled water and a flashlight. They remained in their room's restroom away from windows and exterior walls during the storm. They had filled the bathtub with water before the storm struck and had packed their suitcases to enable a quick departure after the storm, if necessary.

After the Storm

After the storm ceased but before flooding began, there was no available communication in New Orleans such as land and cell phones or radio and television. Marilyn and Chandra had airline tickets for their New Orleans departure on the day the storm struck. After the storm, they contacted the front desk to learn how they might best get to the airport for what they assumed would be delayed but available fights. Front desk staff indicated that it was not possible to hire a taxi and, even if they could, it would be a three hour trip to the airport (the trip was normally less than an hour). The hotel's general manager personally told selected guests that he had tried to obtain buses but no buses were available. The women then resigned themselves to at least another day in the city. To their surprise, when they walked through the French Quarter, two taxi drivers said that they could take them anywhere they wanted to go (there was no traffic) but that airport service had been discontinued.

When the flooding began on the second day after the storm, the New Orleans mayor announced a curfew beginning at 7:00 p.m. Guests were told that they must be in the hotel at that time because doors would be locked and chained (they were!) and that an armed security guard would be patrolling the site to ensure that no one entered or left the property (he did!). Surprisingly, this made many guests feel more secure because of reports of looting and the lack of police control in the city at that time.

Flooding occurred in many parts of New Orleans, but French Quarter hotels were spared because they were on relatively higher ground. Guests and the remaining food from another hotel were transferred to Marilyn and Chandra's hotel, because the other property had received extensive storm and water damage. Some guests were beginning to speculate that hotel managers had information but did not want to provide it for fear that guests would be more terrified than they already were.

For weeks after the storm, news reports provided many anecdotes about people helping strangers during the crisis. Marilyn and Chandra were able to leave town on the second day of the flooding with help from someone they had just met. When they arrived at their West Coast homes later that week, they phoned the hotel's corporate office and learned that all hotel guests had been able to leave the city before the end of the week. Except for a skeleton crew of staff, hotel managers and employees had also vacated the building.

Follow-Up Notes

This case study was written about two months after the storm. During that time, neither Marilyn nor Chandra received any follow-up communication or even an invoice from the property. One of the women had noticed a charge from the hotel on her credit card that seemed excessive. She assumed it included a fee for Tuesday, the day they had left the city, which they had done quickly without informing the front desk. She contacted the property, a copy of the bill was faxed to her, and that charge was deducted from the bill.

Marilyn phoned the hotel's general manager and learned that he and his wife had lost their home, as did about 60 percent of the staff. He didn't know where all his employees were, but he thought some had relocated to other cities. He explained that he was finally able to get two buses late Tuesday night to transport most of the guests to the Houston airport. He had paid $6,000 of his own funds for the buses and had yet to be reimbursed by his organization. He also noted that he was pleased that the property had not suffered greater damage, and he was already addressing the problems that had occurred, including obtaining a large-capacity generator. The general manager thought the changes being made would enable the hotel and its staff to be better prepared in the future, and he was very pleased that all guests were safe and at their homes.

Hotel experts, managers, and security consultants will likely critique the aftermath of Hurricane Katrina for years to better learn what hoteliers should do when natural disasters occur. One important lesson is evident in this case study: Concern for guest safety does not replace the need for careful planning. In fact, concern for guests should be the incentive for the planning that is absolutely essential so that hoteliers can fulfill their primary duty of providing security for their guests.

Fires

Hotel fires are, unfortunately, more common than many people think. In a typical year, about 25 percent of U.S. hotels have a fire that requires a fire department response. These fires are frequently started by cigarettes or other smoking material in guestrooms. However, fires can begin in storage areas, kitchens, and laundries; sometimes they are of suspicious origin. Most hotel fires are small and involve little property damage and few, if any, injuries. Nevertheless, a small fire can become out of control quickly if there is the right combination of heat, ventilation, and combustible materials. Then a fire can spread rapidly from room to room, down corridors, and through ventilation shafts until an entire section or wing of the hotel is involved.

Hotel fires can threaten hundreds of guests who are in unfamiliar surroundings, who often are tired or asleep, and who have widely varying physical capabilities. Guests may be housed multiple stories above the street and well out of reach of fire department ladders.

A hotel fire need not be a major disaster to have a significant effect on the hotel and its employees. Any fire will cause disruption and property damage, and any fire can lead to injuries and lawsuits. A fire of any proportion will generate adverse publicity, sometimes nationwide, and can result in a loss of business and a loss of jobs.

The property's managers and employees are the best fire protection available to the hotel. Managers can provide the appropriate fire safety equipment and can develop exemplary disaster response procedures. As well, they can implement a continuous training program that includes goals of prevention and appropriate response. Employees are the first line of protection, because they work throughout the hotel and can discover hazards, alert appropriate supervisors, and can even deal with a fire in its very early stages (e.g., if they are trained in the use of fire extinguishers).

All reports of a fires should be considered real, should be responded to, and should be investigated immediately. After a possible fire is reported, the following actions should be taken:

- The manager on duty and a security officer should immediately visit the area to determine if the fire is real.
- If there is a fire, the fire department should be contacted immediately.

- If evacuation is necessary, the manager on duty should contact the front desk staff and tell staff to implement the hotel's emergency evacuation procedures. Evacuate the fire floor first, room by room. Initiate a system to keep track of every guest, including those who do not respond to a room call. Assist guests with disabilities. Members of the hotel's emergency response team should assemble in predetermined areas designated in the response plan. After rooms on the fire floor are evacuated, the floor above the fire floor and then below the fire floor should be evacuated.
- Guests should be called and told to evacuate. They should be told to feel the door before opening it and to open it only if it is cool. They should take their room keys with them, should not use the elevator, and if they encounter smoke, they should return to their room and call the front desk.
- If the room door is hot or if guests cannot leave the area, they should remain in their rooms. They should seal all cracks (particularly at the bottom of the door), turn off the air conditioner and fan, hang a sheet from the window to alert the fire department, and fill the tub with water in case that water is needed later to fight the fire.

A hotel employee should be stationed in the parking lot to direct the fire department to the fire's location. Employees should follow their property's crisis plan and assemble at a predetermined place or begin emergency duties such as assisting guests. If it is safe to do so, staff members should be assigned to verify that all guestrooms are vacant. After rooms are checked, an X should be marked on the door to alert fire department personnel that the room is vacant. Chalk supplies should be available at the front desk or another easily accessible and well-known location.

FIRE: WHAT SHOULD FRONT OFFICE STAFF DO?

- Stay calm.
- Phone the fire department.
- Contact the general manager and all department heads.
- Retrieve the room status (occupied rooms) and in-house guest listing emergency reports. Up-to-date reports should be run at least once daily.
- Compile a list of disabled guests who need assistance.
- Phone all occupied rooms and inform occupants of the situation. Instruct guests to feel the door before opening; if it is cool, they should leave the room with their key and follow emergency exit signs (don't use the elevator). If a guest encounters smoke or cannot leave the room, he or she should notify the front desk, seal all cracks under the door, turn off the air conditioner and fan, hang a sheet from the window, and fill the tub with water.
- Keep a list of any room in which guests could not be contacted, and any guests who were unable to leave their room because of smoke or fire.
- Lock the cash drawer and take the key when leaving the area.

Take the room status and in-house guest listing reports and list of guests (with room numbers) who need assistance, along with the guest registration box (the bucket) when leaving the building.

Bomb Threats

When bomb threats occur, they are usually received by the hotel's switchboard or at the front desk. Procedures to manage bomb threats typically require that the first person alerted is the general manager, manager on duty, or director of security. That individual then determines whether local law enforcement or emergency service authorities should be contacted.

The person who phones in a bomb threat may unknowingly provide information that can assist authorities in their subsequent investigation of the call and in their search for the caller. The staff member taking the call can help by remaining calm and by asking the caller questions such as these: When will the bomb explode? Where is the bomb located? What kind of bomb is it? Where are you calling from? What is the reason for the bomb threat? Listening for unique background noises may help determine where the call was made; for example, is there traffic noise, music, or the sound of machinery? The caller's gender, approximate age, race, voice, accent, or attempt to disguise the voice might be noted. All possible details about the call should be recorded to begin tracking the activities undertaken during the response to the threat.

When there is a bomb threat, the front office should contact all department heads immediately. They should then tell all employees to report to a predetermined location and remain available until they are released by a manager. One employee should be assigned to guide police when they arrive and, if the situation dictates, other staff members should keep stairwells, public restrooms, and other public areas under surveillance for unauthorized persons. Staff should not touch, handle, or move any suspicious objects.

Bombs may be hidden in restrooms, large ashtrays, cabinets, equipment rooms, electrical panels, water fountains, and air ducts. If a suspicious package or bomb is found, it should not be moved, touched, or disturbed, and the area should be evacuated. Block off a 300-foot area in all directions and make sure that all doors and windows are open. Assign a staff member to meet the bomb squad outside the building to lead them to the location. Front office employees and their peers throughout the hotel will need to follow instructions provided by law enforcement officials to help ensure their safety.

MODERN FRONT OFFICE ISSUES AND TACTICS

Costly Blackout in Las Vegas

A 3,000-room Las Vegas megaresort, the Bellagio Hotel, was closed for three days during April, 2004, because of a freak power failure. The problem began on Easter morning when, for unknown reasons, there was a disruption of primary power that burned thousands of feet of power lines. Even the hotel's backup power system had to be shut down.

Two thousand employees were laid off with pay for one or more of these three days. The day the hotel reopened, employees were ready to greet approximately 1,200 guests who had reservations to check in to 800 rooms. A crowd of people waited in lines in the lobby to check in. Guests with reservations for another 1,000 rooms were scheduled to arrive on the second day after reopening.

On the first night of the hotel's reopening, food and beverage service was limited. Initially guests were invited to a buffet and full bar in the convention center. Room service, the cafe, lounges, and bars opened later in the evening. Other restaurants opened a day or two later.

The cost of the blackout: at least $3 million per day in revenue and $1 million per day in cash flow.

Adapted from Smith. R. 2004. Bellagio Hotel in Las Vegas opens three days after black out. *Las Vegas Review-Journal*, April 15, Business, p. 1a.

Power Outages

Front office personnel will likely learn about a power outage at the same time as their peers. However, they will need to help protect guests and other employees during the emergency. They may be stationed at the first-floor location of elevators to remind guests that stairways must be used; they may suggest that guests delay visits to their guestrooms, if possible. Front office staff can assist security personnel in ensuring that emergency lighting is operative. If it is not (e.g., on a specific floor), procedures may require that guests in affected rooms be called and given directions to stairwells if they choose to leave the building.

Earthquakes

The first step in preparing for the possibility of an earthquake is to assess the front desk work area. For example, if the workstation is near window or glass partitions, determine where front desk personnel can take cover to avoid being injured by flying glass. If the work area is near temporary walls or partitions, make sure they are securely anchored. If there are materials stored on top of cabinets or shelves, consider moving or securing these items.

There is little or no warning about an earthquake, so there will be no time to alert guests about the emergency. Several actions may be helpful to all persons, including front desk employees and guests in their rooms or throughout the property:

- *Remain calm:* Do not panic or attempt to go outside; protect yourself.
- *Act quickly:* Move away from windows, temporary walls or partitions, and free-standing objects such as cabinets or shelves.
- *Duck:* Stoop or drop down to the floor.
- *Cover:* Take cover under a sturdy desk, table, or other furniture. If this is not possible, seek cover against an interior wall and protect your head and neck with your arms.
- *Hold:* If you take cover under a sturdy piece of furniture, hold on to it and be prepared to move with it.
- *Stay put:* Remain in position until the ground or building stops shaking, and it is safe to move. Stay inside; do not attempt to leave the building during the shaking.

If there appears to be damage after the earthquake such as fallen objects, broken glass, or fallen ceiling tiles, the FOM and other managers should inspect their areas for potentially dangerous situations. They should also plan for aftershocks. It is the responsibility of the ranking manager on-site to provide further instructions based on procedures in the property's earthquake emergency plans. Telephone lines, if operative, must remain clear for emergency communications. If possible, employees need to check all telephones to make sure the receivers have not been shaken off.

Managers should form emergency response teams with no less than two persons per team to check all floors for damage and injuries. Each team needs at least one radio, one fire extinguisher, and one flashlight per person. Team members should provide first aid (or find someone who can do so) to any injured persons. The injured should not be moved unless absolutely necessary. Team members and building managers should have access to basic first-aid kits. As one team checks the water heater and a second team checks the kitchen, a third team should visit the laundry to check for gas leaks. If leaks are detected, the gas should be shut off at the furthest possible point from the hotel itself—from outside the property if possible or from its interior entry point to the hotel if that is not possible.

The hotel's telephone operator should begin informing guests that an earthquake has occurred and that managers are assessing the damage. Guests should be advised to remain calm and stay in their rooms. The operator is responsible for monitoring the local AM or FM radio newscasts and notifying hotel managers of the latest significant news.

Earthquake plans need to specify the nearest exit from all workstations, including the front desk, and the route to reach that exit if an evacuation is necessary. Alternate routes should be defined for use if the first one is blocked or is unsafe.

Hurricanes and Tornadoes

As noted in Figure 14.6, there are three stages of a hurricane, and specific front office procedures are applicable to each. Fortunately, ample time is generally available to prepare for hurricanes, and front office personnel can follow the hotel's procedures for dealing with them. Damages associated with hurricanes include flash floods caused by torrential rain and sea surges (tidal waves). Extremely high winds can damage buildings, uproot trees, break electric power lines and telephone lines, and turn loose objects into dangerous missiles. Lightning associated with hurricanes can cause fires and power failures.

Unlike hurricanes, tornadoes can occur with relatively little advance warning. It is, imperative, therefore, that hotel employees be prepared to warn guests quickly. If practical, telephone calls should be placed to guestrooms:

Hurricane stage	Front office procedures
Stage 1: Alert A hurricane alert is issued when a hurricane is 60 hours or several hundred miles away. Winds are between 38 and 55 mph and, although the storm might appear to be headed in one direction, it may change course.	**For hurricane alert** • Review procedures required for manual check-in and check-out in the event of a power outage associated with the emergency. **For hurricane watch** • Secure all important files and equipment. • Back up computer files and place existing hard copies, account receipts, and other critical documents in secure cabinets away from areas of potential flooding.
Stage 2: Watch A hurricane watch is issued when the storm is 36 hours away and poses a definite threat. The hurricane may still weaken or be diverted. Winds range from 55 to 73 mph.	**For hurricane warning** • Run emergency reports periodically (e.g., in-house guests and/or occupied rooms). • Distribute a list of guests by name and room number to department heads. • Write notices and directional signs on flip charts with markers, if necessary, to provide updated information to guests. • Cover computers, switchboards, and other sensitive equipment. • Take proper safeguards to protect ledgers, records, files, computers, important documents, and cash. • Prepare to implement a fully manual backup system. • Secure cash, records, and keys in safe-deposit boxes.
Stage 3: Warning A hurricane warning exists when the hurricane is up to 24 hours away and is expected to strike land with winds exceeding 74 mph. When a hurricane warning is issued, precautions must be taken immediately.	**After the hurricane** • Assist guests with departure. • Identify damage to major transportation routes and disruptions to public transportation facilities, and communicate that information to the guests. • Advise key tour operators and travel agents about the hotel's status.

FIGURE 14.6   Front office emergency procedures for hurricanes.

Due to severe weather conditions, hotel management requires that all guests and employees report immediately to the (name of area). Please go calmly and quietly, and a hotel representative will direct you further. Thank you.

A list of all occupied guestrooms should be obtained from the front desk and given to members of the housekeeping, front desk, and security departments who should go to each room to make sure that they are evacuated. The manager on duty should inform security officers and other hotel staff to direct guests to the proper, predetermined location. Guests should be instructed to sit cross-legged against the walls with their arms over their heads.

At least one front desk agent should remain at the telephone console for as long as it is safe to do so to handle any communications needs. Other front desk personnel should go to the prearranged emergency location. If evacuation becomes necessary during the night shift, the night auditor should pull the alarm, phone the fire and police departments, secure the cash drawer and guest folio bucket, and remain at the phone for as long as safely possible.

MODERN FRONT OFFICE ISSUES AND TACTICS

Identity Theft and the Front Office

Identity theft is a crime that is affecting more and more people as it becomes easier for criminals to access information that allows them to fraudulently use payment cards, obtain cash withdrawals from bank accounts, and incur debt payable by the victim. Trained front office personnel can help protect their guests from becoming victims of identity theft by following some basic security precautions.

Front office employees must be properly trained about what they should and should not do. For example, the FOM should ensure that only a minimum number of authorized hotel personnel have access to guest data and that these data are not accessible to others. The room numbers assigned to guests should not be publicly announced, and phone calls to guestrooms should not be placed without the caller identifying the name of the guest to whom he or she wishes to speak. For example, the caller saying, "Please connect me to room 313" should be asked, "May I please ask to whom you wish to speak?". Staff members should not provide a room number if asked by a caller or someone who approaches the front desk for this information.

A common hotel practice raises concerns about identity theft: Many properties slide guest folios under the guestroom doors early in the morning of the day of departure. Although this is convenient to guests, folios may be placed under the door of the wrong room, or edges of the paper or envelope may be visible from the hallway and enable the document to be removed. If this occurs, potentially sensitive information such a guest's payment card number or home address might be accessed by others. (Only the last four digits of the guest's credit card number should be imprinted on this or any other document.)

If FOMs retain the services of third parties to audit reservation telephone calls for quality and training purposes, these contractors or their employees will have access to sensitive personal information such as credit card numbers. Contractual language is essential to limit this information to hotel use only.

Criminals act creatively to obtain information that may affect the financial well-being of guests. FOMs must take precautions so that they and their staff consistently do everything possible to protect their guests, even after they depart from the property.

Adapted from Barber, D. 2004. How to safeguard your guests from being the next identity theft victims. Retrieved February, 2004, from http://www.hotel-online.com/News/PR2004_1st/Feb04_IdentityTheft.html.

FRONT OFFICE SEMANTICS

Identity theft: Crime that occurs when someone obtains and uses another individual's personal information to commit fraud, theft, or both.

Terrorism

Hoteliers in a strategic city, an airport, and in facilities that serve large numbers of guests and large group meetings must be increasingly concerned about terrorism. The tragedies of September 11, 2001, and the August, 2003, truck bombing at the Jakarta (Indonesia) JW Marriott show clearly that hotel security procedures must be updated to address terrorism-related concerns. (For a riveting description of the aftermath of the 9/11 tragedy at the World Trade Center Marriott, see the Web site locations noted in the "Front Office and the Internet" section at the end of this chapter.)

Developing the proper response to a terror threat or actual act of terrorism requires concentrated study and changes in the emergency plans and safety procedures of many hotels. Figure 14.7 outlines some tactics applicable to the front office department as the risk of terrorist attacks increase. Recall that door and parking attendants are front office employees. When reviewing Figure 14.7, note that as the risk of terror attacks increases, more stringent requirements are needed. Even though restrictions may have a negative impact on guest service, they are intended to have a positive effect on guest safety. The tactics suggested for times of the highest risk of attack were in use at the time of the bombing at the Jakarta JW Marriott. The vehicle containing the bomb was stopped as it entered the hotel's driveway, about 40 yards from the lobby entrance. The bomb exploded and killed 12 persons. Only one victim was inside the hotel, and it is believed that the restrictive tactics that were in place saved lives.

Will door attendants need training to screen luggage and to assist persons entering the hotel through metal detectors? Perhaps this is a rhetorical question.

Risk of attack	Examples of appropriate tactics
Low ↑ ↓ Severe	• Normal procedures for fire, building evacuation, and bomb threats must be in place and followed consistently. • All front office and other staff require initial and ongoing training in applicable emergency procedures. • Front office staff should be alert for suspicious persons or packages. • All unattended packages and luggage must be identified or security staff must be alerted. • PMS reports of guest listings by name and room number must be generated daily, and these must be available for emergency use. • Parking attendants should not allow unattended vehicles at hotel entrances; all parking at the hotel should be limited to registered guests. Special precautions may be needed for hotels with parking beneath the building (e.g., checking vehicle trunks and restricting access to the garage). • Luggage and packages left by guests for storage should be inspected in the guests' presence. • Hotel entrances should be restricted to hotel guests. • Guest luggage should be scanned; all unauthorized automobiles, including taxis, should be kept away from the immediate vicinity of the hotel; persons entering the hotel must pass through metal detectors.

FIGURE 14.7 The front office and threats of terrorism.

Nevertheless, the question suggests that those on the hotel's safety committee and the FOM must reconsider how front office staff can protect the safety of guests and employees. The "answer" may involve procedures that were not even imaginable only a few years ago.

Maintenance and Engineering Department

Guestrooms must be properly maintained, as well as be cleaned, before they can be made available for guests. In the earlier discussion of the housekeeping department and its interactions with the front office department, you read that the FOM's estimates of guestroom occupancy help the executive housekeeper to make plans for deep cleaning plans. Similarly, occupancy forecasts assist the hotel's maintenance and engineering staff to plan major maintenance and repair work. Maintenance such as replacing wallpaper and painting walls can be done one room at a time. Other maintenance activities will likely make several rooms or more unavailable. Consider the replacement of carpeting in guestrooms: Carpeting for many rooms is brought to the site, and several rooms are recarpeted daily. Sometimes a maintenance task for a single room affects many rooms. For example, older hotels often have plumbing systems designed so that water in an entire wing of rooms must be shut off to service bathroom fixtures in only one room.

MODERN FRONT OFFICE ISSUES AND TACTICS

Automated Preventive Maintenance Systems

Automated preventive maintenance (PM) systems can help ensure that guestrooms are maintained properly, and that guest complaints are minimized and addressed properly. These systems may reduce labor costs, schedule proper PM on equipment at the right time, and reduce the time required to complete work orders. PM systems minimize the number of opportunities for errors, simplify the PM process, and save money by extending the life of assets.

Automated systems also can have a direct impact on cleanliness—a concern of all guests. Although guestroom cleanliness is the direct responsibility of housekeeping personnel, factors such as a guestroom's age, level of maintenance, and decor and lighting influence guests' perceptions about the cleanliness of guestrooms. As maintenance issues are addressed, guest complaints decrease. Then maintenance staff can spend more time addressing PM and less time reacting to problems that could have been avoided if an effective PM program were in place.

Adapted from Hasek, G. 2004. Automated solutions such as Win Track PM add efficiencies to preventive maintenance, rounds, work orders and room inspection processes. Retrieved May 2, 2004, from http://www.hotel-online.com/News/PR2004_2nd/May04_WinTrack Solution.html.

Significant interaction is required between the maintenance and engineering, housekeeping, and front office departments to provide the maximum number of rooms for sale to guests each day. Assume that the housekeeper or a room inspector notes that a television set is inoperative, a faucet in a bathroom leaks, or an electronic mechanism to lock a room door does not work correctly. Housekeeping staff must notify the front desk to put the room on out-of-order status and must also complete and submit a **maintenance request form** such as that shown in Figure 14.8 to the maintenance and engineering department.

Front

**MAINTENANCE
REQUEST**   336695

BY _____   DATE _____

LOCATION _____

PROBLEM _____
_____
_____
_____

ASSIGNED TO

DATE COMPL.   TIME SPENT

COMPLETED BY _____

REMARKS _____
_____
_____
_____

Back

MAINTENANCE CHECK LIST

Check (x) Indicates   Satisfactory Condition
Explain Unchecked In Remarks Section

BEDROOM – FOYER – CLOSET

– WALLS   – WOODWORK   – DOORS
– CEILING   – TELEVISION   – LIGHTS
– FLOORS   – A.C. UNIT   – BLINDS
– WINDOWS   – DRAPES

REMARKS _____
_____
_____
_____

BATHROOM _____
– TRIM   – SHOWER
– DRAINS   – LIGHTS
– WALLPAPER   – PAINT
– TILE OR GLASS   – DOOR
– ACCESSORIES   – WINDOW

REMARKS _____
_____
_____
_____

FIGURE 14.8   Maintenance request form.

FRONT OFFICE SEMANTICS

Maintenance request form: Form used to initiate and document a request for maintenance.

Trained maintenance and engineering personnel know that, of the three potential problems just noted, the problem with electronic door locking is the priority. The room cannot be rented until that repair is completed. Perhaps the television set can be repaired on-site, or it can be exchanged for another set in the hotel's inventory. The dripping faucet probably can be repaired quickly. However, the number of and length of time required to fulfill maintenance requests in other rooms affects the time needed to complete work on a specific room. Typically, the department that initiates the out-of-order room status is the same department that will reinstate the room. For example, if the maintenance department places the room on out-of-order status, it will be responsible for placing the room back in order after necessary work has been completed.

The following PMS reports are of special interest to maintenance and engineering managers:

- VIPs in house
- Due to check out lists
- Out-of-order rooms list

- Work orders initiated summary
- Open work orders list
- Maintenance log reports
- Occupancy forecasts (short and long term)

SECTION REVIEW AND DISCUSSION QUESTIONS

Section Objective: Discuss common ways that FOMs and their staff interact with managers and others in building services departments.

Section Summary: Managers in the accounting department interact with the FOM and his or her staff when, for example, night auditors are trained, room revenues and occupancy information is audited, front desk cash banks are maintained, and guest billing disputes are resolved.

Housekeeping managers alert front desk personnel when guestrooms are cleaned and available for sale. They also accept responsibility for lost and found items and fulfill guest requests to front desk agents for guestroom linens and amenities.

Security staff plan and deliver safety training programs and develop procedures used by front desk personnel as they communicate with guests about safety concerns. They interact with other managers, including the FOM, to develop crisis plans that provide direction in the event of emergencies such as fires, bomb threats, power outages, earthquakes, hurricanes, and tornadoes. Front office staff must be well versed in tactics for building evacuation and alerting the appropriate responders about medical emergencies. They must also be able to respond appropriately to guest concerns about noise, suspicious persons, safety, and other issues brought to their attention.

Maintenance managers help ensure that rooms are maintained in proper condition, and that repairs are made on a timely basis to maximize the number of guestrooms that can be rented.

Discussion Questions:
1. What is an example of how an accounting manager might work with an FOM to reduce expenses incurred in the front office department?
2. In some hotels, new housekeepers are trained carefully, and their work is inspected. Thereafter, rooms are only inspected on a random basis before front desk agents are notified that the rooms are available. In other hotels, all guestrooms cleaned by all housekeepers, regardless of their experience with the property, are inspected. What are the pros and cons of each approach? What would you want to do if you were the executive housekeeper?
3. Some industry observers believe that tactics such as asking for a picture identification, requiring individuals to show a room key before allowing them into a property, and making public areas of the hotel less accessible at night do little to protect guests and property against terrorists acts. What do you think? What,

if any, tactics would you use as a general manager to increase the safety of guests and employees?

4. What concerns might you, as an FOM, have as you provide input to your hotel's crisis plans about the safety of your staff. For example, front desk agents play an important role in guest notification about emergencies, while at the same time they may risk their own safety.

5. What are some things that you would do as a maintenance and engineering manager when you interact with housekeeping managers on a daily basis to minimize the need to declare guestrooms out of order and, therefore, unavailable for sale by front desk agents?

ROLE OF FRONT OFFICE: HUB OF THE HOTEL

When human resources personnel develop training programs for hotel employees, they frequently use a strategy in which trainers (1) tell trainees what they are going to say (preview information), (2) present the training, and (3) tell trainees what they have said (review the information). This book has followed a similar pattern. The first few chapters presented an overview of how the front office serves guests and assists staff members throughout the hotel. All subsequent chapters focused in detail on how front office personnel meet guests' needs and help hotel managers with their planning and

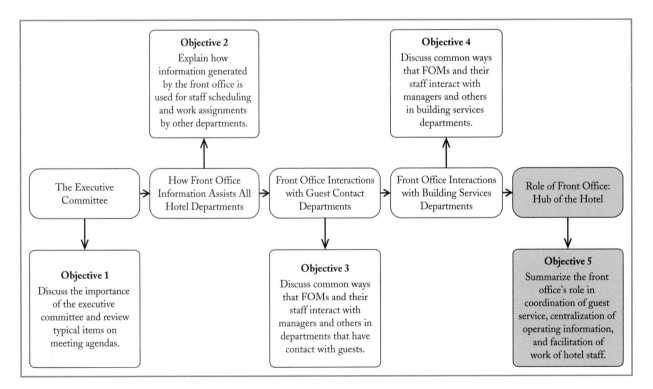

ROADMAP 14.5

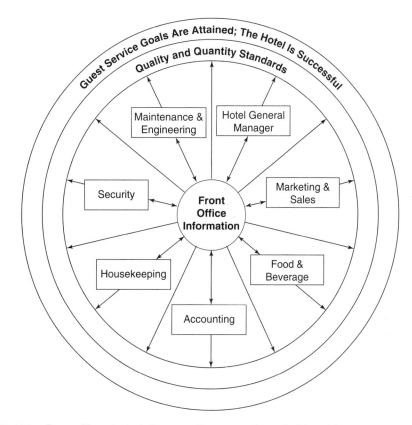

FIGURE 14.9   Front office: the hub that coordinates services of all hotel departments to guests.

operating responsibilities. Now, as suggested in Roadmap 14.5, this section of the final chapter reviews the role of the front office department and its relationship to guests and other hotel departments. A graphic summary is presented in Figure 14.9.

As suggested in Figure 14.9, the front office is the center of the hotel's efforts to collect data and coordinate the dissemination of information used by every department. Department managers use the information as they work toward meeting defined standards of work quality and quantity. As these standards are met, guest service goals are better attained.

The responsibilities of the front office department are threefold:

- *Coordination of guest services.* Front office personnel assist guests as they make hotel reservations and register at the hotel. Service continues as guests' needs are addressed during their visit and when they check out at the end of their stay. From the perspective of guests, the front office is the primary point of contact to obtain assistance of almost any type. Front office personnel represent their peers as they deliver service that reflects the attitude of hospitality that guests desire and deserve.

- *Centralization of operating information.* FOMs, the property's general manager, and staff in all departments need accurate and timely information to make decisions. Much of the data required for short- and long-term decision making is collected by the FOM and his or her team and is distributed to decision makers in PMS reports. Most of the hotel's revenue is generated from room sales, which are affected by interactions among the FOM, general manager, and director of sales and marketing. Using information in PMS reports, they develop tactics to maximize the sale of rooms to transient guests and to groups.

- *Facilitation of work of hotel staff.* Department heads use PMS reports generated by the front office department to develop work plans, to schedule staff members, and to make work assignments. Much of this effort is focused on having guestrooms available that meet the property's quality standards and on providing guests the services they want.

Every department and every staff member—management and non-management—contribute value to the organization. The front office staff serves guests and assists their peers as they work to make each guest's visit as enjoyable as possible. In this way, the FOM and his or her staff contribute to the hotel's profitability, because if guests are satisfied, the hotel can compete successfully with other properties marketing to the same travelers.

The important task of anticipating and addressing guests' needs begins with an attitude of hospitality and genuine concern for doing so. Technology helps managers and staff to deal with the volume of business, but the hospitality "delivered" by the hotel's staff, including those in the front office, remains the critical factor in making the hotel successful.

SECTION REVIEW AND DISCUSSION QUESTIONS

Section Objective: Summarize the front office's role in coordinating guest service, centralizing operating information, and facilitating the work of hotel staff.

Section Summary: The front office department is the focal point of the hotel's guest service efforts. Guests receive and evaluate service as they make hotel reservations, register at the property, make service requests during their visit, and check out. The front office collects much of the information hotel managers need for decision making and distributes it through PMS reports. Managers in all departments use information in PMS reports to make decisions related to (1) the volume of business anticipated, (2) how employees should be scheduled in response to business volume, and (3) the work assignments to be completed by staff.

Discussion Questions:
1. No hotel department is more important that others; all are necessary to serve guests and help the property be successful. How then would you explain the primary contributions made by the FOM and his or her staff?
2. The front office coordinates guest service, centralizes operating information, and facilitates the work of hotel employees. What are important examples of each of these three responsibilities?
3. This chapter emphasized ways that the front office assists other hotel departments. What are some ways that staff members in other departments help their peers in the front office?

The FOM In Action: A Solution

What should the manager responsible for front office activities do when another department is understaffed at a time when significant business volume is expected? Plans to recruit and train new staff members for the affected department must be implemented, but what about the short term?

Teamwork is essential in the operation of a hotel. Employees in the same department and in the same position are encouraged to help each other. Persons in one department are also responsible for working with those in other departments to attain the hotel's goals. For example, interdepartmental teamwork involves housekeeping personnel preparing rooms so they can be rented by front desk staff. Teamwork also means that a person in one position in one department may actually work in another position in another department. Cross-training and job rotation are tactics implemented by

hoteliers to prepare for the situation that Bino, the assistant manager at the Hilotown Hotel, now faces. Bino, other managers, and subordinates in the front office and other departments may need to help clean rooms because there is an insufficient number of housekeepers to work their regular hours and a reasonable number of overtime hours.

Despite the shortage of housekeepers, the hotel must achieve its room cleanliness and other quality standards. The situation is not as simple as one front office employee quickly cleaning a specific room. Instead, the room must be cleaned *properly* so it can be enjoyed by the next occupant in the same way it was experienced by previous guests when the room was prepared by a trained housekeeper. In situations such as Bino's, room inspection after cleaning should receive special attention to ensure that the property's standards are maintained.

From the Front Office: Front-Line Interview

Ada Mary Pêna
Room Controller
Detroit Marriott (1,328 rooms)
Detroit, Michigan

Surviving the Blackout

Ada has been with the hotel in Detroit's Renaissance Center for more than 13 years. She began in the PBX department and eventually became its trainer. In this capacity, Ada trained new staff and coached her more experienced associates. She became the hotel's room controller in 2003. Ada has taken classes from the American Institute of Banking and has participated in many training programs offered by the property since her employment there.

1. **What are the most important responsibilities in your present position?**
   It is important to remain calm and pleasant at all times, and you must have "a smile in your voice" while doing so. It is also important to be able to multitask: Busy front office personnel must do more than one thing at a time. I am responsible for making sure that my guests receive the room types they request and that have been guaranteed. An important part of my position is to interact with them by telephone and in person. I know many of our guests by name, and one part of my job that I really like is to give them a hospitable greeting and to thank them for choosing Marriott!

2. **What are the largest challenges that confront you in your day-to-day work and in the long-term operation of your property's front office?**
   One challenge is to motivate my associates. For example, there should be an obvious sense of urgency if guests become upset, and their issues must be resolved immediately. Each member of our front office team must really have this emphasis on maximizing guest satisfaction.

3. **What is your most unforgettable front office moment?**
   Recently there was a major blackout caused by overloading of an electricity grid that affected the East Coast of the United States and traveled all the way to Michigan. Our front office team worked many hours during that time to take care of our guests and each other.

4. **What advice do you have for those studying about or considering a career in front office or hotel management?**
   My advice is to always remember that when persons have a bad experience, they tell 10 people or more. It is important to work hard to minimize guest-related problems. It is ironic that our vision of great service is not equally acknowledged by all guests. However, we are here to help them, and those considering a career in the industry must recognize the importance of and consistent need to do so.

FRONT OFFICE SEMANTICS LIST

Deep cleaning	Business case	Sleep out
Group resume	Pre-key (guestroom)	Sleeper
Policy	Consortia rate	Defibrillator
Operating costs	Guarantee (banquet)	Identity theft
Flash report	Dram shop law	Maintenance request form
Gateway	Lobby foodservices	

FRONT OFFICE AND THE INTERNET

- To learn about the evacuation of the World Trade Center Marriott during and immediately after the tragedy of September 11, 2001, from the perspective of the property's director of loss prevention who was on-site at the time, go to www.securitymanagement.com/library/001305.html For related stories, type *Marriott Evacuation* into your favorite web browser.

- Many applications of technology can be used by department heads to schedule staff members after the volume of business is known. To review some of these, type *employee scheduling* into your favorite search engine.

- This chapter summarized the primary responsibilities of FOMs: coordination of guest services, centralization of operating information, and facilitation of the work of hotel staff. Use your favorite search engine and type in *hotel front office manager.* Review some of the seemingly thousands of job descriptions. Sort the job tasks that you find into the three categories above. Are there tasks that do not fit into these categories? If so, what are they? Is another classification of work responsibility required?

- You read about identity theft in this chapter and about tactics that front office personnel can use to assist their guests. Type *identity theft* into your favorite search engine; select from the Web sites you find and review their information.

- The U.S. government provides fire safety information for employees who must travel on official business. To view this information, go to www.usfa.fema.gov/applications/hotel/

- To see what guests and other consumers can learn about hotel fire emergencies, check out these Web sites: www.danger.mongabay.com (click on "How to Survive Hotel Fires") and www.christinecolumbus.com/hotelfiretips.asp

- To view a history of hotel fires and to read case studies of several, go to www.iklimnet.com (click on "Fires / Hotel," then click on "Big Hotel Fires" or "Hotel Fire Case."

REAL-WORLD ACTIVITIES

1. If possible, talk with a local hotel's general manager or FOM about the agenda items discussed at a typical executive committee meeting. What role, if any, does information contained in PMS reports play in these meetings? What topics are of most concern to the FOM? Are there issues that point to the relationship between the front office and other hotel departments?

2. Review Web sites for hotel PMS suppliers, including those listed in the "Front Office and the Internet" section at the end of Chapter 4. Do these systems help the FOM schedule front office labor? For example, do estimates of room occupancy interface with systems to schedule front office staff based on the volume of business forecasted?

3. If possible, talk with an FOM about types of group meetings and the impact that the type of group membership has on the types of guestrooms sold. What, from the FOM's perspective, are the pros and cons of guestroom sales patterns of the various groups?

4. Research articles on terrorism. For example, go to www.hotel-online.com and scroll to the bottom of the site. Type *terrorism* into the "Find It Fast" box. Develop a list of tactics that hoteliers may use to best ensure the safety of their guests, employees, and property.

5. If possible, talk with one or more hotel department heads. Ask what information generated by the FOM is of most use to them. What are the most frequent ways that they interact with the FOM?

Glossary

Abandoned property   Property that is given up by someone who does not intend to reclaim it.

Acceptance (contract)   Agreement by the second party in a contract to the terms and conditions of the offer.

Accessible (guestroom)   Guestroom that is designed to accommodate persons with disabilities by removing barriers that otherwise limit or prevent them from obtaining the services that are offered.

Account   Device used to show increases or decreases in the asset, liability, or owner's equity sections of the fundamental accounting equation. Because of the visual appearance of accounts, accountants refer to them as *T accounts* (refer to Figure 11.4).

Accountability   Obligation created when a staff member is delegated duties and responsibilities from higher levels of management.

Accounting   Process of summarizing and reporting financial transactions.

Accounts payable (A/P)   Money owed by a hotel.

Accounts receivable (A/R)   Money owed to a hotel.

Address verification service (AVS)   Company that, for a fee, allows access to its database of current addresses.

ADR index   Ratio measure computed as

$$\frac{\text{ADR of selected hotel}}{\text{ADR of that hotel's competitive set}} = \text{ADR index}$$

Advance deposit   Partial or full payment made for guestroom rental before the guest's arrival.

Advance deposit account   Account used by a hotel to record prepayments by guests.

Aging accounts receivable report   Detailed list of accounts receivable based on the length of time the receivable has been owed. Often these reports group accounts receivable into categories of less than 30 days, 30 to 60 days, 60 to 90 days, and more than 90 days.

All-inclusive (rate)   Special rate that typically includes all guest meals and unlimited beverages as well as the use of specifically identified hotel amenities and services.

All-suite hotel   Lodging property in which all guestrooms are suites.

American Plan (AP)   Special rate that includes specifically identified guest meals (typically, breakfast, lunch, and dinner).

Archive   Process of preserving records or documents (when used as a verb). Records or documents that have been preserved (when used as a noun).

Arrival   An arriving guest. Arrivals are typically counted by the number of individuals. Used as in, "There will be 300 *arrivals* tonight, including 150 children."

Arrival list   PMS report that details the number and names of guests arriving at the hotel during the report period. The arrival list often contains additional information such as each guest's departure date, room type requests, and room rate.

Asset Item owned by a business, for example; cash on hand, money in checking or other accounts, money owed to the business, inventories, property, equipment and furnishings.

Atrium Large, central, and open lobby area of a hotel designed to project an ornate and spectacular reception for guests and others entering the property.

Attorney Trained and licensed person who represents others in issues related to laws.

Attrition Difference between the original room request and the actual purchase of a group. For example, a group might reserve 100 rooms but use only 50 rooms. A hotel's standard contract for group rooms may stipulate that the group must pay an attrition penalty for over-reserving.

Audit Process of verifying records for correctness and completeness.

Authorize payment card To ensure a card's validity and payment ability and capacity.

Auto-attendant System in which incoming calls transferred from the telephone system are answered automatically as they are received. In most cases, callers are asked to select where they want the system to direct (route) their call from a list of options.

Automated wake-up System in which guests (or front office staff) may use the hotel's telephone system to program a prerecorded call to be received in a guest's room at a time requested by the guest.

Availability forecast Estimate of the number of rooms that remain to be sold.

Average daily rate (ADR) Average selling price of all guestrooms for a given time period. The formula for ADR is as follows:

$$\text{Total room revenue} \div \text{Total number of rooms sold}$$

Back-office accounting Process of summarizing and documenting the financial activities and condition of the entire hotel.

Back-office accounting system Automated (or manual) system of data collection and reporting used by a hotel to summarize and document its financial activity and position.

Bar For-profit business serving alcoholic beverages to guests seated at a counter (bar). Limited table service may be available.

Bed and breakfast inn Very small (one to several guestrooms) property owned and managed by person living on-site. These businesses typically offer at least one meal daily. Also called *B&B*.

Bell services attendant Entry-level hotel employee who assists guests with luggage and who may deliver newspapers, dry cleaning, and other guest-related incidentals to guestrooms. Also called *bell staff*.

Benchmarking Search for best practices and an understanding of how they are achieved in efforts to determine how well a hospitality organization is doing.

Best practice Process or practice unofficially considered to be an industry standard that is used by professionally operated properties.

Blackout date Any day in which the hotel will *not* honor a negotiated rate. Blackout dates should be identified at the same time the hotel and the client agree on a negotiated rate. Common blackout dates include New Year's Eve and other times the hotel believes its best interests are served by disallowing the negotiated rate.

Block Rooms reserved exclusively for members of a specific group. A block consists of all rooms held (reserved) by the hotel for the exclusive use of that group. To set aside rooms in this manner effectively creates a "block" of reservations for the group. Sometimes referred to as a *group block*.

Block (funds) Amount by which a card's available credit (if a credit card) or balance (if a debit card) is reduced. Also called a *hold*.

Bona fide occupational qualification (BOQ) Qualification to perform a job that is judged reasonably necessary to safely or adequately perform all tasks within the job.

Bonding Purchasing an insurance policy against the possibility that an employee will steal.

Booking pace Term that refers to the amount of future demand for rooms (or for hotel services such as catering). Often shortened to *pace*.

Bookkeeping Process of initially recording financial transactions.

Bottom-up selling Tactic to first sell the hotel's least expensive rooms.

Brand loyalty   Interest of guests or potential guests to revisit and recommend a hotel (or restaurant).

Brand proliferation   Oversaturation of the market with different brands.

Bucket check   Industry term for a systematic examination of guests' folios to ensure the accuracy of information. Bucket checks typically include rate verification, credit monitoring, and confirmation of departure date and guestroom assignment.

Budget (economy) limited-service hotel   Lodging property within the limited-service segment that offers low-priced guestrooms and few, if any, amenities other than a complimentary continental breakfast or coffee service.

Business case   Advantages that are objectively presented whenever possible in support of a proposal to improve business.

Business plan   Plan of goals and activities that will be addressed within the next 12 months to move the organization toward attainment of its mission.

Business traveler   Person who travels primarily for business reasons. Such guests often have an expense account to defray reasonable travel costs.

Call accounting system   System in a hotel used to establish telephone charges, document calls made, and determine the amount to be assessed to guests for use of the telephone.

Call-around   Telephone "shopping" technique in which a hotel staff member calls competitive hotels to inquire about room rates and availability. The information is used by the calling hotel to help determine room rates.

Call records   Listing of the source, length, and destination of each telephone call made within a hotel during a specific time period.

Camp/park lodge   Sleeping accommodations in parks and other nature conservation areas owned by government agencies and often operated by for-profit management companies.

Cancellation number   Series of numbers, letters, or both, that identifies the cancellation of a specific hotel reservation.

Career ladder   Plan that projects successively more responsible professional positions within an organization or industry. Career ladders allow an employee to plan and schedule developmental activities judged necessary to assume higher-level positions.

Carrier (telephone)   Company providing a hotel's telephone service. In many areas this will be a local carrier (for local calls) and a separate, designated, long-distance carrier. The telecommunications industry continues to consolidate services; thus, some hotels now use the same carrier for local and long-distance calls.

Cashier's drawer   Cash, checks, payment card copies, and other financial records for which an employee (cashier) is responsible.

CAT 5 cable   Category five cable; the preferred cable quality to use when providing certain forms of high-speed Internet access to a standard computer.

Caterer   For-profit business that produces food for groups at off-site locations. Some caterers have banquet space available for on-site use by groups desiring foodservices.

Central reservation system (CRS)   Entity, operated by a franchisor or independently affiliated, that offers potential guests the opportunity to make reservations at the entity's affiliated (branded) hotels by telephone, fax, or the Internet. Used as in, "What percentage of our transient business last month was generated through the *CRS*?"

Centralized accounting system   Financial management system that collects accounting data from one or more hotels and combines and analyzes the data at a different (central) site.

Certified public accountant (CPA)   Designation given to an individual who has passed a national qualifying examination related to accounting practices and principles. CPA designations are granted and administered by state boards of accountancy.

Chapter (association)   Group that is a subset of an association. Chapters are often formed on the basis of geography (e.g., a state association chapter is a subset of a national association).

Chargeback   Payment card charges disallowed (reversed) when a cardholder successfully protests the legitimacy of the charge or because the hotel made an error in processing a charge. When a chargeback request is initiated by a cardholder, the hotel must respond promptly, or else the request will usually be granted.

Check guarantee service Service that ensures checks accepted by a merchant (e.g., hotel) that follows specific procedures will be collectible.

Check verification service Process of matching check writers with databases of acceptable and unacceptable accounts to minimize the acceptance of bad checks.

City ledger Set of accounts used to record charges to and payments from a hotel's nonregistered guests. Examples include persons not staying in the hotel who purchase the hotel's meeting space, food, or beverages.

Civil laws Laws (rules) that are primarily established by governmental edict or legislation. Many civil laws evolved from the time of the Roman Empire.

Commercial foodservice operation Foodservices offered in hotels and restaurants and other organizations whose primary financial goal involves generation of profits from the sale of food and beverage products.

Common laws Laws (rules) that evolved from customs in the Middle Ages in England and that form the foundation for many contemporary laws in the United States.

Comp Short for *complimentary* or *no charge* for a product (room) or service.

Compensatory damages Monetary amount intended to compensate injured parties for actual losses or damage they incurred (e.g., medical bills and lost wages). Also known as *actual damages.*

Competitive set Group of competing hotels to which an individual hotel's operating performance is compared. Often referred to as the *comp set.*

Concierge Individual or individuals within a full-service hotel responsible for providing guests with detailed information about local dining and attractions as well as assisting with related guest needs.

Concierge level Section of a hotel (usually with restricted access) reserved for special guests who pay a higher rate.

Condominium Lodging property in which units are individually owned. In some condominium properties, units can be placed into a rental pool with resulting guest fees split between the owner and the company managing the units. Also called *condo.*

Condotel Hotel with several floors dedicated to condominium units. Condo owners typically have access to the property's amenities.

Conference center Specialized hospitality operation specifically designed for and dedicated to the needs of small- and medium-size meetings of from 20 to 100 people.

Confirmation number Number (or combination of numbers and letters) that identifies a specific guest reservation.

Consideration (contract) Element in a legal contract that relates to money, property, or a promise exchanged for the promise made in a contract.

Consortia rate Room rate given to a guest whose room is booked by selected travel agencies.

Continental breakfast Morning meal that includes coffee, juices, and pastries. An upscale continental breakfast may include additional items such as fruit, hot and cold cereals, and milk and yogurt. Most limited-service hotels offer a complimentary continental breakfast as a guest amenity.

Continuous quality improvement (CQI) Ongoing efforts within the hotel to better meet (or exceed) guests' expectations and to find ways to perform work with better, less costly, and faster methods.

Contract Legally enforceable agreement or promise involving two or more parties.

Contract (express) Contract that involves oral or written words.

Contract (implied) Agreement that is not in writing but that is created by the behavior of both parties who suggest that they are acting under an agreement.

Contract-management company-operated noncommercial foodservices Type of noncommercial foodservices operation in which the program is managed and operated by a for-profit management company.

Controller Individual (or department) in a hotel responsible for maintaining the back-office accounting system.

Convention and visitors bureau (CVB) Organization generally funded by taxes levied on overnight hotel guests that seeks to increase the number of visitors to the area it represents.

Convention hotel   Lodging property with extensive and flexible meeting and exhibition spaces that markets to associations, corporations, and other groups bringing people together for meetings.

Corporate traveler   Guest who is traveling on business or because of his or her job.

Cost per key   Average purchase price of a hotel's guestroom expressed in thousands of dollars. For example, a 200-room hotel offered for $12 million is selling at a cost of $60,000 per key ($12,000,000 ÷ 200 rooms = $60,000). Sometimes called *cost per room*.

Court order   Legal decision made by a court that requires that something be done or not be done.

Credit (accounting)   Accounting transaction that records a change on the right side of a T account in an asset, liability, or owner's equity account.

Credit balance   Amount owed to guests by the hotel. Used as in, "We just got a check to hold the ballroom for next year's Blondstone wedding. When we apply the check to their account, they will have a *credit balance* of $3,000."

Credit card   System by which banks loan money with interest to consumers as purchases are made. Also known as *bank cards*. Merchants accepting the cards for payment are charged a fee by the banks for the charges made by their customers. Examples of credit cards are Visa and MasterCard.

Credit limit report   Comparison of a guest's folio balance to the amount of credit established for that guest. Sometimes referred to as a *high-balance report*.

Credit manager   Person responsible for establishing and enforcing the hotel's credit policies. In smaller properties, this role may be filled by the general manager, controller, or FOM. In larger hotels, credit management policy may be the result of the joint efforts of several individuals.

Credit posting   Entry on a guest's folio that either applies a payment toward the guest's balance that is due or that effectively reduces the total amount due.

Cross-functional team   Group of employees representing different departments within the hospitality operation that work together to resolve problems.

Cross-train   Tactic of training persons for more than one position so that they can assist wherever they are needed.

CTA (closed to arrival)   Term that indicates that a hotel declines reservations for guests wanting to arrive on a specific date.

Currency conversion   Process of accepting payment for charges computed in one currency but paid in the currency of another. A European traveler visiting New York City, for example, who wished to pay a bill in Euro dollars rather than in U.S. dollars, would require a *currency conversion* if the hotel provided this type of service.

Current data   Data related to events that are entered into the PMS but have yet to occur. For example, a room reservation can be entered into the PMS on Thursday for the following Friday night.

Cutoff date   Date on which unreserved rooms held in a group block are returned to the hotel's general rooms inventory.

Daily function board   Place in the lobby and other locations used to post information such as name of function, time, and room number for applicable events scheduled in the hotel on a specific date.

Damages   Amount of losses or costs assessed to the individual or company that was found to be liable for a wrongful act.

Data mining   Using technology to analyze guest-related and other data to make better marketing decisions.

Database   Collection of facts and statistics that provide useful information.

Day of   Short for *day of arrival*. Used as in, "Let's hold the rates at $100 per night for the 22nd but reexamine that decision *day of*."

Day rate   Special rate that typically includes 8- to 12-hour use (but not overnight use) of a room.

Debit (accounting)   Accounting transaction that records a change on the left side of a T account in an asset, liability, or owner's equity account.

Debit card   Payment system in which money collected by a merchant (e.g., hotel) is automatically (electronically) deposited into the merchant's local bank account. As with credit and T&E cards, merchants accepting the cards are assessed a fee for the right to do so.

Decentralized accounting system   Financial management system that collects accounting data from an individual hotel site and combines and analyzes that data at that same site.

Deeded interest (time-share)   Ownership in perpetuity that can be sold or passed on to the owner's heirs.

Deep cleaning   Intensive cleaning of a guestroom, usually including thorough cleaning of drapes, lamp shades, carpets, walls, and other room fixtures and furnishings.

Defect   Outcome arising from a failure to meet standards. A defect can be as simple as an accounting error by a front desk agent or as significant as an agent's failure to take proper action when an obviously intoxicated guest is observed in the hotel's public areas.

Defibrillator   Machine used to deliver an electrical shock to the heart in case of cardiac arrest (i.e., a heart attack) in efforts to reestablish a normal heartbeat.

Delayed check-in   Procedure in which guests are assigned a room, but the issuing of a key is delayed.

Demand   Total amount of a good or service consumers want to buy at a specific price.

Demand generator   Organization, entity, or location that creates a significant need for hotel services. Examples are large businesses, tourist sites, sports stadiums, educational facilities, and manufacturing plants.

Department head   Individual responsible to a higher-level executive such as hotel general manager or resident manager for all property activities related to a specific function such as front office, food and beverage, accounting, human resources, sales and marketing, housekeeping, maintenance and engineering, and security.

Departure list   Report, by name and room number, of all guests scheduled to leave the hotel on a specific date.

Detained property   Personal property of a guest that is held by a hotel until payment is made for the purchase of lawful products or services.

Dialogue training   Teaching employees about what to say in conversations and how to respond to common situations that occur on the job.

Dial-up Internet   Method of Internet connection that uses a standard telephone and telephone call (usually a local or toll-free call) for connection to the World Wide Web. Typically, dial-up systems upload and download data in a slower manner than do high-speed Internet access systems.

Direct bill   Special arrangement that allows a guest to purchase hotel services and products on credit terms because the guest's creditworthiness has been preapproved by the hotel.

Direct report   Employee's immediate supervisor; also called *superordinate*.

Discount fee   Amount (percentage) payment card issuers charge merchants for the right to accept their cards. Discount fees may range from 1 percent to 5 percent of a consumer's total purchase.

Displace (revenue)   To substitute one source of revenue for another.

Distressed passenger   Guest housed at a hotel due to air travel delays. In some cases, the cost of housing is borne by the airline on which the guest was traveling.

Distribution channel   Source of potential room reservations. Sources include the hotel's direct telephone number, its franchisor-maintained Web site, its own Web site, all third-party Web sites advertising the hotel's rates, the front desk (for walk-in guests), and the hotel's sales department.

DOS (director of sales)   Person with overall responsibility for a hotel's sales efforts. Sometimes called the *DOSM (director of sales and marketing)*.

Double entry accounting   System of recording financial transactions in a way that maintains the equality of the fundamental accounting equation: assets = liabilities + owner's equity.

Dram shop laws   Provision in the U.S. legal code that allows an injured party to seek damages from an intoxicated person who caused the injury and from the person who provided the alcoholic beverages to the intoxicated person.

Dump rate   Hotel term for significantly reducing room rates for a given date or dates. Used as in, "We need to *dump the rate* for our suites this weekend."

Duty of care   Obligation imposed by law that requires a specific standard of conduct.

Early check-in   Request by a guest to take possession of a room before the hotel's normally established check-in time.

Early departure   Guest who checks out of the hotel before his or her originally scheduled check-out date.

Economics   Social science associated with the making, marketing, and consumption of goods and services and how the forces of supply and demand allocate scarce resources.

E-distribution channel   Generic term used to indicate all electronic (e)methods of advertising and selling guestrooms. Also known as *e-commerce.*

E-fridge   Cabinet, usually including both refrigerated and nonrefrigerated sections, designed with an electronic processing unit that allows a direct interface with the PMS.

Electronic funds transfer (EFT)   Electronic movement of money from one bank account to another; commonly called *EFT.*

Emergency report   Information and lists that would be critical in the event of a disaster or a PMS crash. Sometimes referred to as a *down time report* because it is most often used when the PMS is down (i.e., crashed).

Employee handbook   Written policies and procedures related to employment at a hotel. Sometimes called an *employee manual.*

Employee-to-room ratio   Number of employees relative to the number of rooms. For example, a 500-room, luxury, full-service property may have 500 employees: a 1:1 employee-to-room ratio. A 100-room, limited-service property may have only 25 employees: a 1:4 employee-to-room ratio.

Employer-of-choice   Concept that the hospitality operation is a preferred place of employment within the community by those who have alternative employment opportunities.

Empowerment   Act of granting authority to employees to make key decisions within the employees' areas of responsibility.

Entry-level position   Position that requires little previous experience in or knowledge of job tasks and whose incumbents do not direct the work of other staff members.

European Plan (EP)   Room rate that does not include guest meals.

E-wholesaler   Room reseller that obtains reduced (wholesale) room prices and inventory commitments directly from a hotel or through an agreement with the hotel's corporate brand managers. The wholesaler then publishes "retail rates" on its Web sites, usually at a mark-up of 20 percent to 40 percent. Examples include Travelocity, hotels.com, TravelWeb, and Expedia.

Executive committee   Short for executive operating committee—members of the hotel's management team (generally department heads) responsible for top leadership and overall administration of the property.

Express check-out   Any number of methods of guest-initiated check-out that do not require guests to be physically present at the hotel's front desk for folio payment.

Extended forecast   Occupancy forecast that projects room demand more than 30 days into the future.

Extended-stay hotel   Mid-price, limited-service hotel marketing to guests desiring accommodations for extended time periods (generally a week or longer).

External recruiting   Tactics designed to attract persons who are not current hotel employees for vacant positions in the organization.

Fade (rate)   Reduced rate authorized for use when a guest seeking a reservation exhibits price (rate) resistance. Sometimes called *flex* rate.

Feeder market   Geographic location that includes a significant number of travelers using a hotel's services. Used as in, "St. Louis is a top *feeder market* for our ski resort."

FF&E   Short for the furniture, fixtures, and equipment used by a hotel to service its guests.

Fiduciary   Relationship based on trust and the responsibility to act in the best interest of another when performing tasks.

Field Data-entry location in a PMS. For example, the reservation screen on a PMS contains a *field* for the guest's name and another field for the guest's telephone number (along with many other fields). Data for these fields are typically entered at the time the reservation is made and may be modified at the time of guest registration. Fields are sometimes referred to as *data fields*.

Fixed labor position Position that involves work tasks not directly tied to the level of business volume. Examples are management positions such as FOM and uniformed services manager.

Flash report Daily information provided to the general manager that reports key financial information from the previous day and, often, accumulated data for the month and/or year to date compared with actual data from previous years. Flash report information is used to determine where, if at all, management attention is most immediately required. Also called *Manager's Daily*.

Flat (organization chart) Combination of positions within an organization to reduce the number of management layers in efforts to improve communication, increase operating efficiencies, and reduce costs.

Folio Detailed list of guestroom and other charges authorized by the guest or legally imposed by the hotel.

Forecast Estimate of future sales activity.

Form of payment Method that guests use to pay their bills (e.g., credit card, debit card, cash, check).

Franchise Arrangement whereby one party (the brand) allows another party (the hotel's owners) to use its logo, name, systems, and resources in exchange for a fee.

Franchisor Company that manages the brand and sells the right to use the brand name. Some franchisors own and operate hotels as well as sell use of the brand name to others.

Free-to-guests Service provided to the hotel guest at no additional charge beyond normal room rental charges. Examples are local telephone calls, use of Internet connections, and access to the hotel's pool or workout facilities. Ultimately, the hotel must absorb the costs of providing these services to guests; therefore, the term does not mean that the services are free to the hotel.

Frequent-guest program Promotional effort administered by a hotel brand that rewards travelers each time they stay at that specific brand's affiliated hotels. Typical awards include free-night stays, room upgrades, and complimentary hotel services.

Frequent-traveler program Program developed to reward a hotel company's guests with free room nights, frequent-flyer airline miles, and other awards as an incentive to book rooms at a property within the brand.

Front-office accounting system Automated (or manual) system of data collection and reporting that summarizes and documents the financial activities of the front office.

Full-service hotel Hotel that offers guests an extensive range of food and beverage products and services.

Full-time employee Staff member who works several days (or more) each week for up to 40 hours each week.

Function room Public space—including meeting rooms, conference areas, and ballrooms (which can be subdivided into smaller spaces)—for banquets, meetings, or other group rental purposes.

Future data Data related to events that have yet to occur and will not be found in the PMS. Although unknown, the data can be estimated.

Gateway Term relating to a location (e.g., airport or hotel) where there is significant activity involving international travelers.

General ledger Primary ledger that contains all of a hotel's accounts used to create its income (profit and loss) statement.

Generally accepted accounting principles (GAAPs) Standards and procedures that have been adopted by those responsible for preparing business financial statements for the purpose of ensuring uniformity.

Global Distribution System (GDS)   System of companies (Sabre, Galileo, Apollo, Amadeus, and Worldspan) that connects hotels offering rooms for sale with individuals and travel professionals worldwide who will potentially purchase them.

Globalization   Condition in which countries throughout the world and communities within them are becoming increasingly interrelated.

GoPar (gross operating profit per available room)   Average gross profit (revenue less management-controllable expenses) generated by each guestroom during a given time period. The GoPar formula for a given time period is

$$\text{Revenue} - \text{Management-controllable expenses} \div \text{Available rooms for that period}$$

Group   Guests who have a hotel reservation as part of a larger, multiguest reservation. Examples include domestic and international tour groups, associations, conventioneers, corporate groups, and individual members of sports teams.

Group (reservation)   Any entity that reserves 10 or more guestrooms at one time.

Group (type of guest)   Large number of guests sharing a common characteristic who are staying at a property at the same time. Groups may receive special rates, amenities, and privileges because of the increased revenue that they generate. Also called *tour group*.

Group history   Number of rooms blocked for and ultimately used by a group during similar events held in the past.

Group resume   Overview of important points about and needs of a group meeting, many of which require interdepartmental coordination.

Guarantee (banquet)   Contractual agreement about the number of meals to be provided at a banquet. A guarantee must be made several days in advance of the event; at that time, the banquet host agrees to pay for the larger of the actual number of guests served or the number of guests guaranteed.

Guest (hotel)   Person who rents a guestroom for a short time period with no intention of becoming a permanent resident. Also called a *transient guest*.

Guest history   Record maintained in the PMS that details information about a guest's previous hotel stay or stays. A useful guest history includes information related to guest name, address, previous dates of stays, room preferences, room rates paid, form of payment, and any other information judged important by the FOM and recordable in the PMS.

Guest ledger   Set of accounts used to record charges to and payments from a hotel's registered guests. Sometimes called the *front office ledger* or *rooms ledger*.

Half-day rate   Special rate that typically includes 1- to 4-hour use (but not overnight use) of a room.

Hard key   Usually a metal key that is not remade each time it is issued. The potential for unscrupulous duplication of such keys makes their use for guestrooms unacceptable in nearly all cases.

HIA (high-speed Internet access)   Technology required to allow hotel guests to access the Internet at download speeds much higher than those that can be achieved with traditional telephone dial-up systems.

Historical data   Data related to events that have already occurred. Sometimes referred to as *actual data*.

Hold   Action taken by a hotel notifying a payment card administrator or issuer that a cardholder will likely be charged for a specific dollar amount. In response, if the card has sufficient credit available (or, in the case of debit cards, sufficient funds on deposit), this amount will be "held" until the charge is either initiated or until the hold is released. Sometimes referred to as placing a *block* or *authorization* on a card. Used as in, "Put an additional $500 *hold* on Mr. Lacey's Visa card because he has decided to stay three more nights."

Hospitality industry   Businesses that provide accommodations (lodging) and foodservices for people when they are away from their homes.

Hospitality suite   Private guestroom of sufficient size to provide meeting space and food and beverage service for a small group of guests.

Host hotel   Property that serves as the headquarters for a group when multiple hotels must be used to house all group members.

Hot spot Wi-Fi area that allows for high-speed wireless Internet access or other data transmission. An analogy is a reception zone for a cell phone.

Hotel For-profit business that rents sleeping rooms and often provides other amenities such as food and beverage services, swimming pools and exercise rooms, meeting spaces, business centers, and concierge services. Also referred to as *motel, motor hotel,* or *motor inn.*

Hotel chain Group of hotels with the same brand name.

Hotel occupancy rate Ratio of guestrooms sold (including complimentary rooms) to guestrooms available for sale in a given time period. Always expressed as a percentage, the formula for occupancy rate is as follows:

$$\text{Number of guestrooms sold} \div \text{Number of guestrooms available}$$

House account Account whose entries are assessed to another hotel entity such as the sales and marketing department, the general manager, or the FOM.

House count Total number of guests staying in a hotel on a specific night.

House phone Publicly located telephone within the hotel that can be used to call the front desk or, in some cases, the front desk and guestrooms.

HVAC system Heating, ventilating, and air-conditioning system.

Identity theft Crime that occurs when someone obtains and uses another individual's personal information to commit fraud, theft, or both.

Incidentals Non-room charges that may include items such as telephone charges, food and beverage purchases, pay-per-view movie rentals, and minibar purchases.

Incremental sales Sales of products and services to guests in addition to those that would otherwise have been generated.

Independent operator Entrepreneur who owns or operates one or a few hospitality properties. Sometimes referred to as owning a *mom-and-pop property.*

Individual call-in reservation Type of reservation in which guests who are part of a group contact a hotel and reserve their own rooms from within that block.

Induction Process of informing new employees about matters related to the department in which they will work. Induction is done after the orientation process is completed.

In-house list Record of all guests, by name and room number, who are checked into the hotel when the list is printed.

Interface Term used to describe the process that allows one data-generating system to share its information electronically with another system.

Intermediary Entity authorized by a guest to make a hotel reservation on the guest's behalf.

Internal recruiting Tactics to identify and attract currently employed staff members for job vacancies that represent promotions or lateral transfers to similar positions in the same organization.

International call Call made to a telephone extension located in a country code outside that of the call's originating country code.

Intranet Designated segment of an organization's Internet site where access and use is restricted to specifically identified individuals (such as employees or managers).

Inventory (rooms) Rooms that are available to be sold by the hotel.

IT (information technology) Broad term used to identify areas of management related to the design and administration of computer-related hardware and software programs.

Job description List of tasks that an employee working in a specific position must be able to perform effectively.

Job specification List of personal qualities judged necessary for successful performance of the tasks required by the job description.

Joint venture Partnership composed of organizations such as corporations, governments, or other entities that is formed to develop a lodging brand or property.

Key packet Envelope or wrapper designed for holding guestroom keys.

Keyword Word or phrase used to find products, brands, services, or information via search engines.

Kiosk   Small electronic unit (machine) located in a hotel lobby that allows guests with proper identification to register or check out of the hotel without the need to interact with a front desk agent.

Late charge   Departmental charges, such as those for food and beverage or in-room vending purchases, that were entered into the billing system late and which are posted to a guest's folio even though that guest has checked out.

Late check-out   Arrangement that allows a guest scheduled to leave the hotel to maintain access to his or her room after the standard check-out time.

Law of demand   Concept of economics that recognizes when supply is held constant, an increase in demand results in an increase in selling price. Conversely, with supply held constant, a decrease in demand leads to a decreased selling price.

Law of supply   Concept of economics that recognizes when demand is held constant, an increase in supply leads to a decreased selling price. Conversely, when demand is held constant, a decrease in supply leads to an increased selling price.

Lawsuit   Legal action in a court of law based on a complaint that a person or company failed to perform a required duty, and that failure resulted in harm to the person filing the complaint.

Leadership style   Mix of attitudes and behaviors that a supervisor can use to direct the work of employees.

Leased interest (time-share)   Right limited to a length of time (e.g., 10 years); when the lease expires, ownership (access) expires.

Least-cost routing (LCR)   System using a preprogrammed, interfaced smart switch to select the telephone route that charges the least based on a call's specific destination.

Legal contract   Contract in which parties to the agreement are of a specified minimum age, parties are mentally competent to understand the contract's terms, and the purpose of the contract does not violate the law.

Leisure traveler   Person who travels primarily for personal reasons. Such guests use private funds for travel expenses and are often sensitive to the prices charged.

Length of stay (LOS)   Number of nights a hotel's individual guests use their rooms. LOS is computed on a per-stay basis. For example, in a hotel that sold 300 group room nights to 100 guests, the LOS would be computed as

$$\text{Room nights sold} \div \text{Rooms sold} = \text{LOS}$$
$$300 \div 100 = 3$$

Liability   Debt owed by a business.

Lien   Legal right of one party to retain or sell the property of another as security for or payment of a lawful claim of charges.

Limited-service hotel   Lodging property that offers no or very limited foodservices; sometimes a complimentary breakfast is served, but there is no restaurant with table service.

Line department   Hotel division that is in the chain of command and is directly responsible for generating revenues (such as front office and food and beverage department) or for property operations (such as housekeeping and maintenance and engineering).

Litigation   Process of suing someone for damages caused by a wrongful act.

Lobby foodservices   Term describing the foodservices offered by many limited-service hotels in their lobby area.

Local call   Telephone call typically made within a small geographic area.

Long-distance call   In general, a call made to a telephone extension located in an area code outside of the call's originating area code.

Long-range plan   Statement of goals and the activities that will be undertaken to attain them that a hospitality operation will use during the next three to five years in efforts to move toward attainment of its mission.

Look-to-book data   Hotel term for the number of bookings achieved relative to the number of hits (looks) on a specific Web site. The best sites have high look-to-book ratios.

Lost property   Personal property that has been unintentionally placed somewhere and is then forgotten about by the rightful owner.

Lounge   For-profit business serving alcoholic beverages to guests seated at tables. A small counter (bar) may be available.

Lowballing (forecasts)   Developing forecasts that are unrealistically conservative (low) for the express purpose of more easily achieving or exceeding them. The practice is most prevalent in hotels that emphasize achieving or exceeding previously budgeted forecasts.

Lowest-rate guarantee   Program that assures travelers that the lowest available rate for a specific room type on a specific date will be found on the franchisor's Web site.

Luxury full-service hotel   Lodging property offering the amenities of upscale full-service hotels and additional features that appeal to clientele who desire the best and are willing to pay premium prices.

Maintenance log   Written record of guest-initiated maintenance repair or service requests received by the front desk and monitored to ensure their prompt completion.

Maintenance request form   Form used to initiate and document a request for maintenance.

Management company   Organization that operates one or more hotels for a fee. Sometimes called a *contract company* or a *contract management company*.

Manager   Staff member who directs the work of supervisors.

Manager's Daily   Summary of a hotel's daily revenue generation that can include additional operating data as requested by the manager.

Market code   Guest types differentiated by sales source. Typical market codes include transient and group.

Market segmentation   Efforts to focus on a highly defined (smaller) group of travelers.

Market share   Percentage of a total market (typically in dollars spent) captured by an industry segment or property.

Marketing plan   Calendar of specific activities designed to meet the operation's revenue goals.

Master bill   Single folio (bill) established for a group that includes specifically agreed-upon group charges. Sometimes called a *group folio* or *group bill*. Used as in, "our group will pay for room and tax on the *master bill*, but any room service charges are the responsibility of individual group members."

Merchant model   Internet sales method in which hotels sell or commit rooms to operators of Web sites. These sites, in turn, allow consumers to enter requested location and arrival dates; consumers are presented with a choice of specific hotels and associated rates available for immediate purchase on the Web site.

Merchant service provider (MSP)   Entity that, for a fee, manages payment card acceptance and collection of funds for businesses such as hotels.

Message on hold   System that eliminates the silence that occurs when guests are required to wait (hold) for their call to be picked up by the party the caller is attempting to reach.

Mid-price full-service hotel   Lodging property offering three meals daily, a lounge, a swimming pool, and limited meeting and banquet spaces.

Mid-price limited-service hotel   Lodging property within the limited-service segment that offers selected property and within-room upgrade amenities for room rates that are higher than budget (economy) hotels within the limited-service segment.

Military time   System of time keeping that does not use the designations a.m. and p.m. to differentiate hours but, rather, identifies hours of the day by the sequence of their occurrence (1–24). For example,

Traditional time	Military time
6:00 a.m.	06:00
6:30 a.m.	06:30
10:00 p.m.	22:00
10:45 p.m.	22:45

Mislaid property   Personal property that has been purposefully placed somewhere but is then forgotten about by the rightful owner.

Mission statement   More focused picture of what the hospitality operation wants to do and how it will do it.

MLOS (minimum length of stay)   Designation that instructs reservationists to decline a reservation request from any guest who will not reserve a room for the minimum number of days allowed as predetermined by the hotel.

Modified American Plan (MAP)   Special rate that includes a specifically identified guest meal (typically one per day—often breakfast).

Moment of truth   Any (and every) time a guest has an opportunity to form an impression about the hospitality organization. Moments of truth can be positive or negative and may, but do not have to, involve the property's staff members.

Motivate   Process of appealing to a person's inner drive to attain a goal.

Move/add/change   Process of reconfiguring or reprogramming a call accounting system to, for example, move an extension from one location to another, add an additional extension, or change a line from one that posts charges for use to one that does not.

Multitasking   Productivity improvement tactic in which an employee does more than one thing at the same time. For example, an employee may read a letter while on hold, awaiting the beginning of a conference call.

Mystery shopper services   Method of product and service evaluation in which a person poses as a guest, experiences the products and services provided, and reports on the perceived quality of products and services received during the visit.

Name recognition   Ability of guests or potential guests to remember and associate with a hotel's (or restaurant's) name.

Negligence   Doing something that a reasonable person would not do, or failing to do something that a reasonable person would have done, in the same situation.

Negotiated rate   Special room rate offered for a fixed period of time to a specific hotel client. Used as in, "What is the *negotiated rate* we should offer to Wal-Mart employees next year?"

Negotiated rate agreement   Document that details the specific contractual obligations of a hotel and client when the hotel has offered, and the client has agreed to, a negotiated rate. Typical agreement content includes start date, room rate to be charged, agreement duration, and blackout dates (if any). The agreement should be signed by a representative of the hotel and the client.

Net ADR yield   Rate (ADR) actually received by a hotel after subtracting the cost of fees and assessments associated with a room sale. The formula for net ADR yield is

$$\frac{\text{Room rate} - \text{Reservation generation fees}}{\text{Room rate paid}} = \text{Net ADR yield}$$

Typical reservation-related fees include those charged by travel agents, the GDS, a hotel's CRS, and operators of Internet booking sites.

Night audit   Process of reviewing for accuracy and completeness the accounting transactions from one day to conclude, or close, that day's sales information in preparation for posting transactions of the next day.

Night auditor   Front office employee who performs the daily review of guest transactions recorded by the front office.

Noncommercial foodservice operation   Foodservice operation whose financial goal does not involve generating profits from the sale of food and beverage products. Also called *institutional foodservices* and *on-site foodservices*.

Nonguaranteed reservation   Room reservation for which guests do not provide payment at the time the reservation is made.

No-show   Guest who makes a room reservation but fails to cancel the reservation or arrive at the hotel on the date of the reservation.

Occupancy forecast   Estimate of future occupancy stated as a percentage of rooms available.

Occupancy index   A ratio measure computed as

$$\frac{\text{Occupancy rate of a selected hotel}}{\text{Occupancy rate of that hotel's competitive set}} = \text{Occupancy index}$$

Occupancy tax   Money collected from guests and paid by a hotel to a local taxing authority. Room revenue (room sales) generated by a hotel determines the amount collected and paid out. In some areas, this tax is known as the *bed tax.*

Offer (contract)   Element in a legal contract that indicates what one entity is willing to do and what that entity expects in return.

Off-the-shelf   Term relating to a generic product (such as a training resource) that is developed for general use rather than for a unique property.

On-call   Agreement between a hotel employer and a staff member that the staff member, although not formally scheduled to work, will remain available to work, to answer questions, or to do both, if necessary, during a specified time period.

On-the-books   Hotel term for cumulative current data. The term is used most often in reference to reservation data. For example, a 300-room hotel with reservations for 200 rooms on a given (future) date is said to have 200 reservations *on-the-books.* (The term originated when hotel reservation data were stored in a bound reservation book rather than in a software program.)

Opaque model   Internet sales method in which consumers "bid" an amount they are willing to pay for a room on a specific arrival date, and the operator of the third-party Web site matches that bid with a hotel willing to sell rooms at that rate.

Operating budget   Financial plan that estimates the amount of revenue to be generated, the expenses to be incurred, and the amount of profit, if any, to be realized.

Operating costs   Costs directly incurred to generate revenue; these costs vary by the amount of revenue (business volume) and are usually within control of the department manager.

Organization chart   Diagram depicting the departments in an organization along with (usually) the management and nonmanagement positions within each department.

Organizational culture   Pattern of shared beliefs and values that affect norms of behavior and that significantly influence the behavior of the organization's members.

Orientation   Process of providing basic information about the hotel that should be known by all of its employees.

Out of order (OOO)   Room that is unrentable for reasons other than routine cleaning. The industry standard notation for this room is OOO.

Over   Situation in which cashiers have more money in their cash drawer than the official revenue records indicate. A cashier with $10 more in the cash drawer than the PMS record indicates is said to be $10 *over.*

Overbooking   Situation in which the hotel has more guest reservations for rooms than it has rooms available to lodge those guests. Sometimes referred to as *oversold.*

Overbuilt   Condition that exists when there are too many hotel guestrooms available for the number of travelers wanting to rent them.

Overflow (hotel)   Guestrooms that are part of a larger group booking that cannot be accommodated by a single hotel. Room rates for overflow rooms are often established at a rate similar to that of the hosting hotel.

Overstay   Guest who checks out of the hotel after his or her originally scheduled check-out date.

Owner's equity   What remains after subtracting what the business owes others (its liabilities) from what the business owns (its assets).

Package   Group of hospitality services (e.g., hotel rooms, meals, and airfare) sold for one price. For example, a Valentine's Day getaway package to Las Vegas offered by a travel agent might include airfare, lodging, meals, and show tickets for two people at one inclusive price.

Paid-outs   Payments made by the front desk for legitimate hotel expenses. Examples include the purchase of minor office supplies, guest refunds, or other expenses authorized by the hotel's FOM and recorded by the appropriate staff member.

Paper trail   Accounting term for trackable, physical evidence that a financial transaction has occurred.

Part-time employee   Staff member who works fewer than 40 hours weekly. Some part-time employees may work on-call and work on an infrequent basis as needed.

Pay-per-click   Arrangement in which a hotel Web site operator pays a search engine operator a fee for each hit (click) on the hotel's Web site that was initiated by the search engine's users.

Pay-per-view   Industry term for a video or audio service, usually delivered on the guestroom television, in which guests are charged for the time they actually use the service.

PBX (private broadcast exchange)   System in the hotel used to process incoming, internal, and outgoing telephone calls.

Peak arrival day   Day for which most rooms in a group block are sold.

Peak night   Night when the most guestrooms for a group are sold.

Per diem   Fixed dollar amount per day that a traveler will be reimbursed for a hotel room, meals, or both; the amount is determined by the traveler's employer and may differ by travel destination.

Petty cash   Small amount of cash available on-site that is not commingled with cash banks for revenue centers and is used to make small, miscellaneous purchases. Funds are usually managed so that the sum of the cash plus invoices for purchases always equals a preestablished amount.

Pickup   Actual number of guestrooms reserved for (or by) individuals. Group pickup is the number of guestrooms reserved for individuals in a group block. For example, if 200 group rooms are blocked for a specific night, and 150 represent confirmed reservations, the pickup would be 150 rooms, or 75 percent (150 ÷ 200 = 75 percent).

Pickup report   Any of a variety of PMS reports designed to summarize reservation activity.

PMS report   Specific set of data or information taken from a hotel's property management system.

Policy   Administrative tool or guideline that establishes parameters to be used when decisions are made.

POS (point of sale)   A location in the hotel (excluding the front desk) at which hotel goods and services are purchased. In many hotels, a POS is interfaced with the PMS.

POS terminal   Computer system containing its own input and output components and, perhaps, some memory capacity, but without a central processing unit. A large restaurant, lounge, or gift shop may have several POS terminals so that servers and cashiers have rapid access to a unit when the operation is busy.

Post   To enter data (including guest charges) into the PMS to create a permanent record of the information. Posting may be done automatically or manually. Used as in, "Please *post* this room charge to Mr. Walker's folio."

Preblocked room   Specific room number that has been assigned to an arriving guest before arrival. FOMs ensure that needed rooms are preblocked to meet guests' requests for specific location or to ensure that guests receive the room type they have reserved.

Pre-key (guestroom)   Making an electronic key for a guestroom before the actual arrival of the guest who will be assigned to that room.

Prepaid reservation   Room reservation in which guests, prior to their arrival, provide payment for their rooms. Sometimes referred to as an *advanced deposit reservation*.

Preventive maintenance   Maintenance activities designed to minimize maintenance costs and prolong the life of equipment.

Professional association   Group of persons who affiliate to promote common interests (which may or may not include business).

Property management system (PMS)   The computer hardware and programs used to record guest reservations and requests and to manage the prices charged for rooms and other services. The system also records and stores hotel sales data and other historical information useful in decision making for effective hotel management.

Pull-out   Industry term for an in-room sofa that converts to a bed. Also called a *sofa sleeper*.

Punitive damages   Monetary amount assessed to punish liable parties and serve as an example to the liable party as well as others not to commit the wrongful act in the future.

Qualifying   Process of asking questions of guests to obtain answers that will better help the hotel salesperson meet the guest's reservations needs. For example, a front desk agent might ask, "Would you prefer one bed or two?"

Quality Consistent delivery of products and services according to expected standards.

Rack rate Price at which a hotel sells its rooms when no discounts of any kind are offered to the guest. Often shortened to *rack*.

Rate (corporate) Special rate offered to individual business travelers.

Rate (government) Special rate offered to the employees of local, state, or federal governments.

Rate (group) Special rate offered to a hotel's large-volume guestroom purchasers.

Rate (package) Special rate that allows a guest to pay one price for all of the features and amenities included in the package.

Rate (seasonal) Increase (or decrease) in rack rate based on the dates when the room is rented. For example, a beachfront hotel may have a seasonal rate offered in the summer with a lower "winter" rate offered in the off-season.

Rate (special event) Temporary increase in rack rate based on a specific event such as a concert, sporting event, or holiday. Sometimes known as *super* or *premium* rack. Examples are rates for rooms during New Year's Eve in Manhattan and during Super bowl weekend in the host city.

Rate integrity (parity) Degree to which a hotel's room rates are comparable regardless of the distribution channel on which they are found. Sometimes called *rate parity* or another term that implies rate consistency.

Rate resistance Refusal to make a reservation because the rate quoted is perceived to be too high.

Rate type Single (unique) rate for a specific type of room that is programmed into a hotel's PMS.

Real estate investment trust (REIT) Public corporation that sells stock to raise money (capital) that is then used to purchase real estate, including hotels.

Reasonable care Legal concept that identifies the amount of care a reasonably prudent person would exercise in a specific situation.

Reasonable cause Knowledge of facts that, although not the same as direct knowledge, would cause a reasonable person knowing the same facts to reasonably conclude the same thing.

Recession Period of downturn in a nation's economy.

Recodable locking system Hotel locking system designed so that when a guest inserts a key card into a lock for the first time, the lock is immediately recoded and entry authorization for the previous guest is canceled.

Recruitment Activities designed to attract qualified applicants for vacant positions within the hotel.

Registration card Physical document a guest signs during check-in. Information contained on the registration card varies based on the specific PMS but always includes the guest's name, room assignment, room rate, and departure date. Often called the *reg card*.

Repeat business Revenues generated from guests returning to the hotel as a result of positive experiences on previous visits.

Reservation, guaranteed Reservation in which the hotel agrees to hold the room until the guest arrives, and the guest agrees to pay for the room even if he or she does not arrive (i.e., is a no-show).

Reservations agent Front office employee whose job consists primarily of taking and entering individual and group reservations into the hotel's property management system.

Resort Full-service hotel with additional attractions to make it a primary destination for travelers.

Restaurant For-profit foodservice operation whose primary business involves the sale of food and beverage products to individuals and small groups of guests.

Retained earnings Profits earned but not paid (disbursed) to the business owners.

Return on investment (ROI) Percentage rate of return achieved on the money invested in a hotel property.

Returned check Check deposited by a hotel into its bank account that, for some reason, is not honored. Checks of this type are "returned" to the hotel. Sometimes referred to as a *bad, bounced,* or *hot* check.

Revenue   Money the hotel collects from the sale of rooms or from the sale of the hotel's products and services.

Revenue manager   Individual within a hotel's accounting department responsible for decision making necessary to maximize the property's long-term RevPar.

RevPar (revenue per available room)   Average revenue generated by each guestroom during a given time period. The formula for RevPar is

$$\text{Occupancy \% } (\times) \text{ ADR} = \text{RevPar}$$

RevPar index   Ratio measure computed as

$$\frac{\text{RevPar of a selected hotel}}{\text{RevPar of that hotel's competitive set}} = \text{RevPar index}$$

RFP (request for proposal)   Official request by a room buyer asking that a hotel quote its rate and contract terms in response to the buyer's specific room and meeting space requests.

Road warrior   Term used to describe business travelers who travel frequently.

Role-model   Act of behaving in a manner that is consistent with the behavior desired of others.

Roll-away bed   Type of bed, usually designed for use by a single guest, that can easily be transported from one guestroom to another. Typically referred to as *roll-aways*.

Room mix   Ratio of a hotel's room types. For example, number of double-bedded rooms compared to king-bedded rooms, number of smoking-permitted rooms compared to nonsmoking rooms, and number of suites compared to standard rooms.

Room night   Single night use of a guestroom. A group using 10 rooms for 5 nights generates 50 room nights. The number is used as an indicator of group size and quantifies the group's importance to the hotel.

Room rate economics   Process by which revenue managers price rooms while considering how consumers may react to the pricing strategies that are used.

Room status   Up-to-date (actual) condition (e.g., occupied, vacant, dirty, or clean) of all the hotel's individual guestrooms.

Room status report   Listing of the current housekeeping status of each available room.

Room type   Term used to designate specific guestroom configurations. For example, smoking versus nonsmoking, king bed versus queen or double beds, and suite versus regular sleeping room. Commonly abbreviated (e.g., K for king and NS for nonsmoking). Availability of the proper room type is often important to guests as they decide whether to rent a room.

Rooming list   Registry of the names of the specific individuals who are part of a group reservation. The rooming list details each guest's arrival and departure dates as well as the form of payment to be used.

Salary   Pay calculated at a weekly, monthly, or annual rate rather than at an hourly rate.

Sales   Number of units (such as guestrooms) sold.

Sales history   Record of past sales activity for a specific period of time.

Search engine   Web site specifically designed for the purpose of directing its visitors to other Web sites.

Search warrant   Written order issued by a judge that directs a law enforcement officer to search a specified place for one or more specified items of evidence.

Seasonal hotel   Hotel whose revenues and expenditures vary greatly depending on the time (season) of the year. For example, ski resorts are busy in winter months and lake resorts in the northern part of the United States are busy in summer months. Many seasonal resorts are open for only part of the year.

Selection   Process of evaluating job applicants to determine those more qualified (or potentially qualified) for vacant positions.

Self-operated noncommercial foodservices   Type of noncommercial foodservices operation in which the program is managed and operated by the organization's employees.

Sell position   Specific placement order of a hotel's information on an Internet booking site. Hotels whose listings are "higher" (appear earlier) on a site are said to have a higher (better) sell position. Each Internet site determines its own listing order requirements, and FOMs should know them.

Sellout Night on which a hotel expects to achieve 100 percent occupancy.

Service (hotel) Process of helping guests by addressing their wants and needs with respect and dignity in a timely manner.

Service recovery Sequence of steps used by hotel staff to address guest complaints and problems in a manner that yields a win–win situation for both the guest and the property.

Settlement (account) Collection of a payment for an outstanding account balance. Settlement may involve the guest paying cash or charging the account balance to a valid payment card or another hotel-approved account.

Share with (room rate) Room rate that is split between (shared with) more than one room occupant.

Shared room assignment Placement of two or more unrelated individual guests into the same sleeping room.

Shift Eight-hour period of time. In the hotel business, the most common shifts are 7:00 a.m. to 3:00 p.m., 3:00 p.m. to 11:00 p.m., and 11:00 p.m. to 7:00 a.m. (sometimes referred to as *night audit* or *graveyard* shift).

Short Situation in which cashiers have less money in their cash drawer than the official revenue records indicate. A cashier with $10 less in the cash drawer than the PMS record indicates is said to be $10 *short*.

Shoulder date Hotel term for a day, or even a season, between two busier time periods. For example, in a specific hotel, Thursday may be a slower shoulder date between the busy week-days (Monday, Tuesday, and Wednesday) and the busy weekends (Friday and Saturday).

Signature authority Right to authorize and incur expenditures on behalf of a group.

Skip (nonpaying guest) Term used to refer to a hotel guest who vacates a guestroom without paying the bill incurred for its rental and for other charges made to the room.

Sleep out Industry term for a room that was paid for and is listed in the PMS as occupied, but in which the bed was not used.

Sleeper Industry term for a room identified in PMS records as occupied (charges are accruing) but that is actually unoccupied.

Smart card Payment card in which user information such as demographics, purchase history, and product preferences is contained within a computerized chip embedded in the card.

Smart switch Device that detects detailed information about the destination of a telephone call when it is made.

SOF (signature on file) Signature obtained from a guest at check-in. If a guest has been properly checked in, the SOF will be on the guest's registration card.

SOP (standard operating procedure) Policy or procedure that is so routine it should be readily known and followed by all affected employees.

Source document Written record that initiates an account debit or credit. Examples of source documents for debits include signed guest checks (for food and beverage charges) and detailed telephone logs (for telephone toll charges). Credit card confirmations for payment produce account credits.

Split rate Room rate that changes during a guest's stay based on room demand.

Staff department Hotel division such as human resources, purchasing, and accounting that provides technical, supportive assistance to managers of line-departments.

Staffing Basic management activity that involves finding the right people for the job.

Standard of care Level of performance that is determined to be reasonably acceptable by the industry to fulfill a duty of care.

Stayover Guest who is not scheduled to check out of the hotel on the day his or her room status is assessed. This guest will be staying and using the room at least one more day.

STR index Comparative measure of a specific hotel's operating performance.

Subordinate Person whose work is directly supervised or controlled by an individual of higher rank or position.

Subpoena Command by a court that a witness appear and testify before it.

Suite   Hotel guestroom in which the living area is separated from the sleeping area.

Supervisor   Staff member who directs the work of entry-level employees.

Supply   Total amount of a good or service available for sale.

Suppressed rate   Term used to indicate that a guest's room rate is not to be displayed on the guest's copy of the folio. Used as in, "*Suppress* the rate on all the folios created for the tour group arriving this Friday."

T&E card (travel and entertainment card)   Payment system by which the card issuer collects full payment from the card user each month. Card companies do not typically assess interest charges to consumers; instead, they rely on fees collected from merchants accepting the cards. Examples of T&E cards are American Express and Diners Club.

Telephone etiquette   Procedures for using the telephone in a professional manner that are respectful of the person to whom one is speaking.

Template report   Standard formatted report from the PMS that may be modified by the end user.

Tenant (hotel)   Person who rents a hotel guestroom for an extended time period with the intent of establishing a permanent residency.

Terrorism   Threat of danger and actual harm caused by persons for political or religious reasons.

THISCO (The Hotel Industry Switch Company)   Now called Pegasus Solutions, this organization is the most frequently used "switch" to interface information from all hotel and airline systems.

Time-share property   Lodging property that sells a part ownership (e.g., one week within a specified time period) in a unit within the property. Also called *interval ownership property.*

Tipped position   Position in which the incumbent routinely receives a gratuity from a guest based on, at least in part, the quality of service that was rendered. The word *tip* is an acronym for "to insure promptness."

Top-down selling   Tactic to first sell the hotel's most expensive rooms.

Track   Hotel term meaning to monitor or to examine.

Track code   Guest types differentiated by traveler demographics. Typical track codes include those related to the purpose of the traveler's trip (such as business [corporate] versus leisure) and those related to LOS (transient versus long-term stay). A track code can be created for any traveler demographic determined important enough to create and monitor a reservation field in the PMS.

Trade association   Group of persons who affiliate because of common business or industry concerns.

Transient (guest)   Guest who is not part of a group. Transient guests can be subdivided by traveler demographics to gain more detailed information about the type of guests staying at a property.

Transnational company   Organization with its headquarters in one country but with company operations in several other countries.

Travel agent   Hospitality professional who assists clients in planning travel.

Travel and tourism industry   All businesses that cater to the needs of the traveling public.

Travel wholesaler   Entity that purchases blocks of hotel rooms and, in turn, sells them to travel agents.

Trend line   Documentation (usually displayed on a graph or chart) of changes in data values. Trend lines may show increases, decreases, or no change in comparative data values.

Trespass   Unlawful entry into or possession of another party's property.

Trial balance   First effort to determine whether a set of debits was posted with a corresponding and equal set of credit postings.

Turnover rate   Measure of the proportion of a workforce that is replaced during a designated time period (e.g., month, quarter, or year). Number of employees separated ÷ number of employees in the workforce = employee turnover rate.

Uniform System of Accounts for the Lodging Industry (USALI)   Standard set of accounting procedures used to record a hotel's financial transactions and condition.

Uniformed services employee   Person in the front office department who provides personalized services to guests. Positions include bell staff (porters), door and parking attendants, van drivers, and in some hotels, concierge personnel.

Unique cancellation number   Number or series of numbers and letters used to identify the cancellation of a single reservation. A unique cancellation number is used only one time to identify the cancellation of only one reservation.

Universal process of management   Concept that, at the most basic level, the principles of planning, organizing, coordinating, staffing, controlling, and evaluating are the same (or similar) in any type of business or organization.

Upgrade   To assign a guest to a more expensive (or desirable) room type than the room type to which the guest was originally assigned.

Upscale full-service hotel   Lodging property offering the amenities of mid-price hotels and additional services such as a gift shop, concierge, exercise facility, high-speed Internet access, and many guest services.

Upscale limited-service hotel   Lodging property within the limited-service segment that offers a wide range of property and within-room amenities designed to provide high levels of comfort, convenience, and elegance.

Upsell   Tactic used to increase the hotel's average daily rate by inviting guests to rent a higher-priced room with better and/or more amenities (e.g., view, complimentary breakfast, and newspaper) than provided with a lower-priced room.

Value   Relationship between what one pays for something and what is received in return. Value is the relationship between the quality and price of the product or service.

Variable labor position   Position that must be staffed according to the volume of business. Examples are front desk agents and staff members working in uniformed services positions.

VIP (very important person)   Term used to identify guests who should receive special treatment or attention during their visit.

Virtual tour   Streaming video located on a Web site that shows sections of a hotel in a 360-degree view.

Vision   Abstract idea about what the hospitality operation would be like if it was ideally effective.

Wage   Pay calculated on an hourly basis.

Wake-up log   Written record of wake-up call requests made by hotel guests.

Walk(ed)   Situation in which a guest with a reservation is relocated from the reserved hotel to another hotel because no room is available at the reserved hotel. Use as in, "We are three rooms oversold tonight, if we don't have some cancellations or no-shows, we will need to decide where we want to *walk* those guests."

Walk-in   Guest wanting to rent a room who arrives at the hotel without an advanced reservation.

Warm-body syndrome   Often used but ineffective selection technique that involves hiring almost anyone who applies for the vacant position, without regard to qualifications.

Wholesome   Fit for human consumption.

Wi-Fi (wireless fidelity)   Internet access technology that does not use a building's wiring system when providing users Internet access.

Wi-Fi certified   Short for wireless fidelity certified. More technically, term refers to any products tested and approved as Wi-Fi Certified (a registered trademark) by the Wi-Fi Alliance and certified as interoperable with each other, even if they are from different manufacturers (e.g., e-fridge and PMS manufacturers).

Word-of-mouth advertising   Informal conversations between persons as they discuss their positive or negative experiences at a hotel.

Work order   Form used to initiate and document a request for maintenance.

Work process   Series of tasks (steps) undertaken to achieve a specific purpose. A typical employee must have the knowledge and skills necessary to perform several work processes.

Wow factor   Feeling guests have as they experience an unanticipated extra during their visit to a hospitality operation.

Write-off   Act of declaring a legitimate debt uncollectible. A write-off can also be the result of a decision that the amount owed is too small to justify significant collection efforts. Used as in, "Tom, we have a $1 late charge from the gift shop that should have been posted to room 231. The couple in that room has already checked out, so fill out a voucher and we'll just *write off* the $1.

X report   Term commonly used to indicate the total revenue generated by a revenue-producing department during one part of a specific time period—typically one shift. The term is used when referring to a point-of-sale or other electronic register or system that keeps a continuous running total of revenues generated. Sometimes called a *shift report*.

Yield management   Demand forecasting system designed to maximize revenue by holding room rates high during times of high guestroom demand and by decreasing room rates during times of lower guestroom demand.

YTD (year to date)   Numbers that include all relevant data for the current year. For example, a YTD ADR of $95 indicates a cumulative average ADR of $95 to this point in the current year.

Z report   Term commonly used to indicate the total revenue generated during an entire time period—typically one day. Producing a Z report includes resetting the continuous total feature of a point-of-sale or other electronic register system to zero to begin recording the next period's revenues.

Zero defects   Goal of no guest-related complaints that is established when guest service processes are implemented.

Photo Credits

Chapter 1

Page 5: Stockbyte. *Page 9:* Lawrence Migdale/Pix. *Page 22:* Tony Freeman/PhotoEdit Inc. *Page 24:* AGE Fotostock America, Inc. *Page 35:* Tom Prettyman/PhotoEdit Inc.

Chapter 2

Page 56: Rob Brimson/Taxi/Getty Images. *Page 60:* Myrleen Ferguson Cate/PhotoEdit Inc. *Page 62:* Photolibrary.Com. *Page 68:* Stockbyte. *Page 81:* AP Wide World Photos.

Chapter 3

Page 95: © Syracuse Newspapers/C.W. McKeen/The Image Works. *Page 100:* © Dorling Kindersley. *Page 110:* Sabina Louise Pierce. *Page 113:* Getty Images, Inc.—Photodisc. *Page 119:* Dennis MacDonald/PhotoEdit Inc.

Chapter 4

Page 143: AP Wide World Photos. *Page 148:* Publicom, Inc. *Page 163:* © Jeff Greenberg/PhotoEdit. *Page 164:* Joan Farre © Dorling Kindersley. *Page 168:* © Jeff Greenberg/PhotoEdit.

Chapter 5

Page 185: Jeff Greenberg/PhotoEdit Inc. *Page 193:* Gunnar Kullenberg/The Stock Connection. *Page 196:* Tyler Malory/AP Wide World Photos. *Page 202:* Chad Ehlers/The Stock Connection. *Page 213:* Stockbyte.

Chapter 6

Page 233: Skip Nall/Getty Images, Inc.—Photodisc. *Page 237:* Manfred Vollmer/Das Fotoarchiv/Peter Arnold, Inc. *Page 243:* Richard Price/Getty Images, Inc.—Taxi. *Page 250:* Phil Mislinski/Omni-Photo Communications, Inc. *Page 260:* David Paul Productions/Getty Images Inc.—Image Bank.

Chapter 7

Page 289: Susan Van Etten/PhotoEdit Inc. *Page 292:* Bill Bachmann/Creative Eye/MIRA.com. *Page 304:* Michael Littlejohn/Pearson Education/PH College. *Page 309:* Toshiyuki Aizawa/Reuters NewMedia/Corbis/Bettmann. *Page 314:* Google Inc.

Chapter 8

Page 333: Alexander Manton/Getty Images Inc.—Stone Allstock. *Page 336:* Martin, Inc., Butch/Getty Images Inc.—Image Bank. *Page 346:* PHOTOMONDO/Getty Images, Inc.—Taxi. *Page 348:* Joshua D. Hayes. *Page 350:* Kraipit Phahvut/SIPA Press.

Chapter 9

Page 373: Jim Pickerell/The Stock Connection. *Page 376:* Getty Images—Digital Vision. *Page 381:* Getty Images Inc.—Stone Allstock. *Page 392:* Tom Stillo/Omni-Photo Communications, Inc. *Page 400:* AP Wide World Photos.

Chapter 10

Page 416: Steven Peters/Getty Images Inc.—Stone Allstock. *Page 426:* Peter Correz/Getty Images Inc.—Stone Allstock. *Page 435:* V.C.L./Getty Images, Inc.—Taxi. *Page 439:* Getty Images, Inc.—Photodisc. *Page 448:* Rob Crandall/The Stock Connection. *Page 451:* Eric K. K. Yu/Corbis/Bettmann.

Chapter 11

Page 467: David M. Grossman/Photo Researchers, Inc. *Page 473:* Laima Druskis/Pearson Education/PH College. *Page 476:* Jeff Greenberg/PhotoEdit Inc. *Page 481:* Getty Images, Inc.—PhotoDisc. *Page 487:* © Chuck Savage/CORBIS. *Page 507:* Double Exposure/Getty Images Inc.—Image Bank.

Chapter 12

Page 519: Gary Conner/PhotoEdit Inc. *Page 526:* Stockbyte. *Page 530:* Spencer Grant/PhotoEdit Inc. *Page 533:* Klaus Lahnstein/Getty Images Inc.—Stone Allstock. *Page 543:* © Tom McCarthy/PhotoEdit.

Chapter 13

Page 559: John Miller/Robert Harding World Imagery. *Page 567:* EyeWire Collection/Getty Images—Photodisc. *Page 575:* David de Lossy, Ghislain & Marie/Getty Images Inc.—Image Bank. *Page 577:* © Trujillo-Paumier/Stone/Getty Images, Inc. *Page 581:* Stockbyte.

Chapter 14

Page 597: Photolibrary.Com. *Page 607:* Stockbyte. *Page 611:* Dan Snipes/The Stock Connection. *Page 617:* www.comstock.com.

Index